Worth the Detour

Worth the Detour

A HISTORY OF THE
GUIDEBOOK

NICHOLAS T. PARSONS

SUTTON PUBLISHING

First published in the United Kingdom in 2007 by
Sutton Publishing Limited · Phoenix Mill
Thrupp · Stroud · Gloucestershire · GL5 2BU

British Library Cataloguing in Publication Data
A catalogue record for this book is available from the British Library.

Hardback ISBN 9-780-7509-4393-2
Paperback ISBN 9-780-7509-4394-7

Typeset in New Baskerville.
Typesetting and origination by
Sutton Publishing Limited.
Printed and bound in England.

This book is dedicated to the memory of my brother, Louis Howard Parsons, who was in many respects a guide and mentor for me, and of whose wit and wisdom I and my family have been prematurely deprived.

Was? keine Frist willst du mir geben
Und überfällst eins ungewarnt
Gar mitten drin im besten Leben?

Contents

The English [word] *guide* is merely borrowed from the French *guider*, and the French *guider* begins with a *gu*, which regularly represents a Teutonic *w*. *Guider* represents a derivative from a Teutonic base *wit-*, which is preserved with sufficient clearness in the Old Saxon verb *witan*, to pay heed to. The idea of 'seeing to' led to that of 'to watch over, to direct, to guide'. The Middle English *witen* had a similar sense, as in the *Ancren Riwle* [*c.* 1200]: 'The vif wittes, that *witeth* the heorte also wakemen' ('The five senses which watch over the heart like watchmen').

Walter Skeat, Notes and Queries, *10th ser.(4 July, 1908), vol. 10, pp. 13–14.*

The old [travel and guidebooks] teach us not to be too arrogant and cocksure in our judgements. We too shall be foolish in our turn.

Aldous Huxley

List of Illustrations

Acknowledgements

A book of this kind – like the guidebooks themselves – is inevitably the product of the many sources on which the author has drawn. Throughout the writing of it, I was acutely aware of the words of that distinguished scholar Richard Krautheimer, in the bibliography for his *Rome: Profile of a City, 312–1308*: 'Nobody has any business trespassing onto fields beyond his ken. But life is too short to become expert in more than one field, if that . . . the only way out of the dilemma for the poor outsider is to purloin shamelessly the findings of those who have thoroughly dealt with the field, and to admit it.' It is in this spirit that I thank the colleagues, friends and acquaintances, as well as people I have never met, who have wittingly or unwittingly helped me with this project. However, the traditional caveat of the acknowledgements page applies even more than usually to this book, with its wide subject matter and vast chronological span: namely that all opinions, as well as misconceptions and errors, great or small, are my own, though I trust I have not misrepresented any authority as a result of quotation, or misleading paraphrase, or inaccurate translation. If this were a guidebook, readers would be invited at this point to write in with factual corrections and updates for future editions. I would welcome any such corrections from people who are similarly fascinated by the guidebook genre.

I would like to extend particular thanks to the Getty Center, Los Angeles. The idea for this book was born there when I was able to use its excellent library and research facilities, despite being a camp-follower rather than a fellow. The Getty Library contains a fine collection of early European guidebooks in English, French, Italian and German, many of them originally from the library of the art historian Ulrich Middeldorf. A number of the fellows who were then at the Getty gave me good advice or assistance, in particular Francesco de Angelis, who allowed me see his unpublished study on Pausanias; Thomas DaCosta Kaufmann, who alerted me to the importance of Pighius and Schott, between them the begetters of the first standard guidebook for the Grand Tour; and Roger Taylor, who was so generous with his time and knowledge. As well as the librarians at the Getty, I would like to thank the staff of the British Library, the London Library and the library of the Royal Geographical Society for their patience, courtesy and help. I am indebted to Frau Bertram of Die Deutsche Bibliothek for tracking down an obscure article by Ludwig Schudt; and to Bridget Cherry, the General Editor of the Pevsner Architectural Guides, for generously supplying material on the history of the eponymous series. Paul Smith and Jill Lomer of the Thomas Cook Archive at Peterborough were extremely helpful in respect of the early history of Thomas Cook & Son. Professor Pauline Fletcher of Bucknell University kindly sent me the volume of the Bucknell Review co-edited by her and containing Inderpal Grewal's interesting study *The Guidebook and the Museum*, which deals with early guidebooks to the British Museum.

Three colleagues have exceeded all conventional expectations of solidarity in their willingness to read and comment on early drafts of individual chapters: Alta Macadam, the compiler of the Blue Guides to Italy, whose knowledge of the descriptive literature of that country is unrivalled; Wolfgang Bahr, whose prowess as an author is only equalled by his formidable rigour as an editor; and Lonnie Johnson, who encouraged me when encouragement was most needed in the early days of what seemed a totally overwhelming project.

Many others have helped me with information, lent me books and articles or made suggestions for research. I list them in alphabetical order and am equally grateful to all of them for their generosity, which in some cases included feasts for the body, as well as the mind: Sarah Anderson, Annabel Barber, Bob and Kati Evans, Jamie Fleming, Tibor Frank, Alexander Fyjgis-Walker, Géza Galavics, Géza and Trixie Hajós, Simon Houfe, Derek Jarrett, Peter and Jean Jones, Helmut and Susan Katzmann, Ágnes Kolben, Walter Krause, Georg and Kristina Kugler, Joshua Large, Karl and Dorothea Nehring, Sándor Radnóti, Al Rieber and Marsha Siefert, Carl and Liz Schorske, Hannes Stekl, Árpad Timár, Peter and Gabrielle Townsend, Mark Thompson, Peter and Marta Urbanitsch, Paul and Kathy Wade.

Separately I would like to thank my agent, Bill Goodman, for sticking with this project through thick and thin; and Christopher Feeney, my unflappable editor at Sutton, together with his efficient colleagues, who have made the realisation of this book possible. In particular I am grateful to Jane Entrican for her work on the illustrations, to Bow Watkinson for redrawing maps and images, and to Elizabeth Stone for her thoughtful and meticulous approach to the editing of the manuscript. For her unfailing support and critical perception, I am once again indebted to my wife, Ilona.

A NOTE ON SOURCES

All the sources directly quoted are recorded in the endnotes to the chapters, and for that reason a separate bibliography has not been supplied. In the case of translations, I have tried to locate the most accessible English version, preferably one still in print. However (as in the case of Pausanias), it has sometimes been necessary to draw on more than one translation, as indicated in the notes. Where translations from French, German or Italian were not available, I have supplied my own. I am grateful to Bob Evans for assistance with Latin.

I am grateful for permission to quote the following material. Excerpts from 'The City' in *The Complete Poems of Cavafy*, English translation published by Jonathan Cape, copyright © 1961 and renewed 1989 by Rae Dalven, reprinted by permission of the Random House Group Ltd; in the USA and Canada by permission of Harcourt, Inc. 'Hymn' by John Betjeman, copyright The Estate of John Betjeman, from *The Best of Betjeman*, edited by John Guest and published by Penguin Books. Reproduced by permission of John Murray (Publishers) Ltd.

Introduction

> A large part of travelling is an engagement of the ego against the world. The
> world is hydra-headed, as old as the rocks and as changing as the sea . . . the
> ego wants to arrive at places safely and on time.
>
> *(Sybille Bedford,* Esquire, *1964)*

'HOW TO USE THIS BOOK'

At the beginning of the second chapter ('Santa Croce without Baedeker') of
E.M. Forster's *A Room with a View* (1908), Lucy Honeychurch enters the famous
Florentine church after being abandoned by her companion for the day, who has
also run off with her Baedeker. As it turns out, crossing the church's threshold at
a moment when she is physically and mentally unchaperoned is a first step
towards a new life for the novel's heroine. It heralds a rite of passage and sets in
motion a chain of events that will determine her fate (or her marriage, which in
the romantic novel is traditionally the same thing). Deprived of her cultural vade
mecum, Lucy falls back on her own instincts, her state of mind hovering between
cultural conformance and liberating defiance: 'Of course it must be a wonderful
building!' she reflects on Santa Croce:

> But how like a barn! And how very cold! Of course it contained frescoes by
> Giotto, in the presence of whose tactile values[1] she was capable of feeling
> what was proper. But who was to tell her which they were? She walked about
> disdainfully, unwilling to be enthusiastic over monuments of uncertain
> authorship or date. There was no one even to tell her which, of all the
> sepulchral slabs that paved the nave and transepts, was the one that was
> really beautiful, the one that had been most praised by Mr Ruskin.[2]

Since the novel was set in the present, Lucy would have been using the 1906
edition of Baedeker's *Handbook to Northern Italy*, by then long established as the
indispensable travel aid for the *Bildungsbürgertum* (the cultivated bourgeoisie),
published in German from the 1830s and in English from the 1860s (the first
edition of *Northern Italy* was in 1868). Together with John Murray's famous
Handbooks for Travellers, which likewise began to be published in the 1830s,
Baedekers were the most respected European guidebooks up to the First World
War, at least for English- and German-speaking travellers. Forster was on record
as admiring these books (he says as much in the Introduction to his own

celebrated *Guide to Alexandria*); his irony is directed at their misuse as a surrogate for thought and a dampener of spontaneity. Their aspirations to objectivity, accuracy and thoroughness were things he could respect without deceiving himself that they could substitute for the reality that lay beyond their brief. Writing to his Classics tutor in 1901, he had remarked: 'the orthodox Baedeker-bestarred Italy – which is all that I have yet seen – delights me so much that I can well afford to leave the Italian Italy for another time.'[3]

This slightly self-mocking observation by Forster suggests a question that otherwise might hardly seem worth asking, namely, what are guidebooks actually for? The question, of course, is related to the far broader issues of why we travel round the sights and what we hope to gain from the inconvenience and intellectual effort that are inseparable from sightseeing. 'Fancy crossing the Atlantic,' writes Evelyn Waugh in a description of a package tour to Egyptian Memphis that he shared with Americans, 'fancy enduring all these extremities of discomfort and exertion; fancy spending all this money to see a hole in the sand where, three thousand years ago, a foreign race whose motives must for ever remain inexplicable, interred the carcases of twenty-one bulls!' Over the eighteen or so centuries in which it has existed as a recognisable genre, the guidebook has made it its business to explain to the sceptic and enthusiast alike, to the willing or merely dutiful traveller, exactly why Waugh's bull carcases (or for that matter the *Mona Lisa*) are indeed 'worth the detour'. And in performing this function, it has also instinctively reflected a series of slowly or swiftly maturing cultural turns. To put it another way, 'what is sacred in one era becomes a curiosity in another; and later, it turns into art'.[4]

The present work follows a narrative thread that runs from the guidebook's sources in antiquity up to the present. The focus of this narrative is on the cultural and social influences that moulded the development of guidebooks, the motives of those who wrote them, and the influence they had on their consumers. By taking a closer look not only at the contents of such books, but also at their compilers and authors, as well as their potential readers, I hope I have been able to supply some fresh insights to those available in the already voluminous literature on travel. Our choice of guidebook, and the ways in which we choose to use one (dutifully, with scepticism, with blind obedience, or even with mockery), reveal a good deal about us and the cultural attitudes we instinctively subscribe to.

A WHITE STICK THAT TALKS: THE GUIDEBOOK AS COMPANION, ENABLER, PROVOCATION

At its best, the guidebook has fulfilled the function of a benevolent, assiduous and not unsophisticated cicerone, one who talks up his theme but avoids talking down to his readers. This stance has allowed it to be an effective intermediary between the high ground of cultural aspiration and the low ground of vulgar curiosity. Although the classic guidebook of the type that was founded and flourished in the nineteenth century was substantially written in a mode that might appear didactic, or at times even apodeictic, it also implied a space for its users to fill with their own (now better informed) reactions. As the great founder of the Baedeker dynasty made clear, whether or not the guide sounded a bit like a schoolmaster, its aim was to be a helpful and tactful companion. While it explicitly demanded good standards of behaviour from the host country towards its tourist protégé(e)s, it also implicitly demanded from those protégé(e)s that they should leave their chauvinism at home and proceed with an attentive and open mind.

My first theme, therefore, concerns the heuristic quality of guidebooks, as agents of inspiration, rather than mere compendia of facts à la Thomas Gradgrind. The novelist Arnold Bennett, who was travelling in Italy in 1910, explains in his *Florentine Journal* how he used his guidebook both as mentor and as a challenge to look beyond its necessarily circumscribed vision: on 10 April he 'went to the Bargello & did it with Baedeker fairly conscientiously!' Later he 'still followed the Baedeker & went to the Ch. La Badia', then on to the Piazza Peruzzi, 'which impressed me deeply, partly for its Gothic-ness, & partly because of the streets round it whose curves (Baedeker) show the lines of the old Roman amphitheatre'. By 19 April, however, he is branching out and developing his own method for sightseeing. 'By dint of taking one room in the Uffizi and resolving to look at every picture in it without exception, I saw things I should never have seen otherwise. Including an Adam & Eve of Cranach, not specially remarked in Baedeker . . .'[5]

Now Bennett was famously unpretentious, both intellectually and culturally, with a refreshing lack of self-consciousness about the gaps in his knowledge. Nor did he pretend to a greater enthusiasm for artefacts than he actually felt (he also remarks, 'I am as interested in "the principal shopping street" of a town as in its antiquities'). Baedeker was therefore his ideal companion, who, like a discreet adviser melting into the background when not required, was always on tap if needed. The guidebook's enthusiasms or exclusions might not always be those of the reader, but they could still stimulate the latter to discover something 'not specially remarked in Baedeker'.

Another novelist, Elizabeth Bowen, talks of being 'unevenly receptive' in Rome to what her 'worthy' guidebooks tell her, but confesses that without them her own narrative of the city would be impossible.[6] The phrase 'worthy guide-books' is rather patronising, but the writers of guides are used to being patronised. Like Forster, the young Henry James could not resist poking fun at Ruskin's *Mornings in Florence*, remarking in 1877 that 'Nothing in fact is more comical than the familiar asperity of the author's style and the pedagogic fashion in which he pushes and pulls his unhappy pupils about, jerking their heads towards this, rapping their knuckles for that . . . Instead of a place in which human responsibilities are lightened and suspended, he finds a region governed by a kind of Draconian legislation.'

Yet, as a recent editor of James's *Italian Hours* has pointed out, the great stylist always carrried Ruskin's volumes with him on his fourteen visits to Italy between

1869 and 1907. The same editor points out that James knew both his Murray and his Baedeker well, despite the scorn expressed for their stereotypic users in two early tales, 'Travelling Companions' and 'At Isella'. And James also relied on the guides written by Augustus Hare, who 'mediated between [the] practical efficiency [of Murray and Baedeker] and the sometimes furious impressionism of Ruskin' by compiling extensive quotations from the more or less famous visitors who had described any given site in the past. 'On the whole,' writes James somewhat condescendingly in a review of Hare's *Days Near Rome*, 'we have not been disappointed . . . It was noticeable in the "Walks" that almost everyone who had written with any conspicuity about anything else in the world, had also written something about Rome that could be made to pass muster as an "extract".'[7]

Elizabeth Bowen and Henry James share an attitude towards guidebooks that is part dismissive and part appreciative (Bowen speaks – felicitously – of the guide's ability to 'direct the imagination' and praises the famous Touring Club Italiano's *Roma e dintorni*). The relationship between the intellectual and his guidebook is often a prickly one, where the scholar's vanity and scepticism are dangerously undermined by his or her need to imbibe knowledge, or at least information, from a mere hack. The classic nineteenth-century guidebook negotiated this problem with tact and generally sought to avoid pre-empting the reader's subjective reactions by adopting a studiedly neutral and authoritative tone inherited from the scientific and scholarly discourse of the Enlightenment. The manner was inseparable from the matter, reinforcing the impression that the latter offered the most reliable facts from the best authorities. Naturally there were plenty of unconscious cultural assumptions lying behind this façade, but the illusion of impartiality based on scholarship was one in which both the compiler and the consumer were happy to connive. Ultimately, however, the guide was to be an aid to the reader's emancipation from itself, the point vigorously made by Aldous Huxley in *Along the Road*. Less modest than Arnold Bennett, Huxley pronounces Baedeker a 'learned, and alas, indispensable imbecile', and complains of being sent 'through the dust to see some nauseating Sodoma or drearily respectable Andrea del Sarto'. But he adds, 'It is only after having scrupulously done what Baedeker commands, after having discovered the Baron's lapses in taste, his artistic prejudices and antiquarian snobberies, that the tourist can compile the personal guide which is the only guide for him.'[8]

The heuristic tradition associated with the guidebook may be traced back through the guides written for the Grand Tour, and especially the serious-minded information-gathering of the Enlightenment (often with a strongly patriotic motive); these in turn grew out of the instructions to travellers, or *ars apodemica* (literally the 'art of being away from home', but generally rendered in modern languages as 'the art of travel') that were produced by the humanist scholars of the Renaissance. And it was Renaissance scholarship that forced a more critical attitude to the mixture of legend, 'religious geography', misconception and downright invention that was often muddled in with ascertainable facts in the earlier guidebooks for pilgrims. These in turn had represented a less scrupulous attitude to dealing with the raw material of guidebooks than is evident in Pausanias' great guide to Greece written in the second century AD. Pausanias takes the validity of religious ritual and the reality of the gods as axiomatic, just as Renaissance guidebook writers were not concerned to disturb the cult of the martyrs. But he also describes the topography of Achaia with scrupulous accuracy and rigorously distinguishes between claims for which he believes there is good evidence and mere anecdote or sensationalism.

IDEOLOGICAL OBJECTIONS TO THE GUIDEBOOK

The most successful (and, by implication, culturally normative) guides of the nineteenth and twentieth centuries have attracted brickbats from contemporary scholars and ideologues, who have tended to view them as exemplars of bourgeois complacency. Typically, the great guidebooks founded in the first half of the nineteenth century stand accused of doing what indeed they did best, namely reflecting the cultural aspirations and preoccupations of their (largely middle-class) target readership. Roland Barthes's coruscating critique of the 1950s Guide Bleu is perhaps the most quoted denunciation of this type. From his aphoristic and witty polemic, the Guide Bleu's discourse emerges as anachronistic, politically reactionary, divorced from the 'real life' of the land it describes (because of its exclusive interest in monuments), and inclined to essentialism or stereotypy. In short, says Barthes, the Guide Bleu 'testifies to the futility of all analytical descriptions, those which reject both explanations and phenomenology: it answers in fact none of the questions which a modern traveller can ask himself while crossing a countryside which is real *and which exists in time*' (emphasis in original).[9]

More will be said on the subject of political bias (witting and unwitting) in the final chapter of this book, but for now it should be sufficient to point out that Barthes's disapproving tone dovetails with Forster's distinction between the 'Italian Italy' and the 'orthodox Baedeker-bestarred Italy', the French scholar having added a radical left-wing spin that is strongly hostile to the middle class's perception of itself. Thus (according to Barthes) the Guide Bleu 'abides by a partly superseded bourgeois mythology', 'suppresses at one stroke the reality of the land and that of its people . . . accounts for nothing of the present, that is, nothing historical, and as a consequence, the monuments themselves become indecipherable, therefore senseless'. Furthermore, 'through an operation common to all mystifications', the Guide Bleu 'does the very opposite of what it advertises', becoming 'an agent of blindness'.

This is a powerful, if sweeping, condemnation of a particular guidebook series in its dotage, a series that had a number of highly successful counterparts in Germany, Britain and elsewhere. Barthes's irritation with the smug, pro-Franco tone of the particular Guide Bleu (to Spain) that he took as his 'awful example' may have led him to overstate his case. Looked at in the political context of their age, Baedekers, Murrays and Guides Bleus could be quite radical at times. Murray's Handbooks (for example, that to Spain (1845) written by Richard Ford, which was radical and anti-Catholic) were not always and automatically conservative or establishment-oriented, even if a certain atrophy had set in by the twentieth century. After all, Murray had been the publisher of Byron! The approach that now appears fogeyish originally reflected a creditable attempt to rise above the partisan conflict of the day – although there were plenty of exceptions to this too, as when Baedeker roundly condemned the removal of the Elgin marbles from the Parthenon. But it would therefore be a mistake to dismiss all apparent attempts to generate more light than heat in respect of contentious issues as simply patronising or deceitful. Furthermore, the sheer volume of information in a Murray or a Baedeker precluded a narrowly essentialist response to the material, even if the overall tone of the works does indeed reflect the outlook of a particular cultural milieu whose intellectual underpinnings actually lie in the Enlightenment. Indeed, as Barthes himself goes on to stress, guidebooks that emerged during the Enlightenment itself did address some of those aspects of society (the judiciary and the penal system, the Paris morgue, institutions of learning and so on) that constituted at least an important framework for a society (if not a countryside) that was 'real' and existed 'in time'.

A secondary point is that all the classic guides responded to the perceived needs and expectations of their nineteenth-century audience, even if the same needs and expectations seemed self-indulgent to a later generation recovering from the horrors of war and genocide. 'It is social geography, town-planning, sociology, economics which outline the framework of the actual questions asked today even by the merest layman,' writes Barthes in the 1950s. Well, maybe. Half a century on, 'culture' (loosely interpreted as anything from the *Mona Lisa* to a theme park) is back with a vengeance: most contemporary guides have even less about the important topics listed by Barthes than did Murray or Baedeker, or even the maligned Guide Bleu. It is true, however, that the authoritative essays on different aspects of the countries covered, which appeared in such guides, were almost invariably written from a historical perspective. Guidebook authors do sometimes resemble the mythical Oozlum bird, which is reputed to fly backwards: not knowing where it is going, it does like to know where it has been.[10] 'History' lent enchantment to the scene, while the present-day inhabitants of the country and their living conditions were more likely to be brought to life incidentally in the context of the 'Practical Information' section, where of course they often appeared in an unflattering light.

And then there is the problem of the 'real' countryside, and indeed its 'real' inhabitants 'existing in time', from which we seem to be farther away than ever, with our pretty 'heritage sites', sanitised industrial museums and other quasi-make-believe representations of blood, sweat and toil. Actually the 'real' life of a country has always been available in a parallel genre to the guidebook, namely the unashamedly subjective one of travel writing, though of course reality emerges in different colours from the pens of different authors. A guidebook may be leavened with flashes of these subjective insights, but generally (as Baedeker himself observed) the classic guide saw its role as providing people with the tools to make themselves independent, physically of course as travellers, but also mentally – hence the distancing perspective of time and the tone of studied neutrality. The project may be illusory, but perhaps no more so than claiming to have discovered what is 'real' and exists 'in time': that discovery, too, unavoidably requires the assembly of ascertainable facts and the perilous task of interpreting them.

GUIDEBOOKS AS BAROMETERS OF TASTE

The second aspect of guidebooks to be looked at in some detail is their ability to reflect changes in taste. Until the triumph of bourgeois society in the nineteenth century, taste in food, fashion and the arts generally percolated downwards in society, from the aristocracy to the bourgeoisie. By the same token, the guides up to the eighteenth century broadly reflect the tastes and needs of the connoisseur, the antiquarian and the gentleman, while the great nineteenth-century ones reflect the tastes and interests of the *Bildungsbürgertum*. Underpinning both, of course, were changing perspectives in aesthetics, or new discoveries of scholars, the intellectual aristocracy whose judgements were concisely filtered through the guidebooks. Many of the guidebooks written for the Grand Tour were indeed written by learned men, usually those who had acted *in loco parentis* for young milords, and who consolidated their knowledge and experience into works such as those of Richard Lassels or the dreary but successful Revd John Chetwood Eustace.

Some guidebooks even appear to have initiated a change of perception, as could be argued in the case of William Gilpin's guides to the 'Picturesque' landscapes of Britain. Significant examples of seismic shifts or stubborn prejudice in aesthetic preference include the rise of the cult of Gothic, or the sustained undervaluation, even abuse, of Baroque, for long a style that lacked a distinguishing taxonomy and was often treated as if it were 'degenerate Renaissance'. Changing perspectives on the monuments of Ancient Rome, on specific artists and artistic styles, and on classic landscape topoi like the Alps, are typically phenomena that guidebooks monitored all the more vividly because they usually did so unconsciously. There were, after all, rather few guidebook writers who deliberately set out to effect a change in attitudes, and those that did tended to be authors moonlighting in the guidebook profession as an extension of their aesthetic ideals – typically, Wordsworth with his guide to the Lake District and Ruskin with his travellers' handbook version of *The Stones of Venice*.

In their reflection of underlying aesthetic assumptions, guidebooks were thus a powerful bulwark of artistic canons; but they also largely invented and made permanent the iconic features of individual cities. Baedeker's star system institutionalised both topographical icons and highlights of the artistic canon, but he was not the first to attempt this, nor did his selection of asterisked items remain unchanged during the eighty or so years when the Baedeker brand was flourishing. Charting the vagaries of artistic taste is a complex matter, but guidebook history does provide some insights into this process. An individual 'celebrity' object, such as the *Medici Venus*, is the focus of changing perception and evaluation, which are vividly recorded in the guidebooks over three centuries. The perceived uniqueness and originality of the *Medici Venus*, what Walter Benjamin has described as 'aura', were based on misconception, but the earlier guidebook writers were unaware of this. Nowadays objects in guidebooks often have a sort of inverted aura based not on authenticity but on the number of people who visit them. This is amusingly satirised in Don Delillo's novel *White Noise*, which features a tourist attraction labelled 'the most photographed barn in America'.

THE MOTIVES AND ASPIRATIONS OF THE GUIDEBOOK WRITERS

The topics mentioned so far chiefly concern the consumers of guidebooks, in so far as they might have used such works to refine their taste and become more cultivated, knowledgeable and rounded invidiuals. However, my final preoccupation in this study has been with the creators of guidebooks – the enthusiasts, tutors, pioneering publishers or even harmless drudges who spent such a large part of their lives toiling on behalf of future travellers. To some extent, the evolution of the guidebook genre can be charted in terms of authors who produced works that had a shelf-life enduring over many generations, a solid text being capable of endless embellishment and revision. On the other hand, Pausanias (see Chapter 2), the first and one of the greatest protagonists of the guidebook, is not in this category, since his manuscript was lost for several centuries. An idiosyncratic and rather shadowy figure, we know him only through his work and the agenda that emerges from it: a celebration of, or a memorial to, the continuity of Greek identity under Roman rule.

In the next phase of guidebook writing (guides for pilgrims in the Middle Ages), authorship is sometimes blurred, and indeed many guides appear to consist of anonymous fragments cobbled together from various sources. Yet there is one famous pilgrim's guide to Santiago de Compostela that is identified with 'Aymericus Picaudus' (Aimery Picaud), a violently chauvinistic Frenchman whose animus against the Spaniards along the pilgrims' route makes for exceptionally lively reading. Holy Land pilgrimage also produced some itineraries written up by colourful personalities, such as that compiled by Antoninus of Piacenza, which gives a vivid impression of what the early medieval traveller to the Holy places would be likely to encounter en route.

The medieval ideal that saw pilgrimage as 'exile from one's native land voluntarily undertaken as a form of asceticism'[11] is succeeded by its secular counterpart conceived and developed by Renaissance scholars, namely the previously mentioned *ars apodemica*.[12] The link with the functions of the guidebook makes these volumes a turning point in the genre, in so far as both the creator and the consumer of the guidebook are here sharing the heuristic experience. These products of the Renaissance spirit were in fact meta-guidebooks, combining a discussion of what a guide should be with examples of the ideas when put into practice. Moreover, the *ars apodemica* looks forward to the consciously educative function of guides for Grand Tourists (the improvement of the individual), and eventually mutates into the patriotic outlook of the Enlightenment, whereby your own land may be improved by conscientiously absorbing and recording the 'best practice' of other countries (the improvement of the nation). The liberal-minded guidebook of the Grand Tour was an actual and symbolic refutation of nervous officialdom's view that knowledge was generally dangerous, unless filtered by the proper religious and political authorities, and of the illogical one that other countries might have something to learn from us, but we had nothing to learn from them.

With the Renaissance humanists the guidebook writer has come of age as a scholar, an authority and even a bestseller. We now begin to know the guidebooks by their author profiles as much as by their purpose. This of course entails a lot of copying and plagiarising by hacks seeking to cash in on an existing text. One such name was François Schott, whose *Itinerario d'Italia* was mostly a compilation from other sources, in particular the itinerary of a German prince whose tutor had written his biography (even though he was only 20 when he died!). The latter work included quite a substantial account of the places in Italy that had been visited before the prince expired prematurely from smallpox. Despite its manifest inadequacies (for example, Florence and Siena did not feature in the early editions, because the young man had died before they could be visited), the book was prized for its 'practical utility as a guidebook'[13] from its first publication in 1600 to its last edition in 1760.

Schott's success marks the hesitant beginnings of the guidebook as a reliable branded product; many of his successors addressing the market for the Grand Tour (Lassels, Keysler, Misson) were to achieve something similar in terms of brand recognition and staying power. Ultimately, of course, the branded author folds into a corporate identity, the transition occurring in the age of Murray and Baedeker, both of which brands emerged from guides originally written by their publishers (John Murray III and Karl Baedeker). Today the brand has taken over, and many guides are no longer even the work of a single author, but frequently that of a more or less anonymous team.

With brands and multiple authorship, the guidebook has reached a point where the framework, or system, of the guide determines the reader's experience of it more than an authorial personality (even a 'branded' personality like Baedeker or Murray.) The apparent impersonality of an expertly produced series like the Eyewitness Guides stems from the fact that the writers are entirely subject to the methodology and required only to fill up spaces between images with the requisite number of words required to fit that space. Yet, as Hayden White has pointed out, 'a mere list of confirmable singular existential statements does not add up to an account of reality if there is not some coherence, logical or aesthetic, connecting them one to another'.[14] Authorial quirks, even prejudices, may well encourage the reader to think rather harder about what is being described than passionless consensual prose.

Hayden White has said of historians that they tended 'simply [to] *assume* a world view and treat it as if it were a cognitively responsible philosophical position'.[15] By the same token, in so far as the guidebook became emancipated from route-maps, road-books or mere taxonomy (e.g. Philo of Byzantium's guide to the seven wonders of the world), it tended to exhibit a more or less identifiable *Weltanschauung*, coherent or less coherent according to the intellectual gifts of the compiler. Such a worldview may be evident not only from what is included, but also from what is left out. Although some guides can be read as polemics (e.g. the handy guidebook version of Ruskin's *The Stones of Venice* or John Betjeman's Shell Guides), the pose of (lofty?) neutrality is more often the one adopted, with the result that underlying cultural or other assumptions emerge only by default.

Does this imply the guidebook writer is a mere swindler trying to impose his or her agenda on 'reality'? It is easy to apply retrospective irony to 'Homeric geography' or Christian cartography, but the practices of postmodernism have given rise to a more indulgent view. It is again Hayden White who has remarked on the professional historian's 'illusion that a value-neutral description of the facts, prior to their interpretation or analysis, was possible'. Homeric geography, which is addressed in the first chapter of this book, is of course at one stage removed from that sophisticated and relatively modern conundrum: here, legend or received tradition had just as important a role to play in shaping the overall import and impact of the work as material acquired through report or autopsy. The truth of the angle of vision supplied by the epic as a whole was more important (and coherent) than the various kinds of 'truth' supplied by its component parts. If Homeric geography – or indeed a guidebook to the Holy Land written by a devout apologist for Christianity – is assessed from this perspective, the dichotomy between truth and falsehood appears less significant than the relative influence of either. To some extent the same applies to the Protestant or Catholic perspective of guidebooks for the Grand Tour, or the solid liberal values of nineteenth-century Baedekers. We are dealing, in John Lukács's happy phrase, not so much with the 'facts of history as with the history of facts'.[16]

PART I
The Ancient World

CHAPTER 1

Beginnings: Antiquity and the Origins of the Guidebook Genre

The describer of distant regions is always welcomed as a man who has laboured to enlarge our knowledge and rectify our opinions.

(Dr Johnson, 1760)

There are no foreign lands. It is the traveller only who is foreign.

(Robert Louis Stevenson)

KNOWLEDGE IS POWER

'The travellers of one age are officials, of another devotees, of another, scholars, of another men and women of fashion.'[1] A generalisation perhaps – one could add migrants, traders, explorers, soldiers and so forth – but this observation by one of the first scholars to deal seriously with guidebooks does highlight the main categories for which they tended to be written before the age of leisure tourism. Nowadays a guidebook is a consumer article like any other, but it started life as an official document, probably even a 'classified' one for restricted circulation. Indeed, one of the earliest topographical documents having elements of a guidebook is the quasi-legal (but also intelligence) report on Palestine ordered by Joshua after the death of Moses and loosely reckoned to have been undertaken at the end of the thirteenth century BC.

Three men from the seven tribes of Israel were to go and survey the promised land and divide it into seven parts, so that they should enter into the inheritance

God had prepared for them (a polite description for land-grabbing): 'Joshua charged them that went to describe the land, saying, Go and walk through the land, and describe it,' whereupon 'the men went and passed through the land, and described it by cities into seven parts in a book'.[2] The Renaissance scholar Jerome Turler similarly looks back to the methodology of this epoch-making survey in his advice to scholarly travellers published in 1575: they are to

> prosecute everie thing most exactlye, imitating the example of Moses, who most diligentlye discovered the differences between Mountaynes, Hilles, Landes, Peoples, Townes, Fieldes and Forestes, adding moreover what is to be considered in them all. For this hee sayde to them whom he sent to view the lande of Canaan: When yee shall come unto the Hilles, consyder the lande what maner one it is, and consyder the people that dwell therein, whether they bee stronge or weake, many or fewe: the lande good or bad. What cyties there bee? Walled or not walled . . .[3]

The ur-colonialism of the children of Israel may serve to remind us that the accumulation of knowledge is the accumulation of power. However, the nexus between knowledge and empowerment can, of course, be viewed at a less banal level than that of mere rivalry between nations. It is at this deeper level that the real origins of the guidebook lie, as an expression of man's desire to understand the world in which he lives, to explore the unknown, to create an intellectual order from an incoherent mass of data, to document, classify and pass on to others the fruits of observation and autopsy. Most of what we instinctively know about how to tackle such tasks was first tried out in the ancient world, and, although many such experiments have been lost or are known only by report, enough has remained to show how curiosity allied to economic (sometimes military) motivation drove men to penetrate far beyond the Mediterranean, to investigate and report, to probe the truth of existing myths and sometimes invent new ones. The systematisation of this body of knowledge, both factual and practical, provided the intellectual foundations out of which the guidebook genre was to emerge. Moreover, these foundations are very varied and include sailing manuals, maps and accounts of voyages or land journeys, as well as the earliest ventures into such fields as anthropology, ethnography, history, geography, topography and medicine. The more striking examples of works in these fields that have a bearing on the development of the guidebook deserve a closer look, which this chapter will endeavour to provide.

SPYING, SURVEYING, SELF-IMPROVEMENT AND SELF-INDULGENCE

The reports of Joshua's spies dovetail with guidebook information in so far as the information could have been useful to the layman for gaining a better understanding of the land he or she was about to enter (and in this case settle). Yet military, diplomatic and political considerations would have been even more important to the commissioners of such a survey, a fact that raises a recurring issue in the history of guidebooks, namely their role in disclosing information to outsiders that more or less paranoid inhabitants, or especially their rulers, might prefer to keep under wraps. On the one hand, a nation's authorities may wish to control its image through the selection of information available to the visitor; on the other hand, rulers and officials are perennially concerned about 'sensitive' information seeping into the public domain (and worse, a domain of foreigners). Context determines the impact of data: apparently harmless and objective information made available to the tourist or scholar might also, when read in a different context, reveal strategic weaknesses or help to narrow a commercial advantage. All knowledge is power, but a lot of power depends on ignorance.[4]

That this was a live issue in the ancient world is reflected in a multitude of different ways. To take a few at random, Xenophon (*c.* 430–*c.* 354 BC) recommends that spies be disguised as merchants, partly because the latter were many and it was an effective disguise, and partly because the merchants among whom they would consort were necessarily among the best-informed people. They needed to protect their interests by being well informed not only about routes, markets and prices, but also about local politics and general social conditions. There were, of course, other sorts of alert traveller, among them itinerant philosophers or scholars, typically the sort of individuals who would bear report or even write down their findings. For example, Thucydides (*History of the Peloponnesian War*, 1.91) mentions the intelligence provided to Sparta, probably by this type of traveller, reporting on the efforts of the Athenians to rebuild their walls.

Then again, the collection of information could be quite open, particularly if you were travelling with a powerful army. Alexander the Great took an entourage of learned men and geographers on his campaigns, including a group of surveyors called *bematistai*, who were charged with writing up the countries through which his conquering army passed.[5] These 'bematists' compiled an archive of key distances in Alexander's empire (not surprisingly, one of them, Philonides of Crete, was famous as a distance runner). Their observations were published as *stathmoi* ('stages'), in which precise distance calculations were combined with reports of fauna, flora and local customs. The descriptions of the local customs have been described as 'outrageous',[6] but the distance measurements proved valuable to the Seleucids, who succeeded Alexander, and they were also drawn on by Eratosthenes (*c.* 285–194 BC) for his geography of Asia. Alexander's campaigns were thus as much exploratory as military, and indeed the king's secretary, Eumenes of Cardia, was charged with compiling a daily expedition report, which unfortunately has not survived.

All this may seem a far cry from the intellectual milieu of even the best-informed guidebooks of today, since the latter aim primarily at the leisure traveller interested in culture, history and the prospects for entertainment or gastronomic pleasures. The Renaissance and Enlightenment writers of travel manuals had other priorities, as we shall see later. Passages from Turler's book cited above have been compared, for example, with Machiavelli's *The Prince*, in which the prospective ruler (one of the specific categories of traveller at whom Turler and similar writers aimed their works) is given, *inter alia*, a list of topographical tasks requiring application and endurance, all of which are to be carried out on the journey. He is instructed 'to inure his body to labour and travel, and learn to know the nature and citation of diverse places, marking the heights of the mountains, the opening of the valleys to admit entrance, and how the plains lie, by this means also . . . [to] know the course of the rivers, their depths and passages, the nature of the marsh grounds, and divers other things'.[7] It is obvious that the future prince's keenness to acquire detailed knowledge about other countries arises from twin motivations of a desire to further the national interest and a love of learning; this was an ambiguity that persisted at least until the Enlightenment, when European nobility on fact-finding tours are to be found complaining of the reluctance of some English manufacturers to allow them to look over their factories. Such surveys originated with the ancient Greeks, who boasted the first literate society with a fully developed system of phonetic writing, which ensured that the interpretation of scripts could no longer be monopolised by manipulative insiders such as priests. It also meant that travellers' reports could, again for the first time, become instruments of 'pure objective research' (not that they always were).[8]

The Greeks, who anticipated us in this, as in so many other things, even formulated the idea of leisure travel, which was possible only in conditions of peace, relative security and at least reasonable communications. As Mary Beard and John Henderson report in their short guide to the classics (though they must be exaggerating about guidebooks), 'the Greeks and Romans were tourists too; they toured the classical sites, guidebooks in hand, braving the bandits, fleeced by the locals, searching out what they had been told was most worth seeing, hungry for "atmosphere"'.[9] It is again Xenophon, writing after the end of the Peloponnesian War, who provides a glimpse of perhaps the earliest systematic tourism. In a papyrus on public finance entitled 'Ways and Means', he drew attention to the advantages of Athens as a tourist centre and the potential that this implied for earning money. Among his suggestions for increasing the flow of visitors was the idea of building hotels to accommodate them, financed by the state.[10] The strict and efficient administration of hotel categories that has always rendered travelling in Greece so pleasurably predictable and economic seems to have had very ancient roots.

HOMERIC GEOGRAPHY

The earliest attempts at purely geographical description are centred on the physical and mental world from which their authors sprang, namely the Greek world of the Eastern Mediterranean and the Black Sea. For centuries the binding element of their vision was what is picturesquely known as 'Homeric geography', an account of territories derived from information in the two great Homeric epics, the *Iliad* (written down *c*. 750 BC) and the *Odyssey* (*c*. 725 BC). The prestige of Homer, as the bard supplying the myth that established a shared self-perception among the scattered Greek settlements, long made it virtually obligatory for writers to reconcile physical realities with Homeric lore. For example, the idea that the earth was a disc, 'exactly round, as if drawn with a pair of compasses, and the Ocean flowing all around it',[11] which Herodotus ridiculed, had long held sway on account of its derivation from the Homeric poems. 'From all we know of the progress of the Greek mind,' writes one historian of geography, 'there can be no doubt that they would be very slow to emancipate themselves from the influence of an error once established upon such authority.'[12] Strabo himself, the famous geographer of the Augustan age, was still sufficiently a Greek to describe Homer as 'the first geographer'.[13] Similar attempts to mould the available information to a revered *Weltanschauung* were to recur in the Christian cartography of the Middle Ages, which usually made Jerusalem the centre of the world and painted dragons on the territories about which little or nothing was known.

From its enduring hold on the Greek mind, it seems fair to assert that 'Homeric geography' was deemed to supply for its proponents a fruitful combination of the cognitive and the mimetic, the twin pillars of an overall Greek-centred vision of the world. And it was fruitful precisely because it encouraged a speculative curiosity that existed in creative tension with empirical observation. In the same way that scientific discoveries often spring from an imaginative insight that surpasses mere ratiocination, so poetry for the ancient Greeks could point the way for science. As Charles Fornara has written: 'Just as genealogical writing was inspired by Hesiodic poetry reflecting a natural interest in what the Greeks conceived to be their heroic past, so the poetry of Homer reveals a natural curiosity about foreign lands, partly real and partly imaginary, that ultimately helped to inspire ethnography.'[14] In the *Iliad*, Greek self-perception is at once symbolic and concrete, for example, in an impressive onomastic recital evoking the Greek homeland, the famous 'catalogue of the Greek ships'. The ritualistic naming of places, which again also features in Hesiod, the other great founding father of Greek literature, may also be seen as a rhetorical adumbration of guidebook practice; furthermore it constitutes the more precise part of Homeric geography covering an area the poet or poets probably knew well either by reliable report or from personal experience. To name a place (even an imaginary one) was at least to assert its contingent reality, to 'put it on the map' as the saying goes (though it might only be a mental map). To name a place within a specific heroic or cultural context already brings it into the purview of the guidebook.[15]

On the other hand, the fabulous islands and territories of Odysseus' wanderings in the sequel to the *Iliad* seem to be purely fictional, and even the identification of Corcyra (Corfu) with Scheria, the land of the easy-going and self-indulgent Phaeacians,[16] has now been largely abandoned by scholars. In early Homeric commentary, it was often claimed that Homer was being *deliberately* vague about the location of his hero's wanderings, a form of mystification that was given the appellation *exokeanismus*. This phenomenon too may be seen as the distant precedent of a recurring subtext of the guidebook, namely its ambivalent relationship with 'the Other'. In John Elsner's subtle analysis, the cultural appropriation of foreign ground vicariously offered to the readers of travel books is counterpointed by that same ground's unknowable and unattainable 'Otherness'. 'Who wants to know what they already know?' asks Elsner rhetorically:

> For the Other to maintain its attraction and to generate the desire of readers to purchase books about the far away, the Other must remain for ever the Other. One of the great tensions of travel writing as a genre is that it is about making the Other comprehensible and yet making sure that it is Other enough to continue generating the attraction of the foreign, to continue to defy total domestication.[17]

Open almost any guidebook and this sort of tension will make itself felt: the exotic experience is tempered by reassurance (perhaps in the 'Practical Information') that it can be obtained within a context of physical security and without threatening the traveller's own identity. Such a tension is often treated with some subtlelty by the ancient Greeks, in whose works startling facts (or fiction) about foreign cultures are counterpointed by the first glimmerings of scientific ethnography, or 'pseudo-scientific "ethnology"' as Paul Cartledge describes it. In a thought-provoking analysis of the Greek sense of the Other, he suggests that homogenised stereotyping of 'barbarians' dates to the mid-fifth century and the traumatic experience of the Persian invasions. Like ancient democracy's underpinnings of slavery, this potentially embarrassing issue for Europeans, who see in ancient Greece the foundation of their civilisation, is now receiving an increasing amount of detailed scholarly attention.

Structuralist social anthropology and the influence of works like Edward Said's *Orientalism* have led to an interest in 'alterity', defined by Cartledge as 'the condition of difference and exclusion suffered by an "out" group against which a dominant group and its individual members define themselves negatively in ideally polarized opposition'. Shorn of its academic camouflage, this is essentially the accusation that the Greeks were racists and cultural supremacists; any for whom the cap does not appear to fit are said to have been the exceptions that prove the rule. A case in point is Herodotus, who was denigrated by Plutarch (*c.* AD 46–*c.* 126) in one of his *Moral Essays* as *philobarbaros*. The expression is provocatively rendered as 'wog-lover' by Cartledge, who goes on to explain how this 'accusation' was as inaccurate as its implications were unworthy.[18]

Generalisations about peoples were also grounded in notions about the influence of climate, as in a celebrated Hippocratic treatise of the third or fourth century BC, *Airs, Waters, Places*. Its latest editor describes this as 'a manual whose chief purpose is to help the itinerant doctor to anticipate the different types of diseases that are likely to occur in cities with different geographical and physical conditions'.[19] The corollary is that the peoples featured (divided into 'Europeans' and 'Asians') are presented largely as products of their climate, though also (and insightfully) of their chosen forms of governance. *Airs, Waters, Places* is therefore primarily inspired by environmental determinism, rather than ethnographical essentialism. It is a 'meditation on the relation of geography, climate and human life',[20] a characterisation that brings it close to one of the core preoccupations of many future guidebooks. Ideas about the influence of climate on national character lingered into the nineteenth century and became discredited by association with racial theorists such as Count Gobineau. However, climate as a *cultural determinant* has resurfaced in the recent spate of books that attempt to account for the political and economic 'success' of early modern and modern Europe by comparison with what is seen as relative 'failure' elsewhere.[21]

This is not the place to venture into the minefield of scholarly debate about the wisdom or otherwise of projecting present-day post-colonial motifs onto the past: suffice it to say that the issues of 'alterity' and climate would resurface in the discussion of nineteenth-century guidebooks such as John Murray's Handbooks and Baedeker. As for the Greeks, it is possible to cite quite striking 'exceptions that prove the rule', apart from the equivocal one of Herodotus. The latter's guiding maxim, as quoted by Cartledge, was that 'custom is king of all'. Or in other words, 'All mankind, that is, Greeks and barbarians alike, are ruled by custom, and all are of the equally unshakeable opinion that their own customary usages are not just the best for them but absolutely morally superior to those of all other peoples.' If this critical detachment makes Herodotus 'not a typical Greek', as Cartledge alleges, the geographer Eratosthenes would appear to be even more untypical, if indeed there really was such a thing as a 'typical' Greek in a culture with so many diverse elements. Eratosthenes disapproved of those writers who divided mankind into two groups, Greeks and barbarians. 'He thought it would be more sensible to divide them according to behaviour, because not all Barbarians were bad any more than all Greeks were noble.'[22]

SCIENTIFIC RIGOUR AND A LITTLE IMPIETY: ERATOSTHENES OF CYRENE

The first geographer to make a clear break with the pieties of Homeric geogaphy combined speculative boldness with an academic rigour not unmixed with irony and irreverence. Eratosthenes of Cyrene (*c.* 285–194 BC) was a polymath who exhibited a scientific spirit that many believe was closer to that of modern scholarship than the works of the later Strabo (*c.* 63 BC–*c.* 23 AD), who was his most hostile and influential critic. Perhaps his greatest achievement was to devise a means of measuring the circumference of the earth, and to come up with a calculation that was no more than two or three hundred miles off the true figure.[23]

While Eratosthenes had no problems with Homeric geography relating to Greece and the neighbouring islands, he was amusingly dismissive of the Odyssean wanderings, the phenomenon described above as *exokeanismus*, characterising Homer's 'intentional' topographical vagueness. '[Eratosthenes] appears to have given especial offence', writes E.H. Bunbury, 'by saying that people will never find out the real localities described in the *Odyssey* – the islands of Aeolus, Circe, Calypso etc. – until they found the cobbler who had sewn up the bag of Aeolus'.[24] Naturally the inhabitants of the regions associated with the jealously guarded Odyssean traditions would not have been best pleased with such a downgrading of their homelands, if and when such negative judgements percolated down to travellers. After all, as Lionel Casson has pointed out, there was a thriving tourist trade in mythological sites even at this early day: the more assiduous travellers could visit anywhere from the exact spot near Sparta, where Penelope made up her mind to marry Odysseus, to the plane-tree in Phrygia where Apollo strung up Marsyas for flaying.[25] The temple of Athene at Lindos on Rhodes possessed an amber goblet that had supposedly been presented to it by Helen of Troy, and in Rome, the ship in which Aeneas voyaged from Troy to Italy was exhibited down to the time of Justinian. There were something like 'package tours' to Ilion in Asia Minor, supposedly the site of Troy, and to Marathon, and even along the route to the East taken by Alexander's army.[26]

Eratosthenes, known as the 'parent of scientific geography,'[27] was a formidable scholar, having spent time at Athens before becoming head of the library at Alexandria; his learning therefore covered the astronomical researches of his immediate predecessors and new geographical data acquired in recent voyages of discovery that have been compared in scale to the first wave of European colonialism in the fifteenth and sixteenth centuries. Unfortunately, the first ever work to be called a *Geographica*, written by Eratosthenes, is known only from the use made of it by later writers. But it is clear that a sea change in perception had occurred by about 300 BC, whereby it had come to be generally recognised that the *oikoumene* (the 'inhabited world', for which more or less detailed information was available) occupied only a relatively small part (about a third) of the northern hemisphere. Furthermore, the new science of geography now adopted the idea that had emerged in varying forms among philosophers, mathematicians and astronomers from Pythagoras to Aristotle, namely that the Earth was a sphere at the centre of the universe, and one which revolved in a twenty-four-hour cycle.

It is worth noting at this point Eratosthenes' independent-minded stance in regard to 'alterity': Strabo quotes him as saying that both the Greek *and* the barbarian (the Indians and the Arians, the Romans and the Carthaginians, 'with their wonderful political systems') should be judged by the unique criterion of morality and not of race.[28] This echoes what can be found (but rather more equivocally) in Herodotus's accounts of the customs of non-Greek peoples written around 200 years earlier. Apart from taking the first faltering steps in what we would now call ethnography and anthropology, Herodotus is most famous for characterising his text as *historie*, which meant 'enquiry', and which thereafter entered European languages as 'history' and its variants.[29] Leaving aside the claims and counter-claims regarding what the 'father of history' may have recorded at first hand, or learned by report, or regurgitated from obviously fantastic tales, parts of his narrative (especially the celebrated Book 2 dealing with the geography, customs, and history of Egypt) have obvious affinities with a guidebook. Indeed, the outlook of Herodotus has frequently been compared and contrasted with Pausanias (see Chapter 2), the author of the first complete guidebook to have survived. The spirit of Eratosthenes' *Geographica*, however, would seem to have represented a further advance on Herodotus, both in terms of scientific detachment and in terms of the accumulation of verifiable data about foreign territories, two elements that were later to be the twin foundations of the well-made guidebook.

STRABO AND PTOLEMY: AUTOPSY, FANTASY AND RECEIVED OPINION

Of Eratosthenes' successors among geographers, two were to have a major impact on the Middle Ages, providing thus a link between the ancient world and early modern times; these two were the previously mentioned Strabo from Amaseia in the Pontic heartland (now Amasya) and Claudius Ptolemaeus (Ptolemy), who was active between AD 146 and 170. Strabo was also an historian (in an age when the lines between academic disciplines remained fluid) whose forty-seven books of *Historical Sketches*, completed in Rome *c.* 20 BC, have been lost. But his monumental *Geographical Sketches*, completed in AD 23, is a major work of human geography, including accounts of the political systems and histories of the peoples he describes. Like most such works, Strabo's geography is a compendium of material, much of it from lost authors. He specifically states (and here is his affinity with the Renaissance *ars apodemica* – see Chapter 5) that he was writing primarily for statesmen, who must get to know countries, natural resources and customs. The earlier authors he most quarried and criticised may thus be seen as also having contributed ultimately to the emergence of the guidebook genre, in particular Polybius (*c.* 200 to after 118 BC), the statesman and historian whose two books on European geography were admired by Strabo.

As with Herodotus, Strabo partly proceeds by autopsy in describing areas he himself knew well or had apparently visited (the Asian shores of the Black Sea, the Caucasus, parts of Iran, Asia Minor, Egypt and parts of Italy). 'You could not find another person among the writers on Geography who has travelled over much more of the the distances just mentioned than I,' was his proud boast.[30] Like Herodotus too, the boundaries between 'autopsy' and other forms of information gathering are of less significance to him than they would be to the modern mind, so he lays no great stress on the fruits of personal experience. Yet that experience must have been crucial. And just as the compilation of detailed and reliable information for travellers and scholars generally presupposes a strong element of prior pacification, so Strabo's later labours were made easier by the stability of Augustan rule from 27 BC.

This helpful stability perhaps accounts for Strabo's decidedly imperial yet pluralist outlook, which sometimes brings to mind the great ethnographical work on the Austro-Hungarian Empire sponsored by Crown Prince Rudolph (himself a dilettante travel writer) in the late nineteenth century.[31] Much of the information given by Strabo would fit into any diligently compiled guidebook – the distance between cities, the principal agricultural and industrial activities of a given region, its political arrangements, ethnographic features and religious practices. Nor are history or natural phenomena ignored; we can learn from him about the Atlantic tides, the volcanic landscapes of Italy and Sicily, or the dramatic rise and fall of the Nile waters. At the same time, the ghost of Homer flits through passages where Strabo struggles to reconcile geographical realities with localities mentioned in the epics (he is particularly concerned to identify the cities mentioned in the *Iliad*). In this way he unites in his work the most ancient traditions of geography with reports of varying up-to-dateness and autopsy.

Of Ptolemy it has been said that his scientific writings 'exercised an influence over succeeding centuries second only to that of Aristotle'.[32] With him we return to mathematical geography and astronomy, his *Almagest* (*c*. AD 150) being the dominant influence in the latter science for Byzantium, the Islamic world and Christian Europe until the discoveries of Copernicus (1473–1543). His eight-book *Geography* consists mostly of a roll-call of places listed with their longitude and latitude, together with the mention of a few salient topographical features. It was probably the first work to employ latitude and longitude coordinates systematically and may have been accompanied by maps, for the scientific preparation of which Ptolemy gives quite detailed instructions. Because Ptolemy relied largely on existing itineraries and *periploi* (sailing information and short descriptions of littorals for mariners), his geography and maps contain many inaccuracies, while imprecise astronomical data seem to have led to a major error in recording the length of the Mediterranean from west to east.

Nevertheless, inaccuracy stemming from inadequate raw materials has not diminished respect for his diligent application of a methodology for map-making, which in turn he made available for his readers to construct their own maps. Despite Ptolemy's clearly stated awareness of the dangers of relying on the sources he was obliged to rely on, his work was held in 'blind, and almost superstitious reverence throughout the Middle Ages',[33] one of the many examples where an author's authority (which might reside in science, ideology or religion) has probably hindered the advancement of knowledge. On the other hand, the same writer stresses that Ptolemy 'certainly possessed information far more extensive and complete' about the British Isles 'than any of his predecessors'.[34] His account is in the habitual form of a *periplous* and contains many place-names and the names of rivers (also for Ireland) that have been identified with reasonable certainty, although he gets the shape of Scotland hopelessly wrong.

Ptolemy's *Geography* was known to the Muslims in Syriac translations and was a model for Arab 'Descriptions of the Earth' (*Kitab surat al-ard*). It was also studied in Sicily under Muslim rulers and their Norman successors from 1060, the latter maintaining a pluralist Islamic-Christian culture to which the unique architecture of the Cappella Palatina in Palermo is eloquent testimony. A translation of Ptolemy became extremely fashionable among the early humanist scholars of Germany and popularised the distinction he made between 'geography', a representation of the whole known world (emblematised by the human head in humanist iconography), and 'chorography' (derived from Greek *khoros*, 'a place'), the detailed representation of a region (emblematised by the eye or ear, organs which, while they form discrete features in the head, are at the same time indispensable elements in the functioning and significance of the whole.) Humanist scholars from Nürnberg are even thought to have interpreted Dürer's marvellous watercolour study of a *Blauracke* (the common roller) as emblematic of the whole avian fauna of Dürer's homeland (its 'geography'), while his separate, and minutely detailed, study of the roller's wing represented its 'chorography'.[35] The implications for the making of a guidebook are clear enough: a text describing a region is composed of detailed parts, the significance of which stands in a reciprocal relationship to the whole. The traveller is helped to see the whole through the parts, but also the parts in the context of the whole.

THE FACTS AND FACTOIDS OF A FACTOHOLIC: PLINY THE ELDER'S *NATURALIS HISTORIA*

It has already been noted above that geographical or topographical studies in the Hellenistic period and under Augustus had been at least partly facilitated and driven by imperial requirements of coercion and exaction as part of the processes of pacification and governance. This tendency became the norm under the Roman Empire, where the *commentarii* ('memoranda') of commanders in the field and provincial governors assumed major significance, although only a small part of such memoranda would have concerned the sort of matter traditionally found in later guidebooks, while some were simply protocols, notes for speeches or even memoirs. The best of Julius Caesar's writings on the Gallic and civil wars represent a sophisticated refinement of this type of literature, combining hard-headed personal observations with ethnographical themes reminiscent of Herodotus. However, they were written to provide the raw material on which later historians were expected to draw, and thus to protect Caesar's reputation for posterity; their geographical or ethnographical information is therefore somewhat incidental. Although a few writers attempted to continue the tradition of practical geography (for example, Pomponius Mela in *De chorographia* (AD 43–4) or Arrian in his *Periplous* (*c.* AD 131) of the Black Sea), geography for the most part became submerged in the encyclopedic genre, whose most notable proponent was Pliny the Elder (AD 23/4–79).

Pliny was an omnivore of facts who boasted in the Preface to the *Historia* that he had culled 20,000 of them from 2,000 books of 100 selected authors ('a severe underestimate' in the caustic view of *The Oxford Classical Dictionary*).[36] This boast, however, also implies his value to posterity, for whom he has rescued a whole world of information that would otherwise have been lost. The fanciful element in that information is just as valuable to a later readership, in so far as it reveals pre-scientific ways of thinking, as are the more accurate (if frequently garbled) accounts of anything from ancient agriculture, medicine and metallurgy to the artistic canon of antiquity. Pliny's 'History of Nature' (*Naturalis Historia*), completed in AD 77, was thus a huge, and hugely intriguing, ragbag of facts that was originally projected as a physical description of the universe itself, but ends up as a magnificent olla podrida 'bearing testimony to the unwearied diligence of its author in the collection of his facts, but showing at the same time an almost total want of critical judgement or philosophical arrangement'.[37]

The derivation of the title of this sprawling work (traditionally, though inadequately, rendered into English as 'Natural History') may serve to illustrate its significance for the guidebook genre. As mentioned above, the Greek word *historie* was adopted by Herodotus in the sense of 'enquiry' or 'research', and Pliny's approach to his material is often similar to that of the so-called father of history. It has been pointed out that both writers 'are avid cataloguers whose approach is often ingenuous and uncritical'. Nevertheless, Pliny clearly saw it as a *particular kind* of enquiry, one that ignored the traditional framework of the liberal arts that had become bogged down in scholastic commentary. The adjective *naturalis*, with which he chooses to qualify his *historia*, may be rendered as 'belonging to nature', or 'belonging to the nature of things'. Pliny's latest English translator takes the view that Beyet's title for his French translation (*Recherches sur le monde*) 'more accurately reflects the scope of the work and accords with Pliny's own definition of his subject as "the natural world, or life"'.[38]

The *Historia* anticipates thereby some of the subject matter later to be a staple of guidebooks, not only in its topographical or geographical matter, but in its treatment of zoology (which begins with 'man' himself), of botany, natural resources, architecture, painting and sculpture. It has even been suggested that the work was intended as a vade mecum for provincial governors, in the spirit of the *commentarii*, but it seems clear that its scope is far more ambitious than that. In his Preface, Pliny remarks in justification of the length of his work (which has thirty-seven parts) that we 'need works of reference, not books'. 'First and foremost,' he writes, 'I must deal with subjects that are part of what the Greeks term an "all-round education" but which are unknown or have been rendered obscure by scholarship'; and elsewhere, with considerable chutzpah, he underlines his populist aim: '[I am writing] for the masses, for the horde of farmers and artisans and, finally, for those who have time to devote to these pursuits'.[39] Even taken with a pinch of salt, it seems clear that such statements reflect a desire to reach a wider audience than that of scholars alone, and in this too, Pliny's pioneering attempt to popularise learning looks forward to an important feature of guidebooks.

On the other hand, Pliny can hardly be said to have made things easy for his readers. The long excursus specifically devoted to geography in the *Historia Naturalis* is one of the most jumbled parts of the whole work, with dessicated catalogues of the names of cities, tribes, rivers or mountains sometimes related to identifiable coastlines, but often enumerated in alphabetical order or no order at all. Even Spain, which Pliny knew well, having served there as *Procurator* (civil governor), features as no more than a statistical and onomastic enumeration, though there is some account of its rivers. All this makes the *Naturalis Historia* one of the most exasperating and delightful works ever written, resembling at times an out-of-date guidebook, at times a learned discourse leavened with sarcasm, and at times a schoolboy essay where diligent plagiarism has been marred by inaccurate copying. This last feature was to become a particular hazard of later guidebooks, whose compilers were seldom so up-front about their sources as Pliny. 'When I compared authorities,' he writes, 'I found that writers of bygone times had been copied by the most reliable modern authors, word for word, without acknowledgement.' In contrast he offers 'as proof of my professionalism, the fact that I have prefaced these books with the names of my authorities. In my opinion such acknowledgement of those who have contributed to one's success – unlike the practice of most of the authors I have mentioned – is a not ungracious gesture and abounds with honourable modesty.'[40] As T.S. Eliot once observed of poets, the poor ones imitate, the good ones steal.

THE NUMBER MAKES IT REAL: MEASURING HEIGHTS AND DISTANCES

One of the areas in which Pliny is acknowledged to have provided interesting and intermittently accurate information is in the measurement of distances, although his data are all taken from earlier sources, such as Marcus Vipsanius Agrippa's geographical commentary on the Roman Empire or the various extant *periploi*. Supplying plausible (and preferably accurate) measurements is of course as crucial to the traveller's handbook as it is to the encyclopedia; indeed it was to become a staple of nineteenth-century guidebooks with their paraphernalia of route plans, mountain heights and sea or lake depths, as well as population numbers or figures relating to the economy. Dicaearchus of Messana (Messina) was apparently not only one of the first writers to attempt mathematically based measurement of the heights of mountains, but also established with some degree of accuracy 'the main parallel of latitude from the Straits of Gibraltar to the Himalayas and the assumed Eastern Ocean'.[41] How Dicaearchus arrived at his figures for mountain heights is not known for certain, but scholars believe that he used triangulation with the help of a simple instrument for measuring angles. Triangulation was well known in antiquity as a method of finding the height of trees and buildings, its discovery being attributed to the great seventh-century philosopher Thales of Miletus, who is credited *inter alia* with calculating the height of the pyramids by the length of their shadows.[42]

A distinguished polymath and star pupil of Aristotle, Dicaearchus flourished between 326 and 296 BC. Sadly, only fragments remain of his *Periodos Ges* (the so-called Tour of the World), which included a topographical description of Greece in which the measurements of its mountains appear, and apparently also maps. The measurements obtained by Dicaearchus (the fieldwork for which may have been commissioned by the rulers of Macedonia) were largely adopted by Eratosthenes, who further asserted that the highest mountains in the world could not exceed 10 stadia in elevation. This figure was in turn revised by Posidonius (*c.* 135–*c.* 51 BC), by whose time the Greeks had learned more about the Alps; he claimed that the greatest possible mountain heights were 15 stadia and the maximum depth of the sea was likewise 15 stadia[43] (as has frequently been pointed out, symmetry was an important element in the scientific perception of the ancients).[44] Stadia were also used to measure distances across land and sea; thus the *Periplous* of Pseudo-Scylax and other *periploi* reckoned a day's voyage at 500 stadia, equivalent to 50 Greek miles. Obviously the measurement of a day's (or a night's) voyage was somewhat unstable, not least because allowance had to be made for variables such as weather, wind and currents. Nevertheless, both Ptolemy and one of his most important sources, Marinus of Tyre, apparently accepted the view of an obscure seafarer named Theophrastus that a single day's sailing 'under favourable conditions' covered 100 miles. Eratosthenes' excessive measurement of the length of the Mediterranean at 26,500 (6,121.5km) stadia is again based on *periploi*, since it adds up point-to-point journeys, rather than following a single line of latitude, which anyway would be impossible to sail. Despite this, his figure implies a better approximation than that of Ptolemy and even of most geographers up to the seventeenth century.

THE WORLD TOUR, PERAMBULATION AND COASTAL VOYAGE (*PERIODOS GES, PERIEGESIS, PERIPLOUS*)

Around the turn of the sixth and fifth centuries BC Hecataeus of Miletus wrote a geographical work ambitiously titled *Periodos ges* (or 'Tour Round the World'),[45] which divided the latter into two huge blocks, Europe and Asia (the latter including Africa, referred to as 'Libya'). In many respects the work, of which only fragments survive, seems to have been a hybrid between two genres that later flourished, the land-based perambulation (*periegesis*, which literally means an 'outline' in the sense of 'description') and the accounts of coastal navigation known as *periploi*. Like the majority of the latter, it traced the Mediterranean and the Black Sea clockwise, starting with the 'Pillars of Hercules' (that is, the Straits of Gibraltar) and finishing with the Atlantic coast of Morocco, but including also material on the Mediterranean islands, Scythia, Persia, India, Egypt and Nubia. More than a mere enumeration of names, it foreshadowed the guidebook with its formula for describing a particular land, the dynastic succession of its rulers, the 'wonders' of a locality and the customs of the inhabitants.[46]

Hecataeus' worldview adhered to the notion that Greece was the centre of the world, and that Delphi, its most important cult location, was the centre of Greece. This was also the underlying assumption of the *periploi*: they reflected the focus of Greek (and especially Ionian) civilisation spread around not only mainland Greece and Asia Minor, but also across many colonies along the rest of the Mediterranean littoral and the Black Sea. A *periplous* described the coastlines, plotting a course from headland to headland, or settlement to settlement, and giving distances in terms of days' sailing. It was as much the ancestor of the medieval *portolan*, which was a compass or rhumb chart for pilots,[47] as it was truly a guide, but at least some of them supplied quite useful information about the hinterland, its trade, natural resources and the local populations.

A seminal *periplous* is attributed to one Scylax of Caryanda who was sent by the Persian king, Darius I (d. 486 BC) to explore the course of the Indus river, and who reappeared after two and half years (according to Herodotus) at the Gulf of Suez. His report has not survived but is quoted by Hecataeus, Aristotle and Strabo among others. Confusingly, his name was tacked onto a somewhat later work of the fourth century BC that *has* survived (the so-called *Periplous of the pseudo-Scylax*), and which was itself probably a compilation from earlier *periploi*. Dilke describes this as 'a verbal map with a selective guidebook',[48] and it could not have been compiled before 380 BC because it mentions Greek settlements on the Adriatic not founded before that date. It follows the same Hecataean pattern in beginning with the Pillars of Hercules and following the Mediterranean, Black Sea and North African coasts clockwise back to its starting point. It reckons a day's voyage at 500 stadia (*c.* 92km) and its most accurate part is that covering the stretch from the Egyptian frontier to Carthage. An uncharacteristic section appears to relapse into Homeric geography with an account of an island of Lotus-eaters, now identified as Djerba off the Tunisian coast.

There are several other well-known *periploi*. They range from the severely practical, like the *Stadiasmus Maris Magni* ('Circumnavigation of the Great Sea'), which is closer to a pilot pure and simple,[49] to the more discursive guide for the Red Sea and beyond (*Periplous Maris Erythraei*, of the first century AD), an invaluable source of information about the trade routes down to southern India and East Africa, which was thought to contain the first mention in the west of China (called 'Thin'). Around 25 BC Menippus of Pergamum wrote *periploi* of the Mediterranean and the Euxine (the Black Sea). More literary is the *Periplous of the Euxine* addressed to the Emperor Hadrian in the form of a letter by the distinguished historian Lucius Flavius Arrianus (*c.* AD 86–160). And most fascinating of all is the voyage of discovery made by the mysterious Pytheas of Massalia (the Greek colony at Marseilles), whose lost work *On the Ocean* (*c.* 320 BC) recounted his fantastic journey past the Pillars of Hercules into the unknown world beyond. He visited St Michael's Mount in Brittany and the tin mines of Cornwall, before circumnavigating Britain (a feat not emulated for another 400 years until Agricola repeated it). Possibly he visited Iceland (which could be what he calls 'Ultima Thule')[50] and may have seen the precious amber deposits of Heligoland. No one believed his tale of course, but his stock began to rise when later scholars such as the great Eratosthenes of Cyrene began to exploit his work.

In a marvellously evocative recent study,[51] Barry Cunliffe has hailed Pytheas as 'the man who discovered Britain' (for the Greeks that is), and argued that he may have followed a well-established overland and river trade route northwards through Gaul to emerge at the Bay of Biscay; from there he would have embarked on his epic voyage round Britain, and then to the German coast and Jutland. On the evidence of surviving quotations, *On the Ocean* seems to have dealt with astronomy, the Atlantic Ocean and the geography of north-west Europe. Although hardly a guidebook, it contained much information that was later exploited by geographers and the writers of *periploi*.

Pytheas' commentators have done their best to bury his reputation, at the same time not scrupling to plagiarise him. Perhaps the most comprehensive attempt to rubbish his work was made by a fellow-Greek, Polybius (c. 200–c. 118 BC), who wrote a major history recording Rome's rise to world dominion, and who himself made an exploratory Atlantic voyage in 146 BC. On the strength of this, he considered himself an authority on the regions of the West and worked hard to diminish the reputation of other writers (principally Timaeus of Tauromenium (Taormina)), who had hitherto been regarded as authoritative). Cunliffe suggests that a further and concomitant irritant was Polybius' discovery in the library at Alexandria of Pytheas' *On the Ocean*, which upstaged his own voyage by over a hundred years. 'His venomous attack on Pytheas's veracity', suggests Cunliffe, 'has all the hallmarks of intense academic jealousy.' And so, like Herodotus before him, and Pausanias after him, Pytheas was malevolently branded a liar, which was not a good omen for guidebook authors. The backhanded compliment of exploiting the material, while busily disparaging its author as an insignificant, muddled and untruthful drudge, is something that guidebook writers and other popularisers would have to learn to live with.

THE BUSINESS OF EMPIRE: ROMAN MAPS AND ITINERARIES

It has already been remarked that Rome concentrated on the practical application of geographical knowledge for the purposes of governance, which is underlined by the Emperor Augustus' collection of military, political and commercial information. Having ordered a detailed survey of his empire[52] from his son-in-law, he had all the resulting maps and their related data locked in the vaults of his palace, partial copies being distributed on the basis of need to generals. At the same time, he also had some issued for educational purposes to schools in the provinces, which seems rather illogical.[53] It was Augustus, too, who instituted the *cursus publicus* or government post, a basic tool of governance that is said to have existed in Mesopotamia as early as the third millennium BC, and achieved high levels of efficiency under the Persians in the fifth century and the Chinese Han dynasty (third century BC). The privileges of the *cursus* were reserved for those carrying an official *diploma*, indicating they were on imperial business and entitled to use the government-maintained facilities along the way. Officially, persons travelling in a private capacity were not allowed to use such privileges, but inevitably a black market in *diplomae* developed, evidently becoming so widespread that the unauthorised sale of them was eventually made punishable by death.[54]

There were many *itineraria* based on the *cursus publicus*, the most famous to survive being the so-called *Tabula Peutingeriana*, an elongated parchment 13in (0.34m) high and 22ft (6.75m) long. The name of this remarkable road map of the Roman world (a medieval copy, with one sheet missing, of an original dating to *c.* AD 365)[55] derives from its last-known owner before it ended up in the Habsburg collections, an Augsburg humanist called Konrad Peutinger. The

Tabula is schematic, consisting of lines showing routes, the names of towns, cities or other stopping places along them and the distances between them. These are given mostly in Roman miles (1 Roman mile equals 1.5 km), but in leagues for Gaul (1 *leuga* equalled 1.5 Roman miles) and in parasangs for former areas of the Persian Empire (1 parasang equalled 3–4 Roman miles). It represents the known inhabited world, from the Pyrenees and Britain to India, though the Mediterranean Basin occupies five sixths of it, of which a third is Italy. The section for the Iberian peninsula has been lost. An interesting feature is its use of coloured symbols beside each station marked along the routes to indicate the quality of the facilities available. As Lionel Casson puts it: 'These serve the same purpose as the surprisingly similar symbols in the *Guide Michelin* or other modern guide books.'[56] Colour is also used to distinguish such things as cities and roads (red), mountains (grey, yellow or pink), or seas and rivers (green). Dilke points out that this was evidently a map for use by civilians, since it lacks references to military installations; while agreeing that the *cursus* may have inspired it, he maintains that it is untypical of Roman maps, but rather resembles the 'topological model' of plans for the tube (subway or metro).[57]

Some scholars[58] have suggested that the *Tabula Peutingeriana* was based on the previously mentioned *orbis pictus* (or *orbis terrarum*) made for Emperor Augustus by Marcus Vipsanius Agrippa, which itself may have been based on Eratosthenes' map. Among Agrippa's many public works, which included the building of aqueducts, baths, a granary, the original Pantheon and a new bridge over the Tiber, was a project for a huge map based on his imperial survey to be displayed in the Porticus Vipsania to the east of the Campus Martius. According to Pliny, construction of the portico was begun by Agrippa's sister after her brother's death, and completed by Augustus [between 7 and 2 BC?],[59] using Agrippa's data.[60] Its origins in a scroll probably accounted for its elongated form, supposedly a device to make it easier for passers-by to read. The map has been characterised as a triumphal monument to imperial governance and universalist aspirations, an interpretation reinforced by Pliny's claim that the intention behind it was 'to show the entire world (*orbis*) to the city (*urbs*)'.[61] The alliterative and rhetorical play with the words *orbis* and *urbs* seems indeed to have become a literary topos at the time of Augustus, surviving in the papal blessing *urbi et orbi* ('to the city and for the world'), whereby the whole of Christendom implicitly looked to the holy and eternal city of Rome for spiritual inspiration.

Both the *Tabula Peutingeriana* and the map in the Porticus Vipsania belonged to the tradition of *itineraria picta*, where the illustrative element allied them to rudimentary cartography; but there were also numerous *itineraria scripta* or *adnotata*, that is, 'written' or 'annotated' itineraries. These consisted of sequential lists of stations on a route and originated with plans for the expansion of the Roman Empire through road-building, the itineraries' arrangement of convenient stages of the journey making them the terrestrial equivalent of the seafarers' *periploi*. The best known of this type is the Antonine Itinerary (*Itinerarium provinciarum Antonini Augusti*) of the third century, which was military in purpose and covered the entire Roman territories.

Such itineraries remind us of the unique achievements of Roman road-building, with its repertoire of bridges, viaducts, dams and tunnels, and its tradition of straight roads underpinned with flexible wooden frames over soft terrain, slightly raised at the centre for drainage, and sometimes even supplemented with parallel pedestrian pavements. Under Diocletian (AD ?240–305) a survey recorded 373 roads covering 53,000 miles, divided between 'military', 'public', 'local or connecting' and 'private access' roads. The extraordinary comprehensiveness of this system, compared with anything previously attempted, allowed for itineraries with different purposes – the forerunners of specialised guidebooks. There were even some that seem to have been chiefly intended for those wishing to visit spas – the ancestors of a sub-category of the genre that was later to flourish.

AN ARMCHAIR GUIDEBOOK

The next chapter of this book is devoted to the one fully fledged guidebook that has survived from the ancient world, namely that compiled by Pausanias in the second century AD. However, as Lionel Casson has pointed out, his was by no means the first to be written and we have sufficiently numerous reports of others to suggest that such books existed at least by Hellenic times.[62] In the late fourth century BC an obscure Diodorus is said to have described the towns and monuments of Attica. Two centuries later (150 BC?) Heliodorus wrote about the works of art on the Athenian Acropolis, in effect compiling the first museum guide. His near contemporary Polemo(n) of Ilium (*fl.* 190 BC?), also concentrated on works of art in his accounts, *The Athenian Acropolis, The Sacred Way* and *The Painted Portico in Sicyon*. Anticipating the craze for inscriptions on the part of travelling antiquaries in the eighteenth century, Polemo rushed around copying from stelae (grave-markers or slabs showing epitaphs, decrees or other inscriptions), and became so notorious that he was nicknamed *stelokopas*, or 'devourer of stelae'. Some have seen Polemo as the first art critic, but his writing also seems to have extended to history and culture generally. It would be wonderful to know what the *Guidebook to Troy* credited to him actually contained.

Polemon was interested in Greek artistic achievements, but tourism in antiquity was of course not limited to a perambulation of Greek sights. The most striking constructions of the civilised world were entered in a canon of world wonders, though such a canon was not compiled purely for the benefit of tourists. The earliest such list, written in Greek, was rescued by Berlin archaeologists in the early twentieth century from the wrapping material for an Egyptian mummy. Included with those of the world's most important lawgivers, painters, sculptors, architects and engineers, as well as the largest islands, mountains and rivers, was a list of the seven greatest 'sights'. The manuscript, named the *Laterculi Alexandrini* after its first editor, has been dated to the second century BC and three of the 'sights' it celebrated are still decipherable (the temple of Artemis in Ephesos, the Pyramids at Gizeh and the Mausoleum of

Halicarnassus). It has been remarked that 'already in this combination [of "sights"] art, technology and wonders of the world are brought together';[63] or, in other words, the core elements of future guidebooks occur, perhaps for the first time. The earliest complete list of the seven world wonders to have survived is found in a manuscript of poems (the *Anthologia Palatina* in a Heidelberg library) and is attributed to an epigrammatist of the late second century BC, Antipater (or Antipatros) of Sidon. His list is thought to date to *c.* 140 BC.

These two lists, then (assuming they were identical), are the earliest known examples of monuments being given canonical status, something that was to become the stock in trade of guidebooks, but which also seems to have featured in the oeuvre of Ptolemy, who compiled a *Canon of Significant Places*. But why seven? And why these particular sights? Seven, apart from one, the only integer of the first ten that is neither a factor nor product of any of the others, was considered to be of particular significance in antiquity. The significance differed from people to people (it was an ominous number for the Babylonians, Sumerians and Egyptians, an apocalyptic one for the Jews); however our list compilers were Greek, who perhaps saw these seven spectacular architectural achievements as counterparts to their notion of the 'seven sages' or 'philosophical pleiad', a canon that, like that of 'wonders', was also subject to modification over the years.

And the word 'canon' itself is slippery: Greek in origin, it implies the exemplary criteria that certain (chiefly literary) works are regarded as embodying, and against which the quality (or authenticity) of other works may be measured. While the recurring designation of the same seven buildings or monuments as 'wonders' is hardly a canon in that sense, what was important about these sights was their supposed uniqueness, or superiority, over all other architectural creations in their genre. The descriptions of them have some affinity with the Greek genre of paradoxography, which was concerned with the unexpected or incredible in geography, zoology and human culture. The third-century Greek poet, Callimachus of Cyrene, who dabbled in paradoxography, wrote about 'wonders in the world'. While he did not reproduce the 'canonical' seven, he did leave a detailed account of one of them, the statue of Zeus at Olympia. His description of it is evidently aimed at a tourist audience, which would have pleased Pausanias, who complains that 'Greeks are apt to regard with greater wonder foreign sights than sights at home. For whereas distinguished historians have described the Egyptian pyramids with the minutest details, they have not made the briefest mention of the treasury of Minyas and the walls of Tiryns, though these are no less marvellous.'[64] It is a complaint that has echoed down the ages, and even today there are those who lament that holiday-makers are more familiar with the top tourist sites abroad than with the outstanding monuments and beauties of their own country.

Foreshadowing the cultural vicissitudes that would later make guidebooks a barometer of changing taste, the list of the seven fabulous 'sights' varied through Greek and Roman times, though some elements (for instance, the Pyramids and the Colossus of Rhodes) were almost always featured.[65] Later, the lighthouse of

Alexandria, first introduced by Pliny, also became a fixture. The specific phrase
'wonders of the world', coined in the first century BC by the Roman scholar
Marcus Terentius Varro (116–27 BC) may itself have marked a shift in perception,
whereby the tone of references to ancient marvels modulates from the
celebratory to the elegiac. The poet Propertius (c. 50–c. 16 BC) is soon exploiting
the decay of the Seven Wonders to emphasise the transience of material things
compared with the eternity of his verses eulogising his beloved. The younger
Seneca (c. 4 BC–65 AD) went further and took them as examples of the transience
of all earthly things. A later rhetorical use by the poet Martial (c. 40–c. 104 AD)
paraded the seven wonders in order to contextualise an eighth of his own
choosing, the Colosseum in Rome; and, finally, Rome itself becomes one of the
wonders. An interesting melange of multiple 'seven wonders' was produced by
Francesco Alberti in the early sixteenth century, whereby the author combined
those of the world, of ancient and modern Rome, and (for good measure) those
of his native Florence all in one volume.[66]

This reinterpretation opened the way for Christian apologists, who had
struggled with a list of purely pagan wonders and now began adding biblical
items such as Noah's Ark or the temple of Solomon. They also tentatively
identified the Pyramids with Joseph's granaries,[67] or simply replaced a pagan
monument (the temple of Artemis) with a Christian one (the church of Hagia
Sophia in Constantinople). Dumping the temple of Artemis was perhaps
significant: one recalls the celebrated passage in the Acts of the Apostles where
the silversmiths and other craftsmen of Ephesus, fearing for their trade should St
Paul's preaching lead to a downgrading of Artemis (Diana), instigated an uproar
against him.[68] Nevertheless, the medieval inflation in world wonders was by no
means limited to propaganda for the faith – even an anonymous list in a Vatican
codex of 1300 has no Christian monuments among its twenty-nine wonders; local
patriotism was more likely to influence the authors, as lists of the seven wonders
of Rome or Constantinople continually testify.

The endurance of the basic canon of 'wonders', however, makes it not so
surprising that they inspired a guidebook, albeit an armchair one. This work
seems to have surfaced some time in the fourth century AD, when its authorship
was wrongly attributed to a writer on technology called 'Philo(n) of Byzantium'
(fl. c. 200 BC). It is modern scholarship that has dubbed it a 'Guidebook to the
Seven Wonders of the World',[69] and the author does indeed offer his readers a
guide that will spare them the wearisome business of travelling over a large part
of the Near and Middle East. In a disarming introduction he writes:

> Everyone has heard of each of the Seven Wonders of the World, but few have
> seen all of them for themselves. To do so one has to go abroad to Persia,
> cross the Euphrates river, travel to Egypt, spend some time among the Elians
> in Greece, go to Halicarnassus in Caria, sail to Rhodes, and see Ephesus in
> Ionia. Only if you travel the world and get worn out by the effort of the
> journey will the desire to see all the Wonders of the World be satisfied, and
> by the time you have done that you will be old and practically dead.[70]

In a bold justification of his work, the author points out that actually visiting the places described is less likely to imprint them on the mind than studying a book such as his: 'if a man investigates in verbal form the things to wonder at and the execution of their construction, and if he contemplates, as though looking at a mirror image, the whole skilful work, he keeps the impressions of each picture indelible in his mind. The reason for this is that he has seen amazing things with his mind.'[71] He goes on to underline that the seven wonders are different in kind from other sights, putting them all in the shade ('For beauty, like the sun, makes it impossible to see other things when it is itself radiant.'). In other words, these monuments are claimed to have a unique aura. The 'guidebook' of course confirms, or even establishes that aura, in this case for a canon of 'wonders' laid down (perhaps) by Antipater and still valid for 'Philo' four centuries later. It consisted of the Hanging Gardens of Babylon[72] and the walls of Babylon (two secular marvels), the Pyramids in Memphis, the Colossus of Rhodes, the statue of Olympian Zeus, the temple of Artemis at Ephesus and the Mausoleum at Halicarnassus (five sacral or necrological monuments inspired by religious awe.) The canon of sights, John Murray's weak canon ('things peculiar to this spot') or Baedeker's strong canon (the 'star' system identifying outstanding sights), were to be a hallmark of guidebooks in the future, and indeed the shorter guides eventually offered their readers a canon of 'must-sees' and little else.

CHAPTER 2

Pausanias:
The 'Baedeker of the Ancient World'

Pausanias was an impostor.

(August Kalkmann)

His testimony stands and carries great weight. Unlike those who contradict him, and one another (occasionally themselves), he walked on firm ground, and in the light of day.

(R.E. Wycherley)

Some time in the mid-second century AD a prosperous Greek from Lydia embarked upon a series of journeys in mainland Greece. His tour has variously been characterised as an antiquarian ramble, an historical and ethnographical fact-finding mission, or a pagan pilgrimage. The common theme in all these is the idea of an 'intellectual itinerary', an 'historical reading of the landscape',[1] or, more specifically, a quest for the rediscovery of Greek identity. Pausanias, like Baedeker's guide to Greece seventeen centuries later, conjures a picture of a depopulated, even desolate terrain full of ruins which yet breathes the spirit of glories past. Of course this was a partial view – the Greece of Pausanias' day had undergone something of an economic and cultural revival under philhellene emperors; but it was true enough to suit his purpose. While Baedeker (1st edition 1882)[2] prints a passionate quotation from Byron on the title verso – 'Sacred ground is here, where you also tread, / Dust, which never bore anything mean' – Pausanias' rhetoric is that of the scholar and stoic: his description will allow the facts to speak for themselves.

The retrieval of those facts, the sifting of the grain from the chaff, the unemotional report of sanctuaries violated or cities pillaged, or of the wounds the Greeks inflicted on themselves through the internal strife that has brought them low, or finally the studied recall of an heroic past that is still present in the whispering ghosts he describes at Marathon – all this constitutes the author's homage to an idea and an ideal.[3] But the data alone would be valueless if not weighed in the context of a greater truth. 'The English', said Oscar Wilde, 'are always degrading truths into facts. When a truth becomes a fact it loses all its intellectual value.' This insight is not alien to the spirit of Pausanias, as we watch him patiently sifting through the encrustation of myths and folk traditions to arrive at a core of meaning, clearing a way through lumber that the Greek psyche has accumulated and hoarded for two millennia.

Pausanias tells us that the object of his work – probably carried out between 150 and 180 AD – was to report on 'all things Greek' (or, in another translation, 'the whole of Greece'). What he in fact describes in the ten books of his *periegesis* (descriptive itinerary)[4] is most of the Roman province of Achaia, omitting Aetolia and the Islands. His coverage therefore includes Attica, Boeotia and Phokis in Central Greece, the Argolid, Achaea, Elis, Arcadia, Messenia and Lakonia in the Peloponnese. Despite its puzzling omissions (Macedonia, Thrace, Aetolia, Acarnania and the Islands) this itinerary includes the places that Pausanias obviously regarded, and later generations have concurred in seeing, as the touchstones of Greek identity: Delphi, Athens, Olympia above all, but also Corinth, Sparta and Thebes. Only Delos is missing, but in fact he makes numerous references to Delos as well, for example, when dealing with the cult of Apollo elsewhere, or describing the decline of formerly bustling centres. In treating of these locations so redolent of Greek history and achievement, he has two major preoccupations, namely the cults, rituals and beliefs whose observance they preserved, and the monuments (chiefly sculpture and painting, to a lesser extent architecture) of the Archaic and Classical periods. With a few exceptions, he is little interested in either history or monuments later than the mid-second century BC, and his cultural 'archaism' in this respect shows that he shared the tastes of the revived Hellenism of his day.

In locating Greek identity in its beliefs and folk traditions, Pausanias naturally treated art as an adjunct to, or an expression of those traditions: this was perhaps what made him so attractive and intriguing a figure for Sir J.G. Frazer, the author of that sprawling anthropological miscellany, *The Golden Bough*. But Frazer began life as a Classicist and his translation and commentary on Pausanias remains a marvellous example of the scholarly and critical ideal that combines empathy with analysis. As Ernest Gellner has pointed out, the study of Pausanias awakened the anthropologist in him. 'Classicists are, generally speaking, intellectual snobs,' writes Gellner. 'What attracts them in the classical world is its excellence – one might say its miraculous excellence. They are attracted by its outstanding achievements.' Yet Pausanias, he claims, 'focused not on the miraculous intellectual achievements of the Hellenes, which distinguish them from almost anyone else, but, on the contrary, on that superstitious underside of Hellenic culture which does not greatly distinguish the

Greeks from anyone, if indeed it distinguishes them at all.'[5] This is a sharp insight, but it is unlikely that Pausanias would have seen the force of it. He does not, unlike later guidebook authors, write as an outsider assessing some sort of Greek 'contribution' to the world, but as an insider who seems to want to remind the Greeks of who they are and where they came from. It is this aim that resonates with that of the pilgrim, 'a journey into one's identity in its topographic, cultural and spiritual resonances', as Elsner puts it.[6]

Perhaps this is the reason that ghosts, visions and dreams play a significant role in Pausanias' 'landscapes of memory', especially in his treatment of defining moments for Greek identity, such as occurred during the Persian Wars. At Marathon (site of the famous victory of the Athenians over a hugely superior Persian army in 490 BC) he says that 'every night you can hear horses neighing and men fighting. No one who has expressly set himself to behold this vision has ever got any good from it, but the spirits are not angered with such as in ignorance chance to be spectators.'[7] This passage leaps from the page precisely because Pausanias' description of this site, so crucial to the Greeks' perception of themselves, their role in history and their perception of the other, is otherwise so circumstantial, analytical and dispassionate.

'Marathon', he states laconically, 'is where the barbarians landed in Attica, were beaten in battle, and lost some ships as they retreated. The grave on the plain is that of the Athenians [the burial mound is there to this day]; there are stones on it carved with the names of the dead in their tribes. The other grave is that of the Plataians, Boiotians, and slaves; this was the first battle in which slaves fought.'[8] The complete self-effacement of the author in this passage, his discretion and absence of emotional intensity is typical of him. It is from his selection of topics for a highly selective account that we learn about his real preoccupations, down to the intriguing historical detail that Marathon was the first battle where slaves fought alongside their masters. And in this too he looks forward to the ostensibly 'neutral' texts of future guidebooks, especially those aimed at the culturally aware and historically literate (Baedeker, Guide Bleu or the English Blue Guides), where the 'neutrality' itself is part of the author's strategy of persuasion. As Susan E. Alcock puts it: 'such a presentation can be perceived as a rhetorical authoritative stance, designed to give Pausanias' personal and select narrative the status of an unchallengeable account'.[9]

PAUSANIAS' GUIDEBOOK: ITS METHODOLOGY AND SELECTION OF MATERIAL

The form of his work is undoubtedly that of a guide: the individual books (ten in all) begin with an account of the focal point of the region dealt with; this description is then generally followed by those of alternative routes away from that point, although Pausanias would nowadays be getting letters from irate readers, since he fails to say when he has silently retraced his steps to the centre in order to start a fresh excursion. This method has led scholars to suggest that the Book(s) were intended to be used on the spot, while others point to the fact that the work would have been 'handwritten on relatively thick papyrus or leather sheets . . . too bulky for carrying around, to say nothing of being too valuable'.[10]

Whether it was designed to be read in a library before departure, or to be perused on the spot under a sunshade held by a slave, the guide adopts a topographical method that conforms to contemporary literary convention. Pausanias, however, supplies a content for his form that is startlingly novel, in so far as it has been substantially obtained by 'autopsy' (personal research). Scholarship has vindicated his claim that he actually visited the places he describes, instead of copying his accounts from other sources; and we may surely take his word for it that he interrogated the locals about their customs and traditions, if only because of his crusty asides about the frequent unreliability of their answers. Indeed, he was probably more candid than his modern counterparts, in that he frequently tells us when he has not visited a place. Several of these flashes of honesty concern opening times, then as now the bane of guidebook writers and their readers. In Pausanias' day they had already set the pattern for inconvenience,[11] not so much on the grounds of cuts to curatorial budgets in ancient Greece, but because most of the sights to see were invigilated by priests. For example, Pausanias complains he was unable to see the remarkable image of fishtailed Eurynome above Phigalia in Arcadia because her sanctuary was opened on only one day a year, and that was not the day he happened to arrive.[12]

Where he is offered varying explanations of the origin of a place or its name, Pausanias often conscientiously relates all the plausible ones, only reserving his scorn for any that he clearly regards as ridiculous. Thus the most ancient shrine of Apollo at Delphi is said to have been built

> with branches brought from the bay-grove at Tempe . . . the Delphinians say the second shrine was made by bees out of bees' wax and feathers [*ptera*], and sent by Apollo from the remote north. There is another legend that a Delphinian called Pteras [i.e. 'feathers'] built this shrine, so that the shrine was named after the builder . . . As for the story about feather-grass [*pteris*] growing in the mountains, and how they knitted a shrine out of this when it was still green, I shall not even begin to tell it.[13]

His massively detailed description of Delphi is as good an example as any of the way Pausanias, after lengthy preliminaries on the people and legends associated with the cult of Apollo, together with descriptions of the Pythian games and the Delphic eisteddfods, takes the reader by the hand and leads him around the sights (beginning at Book X, 4). Systematically he identifies temples, treasuries, statues and other artefacts, in most cases relating the events that prompted their sponsors to place them at Delphi. His account is leavened with vivid detail: how the Corfiots learned the art of tunny fishing after a bull stood roaring on the seashore when the tunny swarmed in;[14] or how the Paionians captured and domesticated bison by herding them into stockades paved with slippery hides, which prevented them from standing up.[15] Reading him, we become aware of the incredible extent of piled up votive offerings that could have been seen at Delphi in its heyday, which Pliny says amounted to over 3,000 statues of men, heroes, gods and animals, and of which a good deal remained for Pausanias to see, despite earthquakes and Nero's plundering of some 500 images. He describes what is extant, but also what is reported to him about the ruined, destroyed or stolen artefacts and monuments.

As with all guidebook writers, selectivity is nevertheless unavoidable. At a certain point he remarks that he will record 'those dedications that seemed [to him] most memorable' and ignore those to 'athletes and obscure musicians',[16] though even so he deals with a large number of inscriptions, many of them still fascinating for the modern reader.[17] Indeed, the French statesman Jean-Baptiste Colbert, who was anxious to make sure that France did not lose out in the race to acquire Greek antiquities, wrote (c. 1679) that travellers to Greece should always have Pausanias with them 'to find the remarkable things that he found when he made this journey long ago', and in order to 'bring back as many inscriptions as possible'.[18] Colbert's advice was endorsed, though with less rapacious intent, by the great Johann Joachim Winckelmann (1717–68), who was substantially responsible for the eighteenth-century cult of Greek art and who formulated a project, never carried out, of systematically researching the sanctuaries of Greece, following Pausanias' example. Such plans testify to the astonishingly vivid account that Pausanias provides: it is one that can still be used profitably for a tour of Delphi in conjunction with the explanatory footnotes of modern scholarship, even though a vast amount of what he could still see has vanished.

In the ensuing perambulation of Delphi that continues to the nineteenth chapter of Book X, Pausanias manages to provide multifarious and rich insights into the lore and customs of most of the peoples of the different areas of Greece. At that point (Book X, 19.4) however, he suddenly embarks on a long account of the 'Gaulish' (Celtic, La Tène) invasion of Greece in 279 BC, which he states he has included in his account of Delphi 'because this was where the Greeks did most against them'.[19] In fact the relevance of this matter to Pausanias' discourse here is indisputable, since one band of Celts is known to have raided Delphi. The historical digression (to chapter 24), lively and detailed as it is, obviously relies on a primary source (Levi tentatively suggests Timaeus or Hieronymus of Cardia), and would nowadays be printed as an information panel, the typographical device used by modern guidebooks to add background information that extends the purely indicative text. The digression ends as abruptly as it began, with the remark 'I assure you that is how it happened'.

The tour then resumes with a description of two huge murals by Polygnotus (active in the fifth century BC) featuring the *Fall of Troy* and *Odysseus Visiting Hades* (*Odysseus's Invocation of the Dead*), which were located in what Pausanias calls the 'club-house' [*Lesche*] for the Cnidians.[20] This work was evidently a marvellous example of realistic history painting that covered the entire internal walls and was already 700 years old when Pausanias described it. His delineation of it may serve to illustrate the nature of his considerable interest in art as a vehicle of instruction and controlled memory. In a minutely detailed account over eight chapters, Pausanias identifies every character featured in the painting and comments on his or her role in the Homeric story. As Jacques Lacarrière has pointed out, the lost painting, which was probably done on wooden panels attached to the walls, constituted 'a kind of pictorial credo drawn from the whole of antiquity, in which everyone could recognize the familiar figures and situations, and even moral instances'.[21] One recalls the analagous role of the so-called *Biblia Pauperum* ('Poor Man's Bible'), itself a kind of visual guide, in making familiar narrative images available to the laity (or preachers) through scenes painted on the walls of medieval churches.

Pausanias' remarks occasionally reveal that he was aware of a learned literature concerning this obviously iconic work (there is a hint that it employed some innovative elements in perspective, in the groundline, and in the distribution of figures), but mostly he concentrates on identification and explanation of the mythical background, making little comment on its aesthetic impact as such. As with the digression on the Gaulish invasion, it is the representation of the Greeks in history and their collective memory that seems to be his prime focus of interest. This task is best performed by inventory-making, and Pausanias' indefatigable zeal in recording the material (but also spiritual) heritage of Greece is perceptively compared by Lacarrière to our modern obsession with rescuing the past. We too are concerned 'to make an inventory of our monuments, to draw up an architectural and aesthetic balance sheet of the past, as if these buildings, indeed our culture itself, was threatened with extinction.'[22] Like Pausanias, we shore these fragments against our ruins . . .

PAUSANIAS AND HIS MANUSCRIPT

Reading his account of Delphi and the modern scholarship on the site, we have every reason to believe that Pausanias was an honest reporter, even if, like all honest reporters, he also had an agenda based on deeply held assumptions about the world. What more do we know about this obviously patriotic and perhaps quixotic Greek, who completed a work that seems to have found no echo among his contemporaries? The answer is, very little, and what we do know is entirely gleaned from the internal evidence of a work whose author (like some of the successful later guidebook writers) for the most part wears a mask of authoritative, unemotional impartiality. The only reason for calling him Pausanias in the first place is that a Byzantine scholar subsequently plundered his work for topographical references and refers to its author by this name. Pausanias was a very common name in antiquity, and efforts have been made to identify him with other writers of the same name, but there is no evidence to connect him with anybody else. The exploitation of his work in the reign of

Justinian (AD 527–65) remains, therefore, the first recorded surfacing of Pausanias and his guidebook in European scholarship. Nearly four centuries had passed since his death around AD 180, centuries in which neither book nor author seems even to have been known, still less read or used.

It also appears that, among Pausanias' contemporaries, not even his prospective audience of intellectual travellers was acquainted with his *opus magnum*. It is true that some readers have detected a nettled defiance of the critics of his project in Pausanias' occasional restatement of his methodology in the later books of the *Guide*, and a single remark about his refusal to share the fruits of his researches on Homer and Hesiod hints at ongoing warfare with the literary establishment ('knowing as I do the carping disposition of some people, especially the professors of poetry of the present day').[23] Nevertheless, the general impression is that he set himself a lonely task, carried it out with great diligence, but possibly in vain. Since conspiracies of silence do not appear to have been part of the armoury of sophistic writers of the second century – on the contrary, the tribe of scribblers, what Rabelais was later to describe as 'little envious Prigs, snarling bastard puny critics', could seldom be restrained from rushing out an opinion of rivals' work – his low visibility is especially puzzling.

One suggestion to account for this is that there may have been but a single holograph of the *Guide to Greece* buried in one the libraries of antiquity. This manuscript, or a later copy of it, must somehow have found its way to the shores of the Bosphorus, where Stephanus of Byzantium (the scholar referred to above) discovered it in the sixth century. Under the Palaeologan emperors (1259–1453), Pausanias gradually acquired the status of a classic in the Greek-speaking culture of Byzantium, but it is the businessman and amateur scholar, Cyriac of Ancona (sometimes known as the 'medieval Pausanias'), who is credited with first bringing knowledge of his work to the West. At any rate, the earliest surviving complete manuscript, itself a copy, but the one upon which all other versions are based, was located in Florence in the fifteenth century. Like many other manuscripts in Byzantine libraries, this one had been brought to Italy in anticipation of 'the last day of the world', namely the day when Constantinople would fall to the Turkish armies, as it did on 29 May, 1453.[24]

Pausanias was saved, but the interest in him was relatively limited until the seventeenth and eighteenth centuries, when he began to appeal to a new breed of travelling antiquarians and scholars who were tracing the lineaments of ancient Greek civilisation on the ground. Their view of him is summed up in the sub-title of a translation (1731–3) into French by Gedoyn de Beaugency, who calls the *Guide to Greece* a '*voyage historique, pittoresque et philosophique*'. In the nineteenth century there was a veritable Pausanias boom, especially in Germany, where no less than seven critical editions appeared between 1818 and 1903. The work was now subjected to rigorous textual, comparative and linguistic examination, which was followed around the turn of the century by massive volumes of commentary. Finally, it entered the mainstream of literature for the non-specialist with the Loeb edition translated by W.H.S. Jones (1918–35). The self-effacing Greek pedant had become famous – or, for some, notorious. Scholars fought pitched battles over his corpus, travellers set off to Greece with him in their luggage; he was interpreted and bowdlerised (one edition 'purged' the text of all historical and mythological passages, the very part to which the author clearly attached the greatest importance). With fame comes resentment, and Pausanias became the target of abuse and ridicule as well as admiration and appreciation. As with Shakespeare, the anti-lobby did its best to cast doubt on his very existence, scratching around for plausible candidates to have written his admirable work. Like Shakespeare, he has survived these onslaughts and it is his critics, the 'earth-creeping minds' of which Shelley speaks, who have sunk into obscurity.

The fact is that, while there were *periegeses* and descriptions of Greek topography and artefacts before Pausanias, the fragments of them that survive are nothing like his work, which is indeed *sui generis*. Sir James Frazer makes the point neatly when he compares some surviving extracts from a description written perhaps 300 years before Pausanias, but falsely attributed to the Messenian writer and polymath, Dicaearchus, a pupil of Aristotle. The approach could hardly be more different from that of the venerable author of the *Guide*: it is gossipy, colourful, frequently scabrous, and concentrates very much on the Greece and Greeks of the writer's own time, rather than on an idealised past. Idealisation does not come into it: the Atticans are 'gossiping, slanderous, given to prying into the business of strangers, fair and false. The Athenians are high-minded, straightforward and staunch in friendship. [Their] city is infested by a set of scribblers who worry visitors and rich strangers.' Athens 'far surpasses all other cities in the pleasures and conveniences of life . . . but a man must beware of the courtesans lest they lure him to ruin.' As for Oropus, it is a 'nest of hucksters. The greed of the custom-house officers here is unsurpassed, their roguery inveterate and bred in the bone. Most of the people here are coarse and truculent in their manners, for they have knocked the decent members of the community on the head.' At Thebes, 'the soil is dark. In spite of its antiquity the streets are new, because, as the histories tell us, the city has been thrice razed to the ground on account of the morose and overbearing character of the inhabitants. It is excellent for the breeding of horses.' And finally, 'The Boiotians have a saying about their national faults to the effect that greed lives in Oropus, envy in Tanagra, quarrelsomeness in Thespiae, insolence in Thebes, covetousness in Coronea, braggery in Plataea, fever in Onchestus and stupidity in Haliartus. These are the faults that have drained down into Boiotia as into a sink from the rest of Greece.'[25]

This cheerfully abusive piece of reportage is of course heightened for satirical effect, a rhetorical entertainment for the literati, rather than an exercise in analysis. It contrasts sharply with Pausanias' studious and plodding manner, his patient enquiry and reluctance to judge. Indeed, the Greeks of Pausanias' own age hardly exist as people of flesh and blood in his pages. In a superbly eloquent passage Frazer writes:

Greece might almost have been a wilderness and its cities uninhabited or peopled only at rare intervals by a motley throng who suddenly appeared as by magic, moved through the streets in gay procession with flaring torches and waving censers, dyed the marble pavements of the temples with the blood of victims, filled the air with the smoke and savour of their burning flesh, and then melted away as mysteriously as they had come, leaving the deserted streets and temples to echo only to the footstep of some solitary traveller who explored with awe and wonder the monuments of a vanished race . . . Yet, as his work proceeded, Pausanias seems to have wakened up now and then to a dim consciousness that men and women were still living and toiling around him, that fields were still ploughed and harvests reaped, that vine and the olive still yielded their fruit, though Theseus and Agamemnon, Cimon and Pericles, Philip and Alexander were no more.[26]

PAUSANIAS THE MAN

About Pausanias' own life and personality, his *Guide* is only intermittently informative. His unwontedly lyrical references to the area around Mount Sipylus in Lydia, one of the territories of Asia Minor (Ephesus and Smyrna – now Izmir – are not far away) have led to the belief that he came from there, perhaps from the city called Magnesia. 'He had seen', writes Frazer,

> the white eagles wheeling above the lonely tarn of Tantalus in the heart of the hills; he had beheld the stately tomb of the same hero on Mount Sipylus, the ruined city at the bottom of the clear lake, the rock-hewn throne of Pelops crowning the dizzy peak that overhangs the cañon, and the dripping rock which popular fancy took for the bereaved Niobe weeping for her children. He speaks of the clouds of locusts which he had thrice seen vanish from Mount Sipylus, of the wild dance of the peasantry, and of the shrine of Mother Plastene, whose rude image, carved out of native rock, may still be seen in its niche at the foot of the mountain.[27]

All this evidently tugged at his heartstrings, even though we also learn that he was a well-travelled man of the world, having visited not only the rest of Asia Minor, but also Syria, Palestine, Egypt, Byzantium, Rhodes, Rome and other parts of Italy. These trips, no doubt undertaken in the interests of learning rather than for pleasure, would have required a great deal of money, so it seems that he came from what Frazer calls the 'municipal aristocracy'. It is perhaps an exaggeration to say that he did the Grand Tour of his day, but certainly his visits to the main cultural centres of the Mediterranean littoral presage similar types of journey by Renaissance scholars doing the rounds of Western European seats of learning.

Pausanias' attitude to landscape and topography may provide other clues to the sort of man he was. In a rather moving passage, his translator, Peter Levi, evokes a person quite different from the dry pedant on view in the passages of historical digression and the sometimes wearisome genealogies: 'He was perhaps, like his greatest editor, Sir James Frazer (whose entire lifework had its roots in

Pausanias), in that all his scholarship and topography and encyclopedic curiosity were a burden undertaken in the attempt to satisfy a deeper anxiety which had been apprehended in religous terms. The collapse of ancient religion or some deeper collapse was the unspoken object of his studies.'[28] What might have triggered such a collapse during the twenty mid- to late century years when Pausanias was active? We can only speculate, but it is known that Greece was ravaged at that time by a barbaric tribe referred to as Costobocci, who sacked the site of the Eleusinian mysteries in 170–171, a sacrilege that would have horrified Pausanias. Then again, during the reign of Marcus Aurelius, a devastating 'plague' (smallpox?) spread through the Greek and Roman world after 165, causing so much damage that the nineteenth-century historian Barthold Georg Niebuhr considered that the ancient world never really recovered from the chaos it left in its wake.[29]

Perhaps it is just coincidence, but it is nevertheless intriguing that Levi thinks Pausanias may himself have been a doctor of medicine, because of the special interest he shows in the shrines of Asclepius (Latin: Aesculapius), the god of healing. Such speculation helps to build a plausible human portrait of Pausanias out of the few dry bones we have, as does Levi's engaging aside describing the crusty scholar in his advanced years: 'when he was old he became addicted to birdwatching and complained about steep hills and bad roads'.[30]

About his attitude to landscape and topography opinions differ sharply. Domenico Musti, in disputing the claim made by Frazer and others that Pausanias was largely indifferent to natural beauty, ends up by implicitly supporting the basis of their point of view when he writes:

> One must recognise that the image of the landscape is, as it were, filtered into the consciousness of the reader in antiquity, but also into that of the alert modern reader, through the mythology that is written into that landscape, and which at the same time expresses it through the descriptions of cults that are bound up with the nature of the places themselves, and the narration of an anecdote or detail which has something of the extraordinary or miraculous about it.[31]

If this is right, what is the *pittoresque* element in Pausanias identified by the French eighteenth-century scholar quoted above? The word surely better reflects the attitudes of the writer and his age than it does the actual content of Pausanias. A clue to this paradox is provided by the attractive *veduta*-like illustrations that accompanied Beaugency's translation. Delightful as they are, they evoke idyllic scenes reflected through the idealising prism of eighteenth-century scholarship, and to some extent anticipate both the normative heroisation of classical Greek culture by Winckelmann and the pre-Romantic taste for the picturesque. For example, the illustration of the Hippodrome at Olympia features a well-attended chariot race in full swing, with elegant staffage figures in the foreground. There is a magnificent wild background of rolling mountainous terrain, noble buildings nestling in valleys and finally (to the

north-west) bald and rocky cliffs dropping into a fishing boat-bobbing sea.[32] Now
it is true that Pausanias devotes a good deal of space to the Hippodrome, but he
is principally interested in the complicated starting mechanism for the races and
follows his account of that with a long and characteristic digression on the origin
of a ghost that scares the wits out of the horses at a point halfway round the
course. His remarks ('the horses . . . suffer extreme panic from no visible cause,
the panic puts them into confusion, the chariots are smashed up and the drivers
injured')[33] stand in rather stark contrast to the stately prancing on view in the
illustration; but leaving that to one side, he shows no interest in the natural
setting, which must have been as impressive to the human perception then as it
still is today. That in itself did not make it worthy of comment, of course. The
Pausanian preoccupation was with human activities and those of their decidedly
anthropomorphic gods.

PAUSANIAS' RELIABILITY

Any consideration of Pausanias' actual reliability as a guide must start from the
premise of what he was trying to achieve for his readers, which itself determines
his selection of topics and the space he devotes to each in his narrative. It has
already been said that he was an 'archaist', primarily interested in the Archaic
and Classical periods of Greece, and that he was especially concerned with Greek
religious beliefs in all their aspects and manifestations. This concern implies his
larger purpose, that of restoring the Greeks' pride in their cultural heritage and
reminding them of what made them 'Greek'. Susan Alcock has written: 'Control
of social memory bears directly upon issues of hierarchy and authority, and not
surprisingly it is thus articulated and enforced in countless ways: not least by the
writing of histories and guidebooks.'[34] Nevertheless, in the last resort, a
guidebook, however entertaining or full of out of the way lore, will stand or fall
on the accuracy of its factual detail, whether or not this has been selectively
adduced. Those of us who write guidebooks hardly need reminding that the
letters of complaint we receive seldom comment on the sweep of the book as a
whole, but direct a sort of angry self-righteousness at what the writer regards
(sometimes mistakenly) as a factual error. On the other hand, it is a fact that
'facts' themselves exist on several levels. On the most fundamental level – the
actual existence of individual buildings, monuments and their locations –
Pausanias (or rather archaeology) has repeatedly confounded his critics. On
historical figures and events, as verified by modern scholarship, he also performs
well, evidently aided by his ability to use his sources discriminatingly.

This ability was also applied in his field research, where his informants were
often the priests at the sanctuary or local guides. Some of the latter were
distinguished, or at any rate knowledgeable, but many must have been like those
satirised by Pausanias' near-contemporary, Plutarch, in a sophistic dialogue[35]
about the Pythian oracle at Delphi: unsuspecting visitors were seized upon by
these, the original culture vultures, and subjected to an unending and

undiscriminating spiel that gushed from them like a broken main, rather like a football commentary today. It was impossible to stop them, and questions (to which they would anyway not have known the answers) were simply ignored. Plutarch would certainly have experienced the full awfulness of their unrepentant misinformation, since he was himself a priest at Delphi for thirty years. As for Pausanias, not untypical is his remark, evidently made more in sorrow than in anger, that the Argive guides 'are aware that not all the stories they tell are true, yet they stick to them, for it is not easy to persuade the vulgar to change their opinions'.[36] Whereby it is characteristic that he seems to blame the credulity of the audience as much as the vulgarity of the guides, who are only supplying their listeners with the sort of stuff they want to hear.

Other observations by him echo Herodotus, who, like Pausanias, was a scholar from Asia Minor. Herodotus had also been an early exponent of autopsy as a basis for research, although unfortunately, and in notable contrast to Pausanias, he failed to make it clear where his autopsy ended and his fantasising began. Nevertheless, our author sometimes speaks with the voice of Herodotus, for example, when he points out the impossible chronology of the local tradition at Olympia in respect of the famous runner Oibotas, and concludes crisply: 'I am bound to tell the stories that are told by the Greeks, but I am not bound to believe them all.'[37] Seventeen centuries later, Norman Douglas was still having the same difficulty in extracting reliable information from an elderly and recklessly untruthful custodian as he perambulated Calabria: 'And that Sir, is the King's tower.' 'But you said just now, it was the Queen's tower!' 'Just so Sir, the Queen, she built it . . .'.[38]

It has been said that truth is anonymous and error is personal. Pausanias, like all guidebook writers, is by no means infallible, but his errors or muddles have proved to be remarkably few in a text stretching to around 1,000 pages in the two-volume Penguin edition. Why then has he attracted such opprobrium in certain quarters, and more specifically, been denounced as a plagiarist who wrote up an earlier periegetic work and passed it off as his own, as well as being called a liar (*omnium Graeculorum mendacissimus*,[39] in the words of one critic) who never visited most of the places he claims to have visited? Alone the language in which the attacks on him were couched – at once mincing and violent – says more about his attackers' state of mind than they say about Pausanias' integrity.

For example, in accusing Pausanias of lifting from an earlier writer (Polemon of Ilium, *fl. c.* 190 BC), one of the most hostile witnesses writes bizarrely that Pausanias concealed his theft under 'a little Rococo cloak of sophistical ingenuousness and childish imitations of Herodotus'.[40] J.G. Frazer subsequently took the trouble to compare systematically each of the passages complained of in order to demonstrate that the charge had no substance. In another instance, the same accuser, evidently in some desperation, developed a confused argument[41] that Pausanias had described the location of a certain Spring of Freedom correctly, but only by mistake. Frazer was devastating in his examination of this effort: 'It would thus appear, on [the author's] own showing, that the book from which Pausanias copied made a mistake, and that Pausanias, in copying it, made

another mistake, which fortunately cancelled out the original error of his
authority, with the net result that he finally blundered into placing the water
correctly . . . It requires less credulity to suppose that Pausanias saw the water
himself.'[42]

To understand the background to these charges it is necessary to understand
the scholar with whom they originated and his particular animus against the
unfortunate *periegete*, who was in reality no more than a lightning conductor for
his attacker's wounded vanity. For what follows I am heavily indebted to a leading
Pausanias scholar, Christian Habicht, whose restrained but feline account[43] of how
a pompous Prussian professor painted himself into a corner on the issue entirely
makes up for the fact that, in the whole of Pausanias' *Guide to Greece*, there are no
jokes whatsoever. The story begins with a trip round the Peloponnese in the
spring of 1873 led by an aristocratic and very promising young academic (he was
25) whose name (Emmo Friedrich Richard Ulrich von Wilamowitz-Moellendorff)
was as weighty as his scholarship. Von Wilamowitz had agreed to conduct a party
of German nobility on part of its Grecian tour, and having mugged up his
Pausanias, he set off with them to follow the *periegete*'s route, as he took it to be,
between Olympia and Heraea in Arcadia. Unfortunately, nothing seemed to fit
the young man's explanations, which were therefore delivered with ever
decreasing confidence, and one can well imagine his embarrassment and the
accompanying aristocrats' gentle irony at his expense. Wilamowitz even says in his
diary that his hostility to Pausanias dates from this fiasco, despite the fact the
mistake was entirely his and not that of Pausanias. (Later he realised – as others
had known for some time – that Pausanias describes[44] this route as if travelling to
Olympia from the south and that the Pausanian description, despite its sporadic
vagueness, does in fact tally.)

An error in such a matter is understandable and all would have been well if
Wilamowitz had simply chalked the Peloponnesian debacle up to experience.
Unfortunately, however, Pausanias seems to have become tangled up in his mind
with the fortunes of his *bête noire*, the businessman and amateur archaeologist
Heinrich Schliemann. From the point of view of the professional academics, this
son of an impoverished pastor had committed various unforgiveable sins, chief of
which was being right when the academics were wrong and discovering Troy.
Then, in 1876, he uncovered the graves of Atreus and Agamemnon, and did so
by a more careful reading of Pausanias than the overbearing armchair scholars of
Germany had managed. He realised, from Pausanias' positioning of the famous
Lion's Gate 'in the wall', that the guidebook's references to the graves 'within the
walls' could only mean that they were within the walls of the *acropolis*, not the
outer walls of the city, as was commonly supposed.[45] In any case the reference was
regarded by all the leading scholars of the day as purely mythical, so Pausanias,
from beyond the grave, had overturned the applecart on two counts: first he had
once again been caught out telling the truth; and secondly he had assisted the
detested Schliemann to further fame and greater humiliation of academe. This
was too much. As readers of the correspondence columns of academic journals
will know, few scholars on the losing end of a controversy have ever understood

or acted on the maxim 'if you're already in a hole, stop digging', which might be deemed particularly apposite in this case. Accordingly, Wilamowitz's attacks bred an entire school of anti-Pausanias scholarship, somewhat akin to that body of learning devoted to proving that Shakespeare (a) never existed, or (b) (fall-back position) if he did exist, he was someone else, and (c) (anyway) the whole of anteriority, at home and abroad, is grotesquely mistaken in thinking that he is anything but an illiterate scribbler/drunken plagiarist – and so forth.[46]

This controversy dragged on through the second half of the nineteenth century, but by 1890 it was clear that Pausanias' supporters had won the day. In that year, a learned reviewer in the *Atlantic Monthly*, discussing a new translation of part of Pausanias' guide, states unequivocally: 'It is well known that the Germans who excavated Olympia were guided, almost step by step, by Pausanias' detailed accounts of temples and monuments standing in his time. Whoever shall have the glory of laying bare what may yet remain of the Delphic sanctuary will be almost equally dependent upon every word of the much-abused Periegete.'[47]

PAUSANIAS' ATTITUDE TO THE GREEKS AND ROMANS

Pausanias' ambivalent attitude to the Greeks of his day is seen most clearly in his accommodation with the Roman hegemony. As already observed, his life would seem to have overlapped with the reigns of three decidedly philhellene emperors, Hadrian, Antoninus Pius and Marcus Aurelius (who wrote his famous *Meditations* in Greek). The implication of some of the commentary on Pausanias is that he was a quietist in matters political, a trimmer even; on the other hand, others have tried to make him an intellectual radical, strongly opposed to Roman rule. Both these extreme viewpoints seem to me to mistake the nature of his work and also to misunderstand or misrepresent the circumstances in which he lived. Although all victorious nations absorb elements of the cultures of the populations they have subdued, the later Roman Empire is unique in seeing itself as the heir and beneficiary of a culture it openly proclaimed as a model for its own. Perhaps the most famous quotation illustrating this attitude, which has wittily been described as one of 'reverse cultural imperialism',[48] comes from one of the letters of Pliny the Younger (*c.* AD 61–*c.* 112), who died perhaps a decade or so before Pausanias was born. Addressing a colleague setting off to take up the post of *corrector* (overseer) of the nominally free cities of Achaia, he admonishes him to

> remember that you are sent . . . to the pure and genuine Greece, where civilisation and literature, and agriculture too are believed to have originated . . . Pay regard to their antiquity, their heroic deeds, and the legends of their past. Do not detract from anyone's dignity, independence or even pride, but always bear in mind that this is the land which provided us with justice and gave us laws, not after conquering us but at our request; that it is Athens you go to and Sparta you rule.[49]

Even blunter is the aphorism taken from an epistle of the poet Horace (65–8 BC) addressed to the first Roman Emperor, Augustus, which begins: '*Graecia capta ferum victorem cepit* . . .' ('Fierce Rome had been captured by captive Greece . . .').[50]

Shortly after Pliny was born, the philhellenic but vicious Emperor Nero spent fifteen months in Greece in AD 66 participating in panhellenic and civic festivals. The four great festivals at Olympia, Delphi, Nemea and the Isthmus were telescoped into a single year, so that Nero could compete in the dancing and singing, and of course carry off most of the prizes. 'The Greeks are the only people who understand how to be an audience,' remarked the gratified genius at the end of it all. He was so pleased that he 'liberated' Greece from Roman administration and taxation in AD 67, as well as ordering work to begin on a Corinth canal. These bombastic gestures, however, had more to do with Nero's vanity than with any real change in the situation of the Greeks; at any rate Pausanias is clear-eyed about it, offering the barbed comment: 'When I consider this action of Nero, I think that Plato was telling the purest truth when he said that the greatest and most daring crimes are not the product of ordinary men, but of a noble spirit corrupted by a perverted education.'[51] It grieved Pausanias that Nero took the opportunity to loot no less than 500 art works from Delphi, an early example of the *Kunstraub* that British and other European aristocrats were later to turn into a favourite pastime. In the same passage, Pausanias continues with the observation that the 'Greeks were not to profit from that gift [of Nero]: Vespasian succeeded [him] and civil war broke out in Greece, and Vespasian reimposed taxes and obedience to a governor, saying that the Greeks had forgotten how to be free.'[52]

Remarks of this kind well illustrate Pausanias' greatest strengths as a writer and commentator: he has a consistent standard of judgement for persons and events, namely what preserved or destroyed his idealised vision of Greek identity. It follows that he can be as critical of the Greeks as he is of the Romans, where their actions (for instance, in the Peloponnesian War) contributed to the destruction of the ideal. By the same token the Romans, who are generally not represented as the 'other' in the sense of 'barbarians' (for example, the Persians), are never condemned *qua* Romans (the notion of collective guilt is refreshingly absent), but only in terms of the actions of specific individuals. Violation of the sanctuaries and the looting of statues were the most heinous crimes in the eyes of Pausanias, since such actions struck at the heart of an identity vested in Greek religious observance and hero-worship.

It is this impiety that he highlights in his treatment of the notorious sack of Corinth by the Roman general Mummius in 146 BC, which heralded the subjection and humiliation of Greece. Symbolically at least, this subjection only began to be reversed with Corinth's refoundation by Caesar just before his assassination in 44 BC.[53] Even more revealing is Pausanias' scrupulously laconic treatment of the brutality of Sulla towards the Athenians in 86 BC: 'Sulla came back into Attica, imprisoned the Athenian opposition in the Kerameikos, and had one man in every ten chosen by lot for the death penalty.' He adds the intriguing comment: 'Sulla's behaviour to most of the Athenians was more savage than you might credit in a Roman, but I hardly believe this brought him to his bad end: surely it was the anger of Zeus of Suppliants because he murdered Ariston in [the] sanctuary in the temple of Athene.'[54] Physical brutality is more or less an inevitable accompaniment of war, he seems to imply, but the gods themselves will punish the impiety that strikes at the very heart of Greek self-perception as expressed through their cults.

Pausanias lived at a time when a revival of Greek consciousness, generally subsumed under the heading of the Second Sophistic, was being promoted by Greek intellectuals, who took their cue from the enthusiastic philhellenism of the Emperor Hadrian. This Greek Renaissance was not an entirely unmixed blessing – it actually encouraged the removal of works of art and manuscripts from Greece by Romans, a form of conspicuous consumption indulged in by *arriviste* officials. Its emphasis on declamation and revival of the Attic dialect inevitably also encouraged affectation and charlatanism disagreeably reminiscent of the excesses of postmodernism.[55] Except in so far as the Sophist technique of *ekphrasis*, or set-piece descriptions of imagined scenes, may have had a marginal impact on his work, Pausanias appears to be little influenced by the literary mores of the Second Sophistic; on the other hand, it is clear that he is a child of his time in terms of its historicising idealisation of the Greek past. That idealisation was given concrete form in Hadrian's foundation of a loyalist organisation of eastern cities in 131/2, known as the Attic Panhellenion, whose Panhellenia festival is attested up to the 250s AD. After Hadrian's death, the Panhellenion became 'a cultic organisation . . . centred on the worship of its deified founder, "Hadrian Panhellenicus"',[56] which evidently contributed to economic and cultural revival in Greece, though how directly and to what extent is not clear. Pausanias, who is generally not interested in contemporary monuments, mentions several to Hadrian and is notably sympathetic to an emperor who, like him, had been initiated into the Eleusinian mysteries, had indulged in the sort of 'heritage' architecture that would have pleased the current heir to the British throne, and had initiated public works of great benefit.

PAUSANIAS' AUDIENCE

The enthusiasms of Hadrian brings us back to a fundamental issue regarding Pausanias the guidebook writer, namely his intended readers. Hadrian has been described as a sort of super-tourist, restlessly traversing his realms in search of knowledge, aesthetic gratification, numinous experience and of course souvenirs. Pausanias himself, it has been observed, 'should be viewed as part of an upsurge of visitors from overseas (Asia especially) drawn to Greece in the wake of Hadrianic initiatives and providing [him] with his envisaged readership'.[57] Heritage architecture and the 'invention of tradition' were part and parcel of the tourist boom in the long period of peace that Greece enjoyed in the second century. The tourists were wealthy, aristocratic and learned, and their tours took in artworks, monuments, and a few famous natural phenomena, as well as affording opportunities for overseas study, thermal or other cures and attendance at oracles and sanctuaries. Favourite destinations were Athens and Sparta in Greece, and Memphis, the Fayûm, Thebes and the Valley of the Kings in Egypt (the colossi of Memnon and other pharaonic monuments are encrusted with tourists' graffiti from this and earlier periods).

Just as there is today, a certain mismatch is apparent between the tourist's reductive essentialism and the native's experience of a living complexity; as today also, marketing of one's own country required a certain complicity in this essentialism, if the tourists were to come and money was to be made. One result of the tourist boom was that ancient '*ephebic*' spectacles[58] (endurance contests for youths) were revived at Sparta, together with festivals such the Hyacinthia and Gymnopaedia, which were 'modernised' with sexy elements to draw the spectators (the participation of girls in sports such as wrestling, for example). Guidebooks and analogous literature would inevitably have been part of the overall marketing effort, including even some works that were not very flattering. A British prime minister once opined that 'all publicity is good publicity', which proved to be spectacularly untrue as far as his government was concerned; but perhaps it was true, within certain limits, of a country that has been described as one 'learning how to be a museum', and which was greatly admired for what she once had been,[59] as much by cultivated Romans as by her own cultivated inhabitants.

Pausanias' work, however much it may have been stimulated by the contemporary climate of nostalgia and perhaps even the *euergetism* (ostentatious patriotic and civic philanthropy) of his contemporary Herodes Atticus (some of whose munificent benefactions he mentions),[60] is in some respects a guide to that museum. But it is also an attempt to 'connect the past to the present',[61] in a meaningful and therapeutic way. The great Hungarian patriot and moderniser Count Istvàn Széchenyi (1791–1860), famously exclaimed at the end of his book *On Credit*, 'Many people think: "Hungary once was"'; I want to believe "she will be!"' Pausanias' memorial to Greece as she 'once was' is also a statement about her aspirations to a present, and a future, fully worthy of her past. His interests may seem anachronistic, but he seems to have had a profound understanding of the idea that a people that has forgotten its history is like a people without a history, naked before the world.

THE *PERIEGESIS* AS PILGRIMAGE, THE *PERIEGETE* AS PILGRIM

The *Periegete*'s preoccupation with history suggests the context in which his choice of topics, his method of description and his mixture of analysis seem most meaningful. There is much in Pausanias that we have come to expect from a guidebook, including specific route directions, notes on history and topography and descriptions of artworks. His taste in the latter probably reflects that of the Second Sophistic; although he does make the occasional aesthetic judgement, it is seldom more than a bald statement of an object's high quality: what interests him is its iconic value, as well as its material substance and size.

As noted above, it is from Pausanias that we derive our knowledge about the monumental wall paintings by Polygnotus at the Cnidian Hall of Delphi, which featured *The Fall of Troy* and *Odysseus Visiting Hades*. His oft-remarked-upon preference for the 'Old Masters' is demonstrated by the fact that he treats of no individual artists later than the sculptor Damophon, active in the early second century BC. Interestingly, the latter seems to have been ignored by other connoisseurs, but it is not difficult to see his appeal for Pausanias, since he was an 'eclectic neoclassicist who attempted to update the style of Phidias while paying close attention to the needs of the devotees of the cult [of Zeus at Olympia]'.[62] And for Pausanias, Phidias (active *c.* 465–425 BC) was the greatest sculptor of all, the most monumental, the most beautiful, the most eloquent protagonist of Greek cultural values; a typically laconic, yet memorable, aside[63] in his description of the Athenian acropolis tells us that the spear-tip and and helmet-crest of Phidias' colossal (40ft high) bronze statue of the seated Athena Promachos ('Athena Who Fights in the Foremost Ranks') were visible to sailors rounding the point of Attica at Cape Sunium (Sounion) 30 miles away. She dominated the landscape as Athens had once dominated her allies.

And the glint from this colossus (we may reasonably imagine) would have marked the beginning of Pausanias' own pilgrimage to the heart of Greekness, for his first book starts abruptly with his ship rounding Cape Sounion, no doubt with thoughts of Theseus and his tragic homecoming already in his mind.[64] The opening passages of his account are typical of the man. There is no nonsense about picturesque cliffs or wine-dark seas; instead we are plunged headlong into his matter in a manner that suggests that this book, and indeed the entire work (which lacks a prologue), might just as well be prefaced with the words 'As I was saying . . .':

> Cape Sounion is part of the territory of Attica projecting from the mainland of Greece and facing the Aegean and the Cyclades. Sail round the cape and you come to a harbour; on the point of the cape is a temple to Athene of Sounion. Sailing further on you will make Lavrion where the Athenians once had silver mines, and quite a small deserted island called after Patroklos, who built a camp on it and constructed a wall. He was admiral of the Egyptian galleys that Ptolemy sent to help the Athenians at the time when Antigonos at the head of an invading army was devastating the land and pressing in with his fleet from the sea.[65]

Of course the modern reader needs a commentary to explain the references that Pausanias obviously assumes were common ground between him and his intended audience. But the nature of the intellectual journey is immediately established, with its topographical precision and historical detail; and by chapter 3, only 15 lines below, we have already arrived at the first sanctuaries at Piraeus, Athene and Zeus, then Aphrodite, with their images and paintings, the peculiarities of their cults and histories.

It is this intellectual pilgrimage[66] that marks Pausanias out most clearly as the father of the modern guidebook. His preoccupation with the history and practices of the shrines (some, admittedly, too secret to be written down),[67] and with the images that support them, looks forward to the age of Christian and Jewish pilgrimage (the latter already flourishing in his lifetime), which generated a discrete literature of the guidebook. The devotional and aesthetic commentaries of the two, pagan and non-pagan, are of course sharply distinguished, since Greek piety ('*eusebeia*' – significantly there was no word for religion as such) was quite different from the monotheistic and dogmatic mentality of Jews and Christians; but the cathartic and redemptive elements of the journey are already in place, reinforced in the case of Pausanias by the genealogies and historical digressions that establish the notion of a Greek identity, legitimise it even in defeat, and above all (*pace* Gellner) distinguish it from the non-Greek. Pausanias, says Lacarrière in a striking phrase, 'was the discoverer, indeed the creator (in the ancient sense) of his fatherland'.[68]

But all later guidebooks, to a greater or lesser extent, respond similarly to needs that are spiritual, cultural and aesthetic, as well as practical. Naturally every age understood these needs in its own way, whether they were those of the simple Christian on the road to Santiago, the Renaissance scholar touching the bases of learning, the patriotic traveller of the Enlightenment improving his expertise for the advancement of his country, or the nineteenth-century tourist, Baedeker in hand, observing the bourgeois cultural ritual of truth–beauty. 'In effect,' writes John Elsner, 'travel-writing is always an act of cultural appropriation',[69] although in the case of Pausanias the writer, as a Greek, is reappropriating what is already his, a Greek identity in danger of being lost, perhaps through trivialisation by the very Sophists who claim to promote it, as much as through foreign domination. Pausanias is the Recording Angel of the Greeks, and all his material – the sanctuaries with their temples and cults, the battlefields, the thriving or decaying cities – is selected for the record. But over the succeeding centuries, shrines, relics and monuments were to move from the sphere of the primarily devotional into that of the primarily aesthetic, until we arrive at a situation today where cathedrals seem to be museums for tourists (some of them complete with entrance charges) and museums are secular sanctuaries of art where the cultural pieties are assiduously observed. Still, it is the journey not the arrival that matters, or rather, as the poet says, the end of all our exploring (Pausanias or Baedeker in hand) is 'to arrive where we started / And know the place for the first time.'[70]

In my Grecian rambles, says Lacarrière, 'Pausanias was my ever-present friend and guide, patiently, passionately and devotedly guiding my steps through Greece, into the land of the living shadows.'[71]

PART II

Late Antiquity and the Middle Ages:
The Pilgrims' Guides

CHAPTER 3

The Pilgrim's Way:
Guides for Pilgrims to the Holy Land

And going from there into Golgotha there is a great court where the Lord
was crucified. There is a silver screen round this Mount, where the Cross of
the Lord has been displayed, adorned with gold and gems and a dome
above . . . And the plate is there on which was carried the head of St John.
There is the horn with which David was anointed. There Adam was formed.
There the Lord was crucified.
(An early amalgamation of scriptural sites in the Jerusalem Breviarius, c. *AD 550)*

The treatment of the holy places is infused with an astringent spirituality
which makes it difficult for readers to remain on the surface of sites
associated with Jesus, both in Galilee and in Jerusalem. They are gently but
firmly helped to give these places meaning in terms of their own lives by
profound, pointed questions, key words designed to focus reflection, and
suggestions for prayer. It would be hard to imagine a more effective antidote
to the mawkish sentimentality that claims to evoke, but only succeeds in
masking, the reality of Jesus' struggle.
(Jerome Murphy-O'Connor introducing the Living Stones Pilgrimage Guide, *1999)*

THE DEVELOPMENT OF HOLY LAND PILGRIMAGE

Until the middle of the second century, when Bishop Melito of Sardis came to
inspect 'the places of [Christ's] preaching and acts' (AD 160),[1] we seldom hear of
pilgrims writing up their tours of the Holy Land, although this certainly does not

mean that there were none.[2] The first well-documented pilgrimage boom, however, was stimulated directly and indirectly by the Emperor Constantine, who furthered Christianity in the Roman Empire by promulgating official tolerance with the Edict of Milan in 313. A further impetus was to be provided by retrospective claims concerning his mother's 'discovery' of the True Cross on her visit to Palestine. Although Jerusalem had been sacred to Christians before Constantine, his endowments helped to intensify the focus on what became Christianity's principal *lieux de mémoire*, while the legacy of his mother's visit in AD 326 was even more powerful; so much so, that a tradition grew up that attributed the founding of almost all the churches in the Holy Land to 'St Helena'. (In fact she founded just three basilicas, although she also saw to it that the existing pagan shrines were removed from Golgotha and the Holy Sepulchre.)

During Constantine's reign, the biblical lands also enjoyed the advocacy of an industrious and eminent protagonist in Eusebius (*c.* 260–339), Bishop of Caesarea. He was a strong influence on the emperor and the illustrious author of the first history of Christianity from the apostolic age up to his own day. However, Eusebius was also a follower of Origen (*c.* 185–*c.* 254), the controversial theologian and biblical exegist, and the latter's influence may be seen in Eusebius' promotion of Jerusalem as the navel (*omphalos*) of the world, a distinction that antiquity had awarded to Delphi.[3] This view found little favour with Constantine, who had determined to make Constantinople the centre and focus of a great Christian empire.[4] But scriptural authority and local tradition were indeed powerful counterweights to imperial ambition: had not the Prophet Isaiah foretold that, on judgement day, all the saved peoples of the earth would stream towards Jerusalem?[5] In the seventh century, Arculf, a bishop from Gaul, reminds the readers of his guide that Jerusalem is called the 'Navel of the Earth'. As late as the twelfth century, the itinerary of an Icelandic pilgrim was still claiming that Jerusalem was 'the centre of the world, where the light of the sun falls vertically to earth at the summer solstice';[6] and at this time, too, the Anglo-Saxon Saewulf was still pointing out the so-called *compas* within the walls surrounding the Holy Sepulchre, where Christ himself had located the centre of the world[7] (or, according to others, his body had marked the same when Nicodemus took it down from the cross).[8]

Spiritually and symbolically all roads no longer led to Rome (nor yet to Byzantium), but increasingly to Jerusalem. Furthermore, Origen had conveniently fixed the location of Adam's grave on Golgotha, a tradition reinforced by St Jerome and later a commonplace of guidebooks and itineraries. These gradually located other symbolic events on or around the same site, now encompassed within the church of the Holy Sepulchre (for example, the creation of Adam, Abraham's sacrifice of Isaac and the murder of Zachariah, the father of John the Baptist). Today's guides show the church as embracing the last five Stations of the Cross, as well as numerous chapels relating to people and events connected with Christ's Passion. A potentially confusing factor for the guidebook writers is that in some cases locations are a matter of dispute between the different confessions (the Armenians, for instance, revere the place where Jesus's mother, her sister and Mary Magdalene stood by the cross at a spot that is unique to them).

In view of the steadily increasing count of places said to have biblical associations, it is not surprising that 'biblical tourism' to the Holy Land flourished during the three centuries of Byzantine rule (330–614). From this period, a fair number of pilgrims' reports, itineraries and topographies have come down to us. In many cases such works are of mixed genre, combining personal report, material copied from other sources, a road book and devotional topography. While perhaps only a few can be described as purely guidebooks, many include elements of a guide and would appear to have been used as such.[9] The pilgrim traffic to which they catered continued until 614, when the Persians overran Palestine and captured Jerusalem. They removed most of the ecclesiastical treasures, massacred many of the inhabitants and destroyed some of the churches. During the siege there appears also to have been a massacre of Jews by Christians, the former being suspected of favouring the Persians after suffering years of Byzantine repression. When the Persians entered the city, the surviving Jews (according to the account of one Strategius) began burning Christian churches in revenge. However, in an extraordinary reversal of fortune, the Persian King Chosroes, when these events were reported to him, ordered his general Razmiz to have the city rebuilt and the Jews expelled. The overall damage appears to have been less than the outraged reports suggest – at any rate Abbot Modestus, left in charge of the city by the Persians, was soon writing to an Armenian colleague claiming that 'all the Jerusalem churches' had been restored. In fact some churches are never again mentioned by guides or itineraries after 614, and so must have fallen victim to either Persian or Jewish action.[10]

In the same letter to the Catholikos of the Armenian Church, Modestus welcomes the fact that the annual Armenian pilgrimage had taken place as usual. For these Armenians a contemporary guide, *The Churches Built in Holy Jerusalem, their Number and Position*, has survived written in their language (though it is possibly a translation from a Greek original). The subjects dealt with, as outlined in the title, may be seen as a very basic summary of the most important sights for a pilgrim of the mid-seventh century who needed to make a brief tour. The guide includes Christ's tomb, the Calvary and Adam's tomb, the church of Sion, the palace of Pontius Pilate, the prison in which Christ was held (which thereafter drops from view until the late eleventh century); then leaps erratically to the tomb of the Virgin at Gethsemane, the church of the Ascension on the Mount of Olives; then another leap brings us to Bethlehem, the Nativity sights and the adjacent 'martyrium in which were kept the remains of the children murdered by Herod';[11] and finally, the guide ends abruptly at the River Jordan and the place of Christ's baptism.

Twenty-two years after the Persian victory, and following a brief Byzantine interlude, Muslims from Arabia (Saracens) conquered Palestine, Jerusalem being surrendered by the Patriarch Sophronius in 638. Under the Arab Umayyad and

Abbasid dynasties, pilgrimage was allowed to continue and both Christians and Jews were free to practise their religions provided they paid the poll tax. With the erection of the magnificent Dome of the Rock mosque between 687 and 691 over the supposed site of Muhammad's ascent to heaven,[12] Jerusalem became a centre of Muslim worship too: it was intended that the mosque surpass the surrounding Christian edifices. Muslim tolerance ended under the unstable Caliph al-Hākim (996–1021) of the Egyptian Fatimids, who ordered the demolition of the church of the Resurrection in 1009 and a general destruction of churches ten years later – this notwithstanding the fact that (or perhaps because?) his own mother was of the Christian faith.[13]

This abandonment of tolerance, continued under the Seljuk Turks from 1070, gave impetus to calls for crusades to 'reconquer' the Holy Land for Christendom. In 1099 the Crusaders took Jerusalem, lost it again to Saladin in 1187, but obtained access for Christians to the city by a treaty with Saladin in 1192. From then on, until the last Crusader enclaves were evacuated in 1291, periodic attempts were made either to control Jerusalem or to ensure free access to Christian sites; however, it appears that pilgrims were obliged to pay a toll to visit the Holy Sepulchre, perhaps from as early as 1217. Eventually agreements were reached whereby the Dominicans, later the Franciscans, were officially empowered to tend the sepulchre and the Bethlehem Nativity Church; the latter order also raised money in the West for the restoration of the holy places and in modern times have commissioned authoritative guidebooks to them.

MOTIVES FOR PILGRIMAGE

The numbers of pilgrims rose steadily throughout the Middle Ages. Many headed to the Holy Land after the First Crusade of 1099; to Rome from at least the mid-eighth century, when the *Liber Pontificalis* tells us that Pope Zacharias (741–52) was ordering distribution of provisions to 'the poor and the pilgrims who doss at St Peter's';[14] and not least to Santiago de Compostela, from the late ninth century onwards, as the cult of St James began to spread round Europe. The urge to embark on a pilgrimage is one that is older than Christianity, and perhaps as old as civilisation itself. It constitutes a fundamental element in the higher religions[15] whose sacred places (Benares for Hindus, Mecca for Muslims, Jerusalem for Christians) became its objects, but it existed for the pagans of antiquity as well. For example, Jas Elsner has presented Pausanias, the subject of the previous chapter, as a pilgrim visiting shrines in search of the ritualistic basis of Greek identity. Pausanias' *Periegesis*, he writes, 'is not only a journey through topography, but also a careful mytho-historical interpretation of the meaning of that topography'.[16] For Christians, pilgrimage was a convenient metaphor for life itself, for the journey through this vale of tears from birth to death; but it also represented a quest to endow that life with meaning and purpose, the route that is voluntarily[17] chosen in fulfilment of a vow or as an act of penance. The traveller Robyn Davidson has rather beautifully remarked that 'the metaphor of the journey is embedded in the very way in which we conceive of life – a movement from birth to death, from this world to the next, from ignorance to wisdom'.[18] The two came together in the ascetic ideal of Celtic monks from the sixth century, whereby many embarked on perpetual pilgrimage for the love of God, an ideal that accounts for the widespread influence of proselytising Irish monks in Western Europe. The perpetual pilgrim needed but a single compass for his soul, which his faith supplied; but the pilgrim who pursued specific devotional aims, or sought absolution, increasingly relied on cicerones and guidebooks for the holy places or the routes thereto.

The earliest such literature was written in Greek or in (often very shabby) Latin, the terminology of pilgrims and pilgrimage being taken from the latter language, where the word *peregrinus* simply meant a resident alien. *Peregrinatio* implied wandering (*peregrinari*) far from one's place of origin, so Abraham could be seen as the first ever pilgrim in his quest for the Promised Land.[19] The biblical notion that Christians were 'strangers and pilgrims on the earth' was a resonance that overlaid the word in the subsequent Christian culture; it achieved profound and beautiful expression in Dante, himself an exile for long periods. Classical authors also used the adverb *peregre*, adopted by medieval authors in phrases that described people setting out on pilgrimages (*peregre iter arripuit*). The original sense of 'foreigner' lingered on, and not all those referred to as *peregrini* were actually pilgrims as we understand the term now. On the other hand, those who set off on the First Crusade in 1095 were collectively referred to as *peregrini* by their contemporaries, non-military travellers and Crusaders alike. The emblem of these 'pilgrims' (with or without a sword in their hand) was the cross stitched to their clothing, and their designation thereafter became *crucesignatus*, that is, 'one signed with the cross' – whom we identify as 'Crusaders'. While this terminology applied to the Holy Land, pilgrims to other shrines acquired their own nomenclature: a *Jacobipeta* for a pilgrim going to Santiago de Compostela, *Thomipeta* for one going to Canterbury, a *Romipeta* for one going to Rome (though the last-named could also mean just any pilgrim).[20]

Originally there was a distinction, which is now largely lost, between two types of pilgrimage. One involved a spiritual attitude that implied perpetuity (as in the aphorism *Vita est peregrinatio*) and the other a journey, often institutionalised by the Church on a regular basis, to a particular shrine for a particular purpose (repentance, fulfilment of a vow, to effect a cure or even collect an indulgence).[21] In the latter case the pilgrim would certainly return home, while in the former case he would not; indeed many who embarked on such a journey intended to wander indefinitely, or alternatively to live and die (as St Jerome did) near the shrine of their choice. Specific pilgrimages could of course become completely secularised: one need only think of the cult of Shakespeare, attracting hordes of tourists to Stratford-on-Avon from the eighteenth century onwards, or indeed that of Lenin's remains in the Kremlin. It was above all this sort of pilgrimage that generated guidebook literature; the latter was a necessary adjunct to the experience of autopsy, whereby the pilgrim strove to create his own psychic and spiritual interface with the deceased saint, writer, political leader or whoever. For Christian pilgrims, relics played a vital role in such encounters, and guidebooks were usually assiduous in mentioning them.

Naturally, demand for relics outstripped supply, leading to fraud, theft and unseemly disputes which the Church authorities were largely powerless to prevent. 'What shall we say of the foreskin or umbilical cord which were severed from [Christ's] body at birth?' complained Pope Innocent III (1198–1216); 'Were they too resurrected?' Evidently so, if popular belief, pandered to by the unscrupulous or naive lower clergy, was to be believed. The foreskin on show in the Lateran basilica from the eleventh century was apparently a gift from Charles the Bald, who brought it from Aachen, to which it had originally been delivered by an angel as a gift to Charlemagne. It was viewed by generations of pilgrims until it disappeared in the Sack of Rome in 1527.[22] Such a valuable attraction as Christ's foreskin was unlikely to go unchallenged, and indeed there were subsequently no less than four rival foreskins on show at Charroux in Poitou, at Coulombs, at Boulogne and at Antwerp. Occasionally the same relics were claimed by more than one culture: the bones of a sea monster preserved at Joppa (Jaffa) in Palestine had been regarded by the Greeks as those of the dragon slain by Perseus in the course of his dramatic rescue of Andromeda. To the Jews this was fanciful nonsense: they knew that these were the bones of the whale that had swallowed Jonah![23] The multiplication of both saints and their relics surged at the turn of the fourth and fifth centuries, following on the most spectacular relic discovery of all, that of the True Cross. This was supposedly found by Helena, the mother of the Emperor Constantine, who had visited Palestine in 326; but like almost all relics, the circumstances of its discovery are decidedly dubious. Eusebius (d. 339), the greatest propagandist for the holy places, does not report on it, and the momentous find only surfaces a quarter of a century later in 351, when Bishop Kyrill of Jerusalem mentions it in a letter to Emperor Constantius II.[24]

The laws of supply and demand hardly left space for scientific or historical analysis of relics: churches needed them to legitimise their foundation, a requirement even made mandatory by the Council of Nicaea in 787.[25] Kings and emperors avidly collected relics, especially the Byzantine rulers, who stuffed the churches of Constantinople with them, much to the delight of the 'Crusaders' who plundered them in 1204. While princes bought or plundered, the humble pilgrim tried to filch some small piece of a relic as a wonder-working souvenir: as early as 385 the True Cross in Jerusalem had to be surrounded by armed deacons to prevent pilgrims biting splinters out of it. If thwarted in this, the pilgrim could fall back on the souvenir trade, staples of which were bottles of water from the River Jordan or the palm of Jericho that many pilgrims brought home. The latter souvenir has supplied us with the word 'palmer' and was a symbol of the victory of faith over sin. Pilgrims were routinely supplied with 'relics', consisting of objects that had been in contact with a shrine, which fulfilled a function somewhere between talisman and souvenir. The Russian Abbot Daniel, who visited Jerusalem in 1106, tells how the warden of the Holy Sepulchre actually broke off a piece of its sacred stone and gave it to him, 'adjuring [him] not to mention it to anyone in Jerusalem'.[26]

Topographical autopsy, the numinous or cathartic moment in the presence of relics, the collection of souvenirs and the witnessing of ritual, processions and the like: all these formed the experience of pilgrims and found their way into the literature of itineraries and early guidebooks. Largely lacking, on the other hand, is any attempt at aesthetic evaluation or judgement of buildings or landscapes. Such things exist for the first guidebook writers only as inspirations for the faithful or vital elements of historical autopsy. The deepest aesthetic judgement ever likely to be made about them in such literature was the very occasional use of the word 'beautiful'. This aesthetically unembellished focus on biblical locations meant that much of the literature was considered appropriate for what has been called *peregrinate in stabilitate*, the mental voyage of the monks and nuns who remained in their cloisters but experienced a pilgrimage through their libraries: 'Turning from St Jerome's list of locations in the Bible, to Adamnan's account of Arculf's actual journey to Jerusalem, to Beatus's "*Book of Fire*", which showed Apostles's journeys, poised between Creation and the Last Judgement, the would-be travellers could launch themselves in spirit at least, leaving the body behind.'[27]

Of course, not only the consumers, but the authors of such literature could be dealing vicariously in 'virtual experience': as late as 1358, the poet Petrarch composed an itinerary for pilgrims to the Holy Land, complete with route instructions, warnings of dangers along the way, descriptions of the sights and other practical information. Yet Petrarch had never undertaken this journey himself and compiled his work entirely from other travel reports. As he disarmingly explained in his Foreword, he himself preferred a quiet life, rather than travel, and in any case he suffered from seasickness. Why, therefore, should he embark on such a voyage with its attendant discomfort?[28]

On the other hand, the medieval guides already reflect the motif of a study tour, the intellectual and spiritual self-improvement of the guidebook consumer that became such a staple of the genre in the Renaissance. 'At the beginning,' writes Rolf Legler, 'all pilgrimages [were] really study tours[29] to the holy places of Palestine, for pilgrims to check what had been handed down at the source of truth itself and to strengthen themselves in their faith.'[30] However, the expansion of pilgrimage destinations in the Middle Ages eventually left pious Europeans spoiled for choice in regard to shrines, each offering its particularist solace, absolution or cure. And even if very many shrines were dedicated to the Virgin Mary, that did not release the individual penitent from the necessity to visit a specific one ('Our Lady of Chartres, Our Lady of Soissons . . .'), as his vision or confessor demanded. In one case, Gregory, Bishop of Tarsus, following his release from bondage to a Middle Eastern slave owner, toured all the principal shrines of Europe in an effort to discover which saint at which shrine had secured his freedom.[31] In the late Middle Ages, the wills of prosperous citizens of Lübeck provided money for pilgrimages to be made on behalf of the deceased. Some forty-two shrines are featured, with Jerusalem, Rome and Santiago unsurprisingly in demand; but there are even more requests for Aachen or Thann in Alsace (the mysteriously popular shrine of St Theobald), and Wilsnack

(Brandenburg), with its more than usually suspect Holy Blood. There are also curious minority choices, such as Beverley or Bridlington in England, or Trondheim in Norway.[32] Many of these places generated a basic tourist infrastructure, perhaps including local guides and modest descriptive literature. The major sites, like Delphi in the ancient world, had a veritable tourist industry.

With the passing of time, the motives for pilgrimage became as varied as the shrines available, not without provoking satirical comment from Chaucer, Erasmus and others. Norbert Ohler speaks of a seamless transition from pilgrimage to leisure journey, the latter being anything from a nobleman's jaunt to a spa visit, or even a sexual odyssey. There were still pilgrims anxious to strengthen their faith and scholars anxious to deepen their knowledge, the two often being combined. Yet even such journeys were increasingly rationalised or pragmatic ('one still travelled to Rome; yet the main interest had become the great remnants of antiquity – which did not exclude a visit to the graves of the apostles').[33] 'By the end of the fifteenth century', writes Jonathan Sumption, it is being claimed that 'the motives for pilgrimage were "curiosity to see new places, and experience new things, impatience of the servant with his master, of children with their parents, or wives with their husbands".'[34]

DANTE AND THE SEARCH FOR ILLUMINATION AND KNOWLEDGE

Pilgrimage as a broad and complex metaphor is seen at its most sophisticated in the greatest medieval poem, Dante's La Divina Commedia ('The Divine Comedy', begun about 1307), in which the poet (who is referred to as 'the pilgrim') has a vision of a journey through Hell, Purgatory and Paradise. His guides on the way are the poet Virgil (for Hell and Purgatory), the object of his pure passion, Beatrice Portinari, and finally St Bernard of Clairvaux (for Paradise). The whole elaborate and many-layered description of this 'pilgrimage' works also as an intellectual and spiritual guide to Dante's envisioned world.

A huge amount of commentary has been written on the Divine Comedy, but only its exploitation of figures and metaphors that deal with the acquisition of knowledge and the enrichment of the individual concern us here. Of particular interest is the treatment of Ulysses in the Inferno, where he appears burning constantly like a tongue of fire. The insatiable fire is a metaphor for the Greek traveller's restless desire to extend the bounds of knowledge, and more specifically for his hubris (according to Dante) in going beyond the Pillars of Hercules,[35] a presumption that is made analogous to Eve's breaking of the command not to eat of the tree of knowledge. Ulysses rouses his crew to sail westwards, saying that they should not deny themselves experience of the unpeopled world beyond the sun, and should recall that they are 'not formed to live like brutes, but to follow virtue and knowledge'.[36] They sail on until they can see Mount Purgatory in the distance, whereupon a huge storm breaks over them and the ship goes down.

As R.W.B. Lewis has pointed out, Dante has a good deal of fellow-feeling with Ulysses and his cammino errato, or erroneous path, for Dante too had abandoned home, wife and children (admittedly his exile had been an enforced one); and he too had gone in search of 'virtue and knowledge'.[37] In his guided tour of the Inferno, Purgatorio and Paradiso, the pilgrim Dante is offering, *inter alia*, a spiritual and ethical tour through the history of man from the ancients up to the medieval present. The extraordinary power of Dante's description reifies an entirely fictive world, so that his 'guidebook' to Hell, Purgatory and Paradise achieves the kind of virtual reality we might associate with the images of a modern computer. Its unreality, we feel, is surreal, more powerful than reality itself. But this tour is by no means designed to be purely sensational, a horror film exploiting atavistic fears; rather, it keeps before us the search for 'virtue and knowledge', that search which was interpreted in religious terms by medieval pilgrims visiting sites of Christian significance in the Holy Land, and then in humanistic terms by the scholars of the Renaissance, as they wrote their own guidebooks. 'Much of the information amassed by the laborious compilers of encyclopedic works (especially Brunetto Latino)', writes one scholar, 'was fused by the poet into the *Divine Comedy* and molded into his various prose writings. The universality of Dante's knowledge embraced the geography and cosmography of his age.'[38]

That search is a major theme in Dante's remarkable work entitled *Il Convivio*, written between *c.* 1294 and *c.* 1307, and ostensibly a learned commentary on the literary value of the *canzone* form. It is, of course much more than that. To quote R.W.B. Lewis again: 'The *Convivio*, as its title indicates, is a banquet, a feast of knowledge in which all men of goodwill are invited to participate – on the assumption that Aristotle was right when he said at the start of the *Metaphysics* that all men by nature desire to know.'[39] Here we find that emphasis is placed as much on the *cammino mostrato* (that is, the way that is shown for others to follow) as on the *cammino errato* of the unfortunate Ulysses. In an elaborate parable Dante conjures two figures: one who shows the way to true knowledge, and one who is too incompetent to follow his lead, misinterprets his guide (the knowledge acquired by his predecessor) and so loses himself. Nevertheless, great emphasis is placed on the value of the *cammino mostrato*, the achievement of a man who, like a proto-guidebook compiler, makes his experience available to those who follow his tracks. Such a man is praised because 'by his own industry, by observation and the resources of intellect, guided only by himself, [he] goes where he intended, leaving the traces of his steps behind himself' (*Convivio* 4.7.7). 'Particularly striking', writes Teodolinda Barolini, 'is the proto-Vergilian image of the the the tracks left for those who come behind, which anticipates the description of the Roman poet as one who "carries the light behind and helps not himself, but after himself makes people wise"' (*Purgatorio* 22. 68–9).[40] These and other broad images in Dante's writing of intellectual and spiritual guidance, of pilgrim journeying and the Christian humanist's lust for knowledge, may serve to remind us of the actual guidebooks available to pilgrims from about the fourth century, and of those that the humanists were to compile (see Chapter 5).

THE EARLIEST BIBLICAL TOPOGRAPHY AS PILGRIM GUIDES

The first three centuries Anno Domini must have presented formidable obstacles to Holy Land pilgrimage. Titus had largely destroyed Jerusalem in AD 70, but its impressive library survived and became a major attraction for Christian thinkers (it supplied the sources for Eusebius' classic history of early Christianity). Christians in the region were persecuted, along with Jews, the latter being expelled from Jerusalem (135) after their unsuccessful attempt, led by Simeon Bar-Cochba, to prevent Hadrian from refounding the city as the Greco-Roman 'Colonia Aelia Capitolina'.[41] A quarter of a century later, in 160, we hear of a visit by the above-mentioned Melito, Bishop of Sardis in Lydia (Asia Minor), which was the first documented 'pilgrimage' in the sense of a journey undertaken for seeing at first hand 'where the gospel was proclaimed and fulfilled'.[42] Fifty-five years later another bishop, Alexander from Cappadocia, made a similar trip 'for the purposes of prayer and researching the [Christian] sights', to be followed in 230 by the great theologian, Origen, who intended to 'learn by enquiry of the footsteps of Jesus and his followers'.[43] However, it was the events of the fourth century that were to be decisive in the creation of the Holy Land as a destination for pilgrims, which in turn generated the first guidebook literature for the orientation of visitors.

Around AD 330, Eusebius, already mentioned as an able propagandist for the faith, completed his *Onomasticon of Biblical Place-Names*, the fourth part of which was a sort of gazetteer that had both topographical[44] and historical elements, as well as giving distances in Roman measures. The first three parts have not survived but are known to have contained the ethnological terms in the Hebrew scriptures, a topography of ancient Judea and plans of Jerusalem and the Temple. In the surviving part, Eusebius appears as the father of Holy Land guidebooks, in so far as he frequently gives the contemporary (Byzantine) name of a place, describes its current condition (or whether it still exists), indicates what sights may still be seen, whether there is a spa, the character of its inhabitants, whether the Romans have occupied the site, and so forth. In all this he may have drawn on an even earlier pilgrim's itinerary, now lost, as well as official sources.[45] The emphasis is continually on what is 'pointed out' (*theíknitai*), or what is alleged to be still visible (*theíknisthai*), for example, the remains of Noah's Ark on Mount Ararat. An existing tradition of knowledge and guiding is thereby implied, one that already exploited the apologetic potential of biblical sites.[46]

Originally written in Greek, the *Onomasticon* was translated into Latin and substantially corrected (though not all the corrections were correct) by St Jerome *c.* 390. The Old Testament, which features some thousand place-names, is treated as a reliable topographical guide, even when it contradicts itself. Herbert Donner notes that Eusebius, on the authority of Deuteronomy 11: 30, locates Mount Gerizim in the vicinity of Gilgal by Jericho. The location is underlined by Jerome, who gratuitously remarks on the stubborn 'error' of the Samaritans: they insisted on placing Gerizim near their main city of Neapolis. Yet this particular mountain indeed lies near Neapolis (today Nablus) in the heart of the Samaritans' territory, and nowhere near Jericho; not surprisingly so, as it was and is the Samaritans' Sacred Mountain.[47] Behind this competition for mountains lies Jewish resentment of the schismatic Samaritans, a resentment inherited by the first Christian topographers. And frequently Samaria was in fact a problematic region to pass through, as the itineraries sometimes remark. A celebrated passage in an account of the Holy Land by the Piacenza Pilgrim (*c.* 570) speaks of the Samaritans 'burning away with chaff the footprints left by Jews or Christians, this being their way of cursing both'.[48] It is not surprising that the Samaritan inhabitants were hostile both to Christians and Orthodox Jews: both seem to have despised them and the latter indeed regarded them as the alien descendants of pagans settled by the Assyrians after their conquest of the region *c.* 721 BC.

While it would be a mistake to think that the accuracy of claimed biblical locations was a matter of indifference to pilgrims (quite the contrary, in fact), in cases of doubt piety was the test applied, which usually meant appealing to tradition or the scriptures. Nevertheless, about one-third of Eusebius' identifications of biblical place-names with their Byzantine equivalents are borne out by modern archaeology, and many more could be correct. Between a half and three-quarters of the identifications of biblical sites in later itineraries are thought to be right. On the other hand, some sites (particularly under the Latin kingdom that lasted until 1187) seem to have been relocated for devotional rather than historical reasons.[49] Local monks in particular had a tendency to choose a 'suitable' location for several of the twenty-five Holy Land sites featured in the New Testament. The identifying of these was not made easier by the fact that those with traditions most closely associated with them, the Jews, had been banished from Jerusalem by Hadrian when the city was reconstituted as Aelia Capitolana in AD 135. There was also a tendency whereby even correctly located sites were described through the filter of biblical text. Dubbed 'religious geography', this is a recurrent phenomenon, but especially so in the *Peregrinatio* (*c.* 400) of the nun Egeria, who 'looks with the eyes of faith on Sinai . . . and describes the fertility of the land of Goshen, echoing the Bible'.[50] Egeria shows no interest at all in any profane aspects of her routes, that took her through parts of Asia Minor and Egypt, as well as to the Holy Land; as to whether we can regard her valuable and sometimes pathos-filled account, probably written for her fellow-nuns back in Galicia, as a 'guidebook' proper, it has been well said that 'Holy Scripture was the guidebook she took with her',[51] and her account is effectively an ecstatic functionalisation of biblical references.

The central focus of all the guidebook compilers, Jerusalem, itself raised the pressing problem of accurate location. The gospels clearly placed the sepulchre of Christ and the place of his crucifixion (Golgotha/Mount Calvary) *outside* the city walls, but Melito of Sardis was already being shown a spot *inside* the walls by the local Christians when he investigated in AD 160. This change was due to the fact that a new city wall encompassing Golgotha had been built by Herod Agrippa in AD 44, although most of the writers who commented on the matter joined the twelfth-century pilgrim, Saewulf, in explaining the apparent discrepancy by reference to the remodelling of the city by Hadrian as Aelia Capitolana *c.* AD 135.[52] The site in question was thereafter occupied by a temple of Venus, ordered to be demolished by Constantine in 324, at which time the claimed discovery of Christ's tomb was made. The complex of churches and shrines instituted by Constantine enabled pilgrims not only to worship at the stations of Christ's death and resurrection, but also to empathise with other asserted biblical associations (Abraham's sacrifice of Isaac, the place of Adam's creation and his grave), all in one interconnected area. Despite nineteenth-century competition from a Protestant-oriented archaeological school, whereby the Calvary was located outside the Damascus gate of Jerusalem,[53] the Constantinian tradition has so far held its own, although the whole complex had to be rebuilt by the Crusaders. The guidebooks have of course been influential in underpinning and perpetuating this tradition.

PILGRIMS' ITINERARIES, TOPOGRAPHIES AND MISCELLANIES USED AS GUIDEBOOKS

The extent to which such early itineraries were intended, or could be used, as guides varies considerably, but those that give distances and other directional indicators surely anticipated the needs of pilgrims who would follow in their footsteps. While it is true that pilgrims' travelogues generally offer 'little information about the landscape or any travel companions', and despite being 'written in the first person . . . could not be called introspective',[54] they are certainly animated by a desire to set down the framework within which the individual's religious experience may be realised. The earliest such record to survive is the *Itinerarium Burdigalense,* or Itinerary of the Bordeaux Pilgrim, dated to 333. Its unknown author travelled from France through northern Italy and down the Balkans to Constantinople. From there he continued through Asia Minor to Palestine. At Neapolis (Nablus) in Samaria the indications of distance between staging posts cease and a guided tour of the Holy Land begins. On the return journey (for which distances are again given), he made his way back through Greece and Macedonia to the Balkans as far as Aulon (modern Vlora in south-west Albania); thence he took ship to Otranto, and travelled up Italy to Rome, the last recorded stop being Milan.

If the Bordeaux Pilgrim had any trouble en route, we do not hear of it. As a Christian he was everywhere protected by Constantine's recognition of Christianity. This also appears to have afforded our author the privilege of using the excellent *cursus publicus* or imperial post (see Chapter 1), enabling him to be back in his hometown only a year after leaving it. The mileages he gives, though quite often implausible, tend to agree with those in the *Peutinger Table* and the *Itinerarium Antonini* discussed in Chapter One, as do the names of the staging posts and hostels (*mutationes* and *mansiones*) en route. Similarly, we do not learn of the pilgrim's reactions to the sights he saw, nor of wonders, relics and martyrs that were to become the staples of later accounts. 'The Palestine that he describes', says Donner, 'is eerily devoid of human occupation and he perambulates Jerusalem as if it were a seldom visited museum.'[55] As to the character and personality of the author, Donner gives us one intriguing speculation: there are several obscure Old Testament references to which the pilgrim apparently attaches importance; moreover, he goes first to the ruined Temple on entering Jerusalem (all other pilgrims go straight to the church of the Holy Sepulchre); and finally, the only rite he specifically describes is a Jewish one, an early form of the ritual at the Wailing Wall. All these points might suggest that he was a baptised Jew, of whom there were many in the ports of the Mediterranean.[56] If this was the case, one can well imagine how the zeal of the convert inspired him to write an itinerary of the Holy Land that would be useful for fellow Christians.[57]

Not all the pilgrims' itineraries contain much that seems specifically designed as a guidebook for others, though most seemed to have enjoyed varying degrees of popularity as 'background reading' for the pious, some of whom doubtless went on pilgrimages.[58] One work that is unequivocally intended for the orientation of its readers is the *Breviarius* (or topography) *of Jerusalem*, probably compiled in the sixth century with later additions (there are two versions and three extant manuscripts). The point has been made that 'very short books of this kind could of course be carried round in the Holy places themselves. They were like guidebooks.'[59] The same author suggests that books such as the *Breviarius* may have been used as publicity for shipping agents, a sort of early travel brochure, quoting a seemingly publicity-oriented passage from a later work known as the 'First Guide' (1101) that was available in Venice, that runs as follows: 'if anyone from Western countries should wish to go Jerusalem, let him go ever eastwards, and he will find the places of prayer in the region of Jerusalem just as they are here described'. Venice had for long enjoyed a near monopoly on the shipping of Western European pilgrims to the Holy Land – until the sixteenth century, when Marseilles benefited from the decline of Venetian Levantine trade.[60]

How does the *Breviarius* stand up as a guidebook? A prospectus for the Royal Jordanian Airline circulated to travel agencies in 1965 gives a short overview of Jerusalem's sights. If the first paragraph is translated into Latin, it is virtually identical to that of the *Breviarius*,[61] which is the earliest known example of a simple tour of Jerusalem's sights aimed at pilgrim–tourists. The tour (it came to be known as the 'Jerusalem circle')[62] begins with the churches founded by Constantine around Golgotha and Christ's tomb, continues to the Sion Basilica and the House of Caiaphas, then proceeds to the residence of Pontius Pilate and the Temple; finally it arrives at the Mount of Olives via Bethesda. Such a circuit is also implicit in the account of the Byzantine *Archdeacon Theodosius*, written about twenty years earlier. A liturgically and historically determined tour, it followed the locations of events during the final days of Our Lord and was institutionalised by the Crusaders as the 'Way of the Cross'. A later version of the *Breviarius* also supplies a full inventory of the churches of Jerusalem in the sixth century and draws attention to the already flourishing cult of relics by mentioning thirteen of the most important. Apart from relics of the passion, such as the Lance and the Sponge, more exotic items were available to be revered, such as the platter for the head of John the Baptist, the chalice used at the Last Supper, the stone that killed St Stephen the Protomartyr and King Solomon's ring.

The *Breviarius* well illustrates how biblical *lieux de mémoire* were already concentrated around the Tomb and Golgotha, which is now also identified as the spot where Adam was created, a rather implausibly but conveniently located Paradise. The motivation for this was doubtless to distinguish such places from the Jewish tradition, that placed them around the Temple; but a secondary advantage was that it made for ease of 'marketing' a package of sights to religious tourists. As early as 333 the Bordeaux Pilgrim was reporting that the place of the crucifixion lay 'no more than a stone's throw' from the tomb.[63] By the time of Theodosius' topography in the sixth century we learn that 'In the city of Jerusalem, at the Sepulcher of the Lord, is the place of Calvary. There Abraham offered up his son for a burnt-offering . . . above the altar rises a hill . . . there the Lord was crucified . . .', and distances to neighbouring sights continue to be measured in Roman paces.[64]

Although the itineraries and guides differ in detail, many of them share the increasingly stock ingredients of the tour to be found in the *Breviarius*. However, the significance of individual items on the itinerary may change according to the writer's information from local informants, how much he or she has copied from others and the changing religious associations of a given site. An example is the pool at Bethesda mentioned above, called the 'sheep's pool' by Eusebius, evidently drawing on the reference in St John's Gospel to the Jerusalem 'sheep's gate'. A shrine to Asclepius seems also to have been instituted here after Hadrian rebuilt Jerusalem as a pagan city, but Christian writers identified the pool as the place where Jesus healed the lame man ('Take up thy bed and walk', John 5: 2–18). The Bordeaux Pilgrim seems to have some vague intimation of this, mentioning that the sick were healed here and the waters turned red when they began to churn. The redness is attributed by Eusebius to the underlying earth having been stained red from earlier animal sacrifice. A travelogue in the form of a letter written by a Bishop Eucherius in the fifth century mentions the red water and follows Eusebius in describing two pools here, while the previously mentioned topography of the Archdeacon Theodosius (early sixth century) is the only account to assert that the bed of the man healed by Jesus may still be seen. By the time of the *Breviarius*, interest in the pool has largely evaporated and the site is principally associated with the birthplace of the Virgin Mary, to whom a basilica was erected in the first half of the fifth century ('Next to the sheep pool is the church of Our Mistress Mary,' as Theodosius remarks).[65] When the Piacenza Pilgrim writes his account (*c.* 570), the story of the miraculous healing has disappeared completely and the pool has become 'a cesspool in which everything is washed, as necessary for the city'. Yet in 1341, nearly eight centuries later, Ludolph of Suchem again recalls how the waters were once periodically troubled by an angel, and how the sick used to be healed here.

The admirable modern guides for pilgrims produced from 1913 under the auspices of the Franciscan Commissioners for the Holy Land give a dispassionate overview of Bethesda's archaeological history and its various religious associations. From the 1999 edition we learn that there were originally two large pools here to supply water for the Temple, one of which, now filled in and partly a car park, was possibly the pool mentioned by our authors. The biblical notion that an angel periodically stirred the waters, at which time all the waiting cripples rushed into them to be healed, is a symbolic interpretation of something more mundane, namely the system whereby water was periodically drawn off to the Temple by a pipe (alternatively, Donner suggests there may have been a dam and sluice system between the two pools).[66] The association with the Virgin's birth seems to come from the apocryphal Book of James (or '*Protoevangelium*', *c.* AD 150), which first identified Mary's parents as Joachim and Anne, the former being a well-to-do shepherd. The association with the 'sheep pool' was thus tempting, the assumption being that sheep were washed here before being sacrificed in the Temple. Nowadays the remains of a Byzantine Marian basilica can still be seen next to the medieval church of St Anne, which probably fell victim to the anti-Christian destruction wreaked by the fanatical Fatimid Caliph al-Hākim in 1009, mentioned above. The Crusaders revived the healing tradition by erecting a small church dedicated to the 'healing of the lame', and so in a sense the wheel had come full circle. The church of St Anne itself has survived a turbulent history, partly because Saladin turned it into a Muslim seminary. Now back in Christian ownership, its crypt is revered as the birthplace of Mary.[67]

ARCULF'S ACCOUNT OF THE HOLY LAND

Arculf was a bishop from Gaul (perhaps from Périgueux in Aquitaine) who spent nine months in the Holy Land around 680 and was blown off course to Iona on the voyage home. He was received by Abbot Adómnan (or 'Adamnan'), to whom he dictated an account of his tour, which Adómnan then embellished with details culled from his own research. Extracts from this work (*De locis sanctis*) were in turn incorporated by Bede into his *Ecclesiastical History of the English People* some sixty years later. Bede also made a longer digest of the work, a sort of armchair guidebook 'for those who live at a great distance from the places where the patriarchs live, and whose only source of information about them lies in books'.[68]

Arculf, who does not seem to have been hampered by the fact that the Holy Land was by then (from 636) under Muslim control, was particularly concerned to describe the churches, for the first time with some description of their architecture. This represented a major advance on his predecessors, who had generally limited themselves to vague expressions of pious wonder. He also moved the guidebook genre forward in other respects, for example, by showing awareness of the archaeology of the three cities built on the site of the ruins of Jericho; by describing views (for instance that toward the Dead Sea from the Mount of Olives); and by commenting on flora (the pine woods of Hebron, the olive trees of Bethany.) Most remarkable of all are the accompanying drawings and groundplans of churches, such as that of the church of the Holy Sepulchre, made from memory on wax tablets by Arculf himself for Adómnan – which in effect makes this the first illustrated guidebook.[69]

Arculf's text is itself endowed with picturesque elements that combine autopsy, 'religious geography' and the traditions of the prophets, some of which elements endure in Baedeker's descriptions of the nineteenth and twentieth centuries, or those of Bernabé Meistermann's Catholic guides to the Holy Land from 1906. Typically, the shallow cave in Bethlehem, assumed by Arculf to be Christ's birthplace and described by him with topographical precision, has acquired outline plans in Baedeker and Meistermann. While Arculf locates the graves of the three shepherds of the Nativity, the modern guides go further and point out the place where the shepherds saw the guiding star. Meistermann's guidebook indeed fulfills exactly the same function as that of Adómnan/Arculf: the author stresses in his Preface to the French edition (1907) that his work is 'not a mere hand-book for tourists; it is a vade mecum for the pilgrim who, while he is entitled to expect precise information, seeks to increase his faith and piety by his acquaintance with the Holy places'.[70]

GUIDEBOOKS DURING AND AFTER THE CRUSADES

The onset of the Crusades from 1095 brought new waves of pilgrims and travel writers to the Holy Land, among whom a somewhat more critical attitude to traditions and locations is sometimes apparent. In this transitional phase of guidebook compilation, a very precise enumeration of actual appearance and measurements is nonetheless combined with an uncritical rendition of the 'facts' handed down as tradition. Thus the Russian Abbot Daniel, compiling his account in 1106, gives an exact description of how the Calvary rock appeared in the church of the Resurrection, with its 'socket hole . . . one cubit deep, and less than a foot in circumference; it is here that the cross of the Lord was erected'. Beneath this rock, he assures us, 'lies the skull of the first man, Adam'. The symbolic fact of its presence here is underlined by the following passage, which recalls that, in the moment our Lord gave up the ghost on the cross, 'the Temple was rent and the rock clave asunder, and the rock above Adam's skull opened, and the blood and water which flowed from Christ's side ran down through the fissures upon the skull, thus washing away the sins of men'.[71]

One of the most influential guides of the Crusader period was that of an Anglo-Saxon from Canterbury called Saewulf, dated to 1102/3 (its author has been described as 'combining trading enterprise with religious zeal').[72] He was followed by John of Würzburg, whose *Description of the Holy Land*, written between 1160 and 1170, is notable for its Teutonic patriotism in vigorously reclaiming the credit for the reconquest of the Holy Land from the French knights who (he complains) had been hogging it. John assiduously notes the scriptural events associated with each place on the itinerary; yet he is also at pains to point out that 'these same holy places of which we think so much . . . have been overthrown and perhaps altered in form. For this reason our pious care about these sites, which we have described as an eyewitness, must not be thought unnecessary or superfluous.'[73] At roughly the same period (after the Muslim reconquest of 1187), a secular topography entitled *The Condition of the City of Jerusalem* supplies a guide to the city where the religious 'sights' have become just that, as in a modern guide. It deals with the layout of the streets, the location of sacred and secular buildings and institutions (the Exchange, the Hospital), as well as markets and shops for various commodities. If the visitor wanted to know where to buy cheese, fish, cloth or gold, this text told him. Likewise, it took him by the hand and directed him through the streets to the Tower of David, the church of the Sepulchre, the Golden Gate, the Temple, the German Hospital, the Syrian and Latin Exchanges and so forth, often adding tips for shoppers ('In this street the Syrians sell their stuffs and make wax candles. In front of the Exchange they also sell fish.').[74] Some manuscripts of this anonymous *City of Jerusalem* include an early thirteenth-century tour of the rest of the Holy Land that indicates the places that could be visited with permission of Saladin and his successors against payment of a 'toll' (*khafara*).

THEODERICH'S GUIDE TO THE HOLY LAND

John of Würzburg's itinerary shares a number of features with a *Guide to the Holy Land* written *c.* 1172 by a certain Theoderich, thought to have been a monk from Hirsau in the Rhine Valley.[75] The two authors appear to have copied similar passages from an historical and geographical account of the Holy Land known as the 'Old Compendium', a much used collection of such material later superseded by a 'New Compendium', both works that were plundered by numerous authors writing up the pilgrims' way from the time of the Second Crusade (1147) to the close of the Middle Ages.[76] However, Theoderich's guide stands out for its literary and informative qualities, which made him a major source for other medieval authors and renders him still readable today. Most of it is autopsy, the parts 'learned from the truthful tales of others' (for example, descriptions of the Dead Sea, Transjordan or Arabia) being immediately apparent from the manner in which they retail familiar myths (for example, Eusebius' inaccurate account of the sources of the River Jordan).

Theoderich's love of, and considerable skill in describing, architecture has led to speculation that he might have been an ecclesiastical architect himself.[77] He deals in far more detail than his predecessors with the fortifications of Jerusalem, its layout, its stone houses with flat roofs designed to catch rainwater, as well as the design and appearance of the churches he visited, the way in which visits to the holiest sights are invigilated and which Orders are entitled to the income from offerings or have liturgical rights, the inscriptions and mosaics that may be seen, and even the behaviour of his fellow pilgrims. This rich mix of detailed aesthetic description, notes for orientation, 'atmosphere' (for example, the account of the coming of the Holy Fire at Easter in the church of the Holy Sepulchre, a carefully staged spectacle that was still current in the nineteenth century, when Baedeker dismissed it as a degrading conjuring trick), as well as acute human observation, makes Theoderich's text a seminal one for guidebooks. Last but not least, his narrative is sufficiently personal to reveal some of the assumptions of a cleric of his day, in particular the anti-semitism inspired by the teachings of the Latin Church. Slighting remarks or unflattering anecdotes and legends about Jews are sprinkled through the text; indeed the very first page of his description begins with a reiteration of the charge that the Jews had murdered Christ, followed by a comment that the Romans then 'destroyed all the cities and villages throughout Judaea, and drove the murderers themselves out of their own country and forced them . . . to live among foreigners'.[78]

GUIDEBOOKS BY NON-CHRISTIANS AND THOSE WRITTEN UNDER THE TURKISH EMPIRE

It should not be forgotten that there were also Jewish travellers to the Holy Land who left accounts that could be used as guidebooks. The best known is that of Benjamin from Tudela on the Spanish Ebro, who left home in *c.* 1159 for an extended tour that took in Palestine (*c.* 1170) after a leisurely perambulation of southern France, Italy and Greece. His aim was partly to examine the condition of Jews in these countries following the pogroms that the Crusades had helped to provoke; but he also supplies copious details on commerce, politics, monuments and natural features. Naturally he is little interested in the Christian sites (the church of the Holy Sepulchre gets a single sentence), but concentrates on such things as the tombs of King David in Jerusalem and of Sarah, Rebecca and Leah in Hebron. In an aside we learn that there are a mere 200 Jews surviving in Jerusalem and that they have a monopoly of the dyeing trade by grace of the Frankish authorities. He returned to Castile in 1173.

Another famous Jewish account was that of Rabbi Petachia of Ratisbon, whose work, however, was ruthlessly censored by his literary executor, Rabbi Yahudi the Pious, so that much valuable material has been lost. Over the years there were a number of other such travelogue/guides, one of the last being Moses Ben Israel Naphtali Porges Praeger's *Ways to Zion* of 1650. The first section of this guide describes the routes to Israel and the costs of travel and life in mid-seventeenth-century Jerusalem. It is full of vivid observation and tips: how to buy cheap lemons to make lemonade and keep the latter fresh by adding a little olive oil on top, what shoes and clothing to take, the necessity of removing anything green from clothing or prayers shawls, since that is the colour of the Prophet and is strictly forbidden to Jews, and so on. 'And know this every man always, / though the Land of Israel is waste these days / and in ruins by reason of our sins, / yet in every mood it is always good . . .'.[79]

There were of course also Muslim travellers and geographers, beginning with Ibn Khurdadbih, who compiled a work entitled *The Routes* in 864. Islamic descriptive writing flowered with Al-Muqaddesi's remarkable social, economic and topographical *Description of Syria, including Palestine* (c. AD 985).[80] A few lines about the water in Syria may serve to demonstrate its engaging flavour: 'In Syria [the water] is for the most part excellent. That found at Bâniyâs, however, acts aperiently; and the water of Tyre causes constipation. At Baisân the water is heavy and bad, while of a truth we take refuge in Allah from that of Sughar.' Space does not permit detailed examination of these and similar texts, which lie outside the European cultural parameters of the present work, but Jerusalem played an important role in them. It is worth reminding ourselves that Mohammed originally saw his religion as the true descendant of the Jewish Old Testament, that in the early years of his mission he and his followers prayed towards Jerusalem, and only after a later revelation towards Mecca.[81] The late seventh-century Islamic sanctuary known as the Dome of the Rock was supposedly built on the ancient site of the Jewish Temple, in the enclosure of which was the sacred rock from which Mohammed climbed to heaven by means of a ladder.

Although their mood fluctuated according to the state of geopolitical tensions, the Muslims were intermittently much more tolerant than Christians in affording access to the holy places. Indeed, when Saladin entered Jerusalem in 1187, there was no massacre such as the Crusaders all too often indulged in, and many Christians unable to pay a ransom were set free nevertheless. The christianised Dome of the Rock was immediately returned to Muslim use, but the church of the Holy Sepulchre was closed for only three days before access was again permitted for Christian pilgrims.[82] Latterly the Christian powers seemed to have learned from Muslim experience – when General Allenby took Jerusalem in 1917, he announced that the arrangements that the Turkish authorities had worked out for the respective rights and privileges of squabbling Christian denominations in the church of the Holy Sepulchre (the so-called Status Quo, fixed by an imperial Ottoman decree in 1757) were to remain in place.[83]

Two Islamic guidebooks may serve to give a brief indication of the genre. The first is by Abu al-Hasan al-Harawi, who was in Jerusalem in 1173. His account of the church of the Resurrection, while admiring its architecture, gives short shrift to the event the church symbolises. He also cites the Christians' assertions regarding the splitting of the rock on Christ's demise and the grave of Adam under the cross. Finally, he is decidedly underwhelmed by the Holy Fire spectacle at Easter ('As to the descent of the fire, I lived long enough in Jerusalem at the time of the Franks to know how it was done.').[84] Al-Harawi also visited the Dome of the Rock, which was then in Crusader hands, and the likewise christianised Aqsa Mosque, but does not especially remark on the changes made by the Latins, although other Muslim writers are more indignant. It was common ground among most visitors – Jewish, Christian and Muslim – that the Dome of the Rock stood on the site of the 'House of the Lord', originally built by Solomon, while the Aqsa Mosque to the south marked the spot where Solomon's Palace had been. Abbot Daniel is not untypical in praising the structure and decoration of the former, avoiding any mention of its Islamic

features, but noting in passing that 'the present church . . . was built by a chief of
the Saracens named Umar'.[85]

The second Muslim writer of note, al-Fazari (d. 1329), works in the stereotypical
eulogistic idiom that pronounced 'On the Merits of Jerusalem' and laid out an
itinerary for the Muslim sights of the Haram that can be compared to the later
Christian 'Way of the Cross'. Like the books of instruction for Roman pilgrims
seeking indulgences, it lays down for the penitent Muslim where to pray and in
what manner. Indeed a slightly later (c. 1350) anonymous Christian guide
dovetails with this methodology, in so far as it treats several of the Holy Land
sights in terms of the indulgences available.[86] This book, the *Innominatus*, appears
either to have initiated or to have taken over a tradition of liturgical direction that
was still being reproduced in an *Elucidatio Terrae Sanctae* of 1649. Thus, in the
church of the Holy Sepulchre, the exact spots where Jesus raised the man from
the dead, where the Holy Cross formerly stood, where Jesus was chained to a
stone, where soldiers cast lots for Christ's garments, and even the chair from
which Helena directed the search for the Holy Cross (!), all attracted temporary
(seven-year) indulgences, while the chapel marking where Christ was imprisoned
and beaten was privileged with a plenary indulgence (complete remission of sins).
The guidebook, elaborate and vivid as it is, also painstakingly lists the biblical
events associated with each area in the separate pilgrimage routes laid out for
Nazareth, Jerusalem, the Mount of Olives, Bethlehem and Hebron, Bethany and
the River Jordan, the Sea of Galilee and further afield into Syria. The whole is like
a slide-show with subtitles, no individual location escaping its biblical, or
sometimes classical tag. Even Damascus is alleged to have been built on the field
where Cain slew Abel, while Syrian Berytus is precisely the place where St George
slew the dragon 'and rescued a virgin from shameful death'.[87]

With this work (a compendium like so many others) the guidebook reaches a
new maturity and comprehensiveness, with a more systematic approach to
distances and orientation. The more helpful guides, several with illustrations,
soon achieved fame and endured for years. Some indeed appeared to have been
treasured primarily for their illustrations, books such as *Viazo da Venesia al sancto
iherusalem, et al monte Sinai*, which was first printed in Bologna in 1500 with
excellent woodcuts by one Piero Ciza, and periodically reprinted up to 1728. Its
practical information, which originated in a pilgrimage of 1483, was obviously
useless by that date and had anyway always been minimal, but its woodcuts were
timeless. Hard-headed practical information was available in the work entitled
Informacion for Pylgrymes unto the Holy Londe, first printed by Wynkyn de Worde in
1498 and reprinted in 1515 and 1524. The material for this had been lifted
almost word for word from the 'prevysyoun' (provision) for a journey to the East
in an itinerary of a fellow of Eton College, William Wey.[88] Among its observations
and tips is one that must be seared on the heart of every British traveller who has
ever been ripped off by a foreign bank, namely: 'Take none englyshe gold with
you [beyond] Bruges, for ye shall lose in the change. And also for the most part
of the way they will not change it.' Travellers are advised to take three ten-gallon
barrels, two of wine, one of water, as well as a cage for half-a-dozen hens and

chickens. All this suggests the author was not aiming at the most ascetic type of pilgrim. As for the Saracens, they may 'go talking by you and make good cheer', but 'they will steal from you if they may'. Another innovation in this guide is the English/Moorish and English/Greek vocabularies. Finally, there is a curious exposition of a model church in terms of its symbolic elements, whereby the stones represent Christians, its windows the Holy Scriptures, its bells the preachers and so on.[89]

By this time there were quite well organised 'package tours' to the Holy Land, the commercially minded Venetians having seen the potential in the hordes of pilgrims who traditionally took ship for Palestine from the head of the Adriatic. In the late fifteenth century, Agostino Contarini provided one such tour. For the cost of sixty gold ducats (around £2,000 today) he supplied transport to the holy places and back, guides to the sights, and two hot meals a day. This all-inclusive price even allowed for what had previously been burdensome extras – fees, tolls and bribes.[90] As we have seen, it was even possible to take out a kind of life insurance for the duration of the pilgrimage, so over the years religious travel had initiated in embryo form many of the devices and products that were to become increasingly sophisticated from the nineteenth century onwards.

It is perhaps appropriate to conclude this chapter with another aid, or rather a set of admonitory instructions, for pilgrims, as reported by the Dominican traveller Felix Fabri of Ulm in *c.* 1480, and issued by the Franciscan Father Guardian of the holy places. As Fabri pointed out, the Franciscans, appointed by the pope and approved by the Muslim authorities since 1333, were responsible for instructing pilgrims from the West in 'the rules and method of seeing the holy places which they ought to observe while dwelling among the Saracens and infidels in the Holy Land, lest they should run into danger through ignorance.'[91] However, the various heads of instruction recorded by Fabri offer far more than this, beginning with a warning that pilgrims required papal authorisation (which the Father Guardian was empowered to give) even to enter the Holy Land. This was because the pope had in fact excommunicated the entire area, because of the too enthusiastic cooperation of the surviving Christian inhabitants with their Mameluke rulers, in particular their treachery in supplying the latter with military hardware.

On the other hand, pilgrims are warned against showing any form of disrespect, intentional or unintentional, to the religious or legal sensibilities of the Saracens. The multiple instructions for the personal comportment of pilgrims are revealing: they are not to chip fragments from the Holy Sepulchre for souvenirs; noble pilgrims are not to draw their coats of arms on walls; all must adopt a grave and devout bearing (especially because laughter made the Saracens suspect that they were the objects of such mirth); they should not be lured into houses by Saracen women nor give a Saracen wine, which drives him mad and makes him violent. In matters of money the Latin Christians are faced with a hierarchy of deceit, starting with the Saracens, who are obliged by their religion to attempt fraud when dealing with the infidels. Worse, however, are 'the German Jews . . . for their whole object in life is to cheat us'. Yet even they are not as bad as the Eastern Christians, 'for they have no conscience, less even than the Jews and Saracens, and will cheat pilgrims if they can'.

Pilgrims were now supplicants in hostile territory (a Saracen guide was obligatory), and had to behave with humility and caution. An indispensable element of guidebooks emerged as a result, that which tells readers how to conduct themselves abroad, how to avoid offending local sensibilities, how to stay out of trouble (or even out of gaol), and how to emerge physically and financially unscathed from your travels. Today's guides are no different: 'It is not wise to carry valuables or large sums of money. Be especially courteous when dealing with officials. If they decide to help, they can be your best friends and cut though mountains of red tape. But if you upset them, they can be your worst enemies.' (*Bradt's Guide to Iraq*, 2002).[92]

Achieving a balance between xenophobic scare-mongering and justified cautionary advice is something travel guides have struggled with at least since the Enlightenment. The German Carsten Niebuhr, who arrived in the Holy Land in 1766, relates the long litany of horrors to be expected from the Muslim inhabitants as retailed by the Franciscan fathers in the reception centre at Ramle. He soon discovers that exactly the same tales have been in circulation for nearly a century. Moreover, he adds drily, 'although I at length began to believe myself that the Palestinian Arabs were the worst race of people imaginable . . . a closer inspection reveals [to the traveller] that the inhabitants of this region are by no means more malicious than anywhere else'.[93]

CHAPTER 4

Santiago de Compostela:
Legend, Legerdemain and
the Love of God

The whole story [of St James's relics] is so exceedingly unlikely and so
clearly concocted to provide a suitable focus for Christian unity in Spain
against Islam, that it would be easy to dismiss it all as mere legend. But none
of that matters; it is the pilgrimage itself which, from the very moment that
the Saint's grave was discovered . . . has created its own momentum,
rationale and legacy.
(Robin Hanbury-Tenison, Spanish Pilgrimage: A Canter to St James, *1990)*

All the fish, beef, pork of the whole of Spain and Galicia cause illness to
foreigners.
(Aimery Picaud (attrib.), The Pilgrim's Guide, c. *1160)*

SANTIAGO PILGRIMAGE AND ITS LITERATURE

The Donation of Constantine, the *privilegium maius* of the Habsburgs, the
Protocols of the Elders of Zion: history is littered with exposed forgeries that
have nevertheless served their purpose remarkably well; and much the same can
be said of opportunely occurring relics, from the True Cross and the Turin
Shroud to the living relic of the bogus 'Anastasia', youngest daughter of the
Russian imperial family slaughtered by the Bolsheviks at Ekaterinburg. Perhaps
in no case has the will to believe triumphed so completely over the available

historical and scientific facts as in that of the cult of St James at Compostela in north-western Spain. For centuries, the inspiration provided by dubious relics and industrious literary-historical fabrication proved impervious to scepticism or rational analysis. It was an inspiration expressed not only in the minds of those pilgrims who have left accounts of their experience, but also in the Romanesque, Gothic and Baroque architecture that sprung up, not only at Santiago itself, but at numerous places along the pilgrim's routes that led to it.

On the other hand, the *Liber peregrinationis*, the first and most famous pilgrim's guide to the Way of St James and the one with which this chapter is primarily concerned, contains little direct evocation of spiritual or emotional experience. That element is only indirectly conjured by detailed and enthusiastic architectural descriptions of churches on the way to Compostela, or (in chapter VIII, one-third of the whole) by its liturgical exposition of the tombs of saints and relics that should be venerated by every pilgrim en route. While its fairly comprehensive description of the city and cathedral of Santiago as they were between *c.* 1130 and 1135 makes it an invaluable art historical source, it has been pointed out that the guide's purely aesthetic judgements are few and far between: the descriptions exhibit rather the author's rhetorical training than any display of taste or feeling.[1] Its most vivid passages, also a very substantial portion of the whole, are those excoriating the terrible inhabitants of the territories that the unsuspecting twelfth-century pilgrim would traverse before he reached his goal. These contrasting, sometimes clashing, motifs gave the guide its double appeal, whereby the religious jostles with the secular, and official piety suddenly gives way to personal, not to say bigoted, commentary.[2]

Such ambivalence tends to recur, at least in the recent literature of the Santiago pilgrimage, which often seems as much concerned with the picturesque or harsh aspects of travelling as with spiritual experience. Indeed, scepticism about the legends of the St James cult inevitably began to creep into travel reports quite early on. In the late fifteenth century, the gossipy account of Hieronymus Münzer, an Austrian doctor, already somewhat uneasily combines Renaissance scepticism with formal piety. Attending a funeral at the basilica in Compostela in 1495, Münzer was appalled by the accompanying flummery of superstition, the behaviour of the money-grubbing clerics, and the worldly throng in the church that reminded him of a fair.[3] The Renaissance English scholar Dr Andrew Boorde was quite clear that 'not one ear or one bone' of St James was in Compostella – though he does allow that the saint's staff, the chain that bound him in prison and the sickle that sawed off his head are there. However, this is not entirely a result of scholarly scepticism, but rather of the fact that he believes (and claims subseqently to have verified) what an elderly monk tells him, namely that Charlemagne had taken the remains for his planned relics collection at Toulouse.[4] Perhaps more significantly, in his *Viaje Santo* of 1575 Ambrosio de Morales expresses surprise – despite his being engaged in a survey of relics, royal tombs and manuscripts in the monasteries and cathedrals for his counter-reformatory sovereign Philip II – when told that Charlemagne had promoted the shrine at Santiago, seeing as how the great king had died in 813 [actually 814], and the Apostle's body was not 'found' until 835.[5]

Yet, devotionally oriented accounts did of course continue to exist into a more sceptical age, notably that of the Minorite monk, Hermann Künig von Vach, compiled just before the onset of the Reformation, but printed just after it in 1521. *Die Wallfahrt und Strasse zu Sankt Jakob* charts a route from the Swiss monastery at Einsiedeln (a popular starting point for pilgrimages) to Santiago; the outward journey is recorded in one hundred stages, and a return journey to Aachen in thirty-eight. The work was written in rhyming couplets, so that illiterate pilgrims could easily commit to memory its travel instructions and hints on what to see. It is one of the few such guides to survive and reminds us of how route guidance for the medieval traveller was generally passed on verbally, even if it sometimes had a written source. It was also probably one of the last such rhyming *aide-mémoires* to be compiled: as Frances Yates pointed out in her great study of memory, the invention of the printed book and the humanism of the Renaissance marked a shift away from the didactic and schematic use of memory in a medieval religious context. As a roadbook (which was not always reliable: Castrojeriz at Burgos becomes 'Castle Fritz' to the German-speaking monk),[6] a source of practical advice (for example, it tells where nails for fastening the soles of shoes are available), and as a treasure trove of colourful allusions (for instance to the caged chickens of Santo Domingo de la Calzada that had miraculously flown off the spit on which they were roasting),[7] Vach's carefully sectioned guide is a medieval book of instruction for the vulgar. It is a far cry from the scholasticism from which it is ultimately derived, whose most elevated form could be experienced by the reader absorbing the painstaking and spiritually didactic topography of Dante's *Divine Comedy*, where 'Memory [is] the converting power, the bridge between the abstraction and the image.'[8]

Credulous (or loyally faithful) accounts of the Santiago pilgrimage had a new flowering in the nineteenth and twentieth centuries. Piety no doubt received a shot in the arm from the excavation, in 1879, of the supposed tomb of the Apostle in the cathedral at Compostela, leading to the claimed discovery of the remains of St James and his two disciples, Athanasius and Theodore. This 'discovery' was reinforced by the subsequent bold proclamation of Pope Leo XIII in 1884 that the *Translatio* (the miraculous transfer of St James's body from Palestine to Asturias after his martyrdom) was an historical fact.[9] In this way, the harnessing of scientific method on the ground (excavations) to papal authority (the Apostolic Letter *Deus Omnipotens*) certainly breathed fresh life into the cult, about which some nineteenth-century writers had become increasingly sardonic. One such was Richard Ford, whose famously idiosyncratic tome on Spain in the Murray's Handbook series had appeared in 1845 and caused something of a scandal in *bien-pensant* circles because of its anticlerical tone and unflattering view of Spanish mores. Of the St James cult in general he remarks characteristically: 'If . . . people can once believe that Santiago ever came to Spain at all, all the rest is plain sailing.' Yet it is also important to note that his was probably the first guidebook since Aimery Picaud's twelfth-century *Liber peregrinationis* to do real justice to the magnificent architecture of the cathedral. In particular he opened the eyes of his readers to the astonishing artistic achievement of the Compostela cathedral's Pórtico de la Gloria, with its array of deeply impressive 'proto-Gothic' sculpture, regarded by many as the finest such work in Europe.[10] It proved so captivating for the British that a full-sized cast was made in 1866 and placed in the court of the South Kensington (later Victoria and Albert) Museum. In a sense, Ford takes up where Picaud left off, since the triple portal, which is now to be found in the narthex behind the present eighteenth-century façade of the cathedral, just postdates the composition of the *Pilgrim's Guide* (perhaps by less than half a century) and so does not appear in it.

From about the same time as Ford's splendid guide, Spanish works began to appear that exploited the recent scholarship on Compostela, while at the same time providing assistance for the ordinary tourist. The shrine, which had always been a money-spinner for the Church, now embarked on its secondary career as major secular tourist attraction. This type of Spanish literature reached a sort of apotheosis with Freire Francisco Barreiro's *Guía de Santiago y sus alrededores* (1885), a huge 576-page tome that combined a detailed study of the cult of St James with substantial practical information, including helpful tips and advice for the would-be pilgrim, and even train timetables.[11] The devotional and the scholarly could now co-exist in a single volume, reflecting perhaps a broader trend whereby the Church was learning (not without sporadic resistance) to be reconciled to the advances of science and the researches of historians, while still insisting that the central tenets of the faith remained inviolable. This sort of compromise seeped into the Santiago pilgrimage literature; from the late nineteenth century onwards, it often took the form of meditative passages mingled with scholarly, aesthetic and descriptive commentary. In the twentieth century, Walter Starkie's classic *The Road to Santiago*, first published in 1957, combines history, travelogue and personal meditation, providing a sort of template for numerous subsequent experiential accounts, which however are a mere trickle in the great flood of scholarly studies. The Dunn and Davidson bibliography of works dealing with Compostela and the cult of St James runs to 2,941 entries, of which an incredible 2,493 were published in the twentieth century, 1,358 of them since the Holy Year of 1965. A mere 10 per cent of these are labelled 'personal narratives or guides', although this is put in perspective when the compilers remark that they rejected another 500 (!) works ' as being purely touristic'.[12]

The numbers illustrate how the *Camino*, the Way of St James, has hugely increased its allure in recent times, no doubt reflecting a widespread desire to discover personal space for reflection in a world dominated by materialism, shallowness, hypocrisy and sensationalism. This allure, however, is in danger of being tarnished by commercial exploitation, although one should immediately add that commercial exploitation seems to have been just as active in the Middle Ages. Still, the *Camino* is now to some extent all things to all people. The excellent Confraternity of St James (UK) explains on its website guide that the *credencial* (a modern version of the safe-conduct given to medieval pilgrims and entitling the holder to use the pilgrim hostels en route) is in practice available to 'anyone making the pilgrimage in a frame of mind that is open and searching', and that prospective pilgrims will not be asked about their denomination, 'or even whether they are Christian, although of course historically the pilgrimage itself has meant Christian pilgrimage'. The same website gives a dispassionate account of the 'legends' and 'traditions' associated with Compostela, together with statistics showing the sharp rise, since the Holy Year of 1993, in the number of pilgrims receiving the Compostela certificate for completion of their pilgrimage. In 1993, there were 99,439 certificates awarded, and in the Holy Year of 1999 this figure swelled to 154,613. In 2003, a bad year for travel everywhere, there were still 74,614 pilgrims; in 1986, the figure had been just 2,491.[13] By way of comparison with the Middle Ages, be it remarked here that some 6,000 people had obtained the requisite King's Licence over the years 1434 and 1435 to make the pilgrimage from England to Compostella.[14]

All this suggests that what was once a religious phenomenon for the faithful and gullible, carefully manipulated by political and clerical interests, is now rapidly becoming an item of heritage tourism, a postmodern experience where (almost) any or no motivation for following the Way of St James (the *Camino*) is equally valid.[15] Mortification of the flesh en route, though not necessarily embraced by the medieval pilgrim, was originally seen as an emblematic imitation of Christ's own *via dolorosa*, the road to Calvary.[16] It is certainly an optional extra today. An advertisement by a package tour operator in the *Financial Times* for a 'Walking Tour to Sanitago [*sic*] de Compostela' in 2003 reassures prospective participants that 'Accommodation throughout the tour will be in the best available hotels including 5 star historic paradors. The tour also includes a number of outstanding meals in excellent local restaurants, including one listed in the Michelin Guide'! Furthermore, 'a support vehicle is never far from your route', should over-indulgence in those 'outstanding' meals render you incapable of further foot-slogging.[17] In the light of such touristic exploitation, the adoption of the *Camino* by the Council of Europe and UNESCO is a mixed blessing: as the erstwhile Chair of the Confraternity of St James put it recently in a valedictory address: 'The former's commitment has taken the form of a great deal of monstrous sign-posting, rather than action which might have prevented the damage done in the run-up to [the Holy Year of] 1993; the latter's involvement came only after the damage was done, thereby giving it the seal of approval – but they are all we have.'[18]

ST JAMES: A FEW FACTS AND A LOT OF FICTION

In the Budapest Szépművészeti Múzeum may be seen one of Giovanni Tiepolo's more striking works, simply entitled *Saint James the Greater* (1749). It depicts the handsome saint astride a white horse, in his left hand a snow-white banner emblazoned with a blood-red cross; in his right, a dagger held to the head of a cowering dark-skinned foe. It is ironic that he is apparently sitting on an Arab stallion, for the picture celebrates the moment when St James, who had been dead for 800 years, miraculously appeared at the battle of Clavijo in 834 to rescue the Christians in their struggle against Islamic forces. One delayed consequence of the Christian victory was the obligation placed on all the liberated territories of Spain to pay tribute in perpetuity to the church at Compostela in recognition of St James's military services: every acre of ploughed land and vineyard had to contribute a bushel of corn or an equivalent amount of wine, an obligation that survived until 1834, although it was sometimes challenged. Tiepolo's picture, a finely painted late Baroque example of propaganda for the faith, sums up the sheer effrontery of the St James cult and its exploitation. Leaving aside the small difficulty that the battle of Clavijo probably never took place at all, the ninth-century diploma supposedly issued by the Asturian King Ramiro I (842–50), which promulgated the Santiago levies or tax to be paid by a grateful population, was only 'discovered' (that is, forged) at Compostela in the twelfth century. In any case, it could not have been issued by Ramiro following the battle in 834, as claimed, since he did not ascend the throne until eight years later. 'It is a wry thought', writes Edwin Mullins, 'that one of the most magnificent cathedrals in the world . . . should have been paid for substantially out of a fraudulent tax perpetrated by the Church authorities themselves for the entire period of six hundred years over which the present building is spread, from the Romanesque in the 12th century to the High Baroque in the 18th.'[19]

So far as can be determined, *Santiago Matamoros* ('Saint James the Moor-Slayer') never actually visited Spain during his lifetime, though he did put in some forty appearances after his death to help out in various battles, and even skipped across to the New World to assist in the genocide of Indian tribes.[20] The Apostle's career before his death is somewhat less spectacular: according to the gospels, he and his brother John (the Evangelist), the sons of Zebedee, were fishermen on the Sea of Galilee, business partners of two other men casting their nets nearby, Simon called Peter and Andrew, who were likewise summoned by Jesus to become 'fishers of men' (Matthew 4: 19). Jesus called Zebedee's offspring 'Boanerges', the Sons of Thunder, on account of their (occasionally misdirected) zeal, and their evident closeness to him may also lend weight to the belief that they were first cousins to the Messiah.[21] James and John are recorded as being present when Jesus appeared after the Resurrection at Lake Tiberias, but nothing else is heard of James until his martyrdom at the hands of Herod Agrippa in AD 44.

Everything else propagated about James would appear to be legend, starting with the idea that the Apostles divided up the world into spheres for their missions and James was allocated Iberia. *The Golden Legend* of Jacobus de Voragine, a collection of so-called lives of the saints compiled around 1260, stamped with its dubious authority the legend existing since the seventh century that James had in fact preached in Spain, however with startlingly modest success, making just nine converts. He did leave two acolytes to continue his work, Athanasius and Theodore, whose bones were so conveniently discovered with those of the saint himself in 1879. The next part of the legend concerns the *translatio*, whereby it is claimed that St James's followers took his body to the coast and deposited it in a stone boat that was carried by the wind (with a little help from the Angel of the Lord) beyond the Pillars of Hercules (the Straits of Gibraltar) to Padrón, near Finisterre on the north-west Atlantic coast of Spain. Thanks to the assistance of the celestial auxiliary, the voyage took only a week (compilers of legends were always gratifyingly precise about such details); and despite an initially discouraging reception from the local pagan queen, Lupa, the disciples were able, with divine help, to thwart her intrigues against them, so that she converted to Christianity and donated a burial ground for the saint. The spot where his modest mausoleum was built, eventually to be the site of Compostela, then lapsed into obscurity, as did the saint, for 800 years.

In the reign of Alfonso II (791–842), a Galician hermit named Pelayo, guided by 'a big star burning low over a thickly wooded hill near the River Sar', stumbled on a small shrine and sarcophagus. The local bishop was summoned, and after much fasting and prayer – but also assisted by a piece of parchment fortuitously lying next to the remains in the sarcophagus – was able to pronounce that this was the long-forgotten tomb of St James. Alfonso was astute enough to realise that the Christians needed an inspiration as powerful as the relics of the prophet claimed by the mosque at Córdoba, and immediately proclaimed James to be the patron saint of the Spain that had already been wrested from the infidel, and also of the rest of Spain that would be reconquered in the future with the saint's assistance. Alfonso ordered the first church to be built on the site of the discovery of the tomb, soon to be joined by a baptistery, other churches and a monastery. Following Old Testament precedent, Alfonso planned the first shrine as a Levitical city, that is to say, one dedicated to a priestly caste with rights and privileges involving territory and grazing rights.[22] The burgeoning ecclesiastical centre, already with numerous miracles to its credit, was called Compostela (*Campus stellae*) or starry field, after the miraculous circumstances surrounding the rediscovery of the saint's last resting place. That, at any rate, became the tradition.[23]

This basic outline of the story is barnacled with many other stories and legends that mostly do not concern us here, except in one respect, the name of Compostela itself. As we saw from Eusebius' *Onomasticon* and the 'religious geography' discussed in the previous chapter on the Holy Land, nomenclature plays a crucial role for the pilgrim in building and holding together a particular vision of the past and its relationship to the present. However, while Holy Land pilgrims sought to identify the places they visited with those where events were recorded in the scriptures, the evocative name of Compostela proved to be a touchstone for myths and fables, all of which tended to enhance its numinous aura. In modern times writers have been less inhibited in speculating that this aura may have been inherited from pagan times. To borrow Edwin Mullins's lyrical formulation:

Santiago, far away under the mists and Atlantic skies of Galicia, all woods and water in a Celtic landscape of menhirs and lost gods, exerted an appeal that was infinitely pre-Christian. The route to Santiago was a Roman trade-route. It was nicknamed by travellers *la voie lactée*, the Milky Way. It was the road under the stars. The pale arm of the Milky Way stretched out and pointed the way to the edge of the known world where the sun went down: to Cape Finisterre (from the Latin *finis terra* – the end of the earth).[24]

In the Middle Ages, the pilgrim's journey did not stop at Santiago, but continued to the chapel of Nuestra Señora at Finisterre, 'the last finger of land crooked into the ocean . . . Here may have been a journey to heaven more mystical and of a far earlier provenance than the church can have been expected to acknowledge.'[25]

As for the appellation 'Compostela', it has been suggested that its association with a pre-Christian star-led route is one of the reasons why the Santiago pilgrimage has had such a primeval hold over the imagination (after all, there are dozens of potentially successful pilgrimage places that have not caught on in the same way). According to this theory, the pilgrimage's popularity rests on a 'never extinguished folk memory of a starry road that led to the western end of the world, its permanent indicator being the Milky Way . . . This ageless road of the stars led straight to the [pre-Christian, Celtic] sanctuary of the god Lupa, and later to that of the Apostle, James the Great.' The same author adds that the most recent philological scholarship no longer derives the name Compostela from *campus stellae* (an interpolated etymology created to support the Santiago legends), but from *compositum tellus*, meaning an 'ordered region, a fashioned landscape'. This, he suggests, is a reference to the geomantic function of the distribution of menhirs, dolmens and ceremonially significant 'blind springs' exactly in the region where the Santiago cult has flourished, pagan monuments that marked an ancient pre-Christian concentration of atavistic ritual and of spiritual energy such as existed at Chartres and other great Christian sites.[26] This seems more plausible than the Latinists' derivation from the word *compostum* (cemetery), since at the time that the name Compostela first appears in mid-eleventh-century documents, nothing was known of the shrine's underlying ninth-century graves, later to be discovered by archaeology.

The stars of the Milky Way play a significant role in another important legend connected with Compostela, namely that which connected Charlemagne with the discovery of the saint's burial place and claimed that he founded a church there. This story is elaborated in the fourth book of the *Codex Calixtinus* held at Compostela and supposedly written by one Turpin, the Carolingian Archbishop of Rheims, but in fact a fabrication and therefore known as the *Pseudo-Turpin*. This chronicle[27] relates how a sleepless Charlemagne was perplexed by the recurrence of a starry road stretching over the western sky, across France and Spain towards the end of the world. One night he is visited by a phantom who introduces himself as St James and tells him that his (James's) mortal remains lie in Galicia in an unknown tomb in a region where the Saracens oppress the land. Charlemagne's duty is to recapture the road leading to the tomb and rid the land of the Saracens. The starry way that he saw night after night indicated that he would go to Galicia at the head of a great host, and subsequently all the peoples of the earth would follow the same path on pilgrimage, up to the end of time. A relief on the Charlemagne shrine (1215) in the treasury of the cathedral at

Aachen shows the startled emperor lying in bed and being admonished to embark on his Iberian mission. In fact Charlemagne's Spanish campaigns were effectively over by 801, when Barcelona was captured and made the centre of the Spanish March. Linking him with St James was a post-hoc exercise in anachronistic historiography, a propagandist tactic yoking the most famous defender of Christianity to the gathering momentum of the *Reconquista*.

The *Pseudo-Turpin* (written *c.* 1150) harmonised two conflicting traditions of the *Chansons de Geste* and relocated the shrines of the great Carolingian heroes along the two French roads of the *Camino*. In this version, Charlemagne himself became the first of the Compostela pilgrims – quite a feat as he would have been dead for some sixteen years before there was a shrine to visit. A later insertion apparently made by local clerics (chapter 19), conveniently has Charlemagne ordaining that all powers, both ecclesiastical and civil, shall be subject to the see of Compostela. For good measure it commanded that all should pay an annual tithe to Compostela, that there should be no rival bishop of Iria Flavia (as there had been traditionally), and finally that Compostela should be reckoned an apostolic see of equal status with Rome and Ephesus.[28] All this was doubtless an extension of the empire-building begun by Compostela's formidable bishop (1101–49) and from 1124 first archbishop, Diego Gelmírez;[29] but it also turned to useful account the insultingly chauvinistic character of *Pseudo-Turpin*'s glorification of Charlemagne and the French at the expense of native Spanish dignity.[30]

The part of the *Pseudo-Turpin* concerning the *Song of Roland* adds lustre to the tales of Charlemagne's campaigns against the infidel, notwithstanding that Roland and the rearguard of the Carolingian army had in all probability been ambushed and slain by the local Basques at Roncesvalles in 778. The Basques were understandably incensed by the great campaigner's deliberate destruction of the city walls of their capital, Pamplona, in order to deny the enemy a strategic stronghold. There is no trace of all that in *Pseudo-Turpin*, of course: the dastardly Basques have mutated into dastardly Saracens, so it is hardly surprising that the *Chanson de Roland* was favoured for recitation by pilgrims in the later Middle Ages, as they made their way to Compostela. The *Liber Peregrinationis*, or Pilgrim's Guide, which follows on from the *Pseudo-Turpin* as the fifth book of the same codex, capitalises on the Carolingian legacy:

> In the Landes of the Bordelais . . . one should visit the bodies of the holy martyrs Oliver, Gondebaud . . . Ogier . . . Arastain . . . Garin . . . and many other warriors of Charlemagne, who, after conquering the pagan armies, were slaughtered in Spain for the Christian faith. Their companions brought back their precious bodies as far as Belin [Gironde] and there buried them with the greatest care. There they lie all together in one tomb, from which emanates a very sweet fragrance wherewith the sick are cured.[31]

The guide also informs us that Roland's body rests in the basilica of St Romanus at Blaye (Gironde) and his ivory horn, split down the middle by the strength of his blowing, may be seen in St Severin's basilica at Bordeaux.

THE *CODEX CALIXTINUS*, AIMERY PICAUD AND THE *PILGRIM'S GUIDE*

An important boost to the pilgrimage to Santiago was provided in the twelfth
century by the so-called *Codex Calixtinus* (*c.* 1150),[32] parts of which have already
been quoted. Its association with Pope Calixtus II (1119–24) is entirely bogus:
the pope's letter introducing and puffing the whole seems to have been a
marketing ploy by the compiler, thought to have been one Aimery (or Aymery, or
Aimeric) Picaud (Aymericus Picaudus in the Latinised form). A more helpful
description of the codex's contents is implied by its alternative title, namely the
Liber Sancti Jacobi (Book of St James). It is a common view that the five books of
the *Liber Sancti Jacobi* are 'a manual of propaganda, [compiled] in order to boost
the pilgrimage to the tomb of St James';[33] however, as we shall see, the guidebook
part at least could only be 'propaganda' aimed at masochists. Book One of the
codex consists of poems and hymns by various hands for chanting by the
Compostela pilgrims; Book Two contains accounts of Compostela miracles
during the lifetime of the cathedral city's first and most famous archbishop,
Diego Gelmírez; Book Three relates, as if it were fact, St James's evangelisation of
Spain, his martyrdom in Jerusalem and the *translatio*, or miraculous conveyance
of his body from the Holy Land to the north-west coast of Spain; Book Four is the
chronicle of the *Pseudo-Turpin* described above; last but not least, Book Five is the
famous guide for pilgrims (*Liber peregrinationis*) written by 'Aimery Picaud', which
has been described as the first European guidebook.

Not a great deal is known about Aimery Picaud, and it is not entirely clear which
other parts of the *Codex Calixtinus* he wrote (or fabricated), or to what extent he
edited and compiled the rest. What *is* clear is the strong French influence on the
whole: Alfonso VI (1072–1109) of Léon-Castile had embarked on a francophile
dynastic and ecclesiastical policy that led, *inter alia*, to an increase of French clerics
at Compostela. It seems likely that the Benedictines of Cluny played a major role,
not only in the development of the St James pilgrimage, but also in the strongly
Gallic slant of the materials in the *Codex*.[34] In one part of the latter, Aimery Picaud
is described as a French priest from Parthenay-le-Vieux, 30 miles west of Poitiers,
who supposedly made the journey to Santiago with a Flemish lady called Gerberga
(Ginberga Flandrensis in the Latinised form). This lady donated a manuscript of
the *Codex* to the cathedral, where it is still housed, the compilation possibly having
been made at the request of Don Pedro Elias, Archbishop of Santiago from 1149.
However, it seems odd that a priest should travel with a female companion, and in
fact most of the manuscripts feature a Picaud *Doppelgänger* called Olivier d'Asquins
(Asquins near Vézelay), who is a more likely (or at least a more appropriate)
companion for Gerberga. Just to confuse things further, the name 'Aymericus', to
whom chapter IX of the *Pilgrim's Guide* is jointly attributed with Pope Calixtus, has
been identified as the latter's chancellor, an historical figure who died in 1141. A
different 'Aymericus' (possibly) is claimed as the author of chapter V of the *Guide*.
Finally, yet another person has also been suggested as its author, namely Aymeric
the Jerusalem monk, who was in Compostela in 1131 on a mission from the Latin
patriarch.

The audience for the *Pilgrim's Guide*, like its author, was indubitably French, since Spaniards could hardly have been expected to relish the uninhibited abuse of their nation(s) that the book contains. Internal evidence suggests that the compiler, whichever Aimery he was (or none), was not uncultivated, a knowledgeable cleric who was sufficiently well off to travel by horse. He probably made his way along the Paris–Tours route *c.* 1135. One wonders, moreover, how the *Pilgrim's Guide*, written on parchment, was expected to be used. The most likely usage would have been perusal in a monastery before setting out on a pilgrimage. Only the very rich would have taken such a work on a journey with them, and the majority of pilgrims were illiterate. It could therefore have been something that was read out to pilgrims, although its far from encouraging account of the dangers to be encountered on the road hardly constitute the 'propaganda' for the St James pilgrimage some scholars have postulated.[35]

Be all that as it may, Picaud's splendid work is not only the first, but certainly one of the most entertaining European guidebooks ever written. Walter Starkie remarks that it is 'the antithesis to the modern guidebooks . . . because they are designed to give the globe-trotter of today a fine supply of labels, which he may stick on his mind and administer just the right dose of potted knowledge'. In short, they produce the illusion that not a moment has been wasted and the traveller has 'mercifully been spared all adventure'.[36] By contrast, Picaud's text combines its elevated educative purpose with an earthy, and often erratic, Chaucerian commentary on places and people. Renato Stoppani has commented on 'the tendency of medieval religiosity to materialise the spiritual (sometimes at the cost of making it banal)',[37] and the guide does indeed exhibit a curious mixture of official piety and personal prejudice. Another writer has commented that the detailed timetable of feast days for the saints to be honoured en route would almost certainly have implied that a fair was held on the same day, so that 'sacred and secular motivations were appealed to simultaneously'.[38] The most startlingly profane element in the guide is Picaud's chauvinistic attack on the Basques, Navarrese and Galicians who will be encountered along the *Camino*. He is at pains to underline their villainous behaviour and sometimes lewd practices, while losing no opportunity of praising the folk (and especially those of his home region) who live east of the Pyrenees.

Picaud's text is thus a somewhat whimsical mixture of wild prejudice, useful information and exact architectural description – of autopsy combined with tradition and anecdote. As Serafín Moralejo writes in defence of the guide and its author: 'the text as we know it seems to be the end result of compiling notes made from direct observation, memories that were perhaps not as reliable as they ought to have been, and written or oral hearsay that was not always truthful or properly understood'. If we bear that in mind, 'then the Guide's mixture of precision and vagueness, and even its flagrant contradictions, are hardly surprising'.[39] All this however must be viewed in the context of the spiritual and aesthetic values made manifest in detailed description of churches, of relics and (in the lengthy concluding section) of the basilica at Compostela itself. And the author closes with the heartfelt admonition, no doubt born of bitter experience, that pilgrims, whether poor or rich, returning from the abode of Saint James or going there, ought to be charitably received and honoured by all peoples. For whoever will receive them and will attend diligently to their lodging will have not only the blessed James, but also the true Lord Himself as guest. The Lord Himself said in His Gospel: 'He that receives you receives me.'[40]

THE *LIBER PEREGRATIONIS* IN DETAIL

The *Liber Peregrationis* has eleven chapters, a total of some 13,000 words, and is featured in twelve manuscripts, of which the earliest and most accurate is that in the archive of the cathedral of Santiago de Compostela. Scholars have suggested a date between 1138 and *c.* 1140 for this version, and believe it was produced either in France or in Santiago itself.[41] The epilogue to the whole *Codex Calixtinus*, of which the *Guide* is the Fifth Book, claims it was written (or compiled) in various places, including Rome and Jerusalem but 'chiefly at Cluny', which would be no surprise, given its French bias. The first chapter deals with the roads of St James, that is the four roads leading from different parts of France to Santiago. These roads acted as feeders for pilgrims from further afield, for example, the Via Tolosana (from Arles via Toulouse) for those from Provence, Italy, Greece and south-east Europe. This route was also the pilgrimage link between the two apostolic seats, Santiago and Rome, via the famous Via Francigena and traversing ancient Roman roads (Via Cassia, Aurelia and Emilia). The second route in the *Guide* is the Via Podiensis (the route from Le Puy), used by Burgundians and Germans; then comes the Via Lemosina (the route from Vézelay, via Limoges), chiefly for pilgrims from central France; and finally the Via Turonensis (from Paris via Orleans and Tours), which was frequented not only by pilgrims coming from the royal seat, but also those from Flanders and England. These itineraries crossed the Pyrenees either through the Somport Pass (thereafter following the *Camino Aragones* to Compostela), or through the Roncevalles Pass (thereafter following the historically most important route, known as the *Camino francés*, the 'French Way', which united several routes at Puente la Reina). The *Camino francés*, described in the *Pilgrim's Guide*, followed pretty closely the ancient Roman road, which may well have witnessed pagan pilgrimages in Roman and pre-Roman times: its final stretch leads through a menhir-studded landscape to mystical Finisterre, 'the End of the Earth' at the far north-westerly point of Spain.

The starting points of these routes – Tours, Vézelay, Le Puy and Arles – developed into flourishing centres of medieval piety, especially Tours with its St Martin cult, to whose tomb, says Picaud, 'the sick come and are cured, the possessed are delivered, the blind are given sight, the lame are raised up . . .'[42] Fifteenth-century itineraries and travel reports like those of Arnold von Harff or the Swiss monk, Hermann Künig, or the Englishman William Wey's *Informacon for Pylgrymes*, essentially follow Picaud with some variations that may have been caused by local warfare or other hindrances. There seems more than an echo of

Picaud in Künig's 1521 guide covering the route from Einsiedeln in Switzerland and back to Aachen, but with the novelty of being written in 651 occasionally bizarre lines of verse. He warns of deceitful innkeepers, praises the charitable hospitals en route and assiduously counts the miles and the number of bridges, as well as dealing with rates of exchange, customs duties and the like.[43] The purely commercial *Itinéraires de Bruges* features, *inter alia*, the St James route from Paris, a clear indication of its long-standing economic significance. Quasi-topographical guides or travelogues add refinements such as listing the number of stone bridges on the way (Arnold von Harff) or, as in the Bruges *Itinéraire* and *Le Chemin de Paris à Compostelle et combien il y a de lieues de ville en ville*, give the mileages between cities. Picaud is still the basis for the sixteenth-century *Guide des Chemins* and Nicolas Bonfons's *La Nouvelle Guide* (of which there were several editions between 1552 and 1583). A curiosity is a guide of 1603 with anti-Reformation rhetoric, which claims to be 'only for the use of men of good will, and not for grumblers and calumniators, of which there are far too many in these miserable times'. Above all, it is stated, this guide should not to fall into the hands of 'heretics, Lutherans and Calvinists, who accuse us of idolatry, because we honour the saints'.[44]

Chapter II of the *Pilgrim's Guide* is a mere paragraph giving wildly optimistic day's journeys on the Way of St James, for example, thirteen days for the trek (700 km) between Port de Cize to Santiago – whereas a modern French organiser of equestrian trips allows four weeks![45] Chapter III is only slightly longer and concerns the names of the towns on the road of St James, but is justified by the author as helping pilgrims to assess their necessary outlay en route. Chapter IV, again brief, praises the three famous hospices on the classic pilgrim routes: the one at Jerusalem, the one on the Great St Bernard Pass in the Alps for those going to Rome, and the one at Sta Cristina near the Somport Pass for those going to Santiago. Chapter V briefly honours the clerics and rulers who repaired the road of the blessed St James. Chapter VI must be the first guidebook text to assess the quality of drinking water in the rivers en route ('I have described these rivers, so that pilgrims starting out for Santiago may be careful to avoid drinking in those which are fatal and may choose those which are safe for them and their mounts.').[46] Chapter VII is a long, highly prejudiced account of the names of the lands and the characteristics of the peoples on the road to St James, although its generalised abuse may partly be following literary precedents from antiquity. Chapter VIII, also lengthy, meticulously lists the bodies of the saints that are at rest along the road to St James which pilgrims ought to visit (twenty-one French and four Spanish saints, their relics and monuments). The fact that more monuments are described for the Paris pilgrimage route than for the others may indicate that this was the route that Picaud himself took, although he begins at Orleans, not Paris.

Chapter IX begins to look like a chapter from a modern guidebook. It is concerned with the characteristics of the city and the basilica of St James the Apostle of Galicia. It catches our attention for the way in which Picaud mixes science with enthusiasm, uses vague terms like 'nave' for several different kinds of space, such as the transept or aisle, but also employs a number of technical building terms, the meanings of which remain unclear. The measurements given follow Vitruvius in using man as the unit of measurement, the height of a man being 'eight palms'. (Elsewhere, and more romantically Picaud says that, to a man who ascends the mountain at Port de Cize, 'it seems he can touch the sky with his own hand'.) The different parts of the church are also anthropomorphically compared to parts of the human body, the trunk corresponding to the nave. There is an interest in spatial effects or relationships, and evidence of real aesthetic appreciation, as well as awe and wonder. There is also a paragraph on the souvenir trade, explaining that, on the parvis beyond the fountain of St James, practical items for pilgrims (flasks, sandals, scrips, medicinal herbs and so on) are offered for sale, as are memorabilia, including the scallop shell, the famous insignia for the St James pilgrimage, which is here mentioned for the first time in the *Guide* but also in other parts of *Codex Calixtinus*. (The origin of the scallop shell's link to St James is obscure: antiquity associated the shell with Venus, who was allegedly born in a shell and carried across the ocean to Cythera, as in Botticelli's celebrated depiction. Picaud's mention of it reflects its establishment in the twelfth century as a *laissez-passer* for the pilgrims of St James, later for pilgrims in general.) After dealing with these tempting shopping opportunities, the *Guide* resumes its description of the basilical architecture, and of its altars and artistic treasures, concluding with remarks on the stonemasons who worked on it and on the clerical hierarchy of Santiago. Chapter X deals with the number of canons of St James, while, finally, chapter XI deals with how pilgrims of St James are to be received.

The *Guide* is all the more fascinating for its internal contradictions. It is not merely a tale of horrors (we learn that at Estella there is 'good bread, the best of wine, and meat and fish and all good things', and that Compostela itself is 'richest in all delights'), but it is odd that a work presumably designed to encourage pilgrims to make the journey should contain so much that would seem more likely to scare them off. Even if one takes the view that the unevenness of the text is the result of its being the work of several hands, someone must have put the whole together for a purpose, and exactly what that was remains uncertain. To the modern reader the vivid attacks on duplicitous Spaniards are both sinister and hilarious: 'While we were going to Santiago, we met two men of Navarre sitting sharpening their knives [on the river bank]; they are in the habit of skinning the mounts of pilgrims who drink the water and die. When questioned by us, these liars said that it was safe to drink. We therefore watered our horses, and immediately two of them died, which these people skinned on the spot.'[47] There are ferrymen who overcharge and overload boats so that they capsize, drowning the pilgrims and leaving their putative protectors to pick the pockets of the dead. The violent Basques extort illegal tolls. The Navarrese are 'full of malice, swarthy in colour, evil of face, depraved, perverse, perfidious, empty of faith and corrupt, libidinous, drunken, experienced in all violence, ferocious and wild' – and so the tales go on. Moreover, the Navarrese men and women show each other their private parts when warming themselves and the men even 'practise unchaste fornication with animals'. Implausibly, a Navarrese is said to 'hang a padlock behind his mule and his mare, so that none may come near her but himself. He even offers libidinous kisses to the vulva of woman and mule. That is why the Navarrese are to be rebuked by all experienced people.'[48] By contrast the Poitevins (whom we believe to be the natives of Picaud's home region) are 'valiant heroes and fighting men, very experienced in war with bows arrows and lances, daring in the front line of battle, very fast in running, elegant in their dress, distinguished of face, shrewd of speech, very generous with gifts, lavish in hospitality'.[49]

Plus ça change! Seven hundred years later, a review in the *Athenaeum* of Richard Ford's 1845 volume on Spain, one of John Murray's Handbooks, complained bitterly of the author's colourful invective against the unfortunate Spaniards, much of which seems to have a familiar ring if one has read Picaud. For example, Ford describes the Murcians as 'superstitious, litigious and revengeful', the people of Valencia as 'perfidious, vindictive, sullen and mistrustful . . . nowhere is assassination more common; they smile, and murder while they smile'. As for the Aragonese, they are as 'hard-headed, -hearted and -bowelled as the rocks of the Pyrenees . . . they are said to drive nails into the walls with their heads, into which, when anything is driven, nothing can get out.' The reviewer magisterially sums up Ford's faults as a writer and guide to Spain, remarking that 'there is everywhere present [in the book] that fanatical spirit which disregards all candour, and even justice, and is blind to every statement and every fact at variance with its prejudices . . .'.[50]

Chapter VII of the *Pilgrim's Guide* might indeed be vulnerable to the same strictures, at least if the same standards were to be applied to a text of the twelfth century as to one of the nineteenth. Yet, despite that vulnerability, and despite the erratic detours into Mandeville-like fantasy (for example, we suddenly learn that Cornish people, sent by Julius Caesar to Spain to subdue the natives, are a race of men with tails) there is plenty of what appears to be plausible and helpful information for readers. And even though the Basque speech reminds the author of the barking of dogs, and is 'utterly barbarous', he still gives a useful brief vocabulary of Basque words (useful also to scholars, since it is one of the earliest records of the language.) Moreover, the countryside is often praised, even as the inhabitants are condemned: Castile is 'full of riches, gold and silver, blessed with fodder and very strong horses, well provided with bread wine and honey', though of course it is 'full of wicked and vicious people'. These passages contrast with the long and detailed accounts of the shrines along the Way of St James that are to be visited and the miracles associated with them, and with the final careful account of Compostela and its churches and the great basilica. The systematic survey of ecclesiastical architecture and the iconography of the basilica's sculpture (which is unique in the records of the time) gives legitimation to the claims made for the *Liber Peregrinationis* as the first true guidebook in Europe, one indeed that held its own for centuries.

Just how strong the influence of this remarkable work has been may be seen from the numerous translations made of it, and from the constant references to it in the guides to *El Camino de Santiago*, even today. The classic among these modern guides bears the English title *A Practical Guide for Pilgrims: The Road to Santiago* and was written by the founder of the Centro Estudios Camino Santiago in Sahagún, Professor Millán Bravo Lozano. Originally published in Spanish, this pragmatic reconstruction of *el camino francés* is now in its eighth edition.[51] Medieval tradition and modern guidebook practice are here brilliantly combined in a work that guides the user through a spiritual, as well as an aesthetic and historical experience. The topographical part (with excellent facing maps) is supplemented by art, history and legends; and each section is rounded off by an eyewitness comment from Aimery Picaud, often supplemented by those from three later well-known accounts of the route written between the fifteenth and seventeenth centuries.[52] This labour of love, a product of the late twentieth-century boom in Santiago studies, closes the circle between the pilgrim of the Middle Ages and today. The ghost of Aimery Picaud, now a cawing raven of ill fame, now a cooing dove of piety and awe, sits on the compiler's shoulder, and indeed on the shoulder of every reader, whether he goes by car, or by bicycle – but above all as he makes his way on foot. As the author remarks at the beginning: 'The pilgrim's way offers something to everyone, whether it be in respect of a religious or aesthetic experience, or whether it be in terms of self-realisation. The aim of this book is that the pilgrim should understand the nature of this message.'[53]

It is a message that resonates through the ages, in Raymond Oursel's words, '*à travers tout le Moyen Âge, le nom de Saint-Jacques-de-Compostelle résonne comme une harmonie de cloches sonores, exaltantes et joyeuses: l'écho en parvient, lointain, jusque dans les brumes des indifférences et des reniements d'aujourd'hui, les pénètre d'une poésie mélancolique*' ('throughout the entire Middle Ages, the name of Santiago de Compostela resonates like the harmony of sonorous, exultant and joyful bells; remotely the echo reaches us, even through the fog of indifference and denial of life today, infusing it with a melancholy poetry').[54]

CHAPTER 5

All Roads Lead to Rome

It is not the learned nostalgia of a Gibbon that pervades the *Mirabilia*. It is
something more earnest and more naïve, a desire for knowledge without the
means of gratifying it.

(Jonathan Sumption, Pilgrimage, 2002)

After all these great cryers of many wonderful things [i.e. Livy, Marco Polo,
'Sir John Mandeville'] I will follow with a small piping of such strange cities
as I have seen and such strange things as I have heard . . . I shall not write
but that I find in authors, that is the first principle, or else that I saw with my
own eyes, and that is the second; or else what I suppose to be the view of the
best authority.

(John Capgrave (c. 1450) in his account of Rome)

In 20 BC, the Emperor Augustus created the office of *curator viarum*, an official
responsible for the upkeep of the Roman roads. To mark the event, a bronze
column, the *milliario aureo* or 'Golden Milestone', was erected in the Forum
close to the temple of Saturn,[1] from which point the consular roads led off to the
provinces of the Roman Empire: the Via Aurelia, the Via Ostiensis, the Via
Flaminia, the Via Salaria and the Via Appia. On the milestone were gilded figures
recording the mileages from Rome to the various imperial cities. The existence
of this terminus was the origin of the saying that 'all roads lead to Rome', a
phrase that was not only topographically symbolic (any road, if followed to its
source would lead to the great capital city of Rome), but also became
metaphorical by analogy, the idea that 'all efforts of thought converge in a
common centre'.[2] Rome thus became emblematic of an idea realised through
technological proficiency, not perhaps the 'navel of the world' in quite the same
way as Jerusalem (even if Septimius Severus thought otherwise), but the beating

heart of empire.[3] At least by the time the Colosseum, and later the city itself had made it onto the list of wonders of the world, we can imagine that Rome had become the potential focus of secular touristic pilgrimage; with the founding of the papacy, it had also become the focus of religious pilgrimage that continues to this day. Both kinds of pilgrimage generated a need for city plans, itineraries and guidebook literature.

SHOWING THE WAY, DESCRIBING THE CITY

We have already seen how Rome boasted a marble map (*orbis pictus*) of the inhabited world (the *oikoumene*) that existed towards the end of the first century BC (see Chapter 1) and was located at the Porticus Vipsania. To what extent this was a symbolic artefact, like painting maps red to show the extent of the British Empire, and to what extent it was practical (for example, whether it showed a calibration of distances), remains a matter of dispute. However, it is easy to understand the need for the city's inhabitants to to be able to visualise the extent of the vast territories of which they were the beneficiaries, and also their need for some sort of practical and decorative plan of the city itself. The earliest evidence of such is supplied by the surviving fragments of the *Forma Urbis Romae*, whose 151 marble slabs decorated a wall of Vespasian's library adjoining a so-called temple of Romulus[4] and showed the city of Rome after AD 203. It may have been the successor of an earlier such plan erected at this site in the Flavian period. Indeed, Vespasian, the first of the Flavians, in his capacity as joint-censor with his son Titus, is known to have ordered a topographical measurement of Rome in AD 74; doubtless this was a purely administrative measure, but it would have created a useful databank for public information.[5] It also set a precedent for later collections of topographical data ordered by secular rulers, and after them the popes, elements of which were to be exploited by the first compilers of guides to the city.

The *Forma* itself, not completed until 208 under Septimius Severus, was over 18 metres high and more than 13 metres wide.[6] Its scale varied between 1:189 and 1:413, and south was at the top (not unusual in antiquity, unlike modern cartography where north is at the top of a map as you read it). It has been claimed that this was the most accurate plan of Rome until the famous one made in 1748, 1,500 years later, by G.B. Nolli. Nolli certainly drew on the *Forma* and displayed its fragments on the staircase of the Capitoline Museums in 1741. The holes made for its fixing hooks can still be seen in the wall of the Vespasian library,[7] which was converted in the sixth century into the church of Sts Cosmas and Damian, but the remaining fragments have been stored away from public access.[8] This is a pity, as the *Forma* offers unique archaeological evidence of Rome as it was at the beginning of the third century.

If we know rather little about Roman cartography, Roman itineraries survived as a basis for travel information throughout the Middle Ages, a period when map-making in the Christian world often descended into fantasy and superstition. Only with the Renaissance did cartography acquire a degree of scientific authority, for example, with the publication in 1500 of a *Romwegkarte* by a compass-maker of Nürnberg named Erhard Etzlaub. The creation of this route-plan for the roads to Rome was probably motivated by a desire to cash in on the Holy Year at the turn of the fifteenth century. The map was still south-oriented however, with Rome at the top left-hand corner and the rest of the plan being a densely annotated display of routes from Germany to the Holy City. An interestingly novel aid for the pilgrim was the listing of the longest days for each latitude in the left-hand margin, so that wayfarers could more easily reckon the hour by which they needed to arrive at a given city's gates, to avoid being shut out for the night. In Schleswig, the longest day is given as seventeen and a half hours; but in Florence it is only fifteen and a quarter. For the first time since antiquity, distances between towns were quite accurately listed by ingeniously making each dot of the dotted line running between them equal to one German mile (7.4 km).[9] Etzlaub's innovation, therefore, was to enable travellers to plan their route and timetable in advance, taking account also of natural obstacles like rivers and the Alps,[10] much as we might today plan our travels with the guidebook before us on the kitchen table and a glass of red wine at our elbow.

As far as Rome itself was concerned, the origins of topographical and descriptive material lie with official data compiled in the fourth and fifth centuries, material that adopted the division of Rome into fourteen regions. This division goes back to the urban reforms of Augustus (63 BC–AD 14), the *rioni* (districts) becoming *rejoni* in the Middle Ages. They were reorganised in 1789 and again in 1938 under Fascism, but the *rioni* still exist, though now there are twenty-two of them and only the boundary of Trastevere remains much as it was in Roman times. According to the historian Gregorovius, these early surveys (*Notitia*)[11] were forgotten or lost for some four centuries, resurfacing in the time of Charlemagne and later attracting the interest of Renaissance scholars.[12] Another compilation, called the *Curiosum urbis Romae* (of fourth-century origin), dealt with the most significant buildings, public spaces and 'curiosities' in the various regions. Common elements of such texts lived on in the fragmentary topographical guides or itineraries that have survived from the early Middle Ages. A recurrent feature was an appendix consisting of an apparently arbitrary list of the city's topographical, architectural and institutional features, such as obelisks, bridges, hills, basilicas and the like. These often look like bastardised versions of similar lists that had already appeared in the *regionaria*, or administrative gazetteers, of the fourth century, which counted both public and private buildings quarter by quarter. From them one could learn not only how many libraries, baths, aqueducts, granaries or brothels (forty-six!) there were at the time, but also how many golden (eighty), how many ivory (seventy-four) and how many equestrian (twenty-two) statues. Perhaps even more interesting, they also recorded the numbers of houses for the well-to-do (1,790 *domi*), and those for the other classes (44,000 *insulae*, or tenement dwellings).[13] In data such as this many of the principal ingredients of the classic guidebook were already present in embryonic form.

Between the eighth and the eleventh centuries, pilgrims' itineraries involving tours of Rome gradually evolved into the celebrated and often whimsical *Mirabilia Romae* discussed later in this chapter. At least from the tenth century, 'Notebooks', some of them already amounting to brief guides, and often compiled by foreign communities[14] in Rome for use by their compatriots, became increasingly popular. From about 1100, a burgeoning topographical and antiquarian interest is discernible, an aspect of what the historian Charles Homer Haskins, following Panofsky, has dubbed the 'twelfth-century Renaissance'. Franks and Germans began to make notes and sketches as a memorial of their perambulations of the city, which became the distant forerunners of the bulky modern guide, even if their efforts only amounted to a few leaves of parchment. In so far as these dealt with antique Rome, they may have been based on the *Notitia* and *Curiosum*; for the Christian heritage, there were lists of 'stations' (churches of particular liturgical significance), cemeteries and basilicas. The confluence of these discrete categories of information, of the antiquary's scholarly interests and the pilgrim's devotional focus, formed the basis from which sprang the diverse compilations known as *Mirabilia*, that proved to have such remarkable staying power over some four centuries. As in a modern guide, buildings from antiquity began to feature alongside those of the Christian era (or vice versa), and the traditions of the pagan sages mingled with the legends of the saints.[15]

PIETY AND PAPAL GREED: IMAGE AND REALITY IN EARLY PILGRIMS' GUIDES

By the seventh century there were already a number of so-called pilgrims' guides to Rome, one such being the *Notitia ecclesiarum urbis Romae*, which probably dates to the pontificate of Honorius I (625–38). Although loosely called a 'guide', and perhaps used in this way, the *Notitia* was more probably written up originally as a record for the ecclesiastical authorities of what was being visited by the pious, rather than as a vade mecum for the latter.[16] It is indeed no more than a sparse enumeration of legends attached to certain churches, crypts and a few sites of martyrdom, but it does indicate whether the buildings mentioned are located to the left or right of the indicated route through the city. Not dissimilar was the mid-century *Liber de locis sanctis martyrum quae sunt foris civitatis Romae*.[17] Apparently an extract from a more extensive description of Rome, this begins with St Peter's, where the *Notitia* ends, traverses a similar route as the latter, but in reverse, ending at the Via Flaminia in the north. This is a more colourful text, containing several bold assertions to satisfy the medieval pilgrim's hunger for physical memorials of the faith. It claims, for instance, that an altar in St Peter's was made by the saint himself; and that a rock kept in the oratory of St Stephen the Protomartyr on the Ostia road was used in his stoning; or that elsewhere the actual grid on which St Laurence was burned, and the prison chains that bound St Peter, were still to be seen (the last two items are still on display today).[18]

A third surviving itinerary, inserted into William of Malmesbury's twelfth-century *De gestis regum Anglorum* ('History of the Kings of England', 1120), dates to roughly the same period (seventh–eighth centuries). Its tours begin from the fourteen gates of the Aurelian walls and systematically cover the shrines and cemeteries within their compass.[19] Malmesbury provided a counterweight to the widespread heroising of Rome with a more jaundiced tourist's view of the city, remarking that she seemed 'slight nowadays in comparison with [her] glorious past. And the Romans, whose ancestors wore the toga and and ruled the earth, are now a miserable lazy race who live by selling justice for gold and putting price tags on every canon of the law of the church.'[20] Another Englishman, Walter Map, took a similar tack, wittily making out of the letters R.O.M.E. an abusive acronym, *Radix Omnium Malorum Avaritia* ('Greed is the root of all evil' – this being a reference to the grasping bureaucracy of the papal curia.)[21] Across the coming centuries, the tension between the heroic past and the rent-seeking present, between an intellectual, idealised image and the sordid realities of everyday life where the tourist struggled with corrupt bureaucracy, cheating taxi drivers, rude waiters and swindling hoteliers, was something the guidebook writers would inceasingly have to wrestle with.

GOING BEYOND THE CHRISTIAN HERITAGE: THE ANONYMOUS *EINSIEDELN ITINERARY*

An early mingling of pagan and Christian elements occurs in the famous *Einsiedeln Itinerary and the Collection of Inscriptions,* usually dated to the end of the eighth or the beginning of the ninth century, and so-called because the manuscript is kept in the Swiss monastery of Einsiedeln. It was discovered in the monastery's library in 1683 by the great Maurist scholar Mabillon,[22] and its choice of items seems to denote a first tentative move away from the exclusive focus on Christian memorials in the two earlier texts mentioned above. The manuscript is evidently the work of a Carolingian pilgrim with a considerable interest in antiquity, given the number of imperial and other epitaphs recorded.[23] It is now thought to derive from a monk of the abbey of Fulda in Hesse, who might have visited Italy around the time when Charlemagne was crowned emperor by Pope Leo III (Christmas Day, 800). From his correct copying of the Greek and Latin epitaphs, the anonymous scribe appears to have been conversant with both languages. The particular value of these *Einsidlensis* inscriptions for students of Roman topography lies in the fact that they anticipate the systematic research of epitaphs in the Renaissance by some 500 years, many such valuable clues for the antiquary and historian having been lost in the intervening period. The copying of inscriptions was soon to become an important part of the guidebook writer's job; indeed, in the eighteenth century it developed into a positive mania among learned travellers, who rivalled Polemon, the ancient Greek *stelokopas* ('devourer of stelae'), in their enthusiasm for the task.[24] The related practice of taking brass rubbings lingered on through

generations of schoolboys until twentieth-century mass entertainment killed off
such innocent pursuits.

The second part of the *Einsidlensis* comprises the Itinerary (Pilgrim's Guide or
so-called *Regionar* of the city of Rome). It actually consists of twelve tours that
take in the most important Christian churches and various antique monuments.
These tours appear to combine some autopsy with a good deal of copying from
an existing plan of the city dating from Late Antiquity or the early Middle Ages.[25]
This probability is heightened by the way the distance of the monuments from
the route follows no regular pattern – it is in fact quite erratic – and by the fact
that the guide, as so often with any irritating travelling companion who hogs the
Baedeker, sometimes gets muddled between left and right. Indeed, the twelfth
route (which bizarrely crops up among the Inscriptions, far from its appropriate
place in the manuscript) is thought by scholars to have been extracted from the
original city plan, from which the author liberally helped himself, sometimes
with distortions, when compiling the other eleven.[26] The net result, it has been
remarked, is often frustrating: 'superfluous for those possessing the plan and of
little use to those who did not'.[27] To this extent, the *Einsidlensis* can be seen as an
'awful example' of a guidebook whose readers might well have been better off
with the originals from which the writer had lifted his material, had they but
known it.

Nevertheless, there is some internal consistency in the organisation of the
eleven routes,[28] the items directly on them are mostly correctly marked and the
clear intention is to provide a guided tour for the Rome visitor. The
identification of features along the way reveals the guide as inhabiting a
transitional mental space between antiquity and the early Middle Ages, whereby
the church of S. Maria in Cosmedin is referred to as the 'Ecclesia in Schola
Graeca', emphasising the influx of refugees from Byzantium during the
iconoclasm upheaval that would have been raging contemporaneously with the
Einsiedeln author's visit. On the other hand, the Basilica Constantinia already
bears the appellation 'Basilica S. Iohannis in Lateranis'; antique monuments,
infrastructure or ruins appear either under their classical names, or with their
medieval Latin ones. As with the inscriptions, a good number of objects are
indicated that had totally vanished by the time of the Renaissance, for example, a
huge Elephantus monument at the Forum Boarium or the mills operating on the
Gianicolo hill. The writer's attention is unevenly divided between the secular and
religious, the practical and the symbolic. It has been justly observed that the
guide was therefore 'meant to appeal to a visitor who [was] Christian, but who
had antiquarian interests and knowledge. Ancient Rome reclaims her place in
the image of the city, long turned Christian.'[29]

The substance of the itinerary consists of itemised monuments, structures and
buildings, very occasionally with a brief comment attached, and is of great
historical and topographical interest. Gerold Walser's recent commentary
(1987)[30] painstakingly seeks to clarify each reference (though some remain
obscure and others are a matter of controversy), enabling us to build up a
picture of the historical background to what the Einsiedeln pilgrim saw, or

copied from his route-plan, at the turn of the eighth century. A few items may be worth highlighting: in the first route, for instance, the *umbilicus Romae* is mentioned in the Forum, being a kind of successor to the *miliarum aureum* (Golden Milestone) erected by Augustus, mentioned above. This *umbilicus* was instituted by Septimius Severus as the central point from which maps of the empire were oriented (the remains of it were discovered next to the Severine Arch in 1803). Close to the major landmarks such as the Campidoglio, the Foro Romano and the Arch of Severus, this was the nodal point of city and empire, where the north–south axis crossed the east–west one.[31] Elsewhere we encounter the celebrated Dioskuri ('horse-tamers') sculptural groups, naively described as *cavalli optimi* in the text, and slightly mislocated near the church of San Vitale instead of its actual position at the Thermae Constantini. They are still to be seen today, but on the Piazza del Quirinale where they were brought by Pope Pius VI at the end of the eighteenth century, having been restored on the orders of Pope Sixtus V in 1588. This was one of the most famous Roman copies of a Greek original monument from the fifth century BC, but the *Einsidlensis* probably mentions it chiefly because it was a great landmark, being 5.6 metres high; perhaps also because its subjects, Castor and Pollux (the sons of Zeus), had been revered as protectors of the city from earliest times, as our author must surely have been aware. Here and elsewhere antiquarian, historical and practical preoccupations blend harmoniously into the description of Christian edifices.

The reference to the Dioscuri as '*cavalli optimi*' is one of very few comments on the objects listed. For the Christian there are also extra snippets of information, for example, the words '*ubi ille assatus est*' ('where he was roasted') are written beside the church of St Laurence in Formonso. St Laurence, the deacon who defied Valerian in 258 by distributing church treasure among the poor, and was allegedly roasted on a gridiron for this act of *lèse majesté*, emerges as one of the most significant martyrs for the Christian visitor to ninth-century Rome. The *Einsidlensis* mentions five churches dedicated to him, while (*Sci.*) *Laurentii in Formonso* appears in no less than four of the twelve itineraries, no doubt because it was thought to be built on the site of the saint's martyrdom. It is interesting to compare its prominence in the *Einsidlensis* with its near total absence from the long lists of churches in the Rome guides of today;[32] and this despite the fact that the successor church on the site (S. Lorenzo in Panisperna, renovated in 1576) is not hard to find, being close to S. Maria Maggiore and the main railway terminus. The reason for its invisibility, no doubt, is that S. Lorenzo in Panisperna is not stuffed with major works of art like other Roman churches. There could be no more vivid example of the shift from religious tourism's preoccupation with *lieux de mémoire* in the Middle Ages and the post-medieval tourist's increasing inclination to treat churches primarily as aesthetic artefacts or religious museums.

Although this church of S. Lorenzo, and several other churches associated with martyrs, would have been of special interest to the writer's probable target audience, they do not crowd out the other material in the itinerary. To take one not untypical example of an item for the antiquary, the interest of the learned would have been aroused by the mention in Route II of the obelisk sundial that had probably served as a way sign since the eighth century, and which stood near the church of San Lorenzo in Lucina. It crumbled in the late Middle Ages, but was restored and set up on Piazza Montecitorio in 1792, where it still stands. Emperor Augustus had brought it from Heliopolis in Egypt and presumably it originally functioned successfully as a clock, but the papal engineers of the eighteenth century were never able to figure out how.

The author of the guide indeed shows considerable interest in infrastructure generally, mentioning aqueducts (which he calls *Forma*) on several occasions, as well as the Gianicolo mills already referred to. (The latter, however, were in fact destroyed by the Goths and substituted by Belisarius with floating mills in the Tiber, so either they were repaired in the early Middle Ages or mention of them indicates borrowing from the older text.) Our author of course also alludes to several *thermae* (baths), and most famously, in an appendix to the itinerary that minutely describes the Aurelian city walls renovated by Emperor Honorius[33] in a vain attempt to keep out the Goths, he records 116 *necessariae*. These were evidently latrines set just outside the city's fortifications for use by the sentries. Their substantial number indicates the heavy defence required for Rome at the time, as does the painstaking enumeration by the *Einsidlensis* of turrets, battlements and so on (383 *turres*, 7,020 *propugnaculae*, 2,066 *fenestrae*, 5 *posternae*). Nevertheless, despite the fascinating asides on infrastructure and pagan monuments, there is still an overall preponderance of churches on the routes described. For the historian at least, these provide a fascinating glimpse of many that have vanished or changed their names, even if the text as a whole was not unjustly characterised by Gregorovius as exhibiting 'the dry taxonomy of the learned scholar'.[34]

TWO LATER CHRISTIAN ITINERARIES: ARCHBISHOP SIGERIC OF CANTERBURY AND ABBOT NIKOLÁS OF MUNKATHVERA

The trips round the Roman sights contained in the diaries of these two gentlemen have been described, somewhat irreverently, as 'ecclesiastical Cook's Tours'.[35] They are of interest because they reveal a personal selection of the sights worth visiting in Rome that is lacking in the anonymous and impersonal *Einsidlensis*; nor do their texts involve the problems of source and attribution attaching to the latter. When Sigeric went to Rome in 990 to receive the pallium from Pope John XV, a member of his retinue compiled the diary, 'the only complete itinerary of an Anglo-Saxon pilgrim to Rome which we possess'.[36] It may well be that the listing of churches along a route was to be used as the type of vade mecum for visitors already described above, since it begins at the *Scola Anglorum*. This was an area close to St Peter's (today the characterless *Borgo*) and was centred on the church of S. Maria in Sassia,[37] founded by Ina, King of Wessex, in the eighth century. The *Scola* was where the English clerics were lodged and English visitors would have stayed. The tour that was arranged for them lasted over two days and took in the most important Roman churches, with a break for lunch with the pope at the Lateran Palace on the second day. The first day's itinerary goes beyond the city walls, the second stays within them; but since some twenty-three churches are listed, and moreover a distance of approximately 25 kilometres was covered on the first day alone, it must be assumed the trip was made on horseback.[38]

The account of the Icelandic Abbot's perambulation (made *c.* 1154) is more discursive, 'a pilgrim-diary . . . embedded . . . in a sort of geographical miscellany'.[39] Like Sigeric's report, it incorporates an itinerary for parts of the journeys to and from Rome; but Nikolás's document (evidently dictated to a secretary) is spiced with references to landscape, languages, climate – and even the fair ladies of Siena! His itinerary of Rome is unsystematic, yet vivid in its description of relics and traditions (he does not forget to mention such four-star attractions as the prepuce of Christ and the milk from the breast of the Virgin to be seen in S. Giovanni in Laterano). While he takes account of some secular monuments, the emphasis is on the four patriarchal churches. To a fifth 'bishop's throne' (that is, a patriarchal church) he erroneously gives the appellation SS. Stefano and Lorenzo: he means the church of S. Lorenzo fuori le Mura off the Via Tiburtina, traditionally one of seven pilgrimage churches in Rome offering absolution, not least because St Laurence was allegedly buried here. Nikolás's claim of a joint dedication to St Stephen reflects a tradition that the protomartyr's remains lay next to those of Laurence, having been brought from Byzantium in the fifth century. Legends of this kind, assiduously reported by the guides, represented a tidying up operation that concentrated more and more relics and other powerfully symbolic Christian references in Rome, the heir of Jerusalem and rival of Byzantium. As with Abbot Nikolás's report, the itineraries and guidebooks, consciously or unconsciously, played their role in this process of establishing spiritual authority and creating an urban identity convenient to the papacy.

Such details about martyrs, and an evident excitement about relics, imply the itinerary's fundamentally spiritual focus. Yet, perhaps for the first time, some very basic aesthetic comments also occur, a faint stirring of interest in the artistic aspects of a structure surfacing in a commentary that is still almost exclusively focused on commemoration and liturgy. Thus S. Pietro is 'very large and splendid', a statement backed up by measurements: 'four hundred and sixty feet long to the holy altar and two hundred and thirty feet wide'. But some secular buildings also inspire the author's respect: *Crescentius Kastali* (the Castel Sant' Angelo) is 'very handsome', while the famous shopping arcade *portica di S. Pietro*, or Bazaar of Peter the Apostle, connecting the Castello Sant' Angelo to St Peter's, impresses by being 'very large and very long'.[40] Unlike Sigeric, the abbot also has time to notice other parts of the pagan heritage, the Porta Latina, the Thermae antoninianae and St Peter's obelisk. Perhaps Nikolás allowed himself to be momentarily dazzled by striking edifices such as were not to be seen in his native Iceland; or perhaps this is a first sign of a realignment of pagan and Christian elements, a phenomenon that was to become much more pronounced in the *Mirabilia*.

THE *MIRABILIA URBIS ROMAE*

If in the *Einsidlensis* there is a certain ambivalence in the treatment of the heritage of antiquity and that of Christianity, such an ambivalence had long existed in artistic production as well: 'Even in the sixth century and into the seventh . . . classical styles and subject-matter are still found alongside Christian ones,' writes Averil Cameron. 'In general it is misleading to think either of a linear development from classical (equated with "pagan") to Christian, or of a series of classical "revivals", although the latter has been a favourite theory among art historians. Rather, different styles and subjects existed side by side, and are more easily explained in terms of patronage and function than, as still commonly, in terms of increasing spirituality.'[41] The author of this is of course writing about Late Antiquity up to 600 AD; yet it is a useful perspective from which to view the cultural shift moving in the opposite direction, perhaps starting with the Carolingian Renaissance and reaching an apotheosis with the High Renaissance. This time the shift is not from 'classicism' to 'Christianity', but from a primarily Christian ethos towards a form of Christian culture that incorporated or co-opted 'classicism'.[42] One authority on early Christian Rome puts his finger on the interaction between pagan and Christian heritages, beginning in the fourth century, when he writes that 'the extension of Christianity into the public space of Rome [brought] with it the last redefinition of the city in antiquity'.[43] The extraordinary *Mirabilia Romae* reflect the maturity of this process eight centuries later, albeit often arbitrarily and erratically, and following no very obvious masterplan or objective. 'The sources of the discourse', writes Maurilio Adriani, 'were twofold, but the rhetoric (*eloquio*) is all of a piece; and not through the deliberate forging of a unity, but because that is how it naturally develops.'[44] And Christina Nardella has written that 'the *Mirabilia [Urbis Romae]* represents a complete fusion between pagan and Christian Rome as revealed in the many legends where one encounters a Christian element grafted onto an originally pagan story'.[45]

The story begins with a guidebook long thought to have been compiled by one Benedict, a canon of St Peter's, some time between 1140 and 1143. (Recent scholarship has, however, cast doubt on Canon Benedict's authorship.)[46] The guidebook bears the title *Mirabilia urbis Romae*, an accurate reflection of the enthusiasm it shows both for the astounding achievements of ancient architects and builders, and for the stories and legends connected with the individual buildings described, many such legends representing the fictive embroidery of the early Middle Ages. It thus constitutes, in Robert Brentano's happy phrase, 'a sort of palimpsest with one civilisation written over another'.[47] We know that Canon Benedict or the anonymous author, probably drawing on earlier sources such as Late Antique gazetteers, legends of saints, guides for pilgrims like those already discussed above, and the papal chronicles known as the *Liber Pontificalis*, originally included his *Mirabilia* in a longer compilation known as the *Liber Politicus*.[48] The title of that book is not justified by the content, being a discursive collection of documents that contains many elements that might be suitable in a guidebook oriented to pilgrims, and was probably compiled for administrative reasons or as a matter of record. It included, *inter alia*, the *Ordo Romanus*, a description of itineraries involving pontifical ceremonies at various churches during religious festivals, a list of 'Station Days' when the pope celebrated mass at St Peter's, a description of popular religious festivals, the *Curiosum* (the fourth-century list of buildings already mentioned), as well as the *Mirabilia*.[49] However, the first surviving example of the *Mirabilia*, plucked from its context, has come down to us as an entry in the *Liber Censuum*, which was an ongoing register of ecclesiastical institutions, cities and lands that were obliged to pay dues (*census*) to the Holy See. The particular *Liber Censuum* in which the *Mirabilia* makes its appearance was the work of Cencio Savelli (later Pope Honorius III) in his capacity as chamberlain to Celestine III, and its compilation was probably begun in 1192.

The *Mirabilia* begins where the *Einsidlensis* leaves off, with a part of the description of the city walls that had been tacked on to the end of the latter. This third-century wall, originally built by the Emperor Aurelian, clearly had an iconic status for the itinerary writers – indeed, the recurring opening sentence of their works, stating that the 'walls of the city have [316] towers',[50] resounds like a ritualised rhetorical salute to Rome. The Aurelian wall had undergone three major improvements (by Maxentius in 303, by Honorius' great general Flavius Stilicho in the early fifth century and by Theoderic the Great in the sixth century). At a height of 35ft (10.6m) and with over 300 towers placed 100ft (30m) apart, the structure was itself a 'marvel' enclosing other marvels. Unlike the impressive cincture built round the heart of Christian Rome by Leo IV and completed in 853,[51] its ancient masonry was both a bitter reminder of past struggles (it was not very successful at keeping the enemy out, even if this was usually because there were insufficient soldiers left in Rome to man it), and an inspiring symbol, one that recalled the great ages of construction when Rome was still perceived as the bulwark of the civilised world. After dealing eulogistically with the walls, which after all had still been the official boundary of the city until half a century before he was writing,[52] Canon Benedict's text (if it was his) continues with an enumeration of some ancient columns, which he evidently lifted from the old *Curiosum*,[53] before embarking on a descriptive round tour of Rome.

This itinerary eclectically takes in the most important Christian and pagan sights of Rome, starting at St Peter's and including the Castel Sant' Angelo, the Mausoleum of Augustus, the Pantheon, the Capitol, Trajan's Forum, the Via Sacra as far as the Arch of Titus, the Palatine, the Colosseum, and the Circus Maximus. It then visits the Celian, Esquiline, Viminal, Quirinal and Aventine hills, ending up back at the Ponte Sant' Angelo, with a final excursion to Trastevere. This lengthy enumeration represents the 'most ancient essay of erudite Roman topography', dealing at greater length with monuments hitherto only mentioned in passing in official documents such as the *Liber Pontificalis*.[54] But even though the author was the first to apply himself systematically to coverage of Rome's ancient monuments, he also introduced that erratic quality for which the *Mirabilia* became notorious. This whimsical character of the material may partly have arisen from an undiscriminating use of sources such as Ovid's *Fasti* ('Calendar' or 'Almanac'), where observations by the Muses claimed equal billing with those of a more scientific nature; but it also reflected a willingness to make things up if necessary. As M. Paul Fabre tactfully puts it: 'where the documents were unable to help him, our author didn't fail to pluck the missing information from his imagination'.[55] In this way, mystification and popular legend crept into otherwise learned descriptions – which is no more than to say that their author was a man of his time. Yet it is possible that another factor influenced the *Mirabilia*'s enthusiasm for Rome's antique heritage, especially when one considers that the origin of the work probably lay in the period virtually contemporaneous with an insurrection against the nobles and papacy led by Arnold of Brescia and the proclamation of a (new) Roman Republic in 1143. In Arnold we already have a figure who aptly symbolises the city's anticlerical, anti-papal tradition that has continued up to the present. The papacy's claim to secular domination over Rome's citizens as unqualified as its spiritual domination was being challenged. The heritage of antiquity eulogised in the *Mirabilia* had a certain propaganda value for the struggle in the present.

It is hard to judge the extent to which this guide, with its frequent references to 'the time of the consuls and the senators', was intended as propaganda. But in describing the Capitol as the *caput mundi*, where the senators and consuls once sat and ruled the world,[56] the author is striking, perhaps for the first time in a guidebook, the elegiac tone that was to become a topos of later works in the genre, and which invariably led to unflattering comparisons with the shabby, diminished ethos of the author's own day. Ruins, relics of a glorious past, begin to exert their rhetorical power in the present through the good offices of the guidebook. Yet, even as we are beguiled by the author's local patriotism and fertile invention, we have to keep in mind that his book was inserted in an official papal record, the *Liber Censuum*; that its presumed author was himself a man of the cloth (as, incidentally, was the monk, Arnold of Brescia); and that an admiration for the monuments of pagan antiquity hardly implied a rejection of the superiority of the true faith. One author even asserts that such admiration was actually used to bolster the faith: '[The *Mirabilia*] treated surviving works of art as vehicles for allegorical commentary,' he writes, 'and in so doing negated the pagan aspect of antiquity for Christian pilgrims.'[57] On the other hand, it is not inconceivable that the author was simply a dissident cleric, who inserted his archaeological promenades in the *Liber Censuum* in order to provoke his employers, or a vain scholar who simply wanted to exhibit his knowledge and literary skills; or did the work become a fixture in the books of the Roman Curia,[58] because the popes themselves hoped to appropriate thereby the lustre of antiquity? We do not know, and there seems no obvious reason why such a heterogeneous document should be inserted into a list of property titles of the apostolic holy seat. 'It is as if, in the middle of a geometry lesson, the professor suddenly started whistling an operatic aria,' remarks 'Benedict's' editor.[59]

THE *GRAPHIA AUREAE URBIS ROMAE* AND LATER VERSIONS OF THE *MIRABILIA URBIS ROMAE*

Subsequent versions of the descriptive tours subsumed under the generic title of *Mirabilia* have been divided into six periods of production between the twelfth and fifteenth centuries, with two sub-types straddling the fourteenth and fifteenth centuries.[60] This proliferation of versions has earned it the reputation of being 'the standard guide book of the more learned visitors to Rome from the twelfth to the fifteenth century'. Moreover, 'its statements were received with the respect due to a work of authority and their influence may be traced in the writings of many of the authors who flourished during that period'.[61] Even when more precise knowledge rendered it of less interest to scholars, its popularity among laymen endured into the age of printing, when several further editions appeared. Except in the *Graphia* version discussed below, there was a basic form that, though sometimes embroidered or otherwise obscured, forms a leitmotif running through the *Mirabilia*'s publishing history. Its three parts usually began with a simple list of buildings, monuments or objects arranged under various themes; then came a collection of legends associated with selected Roman monuments; and the last part was a perambulation of the ancient city, which began at the Vatican and ended at Trastevere.[62]

Revisions to the early *Mirabilia* were not slow in coming, the most significant of these being discovered in a thirteenth-century manuscript in the Laurentian library in Florence under the title *Graphia aureae urbis Romae*.[63] This version seems to have had wide currency, for example, supplying the basis for a description of Rome in a mid-fourteenth-century poem (*Il Dittamondo*) by Fazio degli Uberti,[64] while a large chunk of it was lifted by the English chronicler Ranulf Higden for his *Polychronicon* (completed *c.* 1350). After all, this was an age when 'men had neither pride in originality nor scruples about plagiarism'.[65] Despite the relatively late date of the manuscript, the *Graphia* (probably a fusion of three different sources) appears to hark back to more ancient roots than the *Mirabilia* and is certainly more generous in its coverage of temples and cemeteries. It also has a different conclusion, an account of institutions, manners and ceremonies in which some have detected Byzantine influence. That judgement perhaps arises because it seems to reflect an atmosphere and tone of imperial grandeur, as it was in the past, as it might be again. The Rome of the *Graphia* is still the Golden City of yore, written before an elegiac tone crept into the descriptions of the city at the turn of the century, for example, in the celebrated verses by Hildebert of Lavardin (1056–1133), one of many who were influenced by the dreadful destructions of the previous hundred years.[66]

By the time at which the *Mirabilia* was compiled, the identity of many ancient structures had been forgotten or become encrusted with myth, while even large piles of rubble, the result of the population's ongoing plunder of ancient ruins for contemporary building materials, were sometimes dignified with the name of a building that had never existed. While the *Mirabilia* inevitably reproduced much of this fabrication, it also represented that revived pride in Rome's past that has already been adumbrated, as well as a new and marginally deeper scholarship designed to bolster that pride. The *Mirabilia* also helped thereby to introduce the notion of conservation and preservation of the architectural heritage – though, with historically minded popes, this often took the perverse form of plundering the ancient ruins for columns and pillars to adorn the churches they were having constructed.[67] Such actions well illustrate the creative tension between pagan and Christian priorities in the guide itself, which, while it 'retraced the footsteps of Peter and Paul and the other Christian martyrs', was also 'a paean to the monuments of Roman civic life'; finally, it was also a 'learned treatise on the historical traditions of the city itself, its art and architecture'.[68] Yet, when we recall Charlemagne's desire to create a sort of theme park replica of Rome at Aachen and the papal moves to set up an open-air museum for the display of antique monuments in front of the Lateran Palace, we are reminded that this tradition was a very ancient one.[69]

Browsing in Francis Morgan Nichols's compilation of the *Mirabilia*, today's reader finds much that is entertaining (though not necessarily in the way its author intended), and much that is of historical and cultural interest. Most versions of the *Mirabilia* had three distinct features, a sketch of the historical (or mythical) background to the rise of Rome, fantastic legends associated with famous sites and, lastly, a narrative itinerary for tourists. The first section of Nichols's reprint jumbles together a splendid confusion of ancient heroes, gods and biblical figures (starting with Noah) who, it is claimed, were associated with the origins of Rome. The survey ends on a triumphant note, a rhetorical assertion that Rome is the city of cities, the cynosure of the world: 'And in Rome Etrurians, Sabines, Albans, Tusculans, Politanes, Telenes, Ficenians, Janiculans, Camerians, Capenates, Faliscans, Lucanians, Italians, and, as it could be said, all the noble men of the whole earth, with their wives and children, came together to dwell here.'[70] There follows the now all but obligatory listing of the features of the (old) city wall and its gates, which adds some details of castellations and arches not in the *Einsidlensis*. The emphasis is predominantly on the antique, but Christian motifs are mixed in to the description, together with colourful legends that made the work such lively reading for contemporaries:

> The gates of the famous city are these: the Porta Capena, which is now called Porta San Paolo, near the temple of Remus; Porta Appia, at the church of Domine Quo Vadis, . . . where the footsteps of Jesus Christ are seen . . . the Gate of Tivoli . . . is called the Bull Gate because there are carved on it two heads of bulls, one of them lean and the other fat. The lean head on the outside signifies those who come with slender means into the city; the fat and full head on the inside signifies those who leave the city rich . . .

This listing of hills, baths, theatres, bridges and columns ends on a Christian note with an enumeration of cemeteries and 'the places of martyrdom'.

The second part deals with the legends behind Rome's monuments, again mixing pagan and Christian motifs (the order of Emperor Octavian and the Sibyl's answer, descriptions of the Pantheon, the Colosseum, and of 'the passions of Saints Abdon and Sennen, Sixtus and Laurence'); and again ends on a Christian item ('Constantine's Three Great Churches of Rome'). The third part is the perambulation of the city, the guide proper if one will, covering sixteen items in a logical topographical order, but without the directions of the *Einsidlensis*. The 'Conclusion', a sort of mission statement that reveals the compiler's aesthetic and historical preoccupations, is worth quoting in full:

> These and more temples and palaces of emperors, consuls, senators, and prefects were inside this Roman city in the time of the heathen, as we have read in old chronicles, have seen with our own eyes, and have heard the ancient men tell of. In writing we have tried as well as we could to bring back to human memory how great was their beauty in gold, silver, brass, ivory and precious stones.[71]

It is indeed a conspicuous aspect of the perambulation, that Christian monuments serve only as locators for those of antiquity ('At Santa Maria Maggiore was the temple of Cybele. At San Pietro in Vincoli was the temple of Venus. At Santa Maria in Fontana, the temple of Faunus.').[72]

The author of the *Mirabilia* is fond of etymologies: 'the Basilica of the Vatican . . . [is so-called] . . . because in that place the *Vates*, or priests, sang their offices before Apollo's temple'; 'the Capitol is so-called because it was the head of the world where the consuls and senators met to govern the world'.[73] He is also interested in practical matters like hydrology, telling us that water from the Sabbatina Aqueduct flowed to the emperor's bath, and remarking on the drainage for Nero's Terebinth ['turpentine tree'] monument. Over all, however, he strives to provide the various monuments with a context of historical facts, even if the latter, in accordance with the medieval way of looking at the world, are often indistinguishable from legends. And he wants to impress upon us their past splendour, which indeed reflected that of Rome itself and its empire. We have been told in the second part of the *Mirabilia* that the Colosseum was the temple of the Sun, in the middle of which dwelled Phoebus who, 'with his feet on the earth . . . reached to heaven with his head and held in his hand an orb that signified that Rome ruled over the whole world'. The perambulation, while more soberly factual in tone, draws on literary sources such as Ovid's *Fasti*, or historical sources like the old gazetteers, to flesh out the legends of the previous section in terms of surviving images. Thus we are now told that the image of Phoebus was located on the top of the Colosseum, that the god wore a golden crown decorated with gems, and that 'the head and hands [of this statue] are now in front of the Lateran'.[74] Rhetoric, literary allusion and antiquarian (or pseudo-antiquarian) exegesis all play a part in this lively genre.

MASTER GREGORY'S *MARVELS OF ROME*

One of the most fascinating texts probably influenced by the *Mirabilia* is a work by an English clerk written in the early the thirteenth century. If, as mentioned above, an elegiac tone is already present in Hildebert of Lavardin's remarks about Rome, it is a fair way to becoming a topos in the *Narracio de Mirabilibus urbis Romae* of 'Magister Gregorius', composed perhaps between 1226 and 1236.[75] The ruins of Rome, he muses in a Gibbonian passage, 'make it awesomely clear that all temporal things soon come to ruin, since the head of all things temporal, Rome, slips daily languishing away . . .'[76] However, Master Gregory proves a refreshing guide after the credulous authors of the traditional *Mirabilia*. As one of his translators has observed, his 'unabashed antiquarian curiosity' and healthy scepticism in an age 'better known for its unquestioning faith' make him seem 'little different from many modern art historians: scoffing at the tales told by the local guides, measuring buildings and returning three times to study a statue [of Venus] which appealed to him'.[77] His scorn for the local guides pales beside his contempt for the superstitions of pilgrims. Their belief that the 'pyramid' (tomb) of Romulus near St Peter's was the apostle's heap of grain, which turned to stone when Nero confiscated it, he dismisses as 'most certainly a stupidity, and the pilgrims abound in such stupidities'.[78]

For the first time, aesthetic appreciation and an interest in the protection of ancient monuments appear to be paramount in a text written for other sightseers, even if it is hyperbolic to call Gregory 'the first connoisseur of ancient art'.[79] Certainly he comes close to outright denunciation of Gregory the Great for transferring the column with Marcus Aurelius's statue from the emperor's villa to S. Giovanni in Laterano in the sixth century, and for the pope's indiscriminate destruction of other pagan statues. As a guide, his aesthetic and scientific enthusiasms reveal an individual personality that is lacking in the vast majority of previous guidebooks or itineraries. It is typical of him to complain that Diocletian's 'palace' (by which he means the baths) was so high that no one could throw a pebble to the top of it – a complaint that immediately conjures a picture of Gregory himself attempting, and failing, to get results with this less than satisfactory technique of measurement.

Despite his disdain for the retailers of legends and myths, Gregory is himself not lacking in credulity at times; indeed, the main body of the work begins under the heading: 'Here begins the narration of the marvels of Rome, whether realised by magic art or human labour.' There is also a specific and inbuilt tendency to fantasise, in so far as he attempts to shoehorn the marvels he finds in Rome into the framework of a medieval treatise on the seven wonders of the world that had evidently taken his fancy.[80] Naturally this leads to some abrupt moments, while his habit of leaping from one object to another because it occurs to him they have something in common, even if stimulating for the armchair reader, must have earned him opprobrium from those trying to use his work on the ground. For example, he passes blandly from an account of Caesar's remains and ashes placed on top of a wondrously high 'pyramid' (actually obelisk) to a totally irrelevant and longish description of the lighthouse at Alexandria, evidently on the grounds that it is 'another marvel'. When he sticks to the point, however, his focus is entirely on pre-Christian Rome, S. Pietro and S. Giovanni in Laterano being mentioned only in passing together with only one other church, S. Maria Rotonda – and that because it was the christianised Pantheon.[81] The bones of the martyrs, so prominent in other itineraries, do not interest him, but the whereabouts of the remains of Julius Caesar does. All this suggests that Gregory was a man of broader culture than his predecessors and contemporaries who compiled the *Mirabilia*, a clerk who wrote fluent Latin with rhetorical turns (though he confesses to difficulty in reading abbreviated antique inscriptions), and cited the ancient authors (silently or by name) from first hand, rather than from the texts customarily filtered through Christian writers.

Little is known about the enigmatic Master (*Magister*) Gregory, whose title implies a man with scholarly training.[82] It has been suggested he was the Magister Gregorius who was granted a pension by Henry III in 1238, and who is described as the chancellor of Otto of Tonego, the papal legate to England between 1237 and 1241. The pension was to be paid from the funds of the bishopric of Norwich, from whose bishop, recently deceased, Gregory had apparently been receiving financial support. This benefactor may have been the *dominum Thomas* saluted as a colleague in the Prologue to the *Marvels*. Apart from these meagre facts, we can only surmise Gregory's character from the evidence in his work. Here he appears as a proto-humanist, a sceptic (at least in respect of the semi-christianised myths adhering to the monuments of antiquity) and an individualist. He does not follow the well-worn path of the *Mirabilia*, which he would certainly have known, but selects objects to discuss and frames his descriptions in a personal way with much more attention to the aesthetic dimension than heretofore. He is something of a pedant and *Besserwisser* or know-all (becoming such is an occupational hazard for guidebook writers);[83] and like many such he is quite capable of substituting one error for another. A scholar himself, he perhaps had an exaggerated respect for the scholars of the papal court, whom he tells us he consulted; at any rate they seem to have fed him a good deal of information, much of it wrong.

About one-fifth of his *Narracio* is taken up by a single monument, which we now know to be the equestrian statue of Marcus Aurelius, the most impressive bronze remnant of Roman antiquity.[84] The statue had survived the plunder and destruction visited upon other pagan monuments both by the popes and the populace of Rome, for the simple reason that in Late Antiquity and the Middle Ages it was thought to represent Constantine, thus making it acceptable to Christian propagandists. By the time of Master Gregory's visit, this identification was already in doubt and Renaissance scholarship subsequently discovered the correct one. Gregory's description is located between earlier myth and later reality, Rabbi Benjamin of Tudela having been the last writer, in 1170, to refer to the statue confidently as that of Constantine. Gregory is just as dismissive of the view held by foreign visitors that the statue represented Theoderic as he is of the Romans' determination to preserve the Constantinian tradition. Instead, he relies again on the scholars of the curia, who offered two somewhat complicated heroic legends connected with the monument, one concerning a certain 'Marco' and the other featuring a 'Quinto Quirino', both of which he relates at length.

Gregory is just as interested in the statue's aesthetic aspects however, as indeed he is in statues generally ('of all the marvellous works that were once to be seen in Rome, the great quantity of statues was the most astonishing').[85] They provide fruitful material for historical exegesis, so it is not surprising that much space is also taken up with an account (again largely taken from his 'Seven Wonders' source, the pseudo-Bede) of the seventy mythical statues once situated on the Capitoline Hill that represented the various peoples under Roman rule, and were said to possess magical qualities. Known collectively as the *salvatio civium* or *salvatio Romae*, each of them, according to Alexander Neckam's *De Naturis Rerum* (*c.* 1180), had a silver bell hung on it; as soon as the people it represented revolted, the statue moved, causing the bell to ring, whereupon the watching priests hastened to convey the news to the emperor. Gregory also reports that a bronze soldier on horseback located above the statues was apparently synchronised to their movements, directing his lance towards whichever one was sounding the alarm about a distant rebellion. This ancient commonplace is vividly related, but Gregory does not say it is true, only that people claim it is. Nevertheless, his Christian faith emerges towards the end of his discourse, when he passes on the legend that the bronze soldier fell from his perch the night that Christ was born; moreover, the eternal flame next to the *salvatio civium* was also extinguished 'when the true and eternal light arose'. 'It is credible', he adds, 'that the evil one also lost his power to deceive the people at the moment when God became man.'[86] This, however, is the only reference in the whole *Narracio* from which it could be inferred that the writer was a practising Christian.

As a protagonist of the twelfth-century Renaissance, Master Gregory has been of continuing interest to scholars. As far as the history of the guidebook is concerned, he stands at the threshold of a more pragmatic, informative and sceptical approach to the description of sights, even if his information (how could it be otherwise?) is no better than his often unreliable sources in the curia or the pseudo-Bede. His fascination with the technical and aesthetic achievements of the anonymous antique builders is refreshing, as are his outbursts against plundering popes and the shameless looting by the Roman populace itself. It is true that he still has a weakness for a good story, which sometimes leads him to see things that are not there. The tuft of hair between the ears of Marcus Aurelius' horse is asserted to be a bird, a conceit to fit the Quintus Quirinus story with which he has been lumbered by the papal scholars (the hero Quirinus was said to have sacrificed himself to save the city from plague by riding his horse into a chasm spewing fire that had opened up in the streets, whereat a cuckoo flew out, the chasm closed and the plague receded). Then again, his bizarre account of the *Spinario*, a celebrated sculpture of a boy plucking a thorn from his foot, now in the Capitoline Museum, arises from a source claiming that the sculpture represents Priapus. It is, says Gregory, ridiculous as a work of art and goes on to imply that it is made all the more so by the disproportionate size of the boy's virile member, an assertion wildly at variance with the facts. Yet at other times his reader is better served, for example, with his detailed researches into the origins and intended representation of the Colossus, or his susceptibility to the eroticism of a statue of Venus[87] to which he returned three times, and which, in a conceit to be reprised by later guidebooks describing the *Medici Venus*, he imagined to be slightly red, as if the goddess blushed for her nudity. These and other touches look forward to the opinionated guidebook writers of a later age.

INDULGENTIAE AND THE CONTINUING CHRISTIAN TRADITION

While Master Gregory's description of the marvels of Rome suggests an incipient secularisation of scholarship and perhaps an increased desire on the part of the popes to promote their role as temporal rulers who had inherited the mantle of the emperors, other guidebook literature reminds us of the city's continuing role as the spiritual hub of the Christian West. Indeed, with the Holy Land lost to Islam and Constantinople left in ruins by the Fourth Crusade, the Rome of 414 churches[88] became the medieval pilgrimage centre par excellence, rivalled only by Santiago de Compostela. Its hoard of relics could only enhance its prestige: 'on every day of the calendar (so it seems) some church was lighted to celebrate the feast of the saint of whom it held some fragment'.[89] One of the most popular relics was the *Veronica (sudarium)* held at St Peter's, but there was also the True Cross brought to Rome by St Helena and kept at Sta Croce in Gerusalemme, while Sta Prassede held the column of Christ's flagellation brought from the Holy Land by a Colonna prince.[90] Such 'sights' stimulated pilgrimage, in fact religious tourism, whose participants were known as *Romipetae*, or 'Rome-seekers'.[91] The jubilees instituted by Pope Boniface VIII in 1300 could but increase the flood: the Florentine chronicler Giovanni Villani suggested there were 200,000 pilgrims in the city at any one time. The crush was commensurate, to the extent that an English Benedictine was so badly mauled by crowds jostling to see the *Veronica* that he died of his injuries.[92]

The Holy Years, when a plenary indulgence, or jubilee, was granted to pilgrims, generated their own guidebook literature, the *Indulgentiae ecclesiarum Urbis*,[93] which supplied lists of indulgences that could be obtained by the pilgrim at particular shrines. Not surprisingly, the bifurcation of the *Mirabilia Romae* genre into *Mirabilia* and *Indulgentiae* appears to date from the proclamation of the first Jubilee Year on 29 June 1300 by Boniface VIII.[94] *Indulgentiae* also existed for other pilgrimage centres, but the majority so far discovered by scholars relate to Rome.[95] Such lists were compiled despite the Church's sporadic attempts to ban catalogues of indulgences because of their abuse and the difficulty of checking their authority in ancient documents. Plenary indulgences for the remission of all the temporal punishment that was the result of an individual's sins were offered under certain circumstances (for example, Urban II made such a concession to the Crusaders in 1095); but odd indulgences, like those of 1,000 years or more, seem never to have been officially authorised by the Church, though they were proclaimed and must have proved a powerful magnet for pilgrims. In the thirteenth and fourteenth centuries, officially recognised indulgences were seldom for more than five or seven years, and often only for a few days. But when we hear that the unlucky

Pope Pius VI had two stones removed from the entrance to the relic-rich Sta Prassede in 1775 (!), because they advertised an indulgence of 12,000 years, the huge gap between the Church's official line and the individual's expectations becomes apparent.[96]

There were forty-four Latin editions of *Indulgentiae* between 1475 and 1523, as well as twenty editions in German and others in Italian, French and Spanish.[97] An idiosyncratic metrical version was available to English readers under the title *Stacyons of Rome*. This edition claims that those who travelled to Rome to see the *Veronica* qualified for 12,000 years of remission of their sins (the Romans themselves, on the other hand, received only 3,000 years.)[98] There are signs that Rome was concerned to acquire a marketing edge in the pilgrims' market – at any rate, the *Stacyons* says that going to the church of S. Paolo every Sunday in the year was worth as much remission as a pilgrimage to the shrine of St James. Other *Indulgentiae* similarly promote the remission potential of Rome over that offered by its two main rivals, Santiago and the Holy Land.[99] Indeed, the whole idea of a plenary indulgence, previously the exclusive reward of Crusaders, may have been an attempt by Rome to usurp the authority of the Holy Land, and to bolster the city's claim to be the 'New Jerusalem'.[100] The *Indulgentiae* usually opened with the seven principal churches of Rome, always beginning with the Lateran Basilica,[101] then visited a selection of the others in one or two circuits. A few are illustrated with a symbolical frontispiece, an illustration of the display of the *Veronica* and figures of the saints to whom the seven main churches are dedicated. The numerous printings of the *Indulgentiae* betoken their popularity, eventually usurping that of the *Mirabilia* in the sixteenth century,[102] by which time the latter was gradually being marginalised by Renaissance scholarship.

JOHN CAPGRAVE'S *SOLACE OF PILGRIMES*

If the *Indulgentiae* existed in a symbiotic relationship with the *Mirabilia*, the latter was clearly an important source for a very substantial description of Rome dating to *c*. 1450. It was written in Middle English by an Austin friar called John Capgrave, who gave it the title *Ye Solace of Pilgrimes*, which emphasised the intended audience. Capgrave tells us that Rome was extremely crowded during his visit, which suggests he was there for the jubilee of 1450.[103] He is a vivid and scholarly writer, and his humanity is evident from his rejection of the slanderous reasons given for excluding women from the viewing of relics, these being 'many lewd causes to which I will give no credence'. More likely, he thought, it was because of the danger that frail or pregnant women would be crushed to death in the throng, as had indeed happened to a pregnant lady in 1388 in a crowd gathering to see the head of St Martial.[104] However, notwithstanding his generally judicious tone, the first section of his guide, covering the foundation of Rome and its topography, obviously relies heavily on the *Mirabilia*, inheriting the latter's tradition of beginning the tour with an enumeration of the ancient city walls and their towers. As in the *Mirabilia*, pagan, Christian and christianised monuments are jumbled together; and although the author refers to a city plan, we do not know which. The book is divided into three parts, three being the sacred number of the Trinity as Capgrave is careful to remind us. In Part I, there is an initial chapter on the founders of Rome, then twenty-three chapters dealing with the most famous sights, and finally two chapters on the rulers of Rome from Romulus to Frederick II. Part II begins with the seven principal churches of the city (S. Giovanni in Laterano, S. Pietro in Vaticano, S. Paolo fuori le Mura, Sta Maria Maggiore, S. Lorenzo fuori le Mura, S. Sebastiano and Sta Croce in Gerusalemme). This is followed by forty-six 'stations' (that is, churches where the pope celebrated Mass on certain days as marked in the Roman Missal). Part III, which is not complete, deals with thirteen churches dedicated to the Virgin Mary.

Capgrave may be said to offer a package deal of *Indulgentiae* with the ingredients of the *Mirabilia*, though considerably enhanced and refined, thrown in, the latter presumably designed to entertain the pilgrims once their religious duties were over. Although his topography is remarkably accurate, the information is not presented as a round tour, but as a sort of gazetteer, with objects listed under genre rather than in a single alphabetical list. In an interesting section he gives some dozen examples of Christian edifices built on former pagan sites, promising to return to this theme in Part II; and elsewhere he lists 'divers temples of false gods turned to the service of saints'.[105] In his description of the ruins on the Capitol, he takes issue with the people of Rome, who apparently claim that they have never prospered since the coming of Christianity (an interesting example of the local population's nostalgia for antiquity); scornfully he proclaims that he will demonstrate to them that they were 'conquered by other nations long before Christ was incarnate'.[106]

Capgrave is no nearer to identifying the statue of Marcus Aurelius in front of the Lateran than was Master Gregory, though he does reject the popular attribution of Constantine out of hand; instead, he relates a long legend about the fabled hero represented by the statue, which has some affinity with Master Gregory's tales from the papal scholars. However, his lengthy discussion of the legends and identification of this and other objects puts him in a class of his own in terms of research and information; and also in terms of lively description, particularly of relics. We learn that St Peter's head is 'broad . . . with much hair on his beard, which is of a grey colour between white and black'. The head of St Paul 'has a long face, balled with red hair, both beard and head'.[107] And elsewhere he saw 'a piece of the flesh of St Laurence and coals joined thereto right as they fried in his passion . . .'. Or again 'three stones, all bloody, which were thrown at St Stephen'.[108]

The meat of the book for pilgrims lies in the lengthy last two sections. Following tradition, Capgrave attributes the appointing of 'station churches' for papal Masses on 'station days' (all in Lent, according to him) to Pope Gregory the Great; but the real interest for his readers lay with the claim that Gregory granted 'to that church where the station is, as much pardon as is in all Rome as [*sic*] for that day'.[109] In other words, the 'stations' offered a highly convenient way of collecting substantial amounts of indulgences without having to visit too many churches ('And this is the cause, as I suppose, that few Romans walk the circle, but the stations, as a man may plainly see.').[110] Capgrave also offers a calendrical reckoner for the collector of indulgences and surveyor of relics: 'the Thursday before the first Sunday of Lent is the station at a church of Saint George, where his head is showed, his ensign and the lance with which he killed the dragon. The head is displayed on an altar on that day, in a tabernacle of silver and gilt, so made that a man may lift up a certain part thereof and touch and kiss the bare skull.'[111] This exemplary exactitude regarding relics was indispensable for his pilgrim audience. (Interestingly, such needs were still being met into modern times: for example, in the late nineteenth century, St George's head, which was displayed in the church on station days up to 1891, is still featured in Chanoine de Blesser's *Guide du Voyageur dans la Capitale du Monde Chrétien*.) Another attraction for the pilgrim armed with Capgrave's information was that he could participate in the spectacular processions of clergy and people that were associated with station days, one of the more enjoyable aspects of religious tourism.

The last part, covering the churches dedicated to the Virgin Mary, 'specially those on which anything notable has been written',[112] is very much like a traditional guidebook, displaying the author's antiquarian and aesthetic preoccupations. Above all it provides historical background and lore, naturally with a degree of Christian uplift, as in his detailed account of the transition of the pagan Pantheon into the church of Sta Maria Rotonda. He is the first English writer to give a reasonably detailed account of the catacombs, which he graphically describes as 'grete voutes and mynes undir the erde in which seyntis dwellid but now be desolate for horrible derknesse and disuse of puple'.[113] This final section satisfactorily rounds off the material of the other two parts, so that the pilgrim could feel he had, in a single text, a complete devotional, cultural and historical guide to the city, covering everything from antique inscriptions to lists of relics and indulgences. Moreover, as his editor remarks, Capgrave is 'most careful not to put down a thing unless he has seen it himself, or has in his opinion the best authority for it'.[114] Disarmingly, he sometimes confesses that he did not take the trouble to find something out, or failed to find a monument, or could not copy down information because the throng was too great. His candour is not, alas, too often reflected in subsequent guidebook compilers, and of course his information is frequently inaccurate or wrong because he was led astray by his sources. We even know that he occasionally had second thoughts: for instance, he struck through the reference to a relic (an arm) of St Thomas Becket that was claimed to be in Sta Maria Maggiore, presumably because he had come to realise that English guides shamelessly transferred the association of the church with the Apostle Thomas to Thomas Becket, since this was what their audience wanted to hear.[115] Capgrave was made of sterner stuff: he strove to be accurate, and in so doing contributed something notable to the guidebook tradition.

WILLIAM BREWYN'S *GUIDE TO THE PRINCIPAL CHURCHES OF ROME*

That men of the cloth were also antiquaries, and tempted to become collectors, we know from numerous surviving references to scholarly looting. As early as the twelfth century, the great Abbot Suger of St-Denis had expressed his frustration at being unable to remove attractive columns from Rome (he had in mind, *inter alia*, all those of Diocletian's *thermae*, which would have been a huge operation for the time); and the canons of Durham cathedral are on record as asking pilgrims to obtain sufficient marble from the Holy City to pave the floor of their church. Henry of Blois (d. 1171), Bishop of Winchester and King Stephen's brother, created a stir with his acquisitiveness: John of Salisbury records the astonishment of papal courtiers who observed him, 'conspicuous by his long beard and philosophical solemnity', as he bought up 'idols carved by pagan hands'.[116] It is therefore all the more remarkable that William Brewyn, an unbeneficed secular priest who lived for a long time in fifteenth-century Rome during the pontificates of Paul II (1464–71) and Sixtus IV (1471–84), although 'well known as a diligent investigator of the antiquities of the city, and . . . the author of a little book of some merit on the Seven Principal Churches of Rome',[117] still shows no signs of the Renaissance critical spirit. His useful 'little book' indeed combines detailed information about the holy places of Rome with practical advice regarding the journey thither; but its author 'repeats the most extravagant of [the] legends [of the *Mirabilia*] with the same unquestioning faith as his predecessors'.[118] The primary focus of his work is the meticulous recording of the indulgences pertaining to each and every shrine.

Brewyn's credulity has its entertaining side, for example, his solemn account of the inspection of the pope's manhood at his enthronement to avoid the embarrassment caused by the (mythical) Pope Joan, who, according to a legend originating in the thirteenth century, had succeeded Leo IV in 855 and gave birth to a child during a procession to the Lateran. Brewyn's more practical side is seen in his advice for an itinerary from Calais to Rome for English pilgrims who wished to avoid the war then threatening between England and France, and by his reproduction of Paul II's Bull of 1469 excommunicating all who should attack or molest pilgrims during their stay in the city. This was the contemporary equivalent of travel insurance. He also supplies an astonishingly complicated Table of Exchange (in Rome he got two ducats in exchange for nine English shillings) and recommends that pilgrims carry plenty of papal groats, bemys, blaffords, crucers and Cologne pence as being the most useful money for the journey. Interestingly, Brewyn himself made use of a letter of credit drawn on the London branch of the bank of 'Jacobo de Medici'[119] and he also speaks of changing money en route in a Bruges bank. His is thus one of the earliest guides to address the problem of money in detail, though whether the average pilgrim could have worked with a list of some twenty-seven different coins, with no indication as to whether the exchange calculations are from one currency to another, or divisions of the same one, must be open to doubt. He would have had to deal with (English) ducats, Rynysh guilders, old and new plackets, colenpens, Cologne pennies, hallers, Bemes, feras, blaffordys, lylyards, old groats, Papal groats, Venetian groats, Phylypp pens, stivers, Stotyrs, crucers, beaukos, bolendyns, feras and Kateryns. By comparison, the transactions of today's hedge funds dealing in currencies seem mere child's play.

Brewyn's book is a fairly late example in a long line that progressed unevenly from sparse itinerary through sensationalist legend-packed description and pilgrim-oriented utility to the antiquarian and scholarly guides of the Renaissance. While the invention of printing gave a new lease of life to the *Mirabilia* – versions of which actually lasted into the sixteenth century and beyond – by 1510 the Florentine Francesco Albertini's *Opusculum de mirabilibus Novae et Veteris urbis Romae*, despite retaining a *Mirabilia*-like title and being in many respects a reworking of the same,[120] already shows the influence of the new learning, including some remarks on contemporary art and architecture. This is a work that exhibits an engaging chauvinism in the prominence it gives to the artistic achievements of the author's fellow Florentines,[121] and it also heralds a new type of guidebook, to which we shall now turn.

PART III

From the Renaissance to the Enlightenment: Scholars, Moralists and Men of Taste

'The Art of Being away from Home': The Scholar or Patriot's Guidebook from the Renaissance to the Enlightenment

Some light-minded and inquisitive persons go on pilgrimages not out of devotion, but out of mere curiosity and love of novelty.

(Jacques de Vitry, thirteenth century)

The word, not the image, the ear and the tongue, not the eye, stand at the center [of humanist treatises on travel]. Any sightseeing which takes place remains at the service of textual authority.

(Judith Adler, 'Origins of Sightseeing', 1989)

THE AMBIVALENCE OF HUMANISM

We are accustomed to think of the advance of humanism as being rooted in the rediscovery and study of the texts of antiquity, which inevitably led to a fresh assessment of pagan philosophy. At the same time, the unveiling of a new continent, the opening up of trade routes to the East and a more scientific approach to geography and cosmology began to make 'local certainties seem wrong or parochial'.[1] The spirit of analytical and empirical enquiry that characterised the first phase of humanism in Italy was potentially inimical to religious dogma; in reality, a symbiotic relationship between faith and scholarship developed. Montaigne, in many ways a quintessential Renaissance figure, demonstrates in his *Essays* the way in which a 'balance between religious certainty and rational doubt and inquiry'[2] could be struck, without obvious damage to either.

Indeed, the humanist antiquaries of Rome – many of them princes of the Church – found ways of harnessing the reflected glory of ancient Rome to the notion of modern Rome as the cynosure of Christendom. This is also the spirit of Joachim du Bellay's sonnet that refers to the '*Nouveau venu qui cherches Rome en Rome*', or the eighth book of Petrarch's epic poem *Africa*, which attempts an accurate recreation of the Rome of the Punic Wars. Petrarch had used the *Mirabilia* as a guide during his visit to Rome in 1337, but was one of the first to adopt a critical spirit towards that work, correcting some of its identifications by reference to his own reading of the ancient authors.[3] At the same time, other writers attempted to allegorise the figures of antiquity with a Christian message, whereby Socrates' self-sacrifice becomes analogous to that of Christ, and Seneca's suicide likewise recalls Christian martyrdom. More concretely, the researches of humanists in the city did little to disturb the cult of the martyrs, 'the witnesses' of the faith, whose relics were seen as providing a physical continuity between pagan and Christian Rome.

While the Catholic humanism of Italy helped to 'modernise' the Church (as we would now say), rather than working to undermine it, the humanism of northern Europe, most notably that of the Netherlands and Germany, was often associated with the ideas, or at least the spirit, of the Reformation. Humanism everywhere was text-oriented, but the rigorous systematisation and theorisation of travel pioneered by scholars in Switzerland (Basel) and northern Europe suggests the bifurcation of Christian culture in the West. While pioneers of *ars apodemica* ('the art of travel'), such as Theodore Zwinger, laboured to achieve a methodology for making a guidebook that largely ignored sensual experience, the humanists of Rome were far more attuned to the kind of truth that could be communicated better, or at least as well, through art, sculpture, music and poetry. The difference in attitude is perhaps best expressed in the distinction that German scholarship makes between *die Kultur des Wortes* ('the culture of the word') and *die Kultur der Sinne* ('the culture of the senses'). While this useful distinction should not be pressed too far (in poetry and prose it can vanish altogether), it is clear that a subtext of iconoclasm especially marked in early Protestant culture stands against the sensuality of the Baroque. The latter was conceived (principally by the Jesuits) as a deliberate attempt to woo hearts and minds through the senses, though we should not forget the carefully worked out iconography that stood behind Baroque images.

FROM SUPERSTITION TO SCIENCE: THE SECULARISATION OF THE GUIDEBOOK

The most notable feature of what the humanist scholar and chorographer Konrad Celtis dubbed 'the commonwealth of letters' has been aptly described as 'learned itinerancy'. The phrase implies the exchange of scholarship across Western Europe, both through international communities of students at the great universities, and through letter-writing and reciprocal visits between the celebrated minds of the age. Celtis in fact wrote a poem in praise of the vagabond life dedicated to pursuit of knowledge, and John Hale describes him as 'spending ten precarious years [he had run away from home] flitting from school to school and university to university and, indeed, mistress to mistress'. Likewise the great Paracelsus spent years as a peripatetic scholar in Central Europe, ranging also as far afield as Spain and England. He says he did not limit his inquiries to scholars of medicine, but consorted also with 'barbers, bathkeepers, learned physicians, magicians and women'. 'While these travels helped to form the independence of his views,' observes Hale drily, 'his taste for drink and low life and his combative nature also delineate him as a learned *picaro*', the sort of person, in short, who was often to be either a writer or a consumer of guidebooks in the coming centuries. An Italian author fixed the type in 1591 as a man 'on whom a certain decree of the heavens has imposed a life of wandering about the provinces of the world'.[4]

Humanist scholarship and its polite vagabondage impacted either directly or peripherally on the guidebook genre in at least four ways: through the rise of scientific cartography, through the practice of topography and chorography (that is, the analytic description or mapping of regions), through the production of treatises on the 'art of travel', and finally through formal panegyrics of cities, such as Leonardo Bruni's *Panegyric of the City of Florence* (1403–4),[5] or Konrad Celtis's poem in praise of Nürnberg. Not surprisingly, since we are in the Renaissance, such works recall the distant roots of the guidebook in antiquity, as discussed in the first two chapters of this book. 'Chorography', for example, is a word invented in the sixteenth century and is derived via Latin from Greek 'khorographia' ($\chi\omega\rho\omega\gamma\rho\acute{\alpha}\psi\acute{\iota}\alpha$) and khora ($\chi\acute{\omega}\rho\alpha$), meaning a region or town – a word familiar to anyone who has holidayed on Greek islands with village names like 'Palaiokhora'. Such chorographic and panegyrical writings were founded in local patriotism, albeit one routinely measured against the city, region or country's prominence and valour in the annals of the Roman Empire. Imitative of the epideictic oratory of antiquity, which was designed to show off the speaker's skill in arousing feelings of awe and admiration, they were often as much exercises in classical rhetoric as they were empirical works of practical use.

The city panegyric gradually evolved into the city guide, for example, Philipp von Zesen's illustrated *Description of Amsterdam* (1664). The latter was written in verse and has been described as 'the first modern European guidebook'.[6] Von Zesen (1619–89) was a German who lived in Holland for twenty-two years, and this work was his declaration of love to the city, written in the Dutch he had mastered so well that he could write poetry in that tongue. The book praises the extreme cleanliness of Dutch dwellings, the splendour of the patrician houses on the Keizersgracht and the prettiness of the Dutch girls. Von Zesen was not untypical of humanist scholars in being totally devoid of a sense of humour (Erasmus was the exception). When his students ceremonially presented him with a poem that parodied his flowery diction *ad absurdum*, he happily took it as another instance of the extravagant flattery to which he had long been accustomed.[7] A Lutheran Pietist who translated Catholic devotional works into German from Spanish, French and Italian, Von Zesen exemplified the parallel intellectual worlds inhabited by north European humanist intellectuals. Despite the Baroque pedantry of his learned works, something of his independence of mind was transferred to his guidebook, allowing it to break away from the increasingly stale models of the panegyrics. His fellow-feeling for Dutch Protestantism, his success with the Amsterdam ladies and the gratitude he felt for being made an honorary burgher of the city all contributed to a spontaneity in his text that ensured it greater popularity than its fustian models.

ARS APODEMICA

Also with their roots in the rules of rhetoric were the scholarly humanist treatises on travel known as *ars apodemica*. The expression was a contemporary coinage, the literal translation of which is 'the art of being away from home', but customarily rendered as 'the art of travel'.[8] It had a counterpart in the so-called *Hausväterliteratur*, which gave advice on the tasks of the paterfamilias – the art of being at home, so to speak.[9] Methodology was paramount in such manuals: it is no surprise that they were the product of Germanic, and almost entirely Protestant, humanism, with its characteristic mania for didactic taxonomy. While Italian humanists had less use for such works (after all, they lived in the areas that everybody else was travelling to see), the genre had an astonishingly prolonged shelf life in Germany, Holland and England. The eye-watering tedium of *ars apodemica* treatises should not therefore blind us to their influence, nor to the reasons for it. And one reason for their popularity may have been that a methodology of travel that anyone could apply (as long as they could read and write) was both liberating and democratic. By the same token, *ars apodemica* displays an affinity with the levelling effect of '"Protestant inwardness", the notion that access to the kingdom of heaven is open to everybody individually, not mediated through the Church, but through Christ'. In such treatises, but also in the great wave of travel literature from the late fifteenth century onwards, the humanist scholars and explorers transformed a non-empirical account of the world controlled by clerical authority into an exploration of external reality,[10] or at any rate a methodology for such exploration.

Furthermore, writing one's own guidebook according to scientific principles of organisation represented a rather different philosophical and doctrinal approach to the individual's quest for knowledge than subjecting oneself to the vagaries of anachronistic guides written by others. In the sixteenth century, such guides still mingled fact with fable, dogma with hypothesis and plagiarism with autopsy. It was not that such a liberation of the individual encouraged subjectivity – rather, its opposite. As Justin Stagl puts it:

> Method is a democratic concept. Whoever applies it to the same initial situation must arrive at the same result; his personality, his inspiration, do

not matter. By its claim to universal validity, [the] method implicitly denied privileged sources of knowledge, such as the Bible, classical antiquity, or individual genius, and instead aimed at the accumulation of all knowledge by the exertions of many likeminded researchers working in different fields.[11]

As he settled down to his report, the earnest young scholar who sought to follow the tyrannical demands placed upon him by *ars apodemica* was more of a Nibelung than a Siegfried . . .

The method referred to above is that of Ramism, which strongly influenced the major works of *ars apodemica*, such as Theodor Zwinger's *Methodus apodemica* (1577), Hieronymus Turler's *De peregrinatione* (1574) and Hilarius Pyrckmair's *Commentariolus de arte apodemica* (1577), not to mention their many imitators in Latin or the vernacular.[12] Petrus Ramus (Pierre de la Ramée, 1515–72) was an enormously influential scholar of the day (Zwinger was his pupil) who devised a universal method for organising both empirical and non-empirical knowledge. Applied to the *ars apodemica*, his method produced, by means of standard questions the traveller should ask, a sort of tree of knowledge or hierarchy of propositions. These descended from the general to the particular through endless subdivisions until (at least according to Ramus) no further subdivisions were possible and one had arrived at the essential nature of things.

Ramism's epistemology reminds one of Bertrand Russell's genial account of the Indian philosopher who asserted that the world rested on an elephant. Asked what the elephant rested on, the philosopher said a tortoise. And asked what the tortoise rested on, he said 'Suppose we change the subject?' Nonetheless, Ramus, who was not one to hide his light under a bushel, roundly asserted that his system was universal, applicable to all the arts and sciences – a display of hubris that brought him as much denunciation as fame. The controversy was at least in part religious: Ramus died a Huguenot in the St Bartholomew Day's massacre; and his system appealed to the Protestant mind because it replaced traditional memory techniques, which exploited memorable images, with 'an abstract order of dialectical analysis'. It provided, says Frances Yates in a happy phrase, 'an inner iconoclasm, corresponding to the outer iconoclasm'.[13] A guidebook produced under its aegis would necessarily be devoid of imagination and image, or precisely the curious spectacles and sights that turn the wheels of the tourist industry. One envisages a minute description of the origin, materials and function of the tower of Pisa that omitted its most salient characteristic.

On the other hand, his method's universality was of course its great selling point for scholars. It appeared to combine complete flexibility (applicability to any topic) with absolute rigidity (all knowledge had to be subsumed into the same given framework), and offered the kind of self-referential, closed system of thought to which careerist academics are notoriously attracted. 'In view of the immense expansion of the cultural horizon in the sixteenth century,' to quote Stagl again, 'Ramism gave its adherents gratifying security.' Its main drawback was that the ability to subsume reality and experience in such a system was beyond the talents of most travellers, even when they conscientiously tried to follow the rules of *ars apodemica*, with its endless lists of questions to be asked and conceptual categories to be applied. A gifted Hungarian, Márton Szepsi Csombor, came quite close to half-succeeding with his *Europica Varietas* (1620), but the writing of it consumed so much time he was dismissed from his post as a schoolmaster for neglecting his duties. The final work, a digest of autopsy material from other authors and information gleaned from his correspondence, has been described as 'the first work of Hungarian descriptive statistics'.[14] Significantly, Csombor wrote a further book on the education of young noblemen, a genre from which a far more successful type of guidebook would soon arise, written for use on the Grand Tour.

Although there was a real danger that the *form* of *ars apodemica* would become an end in itself, while the *content* would self-destruct like a New Labour project in a frenzy of box-ticking, the issues it engaged with were often of real interest and of great significance for the guidebook's future development. The analysis of travel in a typical *ars apodemica* treatise inevitably began with a *definition*, which might seem superfluous to the modern mind, but typically such a definition ended with the idea that the traveller travelled in order 'to acquire . . . some good . . . which could be useful either to the fatherland and . . . friends . . . or to ourselves'. This anticipated what is now called 'field work' or 'social research'; it also introduced the notion of the 'patriotic traveller', a classic example of the latter being Leopold, Count Berchtold, whom we will come to shortly.

In Zwinger's 400-page treatise, ominously described by Stagl as 'more praised than read', the topics listed under the general heading of travel are endlessly subdivided: 'a single idea', observes Clare Howard in some desperation, 'is made to wend its tortuous way through folios'.[15] Nonetheless, an underlying intellectual order is provided by squeezing the didactic material into the framework of the four Aristotelian 'causes' that govern phenomena and their potentiality. The kinds of person who travel fall into the category of the 'material cause' or matter; the physical, material and spiritual powers that travellers should dispose of are identified with the 'formal cause' or form; the means by which they travel are the 'efficient cause' or action. (Here, beside the obvious options of land and water, Zwinger prophetically includes air, reminding his readers that this was the mode of conveyance preferred both by Daedalus and Philip the Evangelist, the latter having once been rescued from Samaria by a posse of angels.) Lastly, travel logistics (destination and routes etc.) represent the 'final cause' or purpose.

Zwinger then turns to the debate about travel, which continued the arguments for and against pilgrimage, or its abuse. More particularly, it adumbrated a large body of didactic literature centred on the Grand Tour and concerned with the question of whether the latter corrupted the young gentlemen who undertook it as much as it polished them. This was followed by medical advice, which had an even more ancient provenance in the Hippocratic writings discussed in Chapter 1 above. *Ars apodemica* invariably adopted the latter's doctrine of climatic influence on racial types, besides repeating sensible health advice of the sort that still features in the guidebooks of today. There was also some room for religious advice, whereby the authors had to deal with the difficulty that most of their readers were Protestants who travelled to Catholic countries. No less important was practical advice, including how to gain access to important men (*viri illustres*) abroad, and how to be open to foreigners and learn from observation. This last was rather undermined by the customary short descriptions of Europe's principal nations that followed, and which usually reverted to stereotypes. Finally there would be material on how to use the method to observe, record and evaluate all that was learned en route.[16]

THE DEBATE ABOUT TRAVEL

The travel literature of the Middle Ages was much concerned with wonders and exotica. Like the boulevard press of today, medieval texts made little distinction between what was known, however inaccurately, about other parts of the world, and grotesque fantasies introduced to titillate their readers. This genre may be traced back to antiquity, to Herodotus and Pliny, for example, but also to the tradition of paradoxographers mentioned in Chapter 1. The Renaissance voyages of discovery and the development of scientific cartography, themselves the consequence of an outward-looking, inquisitive mentality that replaced the inward-looking superstition and spirituality of the Middle Ages, brought about a 'cultural shift' in the Western European perception of the world. It was a shift that undermined not only the medieval romances but also the prerogatives of medieval religion. Critics of the change in attitudes deplored the fact that the *pietas* of the traditional pilgrim was losing ground to *curiositas*, 'a fastidious, excessive, morally diverting interest in things and people'.[17] Travel itself, and mobility, had long been associated by conservative Christian moralists with undesirable curiosity, with 'a wandering, unstable state of mind'. This sort of a mentality was dangerously opposed to the appropriate *stabilitas* anchored in the true faith, and to a fixed position in the God-given social dispensation of the Middle Ages. It now seems odd that travel should need justifying at all, but the humanists departure from convention, their application of standards of analysis that could challenge the authority of religion to provide a comprehensive explanation of the world, were part and parcel of their philosophy of travel.

Such a change in attitude does not occur overnight, nor did the new empirical travel reports entirely eschew the employment of useful, or sensational, fictions. The debate continues as to how much autopsy is implied by Marco Polo's *Il milione*, the title itself possibly an oblique reference to the genre of the 'tall story'.[18] Likewise, the famous account of a journey to China in the early fourteenth century made by the Friulian monk Odorico da Pordenone hovers between actual and imagined geography.[19] The fate of that great medieval bestseller *The Travels of Sir John Mandeville* is instructive: following its first circulation in the mid-fourteenth century, it was considered a reliable source of solid geographical information for over two centuries. A recent editor of

Mandeville points out that Columbus perused *The Travels* for information on China and Frobisher had a copy by him as he lay off Baffin Bay in 1576. But by the early seventeenth century, Bishop Joseph Hall is castigating *The Travels* for its bad influence, and a satiric comedy called *The Antipodes* had been written with the sole purpose of ridiculing the author and his 'lies'. It is probable that Mandeville has the last laugh in this debate, both on the credulous and the sceptics (does he not slyly inform us: 'Of Paradise I cannot speak properly, for I have not been there; and that I regret'?); but the shift in attitudes towards travel reports is a shift from the fabulous perceived as fact to the factual perceived as utilitarian.[20] A century later Samuel Johnson summed up the matter in characteristically apodictic manner when he stated that 'the use of travelling is to regulate imagination by reality', arguably the opposite of Mandeville's literary project.

While the Renaissance was a time of energetic travelling by the learned (for example, the Cambridge don Fynes Moryson, who was able to take five years 'study leave' between 1590 and 1595 for his subsequently famous tour of Europe), there were those who believed that tourism was 'a training school for patriotic irresponsibility and vice and instead advocated a *Wanderjahr* in the head'.[21] Indeed, in 1600, one Samuel Lewkenor published a work brazenly entitled *A Discourse . . . for Such as Are Desirous to Know the Situation and Customes of Forraine Cities without Travelling to See Them*. From the proliferation of analogous works we can see that the debate about travel began in earnest in the Renaissance and continued into the age of the Grand Tour. It was a debate infected with the struggle for intellectual supremacy between Protestantism and Catholicism, to which arguments about the perils of travel, physical or ethical, were often subordinated. The disputes about patriotism cut both ways: probably the majority of English travellers to Rome in the late sixteenth and early seventeenth centuries were recusants, to a greater or lesser extent political dissidents or refugees whose embrace of the culture of Catholicism and recognition of the authority of the papacy was threatening to the establishment at home. On the other hand, and progressively as we move towards the period of the Enlightenment, the concept of the 'patriotic traveller' gained ground, culminating in Count Berchtold's celebrated book of that title. Sir John Stradling, quoting Iustus Lipsius, expressed a widespread view when he wrote: 'Many countries it is good to see / So that we keep our honestie.'[22]

THE PATRIOTIC TRAVELLER

The eponymous protagonist of such a work visited other countries to see and record what his own could learn from them; the particularism often implicit in Renaissance panegyrics (albeit subordinate to an overarching perception of the supremacy of Greek and Roman culture) faded into a universal vision of moral and material progress in which all could learn from each other. 'Travelers as carriers of enlightenment, or – in Bacon's phrase – "merchants of Light," eventually made it plausible to order objects in terms of their moral claim to attention.'[23] Count Berchtold is the most vivid protagonist of this last idea, combining a Renaissance attention to methodology with a Josephinist sense of *noblesse oblige* and the public spirited rationalism of the Enlightenment.[24] The two-volume *Essay to Direct and Extend the Inquiries of Patriotic Travellers with Further Observations on the Means of Preserving the Life, Health and Property of the Unexperienced in their Journies by Land and Sea* (1787–9) is the *ne plus ultra* of travel instruction – and obviously a literary and methodological fossil in its age. In Berchtold's scheme of things, the preparation alone for a journey would imply a more than liberal education, requiring studies in mineralogy, metallurgy, chemistry, mathematics, mechanics, hydraulics, navigation, shipbuilding and even swimming and medicine. Not only proficiency in shorthand was indispensable, but also mastery of a secret alphabet 'in order to conceal such important matters as may be improper for the inspection of prying or designing persons'.[25]

Here the traveller comes dangerously close to being a spy, and in fact industrial espionage was an ongoing concern of host countries, particularly England during the Industrial Revolution. The reception given to 'patriotic' travellers was therefore mixed. Goethe, who believed strongly in the catalytic value of the Italian experience for cultivated Germans, was almost arrested as an Austrian spy at the beginning of his Italian journey for sketching the castle at Malcesine on Lake Garda. His delightful account of the incident turns a simple misunderstanding into an amusing account of cultural dissonance, when he remarks to his accusers that 'he had not realised these ruins were a fortress', as claimed, and endeavours to justify an enthusiasm for the picturesque that is incomprehensible to the locals.[26] On the other hand, Gabriel-Jean Jars, in his *Voyages métallurgiques* (1774–81), relates that he was well received in many foundries and forges in the north of England, and as a result was able to carry off valuable information to his patrons in France. Then again, Arthur Young complained of the impact that French espionage had had on the less accommodating craftsmen of Birmingham, who engaged in what David Landes delightfully calls 'rational paranoia'.[27] Perhaps it is no accident that Hieronymus Turlerus, whose *De Peregrinatione* (1574) was translated into English the following year as *The Traveiler of Jerome Turler*, had only three other known works to his credit – and they were translations from Machiavelli.

Berchtold was a man of astonishing energy and benevolence; like the famous English agronomist Arthur Young, whose close friend he was, he was allied with the physiocratic tendency, which embraced laissez-faire economics based on flourishing agriculture and fair treatment of the agricultural labourer.[28] His benevolence bordered on the eccentric: not only did he test a prophylactic against the plague by working in the plague hospital at Smyrna, in Algiers he collected the details of Christians who had been enslaved by barbary pirates and published them in order to raise money for their redemption. As he might have foreseen from his study of laissez-faire economics, the immediate result of this was to force up the prices demanded.[29] But the few such failures are far outweighed by the endless stream of reforms, charities and good works he initiated from his model estate at Burg Buchlau in Moravia (now Buchlov in the Czech Republic.) The regimen he set for travellers reflected his own workaholic schedule and would have been far beyond the powers of lesser mortals, but it proposed a gold standard for the use of travel as a means of instructing not only the individual, but also his and other nations. 'A philosopher traveller looks upon his country as a sick friend, for whose relief he asks advice of all the world' is a typical sentiment; and 'the principal work [of the traveller] is to see how far the ideas we had formed of an object were founded on reason during anticipation' seems to echo Dr Johnson.

There were of course many other works that justified, attacked or methodologised travel, but the majority of those in English concerned the benefits or dangers of the Grand Tour, and a discussion of them belongs in the next chapter. Josiah Tucker's *Instructions for Travellers* (1757) straddles both categories, but his embrace of free trade and advocation of low taxes places him in the same tradition as Berchtold. His liberal and enlightened attitudes did not endear him to everyone: his advocation of the naturalisation of Jews caused him to be burned in effigy with the offending pamphlet, and his bishop remarked that the Rector of St Stephen's in Bristol (Mr Tucker) 'made a religion of his trade and a trade of his religion'. Generally speaking, the English contributions to the debate about travel (Joseph Hall, 1617; James Howell, 1650; Tucker, 1757; Richard Hurd, 1759) were less concerned with grand methodology in the excruciatingly detailed and rigid German manner, and more concerned with concrete problems and Protestant polemic. *Ars apodemica* lingered on in Germany long after it had come to seem old-fashioned elsewhere. Indeed, under the influence of men like August Ludwig Schlözer, author of *Entwurf zu einem Reise-Collegio* ['Outline for a Book of Advice for Travellers'; Göttingen, 1777], it was brought into the university curriculum. Eventually it was subsumed into the disciplines of statistics, political science, sociology and even ethnology.

Schlözer's efforts imply an *embourgeoisement* of both the theme and actuality of travel and is aimed at the needs of young scholars of limited means. It concentrates on the preparative study to be undertaken before travelling and how to behave during the journey. Prior study is considered to be so important that one begins to wonder whether the journey needed be undertaken at all: at any rate, the example of Lalande[30] is paraded as worthy of emulation, with Schlözer applauding the fact that he 'wrote up his journey to Italy *before* . . . [it] took place'. This is even more extreme than Montaigne's behaviour during his tour of 1580, when he lost patience with the bottomless ignorance of his local guides. According to his secretary, he decided to become his own cicerone 'with the help of various books and plans which he studied in the evenings, while during the day he served apprenticeship on the spot, so that in a short time he himself could have guided the guide'.[31] Montaigne was in fact a typical Renaissance traveller, in that he travelled intellectually and selectively, ignoring the drama of nature that ravished the Romantics. Attilio Brilli quotes the great essayist's significant observation that the traveller finds himself in the same situation during a journey as those who, having committed themselves to reading a book, are seized with the anxiety that it could end too soon.[32] For Montaigne, the adventure in the mind is just as real, or even more real, than the physical adventure of travel. Accordingly, in making his own guidebook, he disparaged much of what a modern guidebook contains. The purpose of travelling, he sniffed, was not just to count *'combien de pas a "Santa Rotonda"'* (presumably referring to a circuit of S. Maria Rotunda, as the christianised Pantheon was called for many years) or to compare how one image of Nero on a medallion is taller or wider than another, but 'principally to report on the temperaments and ways of [other] nations, and to polish and sharpen our wits against those of others'.[33]

Probably the attentive reader of Franz Posselt's vast and windy two-volume *Apodemik oder die Kunst zu reisen* (1795) would have arrived at a similar conclusion. This last great work of *ars apodemica* was also its tombstone, a trawl through all the traditonal topoi of travel advice from the Renaissance onwards. Like all its predecessors, *Apodemik* was strong on categories and silent on particulars, so the traveller decided himself what individual object was worthy of note. The rise of the bourgeois guidebook may perhaps be traced to the difficulty that most people experienced in making such decisions and the relief they felt when the guidebook authoritatively made the choices for them. What remained of *ars apodemica* was incorporated into the section on 'Practical Information' in later guidebooks. Nor were the literary results engendered by the *ars apodemica* methodology encouraging. Stagl quotes a not untypical example, Friedrich Nicolai's *Beschreibung einer Reise durch Deutschland und die Schweiz im Jahre 1781*, which was scheduled to appear in a mere twelve volumes between 1783 and 1796. Greeted enthusiastically at first, it eventually had to be discontinued because of hostile reviews and dwindling sales to an exhausted readership. 'Famous travel reports like Carsten Niebuhr's *Beschreibung von Arabien* [1772]', adds Stagl, 'owed much of their success to the fact that [their authors] had had the common sense to disregard much of the advice of the methodologists.'[34]

SOME QUASI-GUIDEBOOKS OF THE RENAISSANCE

In the sixteenth century 'the guidebook' was still a fragmented genre, including advice for seafarers that could be traced back to the *periploi* of the ancient Greeks discussed in Chapter 1, pilgrim's guides that were split between itineraries and devotional instruction, books of medical advice that have a distant ancestor in *Airs, Waters, Places* (see Chapter 1) and road-books that are descended from Roman itineraries. These last catered to a rising merchant class, one of the oldest printed road-books being Jörg Gail's modest *Raiß Büchlin* (Travel Booklet) printed for the traders of Augsburg in 1563.[35] Before printing was invented, however, a more interesting work was compiled *c.* 1340 by the Florentine merchant Francesco Pegolotti, entitled *Advice to Merchants Bound for Cathay*. This fascinating document is particularly detailed on money matters, including the costs of the journey, the paper money given by the Chinese ruler in exchange for silver or merchandise, and the opportunity the Genoese and Venetians had of exchanging their speciality linens in return for funds to finance the return journey. The author, an agent acting for the great Florentine banking family of the Bardi, fully justifies his claim of providing not only a description of the countries that must be crossed on the Cathay route, but also the 'measures employed in business, and . . . other things needful to be known by merchants of different parts of the world, and by all who have to do with merchandise and exchanges . . .'[36] This was perhaps the first businessman's guidebook, a genre that did not really flourish again until the twentieth century. It reflects the burgeoning trade contacts with the East and the increasing security of travel in hitherto highly dangerous regions. Dated to the mid-fourteenth century, it lent credibility to the contemporary claim that 'on the orient caravan route, a virgin alone, riding a mule loaded with gold, could traverse the territory of the Great Khan without danger'.[37]

A number of humanist travel writers and travel theorists were doctors of medicine, such as their mentor, Theodore Zwinger; and some offered their experience to travellers in printed manuals of advice. Georg Pictorius (namely, Jörg Maler (c. 1500–69)) was one such and wote a *Raise Büchlin* giving rules for those who wished to protect their health when travelling in unknown lands.[38] Although its diagnosis is still based on the four humours, the advice is often familiar and efficacious – for example, the recommendation of rhubarb for constipation. There are remedies for the traveller's most common afflictions, including lassitude, headaches, excess wind, diarrhoea, chillblains, fever, nausea, inflammation of the bladder and nosebleeds. Pictorius was personal physician to a European princeling, but another travelling doctor, Andrew Borde (c. 1490–1549), seems rarely to have practised, except for a brief spell in Glasgow. Although he did publish a work called the *Dyetary of Helth* (1542?), which was hailed as even more impressive than his seminal *Treatyse upon Beardes*, he is best known for his *First Book of the Introduction of Knowledge* (c. 1547), considered the first continental guidebook in English. Much of it is written in doggerel and the author wears his patriotism on his sleeve, perhaps not surprisingly, since he seems to have been used as an informant and diplomat by Thomas Cromwell to gauge reaction on the Continent to the policies of Henry VIII.

As a guide, Borde is ambitious, but erratic. He travelled all over Europe, Byzantium and North Africa, indicating the vital statistics of each country visited, with something of its geographical features and the splendour or otherwise of its cities. He is particularly interested in languages and supplies phrases for foreign travellers in Wales and Ireland, but is defeated by the 'spech of Hungary', which is 'corrupte Italian, corrupte Greke and Turkish'. Nor are the languages any more comprehensible in the Scandinavian countries, where 'in stede of bread they do eate stockfish and they will eat raw fish and flesh; they be beastly creatures, unmannerly and untaught'. A former Carthusian monk, Borde obviously decided to make up for lost time after releasing himself from his vows. His suggestion in his *Dyetary* that nutmeg dampens sexual desire seems to have reflected a misplaced optimism in his case. At any rate, as Giles Milton has observed, Borde of all people should have kept taking the nutmeg, for he ended up with a reputation for scandalous living: 'Under the colour of virginitie and of wearing a shirt of hair [he kept] three whores at once in his chamber . . . to serve not only himself but also to help the virgin priests about in the country.'[39] As to his pioneering works, they evidently made a considerable impact, as Borde himself must have done on those who met him. He 'seems to have courted popularity by the jocoseness of his style, which', sighs his modern editor, 'often degenerates into buffoonery'.[40] On the other hand, there have been many guides that could have done with a little more of Borde's chutzpah. Sadly, he died in the Fleet Prison.

Another scholar in the service of Henry VIII was John Leland (1506?–52), more of a topographer than a guidebook writer, but one whose task of making inventories of the English monasteries' manuscripts and antiquities had implications for the aesthetic matter of future guides. Of course his 1533 visitation of the religious foundations was hardly disinterested, since his royal patron was probably looking for things he could lay his hands on, prior to the dissolution of the monasteries that began three years later. In his defence, Leland claimed he was saving manuscripts *inter alia* from young German scholars, who were everywhere taking advantage 'of our desidiousness and negligence' and not only purloining the most valuable ones but also bowdlerising others and 'publishing the extracts as relics of the ancient literature of their own country'. However, his allegiance to Henry in the very year when the latter outraged the Church by marrying Anne Boleyn no doubt accounts for the hostile reception he sometimes received. At Oxford he had to wave the king's commission in the face of the recalcitrant Grey Friars, and 'came very near to using force'. Nevertheless, he was clearly a patriot with a consuming passion for his homeland, its archaeology, topography and history.

In pursuing his five itineraries across Henry's realm, Leland appears as one imbued with the principles of *ars apodemica* before its time. He made astonishingly copious notes, both on the road and about each town he reached, its location, walls, gates, castle, parish church, streets, markets, the finest houses, its river (if any) and bridges over the same, its suburbs and staple industry; finally its archaeological remains with perhaps a reference to local folklore and musings on the etymology of the town's name. 'His supreme antiquarian merit resulted from his resolution to go to look at places of interest instead of merely reading about them,' wrote Sir William Kendrick, which sharply distinguishes him from his predecessors, whose travels/topographies were mostly works of the study. Leland's book indeed paved the way for William Lambarde's more limited *Perambulation of Kent* (1576), John Stow's *Survey of London* (1598), which drew heavily on Leland's notes, and William Camden's massive topographical work, *Britannia* (1586). According to the *Dictionary of National Biography*, Leland claimed to have visited 'almost every bay, river, lake, mountain, valley, moor, heath, wood, city, castle, manor-house, monastery and college in the land'. Though a man of his time, 'he nevertheless understood and was fascinated by the medieval world, which his own world was displacing, and was able to spend its last crucial decade describing its death-throes in meticulous detail. On virtually every page of the *Itinerary* we feel the sense of the old world giving way to the new, the clock striking midnight.'[41] Eventually he suffered a breakdown from overwork and was committed to the care of his brother with the income from two benefices to finance his keep. The grant of commitment described him as 'mad, insane, lunatic, furious, frantic, enjoying drowsy or lucid intervals, so that he cannot manage his affairs', a sad end for the great English peregrinator.

One last example of the Renaissance proto-guidebook is worthy of notice, namely William Bourne's *The Treasure for Travelers . . . either by Sea or by Lande* (1578), another edition of which appeared under the title *A Mate for Mariners* in 1641. Bourne was a mathematician who had also written on navigation and designed a submarine; of the five sections in his *Treasure for Travelers* four are concerned in some way with mathematical measurement ('Geometrie perspective', 'Cosmography', 'Geometrie general', 'Statick' and 'Naturall Philosophy'). The influence of *ars apodemica* is seen in the discussions of what type of person should embark on travel, and what type of thing the traveller should note. However, his main matter is practical: how to use an astrolobe, how to work out your position using longitude and latitude, how to measure surfaces and solid bodies, how to calculate the displacement of a ship. The last book explains the origins of sand and rocks, why the sea is salty and sundry other such puzzles. Interestingly, Bourne, who describes himself as being 'altogether unlearned', is evidently not writing for scholars but 'to teach them that are simple and unlearned'. He embraces the Protestant view that the common folk are to be empowered through knowledge and couples this with a violent attack on the clergy of his day, 'who should be as Lanternes . . . to leade us unto vertue', but who rather light the way to vice. There follows a coruscating attack on Catholic icons and ritual, as also on the behaviour of the indolent and licentious gentry, but all this is rounded off with a paean of praise for the governance of Elizabeth I.

Despite this quasi-puritanical introduction, Bourne is at heart a scientifically minded Renaissance man. He stresses the civilising benefits of travel, while warning that these will not occur unless the traveller is a mature person of good judgement (actually 'betweene the age of 40 and 56 or 57 yeares'). There then follow the usual lists of tasks for such travellers, as can be found in Turler, Pyrckmair and the other protagonists of *ars apodemica*. *The Treasure for Travelers* offers thus an interesting mix of practical instruction and polemic, of piety and patriotism, of perceptiveness and prejudice. It might be thought odd by the modern reader that sententious moralising should sit easily in the same text with instructions on using an astrolobe or measuring distances, but that was the temper of the age. In the same way the mathematician Bourne had an endearingly human capacity for error, or so we learn from a document produced in Gravesend in 1571. This reveals that he was one of fourteen 'Innholders and Tiplers that were amerced in that year for selling Beer and Ale in Pots of Stone and Cans not being quarts of full measure'. Bourne was fined 'vi d'.[42]

ROME AND THE HUMANIST GUIDEBOOK

Around 1431, Poggio Bracciolini, the humanist secretary to the papal *curia*, was accustomed to walk with a fellow scholar round what he called the 'wastelands' of the city of Rome. His meditations on these excursions were subsequently written up in the form of an essay bearing the portentous title 'On the Inconstancy of Fortune', essentially an account of the conversations held during their rambles between Poggio and his companion, Antonio Loschi. Surveying the city from the Capitoline Hill, Antonio laments 'how different these temples and citadels are, Poggio, from those which our Virgil celebrated in verse: "Now glittering like gold, once bristling with woody brambles". Indeed that line could be rephrased: "Gilded once, neglected now, massed with thorn-thickets and briars".' Notwithstanding the pervasively elegiac tone of this conversation, it also indicates the determination of the learned local patriots of Rome to begin the work of recovering its ancient glories, of retrieving the past to make it serve the present.

The conversation turns into a description by Bracciolini of what he has been able to discern of ancient edifices among the 'thorn-thickets and briars', such as the public salt supply on the Capitoline Hill, or the tomb of one Gaius Publicius Bibulus, a bridge over the Tiber, a Tiburtine stone arch over the road between the Aventine and the riverbank, the Cimbrian temple, and a pyramid near the Ostian gate.[43] He had also just discovered a manuscript concerning the city's water supply under Nerva (AD 97). Much of this knowledge had been acquired by diligent reading of inscriptions, for which Bracciolini is congratulated by his friend: 'You have searched in many places both within the city and outside it, and having gathered together those same [inscriptions] on both public and private buildings in a small volume, you have bequeathed them to be read by scholars.' These 'small volumes' (1430) of both pagan and Christian inscriptions were a genre of literature known as *sylloges*, which had been invented by Bracciolini.

In Loschi's pregnant remark may be glimpsed the dawn of the humanist guidebook, with its particular fascination, one might even say obsession, with inscriptions. These were still being collected diligently by such English travellers as the essayist Joseph Addison over 250 years later. Here too we have an early encounter with scholarly one-upmanship, a critical spirit that supplants the former wholesale incorporation of long discredited claims into generations of guidebooks. Speaking of the funeral monument of Gaius Cestius, a priest of ancient Rome responsible for organising the banquets of the gods, Bracciolini pounces on some sloppy scholarship in one of Petrarch's letters, where this tomb (he claims) is wrongly identified: 'As [the] inscription is still extant, the more I wonder why Francesco Petrarca, that most erudite of men, writes in one of his letters that it is the tomb of Remus. I believe . . . that he did not go to much effort in carefully examining an inscription hidden by vegetation. Those less learned who have followed afterwards have shown more diligence in reading these inscriptions.' This was written at a time when 'ordinary Romans handed out misinformation to all comers, identifying every large building in the city as a bath', and the scholar's main weapons against such error was still 'more textual than empirical'.[44] Archaeology as such did not exist, and indeed, as we shall see in Palladio's accounts of the martyrs, Renaissance scholars were not above drawing information from 'medieval guidebooks, from earlier collections of inscriptions, and from the oral traditions that lived on among the few thousand inhabitants who still haunted Rome's narrow porticoed streets'.[45] On the other hand, scholarship made significant innovations in methodology, which in itself progressively engendered a more critical approach to the sources.

Passing lightly over the fact that Bracciolini himself makes some errors in his own descriptions,[46] we may observe another more ominous remark concerning the temple of Concord in the Forum: 'When I first came to the city I saw this almost whole and completely radiant with marble. The Romans have since demolished the whole temple for lime, as well as part of the portico, and the columns lie dashed to pieces. The letters S.P.Q.R. . . . on the portico have been consumed by fire and are to be re-instated.'[47] From at least the eleventh century, the people of Rome had been stripping the marble from ancient buildings and burning it in limekilns for re-use as building material. Priceless statues were burned and ground in the smoky shops between the Capitol and the Tiber in a street still known as the Via delle Botteghe Oscure. Subsequently, the re-ordering of the urban landscape and the great building boom under the Renaissance popes was to have an even more devastating effect on the fabric of the ancient city. Indeed, Bramante, who began the demolition of Constantine's (already much ruined) basilica on the orders of Julius II in order to build the new St Peter's, was the butt of a coruscating satire that dubbed him 'Bramante Ruinante'.[48] On the other hand, Bracciolini's reference to the rescuing of the letters S.P.Q.R. suggests the influence of the scholars, who would help to create a new synthesis of a noble past and a glorious present, ancient landmarks and splendid palaces and churches. Guidebooks to the city tended to be what economists call a 'lagging indicator' of this kind of change; and when they did begin to reflect it, the Middle Ages, which did not fit comfortably with the new Janus-dynamic of the city, fell into a sort of historical black hole, ignored by the vast majority of compilers, though there were exceptions.

By the sixteenth and seventeenth centuries, a different and differentiated perception of Rome began to make itself felt in the literature for travellers, even if the old *Mirabilia* also continued to be published in new editions. Some of these, either out of commercial pragmatism or sheer indifference, came to terms with new material grounded in humanist scholarship simply by adding it as a separate section, for example, Palladio's celebrated *L'antichità di Roma*. Humanist topographies, such as Flavio Biondi's *Roma Instaurata* ('Rome Restored' (1481)) or Giovanni Dondi's fourteenth-century antiquarian notes taken on a journey to Rome (*Iter Romanum*), assiduously chipped away at layers of legend, just as amateur archaeologists like the subsequently notorious Cola di Rienzo (1313–54) spent days scraping away the grime of centuries to get at buried inscriptions and fragments of buildings. The most happy marriage of Christian observance and pagan antiquarianism is exemplified in the daily routine of the Florentine Giovanni Rucellai, who wrote his *De Urbe Roma* during the Jubilee Year of 1450.

The mornings he spent visiting the four main basilicas to comply with his obligations in respect of indulgences in a Holy Year; and in the afternoon he rode out to view different antique sites for his own edification and pleasure.

ROME'S TOURIST INDUSTRY EXPANDS

The biggest single impulse to the Roman tourist industry was given by the institution of Jubilee Years by Boniface VIII in 1300. Since pilgrims could obtain a plenary indulgence (the remission of all temporal punishment incurred by an individual's sins) by coming to Rome in a Jubilee Year and visiting the required churches and relics according to a prescribed schedule, it is not hard to gauge the Jubilee's potential for commercial gain – and of course for publishing guides. Commentators like the above-mentioned Rucellai were indeed alert to the Holy Year's impact on Rome's economy, noting that there were 1,022 hostelries in the city with signboards, and a further large number without.[49] It helped that Jerusalem, until the return of the Franciscan mission in 1335, was no longer very attractive to all but the most intrepid pilgrims, being under Mameluke control. An idea of the numbers of visitors to Rome in the first Jubilee Year is conveyed by commentators like Giovanni Villani, and among those of high or low estate who thronged the streets of Rome was his fellow Florentine, Dante Alighieri.[50] The fabric of the city was not equal to this assault, as became evident in 1450, when a stubborn mule obstructed pilgrims returning across the Ponte Sant' Angelo from St Peter's, causing a panic-stricken crush in which over a hundred died, either trampled or drowned in the Tiber.[51]

Jubilees had their origin in Mosaic Law (*imprimis* in the seventh day of rest decreed at the creation, then, by extension, the seventh 'sabbatical' year, when slaves were released and appropriated land restored to its owners.) A socially more acceptable formula had evolved of seven times seven (49) years being followed by a fiftieth one, the Jubilee. Boniface simply doubled this period to 100 years for the proposed Christian Jubilees or 'Holy Years', but it was soon realised that many Christians would not live long enough to experience one; so in 1343 the interval was restored to that of the Jewish fifty years, reduced to thirty-three years (the supposed term of Christ's life) in 1389, and finally to twenty-five years from 1475, the most recent Holy Year having been in 2000.

The literature produced to cater for the Jubilees was diverse, perpetuating a tradition of writing designed to attract pilgrims to Rome rather than its rivals. For example, it has been said of the English poem *The Stacyons of Rome* that it was 'simply a puff of the merits of the Papal city as a place for getting pardons and indulgences, in comparison with Santiago and Jerusalem'.[52] The work was evidently popular and exists also in prose form, having much in common with the *libri indulgentiarum* discussed in the previous chapter, which were among the earliest printed books. The latter were indeed booming, the *Indulgentiae ecclesiarum Urbis*, as previously remarked, going through forty-four Latin editions between 1475 and 1523, as well as twenty in German and others in Italian,

French, Spanish and Flemish.[53] The *Stacyons*, however, is more interesting, in that it departs from the traditional method of organisation, whereby the five or seven principal churches are listed with their relics and indulgences, and are followed by a few notes on other churches. It begins its discussion of Rome with St Peter's and thereafter follows an order evidently dictated by topography and the actual pilgrim route, making it much more practical as a guidebook. Since pilgrims moved in groups, one of whose number would know the way, the traditional pilgrim guides dispensed with precise route directions. The 'stations' of the poem's title referred to solemn papal processions, mostly during Lent, Holy Week and over Christmas, to some forty Roman 'station' churches where the Pontiff (later his representative) would celebrate Mass.

Indulgences were one of Rome's main selling points in the late Middle Ages and early Renaissance. The *libri indulgentiarum* promoted them as heavily as sunshine and sea on today's tourist brochures; and just as such brochures do not always reflect the unvarnished truth, the *libri* did not always reflect what the Church as an institution officially licensed in terms of indulgences. Yet the persistence of the indulgence cult can be seen from the necessity of removing two marker stones promising generous indulgences from outside S. Prassede late in the eighteenth century.[54] Removing spurious information was one thing, inculcating correct behaviour and inspiring a proper spiritual motivation in pilgrims was another. Sebastiano Fabrini's *Declaration of the Jubilee Year* (1600) tried to do just that: not only does it make the physical suffering of the pilgrim inseparable from the spiritual rewards of pilgrimage, it also seeks a measure of social justice, allowing poorer pilgrims to complete their cycle of devotion at the main basilicas in a single day, so that they could save on lodging. Fabrini exhibits two other aspects of Counter-Reformatory severity, denouncing non-Catholics who come to Rome merely to slander Catholicism, and (revealingly) condemning those who are only interested in antiquities: 'It must be warned that there is no need to go to Rome only or principally with the intention of seeing antique things and marvels of this city, such as the baths, circuses, amphitheatres, the extremely tall columns, the marvelous pyramids, or the obelisks, the Campidoglio, [H]adrian's tomb, and other curiosities . . .'.[55]

ANDREA PALLADIO'S CONTRIBUTION TO ROME TOURISM

Forty-six years before Fabrini eloquently highlighted the tensions between spirituality and tourism – that is, between devotional and antiquarian motivations for travel – no lesser figure than Andrea Palladio reconciled the two in a couple of booklets, both published in 1554. By far the better known is his *L'Antichità di Roma*, a work based on autopsy and humanist scholarship, which Palladio says in his Preface should be studied diligently by any reader who wants to experience 'that delight and marvel, which one chiefly feels in understanding clearly the great things of such a noble and famous city as Rome'. The author emphasises his break with previous standard guidebooks, remarking that he had written

L'Antichità precisely to correct the myths and legends spread by 'a certain book . . . entitled Le cose maravigliose di Roma,' which, he says, is crammed full of the most bizarre falsehoods ('tutto pieno di strane bugie'). As noted above, it is one of the more delightful ironies of guidebook history that it was precisely to later editions of this very book that L'Antichità was subsequently attached![56] Moreover, strane bugie emerges as a somewhat relative term, when one considers the hagiology complacently retailed by the same author in his account of Roman churches . . .

In fact Palladio was not the first to attempt an assault on the strane bugie of the Mirabilia Romae; Leon Batttista Alberti, the celebrated architect and author of a great architectural treatise De re aedificatoria (1452), had composed a Descriptio urbis Romae (c. 1432–4); though it does not advance much on Giovanni Dondi's Iter Romanum already mentioned, it was important because Alberti published thereby the polar coordinates of ancient monuments established by his newly invented astrolabe. This first attempt to establish the spatial dimensions of the city was at least an improvement on the hopelessly arbitrary sketch maps of existing guides and we may perhaps see in it the distant ancestor of the sophisticated aids to orientation that we now take for granted in the cartography of modern guidebooks. Scholarship took a more decisive step forward when Cardinal Della Rovere, the nephew of Julius II, complained about the fables in the Mirabilia and asked the Florentine scholar-priest Francesco Albertini to do something about it. Albertini's response to this ukase, the Opusculum (1510) on 'new and old wonders', enjoyed wide currency in Rome and abroad (Basle, 1519, Lyons, 1520).[57] Likewise, the same author's Seven World Wonders and those of the Cities of Rome and Florence overtly linked past glories to the those of the present, making no invidious or doctrinal distinction between the splendour of a church such as Sta Maria Maggiore and that of the Pantheon. Notwithstanding the popularity of these works, it was Palladio's guide that established itself (together with his Le Chiese di Roma), going through innumerable editions over the 200 years between 1554 and the mid-eighteenth century.[58] Doubtless this was because it had at least some of the properties of a modern guidebook: the leading Palladian scholar has called it 'definitely Baedekerian rather than Antiquarian',[59] although it is in fact organised as a gazetteer. It begins with a concise history of Rome, follows up with an enumeration of the city's seven hills and then deals with other urban features, gates, streets, bridges and so forth, the whole amounting to a 'lucid description of the topography of ancient Rome, based on contemporary scholarship as well as ancient authors'.[60]

Palladio's Descrittione de le Chiese, Stationi, Indulgenze & Reliquie de Corpi Sancti, che sonno in la Citta de Roma might appear, from its title, to be a reversion to the old pilgrims' guides with their inaccuracies and propaganda.[61] However, it claims to be informed by the same spirit as L'Antichità, as the author stresses in his address to the reader, where he again says that what has been written from memory about the city's sacred buildings and sites in most of the available guides does 'not correspond to the truth', many such sites having been ravaged by war and fire. Despite his proclaimed scepticism, scholars are of the opinion that he nevertheless borowed from a number of earlier guides, and in particular from the 1550 edition of *Le cose maravigliose di Roma*.[62] Still, he considerably enlarged the material of the latter, which dealt with eighty-four churches, while Palladio mentions 121, and his book was also produced in a pilgrim-friendly octavo format. The well-thumbed six copies that survive, all with extensive marginalia, show it was generally used as a companion guide en route, rather than being stored in a library. 'Palladio seems to have been a deeply religious man,' writes Deborah Howard, 'but his approach is once again matter-of-fact and instructive.'[63] Moreover he promises a new, conveniently organised tour of the city, beginning with the seven principal churches, passing from Trastevere through the Borgo, then to the Piazza del Popolo and from there to the Campidoglio, thence covering the seven hills of the city and its most ancient regions in a strictly clockwise direction. The itineraries effectively quarter the city, and interestingly the Capitoline Hill retains its 'geographical and symbolic importance'[64] as the hub of three out of the four routes, while the fourth one connected Trastevere sights with those of the Vatican Borgo.

The meat of the book lies in the details of churches, their foundation myths or history, their relics, their various privileges, which of them were 'station churches' (where, as already described, and as laid down in the Roman Missal, the pope was supposed to celebrate Mass on certain days), and finally the indulgences they offered. These last are as extravagant as ever, though Palladio claims that they are 'licenced by the Supreme Pontiff'. There is even a hint that Palladio is doing his bit to uphold the claims of Rome against the competition, which was after all competition for pilgrims' money. After listing the 28,000 indulgences available at S. Giovanni in Laterano on the Day of St John the Evangelist, he adds gratuitously that 'there are still infinite indulgences [i.e. at S. Giovanni], which means in particular that there is no need to go to the Holy Sepulchre of Christ or to St James Campostella'.[65] Six thousand years' remission are on offer at the twelve most important churches, and even more elsewhere; for example, at Sta Bibiana, 'where five thousand martyrs are buried, not counting women and children'(!), 9,000 years are on offer; and at the same church on All Saints Day, no less than 600,000 years. Sta Bibiana, today a church largely ignored by the mainstream tourist guides, was also a 'station church', but Palladio leaves unspoken the fact (if he knew it) that its association with thousands of martyrs was spurious. His guide helped it to maintain its prominence and it was still considered important enough in 1624 for the young Bernini to be given the commission (his first architectural one) to supply it with a Baroque façade.

Palladio's book in fact relates all the traditions attached to the churches he covers in assiduous detail, a labour of scholarly diligence; yet he is not minded to examine critically any of the legends he retails, nor the authenticity of relics, nor that of architectural fragments said to be from the time of Christ, and brought from the Holy Land to Rome. In this respect his work on the churches is of its time and forms a natural counterpart to *L'Antichità*: it presents a collection of Christian lore and legend that is *sui generis* and not considered susceptible to rational analysis, especially since its value chiefly resides in its symbolic significance. There is perhaps a hint of scepticism in the formula 'they say that', as in 'they say that the angel Gabriel entered through [the marble window of the Chapel of St Silvester at S. Giovanni] when announcing the Incarnation of the Son of God'. And elsewhere Palladio notes that 'it is said' that 'the two porphyry seats which are outside the Chapel of St Sylvester[66] . . . were ordered after that woman was made pope to confirm the testicles of new popes'.[67] Perhaps he entertained doubts as to the truth of this ancient Roman folktale about 'Pope Joan'[68] that even the philosopher Leibniz was still treating as established fact more than a century later? At any rate he continues: 'The latest deacon performs this office. But [Bartolomeo] Platina in *The Lives of the Popes* [1479] says otherwise.'[69] However, the text is also larded with genuinely 'historical', but not necessarily accurate, information. Into this category presumably falls his remark that Rome had previously had 3,000 churches, 400 of them dedicated to the Virgin Mary, of which the greater part is now in ruins. He concludes his address to the reader with a paean of local patriotism, combining pride in the Rome of antiquity with pride in its role as the focal point of Christendom.[70]

The Palladio of *Le Chiese di Roma* thus appears as a quintessential Renaissance figure, one who had taken his assumed 'humanist' name from a pagan goddess, Pallas Athene,[71] while maintaining a devout Christian allegiance as a builder of churches – and indeed as a guidebook writer. It was said that the harmonious impression of his architecture (not only his churches) was divinely inspired; but it was equally characteristic that his belief that architectonic proportion was derived from musical intervals could be traced to pagan antiquity, and in particular to Pythagoras.[72] Moreover, his studies of the (then still vaulted) baths of antiquity in Rome influenced his design for churches such as the Redentore in Venice; and it has been well said that he wanted 'to enlist mathematics in the service of worship'.[73] Hart and Hicks in the Introduction to their new translation stress that both *L'antichità* and *Le chiese* 'far from being unrelated as some commentators have maintained . . . can be seen to form part of a single Christian vision, emphasizing the compatibility of the ancient pagan city with the modern Christian one'.[74] The ambivalence at the heart of Renaissance piety, its scientific secularism married to religious inspiration, its twin celebration of Rome's pagan past and its Christian present in the notion of *caput mundi*, the first city of the world, are summed up in the personality of this remarkable man whose little guidebooks enjoyed such a long shelf life.

SENSUAL JOYS AND ANTIQUARIAN INTEREST

By the mid-sixteenth century, tensions between secularism and spirituality were evident at the top echelons of the Roman Church. Some popes were extremely worldly, both in their taste for profane art and their penchant for nepotism; others were decidedly hostile to ancient culture. The della Rovere pope, Julius II (1503–13), was one of the more worldly pontifexes and proudly claimed descent from Julius Caesar. When the celebrated sculpture of the *Laocoön* group was discovered close to the remains of Nero's Domus Aurea in 1506, he sent the architect Giuliano da Sangallo with the great Michelangelo to inspect it; and when they confirmed that it was indeed as superb as Pliny had claimed, della Rovere promptly acquired it and moved it to the Belvedere court in the Vatican. But some later popes, such as Hadrian VI (1522–3) and Pius V (1566–72), deplored this enthusiasm for pagan art. Both of them locked the doors of a now much expanded Belvedere collection, which included the so-called *Apollo Belvedere*, and even sold off some of the statues.[75] Even humanist popes could be alarmed by what they regarded as excesses in intellectual adventure: Paul II imprisoned members of Pomponio Leto's Roman Academy, suspecting its adherents of 'republican conspiracy, sexual immorality and pagan irreligion',[76] while the scholarly Urban VIII, Bernini's greatest patron, was also the pope who had Galileo condemned.

A completely different view of Rome's treasures and intellectual life was taken by the increasing number of Protestant visitors to Rome, who might often have antiquarian interests, but were likely to be hostile to the burgeoning Baroque splendour of Rome's churches in the seventeenth century. At the height of the Reformation, Calvinists had violently attacked pilgrimage as a superstitious practice, not surprisingly reserving especial venom for relics. On the other hand, the attitude to relics of local humanists (as we have seen with Palladio) was uncritical, if not enthusiastic, since they viewed them as physical links with the history of the early martyrs and as important topographical markers in the psycho-spiritual landscape of Rome. The popes had from earliest times struggled to bring order and discipline into the cult of relics by dedicating sumptuous buildings to those regarded as of real significance, notably at S. Giovanni in Laterano and St Peter's. But ambivalence remained: the Holy Year instruction books lauded the magnificence of the 'A List' shrines, while simultaneously warning pilgrims against being seduced by the sensual pleasures of spectacle.[77]

It is against this background that the significance of the first guidebooks principally or entirely dedicated to works of art should be viewed. A key text was Giulio Mancini's *Il Viaggio per Roma*, which he probably compiled in 1623–4, and which was never published, though it clearly became a source to be plundered by others. While Mancini makes some use of the best of the existing guides, and specifically Felini's much amplified version of the *Mirabilia* referred to below, and (for the medieval material) Ugonio's 'History of the Stations [of Rome]', in every important aspect he is his own man. He is the first to concern himself exclusively with monuments and works of art per se. This is all the more remarkable when one considers that his itinerary primarily deals with churches. His editor, Ludwig Schudt, writes of him: 'In the description of churches [of which he mentions a hundred, but only fifteen palaces], for the first time, all fabulous tales regarding indulgences, relics, foundations and founders, or generally of a hagiological nature, are completely ignored and only the monuments are discussed.'[78] Another pioneering aspect of his work is his willingness to include art from any period in his critique, including that from the then usually neglected medieval era. The guidebook part of his manuscript was in fact the prefatory matter to a treatise on writing about art, in which he does not spare the opposition: for example, he dismisses Vasari's life of Giotto as 'half a fiction' – though he does not say which half. Significant for the genre was Mancini's insistence, argued in one of his treatises on art and the appreciation thereof and echoing Cicero's *De Oratore*, that a non-artist had a perfect right to criticise or comment on painting. This debate, which has never quite disappeared, reminds us of a certain ambivalence in the role of guidebooks: do they, or should they, reflect the public taste of their time, or actually form it? They have always done both, of course, depending largely on the author, whether he was, so to speak, a Baedeker or a Ruskin – or a Mancini.

Mancini had studied medicine and astrology at Padua and from 1623 was the personal physician to the Florentine Pope Urban VIII, Maffeo Barberini. It has been noted that guidebooks proliferated under the latter's tenure of the papacy (1623–44), presumably meeting a need caused by the extensive building activity that he initiated in Rome. Besides the enlargement of palaces and monasteries and the founding of churches, whole new streets and piazzas were laid out. The city's centre of gravity began to shift away from areas like the fever-infested Tiber banks and towards the more salubrious Piazza di Spagna. Indeed, this iconic location (later to be embellished with the celebrated 'Spanish Steps'), received its name at this time, when the Spanish Ambassador took up residence here.[79] Perhaps it was the continuous embellishment of the city that attracted an increasing number of elegant sightseers and connoisseurs, not just the traditional hordes of, generally, impoverished pilgrims. At any rate, cicerones flourished, along with the written guidebooks, and one of Urban VIII's Swiss guards made a name for himself as the best informed guide on the ground. Adopting the professional name of Giovanni Alto (a humanist joke – he was in fact a German Swiss from Lucerne called Johann Hoch), he capitalised on his fame by publishing a guidebook in 1641 in Latin, Italian, German and French. Its overlong title leaves no doubt as to its secular, antiquarian emphasis, claiming to cover 'all the principal temples, theatres, amphitheatres, city walls, artificial basins for staging mock sea battles (*naumachie*), triumphal arches, obelisks etc., together with the most impressive gardens of the ancient and modern Romans'. Just as important as its emphasis on non-Christian edifices and monuments was the fact that this work was richly illustrated with 166 engravings by Alto's friend Jacobus Laurus (Giacomo Lauro),[80] a portent of the increasingly romanticised images that were to become so popular in the eighteenth century.[81]

If we compare Alto's with Mancini's work, a new fault line appears in the approach to writing descriptive guides: an antiquarian, like Alto, is a compiler of monuments, a copier of inscriptions and a collector of, or dealer in, antiquities; an aesthete, like Mancini, seeks a critical confrontation with the art of his day and earlier times, and with other commentators or critics. Mancini was fifty years ahead of his time in this approach to guidebook-writing, and his work was never put to the test by consumers. His manuscript is considered one of the earliest sources for reliable art history, documenting in particular the rise of Roman Baroque, as well as the careers of his important contemporaries such as

Caravaggio, and members of the Bolognese school such as Guido Reni and Domenichino. The first guidebook overtly to emulate Mancini did not appear until 1673, the *Studio di pittura* by Abbate Titi, although this still ignored the Middle Ages. Schudt says that Titi's work 'marks the end of the first great era of Roman guidebook literature'. Its author was objective and scholarly, dealing systematically with all artwork in the churches described.[82]

GROWING PAINS OF THE GUIDEBOOK

History does not progress in a straight line, especially not the history of guidebooks. Throughout the sixteenth and seventeenth centuries guidebooks to Rome continued to produce what were little more than anachronistic rehashes of existing material. It was a time when ignorance, religious superstition and fabulosity coexisted with amateur archaeology, humanist scholarship and genuine piety. Clearly, money could be made from the sale of guides to the city, however questionable their accuracy, just as money could be made by the cicerones, some of whom may have been no better than the 'old and untruthful custodian' encountered centuries later by Norman Douglas in Calabria. Even humanist scholars seem not to have been above temptation: Pomponio Leto, on his guided tours of the city, was accustomed to point out the tower from which, he claimed, Nero gleefully watched Rome burn as he twanged his lyre (this was actually a defensive tower erected in the thirteenth century under Pope Gregory IX, but what guide could resist such a story?).[83] Nevertheless, a gradual desire of guidebook compilers to distance themselves from the more unlikely tales does become apparent as the genre slowly evolved from an exercise in the gratification of the credulous into one designed to part them from treasured, but erroneous beliefs. A good story could still find a place in the text, of course; all the compiler had to do was to preface it with a health warning.

Three other guides established a market in the fifteenth and sixteenth centuries, and deserve to be briefly mentioned. The first is *La guida Romana* (1557) by an Englishman enigmatically recorded as 'Schakerlay Inglese', who has only recently been identified as the English musician Thomas Shakerley, a papal organist also in the employ of the Cardinal of Ferrara. In his address to his readers Shakerley says his book is aimed at foreign visitors who come to Rome full of enthusiasm for sightseeing, but end up only seeing one-third of what they wanted to see. His three-day tour through the city starts at the well-known Albergo del Orso by the Campo Marzio, where many foreigners stayed, and is weighted towards ancient monuments, as well as containing descriptions of the former gardens of imperial or republican villas that were dotted with Roman fragments and referred to as '*vigne*', though not all included vineyards.[84] A list of the popes closes the book. Like Palladio's *Antichità*, the *Guida Romana* was tacked onto many of the compendia of *Le cose maravigliose* (from 1557), and (from 1563) frequently added to.[85]

Although Shakerley's name and origin were dropped from all editions of the *Le cose maravigliose* subsequent to 1562, the text was still frequently and anonymously attached to that of the *Mirabilia*, and indeed updated from time to time (for example, to take account of Pius IV's changes to the layout of Rome in the early 1560s). The author, says Eunice D. Howe, 'appears alternately apologetic and ill-tempered about having assumed the awesome task of compressing the tour of ancient Rome into two and a half days',[86] and indeed the itineraries become progressively less taxing, until he remarks at the end 'I, for certain, can no longer walk'. The first modern instance, then, of the dreaded grumpy guide, a tribe that was known in antiquity and periodically re-emerges – for example, as the whey-faced propagandists of Communist times, like the unpleasant Serb woman who once took me round the Biliarda Palace in Cetinje, mixing Serb government propaganda with a listless recital of what she had mugged up, any questions being met with a stony glare. Shakerley, says Howe, is 'knowledgeable but not learned', which could almost be a definition of the rote-prepared city guides who mumble into microphones on tour buses; however, his descriptions of ruins suggest that his work was the fruit of autopsy, and despite many errors the usefulness of the guide and its amusing human touches ensured its popularity.

In the late 1580s the major changes initiated to the layout of Rome during the papacy of Sixtus V (1585–90) began to appear in the guides, among the most successful being those printed by the Franzini dynasty, which was of Venetian origin. The popularity of this work lay in its large number of woodcuts, making it the first systematically illustrated guide to the city. By now, the elevation of the church of Sta Maria del Popolo, which was lavishly restored by Sixtus IV, is placed in the Franzini guides immediately after the seven principal churches; also, fairly extensive accounts of the building of Il Gesù and other new foundations are given, while (hitherto a rarity) a number of artists and their works are mentioned by name. In 1610 the Franzini published a major revision by the Servite monk Pietro Martire Felini that includes some 300 churches, the ordering of which became canonical for subsequent publications up to the eighteenth century.[87] The book was a bumper package, including the *Guida Romana*, an updated *Antichità* and several new woodcuts. It more or less knocked out the competition from the little altered versions of the *Mirabilia Romae*, both for its topicality and its interest in artefacts. This latter quality was even more evident in a later work by Caravaggio's arch-enemy, Giovanni Baglione, which was limited to *Le nove chiese di Roma* (1639), but quite thorough in treating of art and architecture in the manner of a highly cultivated and well-informed connoisseur.

Finally, two much reprinted guides dominated the field in the second half of the seventeenth century, Pompilio Totti's *Ritratto di Roma moderna* ('Portrait of Modern Rome', 1638) and Fioravante Martinelli's oddly titled *Roma ricercata nel suo sito e nella scuola di tutti gli antiquarii* ('In Search of Rome on Site and in the School of All Antiquarians', 1644').[88] Totti was perhaps more of an editor than an author (Schudt speaks of his 'naïve plagiarism' of Ottavio Panciroli's 'Hidden Treasures of Rome' (published for the Jubilee of 1600)), but he added extensively to what he took and almost all important contemporary painters appear in the work. Valuable also are the copper engravings, a great improvement on the woodcuts in Felini's guides and a valuable source for art history. Totti's guide also marked a new departure in itineraries, whereby each day's tour covered two to three of the *Rioni*, starting with the Borgo and Trastevere on Day 1 and ending with Monti on Day 6. Enlarged with new material and an increased number of illustrations, Totti's work survived into the eighteenth century as the *Descrizione di Roma Moderna* and *Roma sacra antica e moderna*.

Martinelli's *Roma ricercata* was, if anything, even more successful than Totti's *Ritratto*. It was originally a tiny pocketbook of modest length that was ideal for tourists moving rapidly round the main sights. Its other tourist-friendly aspect was its division into ten daily walks based on a cheap hotel, l'Albergo dell'Orso. It was reprinted repeatedly under Martinelli's name and in a larger format (1658) until 1771,[89] and translated into English by Henry Cogan in 1654,[90] while the Italian edition astonishingly lived on under another title until well into the nineteenth century. Although most commentators find it pretty dry stuff, it is discursive on the architecture of Borromini, who was evidently a personal friend of Martinelli, and on the works of Bernini, who was at the height of his fame when the book was written. From 1658 the book appeared with good engravings, especially of Borromini's oeuvre, but what looks like a cheaper edition with inadequate woodcuts appeared from 1687. This popular edition, says Schudt, was 'evidently the bestselling and cheapest guide to Rome' in the early eighteenth century. By this time the (now) nine principal churches of Rome are no longer handled separately, as heretofore, but integrated into the tours in their appropriate places.

ROME'S PRINCIPAL CHURCHES

Since travellers' visits to Roman sights remain heavily oriented to churches even in the secular twenty-first century, it is worth briefly recapitulating the significance of the principal churches, whose gradual increase in numbers the guidebooks reflected. There were originally four, all basilicas, and each one associated with a Patriarch. S. Giovanni in Laterano was reserved for the Patriarch of the West, that is, the Pope; S. Pietro in Vaticano was associated with the Patriarch of Constantinople; S. Paolo fuori le Mura with the Patriarch of Alexandria; and Sta Maria Maggiore with the Patriarch of Antioch. The title of 'patriarch' dates to the sixth century and was applied to the bishops of the five governing sees of Christendom: Rome, Alexandria, Antioch, Constantinople and Jerusalem. A little later S. Lorenzo fuori le Mura was also appointed a 'patriarchal' basilica for the hitherto unrepresented See of Jerusalem, bringing the number up to five, a figure frequently mentioned in early guidebooks.

A pilgrimage custom grew up of visiting all five basilicas within one liturgical day, in other words, between the vespers of one evening and the next. Over the years, the number of 'principal' churches recorded by the guidebooks creeps up to seven, with the additions of S. Croce in Gerusalemme and S. Sebastiano fuori le Mura (at the catacombs on the Appian Way). The latter was originally known as the Basilica Apostolorum, a reference to the belief that the remains of Saints Peter and Paul had been moved here during the Valerianic persecution of 258. The canonical 'seven churches of Rome', given official status as a route for the absolution of pilgrims by Boniface VIII in the Jubilee Year of 1300, seems to have been arrived at largely because the two additional churches lay respectively on the routes between S. Giovanni and S. Paolo; moreover, they contained, between them, important relics of Our Lord's Passion, and (possibly) those of the two Apostles.

In the ninth century the Basilica Apostolorum was consecrated to S. Sebastiano, a Roman soldier martyred under Diocletian. The church's chapel of relics in the rebuilt seventeenth-century church (1608) was said to hold one of the arrows that pierced the saint, and which are so graphically featured in this most beloved theme of Renaissance and Mannerist painters. The Via delle Sette Chiese, which is still so-called, runs between S. Paolo and S. Sebastiano and takes its name from a devotional route established by S. Filippo Neri in 1575, the year of the Jubilee of the Counter-Reformation. The zealous Counter-Reformatory Pope, Pius V (1566–72) said of the seven basilicas that they were 'celebrated for their antiquity, their religious services, the relics of the martyrs venerated therein, the indulgences gained, and finally, for the mystical significance of the number seven'.[91] The liturgical and mystical import of the number seven was, of course, a commonplace: Gregory Martin in his *Roma Sancta* (1581) defends the belief in its inspirational power against the charge of superstition levelled by Protestants, citing biblical and liturgical authority: the washing of Naaman [the leprose Syrian commander-in-chief] seven times in the River Jordan, the resting of Almighty God on the seventh day of the Creation, the seven virgins with their seven lamps, the seven '*eies*' [*sic*] of the prophets, the Seven Churches and seven candlesticks, the seven Angels in the Apocalypse, the Seven Deacons and the Seven Gifts of the Holy Ghost.[92]

While the seven churches remained canonical,[93] some guidebooks began adopting a palette of nine, as in Giovanni Cavalier Baglione's *Le Nove Chiese di Roma* (1639), which added the Abbazia delle Tre Fontane (on the Via Laurentina) and S. Agnese fuori le Mura to the list, both of them sanctuaries revered by pilgrims in early times. The name 'three fountains' refers to a legend according to which, when St Paul was martyred, streams flowed from the three spots where his severed head bounced before coming to rest. S. Paolo fuori le Mura nearby is built on the spot where his remains are supposedly buried. These additions were not constant however, and more recent glories of papal or Jesuit patronage, such as the Gesù or S. Maria del Popolo, soon replaced them.

GUIDEBOOK COMPETITION

The broader significance of Totti's and Martinelli's guides is the light they throw on the 'internal struggles for the right to represent Rome'. Written by 'professional intellectuals', they were in market competition with Counter-

Reformatory guides that 'sought to regularise pilgrimage practices'.[94] Bringing a semblance of order to the Rome visitor's tour, or in other words, offering a systematic and normative approach to the sights, is what these guides are moving towards. This was necessary, says Martinelli in his prefatory remarks, because foreigners without a guide 'often wander dazedly through the city, departing from it confused due to the magnificence of chaos'. Martinelli's and Totti's guides seek to order that chaos, which is both a physical one on the ground and an intellectual one in the head. On the ground, the *Portrait* organises a tour in terms of the current administration of the city (the *Rioni*), while *In Search of Rome* offers a logical topography of the ancient and artistic sites. Intellectually, Rome is presented as the 'personification of both Roman and Catholic empires'.[95] This formula offered a resolution of the ancient tension between, and undecidedness towards, the relationship between pagan and Christian, between ancient and modern, and between secular and spiritual claims on Rome's *lieux de mémoire*, an escape from 'the ceaseless oscillation of irreconcilable perspectives'.[96] Modern also is the element of 'social research' in Martinelli, whereby he identifies and describes institutions, and especially areas of commerce, such as the Campo de' Fiori: 'Here reside shoemakers, armourers, retailers of old clothes, the excisemen of custom on horses and straw. Here grains, corn, horses and asses are brought to be sold, and justice is carried out on those condemned to death for reasons of religion.'[97]

This last laconic observation may be compared with *The Portrait of Rome*'s treatment of the Jewish ghetto (which is dismissed in a single sentence by Martinelli). Totti describes its origin under Paul IV, what he sees as the Jews' abuse of their privileges and Pope Paul's ordinances against them. He ends by observing that the segregation law is now honoured in the breach thereof and 'in part the rigour against [the Jews] has disappeared'.[98] While full of anxiety about money-lending and so forth, Totti's account lacks the indiscriminate calumny of a medieval account and the rabid theologically inspired anti-semitism of the Counter-Reformation. It offers a slightly more balanced perspective on the subject (even rather unctuously pointing out that the pope treated the Jews far more leniently than the Kings of France and Spain). The more differentiated picture speaks to the broadly tolerant class of intellectual from which Totti came, and to his anticipated audience of a similar cut. If the Enlightenment spirit is not yet present in his book, nor in that of Martinelli, the love of learning certainly is. Both wanted to bring order into chaos and made a good stab at it, which later guides could build on. If Martinelli is rather a dry old stick, he could not have anticipated that one day an audience of guidebook readers influenced by the *Zeitgeist* of Romanticism would actually demand the very 'magnificence of chaos' against which he had laboured.

CHAPTER 7

The Long Tutorial:
Bear-Leaders, Antiquarians and
Connoisseurs Write up the Grand Tour

From school to Cam or Isis, and thence home:
And thence with all convenient speed to Rome.
With reverend tutor clad in habit lay,
To tease for cash and quarrel with all day:
With memorandum-book for every town,
And every post, and where the chaise broke down.
(William Cowper, The Progress of Error, *1782)*

It is said that the historian should have neither fatherland nor religion; it is
equally justified to demand the same of a travel writer.
(Johann Jacob Volkmann, Historisch-kritische Nachrichten von Italien, *1770–1)*

CUNNING AND EXILE: THE METAPHOR OF ULYSSES

In his *Itinerary* (1617), Fynes Moryson describes his homecoming in 1595, after
four years in foreign parts:

When I entered my sister's house in poor habit a servant answered that my
sister was at home, but when he did see me go up the stairs too boldly (as he
thought) without a guide, he not knowing me did furiously and with
threatening words call me back and surely would have been rude with me

had I not gone faster than he could follow me, and he had taken hold of my old cloak, which I willingly flung off to be rid of him. Then by my sister's embraces he perceived who I was and stole back as if he had trodden upon a snake.[1]

The pathos of this moment, the return of the master whom no one recognises, recalls the parallel scenes towards the end of the *Odyssey*, although the situation has been inverted: in the *Odyssey* it is Odysseus' old nurse, Eurycleia, who first recognises the wanderer. The echo of the *Odyssey* is probably nonetheless intentional, since the voyaging of Odysseus/Ulysses was a metaphor that symbolised for Renaissance theoreticians of travel the journey of intellectual discovery that they advocated and systematised. In the mid-sixteenth century, however, the emphasis began to shift from the purely scholarly traveller to the gentleman or young nobleman seeking to refine his manners and improve the governance of his country, for which purpose the Italian city-states were regarded by many as idealised models of *ratio gubernatoris*. The celebrated opening lines of the *Odyssey*, quoted in *The Scholemaster* (1570) by the much travelled Elizabethan scholar Roger Ascham, seemed to suggest this change of emphasis and soon became a topos of travel commentary: 'Tell me Muse, of that resourceful man who was driven to wander far and wide after he had sacked the holy citadel of Troy. He saw the cities of many people and he learnt their ways.'[2]

Sir John Stradling's 1592 adaptation of Iustus Lipsius indeed makes the Ulysses metaphor central to his argument that the lordlings to whom his treatise was addressed should seek, like the antique hero, to acquire wisdom ('pollicie'), knowledge ('learning') and manners ('behaviour'). We have moved from Dante's medieval spiritual outlook, an ambivalence about the hubris of Ulysses who ventures towards the setting sun and is punished with shipwreck, to Ulysses as role-model for the enquiring mind. Moreover, at least in the opinion of the seventeenth-century diarist John Evelyn, that mind should be concentrated on much more than just ticking off the sights: 'It is written of Ulysses, that hee saw many cities indeed, but withall his remarks of mens Manners and Customs, was ever preferred to his counting Steeples, and making Tours: It is this Ethicall and Morall part of Travel, which embellisheth a Gentleman.'[3] The Classicist tutors, finding themselves unenviably *in loco parentis* to the young gentlemen that Evelyn had in mind as they navigated what became known as 'the Grand Tour', would have had cause for wry reflection on the 'Ethicall and Morall part of Travel'. They might have recalled that Ulysses was unable to honour his promise to bring his comrades home, for 'in their folly they devoured the oxen of Hyperion the Sun-god and he saw to it that they would never return'.

These bear-leaders, as the tutor/guardians were rather unflatteringly called, had not only to preserve their own integrity in sometimes precarious circumstances, but see to it that their charges imbibed the best from their new surroundings and did not succumb to the worst (which usually meant vice and false religion). William Cecil, Elizabeth I's great minister, Lord Burghley, spoke for many who feared the dangerous consequences of what was supposed to be educational travel, especially in Italy. His view may have been unduly jaundiced, because of the effect that Italy had apparently had on his son-in-law, Lord Oxford, who was reported to have become a drunkard, a homosexual and an atheist under Italy's sunny skies. 'Suffer not [your] sons to pass the Alps,' he wrote, 'for they shall learn nothing there but pride, blasphemy and atheism. And if by travel they get a few broken languages, that shall profit them nothing than to have one meat served in diverse dishes.'[4] Yet, although there were awful examples enough of young men going to pieces like Lord Oxford, or worse still, being seduced into the Catholic faith by the wiles of the Jesuits, the stream of English travellers continued through the most dangerous times and then swelled to a flood in the golden age of the Grand Tour.

NEW TRAVELLERS AND AMBIVALENT ATTITUDES

While the scholar and pilgrim still travelled their particular routes with their particular aims in this period, most of the literature catering for seventeenth-century travellers no longer reflects the schematic aridity of the Renaissance *ars apodemica* or the pilgrims' obsession with indulgences, but rather the preoccupations of young noblemen being groomed for a career in politics or diplomacy. In the eighteenth century, the Grand Tour may still have performed some of these functions for its participants, but there is an obvious shift towards the interests of antiquaries and connoisseurs on the one hand, and the acquisition of a background of broad cultural knowledge on the other. This might mean collecting aesthetic experience as much as it meant collecting objects. Eventually these motivations were to become part of a more general concept of leisure travel, which became available to a prosperous middle class in the nineteenth century.[5] The character of the guidebooks was to change yet again to reflect this social and economic shift, and, even before the last book aimed at the Grand Tour had appeared, Mariana Starke had produced the prototype of a 'bourgeois' guidebook, from the concept of which today's guidebooks are directly descended.

By far the greatest number of Grand Tourists came from Britain and Germany. Their ethnic backgrounds had implications for their travel experiences that were both religious (especially for the British, since the travellers were both recusants and Protestants) and national (especially for the Germans, whose attitudes tended to hover between obeisance to the cultural values of ancient Rome and something approaching contempt for the corruption of contemporary Italian society). Konrad Celtis is a prominent example of German ambivalence about Italy that lasted into a later age, almost a love–hatred in fact. He was extremely sensitive to the charge of barbarism that had dogged his fellow Teutons ever since they had first traversed the Alps to lay waste a decaying Roman Empire, and was still being repeated by Petrarch in the fourteenth century. On the other hand, Celtis's celebrated *Ingelstadt Oration* of 1492 lambasted the Germans themselves for their supposed backwardness: clearly he is still smarting from his own experience of Italy where he was patronised by those who thought humanists from north of the Alps were (in Celtis's words): 'mere mannikins, born in the midst of barbarism and drunkenness'. When he actually reached Rome, however, he was disillusioned by the huge discrepancy between 'the ancient traditions symbolised in the ruins of the imperial city' and 'the racketeering modern reality'.[6]

Ambivalence about both France and Italy took a slightly different form for Englishmen. The young gentleman's sojourn in France was principally designed to knock the edges off him, to teach him social graces and proficiency in such noble pursuits as fencing, riding and dancing. Successful acquisition of these skills did not protect him from being mocked at home, however, if he returned with Frenchified airs and linguistic affectations. Nor were the great minds of the day unanimous about the benefits of all this training: the philosopher John Locke was particularly scathing about fencing, which he said had little relevance to civil life and still less to actual warfare. Moreover, he (and others) shrewdly pointed out that, if a man was so young as to need a guardian, he was unlikely to be admitted to the very company he was supposed to keep in order to learn how to behave, and in the end would spend the time quarrelling with his guardian or tutor. In a large number of cases, this is indeed what happened.

The guardian, typically the family chaplain, was in an invidious position, simultaneously a servant and a spiritual mentor acting *in loco parentis*. In the seventeenth and eighteenth centuries, such ill-matched couples of the leader and the led became an object of ridicule in Europe and at home. Goldoni had fun at their expense in his comedies, and so did Cowper in *The Progress of Error* (1782):

> Surpris'd at all they meet, the gosling pair,
> With awkward gait, stretched neck, and silly stare,
> Discover huge cathedrals, built with stone,
> And steeples tow'ring high, much like our own;
> But show peculiar light by many a grin
> At popish practices observ'd within.

On his return, the young lord is hardly an advertisement for the Grand Tour:

> Returning he proclaims, by many a grace,
> By shrugs, and strange contortions of his face,
> How much a dunce that has been set to roam
> Excels a dunce that has been kept at home.

Congreve said that young gentlemen travelling with their crushed clergymen tutors returned home as much refined as 'a Dutch skipper from a whale-fishing'.[7] This hardly seems an exaggeration if the accounts of licentious student life in Padua and Venice are to be believed. Moralists such as Turler complained that young men often brought home from Italy only three things, 'a naughty conscience, an empty purse and a weak stomache'.[8] An Italian saying that first came into vogue in Elizabethan times expresses the alarm that many felt, and for which there was distressingly ample evidence: 'An Italianate Englishman is the devil incarnate' ('*L'Inglese italianato, è un diavolo incarnato*'). It is again Roger Ascham who quotes this in *The Scholemaster*, before reverting vividly to the Ulysses metaphor: the task of the tutor, he stresses, was to keep his charge 'safe and sound, in the fear of God, in Christ's true religion', just as Ulysses was prevented from running 'headlong into many jeopardies . . . if *Pallas* had not always governed him: if he had not used to stop his ears with wax: to bind himself to the mast of his ship: to feed daily, upon that sweet herb *Moly* with the black root and white flower, given unto him by Mercury, to avoid all the inchantments of *Circes*'.[9] Often one gets the impression that a young English traveller to seventeenth-century Italy was simultaneously expected to open his mind and keep it closed, to imbibe and resist in equal measure.

Notwithstanding their precarious position, a number of 'bear-leaders' took their duties seriously enough to codify their knowledge in guidebooks intended for others embarking on the Grand Tour, a phrase that gained currency after being made the leitmotif of the first such work by Richard Lassels (1670). We shall come to his pioneering and trend-setting guidebook for Grand Tourists shortly, but here it may be observed that his 'Preface to the Reader' gives vivid insights into what many bear-leaders had to contend with, as they tried to instil learning and manners into their lordlings. Sometimes they were personally at risk from the Inquisition if they were too free with 'heretical' opinions, and the advice to them and their charges was to keep their eyes open and their mouths shut. In the worst case of persecution, the unfortunate John Mole, tutor to Lord Roos, was arrested in 1608 in Florence for criticising Catholicism, and spent the rest of his life of over thirty years in a Roman prison, where he died. What made this case particularly unsavoury was that young Lord Roos, who had become a Catholic, connived at the arrest of his Protestant tutor.[10] But Lassels is also free with horror stories concerning the behaviour of the guardians themselves, who abused their positions for financial gain, or in other ways betrayed the trust placed in them and neglected their charges. Clearly he was not one of these (he would scarcely have bothered with his guidebook if he had been), and nor was Franciscus Schottus, who wrote the first guidebook directly aimed at the young northern European noble on the Grand Tour, and whose work had an astonishingly enduring shelf life long after it was so out of date as to be almost useless.

GUIDEBOOK NOMENCLATURE

By the end of the eighteenth century the guidebook genre, which had not yet settled under that all-embracing nomenclature, was sailing under a variety of descriptions, each of which to a greater or lesser extent defined its individual focus. At the most basic level were the road-books, which did not aspire to do much more than map the negotiable routes and were usually based on the post, as they had been from Roman times onwards. One of many examples was Richard Rowlands's *The Post for Divers Parts of the World* (1576), something between a road-book and an itinerary, which seems to have been plagiarised from Cherubino di Stella's *Poste per diverse parti del mondo* (Lyons, 1572). It included a 'description of the antiquitie of divers famous cities' and claimed to be 'very necessary and profitable for Gentlemen, merchants, factors, or any other persons disposed to travail'. Perhaps because of the centralising efforts of the French monarchy, France had produced more of this type of literature than existed elsewhere. As early as 1552, Charles Estienne's monumental *Le Guide des Chemins de France*, based on the pilgrimage routes to Santiago de Compostela, offered assistance for all those 'coming and going in all the regions of the French kingdom'. More than a century later something less ambitious appeared in Britain based on the earliest official (royally sanctioned) topography-cum-itinerary,[11] Ogilby's *Britannia*[12] of 1675, and called *The Infallible Guide to Travellers* (1682). It consisted of four annotated itineraries for 'Direct Independants', starting from London and heading for Aberystwyth, Arundel, Berwick and Bristol. Bristol is summed up as 'large and populous and well built, esteemed the second [city] of the Kingdom for Trade and Traffiques . . . . [containing] 18 Parish churches, besides the Cathedral . . . an Episcopal See . . . wall'd about, Govern'd by a Mayor . . . sends Burgesses to Parliament, and gives Title to the Right Honorable George Digby, Earl of Bristol'.

Early road-books usually had a secular function, for example, the printing of the dates of commercial fairs and the routes, together with other tips useful for itinerant traders. The French tradition of such useful publications reasserted itself with *L'État des Postes* published officially under Napoleon and translated into English as 'The Post Roads of Europe'.

'Itineraries' also have a very ancient history, again stretching back to Roman times at least – witness the *Tabula Peutingeriana* (mentioned in Chapter 1), and including the pilgrim's *Itinerarium Burdigalense* (described in Chapter 2) and the medieval *Bruges Itinerary*, probably compiled for merchants. Itineraries resemble road-books, but offer more information, and some, like Paul Hentzner's *Itinerarium* (1612) are virtually guidebooks. (Hentzner was bear-leader to a Silesian nobleman.) Indeed, the first recognisable guidebook to France is the *Itinerarium Galliae*, a modest volume designed for Germans residing in France and compiled by Jodocus Sincerus (Justus Zinzerling), which was translated into French in 1639.[13] A product of the Renaissance was a compilation of information derived from different itineraries, the *Variorum in Europa itinerum deliciae* (1594). Compiled by Nathan Chytraeus, a humanist scholar from Rostock, this was a European travel lexicon following the elements of *ars apodemica* under six headings. Louis Dutens's much-used *Itinéraire* (1775), discussed below, clothed the skeleton of practical information on routes, mileages, journey times and the price of post-horses with more expansive advice (on inns, money and measures), as well as sociological and touristic observations on populations or 'curiosities'. Dutens's book only differs from the guidebook of today in respect of the allocation of space that he chose for each of these topics. Another pioneering aspect of his publication was a dual language edition with French and Italian on facing pages ('*La vera guida per chi viaggia in Italia*'), also published in 1775. In Britain, *Paterson's British Itinerary*, later known as 'Paterson's Road Book', established itself from 1785 and reached eighteeen editions by 1826. John Cary (1755–1835) was appointed surveyor of roads to the General Post Office in 1794, and produced a *New Itinerary* in 1798, which included authoritative measurements made with a perambulator.[14] The *ne plus ultra* of itineraries were the twelve published between 1637 and 1674 by the Styrian[15] Martin Zeiller, which included regions relatively unvisited at that time, such as Spain and Portugal – and even Poland and Lithuania. His quasi-guidebook of 1651, *Fidus Achates; oder Getreuer Reisgefert* (the classical allusion is to Virgil's Aeneas) has sixty pages of advice for travellers and indications of European routes, one of the many books over the years to be claimed as 'the first Baedeker'.

By the time we get to Reichard's *Itinerary of France and Belgium* (1822), the itinerary is a fully fledged guidebook, though one that concentrates on practical information. The style of his entries foreshadows Michelin. For instance: 'Pont Saint Maxemce on the Oise: This town trades in corn and flour; it has manufactures for combs and for dressing buck-skins and chamois leathers. Population 3,000.' He goes into detail as to how letters of credit may be used by travellers, warns against taking too much baggage and gives an impressive account of the security and honesty of the highly regulated posts of the Continent; for example, there was a regulation that travellers hiring a saddle-horse *must* by law be accompanied by a postilion to act as a guide. Where the text is not concerned with the practicalities of travel, it is largely confined to potted histories and scenic wonders.

We have seen that the *Mirabilia* of Rome (or their Italian successors, *Le cose marivigliose . . .*) became synonymous with the concept of a 'guidebook' for that city, while the *Indulgentiae* were likewise identified with a specific type of the same for pilgrims. Between 1475 and 1600, 127 guides had been published for Rome, and in the next four quarter centuries respectively 66, 103, 95 and 117 appeared.[16] Giles Barber asserts further that 'most major Italian towns had their guide by 1660, other capital cities such as Amsterdam, Paris and London being covered in the next 40 years', while guides to whole countries begin in earnest with Schott's *Itinerarium Italiae*, discussed below.[17] Many books bearing the title 'A Tour through . . .' were either guidebooks (like John Chetwode Eustace's book, the last great guide for the Grand Tour) or usable as such; and other broad titles ('Descriptio', 'Diarium', 'Picture' and so on),[18] like John Moore's *A View of Society and Manners in Italy* (1781), were guides in all but name. They provided the broader socio-political context, as Dr Charles Burney's account of musical life in Europe published in 1771 and 1773, and the agronomist Arthur Young's influential *Travels in France* (1792). Moore's kind of commentary had its roots in Renaissance methodologies of travel in so far as it highlighted what could profitably be learned from (or also avoided) in foreign countries. An important work that straddles Renaissance didacticism and that of the Enlightenment is Sir

Robert Dallington's *The View of France* (1604), which was accompanied by a twelve-page supplement containing 'A method of travel'. Besides being prescriptive about the traveller's aims, this also contained practical information about dress and money. A final efflorescence of didacticism in relation to travel may be seen in Richard Lassels's lengthy and sometimes irreverent Preface to his guidebook, discussed below.

In regard to Italy, the same Dallington prefigures John Moore's informative *View of Society* with an outspoken work entitled *A Survey of the Great Duke's State of Tuscany in the yeare of our Lord 1596* (1605). This clear-eyed report documented the decline of humanistic scholarship in Florence, the rampant poverty (especially among the Tuscan peasants), and the increasing despotism of the once civic-minded Medici. He concluded his observations with a savage pun: '*Qui sub Medicis vivit, misere vivit*' ('he who lives under the Medici (or is "under" the doctors), lives miserably'). Publication caused a scandal and Grand-Duke Ferdinand I demanded retribution from Britain's King James I, who was in debt to the Medici bank. James had three copies ritually burned in St Paul's Churchyard in the presence of the Tuscan Resident, but a second edition immediately appeared. Dallington, who acted as tutor and guide to the Earl of Rutland on his Tuscan tour, wrote admiringly of the beauties of Florentine architecture and the city's bridges, and is interested in the curiosities of the Uffizi; but even here he is radical, being one of the first to point out the human cost, particularly in terms of oppressive taxation, that often lay behind great architectural achievements, such as the repairs to the Baptistery at Pisa after a fire in 1595.[19] This is a matter – the circumstances in which great projects that are on every itinerary were financed at the time they were built, and the human cost often involved erecting them – upon which even modern guidebooks, awash with aesthetic superlatives, often choose to remain discreetly silent.

The French favoured the word *Voyage* for a guidebook, as in Cochin's *Voyage d'Italie* (1758), La Lande's popular, multi-volume, guide to Italy (1769), or *Le Voyage de France* of 1639. This was the word also adopted by Lassels for his guide *The Voyage of Italy*, and likewise by Misson, with his *Nouveau voyage d'Italie*, both discussed below. There was also the Germans' *Italienische Reise*, but their works tended to be more discursive; the most celebrated was of course Goethe's *Italian Journey*, undertaken between 1786 and 1788, but not published until thirty years later (1816–17). Finally, many guidebooks from the seventeenth century onwards appeared as *Deliciae* ('The Delights of . . .', or perhaps better, the 'Pleasures of . . .', as in Rose Macaulay's charming twentieth-century travelogue *The Pleasure of Ruins*). Examples of such cherry-picking works are Matthias Quadt's *Deliciae Galliae* (1603) or *Les Délices d'Italie* (1706). The last named work did not impress La Lande, who described it as merely a 'rhapsody on everything that can be found in dictionaries', with city plans that were 'useless'. The first *Deliciae*, a collection of itineraries for Germany, France and Italy, was compiled by Matthias Quadt and Cyprian Eichoff between 1602 and 1606. Thereafter the *Deliciae* developed into gazetteers, a now discarded form of packaging for travel information (except for the post-war Baedekers) that enjoyed a certain vogue when motoring made frequent and selective travel a possibility.

Finally, one or two formulations for guidebooks are decidedly idiosyncratic, such as the delightfully named *Ulysse Belgico-Gallicus* (Leyden, 1631, 1655) written by one Abraham Göllnitz of Danzig, or the *Mercurius Italicus* (1625) of J.H. von Pflaumern. Many of the authors of such works 'borrowed widely, supplemented from other sources, and also made things up'. The 'minefields of information' they produced were 'counterfeited, copied or republished without the permission of the author [and] translated into many foreign languages'.[20] The temptations of embellishment were always present for guidebook compilers, as they were for travellers who brought back tall tales to impress a gullible public at home. Nowadays a guidebook sees it as its task to dispel myths, however venerable, rather than propagate them, and lays claim to dispassionate accuracy. This attitude began with the Enlightenment and is certainly harder work for the writer. As Etienne Rey elegantly puts it, an author is 'master of the lie and the slave of the truth . . .'.[21]

THE *ITINERARII ITALIAE* OF FRANCISCUS SCHOTTUS

Some seven decades before Lassels's first recognisably modern tour guide to Italy, the humanist François Schott of Antwerp (1548–1622)[22] published his itinerary[23] of the country's sights. The genesis of this first guidebook evidently written for the edification of Grand Tourists (not yet called that) was as remarkable as its publishing history, which began with a Latin printing in 1600 and continued through numerous translations to the last edition of 1761. Not least curious was the fact that its core material had not been supplied by Schott at all, but was based on selective plagiarism from the necessarily short biography of Prince Friedrich Karl von Cleve by his tutor and travelling companion, a scholar named Stephan Wynandt Pighius.[24] It was 'necessarily short' because the young traveller unfortunately died of smallpox in Rome in 1575 after having seen only a relatively small part of Italy. This meant that Tuscany, Florence, Siena, Livorno, Lucca, Pisa and the whole of Liguria and Piedmont were lacking from Pighius' account of the tour, death having intervened before they could be visited. Schott's work was initially lop-sided in the same way. Of course plagiarism was not viewed in the seventeenth century as it is now, and indeed hardly existed as a literary sin, especially in this kind of literature. All the same, there is a certain irony attached to a work in which the plagiarism partly consists in omissions. A further irony is that Schott's work itself suffered the indignity of a botched up piracy in the form of a corrupt English translation by Edmund Warcupp (1660), in some versions of which the name of the original 'author' (or plagiarist) is not even mentioned. The translation is so bad, observes E.S. De Beer, that 'it is frequently unintelligible without recourse to the original' (an Italian printing of 1654).[25] For good measure, Warcupp stuffed in some poems by Waller and chunks lifted from the *Mercurio Italico* by John Raymond.

Schott was himself quite eclectic in helping himself to existing texts for his compilation. From Pighius, he took details of the journey from Venice to Milan, thence to Bologna and Ferrara to Ravenna on the Via Emilia, and on to Ancona and Rome on the Via Flaminia. The same source supplied the descriptions of Naples, Vesuvius and the Phlegraean Fields, so that Books 1 and 3 of his *Itinerary* are little more than regurgitations of Pighius. For his account of Rome he borrowed from a 1592 work by Lorenz Schrader called *Monumentorum Italiae*,[26] on which he relies for the seven principal churches, together with details on the Tiber floods and Roman wines. Then he pillaged a popular German guidebook by J.J. Boissard,[27] offering a four-day tour of Roman sights, and said to be the only such work easily available to Germans at the time of its publication in Frankfurt in 1603. Finally, he copied out material on the cemeteries of Rome and the Vatican Library from the writings (1570) of Onofrius Panvinius. The only actual research by autopsy appears to have been supplied by his Jesuit brother, Andreas Schott, who, because of his calling was much in Italy, while for the maps Schott relied on his compatriot Abraham Ortelius, who had pioneered the modern world atlas with his *Theatrum Orbis Terrarum* (1570).[28] The lack of originality is worth stressing because it highlights the fact that a thoroughly successful guidebook, the first in the Grand Tour genre, owed its success neither to autopsy nor comprehensiveness, but to adroit use of some of the best materials available at the time; and also to the fact that it filled one of those niches of which publishers dream but which so seldom manifest themselves until the right book has shown it existed.

Like so many successful authors, Schott did not set out to write a bestseller. In fact his guidebook miscellany of history, geography, topography, and extracts from ancient and modern authors was put together for his nephew, who intended to visit Italy in the Jubilee Year of 1600. Thus, by a happy coincidence, the book became available at a prime selling time, when pilgrims and scholars alike were streaming to Rome. Subsequently it tended to be reprinted, revised or not, in Jubilee Years, no doubt because it conveniently combined the requisite coverage of churches with secular and pagan monuments. Although the *Itinerary* is a product of the *Kultur des Wortes* ('the culture of the word') rather than the *Kultur der Sinne* ('the culture of the senses'), its learned evocation of antiquity and its background information on monuments and buildings proved congenial to its users. And almost immediately some of its lacunae were remedied in a revised edition (Vicenza, 1601) by the Dominican monk Fra Girolamo da Capugnano, who indeed added an element for 'the senses' by expanding the comments on artworks, as well as supplying a good deal of material that was missing in Pighius. It was really this edition (which also drew on Fra Alberti's encyclopedic *Description of Italy*)[29] that launched Schott's work as a serviceable guide, despite its almost total lack of 'practical information' on transport, inns and the like. From 1601 most editions partially compensated for that deficiency by attaching a road-book and map for Italy, together with some sketchy town plans and a few plates. In 1610 the book first appeared in Italian, with many subsequent editions, and a French version appeared in Paris in 1627. No serious revision to the core text was undertaken, however, until 1737, when the guide was finally freed from the shackles of Pighius' original scheme.

Despite its obvious deficiencies, Schott's *Itinerary* seems to have been the most popular guidebook of its day, at least for those who were not travelling solely as pilgrims. The latter may still have preferred the *Mirabilia Romae*, the last edition of which (in Spanish) appeared as late as 1769, eight years after the final edition of Schott. The *Itinerary* introduced more systematisation into the material, though this was partly in the form of a table derived from *ars apodemica*, which instructed the reader how to set about his exploration of the country. From this it is clear that history, geography, topography, economy and governance prevail over coverage of art objects and monuments (the principal preoccupations of a modern guidebook), which indeed fills only one section out of six in the table's list of 'what is to be observed during the journey'. Architecture is given more prominence however, because Schott is interested in the overall impression of a city, with particular emphasis on its defences. The focus is on technical achievement, rather than aesthetic effects: Domenico Fontana's feat in erecting the Egyptian obelisks in Rome, Brunelleschi's dome for the Duomo in Florence and above all Palladio's sophisticated Redentore church in Venice receive the highest praise in this respect.

These encomia are combined with a relatively naive approach to works of art and the interior decoration of churches. Those considered the most famous artworks made since the Middle Ages, including Leonardo's *Last Supper*, Michelangelo's *Pietà* in St Peter's and Giotto's frescoes in Padua, are formally but uninformatively applauded, as are works by Raffael, Correggio and Titian. The Mannerists, some of them Schott's near-contemporaries, receive respectful recognition, for example, Giulio Romano's astonishing decoration of the Palazzo del Te and works by lesser masters such as Lomazzo, Campi and Zuccari. On the other hand, it is notable that the name of Sansovino occurs nowhere and Michelangelo's Sistine ceiling is all but ignored.[30] Since the existence of the ceiling and Michelangelo's work on it was certainly well known, the absence of any reference to it is odd; but it could be because it was difficult to see the ceiling properly if the time of day was not favourable for illumination by natural light, so many visitors had no memorable experience of it. Moreover, the Sistine was the pope's private chapel, which may have been of limited access. Some later guidebooks (Lassels's, for example) are also curiously uncommunicative on the subject of Michelangelo's great work, which is now the highlight of any visit to the Vatican and attracts commensurate space in any guide.

Schott's achievement, however uneven and sometimes misleading (as in some confident references to non-existent pictures), is undeniable, and inspired imitators such as J.H. von Pflaumern (*Mercurius Italicus*, 1625) and Martin Zeiller (*Itinerarium Italiae*, 1640), Zeiller being the author of the 'first German Baedek' (*Itinerarium Germaniae* (1632)). But it held its own as a useful primer for the Grand Tour, whereby lordlings in their gap years could compare forms of governance among the Italian city-states, immerse themselves in the roots of Western culture and the processes of history, as well gaining exposure to the greatest works of art and architecture made from antiquity up to their own time. If it was short on the practicalities and the indulgence of pleasures that we now expect from a guidebook, it was certainly the best available companion for a study tour. At least its later editions do not merit the contemptuous retrospective comment of J.J. Volkmann, who wrote his own book on Italy in the eighteenth century and who described Schott's work as a 'an absolutely miserable concoction'[31] only good for artisans to find their way from city to city. In fact it provided the bridge in guidebook-writing between the outlook of sixteenth-century humanism and that of the Enlightenment that Volkmann represented, and its success spoke for itself. Nevertheless, Volkmann's complaints about Schott's undigested and indigestible slabs of Church history, his fondness for miracles, his inventory of artworks with no element of selection or taste, all serve to show how the expectations of readers were to change in the course of a century.

RICHARD LASSELS (C. 1603–68)

The characterisation of Italy by Protestant moralists as a nest of false religion and stew of vice mostly failed to dampen the English passion for the country, which was apparent as early as William Thomas's *History of Italy* of 1549. Thomas, remarks a recent editor of his work, 'opened the way [that is, for the English] . . . to the Italian nation, which seemed to flourish in civility most of all other at this day'.[32] The ground-breaking book was itself partly a guidebook with extensive descriptions of Rome, and shorter ones of Venice, Naples, Florence, Genoa, Milan, Mantua, Ferrara, Piacenza, Parma and Urbino. Its value for posterity lies in it being the first work to describe what contemporary Italy *was like* as a society, rather than simply treating it as an historical tableau with which the everyday reality seemed out of kilter. Thomas is a good Protestant (indeed he published an imaginary dialogue between himself and some Italian gentlemen, in which he triumphantly defended Henry VIII against their indictments); yet he does not let his religious convictions interfere with his judgement in describing Italy's successes in governance (for example, of Venice), or in agriculture and trade. The effect on the reader is rather like a rollercoaster, with exclamations of admiration following hard upon violent denunciations – for instance of the licentiousness of the Roman prelates, who, he says, maintained some 40,000 harlots for their use in the city.[33]

The attitude of basic, yet not uncritical, sympathy and admiration for Italy, may have waxed and waned according to political and religious circumstances; but it is nevertheless a staple of guidebooks for the 'Grand Tour' – a phrase that had first appeared in the early seventeenth century with reference to a tour of the French provinces,[34] but had become associated with a more extensive European tour focused on Italy by the time it appeared in Richard Lassels's guide (1670) to that country. The British enthusiasm for Italy even survived virtual or outright bans on travel there (and especially in Spanish-controlled Italy), as imposed by the Privy Council in the last three decades of the seventeenth century[35] – precisely when Lassels was compiling his book. While the nobility would be dependent upon Privy Council approval, others such as the 'gentleman, merchants, factors' for whom Rowlands compiled a road-book in 1576,[36] or the 'intelligencers [diplomats-cum-spies], craftsmen, divines, soldiers, lawyers',[37] or even jewellers, physicians and 'schollers pregnant'[38] mentioned in seventeenth-century essays on travel, continued to enjoy the forbidden fruit of Italy. Travel literature often took their motives for travelling into account, albeit haphazardly. For example, James Howell, the author of *Instructions for Forreine Travell* (1642), first toured Europe when he was sent to Venice to recruit craftsmen on behalf of the London glass manufacturer for whom he worked. He took six months to get there, travelling via Amsterdam, Paris and Spain![39] Women, of course, were expected by the seventeenth-century travel moralists to stay at home: Sir Thomas Palmer even classified them, with the sick and deranged, as unfit for travel.[40] From the mid-eighteenth century, however, well-born English ladies and bluestockings increasingly made their own 'Grand Tours' and wrote up their experiences in diaries and letters.[41]

With Lassels, the sympathy for Italy and Italians becomes even more pronounced: as a prominent Catholic exile, he was in Rome for extended periods, and was of course untroubled by the aesthetic or doctrinal inhibitions exhibited by his Protestant fellow-countrymen. 'Yes, yes,' he writes in the Preface to his *Voyage of Italy* (posthumously published in Paris in 1670), 'it's this great blessing of God, warm Sun, which has so thoroughly baked the Italian wits, that while (according to the observation of Charles V) the French appear not wise, but are wise; the Spaniards appear wise, but are not wise; the Dutch neither appear wise, nor are wise; the Italians only both appear wise, and are wise'. There follow paeans to Italian achievements in literature, philosophy, architecture and the fine arts, whereby, most importantly, the achievements of modern Italians are placed on the same level as that of their forerunners in antiquity. As Lassels puts it: 'They are ambitious still of honours, remembering they are the successors of the masters of the world.'

A highly moral man himself, Lassels also turns the accusation of the influence of Italian immorality on the young on its head, citing a parable of St Ambrose. A young gentleman returning from foreign travel bumps into his former mistress and affects not to know her: 'whereat she wondering, told him that she was such a one: it may be so, sayd he, but I am no more I'.[42] Unlike Thomas, who uses the harlots of Rome to denounce the hypocrisy of the Church, the Catholic Lassels ingenuously turns the argument around. Comparing the whorehouses of Rome with those of (Protestant) Amsterdam, he claims the former are much to be preferred because their inmates are there by choice (!), while those in Amsterdam are confined by force; the Roman prostitutes (as good Catholics) 'do great acts of austerityes and penance', as the blood on the walls of their cells makes manifest, whereas the unfortunate Amsterdam whores 'laugh, and are merry'. 'Here [in Rome] the love of vertue and penance locks up these: there the Vice of Love locks in those, and not true repentance.'[43] Can he be serious? It would be hard to find an argument with more holes in it, but apparently he is.

Lassels visited Italy five times between 1637 and his death in 1668, and indeed he gives five possible approach routes over the Alps in his guide. He was a Roman

Catholic priest – a recusant – who made a living as tutor and guide to English nobility on the Grand Tour. An earlier manuscript was an account of an Italian journey he undertook at the request of Lady Catherine Whetenhall, the married daughter of the Catholic Earl of Shrewsbury, in the Holy Year of 1650.[44] His other role was as agent (using the alias of 'Richard Bolds') for the English Chapter negotiating with the Holy See over the status of English Catholic prelates, a thankless task bedevilled by intrigue and caprice. He wielded his pen in both capacities, as the author of *An Apologie for the Roman Catholicks* and of *The Voyage of Italy*, which was itself the offspring of at least two earlier writings (1650 and 1654) exploiting his experience as a cicerone. With its utilitarian pocket format (6½ by 4 inches), its practical itineraries, its much more extensive coverage of monuments and works of art, as well as observations on society, government and economy, it has been claimed as 'the first true guidebook in the English language'.[45]

While the book easily eclipsed its only potential (but already faded) English rival, the *Itinerary* ['*Il Mercurio Italico*', 1648] written by a young Royalist called John Raymond,[46] in due course it attracted competition in the form of *Some Letters. Containing an Account of what seemed most remarkable in Switzerland, Italy &c* (1686), written by the prolific, bustling and very political prelate Gilbert Burnet. *Some Letters* (followed by two books of continental travels) was avowedly written to expose 'popery and tyranny', so that the guidebook genre now began to reflect the ideological fissure between Protestant Whiggery and Catholic Toryism. Yet it is fair to say that neither writer was ultimately an extremist in his cause, Burnet because he was a natural politician and conciliator, and Lassels because he was a cultivated and much-travelled man of the world. Still, the second edition of the latter's *Voyage of Italy*, published in London, was purged of its 'more objectionable references to Protestantism', such as the remark that Luther had been the 'great corrupter of religion' (as Machiavelli had been of 'policy', and Cesare Borgia of 'manners'); and that Geneva 'like a good sinke' was 'fit to receive into it the corruption of the Apostates of the Roman church'.[47]

While Lassels has his waspish moments, one should remember that the anti-Catholic rhetoric was generally far harsher. The subtitle of a tract-cum-guidebook published to mark the Jubilee of 1700 describes it, *inter alia*, as: 'An Account of . . . Ridiculous Religious Processions and Ceremonie . . . Likewise the Debauch'd Lives, and Amorous Intrigues of Lustful priests, and Leacherous Nuns . . . Reflections upon the Superstition and Foppish Pageantry of . . . the last Grand Jubilee at Rome.'[48] This was a guidebook (just about) for bigots, and seems to have been quite seriously intended, although its users would of course have derived from it virtually nothing of value about Italian culture and society.

THE VOYAGE OF ITALY AS A GUIDEBOOK – LASSELS'S PRECEPTS

The lively and sometimes witty Preface to Lassels's *Voyage* by no means justifies De Beer's curmudgeonly judgement (later revised) that 'his style is tawdry, he himself flippant and half-educated'.[49] Serenely anticipating such charges, Lassels says a little levity 'makes a bad dinner go down and a bad horse go on'; and as to his language, that is adapted to the subjects he treats, whereby it has been remarked that Lassels considerably enlarged the aesthetic vocabulary of the average English traveller by using technical terms for works of art culled from his reading of Vasari. He was something of a connoisseur and friendly with the great Italian antiquarian and theoretician of art Giovanni Pietro Bellori, who had himself written a Vasari-like work on modern painters, sculptors and architects.[50] Of his competitors Lassels observes that 'the one writes much of Italy, and saies little: the other writes little and leaveth out much; which I impute to the ones [*sic*] writing out of old Geographers, long after he had been there'. His gibe was only too justified as numerous writers (even the famous diarist, John Evelyn, who indeed pillaged Lassels's book) made limited notes en route and then silently padded out their efforts with plagiarsm from other works. Finally, his Preface represents the apotheosis of the vindication of travel against its critics, adducing for the last time the Ulysses metaphor to underline his remark that 'he that will know much of this great book, the world, must read much in it'. The target of his rhetoric is the insular English country gentleman who 'can scarce go to London without making his will, at least without wetting his handkerchief'.

While all the usual arguments are employed in favour of travel, which is described as taking 'any young nobleman four notches lower in his self-conceit and pride' (that is, through exposure to the sophistication of other cultures and the hardships of the journey), he also has a lengthy discourse on the qualities required of a good bear-leader. From this it is evident that there were plenty of corrupt ones, though the Catholic Lassels includes in his condemnation those who take their pupils to Geneva. Particularly reprehensible are those who '[dally] in the country where they had a mistress', or inveigle their charges into Academies where they get a fat commission from the teachers. Worse still, 'others I have known who have locked their pupils in a chamber with a wanton woman, and taken the key away with them', a practice, one would have thought, more appropriate to the mating of dogs.

Lassels also has clear ideas about the best organisation for a Grand Tour. First, the young man should go to Italy at the age of 15 or 16 'to season his mind with the gravity and wise maximes of that nation, which have civilised the whole world, and taught Man Manhood'. After two or three years there, he should spend another three in France learning to fence, ride, vault, handle his pike, musket and so on. In between he should acquaint himself with Germany, Holland and Flanders. In Germany, overexuberant hospitality was the main problem: 'I like well them shaking hands with you when you first enter into their houses; but I like not their quarrelling with you for not pledging a health of a yard long, which would ruin yours.' As to the Dutch, their 'clownish hatred of Nobility' is held against them, together with their obsession with a spotless home, so that they 'stand in such awe of [their hearths] as not to dare to make a fire in it'.[51] Such remarks reflect the author's Englishness, as well as his Catholic Royalist sympathies, but they generally rise well above the level of mere prejudice. This may explain why Lassels, required reading for the many English

Catholics on the Grand Tour or in exile, was also much used by Protestants (if admittedly purged of a few excessively anti-Protestant remarks). As Chaney remarks: 'How much more appropriate, after all, even if you were not one yourself, to have a Catholic priest inform you about Baroque Rome rather than an "enlightened"' Whig who would in any case be more concerned to persuade you of the necessary link between popery, tyranny and economic decline, than to praise papist painting and sculpture.'[52]

FRANÇOIS MAXIMILIEN MISSON AND THE *NOUVEAU VOYAGE D'ITALIE*

The ability 'to praise papist painting and sculpture' grew with the eighteenth-century development of a canon of taste that is wholly absent in the earliest guidebooks. John Raymond, it is true, does devote a good deal of space to architecture, sculpture and painting, but he has no aesthetic vocabulary. In keeping with the *Zeitgeist* he is chiefly interested in the impression of splendour and wealth that princely collections create; in Rome he simply refers the reader to the numerous specialist guides available, for example, works such as Totti's now much expanded and altered *Ritratto di Roma moderna* discussed in the previous chapter. Lassels advances the position, but not by much, still writing a description of the Sistine chapel that leaves out Michelangelo's ceiling! (In fairness one should say again that it was rather hard to see before the invention of electric light.) Typically, he clinches a fairly detailed description of a table with *pietre dure* inlay displayed in the Uffizi by saying: 'You'll conceive better of this table when I tell that it is worth a hundred thousand crowns, and that it was fifteen years in the making, and yet thirty men wrought at it daily.' Nevertheless, he begins to show an interest in individual artists and their styles (his opinions heavily influenced by Vasari), the kind of thing we now think is a sine qua non of a guidebook but which was then quite new. It is a considerable irony that the Huguenot, Maximilien Misson, who discreetly exploited Lassels's book for his own bestselling guide – while losing no opportunity for denouncing the latter's 'Unexactnesses, Puerilities [and] gross Ignorances' – exhibited a remarkable sympathy, given he was a Protestant, for Neapolitan baroque.[53] Perhaps the Grand Tourist's demand to have his or her curiosity satisfied about individual sights was beginning to take precedence over the religious preoccupations of the author? Nevertheless, even today, Misson's guidebook still gives rise to denunciation as being 'virtually useless for Grand Tourists seriously interested in art and antiquities'.[54]

Misson had been one of the Protestant judges appointed to the Parlement in Paris before the Revocation of the Edict of Nantes in 1685, when he was obliged to flee to England. Naturalised there in 1687, he accompanied Lord Arran on the Grand Tour in 1687–8, starting at Rotterdam and travelling through Germany and the Austrian Crown Lands, before visiting the Veneto, Loreto, Rome and Naples. The return route took in Bologna, Milan, Genoa, Turin, Geneva, Strasbourg and Brussels. This covered virtually all the Grand Tour highlights except Florence and Tuscany, and the text of his subsequent guidebook is full of intriguing first-hand observation written generally from a Huguenot perspective. Misson also wrote a vivid descriptive dictionary of England[55] dealing in some depth with its cultural and social peculiarities. Notwithstanding these successes, the author acquired a reputation for exaggeration, and even forgery in the case of an account of François Leguat's Indian voyage (1708). The work was represented as original with his own introduction, but it appears that Misson in fact wrote the whole (it is thought to have been one inspiration for Defoe's *Robinson Crusoe*). The picture that emerges of Misson is of a somewhat erratic personality: '*Il y a beaucoup d'érudition, mais mal digérée,*' and '*l'auteur est d'ailleurs très partial*', says the *Biographie Universelle* of his guidebook. Not only did he exhibit unbounded zeal for reforming society, he could also be somewhat naive, even fanatical, as his dealings with the ecstatic and rebellious Camisards of the Cévennes would suggest. Under their influence, he is said to have contemplated trying to convert both the pope and the sultan to Protestantism! These characteristics may account for the dogged attempts to disparage him and his works, including the guidebook, by Freschot, a Benedictine scholar from the Franche-Comté, who exposed the forgery of the Leguat book and pursued Misson mercilessly over the years. His anti-Catholic stance also attracted brickbats from several other French authors such as Père Labat and Blainville, who were clearly irked by the hold that Misson had over the guidebook market. The mud stuck, so that by the nineteenth century, John Pinkerton's bibliography of travels is warning readers that the *Nouveau voyage* is 'replete with the grossest misrepresentations of the religious state of Italy'. However, Percy Adams sums up the Huguenot's reputation thus: 'If all the praise of Misson and all the complaints about him could be gathered, one would have materials for a small volume, but the complaints would be either unimportant or inspired by religious differences.'[56]

In stealing Lassels's title for his own book, Misson was also paying his predecessor a backhanded compliment, though it might also be seen as an attempt to cash in on the reputation of a work that was now international, with French editions from 1671 and German ones from 1673. That Misson had a Protestant axe to grind can be seen from his sensational account of the fictitious female Pope Joan, a story few Protestant writers could resist, and which was almost certainly inserted as a counterblast to Lassels's scholarly discrediting of this ancient fable in the *Voyage*.[57] While some Protestants evidently used Lassels, few Catholics seemed to have used Misson. A Scottish nobleman, writing to his young sister in 1695, was expressing a widespread view when he said: 'If you see Misson, do not believe one word he says, for he is the most infamous lyar in nature.' And later: 'If you have Lassels by you, you may save me the trouble of a long letter. I shall only direct you to him . . .'.[58]

Like many Huguenots, Misson was an anglophile and in fact his book appeared in English (as *A New Voyage to Italy*, 1695) shortly after the two-volume French original (The Hague, 1691),[59] something which may also reflect the commercial reality that far fewer Frenchmen undertook the Grand Tour than

did the English and Germans. His work became the standard guide for half a
century, running through five editions before 1739. This was despite the fact that
its eventual four volumes hardly made a handy travelling companion, unlike
Lassels's pocket-sized book, while it also adopted the common strategy at that
time of arranging the material in the form of fictive letters to a friend.[60] Its
content, however, which Misson was careful to stress in his 'Advertisement' was
the product of autopsy and consultation of the best authorities, was directly
aimed at the Grand Tourist. His authorial stance – echoed later by La Lande and
others, who warned of the excessive praise lavished by the Italians on their own
artistic achievements – was one of judicious scepticism (*'j'ay examine les choses de
sang froid, en laissant les admirateurs s'évaporer en loüanges & en exclamations sans me
laisser surprendre à leurs termes pompeux & superlatifs'*). However, as we have seen,
this does not prevent him from swallowing the tale of the female pope,[61] and
likewise his claim that he has consulted no other book is, to say the least, a
generous interpretation of the truth. His detailed letters cover Holland,
Germany and Italy, with some material also on Switzerland, which was about to
begin its ascent in the popularity ratings.

Not surprisingly, Misson found that librarians were reluctant to show him
material from which he might '*tirer quelque avantage contre la Religion Romaine*', and
indeed was denied sight of a history of the papacy in the Library of
Sant'Ambrogio in Milan when he refused to reveal what faith he followed. It was
necessary, he remarks sarcastically, not only to cultivate the librarians, but also the
sort of 'concierge[s] who [were] impatient only for the tip they expect upon your
departure' (applied to anything from toilets to temples, this was to become a
fairly standard lament of guidebooks). While Lassels says: 'I cannot speak of
Rome, but I must speak of Relicks, Ceremonies and Religion. Yet I believe I give
my reader a full draught too of prophane antiquities, mascarades, shews, dressings
and pastimes,'[62] Misson often sees a religious tradition as an opportunity for irony.
For example, after telling us that the election of a bishop to succeed St Apollinaris
of Ravenna was facilitated by the Holy Spirit appearing in the form of a dove, and
alighting eleven times on the one to be chosen, he adds drily: '*mais depuis ce temps-
là, ils ont fait leurs affaires sans le mesme secours*'.[63] The readability of his text is
likewise greatly enhanced by irreverent asides, such as that describing how gangs
of gondoliers were employed as a claque at the Venice Opera; or his sardonic
characterisation of the type of local chauvinism and provincialism from which he
aims to free the travellers who read his book. In the third edition of the same, he
responds to his critics with aplomb: to a Bernese who had complained that he had
not described some important statues in the church at Bern he retorts that, if he
had been obliged to mention even all the statues that greatly surpassed these in
beauty, his work would have required several more volumes. '*Il faut donc distribuer
les éloges selon le différent mérite. Ainsi, un Paisan qui n' a jamais sorti de sa chaumière,
s'imagine que le soy-disant Chasteau du Seigneur, et la vieille tapisserie qui y pend depuis
cent cinquante ans malgré les rats et les araignées, sont les plus belles choses du monde.*'
Anyway, he adds crushingly, the sculptures so admired by the Swiss are not in the
least esteemed by connoisseurs.[64]

THE HEYDAY OF THE GRAND TOUR: KEYSLER (1740) AND NUGENT (1749)

As the Grand Tour gathered momentum in the eighteenth century, the trickle of books relating to it (journals, letters, reports and guidebooks) rapidly became a flood, of which the bibliography only of those books on Italy and published in English constitutes a formidable reading task.[65] Between 1498 and 1853 some fifty-four guidebooks, or books used at such, appeared from British, French, German and Italian authors, the great majority after 1700. The demand was obviously there: by 1785 Gibbon is writing from Lausanne that 'upwards of forty thousand English, masters and servants, are now absent on the continent'. While 'Grand Tourism', in the sense of travelling purely for pleasure and to gratify personal curiosity, was still confined to the wealthy and (usually) the aristocratic, those who catered to their needs in the form of guidebooks were generally clerks and scholars whose travels were financed by their patrons. Johann Georg Keysler, for instance, who wrote one of the most popular guidebooks of the century, was in the service of Baron Bernstorf's family for more than a decade, following earlier travels in Germany, France and the Netherlands as bear-leader to a couple of lordlings from another family. Like Misson's, his was a four-volume work in the form of letters and provided coverage of France, Switzerland, Germany, Bohemia, Hungary and Austria, as well as Italy. A man 'of excellent morals and uncommon erudition', as claimed in the dedication to his work, 'his observations are no other than become a scholar and a good man to make'. His learning and integrity evidently impressed: on his 'philosophical journey' to England in 1718 he was made a Fellow of the Royal Society in recognition of his works on Stonehenge and a dissertation on the 'consecrated mistletoe of the Druids'. Although he was a Protestant, like Misson, his learning made him acceptable to 'Bandolot, Montfaucon and other learned persons in France' who 'departed from their prejudices against the Germans which that self-conceited nation generally entertains with regard to the rest of the world'.[66]

Still, like Misson, Keysler can be a combative Protestant at times. He comments adversely on the censorship exercised by the Jesuits in Vienna, and is contemptuous of Protestants who convert to Catholicism to advance their careers and 'afterward make show of a mighty zeal for their new religion'. In Hungary he found that men and women could still be burned for witchcraft, an activity hardly exclusive to the Catholic authorities. But Keysler describes a 'papist' who answered his objections on behalf of one victim of this barbarism with the assertion that 'nothing could be plainer than his guilt, for . . . [the accused] was a tall corpulent man, [who] weighed but three ounces and a half'. Keysler enquired sarcastically whether the man had been weighed publicly, and by a pair of scales, but 'soon perceived that it was not proper for me to make any longer stay in that place'.[67] In reality, Keysler was as much a precursor of the Enlightenment as a militant Protestant, which accounts for his splendid way with the anecdotes that fill his book, for example, his description of Magliabecchi, the legendary librarian of the ducal library in Florence that still bears his name. 'The Jesuits and he equally hated each other,' he recalls, the Jesuits sneering that he 'appeared learned among librarians, but a library-keeper among the learned'. Of Magliabecchi's own library, Keysler observes that it

> made a very indifferent appearance, the books lying on the ground in heaps; but by the assistance of his great memory, Magliabecchi could immediately find his books on any subject that was talked of. The books which he frequently consulted bore the marks of snuff . . . and others which had served him for plates, were daubed with yolks of eggs, which were his principal food. By the length of his nails, he resembled a Harpy. He very seldom changed his linen; so that when a shirt was once put on, it remained as long as it would hang on his back. As he lived in this sordid manner and hardly ever washed himself, it is no wonder that the offensive effluvia he emitted could scarce be borne with, but for the pleasure of his conversation.[68]

From examples like this it can be seen that Keysler could simply be read as a travel book; but the systematic coverage he gave of history, manners, laws, commerce, the arts and architecture, as well as things of interest to antiquaries such as ancient coins, meant that his work was appropriate for use as a guidebook. This was certainly what he intended, claiming to illustrate 'the great beauty and advantage of connecting natural philosophy with geographical description'. The weakness of the book as a guide lies in the lack of practical information, something that was put right in Thomas Nugent's Grand Tour (1749), perhaps the most popular eighteenth-century guidebook for the Continent. This is more like a modern guide in that it is a compendium drawn from existing sources and checked against autopsy, offering (as the author candidly says in the Preface) a novelty of method, rather than 'a new discovery of matter'. It is in convenient duodecimo format for travelling, and to some extent anticipates Murray and Baedeker by offering a series of tours based on a capital city and largely following the post roads.[69] Other works, says Nugent, leave travellers at a loss in respect of 'roads, accommodations, the nature and price of carriages, knowledge of various coins [the local currency] and several other articles absolutely necessary in foreign peregrinations'.[70] He goes on to say that his book precisely covered the requirements of the Grand Tour, volume 1 being devoted to the Netherlands, volume 2 to Germany, volume 3 to Italy and 4 to France – a clue to the way a standard tour was actually planned. Although he had intended to add Scandinavia, Spain and Portugal, as advertised on the title page, these have been held over until the reaction to the first edition has been gauged.

While Nugent is by no means such a good read as Keysler, he is more useful on the ground. His hints on travelling in Italy include advice on what to take with you (such as your own bedding), security (how to blockade your door at night), types of transport available, how to avoid those servants who are, in fact, merely thieves, and how to choose guides ('These antiquaries are ridiculously distinguished by the name of Ciceroni, and may be retained for a few pistoles a month').[71] He is also one of the first seriously to attempt to unravel the nightmare of ever-changing distance measurements for his readers. If 69 or 70 English miles constitute one degree,

> the German mile is the fifteenth part of a degree, or better than four English miles. An Italian mile is 1000 paces, of five Roman feet each, which is two thirds of an inch less than the English foot, so that 76 Italian miles are near a degree. A Danish, Swedish and Hungarian mile makes one German mile and a half, or six English miles. A French league is the 25th part of a degree, which is two English miles and three quarters. A Spanish league is four Italian miles, seventeen and a half to a degree. A Russian Werst is little more than three quarters of an English mile.[72]

Only Louis Dutens's popular *Itinéraire*, available in English from 1782, went one better, having calculated the distances in English miles 'by Means of a Perambulator fastened to the Chaise'.[73] Similarly complicated are the four and a half pages Nugent supplies detailing the coinage of each Italian region. Finally, his tips for behaviour show that Nugent, although 'a Protestant and ardent supporter of the Hanoverian constitutional settlement',[74] is far more relaxed than Misson and Keysler in matters of religion, merely remarking that the 'Inquisition is established in several parts of the country', but less severe than in Portugal or Spain. 'Foreigners in general are under no great restraint in point of religion, but are allowed a good deal of freedom in their discourse, and nowhere more than in Rome.'[75]

MANNERS AND SOCIETY IN THE GUIDEBOOKS: MOORE, VOLKMANN AND ARCHENHOLZ

Among the many other guides used for the Grand Tour a rough division can be made between those that concentrated on 'manners and society', such as the much-praised *Lettres historiques et critiques sur l'Italie* (Paris, 1799) by President Charles de Brosses, and those that showed more interest in the fine arts and monuments, such as Charles-Nicolas Cochin's *Voyage d'Italie* (Paris, 1758), though the distinction is not rigid and there is often overlap. A popular example of the former was Dr John Moore's informative *A View of Society and Manners in Italy: With Anecdotes Relating to Some Eminent Characters*.[76] This went through six editions between 1781 and 1795 and enjoyed the backhanded compliment of appearing unacknowledged in a compendium of plagiarism called *The Polite Traveller* (1783). Moore is indeed notably free of the factitious enthusiasm for works of art that had become fashionable among visitors to Italy anxious to pose as connoisseurs, and wrote of the Uffizi that he did 'not prolong [his] visit after [he] began to be tired, merely to be thought what [he was] not'.

On the other hand, a great deal could be learned about Italian governance and society from his discriminating and sober account of such things as the *mezzadria* (sharecropping) agricultural system, which was an instrument of oppression in the Kingdom of Naples but, he claimed, functioned somewhat better in Tuscany under more enlightened rulers. It will be noted that this is the exact opposite of Dallington's view 180 years earlier. However, like Dallington, he is critical of the cruel use of tortures such as *la corda*, where victims were hoisted on a rope and left dangling for hours, then abruptly dropped and jerked up, so that the arms and shoulders were dislocated.[77] And he is enlightening on the background to the widespread phenomenon of *cicisbeismo*, whereby etiquette allowed a married woman to cultivate an escort whose status was often unclear, it being considered bad form for the husband to intervene or enquire too closely into the exact nature of the relationship.

Apart from high sales, as with Moore's book, some evidence of the proven value of individual guidebooks may be gleaned from what the competition said about them. In his survey of other works in the Preface of his *Historisch-kritische Nachrichten von Italien* (1770–1), J.J. Volkmann[78] praises Joseph-Jérôme de Lalande's[79] immensely successful *Voyage d' un Français en Italie, Fait dans les Années 1765 & 1766* (1769 – much used by English travellers, though never translated); magisterially Teutonic, Volkmann kindly remarks that Lalande displays a diligence and thoroughness 'that one would not suspect in a Frenchman . . .'. (In the third edition of his book, published in 1790, Lalande gets his own back, remarking in his Preface: '*Il a paru en allemand une traduction libre de mon voyage, avec des additions, par M. Volkmann, imprimée à Leipzig en 1771 et 1778*'.)[80] Volkmann, echoing Lalande, observes that Misson's book was still the market leader (this in the 1770s!), unhappily so, because that has meant that others have copied his errors, while Bishop Burnet's work, also out of date, is disfigured by misrepresentation arising from his zealous Protestantism. He praises Keysler, although he, and especially English authors, are blamed for 'trying to make fun of the Catholic religion and introducing trivia in order to practise their wit'. The spirit of the Enlightenment further informs not only Volkmann's insistence on rational planning and dispassionate investigation in the guidebook, but also his attitude to relics and miracles. Relics, he says, can be ignored, as they 'are not conducive to the formation of taste', while miracles and hagiography, on the other hand, have to be engaged with 'because the history or the meaning of a picture may be dependent upon them. In this case we present the matter as it is related and leave it to each individual to believe as much of it as he will, without offering a judgement ourselves.'[81]

It can be seen that in matters of religion, Volkmann has arrived at roughly the position of the contemporary guidebook. The vast paraphernalia of relics, wonders, saints, miracles and so forth was staple fare for the medieval guidebook; it survived even the Renaisssance and Counter-Reformation, with critical examination confined to a few scholars, and hostile comment coming only from Protestant commentators. Now it is simply treated as an historical phenomenon, knowledge of which is useful for explaining the cultural context of artefacts: according to Volkmann, 'It is said that the historian should have neither fatherland nor religion; it is equally justified to demand the same of a travel writer'.[82] This secular rationalist approach was pursued by another German, the

Prussian officer Johann Wilhelm von Archenholz, part of whose *England und Italien* (1785) appeared in English as *A Picture of Italy* (1791). In 1797 a translation of the other part appeared as *A Picture of England*, which purported to do for that country what John Moore had done for Italy, but is in fact a remarkable example of the 'Anglomania' of the Enlightenment (Volkmann's own 1781 work on England is far more circumspect).

Archenholz's inferior work is interesting only by comparison with Volkmann's, which was the standard guide to Italy for Germans of the Enlightenment, and whose author achieved similar success with guides to England, the Netherlands, France and Spain, using the same formula. Luckily, we have first-hand evidence of what it was like to use such a book, because Goethe, who took it on his Italian journey, constantly praises it. Perhaps that is because, unlike Archenholz and despite plenty of critical observations, Volkmann is fundamentally in sympathy with the country and its inhabitants, instead of comparing everything adversely to supposedly better arrangements elsewhere. Once in a while, however, Goethe feels obliged to disagree with the 'honest', 'good and ever-useful' Volkmann, and that is usually when the latter is being disparaging. For example, Goethe refutes his assertion that there are 'thirty to forty thousand lazy ne'er-do-wells (*lazzaroni*) in Naples' by ascertaining that all the people he (Goethe) discovered standing around were persons 'whose occupation permitted it at that moment' (carriage drivers, porters, fishermen, rubbish collectors and so forth). He concludes that even Volkmann is guilty of repeating unthinkingly 'the biased view of a person from the north, where anyone who is not feverishly at work all day is regarded as a loafer'. Volkmann was indeed repeating what had become a guidebook cliché: Jérôme Richard, for example, in his *Description historique et critique de l'Italie* (1766) describes the *lazzaroni* of Naples as, *inter alia*, insurrectionist pimps who sold their wives and daughters while they lazed around all day or indulged in petty crime. Lalande (1769) takes his cue from Richard, describing the Neapolitan populace as feckless layabouts who were only controlled by the authorities with food hand-outs, severe punishments and endless festivals. Richard de Saint-Non's guidebook (published in five volumes between 1781 and 1786)[83] simply said that idleness is 'the trait truly characteristic of the Neapolitan nation', and so on.[84] However, Goethe's occasional polite (and empirical) dissent from Volkmann pales beside his devastating judgement on Archenholz:

When one reads it here, it is incredible how such scribble shrinks to nothing. It's as if one had thrown it in the fire, and watched it slowly turn brown and black, till the pages curled and went up in smoke. The author has seen everything, of course; but he knows far too little to excuse his overbearing, contemptuous tone, and, whether he is praising or blaming, he makes blunders all the time.[85]

In truth Archenholz had simply used the 'awful example' of Italy as a foil to highlight the merits of England that he was determined to demonstrate.

CONNOISSEURS, COLLECTORS, AESTHETES: RICHARDSON (1722), WRIGHT (1730), MARTYN (1787)

'Eduardus Wright', as he styled himself, summed up the craze for collecting antiquities that characterised the English visitors to Italy of the eighteenth century in his *Observations* compiled in the early 1720s: 'The Roman [virtuosi][86] . . . have such a notion of English ardour in the acquisition of curiosities of every sort, that they have this expression frequent among them: "Were our amphitheatre portable, the English would carry it off."'[87] Little did they know that, by the end of the century, Lord Elgin was to show that even this was conceivable! While Wright exhibits the familiar Protestant prejudice against the Catholic culture that produced them – he speaks of the '*pious fraud*' used by the priests 'to catch the people with whatever bait will serve best to take them'[88] – he provides quite extensive coverage of 'paintings and modern sculptures', as well as of the sights of antiquity. A glance at his index reveals that aesthetic sightseeing, so superficially addressed in the majority of guides discussed hitherto, was well established by the early eighteenth century and was generating its own corpus of guidebooks.[89] In Rome he deals with fifty-two churches, twenty-three temples, twenty-nine palaces and fourteen villas, besides columns, obelisks, fountains and the like. Under 'masters and their works' appear at least fifty modern painters, besides many minor masters, not excluding Saint Luke.[90] An indication of the taste of the age may be gleaned from the most frequently referred to artists, for example, Raphael receives twenty-nine mentions, 'Guido' [Reni] twenty-five and Titian twenty-four. Lalande later refers to Wright as 'the most esteemed of the connoisseurs'. Wright's book was followed by Matthew Pilkington's much more substantial *Gentleman's and Connoisseur's Dictionary of Painters* (1770), which claims to analyse some 1,400 European painters.

We have seen that Volkmann made an important distinction between sights that were 'conducive to the formation of taste' and those that were not. Several authors produced works in the eighteenth century that were clearly designed to guide the individual in the appreciation of art. Some of these were translations, like William Lodge's popular *The Painter's Voyage of Italy* (1679), a translation of Giacomo Barri's book of 1671, which introduced the English to Guercino, Guido Reni and the Carracci, and whose influence can be detected in the painters singled out for approbation by the guidebook writers. 'To have good taste,' Leibniz had written, 'one must practise enjoying things which reason and experience have already authorised.'[91] Formation of taste had to a degree been institutionalised by the formation of the Society of Dilettanti in 1734 for the study of antiquities by noblemen who had been on the Grand Tour. This process therefore began well before Winckelmann's mid-century establishment of classicism as the dominant component of European taste – and as the foundation stone of the not yet constructed discipline of art history. Winckelmann, however, gradually took the process beyond the kind of empirical analysis of artistic objects that chimed with the scientific spirit of the age, and towards a quasi-numinous engagement with works of artistic genius. The logical consequence was the transmutation of attitudes to art into a form of secular religion. Indeed, Winckelmann ended up by debunking the distanced analytical approach of scholarship that had served him well in his early research, and began to lambast the scholars who 'know everything but see nothing'.[92] One is reminded also of James Howell's amusing characterisation of the unobservant traveller as being like Jonah in the whale's belly, who 'travelled much but saw little'.

In 1722 Jonathan Richardson had published (with his son) *An Account of Some of the Statues, Bas-reliefs, Drawings and Pictures in Italy, &c. with Remarks*, which was as much a treatise as a guide, and in the same year a similarly conceived book by Robert Samber entitled *Roma Illustrata* appeared. The novelty of Richardson's book was that it applied the aesthetic theory developed in the discourses he had written (for example, that on 'How to Judge the Goodness of a Picture') to objects encountered in the field. Scholarship, autopsy and tourism were increasingly being combined. In his Preface, Richardson remarks that there are of course catalogues, prints and copies that document Italy's works of art, 'but these are as the names of towns in a map, or the views of places, neither of which, not even the latter, are sufficient to to give an idea of them; and if some writers have accompanied their accounts with remarks, they are mostly extravagant and undistinguishing general encomiums, or notices of particulars the least considerable'.[93] This was all too true, even if the Richardsons are fairly cavalier themselves, for example, discarding the entire Venetian school of painting on the grounds that the 'people [of Titian, Tintoretto and Veronese] neither look nor act with that grace and dignity as those of Raffaele, Michelangelo, Giulio [Romano], Correggio, Guido [Reni] etc.'[94] Nevertheless, we may believe Richardson when he tells us that he had devoted his life to 'endeavouring to raise and cultivate the love of art by showing its true uses and beauties',[95] and his account represents an early attempt to give the guidebook a truly didactic role in regard to the arts. Moreover, he was the first to insist that the most famous Greek works mentioned in the standard literature had been lost and the extant objects were only copies of originals that had perished.[96]

It is important to keep in mind that this didacticism was not merely regarded as serving the private need for self-improvement of the gentleman tourist. In *A Discourse on . . . The Science of the Connoisseur* (1719) Richardson stressed the improvement of manners that knowledge and appreciation of the arts would bring, ultimately to the whole nation: 'If gentlemen were Lovers of Painting, and Connoisseurs, this would help Reform Them, as their Example, and Influence would have the like Effect upon the Common People. All animated Beings naturally covet Pleasure, and eagerly pursue it as their Chiefest Good; the great Affair is to chuse those that are Worthy of Rational Beings.'[97] This viewpoint dovetailed with that of William Aglionby in his *Painting Illustrated in Three Dialogues* (1685 – chiefly a translation of Vasari's *Lives of the Artists*), where the English revolution is blamed for the country's backwardness in the arts ('whose Quarrel was as much to Politeness and the Liberal Arts, as to Monarchy and Prelacy'). The implication is clear: Englishmen suffered from a cultural deficit. One of Aglionby's main concerns was to persuade the English to regard the painter not as a mere 'Mechanik', but as one with a 'Title to the Liberal Arts'.[98] From this it would be a short step to the cult of artistic genius.

The principle of 'empathise and analyse', while most obviously applicable to works of art, could with profit be applied more widely as part of the touristic experience. In 1702, Bernard de Montfaucon's influential *Diarium Italicum* (English translation, 1712) had encompassed contemporary discoveries in the infant discipline of archaeology, a discipline to which he returned a few years later in compiling his great work on the monuments of France. The *Diarium* indeed begins with France (Vienne, Arles, Nîmes, Marseilles), but the meat of it lies in a systematic treatment of the artistic heritage of Italy, covering everything from manuscripts, inscriptions (then much in vogue), works of art and buildings to 'a noble monument found under ground at Rome anno M.DCC.II'. Into the same category of works fall the many collections of inscriptions, while Joseph Addison's *Dialogues upon the Usefulness of Ancient Medals* (posthumously published in 1721) provides the theory upon which a connoisseur's sightseeing might be based. Addison's protagonist remarks that whole scenes or portraits of emperors on medals can be recovered through the adroit cleaning of them by a specialist. 'I am sorry', says his interlocutor, 'that I did not know this last use of Medals when I was at *Rome*. It might perhaps have given me a greater taste of its Antiquities, and have fixed in my memory several of the ruins that I have now forgotten.'[99] No such failure of retention was likely in the case of Gibbon, who tells us in his autobiography that he prepared for his Rome tour by assiduous reading and note-taking:

> I formed and executed a plan of study for the use of my Transalpine expedition: the topography of old Rome, the ancient geography of Italy, and the science of medals . . . From these materials I formed a table of roads and distances reduced to our English measure; filled a folio commonplace-book with my collections and remarks on the geography of Italy; and inserted in my journal many long and learned notes on the insulae and populousness of Rome, the social war, the passage of the Alps by Hannibal etc . . .[100]

The works by Richardson, Addison and others imply a gradual transition from travellers' preoccupation with uniquely dramatic curiosities to the formation of taste through individual engagement with works of art. Hitherto, writes Judith Adler, the focus had been 'on the strange and the bizarre, natural marvels and monstrosities [as in the princely "*Kunst- und Wunderkammer*"], precious stones, rare coins, medals and other antiquities', as well as 'oddities of social custom'. "Landscape", appreciated for its "beauty" without reference to military or productive uses, lay entirely outside it, as did all the arts (with the exception of architecture).' Joseph Addison, in his *Remarks on Several Parts of Italy* (1705), epitomises the pre-picturesque (let alone pre-romantic) attitude to landscape, when he remarks: 'The greatest pleasure I took in my journey from Rome to Naples was in seeing the Fields, Towns and Rivers, that have been described by so many classic authors, and have been the scene of so many great Actions.'[101] Thomas Hearne, a Jacobite commentator hostile to Addison's Whiggism, exploited this well-known aspect of Addison to rubbish his work, observing that his book was 'very trite, being made up of nothing but scraps of verse, and things which have been observed over and over'. However, in a finely turned backhanded compliment, he allowed that the *Remarks* were well written in a 'clean style, and for that reason will please novices and superficial readers'.[102] The systematic sightseer, however, visited 'palaces, charitable institutions, libraries and curiosity cabinets, catalogues of whose contents were beginning to be published as a sub-genre of the travel guidebook'.[103] Such places of course remained items on the tourists' itinerary through the age of the Grand Tour, but the eighteenth century also saw an aestheticisation of both learning and culture that paved the way for the extreme subjectivity of Romanticism, and gradually altered the sightseeing priorities of travellers.

The phenomenon of collecting, which is a continuum from antiquity, was part of the wider desire to retain something concrete from places visited that should be both symbolic of the individual's achievement through travel and a private negotiation of the ego with the places visited. Medieval pilgrims had chipped (or bitten) off fragments from sacred objects; English milords now bought up wagon-loads of antiquities. It has even been suggested that the Protestant Englishman, denied the Catholic's enjoyment of relics, transferred his acquisitive and devotional impulses to classical art and the relics of antiquity.[104] An extreme example was Sir Richard Colt Hoare, the owner of Stourhead in Wiltshire, who is said to have spent four hours a day for five weeks in Rome looking for antiques with his agent. He also made his own copies and drawings, and once picked up a cache of Canalettos from a Venetian bookseller who was unaware of their worth. At least from the eighteenth century, commerce liberally supplied ersatz versions of antiquities in the form of casts and copies for those unable to afford the real thing; as time went on, the whole process sank into the mass squalor of the souvenir trade that we know today. One could, however, also 'collect' aesthetic *experiences*, rather than original antiques or their copies; and this was something that guidebooks, however hesitantly, began to address.

Before they could do so, unrestricted access to the objects had of course to be possible. In 1783 the modernising Habsburg Emperor Joseph II not only sponsored the first truly scientific catalogue of an art collection for the imperial gallery in the Vienna Belvedere, but also threw open the gallery to the public, who could visit it without payment. And even before the fledgling French Republic turned the Louvre into a public art collection in 1793, Thomas Martyn, in his guide for the *The English Connoisseur* (1766),[105] was praising the French kings and nobility for allowing virtually anyone access to their pictures. 'The polite arts are rising in Britain,' claims Martyn, 'and call for the fostering hand of the rich and powerful; one certain way of advancing them is to give all possible opportunities to those who make them their study to contemplate the works of the best masters, that they may not form a bad taste and a poor manner upon such productions as chance throws in their way'. Not all the English were backward in this respect, he concedes, and praises Horace Walpole, who wrote his own guidebook[106] to Strawberry Hill in 1784, and also prepared a leaflet for prospective visitors. Many of the visitors were expected to become genteel practitoners of the arts themselves, as Martyn is obviously implying. This idea was not in fact new, though now much more widespread: it could be found as early as 1665 in Balthazar Gerbier's *Subsidium Peregrinantibus*, where the identification and analysis of the major works of art is considered crucial for a gentleman's education, that is, the formation of his active taste (as a practitioner) and his passive taste (as a connoisseur.)

Adrian Tinniswood has documented the rising tide of visitors to English country houses in the second half of the eighteenth century. A lovely house like Wilton, for example, could attract 2,324 visitors in a single year (1775). Sightseeing soon needed to be systematised with opening times for the great houses and the issue of tickets, together with the printing of catalogues and guidebooks. Some of these home publications were substantial: the *Copious and Comprehensive Catalogue of the Curiosities of Wilton-House* ran to 150 pages, though interestingly, one clergyman visitor complained that the compilers were too drily historical, and did not expatiate on the *beauty* of the objects.[107] Amazingly, this being England, there were ocasionally guides in foreign languages – in French to Blenheim, in Italian to Wilton. Printed guides were indeed necessary, as otherwise it was usually the housekeeper's job to show people round, and many are the travellers' complaints of insolent, drunken, ignorant or merely grasping retainers. Not untypical is the comment of Lady Beauchamp Proctor on her tour of Raynham, where the property was shown by 'one old witch and a great dog, that attended us all over the house, and saluted every corner that was convenient for his purposes'.[108]

Thomas Martyn was not only the author of *The English Connoisseur*, but also of three volumes of 'Gentleman's Tours' through France, Italy and Switzerland, all published in 1787. His preface states that he had used autopsy as base material, supplemented by the advice of friends and consultation of the most reliable accounts of other travellers. Of these, he lists no less than thirty-two Italian journeys he considers significant, starting with Sandys in 1610 and ending with Henry Swinburne's sojourn in the two Sicilies (1777–80), Moore (1775–6) and Hester Piozzi (1786.) The list includes most of the guidebooks discussed above (Raymond, Lassels, Misson and so forth), but not Nugent; also all the travel reports that were obviously used as guides, including several untranslated French works that were habitually used by English tourists (Lalande, Abbé Richard, Cochin). What more could profitably be added to such voluminous material? Martyn poses the question himself and answers it by claiming (by no means justly) that much of the competition had been written 'to amuse the indolent, rather than instruct the active'; it was bulky 'fireside reading', whereas his work was portable and designed for use on the spot. He not only took over mileage measurements from the previously mentioned indispensable *Itinéraire* of Dutens, but also such things as conversions into English measures from the local ones for silk, linen, cloth and so on, thereby offering the first truly focused shopping guide.

All this practical information (including transport costs, tolls payable at city gates, the opening and closing times of same, the *lascia-passare* for the *dogana*, and even an advertisement – the first in a guidebook? – for banking services) is allied to a systematic inventory of artistic sights ('ample catalogues of everything that is curious in architecture, painting and sculpture'). As this suggests, even at this late date Martyn is still essentially providing an inventory; his method is to describe historical and other features of each Florentine church, while listing in a footnote (without comment) the paintings or frescos that may be seen in it. It is evident that near-comprehensiveness is aimed at, in respect of the artistic sights, but there is as yet no real space either for critical analysis or personal engagement.

GUIDEBOOK ENGAGEMENT WITH A SIGHTSEERS' CLASSIC: THE *MEDICI VENUS*

The concept of ideal beauty, which Winckelmann believed was realised in Greek sculpture, by definition was not to be found simply in the imitation of nature; rather was it an intellectual formulation, conceived as a composite of the best features that nature had to offer. This point is underlined by the antiquarian and aesthetician Giovanni Pietro Bellori (1615–96) in his celebrated lecture to the Accademia di S. Luca in Rome published in 1672. He quotes Raphael's complaint that there is 'a scarcity of beautiful women', so he [Raphael] is obliged to use 'a certain idea that comes to [his] mind'. Similarly, Guido Reni's depiction of Helen is based on an idea – let us not forget, says Bellori, that the real Helen was found to have aesthetic defects, 'so it is believed that she never did sail for Troy but that her statue was taken there instead, for whose beauty the Greeks and Trojans made war for ten years'. (!) And just as Helen 'with her natural beauty did not equal the forms of [the painter] Zeuxis and Homer . . . nor [did] any woman [equal] in beauty the Medicean Venus of Cleomenes'.[109]

He is referring of course to the so-called *Medici Venus* (*Venus de' Medici*), which was regarded as the high point of the tour for those visiting Florence, or indeed Italy, throughout the period of the Grand Tour. The Venus was first recorded in 1638 in the Villa Medici[110] in Rome, but Lalande (and some other guidebooks down to the present) claim that it came originally from Hadrian's Villa at Tivoli. In 1677 it was moved to the ducal collection in Florence by Cosimo III. It was displayed in Buontalenti's rotunda in the Uffizi, the so-called *Tribuna* (1584), which was reserved for the most spectacular items in the collection.[111] Its celebrity in the eighteenth century was roughly equivalent to that enjoyed today (but not then) by the *Mona Lisa* of Leonardo da Vinci,[112] while the now hugely admired pictorial treatment of the *Birth of Venus* by Botticelli did not even feature in most guidebooks or travel accounts. Once the *Medici Venus* had become established as representing the *idea* of feminine beauty, most observers saw in it what they were obliged to see.[113] Despite quite severe restorations, it far outdid similar statues in fame; the inscription on the base, attributing the work to one 'Cleomenes, son of Apollodorus', was correctly regarded as spurious, which allowed eighteenth-century commentators to claim that it was really by Phidias or Praxiteles. As late as 1840, Ruskin was describing it as 'one of the purest and most elevated incarnations of woman conceivable'. Its reputation may be said to have been the product of notions current in the early practice of art history, and it is art history that finally dismantled that reputation, modern analysis deeming it to be an Athenian or Roman copy of the first or second century BC derived from an original that was perhaps made at the time of Praxiteles.[114] By any standards, its decline has been dramatic: the work that Napoleon was so determined to carry off to the Louvre[115] is now described in Martin Robertson's *A History of Greek Art* (1975) as 'among the most charmless remnants of antiquity'[116] – although this is admittedly an extreme view.

There is no mention of the Venus in Lassels, presumably because it was still in Rome at the time he compiled his book, but it is recorded as being in the Uffizi for the first time in Robert de Cotte's *Le voyage d'Italie de Robert de Cotte* of 1689.[117] Maximilien Misson's *Nouveau Voyage d'Italie* is already ecstatic about '*cette incomparable*' statue, sentiments to be echoed for another 150 years. Misson also sets the tone that was to recur in travellers' comments, whereby the Venus is treated as a genteel form of soft porn: '*elle porte la main droite devant de son sein, mais à quelque distance; de l'autre main, si cuopre le parti onde la Donna arrossi, quando si scuoprano; ce qui elle fait sans y toucher non plus.*' Lalande also writes that she '*couvre d'une certaine distance ce que la pudeur ne permet pas de laisser voir*'.[118] Part of this description resurfaces seventy years later in John Northall's guide,[119] the author evidently having used Misson's text. Northall recycles Misson's Pygmalionesque conceit: '*il ne luy manque que la voix et le vermillon . . . et en un mot, ce rare chef d'oeuvre est une parfaite imitation de la plus belle nature*'. Northall, echoing the unisonant opinion of countless other observers, says it was the 'unanimous opinion of all judges' that the statue surpassed 'any piece of sculpture throughout the whole world'. Wright speaks of it being 'well known by the copies in England and all over Europe', and adds: 'To attempt a description of this miracle of sculpture would be to injure it: 'tis enough that it is the most beautiful part of the creation represented in the most exquisitely beautiful manner.'[120]

Hovering between expert opinion and sexual arousal (Pope Innocent XI had supposedly allowed the statue to leave Rome because of the 'lewd behaviour that she excited'), Misson unconsciously adumbrates the tension between the ideal form based on an idea and a desire for naturalistic effects. Winckelmann, writing half a century later, ingeniously resolves that tension by citing the example of Bernini, who was of the opinion that nature was 'capable of bestowing on all its parts the necessary amount of beauty, and that the skill of art consisted in finding it. He prided himself in having overcome his earlier prejudice concerning the charms of the Medicean Venus, since, after painstaking study, he had been able to perceive occasionally these very charms in nature.' Winckelmann continues:

> It was this [Medici] Venus therefore that taught him [Bernini] to discover beauties in nature which he had previously seen only in the statue and which, without the Venus, he would not have sought in nature. Does it not follow then that the beauty of Greek statues is easier to discover than beauty in nature and that thus the former is more inspiring, less diffuse and more harmoniously united than the latter?[121]

Many viewers of the *Medici Venus* might have been secretly inclined to think that Bernini had it right the first time and that Winckelmann's argument was merely perverse. However, the influence of the theoreticians was making itself felt and orthodoxy required a display of the requisite feeling. Even Gibbon, whose 'temper', by his own account, 'was not very susceptible to enthusiasm', tells us how he 'first acknowledged, at the feet of the Venus of Medicis, that the chisel may dispute the pre-eminence with the pencil, a truth in the fine arts which cannot on this side of the Alps be felt or understood'.[122] Richardson's Account of 1722 describes how he spent ten hours in the Uffizi, but kept returning to the Venus; likewise the Professor of Poetry at Oxford and bear-leader to Lord Middlesex, Joseph Spence, says he went to see the Venus one hundred times during his visit to Florence. Richardson of course gives a precise and critical description, including adverse comment on the statue's repairs and replacement parts, which seldom seemed to disturb other viewers, though both Wright and Nugent recycle the contemporary opinion that they are mostly the work of Bandinelli.[123] He adds that Sandraat claimed the Venus stood in the Pantheon, 'but quotes no authority'. Richardson is also the first, indeed the only, contemporary writer to state unequivocally that the greatest statues of antiquity lauded by Pausanias and Pliny could not have survived, because all the discovered statues had other names on them, usually those of copyists.[124]

Eduardus Wright, having repeated the cliché about the unique beauty of the Venus, is moved to write a Latin distich that he sent to a 'learned peer', together with some embarrassing lines in English:

> So just, so fine, so soft each part,
> Her beauties fire the lab'ring heart
> The gentle risings of the skin
> Seem push'd by muscles from within:
> The swelling breasts, with graces fill'd
> Seem easy to the touch to yield . . .

The latter responded with two lines that are reminiscent of the heroic bathos in Wordsworth's unintentionally hilarious salute to 'The Stuffed Owl':

> Charmed, we confess the Queen of Love
> And wonder she forgets to move.

Keysler gives one of the longest accounts (two pages) and helpfully summarises the views of connoisseurs (including Richardson), such a summary certainly being more useful than the dutiful eulogy generally on offer. A rare dissident is the dyspeptic Scots doctor and novelist Tobias Smollett. Not without irony, he remarks that 'it must be want of taste that prevents my feeling that enthusiastic admiration with which others are inspired at the sight of this statue'.[125] 'Smelfungus', as Laurence Sterne unkindly called him on account of his bilious attitude to all things foreign, nevertheless discourses quite knowledgeably about

the Venus and its provenance and mentions that some think it represents
Phryne, the Athenian courtesan who emerged naked from the bath before the
spectators at the Eleusinian games. Of this Sterne remarks in his *Sentimental
Journey* that 'Smelfungus' 'fell foul of the goddess and used her worse than a
common strumpet, without the least provocation in nature'.[126] The goddess was
not lightly mocked, nor was her image to be besmirched by ignoble associations.

By the nineteenth century doubts about the attribution of the Venus and
changes in taste were leading to more sober assessments.[127] Nevertheless, Byron's
rhapsody in *Childe Harold* (Canto IV, 1818) still reverts to Winckelmann, placing
the *idea* and *ideal* of beauty embodied by the statue above everything else:

> We stand, and in that form and face behold
> What mind can make, when Nature's self would fail . . .[128]

On another occasion, the poet characteristically observed that 'all dumpy women
should pray to [the *Medici Venus*] as they pass', a remark quoted by Lady Morgan in
her controversially liberal *Italy* (1821). She feels obliged to defend the goddess from
her critics (obviously growing in number), saying that the Venus has 'felt the breath
of revolutions' and is consequently now obliged to yield her position to a rival
beauty who is 'no goddess, still less saint, just an ordinary woman'.[129] The sublimity
of form transcending naturalism (and therefore vulgar eroticism) is dwelled upon
most eloquently of all by Joseph Forsyth in his guide compiled in 1802–3, despite
his general misconception about colour on ancient statues. His account of the
significance of the Venus is a model of conventional good taste:

> Sculpture admits no diversity of materials; it knows no colour, it knows
> nothing but shape. Its purpose is not to cheat the eye, but to present to the
> mind all the truth and beauty and grace and sublimity of forms. Did the
> excellence of the statue depend on the illusion produced or on the number
> of idiots who mistake it for life, the Medicean Venus would then yield to
> every waxwork that travels from fair to fair.[130]

On the other hand, the author of the first guidebook published by John
Murray, Mariana Starke, is rather down-to-earth and clear-eyed, offering a well-
informed description of the statue, and (like Lalande) quoting Pliny on the six
famous Venuses of antiquity. She is highly sceptical of the attribution to Praxiteles.
Lalande, for his part, although he says it is not possible to decide definitively
which of the Venuses mentioned by Pliny was closest to the *Medici Venus*, favours
the Aphrodite by Praxiteles that stood in the temple at Cnidus (Cnidos, Knidos)
in Carian Asia Minor[131] and was eulogised by Ovid. One suspects that Lalande
singles out this statue partly because of its famed erotic power. Praxiteles had in
fact made a clothed version of the same subject, which was bought by the people
of Cos. The Cnidians opted for the nude one, which Pliny tells us 'many people
have sailed to Cnidus to see'. Lalande quotes an anonymous Greek author who
comments that Venus herself wondered how Praxiteles got to see her naked, since

only thus could he have rendered her so perfectly: 'Paris, Anchises and Adonis saw me nude; I only know of these three: but Praxiteles, where has he seen me?'[132] This reference introduces the element of voyeurism that was to recur in accounts of the *Medici Venus*, for Pliny not only reports on Nicomedes IV of Bithnyia's avid desire to acquire the statue, but also relates a most notorious incident of indecency that has embarrassed Classicists and schoolmasters ever since: 'There is a story that a man who had fallen in love with the statue hid in the temple at night and embraced it intimately; a stain bears witness to his lust.'[133]

Another less than reverent commentator was Anna Brownell Jameson, an amateur art historian and follower of Ruskin. In her *Diary of an Ennuyée* (1826), she satirises the obsession with the statue affected by the writer Samuel Rogers, author of the massive, but leaden, poem entitled 'Italy' (1822–8). The besotted Rogers, she writes, 'may be seen every day about eleven or twelve in *La Tribuna*, seated opposite to the Venus, which appears to be the exclusive object of his adoration; and gazing, as if he hoped, like another Pygmalion, to animate the statue; or rather', she adds maliciously, 'perhaps that the statue might animate *him*'. She continues with an anecdote about a young English prankster who put some verses in the hand of the Venus, in which the goddess entreats Rogers not to come there ogling her every day, because she knew he had come from the other side of the Styx, though 'partial friends might deem him still alive'. Especially she entreated him to spare her 'the added misfortune of being berhymed by his muse'.[134]

And finally William Hazlitt, ever the awkward squad, makes a shrewd point when he writes that 'all the world have already formed an opinion [of the *Medici Venus*] for themselves; yet perhaps, this opinion, which seems the most universal, is the least so, and the opinion of all the world means that of no one individual in it'. He then hazards a conjecture ('for it is only a conjecture where familiarity has neutralised the capacity for judging') that 'there is [in the *Medici Venus*] a want of sentiment, of character, a balance of pretensions as well as of attitude, a good deal of insipidity, and an over-gentility'.[135] Hazlitt was of course a critic in the days when art critics were literary men, and it is ironic that his opinion, give or take a few emphases, is almost the same as that of the learned Martin Robertson 150 years later . . . The *Medici Venus* had fallen to earth, and thereafter many guidebooks began hedging their bets (one way of doing so was by stressing what the Venus had meant to *previous* generations of sightseers . . .).

THE LAST GASP OF THE GRAND TOUR GUIDEBOOK AND THE FIRST BOURGEOIS GUIDES: JOHN CHETWODE EUSTACE, MARIANA STARKE AND JOSEPH FORSYTH

The last guidebook that is obviously devoted to the Grand Tour was the Revd John Chetwode Eustace's four volumes entitled *A Classical Tour Through Italy*, first published in 1813 and in its seventh edition by 1841. Like the first standard work for the Grand Tour by Lassels, this was the work of a Catholic priest. However, Eustace's Catholicism was hardly militant, notwithstanding that he 'is said to have repented later of some of his more liberal expressions of opinion' (*Dictionary of National Biography*); rather the author takes pains to correct common misconceptions, for example, about the papacy, to which he devotes a lengthy appendix recounting its history and contemporary powers. His tour had been made in 1802, when Italy was under French occupation, and he seldom lets slip an opportunity to excoriate the French regime. A typical outburst is his ringing proclamation that 'as long as religion and literature and independence are objects of estimation among men, so long must revolutionary France be remembered with horror and detestation'. His Catholicism and hostility to republicanism attracted criticism, notably from Byron, who mocked Eustace mercilessly in a footnote to *Childe Harold*.[136] Shelley, an ardent Republican of course, wrote to his friend Peacock that he should 'consult Eustace if [he] wanted to know nothing about Italy'.[137] This and other attacks on Eustace's plodding style and general pomposity receive a spirited rebuttal in the Editor's Preface to the sixth edition (1821 – Eustace himself had died in 1815). In truth, some of the criticism was less than fair, accusing the author of failing to do what he never intended.

So what was it that Eustace intended? In his own Preface he writes that his book '[traced] the resemblance between Modern and Ancient Italy, and [took] for guides and companions in the beginning of the nineteenth century, the writers that preceded or adorned the first . . . It must be remembered that Modern history is not classical and can claim admission only as an illustration.'[138] His guide is almost a textbook, with its didactic reading list of ancient authors and musty commentaries on architecture, as well as an admonition that the prospective traveller should attend lectures on anatomy before departure, in order to be able to appreciate sculpture adequately. Unlike those guides and commentators of the seventeenth and eighteenth centuries who believed that British travellers had the most to learn, even from contemporary France and Italy, Eustace exhibits an imperialistic confidence that reflects the British Empire in the ascendant. Nevertheless, while he should not be blind to Britain's 'prosperity' and its 'pre-eminence', the traveller is counselled to 'shew some indulgence to the errors and some compassion for the sufferings of less favoured nations'. After all, as the ancients discovered, Britain too will one day decline, as did their great empires. In the same spirit he warns of religious intolerance, remarking of Madame de Staël's *Corinne, ou l' Italie* (1807), that the author 'though a Protestant . . . speaks of the dignity of Italy with reverence, and treats even superstition itself with indulgence'.

According to Eustace, a minimum of one year was required to complete his tour of Italy, preferably one and a half or two. He follows the Grand Tour's seasonal programme pretty closely (April, May and June in Rome; July and August in the cool of the Alban Hills; September in Tuscany, and the autumn divided amongst the cities of north Italy; December again in Rome; and January to March in Naples). The phrase 'A Classical Tour' in the title of Eustace's book does not in practice mean an exclusive focus on antiquity. Selected modern paintings and sculptures are featured, and many churches are visited, though the

The Pharos at Alexandria *(above) and the* Colossus of Rhodes *(below). Two copper etchings from original drawings of* The Wonders of the World *(1572) by Maarten van Heemsersck* (© Bettmann/Corbis)

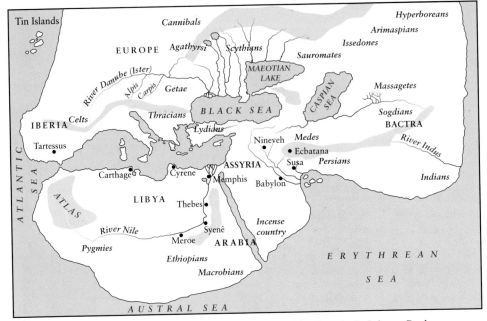

The oikoumene *or inhabited world according to Herodotus. Herodotus included non-Greeks ('barbarians') in his purview, but for many other Greek writers the* oikoumene *was the civilised world (i.e. inhabited or settled by Greeks.)*

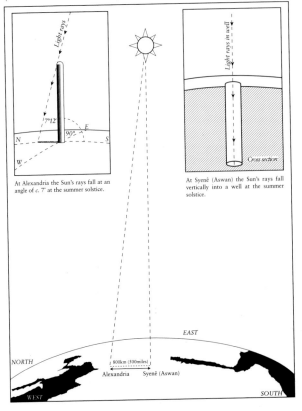

At Alexandria the Sun's rays fall at an angle of *c.* 7° at the summer solstice.

At Syenê (Aswan) the Sun's rays fall vertically into a well at the summer solstice.

Eratosthenes' measurement of the earth's circumference. At noon on the summer solstice the sun's rays fall vertically down a well shaft at Syenê (Aswan), while at the same date and hour they fall at an angle of 7° to the vertical at Alexandria. The known distance between the two cities of 5,000 stadia was thereby calculated by Eratosthenes to be one-fiftieth of a great circle, and from this he extrapolated the circumference of the earth (250,000 stadia.) Because we do not know the exact length of the Greek 'stadium' used by Eratosthenes (276–194 BC), it is not clear how far his final figure was adrift of reality; but his method was sound, and most of the inaccuracies could be ascribed to the imprecision of the measuring tools available to him.

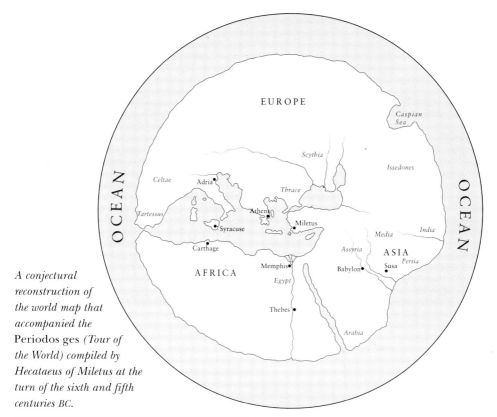

A conjectural
reconstruction of
the world map that
accompanied the
Periodos ges *(Tour of
the World) compiled by
Hecataeus of Miletus at the
turn of the sixth and fifth
centuries BC.*

A romantic depiction of The Raft of Odysseus. 'Homeric geography', based on the wanderings of
Odysseus as described by Homer, had a powerful hold over early Greek geographers and historians.
(bpk/Dietmar Katz)

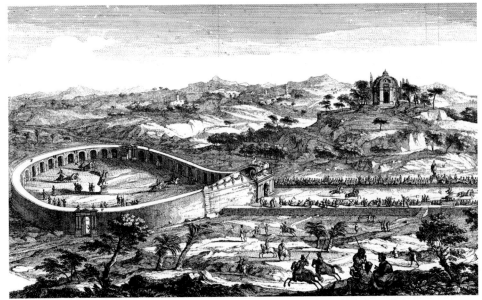

The Hippodrome at Olympia, *engraved by J. Rigaud for a French translation of Pausanias's* Guide to Greece *published in 1731.* (Bibliothèque nationale de France)

The Acropolis at Athens, *romantically evoked in a painting by Leo von Klenze (1846). Note Phidias' vast statue of Pallas Athene looming in the background, while the foreground shows St Paul preaching to the Athenians.* (Neue Pinakothek, Munich/akg-images)

The Madaba mosaic (sixth century AD), a Byzantine topography of the Holy Land. It was discovered in the late nineteenth century during the rebuilding of the Church of St George at Madaba on the Jordanian Plateau and forms part of the floor of an earlier church on the site. This is the earliest extant depiction of Jerusalem as it would have been after AD 70. (British Library, London/ Bridgeman Art Library)

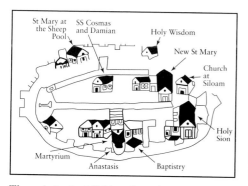
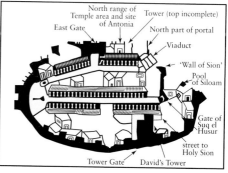

The ecclesiastical (left) and secular (right) buildings of Jerusalem extracted from the Madaba mosaic.

European pilgrimage routes to Santiago de Compostela.

Huelsen's reconstruction of the Einsiedeln *Itinerary for Rome (end of the eighth or early ninth century AD). The itinerary is named after the Swiss monastery where it was discovered in 1683. It may have been compiled by a monk from Fulda in Hesse, who visited Rome for the coronation of Charlemagne (Christmas Day, 800).*

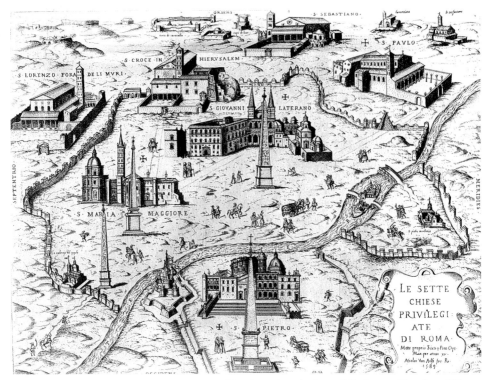

An engraving by the cartographer Antonio Lafréry featuring the Seven Pilgrimage Churches of Rome and made for the Holy Year of 1575. (akg-images)

John Bargrave, Alexander Chapman and John Raymond Studying a Map, *painted by Matteo Bolognini (Siena, 1647). The Royalist John Raymond compiled* Il Mercurio Italico *(1648), an early work aimed at Grand Tourists that combined a travel account with guidebook features.* (Reproduced with permission from the Dean and Chapter of Canterbury)

A statue of the celebrated (or notorious) 'Tribune of Rome', Cola di Rienzo (1313–54), whose intense local patriotism extended to amateur archaeology. He was particularly interested in inscriptions, later to be a staple of guidebooks for learned visitors, and spent many hours scraping monuments, long buried under dirt and weeds, to retrieve the obscured epitaph. (Tristan Lafranchis/akg-images)

Jean-Baptiste Chardin, The Antiquarian Ape *(1726). An obsessed antiquarian is depicted as an ape in a morning robe examining a coin with a magnifying glass. Antiquarians were regarded by some as pedants, or even lunatics, who became ridiculously excited over banal objects from the past.* (Musée du Louvre/Erich Lessing/akg-images)

THE VOYAGE
OF ITALY.

ITALIA

PRINTED·AT·PARIS·
Anno dñi. M.DC.LXX

The title page for the first mainstream guide for the Grand Tour, The Voyage of Italy *(1670) by Richard Lassels. The author was a Catholic priest involved in the politics and diplomacy of Royalist English Catholics on the Continent.* (© The British Library)

S.H. Grimm, The Returning Son *(1770). Young milords who returned with airs and affectations after a couple of years on the Grand Tour were the subject of mockery and satire, as in this caricature.* (British Library, London/Bridgeman Art Library)

Pier Leone Ghezzi, Dr James Hay as Bear-Leader *(1725). The generally thankless task of 'bear-leader' involved chaperoning frequently insolent sons of the aristocracy as they made the Grand Tour. A number of bear-leaders exploited their experiences by writing up travelogues and guidebooks for future Grand Tourists.* (© The British Museum/Heritage Image Partnership)

English tourists studying their Baedeker. (bpk)

'*An essential aid to travel: a good guidebook!*' (bpk)

'Doing' Cologne Cathedral *by Dicky Doyle.*
Doyle was a leading illustrator for Punch,
which often poked fun at literal-minded tourists
and their helplessness without their guidebooks.
(From *The Foreign Tour of Messr. Brown, Jones*
and Robinson (1854))

Cannibal chief, releasing victim: 'Why didn't
you say before you were from Cook's – I'm their
Local Agent.' Early postcard from the Thomas
Cook Archive. (The Thomas Cook Archive)

Sir Nikolaus Pevsner in 1973 with a huge pile of
all forty-six guides to the buildings of England
produced under his auspices. (Allen Lane
Archive/Frank Hermann)

John (later Sir John) Betjeman happily immersed
in an untidy heap of Shell Guide manuscripts.
(Photograph by John Murray)

coverage is usually confined to generalities. Nonetheless, classical allusions are what excites Eustace and little seems to have changed from Addison's *Travels*, where landscape had the function of prompting instances from the classics; one imagines the author, like Eduardus Wright, taking Virgil with him to Pozzuoli to read among the ruins. The real aim of his tour, Eustace says, is 'moral improvement' for the travellers, without which 'knowledge is the amusement of an idle moment . . . Nations, like individuals, have their characteristic qualities and present to the eye of the candid observer . . . much to be imitated, and something to be avoided.'[139] Then as now, many readers must have wandered the streets with their noses buried in a guidebook, in this case Eustace, largely detached from the bustle of contemporary Italian life. One recalls Horace Walpole's snide remark about Addison that he 'travell'd through the poets, and not through Italy; for all his ideas are borrowed from the descriptions, and not from reality'.

While this would be too harsh a judgement with which to dismiss Eustace's labours entirely, one does have the feeling that he often needs the white stick of past writings to guide the visual sense in the here and now. Not untypical is his extraordinary dismissal of the Medici villas in Tuscany (all of them!) as 'inspiring no great interest' and their gardens as displaying 'little or no pleasing scenery, no masses of shade, no expansions of water, no groves or thickets to delight the eye or amuse the fancy. All is art, stiff, minute and insignificant.' But then he recollects their historical associations and adds: 'Yet it is impossible to visit some of them without emotion . . . the retreats of the Medici and once the haunts of the Italian muses.'[140] In these and other passages Eustace exhibits the frustrated romanticism of hundreds of English schoolmasters and academics of his day who were well versed in the classics – epicene, learned and living vicariously with the great authors of antiquity. His tone of voice would have been very much to the taste of such people, which partly explains the success of his book, which, he says grandly, is addressed 'solely to persons of a liberal education'.

Nevertheless, Eustace's guide seems anachronistic, if only because the phenomenon that determined its premises, the Grand Tour, had all but died out as a result of the Napoleonic Wars. At the wars' conclusion, there was an explosion of guidebook activity that excluded France – travel books to Italy appeared at the rate of about nine a year throughout the post-war decade.[141] The wars had also opened new horizons for travellers who had had difficulty traversing the traditional routes because of the conflicts. Greece, made popular by Byron and the Philhellenes and soon to be liberated from the Turkish yoke, now attracted many who, like Winckelmann, would have found the prospect too daunting in the past. From the mid-eighteenth century, Greece had generated a travel literature of its own, though few of the works devoted to it at this early stage could truly be said to be guidebooks. A quasi-exception is Sir William Gell's archaeologically oriented *Itinerary of Greece, with a Commentary on Pausanias and Strabo and An Account of the Monuments of Antiquity at Present Existing in That Country; Compiled in the Years 1801–06* (London, 1810). At the same time, a new type of travel guide for Europe was incubating, one designed for the rising middle class. Two years before Eustace made his tour, Mariana Starke's *Letters from Italy* (1800) had appeared, the fruit of a six-year stay in the country between 1792 and 1798 in the company of her consumptive mother. The multilingual Starke wrote her guide in the now outdated form of letters, but John Murray saw the book's potential and a later edition appeared under his own imprint, the first guidebook from the firm that was to become famous for its 'Handbooks'. Certainly Starke's book continued a long tradition of works that concerned themselves with spas and 'health tourism', but it was much more than that, a cultural, practical and 'wellness' guide all in one.

In her 'Advertisement' Starke says her book is designed to obviate the need for travellers to buy multiple vade mecums to cover everything (post-books, museum guides, gallery catalogues) in the countries she deals with. Such purchases were indeed becoming onerous (for Paris she mentions separate catalogues for the picture galleries and Galignani as a general guide; for Florence, Molini on the gallery and Gargiolli on the city; and for Rome, Vasi's four-volume itinerary with Nibby's update, not to mention 'ten or twelve' guides to Naples and environs). Her thorough coverage of painting and sculpture, with the opinions of Winckelmann and other experts added, as well as her 'attempt to classify works of art as one would hotels'[142] by the use of exclamation marks, established her as the forerunner of the bourgeois-oriented products that were to make both Murray and Baedeker household names. Typically, she lists the vast improvement in facilities for travellers over the previous twenty years – even the introduction of street lamps in Italy, which (she claims) put a stop to 'the dreadful practice of assassination'.

Starke's guide is knowledgeable, vividly written and highly practical, at least in respect of Italy, which she knew well (in the second edition, she unwisely extended her coverage to countries such as Bohemia, which she knew only superficially). She is one of the first to offer the *Geheimtip*, the 'insider's knowledge' that guides now routinely claim to possess (for example, how to secure the best vantage points for viewing the Maundy Thursday ceremony in Rome). She was herself a vivid character of indeterminate sexuality, and known as 'Jack Starke' for the manly garb she affected of a tall hat and riding habit. Barwick notes that her list of things recommended for the traveller to take with him was 'appalling', including a sofabed, a saddle, 'opodeldoc' and Dr James's powder. In her *Travels on the Continent* (from 1824, *Information and Directions for Travellers on the Continent*), which was the John Murray version of her extremely popular work, a new wind can be felt blowing through the guidebook genre.[143] The book went through eight editions and was published also at Leghorn (Livorno) and Paris. The bourgeois tourists were on their way; in another twenty-five years or so, the masses were to follow.

A much more sophisticated book than Starke's, which also serves as a bridge between the material expected in a guide by the Grand Tourist and what the diligent middle-class traveller was coming to expect, was that by a Scotsman, Joseph Forsyth.[144] Of disasters that befell guidebook writers, Forsyth had more than his fair share. Taking advantage of the Peace of Amiens (1802) between

Britain and France, he set off on his Italian tour, but was caught up in the renewed outbreak of war as he hurried home from Turin in the following year. He was to spend the next eleven years in a French prison, passing the time amplifying his travel notes with a close study of Italian culture. His *Remarks on Antiquities, Arts and Letters during an Excursion in Italy* were actually published as an attempt to secure his release by demonstrating (to Napoleon) his disinterested love of the arts and general harmlessness. It failed in its object, notwithstanding that Stendhal (a great Napoleonist) claimed it was one of the best books on Italy ever. Sadly, prison broke its author (his travails had included a forced march in winter over 600 miles to a fortress in the Vosges mountains) and he died only a year after his release.

Forsyth's book extended the Italian tour to Sicily and the south, which had generally been ignored except for two late-eighteenth-century guides that had achieved some popularity.[145] He was at pains to contextualise his information, something which the previous jumbled compilations of sights and facts failed to do.[146] It was his aim to arrange his subject matter in a way that made sense of genre and chronology: 'We make the tour of Italy as we make the circuit of a gallery,' he wrote in his *Remarks*.[147] In fact this comment, suggesting lack of engagement with the native population, is misleading. Forsyth demonstrated an empathy with the host nation that had all too often been lacking in the earlier guidebooks, although Eustace had praised Italians and their culture chiefly as a way of insulting the French through frequent and unfavourable comparison. Mary Shelley amusingly describes Eustace as pretending that 'Italy was the garden of Eden and all the Italians Adams and Eves untill the Blasts of Hell (i.e. the French, for by that polite name he designates them) came.'[148] Forsyth was more rewarding than this: Byron said of him that he understood the *causes* of the Italians' 'misery and profligacy', which he rendered with 'truth and tact'.[149] As to his attitude towards religion, we have moved on from the Protestant/Catholic battles of the Grand Tour guides. As Keith Crook, his recent editor, points out, Forsyth assessed religion largely in aesthetic terms: 'Artistic integrity, rather than belief in the supernatural, guided [his] remarks on the clergy. In his customary manner, he discriminated in his judgements, recognising that the "catholic religion is surely a friend, but an interested friend to the fine arts," which cannot be said of "gloomy Presbyterians" who have pleasure in demolishing beauty (for itself) as well as for its being the focus of idolatry.'[150] Such an attitude already implies a sympathetic attitude, for example, to Baroque architecture, that was rare among British accounts of Italy, even before the calumnies of Ruskin.

Perhaps the most refreshing aspect of Forsyth is his generally tolerant stance and catholic tastes. Although a reviewers' war was waged between the most important cultural journals of the day, the Whig-leaning *Edinburgh Review* and the Tory *Quarterly*,[151] and Eustace and Forsyth were made to stand proxy for Whig and Tory outlooks, this was a rather artificial dispute. Ideologically speaking, it would have been just as plausible if the two reviews had adopted the opposition's protégé and opposed their own mascots. The chief interest of the quarrel lies in the fact that even guidebooks had now been harnessed to partisan politics, even if this seldom rose above crying up 'your man' and knocking down 'the opposition's man'. Forsyth was still a product of the measured and sceptical eighteenth century, who caused offence to one clerical commentator by commenting that the Vatican left the street lights dim in Rome in order to facilitate illicit liaisons in the evenings! But he was also a forward-looking sensitive scholar who had absorbed Winckelmann and was enthusiastic about *Sturm und Drang*, Schiller and Alfieri. He brought to his task, says his editor, 'accuracy and enlargement of views, and sophistication, without trying to parade these qualities'. This is indeed the ideal that almost any modern guidebook would now subscribe to. He could also appeal across the ideological divide between parties by his sympathy for Italian aspirations, which were soon to find expression in the Risorgimento. He was, in short, a modern democrat and a hater of oppression, a North Briton of the Enlightenment, the ideal man to take the broad view. He was also a realist, and unsentimental in his remarks about the disastrous waster 'Bonnie' Prince Charlie, who had died of drink in Rome in 1788, and whose main interest had become the prophecies of Nostradamus. Of the Prince's elder brother, Cardinal York, Forsyth merely says drily that he was a warm-hearted testy old man with little to tell: no sentimentality there.[152]

PART IV

The Bourgeois Traveller and the Beginnings of Mass Tourism

CHAPTER 8

Annexing the Tourist World: John Murray III and Murray's Handbooks

Murray's Guidebooks now cover nearly the whole continent and constitute one of the greatest powers of Europe. Since Napoleon no man's empire has been so wide.

(G.S. Hillard, Six Months in Italy, *1853)*

Baedeker is a guide and Murray a companion.
(W.A.B. Coolidge, author of Swiss Travel and Swiss Guide-Books, 1889)

Queen Victoria came to the throne in 1837, just a year after the firm of John Murray published what was to be the first of a celebrated series of guidebooks.[1] In the next few decades, large parts of the globe became steadily more apprehensible, the experience of them more attainable, for Britain's growing middle class. Imagined terrains yielded to the new dispensation of time and motion, while areas once defined by the interests of wandering scholars and explorers acquired alternative identities in response to the exigencies of tourism. Information travelled faster, people likewise, and there was suddenly a far greater circulation both of the written word and of travellers. Steam, that great engine of democratisation, eventually put destinations undreamed of within the reach of persons who had travelled but little in their own country, let alone in foreign ones;[2] cheap printing, that other great agent of democratisation, inspired readers to embark on journeys to see in person what they had formerly seen only in pictures, if at all, and supplied them with the information they needed to take on the journey. Perhaps the single most remarkable aspect of this transformation was its rapidity. The leisurely and aristocratic convention of the Grand Tour had had its roots in the Renaissance and enjoyed a late boom in the wake of the Napoleonic wars, not least because the 'horrid' Bonaparte had greatly improved the roads in the meanwhile; the middle class educational journey, for which the Handbooks of Murray and Baedeker were to cater, was a phenomenon that expanded within twelve years of their first guides being published to encompass the lower middle class and eventually the working class. Such a radical paradigmatic shift was naturally reflected in the guidebooks themselves: as Robert Gildea has noted, 'the broad middle class which carried so much weight in mid-nineteenth-century Europe was educated but not cultivated. It was greedy for knowledge rather than meaning and consumed culture as it consumed material goods, rather than using it as a means of self-perfection.'[3]

Like all generalisations, this one should immediately be qualified. For a start, it was the definition of self-improvement that had changed, rather than the aim itself. To be well travelled was to be well informed; and to be well informed was both a necessity and a sign of moral worth for the aspirant man of the world. Even leisure activities had to be pursued with a recognisable aim, especially if you were a product of the Weberian Protestant ethos of northern Europe; as Gildea himself says: 'Aristocratic leisure was associated with idleness, and although the middle class had time on its hands, it was God's time and could not be frittered away uselessly.'[4] True, the working class did not have 'time on its hands' at first, but in the second half of the century, it too began to acquire leisure time through Acts of Parliament that limited working hours and entrenched basic holiday rights in law. The zeal with which knowledge and cultural education were pursued lower down the social scale could only increase as new horizons and opportunities opened up. By the end of the century Thomas Cook & Son were catering to institutions like the Toynbee Traveller's Club, an offshoot of the workers's education centre at Toynbee Hall, and the non-profit Cooperative Holidays Association. Their extremely focused members, writes J.A.R. Pimlott, 'like the Grand Tourists before them, saw [foreign travel] as a means of self-improvement . . . Middle-aged ladies who on winter evenings sat at the feet of the Christian Socialist lecturers might be found exploring the Louvre at the heels of a guide, and serious-minded young clerks from the Working Men's College might be seen in their summer vacations at the end of a rope on a Swiss glacier.'[5] (The Alpine Club was in fact formed in 1858, its founders evidently unfazed by an observation in Murray's Handbook of 1852 drawing attention to the 'remarkable fact' that a large proportion of those who had so far ascended Mont Blanc had been persons of unsound mind.)

The experience of travel was challenging, involving energy, expense and some planning; from the start of organised tourism, however, it also represented a diminution of individuality, a degree of submergence in the group, and hence the tendency to authenticate the experience with a stock response as proof of participation. Trivial or absurd information, clichés or stale anecdotes, soon begin to loom large, simply because they are easy to appropriate and recycle. This in turn gives rise to ironic observation on the part of other travellers, who are at pains to disassociate themselves from mere tourists. Remarks by Theodor Fontane in his *Modernes Reisen* concerning a typical tourist outing to a German country house could stand for many such sarcastic references: 'On a visit to Schloss Reinhardsbrunn, members of a small town rifle club are suitably over-awed to learn that Archduke Ernst killed 50,157 head of game over twenty-five years; they write down the imposing figure in their notebooks and gleefully anticipate those future moments when they will have leisure to calculate how many head per day that works out as.'[6]

The people who indulged in the new mobility engendered a whole new terminology, so familiar to us now that we forget its comparatively recent coinage. Reichard's popular *Guide des Voyageurs en Europe* (Vienna, 1793) is one of the first books to feature the word *Tourist* in its original German version (1784). According to Daniel J. Boorstin, the word was originally spelled with a hyphen (*tour-ist*) and its stem, 'tour', was derived from Latin *tornus*, itself descended from the Greek word for a tool describing a circle.[7] The *Oxford English Dictionary* traces the word 'guide' as used for a book, to 1759, while 'guidebook' apparently exists only from 1823, when it appears in Byron's *Don Juan*. 'Sight-seeing' appears a few years later, first recorded in 1847, and 'attraction', used in the sense of a thing that draws the curious, dates from about 1862. In Britain the word 'tourist' seems to have appeared in the late eighteenth century, while 'tourism' is current at least from 1811, neither word originally having the pejorative implications they soon acquired.[8] The great agronomist Arthur Young, whose books on farming in England and on the Continent were hugely influential, was splendidly known as an 'agricultural tourist', although his disparagers were soon referring even to him as a 'mere tourist'. Young also attracted a barrage from a rival travel writer, one Adam Walker, in a book about the Lake District. Walker's complaints already reveal the ambivalence about tourism and its corrupting influence, real or imagined, that continues up to the present; he claimed that Young, whom he rudely called a 'rattling tourist', had blurred and destroyed the local character of places, exciting 'envy and false ideas of happiness among the peaceful inhabitants'.[9]

The years between 1830 and 1870, says Giles Barber in a perceptive lecture on guidebooks, represent the 'high watermark of English tourism', as of 'imperialism through tourism', when Switzerland became the 'playground of Europe', when the British were able to claim that they had invented skiing in the Alps, and when so many '*promenades*' or '*cascades*' in French-speaking countries suddenly became '*des Anglais*' and hotels became '*de Londres*' or '*de l'Angleterre*'.[10] Even Budapest, where British travellers were sighted comparatively rarely, but where Anglophilia, even Anglomania, was a feature of the early and mid-nineteenth century, boasted its own *Szálloda az angol királynőhöz* (Hotel of the English Queen), in which Ferenc Deák, the architect of the 1867 compromise with Austria, kept a permanent suite. The surge of English travellers to the

Continent dismayed long-time English residents abroad as well as self-appointed moralists; many and mournful are the laments from writers as varied as Ruskin, Thackeray or Charles Lever concerning the ubiquitous Brits with their philistine, gregarious behaviour. A good deal of this is pure snobbbery and there were even novels poking fun at the petit bourgeois along the lines of *The Diary of a Nobody*, but somewhat less amusingly. Arthur Sketchley created a character called Mrs Brown, whose social station and foreigner-resistant attitudes are rather ponderously mocked, as in the following: 'When you're in Rome do as the Romans does, as the sayin' is, and so I went all over the place with the rest of the Hinglish.'[11]

JOHN MURRAY: THE SHREWD INNOVATOR

The first publisher fully to appreciate the need for comprehensive and practical guidebooks to cater for the burgeoning market was the distinguished firm of John Murray, founded in 1768. Uniquely, the firm survived as a family business for 234 years until its sale in 2002, having long been one of the last Mohicans of family-run publishing in Britain.[12] During that time it engendered (in so far as such a thing is possible with a publishing imprint) a remarkable 'brand loyalty', not only among authors[13] but also among a particular layer of readers. Such readers especially valued Murrays' always strong and gracefully written list of travel books, a line the business had cultivated almost from its inception. The last (and seventh) John Murray to head the firm before its sale evidently realised that such an avuncular institution, struggling with the marketing costs of much larger firms but lacking their capitalisation, could no longer compete in today's world of corporate feeding frenzies. Even then, the famous Murray shrewdness seems to have paid off with a sale price thought to have been well above the firm's nominal asset value of eight million pounds. Murray was famously Byron's publisher (in his Albemarle Street office the poet's memoirs were burned in 1824), and the firm's shrewd open-mindedness over the years meant that it published authors as diverse as Jane Austen, Gladstone, Livingstone, Samuel Smiles and Charles Darwin (ignoring the professional reader's swingeing rejection of *The Origin of the Species*).[14] Travelogues and travel information have featured consistently in their list – even Byron's *Childe Harold's Pilgrimage* of 1812–17 can be seen as a sort of travelogue: 'Canto IV of *Childe Harold's Pilgrimage*', says Bruce Redford, 'smells not of the lamp but of the guidebook . . . [Byron] has dropped the mask of the pilgrim to tell his own story, the story of a journey from Venice to Rome.'[15] However, the volume most nearly prefiguring their famous series of guides was the previously mentioned Mariana Starke's *Travels on the Continent* (1820). That was followed by her more comprehensive and hugely successful *Information and Directions for Travellers on the Continent of Europe*, which had reached its eighth much enlarged edition by 1832.[16]

John Murray himself was to publish modified posthumous editions of the guide by Starke, a determined and somewhat butch lady, who died in harness at Milan in 1838. It is clear from her text that her audience no longer consisted of aristocrats and connoisseurs, but rather the practical middle class traveller for whom time was money. The very title, *Information and Directions*, is a true reflection of the book's content, with its routes taken from sources such as the post-books published by the French government (and mostly tested by the author herself), and its tips on climate, hygiene, transport, sharp practices by tradesmen and innkeepers, and food. Since her first seven-year stay in Italy had been spent looking after a consumptive relative, Starke is particularly informative on health matters and cheap accommodation; for example, she notes in passing the increase in furnished lodgings in Italy 'owing in some measure to the poverty of nobles, who often let their palaces to foreigners'.[17]

Last but not least, Starke standardised the practice of grading sights, buildings and artworks with exclamation marks, a device (altered to stars) which was to become one of the hallmarks of robustly didactic future guidebooks for the bourgeoisie from Murray and Baedeker in the nineteenth century to Betjeman in the twentieth.[18] This spoon-feeding seemed to justify the most violent prejudices held against guidebooks by those who considered themselves sufficiently cultivated to make their own judgements. 'If there is one thing more hateful than another, it is being told what to admire and having objects pointed out to one with a stick', Francis Kilvert was to harrumph in his Diary (1870–9), adding: 'Of all noxious animals, the most noxious is a tourist; and of all tourists, the most vulgar, ill-bred, offensive and loathsome is the British tourist. No wonder dogs fly at them.' Some half a century later, Aldous Huxley also lambasts the guidebooks in *Along the Road* (1925); however, his argument is subtly different from that of Kilvert: where the former assumes that the consumer of guides is a dreadful philistine and ignoramus who should not be cluttering up the Continent in the first place, Huxley characterises the guides themselves as both useless and (paradoxically) necessary to the traveller; moreover, the latter is here not patronised as the dreaded 'tourist', but assumed to be an autonomous and sentient individual. Huxley asserts that the only useful guidebook 'will be the one [the traveller] has written himself. All the others are an exasperation. They mark with asterisks the works of art which he finds dull and they pass over in silence those which he admires. They make him travel long miles to see a mound of rubbish, they go into ecstasies over mere antiquity. Their practical information is invariably out of date' – and so on. Of Baedeker he complains, not entirely fairly, that he 'has a way of lumping all old things of one class together and treating them as if, being made in the same period, their merit were exactly equal'. Yet Baedeker is nonetheless an 'indispensable imbecile; only after having scrupulously done what Baedeker commands, after having discovered [his] lapses in taste, his artistic prejudices and antiquarian snobberies, [can] the tourist . . . compile that personal guide which is the only guide for him'.[19]

Guidebook writers are probably resigned to brickbats that have been inspired by anything from social and intellectual snobbery to ideological distaste, as also to the fact that many who patronise and denigrate guidebooks in public privately plunder them for information and assistance. But how do the great names in the genre emerge in retrospect – the John Murrays, Baedekers and Joannes who epitomised the cultural preoccupations of an age, and were to some extent also national icons? Chronologically the first book to appear of these famous series was the *Handbook for Travellers on the Continent*, which covered Holland, Belgium,

Prussia and North Germany, with an itinerary along the Rhine to Switzerland. It was written by its publisher, John Murray III (1808–92), who had set out in 1829 to complete his education by travelling on the Continent, and landed at Rotterdam 'unprovided with any guide excepting a few manuscript notes about towns and inns' supplied by a friend. He at once perceived the need for a new type of guide, but like all competent publishers made careful comparisons with any competition worth the name. Starke, which anyway dealt primarily with Italy,[20] we have already mentioned, but there were two other works of some distinction that he describes as relevant to his itinerary, Boyce (for Belgium)[21] and Ebel (for Switzerland).[22]

Ebel's distinguished work put Switzerland on the map for learned tourism. Like Murray, he set out to remedy the defects of existing guides; his itineraries were likewise made up from personal experience, and he had a specific audience in mind for the book, which included 'philosophers, geologists, mineralogists, botanists, doctors and landscape painters'. Boyce's work, which is actually about the whole of the Netherlands, 'Belgium' being under the rule of the House of Orange when he wrote it, is sententious and patriotic. He is at pains to tell us that his work is by no means intended to encourage emigrants, since, excepting in respect of the 'cheap provisions' available in Brussels, 'he is too much an Englishman not to feel that . . . no country can vie with his own native land'. As in Murray's Handbooks, religious tolerance (of which the Netherlands, with its Protestant king and a large Catholic population, represented an estimable example) is applauded. However, the tone is discursive and his opinions openly subjective, while the aesthetic analysis is threadbare (churches are described as 'venerable structures' and their interiors are said to be 'composed entirely of marble'). Generally he is more interested in social matters, particularly brothels, the workhouse and the mercenary character of the Dutch.

It has already been mentioned that Murray's first Handbook (his father, John Murray II, was its nomenclator, no doubt borrowing it from the existing German terminology) appeared in 1836; he went on to write one more volume entirely by himself (*South Germany*, 1837), and two more with collaborators (*Switzerland*, 1838 and *France*, which excluded Paris, 1843). His collaborator on *Switzerland* was William Brockedon, a well-known illustrator specialising in Alpine road-books with picturesque engravings; it proved to be one of the most successful Handbooks, selling 26,000 copies in seven editions. A *Punch* parody of 1859 testified to its success: 'Once I could scarce walk up The Strand / What Jungfrau now could us withstand, / When we are walking hand in hand, / My Murray.'

Murray gave some twenty-six editions of these three guides his personal imprimatur, besides working on two editions of *Scotland* (1873 and 1875). However, on the death of his father in the year of publication of *France*, he was obliged to give up the compilation of new country guides, which involved him in lengthy absences for travel, and settled into the base at 50 Albemarle Street, which had been acquired in 1812, to direct the firm on a day to day basis. He was extremely and rightly proud of the Handbooks he had written, which reflected, he said, his 'tastes, studies and predilections' and the 'results of [his] private reading'.[23] Later volumes in the series did produce a few authorial wild cards such as Richard Ford, but the effect of the multi-authorial collaboration that took place on many of the subsequent Handbooks tended to produce what James Buzard calls 'a levelling of style and tone, Murray's "tastes and predilections" now sinking beneath the placid surface of guidebook prose'.[24] On the other hand, the air of apodictic good sense and authoritative information in a 'Murray' may ultimately be seen as a literary mask like any other, an 'objectivity' that is often based on largely unquestioned and unspoken cultural assumptions. And as Buzard also implies, the continuing and highly personal involvement of the eponymous publishers as editors in chief for most of the guides meant that the sort of 'corporate identity' achieved by Baedeker, which has enabled it to survive up to the present day, ultimately eluded the Murrays. At the turn of the twentieth century, diminishing returns impelled them to to sell out the series to Stanford.

Near the end of his life the publisher reflected on the genesis of the Handbooks in an article in *Murray's Magazine* (1889). A backhanded compliment to Miss Starke may be seen as an indirect reference to the systemisation of knowledge that was the Handbooks' claim to innovation: 'Hers was a work of real utility, because, amidst a singular medley of classical lore, borrowed from Lemprière's Dictionary, interwoven with details regulating the charges in washing-bills at Sorrento and Naples, and an elaborate theory on the origin of Devonshire Cream, in which she proves it was brought by Phoenician colonists from Asia Minor into the West of England, it contained much practical information gathered on the spot.'[25] This, however, was a relatively gentlemanly view penned in retrospect: in 1831 he had written to his father from Munich: 'I am very sorry to find that Mrs Starke has been so precipitate in reprinting her book. The errors in the German part of it are innumerable . . . the latest edition . . . is perfectly detestable – errors in almost every line.'[26] Murray himself, as we learn from Samuel Smiles's *Memoir*, specifically set out to avoid the 'inflated language' of local guidebooks, which indiscriminately heaped up information; rather than 'bewildering [his] readers by describing all that *might* be seen', he aimed to 'point out things peculiar to this spot, or which might be better seen there than elsewhere', and all this in 'the most condensed and simplest style' of description. He then road-tested his routes by having the material roughly set in type and giving the itineraries to friends who would be travelling along them, subsequently incorporating their amendments and taking note of their criticisms. Finally, he did not publish the first guide until he himself had made successive journeys and stayed for extended periods in continental cities, as well as exploring the interstices between his routes and 'various districts into which [his] countrymen had not yet penetrated'.

In short, Murray's work was a labour of love. His letters home during his travels for research give an insight into the privations guidebook writers are, or were, expected to take in their stride: cholera scares in Austria and Bavaria, being turned out of coaches on some windy nowhere in the middle of the night, the hours spent dozing on benches in dingy inns while waiting for transport, scrambles up mountains or down into caves for sights claimed by the locals to be earth-shaking, but which turn out to be a waste of valuable travelling time, highwaymen and robbers in Spain, even a terrifying precipice in the Pyrenees, the ascent of which was flatly refused by his companion, but [Murray's] 'desire to benefit the readers of my Handbook (should there be any readers) prevailed'.[27] And if precipices were terrifying, wardens and caretakers were frequently rebarbative or recalcitrant, the local guides vague, inconsistent or even untruthful.

THE MURRAY HANDBOOKS: AVUNCULAR COMPANIONS

The endurance of all these travails resulted in a new systemisation of knowledge for the traveller with an enquiring mind. The prefatory matter, which might be between thirty and fifty pages, supplied a good deal of practical information (tables of conversion for money, distances, weights and measures, notes on modes of transport and accommodation, observations on topography, scenery and routes, as well as concise analysis of modern administrative districts in historical context and a chronological table of rulers). All such may be found in the introductory information of, for example, the fourteenth edition (1877) of Murray's *Handbook for Travellers in France*, updated to take account of, *inter alia*, the great railway expansion that had occurred since Murray himself had written the first version some thirty-five years earlier. This, however, was the minimum that might be expected of a Handbook – others (particularly after John Murray IV took over) have substantial or extended essays on such matters as government, constitution and administration, the armed forces, religion, commerce and industry, agriculture, architecture, the arts and the ethnic origins of the inhabitants. A list of recommended reading is appended, but 'only such works [are mentioned, for example, in the *Handbook to Central Italy*] 'as may be useful for reference, or in perpetuating the memory of those scenes which frequently survive all other recollections of the journey'.

The topics mentioned above are concisely featured in the *Handbook for Travellers in Central Italy including the Papal States, Rome and the Cities of Etruria*, first published in 1843. By 1899 the spin-off volume dealing only with Rome and the Campagna has hugely expanded the background material, and now has three parts: a Directory, an Introduction and Routes. The Directory (38 pages) is the 'practical information' of today's guides, but includes some intriguing items such as cab fares (prices for an open or closed cab or one with two horses), where to obtain firewood (outside the Porta del Popolo), and where to go fox hunting (in a lengthy entry we are assured that the hunt boasts 'an experienced English huntsman and whip and a stable of English hunters'). It concludes with tabular itinerary divided into mornings and evenings and a list of opening times and charges. The headings of its introduction (pages 39–126, closely printed in double columns), could themselves be the chapter titles of a small book: we begin with an extensive historical topography (including a plan of the walls of Rome) and move on to the churches of medieval and modern Rome and the catacombs; then come learned societies and academies, geology, fortifications and rides in the Campagna; then the history of Rome, the description of a papal election, architecture, sculpture, painting, chronological tables of emperors, of famous men of antiquity, of bishops and popes, and of kings of United Italy; there follows a listing of theological colleges, together with the names of religious orders and the dates of local saints, then the dates of architects, sculptors and painters active in the city, followed by a glossary of technical terms, the coats of arms of famous popes and nobles, and finally a list of routes with their principal sights.

All this, before we have even reached the guide itself! It is solid stuff, reflecting perhaps the leisure time available to those who would read it, but also the perceived need to spend that time industriously improving one's cultural awareness and increasing one's knowledge. Significantly, there is hardly anything on cuisine, although some indignation is directed at Roman hoteliers and restauranteurs for failing to offer the much cheaper local wines from Frascati, thus forcing the traveller to consume expensive wine from abroad or other Italian regions. The text is formulated in a way that assumes an intelligent, averagely cultivated, but not very knowledgeable reader. It definitely also assumes a user who will be in Rome for a protracted stay – a month at least would be needed to to digest the background information and cover about half the sightseeing offered. Some people may even have died before they had thoroughly digested their Murray; at any rate, 'the friends or relatives of travellers who stayed so long they never made the journey home are warned indignantly by [the Handbook] of the "tourist prices" demanded for Protestant burials' in the Holy City.[28]

It is this combination of inventory and description, narrative and reference, but also ultimately of fact and (supposedly objective) opinion, that characterises the classic bourgeois vade mecums of Murray and Baedeker. The Handbooks were just that, wittily combining the German concept of *Handbuch* (manual or reference work) with the notion that the books were designed to be held in the hand as one went round the sights (the little red volumes, closely printed in double columns, measured only seven by four and five eighths inches).[29] But they were also cultural artefacts that carried within their burnt sienna covers a British identity, the comforting white stick amid the potentially confusing shadows of otherness, an authoritative reassuring voice among the babble of foreign tongues, the expression (usually) of a tolerant measured *Weltanschauung* that was even-handed (if a shade patronising) in its treatment of potentially contentious issues. 'The Englishman', wrote a reviewer in *The Times*, 'trusts to his MURRAY as he would trust to his razor, because it is thoroughly English and reliable; and for his history, hotels, exchanges, scenery, for the clue to his route and his comfort by the way, the RED HANDBOOK is his "guide, philosopher, and friend".'

It was important that this 'guide, philosopher, and friend' should not only be, but be seen to be, a sea-green incorruptible. G.S. Hillard, quoted at the head of this chapter, said that eventually 'from St Petersburg to Seville, from Ostend to Constantinople, there [was] not an inn-keeper who [did] not turn pale at the name of Murray'. In later volumes notices appear facing the title page inviting corrections to the text from the travelling public, followed by the magisterial observation: 'No attention can be paid to letters from innkeepers in praise of their own houses.'

There follows a warning to travellers not to import copies of English works pirated by continental printers ('even a single copy is contraband, and is liable to seizure at the English Custom-house').[30] This is followed by a paragraph describing how

> a person or persons have been extorting money from innkeepers, tradespeople, artists and others . . . on the pretext of procuring recommendations . . . in the Handbooks for Travellers. The Editor, therefore, thinks it proper to warn all whom it may concern, that *recommendations in the Handbooks are not to be obtained by payment*, and that the persons alluded to are not only unauthorised by him, but are little better than swindlers.[31]

We do not know whether these swindlers were locals or unscrupulous Englishmen, but the conviction that hordes of continentals (later Arabs, Indians and others) were lining up to cheat the honest British traveller as soon as he stepped ashore certainly does lurk behind much of Murray's prose. The anglocentric outlook of the guides, though tempered with the spirit of the Scottish Enlightenment of which the Murray dynasty was originally a product,[32] may well account for the fact that, unlike Baedeker, they did not greatly lend themselves to translation. John Gretton remarks that 'Murray's French translations were confined to a few foreign piracies in the 1840s',[33] but it appears that there were also some German ones put out at the time when Baedeker opted for outright competition with Murray, thus ending the friendly collaboration of hitherto.[34] The paucity of translations is perhaps not so surprising when one reads some of Murray's strictures on the behaviour of foreign officials, often compared unfavourably with British good sense. In France, he warns his readers, the gendarmes may demand to see your passport not just at the frontier, but in fortified towns, remote villages or on the road. They may 'force themselves into the salle à manger or enter your bedroom to demand sight of this precious document'. And he adds resignedly: 'It is needless to expatiate on this restraint' (having just done so for a whole paragraph!) 'so inconsistent with the freedom which an Englishman enjoys at home, or to show that the police are a pest to the harmless and well-conducted without being a terror to evil-doers; it is the custom of the country, and the stranger must conform, or he has no business to set foot in it. It must be allowed that the police perform their duty with civility, so as to render it as little vexatious as possible.'[35]

FOREIGNERS AND THEIR WAYS

This is quintessential Murray, somewhat inconsistently coupling a highly ironic characterisation of otiose foreign officialdom with a world-weary application of his own injunction to his readers elsewhere, namely that they should leave their prejudices at home – especially 'the idea of the amazing superiority of England, above all other countries, in all respects'.[36] Under serious provocation, however, this genial acceptance of *andere Länder, andere Sitten* is found to have its limits, for instance when discussing (in the *Handbook to South Germany*) the inadequate washing facilities of the inns and the general filth that 'proclaim the nature of German habits . . . and show how easily the desire for ablution is satisfied' in the region. He further expresses the hope that 'increased intercourse with the English will introduce a taste for cleanliness and a greater appreciation of it'. This is quite rich in view of what travellers could expect from the average English inn at the time. Cleanliness and hygiene are indeed something of a leitmotif in contemporary guidebooks, but in fairness one should emphasise that Murray is here comparing the backwardness of southern Germany with the north and the Rhineland, whose excellent hotels he praises. It is perhaps a little too easy to pick out passages that would seem to contradict his laudable aspiration to dispute the 'amazing superiority of England', since one can also point to passages that fulfil it. Besides which, many of the guides published elsewhere in Europe during the long, imperialist nineteenth century share, to a greater or lesser extent, an underlying assumption of the superiority of Western European civilisation when advising their readers on travel in the Near and Far East. As Lynne Withey points out, Murray's view of the Arabs as child-like, but controllable with a firm display of stiff upper lip, reflected the general attitude. 'The robbers of Syria are generally amateurs,' notes the *Handbook for Tavellers in Syria and Palestine*, and the traveller will find that 'by cool self-possession and a determined manner [he] can generally overawe them'.[37]

On the other hand, considering that they were produced in the age of nationalism, the serious nineteenth-century guidebooks preserve much of the spirit of impartial scientific enquiry that was part and parcel of patriotic endeavour to 'improve' the homeland pursued by men like Count Berchtold in the period of the Enlightenment. Man is said to be the only creature capable of standing outside himself sufficiently to examine and analyse the instincts that intuitively guide his behaviour; by the same token, the individual profits from taking the trouble to look at his own race, nation or culture from the viewpoint of others. Murray and many of the later Handbook writers are ambivalent in this respect: 'political correctness' in the modern sense was unknown to them, which often allows for more candour and less mealy-mouthed evasion of unpalatable facts than may be present in many (but not all) modern guidebooks; as against that, there is a risk that the nineteenth-century form of the guidebook, with its innate claim to authority, may tempt the writer into apodictic generalisations that are, to say the least, questionable. Thomas Denman Whatley, for example, writes of the Russian serf that he is 'happy and contented . . . naturally gay, good-humoured and light-hearted', an idyllic picture that doubtless seemed appropriate and consoling to a pompous conservative barrister such as the author. True, his *Handbook to Northern Europe* had to get past the Russian censor, but this seems to be overdoing it somewhat.

The Murray Handbooks, like the guides of Thomas Cook later, are generally written from a Low Church standpoint, yet are at pains to instruct their readers to show respect for differing faiths, including non-Christian ones. Indeed, Christianity itself is not spared when the author believes that certain practices, however popular locally, bring it into disrepute. The 1868 edition of the *Handbook for Travellers in Syria and Palestine* is fiercely critical of the 'Holy Fire' at the church of the Holy Sepulchre in Jerusalem, supposedly a miraculous flame descending from heaven on Easter eve and kindling all the lamps and candles in the sepulchre. The Greek patriarch or his representative alone entered the tomb, but the assembled multitude witnessed the presence of the fire through a hole in the northern wall. Murray does not mince his words: 'The imposture of the Holy Fire is unquestionably one of the most degrading rites performed within the walls of Jerusalem. It is not too much to say that it brings disgrace on the Christian name. It makes our boasted Christian enlightenment a subject of scorn and contempt to both Jews and Mohammedans.' And there is more in the same vein. The objection is primarily to 'fraud' and 'superstition', a traditional Low Church suspicion of wonders and the like, but also to the degradation of religion into a sort of tourist spectacle for pilgrims.[38] These strictures are perhaps sharper than is usual in Murray, and it is not altogether surprising to find that the author of the Handbook concerned was the Revd Josias Leslie Porter, a Presbyterian Minister who had been sent by his church as a missionary to the Jews in Damascus in in 1849.

The most outspoken of Murray's authors was Richard Ford (1796–1858), whose *Spain* appeared in 1845. This was a bowdlerised version of the original work, 768 printed pages of which had to be pulped after the publisher's reader became alarmed by the author's unrestrained comments, *inter alia*, on the Catholic Church in Spain (he was a close friend of the colourful George Borrow, author of *The Bible in Spain*, and Borrow was also consulted on the Handbook). Even so, the supposedly sanitised book was the subject of a diatribe in the *Athenaeum* (30 August 1845). The reviewer is enraged by Ford's 'sneers at the Roman Catholic religion', his 'hatred of everything French', his 'sarcasms against men . . . who are not of the same political, religious and literary creed as the author', his 'ebullitions of party feeling and of personal dislike in regard to Englishmen at home – and [his] inexhaustible self-conceit'. If this was a fair characterisation, the text stood condemned as everything a modern guidebook should not be; yet, after some withering exposure of its historical inaccuracies, the *Athenaeum*'s scribe inexplicably concludes that the 'defects [he has] indicated do not affect the main features' of this handbook, namely 'its value as as a guide for the tourist – its value as a work of reference for home dwellers. That value is very great and renders the book absolutely indispensable.'[39] While posterity has vindicated the last judgement – Ford's book is probably the best known of the Murray guides and the author had an even greater success with *Gatherings from Spain* (1846), which contained much of what had been deleted from the first draft of the handbook – the reviewer's strictures may serve to remind us that different volumes in the same series exhibited widely differing degrees of outspokenness. Though a dispirited Ford complained that he had thrown 'pearly articles into the trough of a road-book', the public recognised the freshness and depth of information in his book. Evidently unfazed by the swingeing invective that upset the anonymous critic of the *Athenaeum* (or perhaps because of it), tourists and armchair travellers rushed to buy 1,389 copies in the first three months of publication – a very good sale for such an expensive work (30 shillings) at the time.

MURRAY'S AUDIENCE

The cover prices of the Handbooks do indeed imply a well-to-do readership: it has been pointed out that the average price of the guides equalled an agricultural labourer's weekly wage in the mid-nineteenth century. Of course, the series on Britain (initiated in 1849 with a book on London) was cheaper to research; covering comparatively small regions (usually two or three coterminous counties treated together), their prices at the turn of the century ranged from 6 shillings for *Cornwall* to 12 shillings for *The Eastern Counties*, while titles in the foreign series might be nearly double the price (*India* cost 12 shillings and Ford's very expensive *Spain* has already been mentioned). Murray did try to go 'downmarket' with a cheaper series of short 'Knapsack Guides' for ramblers, but they failed to establish themselves and had a run of only eight years between 1864 and 1872. Rival products such as Stanford's *Tourists' Guides* and the excellent series by A&C Black at prices ranging from one to four shillings may have crowded them out (these were also illustrated, while Murray's Handbooks usually only had maps). Indeed, Black were probably the only serious competition to the English Handbooks, albeit written in a less mandarin style and more vigorously exploiting the possibilities of cheap rail travel than Murray, for example, with their Picturesque series. Nor should we forget that Black's *Economical Tourist of Scotland* had appeared in 1826, a decade before Murray's first continental guide and more than two decades before his first volume devoted to Britain.[40]

Murray did receive complaints (as did Baedeker in his turn) from persons (usually innkeepers) who felt maligned. The acidulated snob Augustus Hare, who later wrote up his own series of Italian perambulations,[41] was one of Murray's authors on the English series and dealt hoteliers some savage blows. The proprietor of the famous Mitre Hotel in Oxford even had a solicitor's letter sent to the publisher (his establishment, together with all others in Oxford, had been characterised as dirty, comfortless and overpriced). Murray wrote in the margin: 'It is preposterous to think that *Handbooks* should not have the power of praising or condemning hotels,' but nevertheless removed the offending reference. On another occasion, the rector of the village of Wheatley complained that his parish had been dismissed with the simple epithet 'hideous', and pointed out that Dr Johnson, according to Boswell's *Life*, had described it as 'a very pretty country village'.[42]

As time went on, Murray almost inevitably became part of the British cultural establishment[43] and later Handbooks tend to lack Ford's talent for controversy. British spheres of influence such as Egypt and the Sudan were covered by the series from 1847, and the imperial territories of India, Ceylon, Burma, Pakistan and Nepal (in one volume) from 1858. India later appeared as a single volume (1891) that outlived the demise of the parent brand in its home territory, a literary equivalent of the Morris Oxford cars that trundled along Indian roads for decades after they had ceased production in the UK.[44] The 1891 compilers (General Keatinge VC, a hero of the Indian Mutiny, and Sir George Forrest of the Imperial Record Office) stressed in their Introduction that 'a trip to India is no longer a formidable journey or one that requires very special preparation.

The Englishman who undertakes it merely passes from one portion of the British Empire to another.'[45] When the *Handbook to New Zealand,* the last to be published in the foreign series, appeared in 1893, the *Athenaeum* commented that 'Mr Murray has annexed what remained for him to conquer of the tourist world'; tongue in cheek of course, but a clear hint that Murray really had become the bible for the imperial and governing classes. On the other hand, perhaps it was precisely this authoritative status that often enables him to rise above narrowly chauvinistic attitudes. For example, the *Handbook for Travellers to Greece* (4th edn 1872) takes a clear stand on the Elgin marbles. It quotes with approval Sir Charles Trevelyan's assertion that they should be returned to Athens 'for we are now no longer able to plead the importance of protecting [them] from untrustworthy guardians'. The restitution would be an 'act worthy of England, and the sculptures would exercise a greater influence, even upon the taste of the English people, in their glorious original position, than they do now in a dark room in the British Museum'.[46] Baedeker, of course, was even less restrained in his comments on Elgin's removal of the marbles.

MURRAY'S AUTHORS

In general, the Handbooks reflect the aesthetic tastes of educated Victorians, and in particular the classical scholarship of dons and clergymen is strongly represented (a number of clergymen worked on the guides, particularly the English series). While a feeling for the picturesque is evident, there is also a marked interest in the disciplines that were making important advances throughout the century – archaeology, Egyptology, geology, anthropology and the beginnings of art history (as opposed to the connoisseurship of the eighteenth century). Most of the contributors were men, but there were some bluestockings and other ladies who (like Mariana Starke and the successful, if much mocked, travel writer Lady Morgan) had begun their writing careers with plays or romantic novels. Such was a Miss Beeston (*Travellers on the Continent,* 1873/4), the author of *Fair Bruges: A Romance of the Present Day.* 'It is not surprising,' says Lister ominously, 'that she did not try a second novel.'[47] Eccentricity is also to be found among the male authors. The Revd William Augustus Brevoort Coolidge (*Switzerland,* 1891/2) was, says Lister, 'in many respects the Dr Johnson of Alpinism, [but] lacked Johnson's broad humanity . . . he was cantankerous and inclined to hoard grudges against the day when he had time to indulge them . . .'. And, further: 'It was typical of him that his Christmas card should merely consist of his current entry in *Who's Who.*'[48]

The Murrays were adept at handling 'difficult' authors, combining firmness with tact, while keeping their eye firmly on the ball. Their assiduously cultivated social and academic connections can be seen from the contribution made to the Handbooks by members of famous families, or by distinguished scholars and senior military men. Authors included Sydney Courtauld (*Algeria and Tunis,* 1873) of the textile dynasty; the polymath Sir Francis Galton (*Switzerland,* 1865), famous for his work on eugenics and the author of the celebrated *Art of Travel*; Gladstone, whose travel journal was used in the compilation of *Sicily* (1864); Lafcadio Hearn

(*Japan*, 1894), one of the few Handbook contributors to write very much from the point of view of the culture being described (he took Japanese nationality, a Japanese wife and a Japanese name, Koizumi Yakumo). The Handbook to Portugal was written by J.M. Neale, the great hymn-writer, scholar and linguist (he was more or less proficient in some twenty languages), a somewhat tragic figure who was sidelined for his Puseyism at home, though showered with honours from abroad.

North Italy (1842/3) was compiled by Sir Francis Palgrave, the distinguished father of the better known F.T. Palgrave who compiled the *Golden Treasury*. Palgrave's handling of Italian art enraged the newly famous John Ruskin, and Murray asked the latter to rewrite the art section for the 1847 edition of *Italy*. This is an interesting example of how the Handbooks kept up with changing trends in aesthetic taste. For his part, Ruskin obviously derived positive as well as negative stimulation from using the Handbooks, a point explored in J.G. Links's *The Ruskins in Normandy. A Tour in 1848 with Murray's Guidebook* (London, 1968). On the other hand, perhaps because historians, classical scholars and the like tend to predominate among the authors, the lack of a consensus even on art historical terminology is from time to time apparent. If we look again at Murray's *France* (Part 1) of 1877, and specifically at the passage on Chartres, we see that value judgements can be adroitly impersonalised by remarks such as 'the S.W. *Tower* and *Spire* are considered the finest of their period in France', although the compiler was taking few risks in awarding two asterisks to the cathedral itself. The specifics of style, however, can seem decidedly eccentric, if only because they were written before art history had come of age as an academic pursuit and established strict categories of periodisation, provenance and style.[49] Thus the statues of royal saints of the Porte Royale at Chartres are described as 'attenuated figures with formal plaited drapery, characteristic of the Byzantine sculpture of the 12th cent', a description which would no doubt startle the layman as much as the specialist today.

Murray's Handbooks are inevitably prescriptive and didactic, even or especially when preaching the virtues of open-mindedness and respect for other cultures. The homily on 'the English abroad' at the beginning of the *Handbook to France* alludes to the unpopularity of the English on the Continent, partly because of 'ill-conditioned persons . . . who, not being in a condition to face the world at home, scatter themselves over foreign lands', partly to the niggardliness of 'respectable and wealthy' persons, or to an Englishman's apparent sullenness resulting from his incapacity to learn languages, or other reasons such as disrespect for the Catholic religion, arrogance and quarrelsomeness. By the same token, whatever the merits of some of the artistic judgements, it can be said of Murray, as Graham Hough says of Ruskin, that 'he is opening the eyes of an age by whom the sense of sight was left uncultivated as it had probably never been before'.[50] Middle-class culture was primarily a culture of the word, as the huge success of long novels put out by the circulating libraries suggests, and even art criticism, if such it could be called, was mostly in the hands of literary men like Thackeray, whose effusions are rightly described by Hough as 'cheerful philistinism'. Murray was tuned to the needs of his public, and when that public largely disappeared, as it did with the coming of the First World War, the guides disappeared too. In fact the series (excluding *Japan*, which was never Murray's property, and *India*, which was jointly published with a Calcutta firm) had already been sold to Edward Stanford in 1901; increasing costs, and above all competition from English-language Baedekers, was slowly throttling the market for Murrays. Financially speaking, the heyday of the Handbooks was the mid-century when their founder, John Murray III, was able to spend some of the £10,000 of net profit they had made by buying a country house at Wimbledon. He called it Newstead after another of the firm's money-spinners; but most people called it Handbook Hall.

CHAPTER 9

The Baedeker Dynasty: Guidebooks as Agents of Canonicity

To be 'Baedeker-drunk' is more than possible; and the more devoted the admirer, the greater the risk of being dominated by the masterful mind behind the façade of words.

(W.G. Constable, 1953)

Kings and governments may err
But never Mr Baedeker.

(A.P. Herbert, La vie Parisienne, *1929)*

THE SIGHTSEER'S CANON

The ancient world already had a canon of sights that could be seen as the forerunner of today's much expanded list of the absolutely obligatory stops on the tourist's route. Even then, the local inhabitants at these sights were fleecing visitors with the contemporary equivalent of souvenir stalls, fast food and pushy guides. The items in the canon were known as the seven wonders of the world and the oldest (the Great Pyramid of Cheops at Giza, built *c.* 2560 BC) is the only one still standing – and still on the tourists' itinerary. Later there was even a guidebook to the seven wonders,[1] wrongly attributed to a Byzantine engineer named Philon (*c.* 280–220 BC), although this work seems to have been aimed at the armchair traveller. Philon was probably saddled with authorship because the main interest of the anonymous author was less the aesthetic or historical aspects of the sights described, but rather the technical details of their construction.

The task of the earliest would-be guidebook writers was made lighter than that of their successors by the fact that the mystical figure of seven (in respect of the greatest, and therefore canonical, sights) was long adhered to; for instance, one of the first lists of the world's 'wonders' compiled after Christianity became the official Roman religion still had seven items, three or four of which were now Christian (the catacombs of Alexandria, the Leaning Tower of Pisa and Hagia Sophia in Constantinople; and perhaps the Colosseum could also be considered Christian, a site of martyrdom which was indicated by the huge cross erected at its centre). Later, inflation inevitably set in, and Christian authors ended up listing as many as sixteen past and present crowd-pullers, combining traditional and new wonders. They were seemingly undeterred by the fact that many of these, such as Noah's Ark, were no longer to be seen, if indeed they had ever existed.

Previous chapters have devoted some discussion to iconic or canonical artefacts or buildings, as featured by the guidebooks from the Middle Ages up to the era of the Grand Tour. However, with the founding of the two greatest nineteenth-century series of guidebooks, Murray's Handbooks and Karl Baedeker's Handbücher für Reisende, a new contextualisation of the sightseer's canon becomes evident. Aesthetic canons, though still subject to intellectually led swings of fashion (witness the contrasting nineteenth-century reception of 'Gothic' and 'Baroque', the latter a mere term of abuse with no generally accepted taxonomic or stylistic application until 1855),[2] nevertheless become somewhat more stable and gradually reflect the input of the fledgling academic study of art history. Certain views (for example, that of Niagara Falls) or locations privileged by the aesthetic theory of the picturesque or the Romantic poets (for example, the Lake District in the north of England or the temple at Sounion, where Byron barbarously carved his intials) also became canonical, while other places might become so through a combination of such factors with historical and/or patriotic, sometimes nationalistic, associations (Waterloo, Glencoe, Stonehenge).

As Dean MacCannell has pointed out, the process of canonisation is linked to that of sacralisation, whereby certain artefacts or places emerge as having a stronger 'aura'[3] than others. The process is largely self-nurturing: the more people have seen a place or work of art, and talked about it, the more people visit; but it is also helped along by official sacralisation stemming from Parliaments, Congress, English Heritage, Tourist Boards and other official or quasi-official bodies. This phenomenon began in the nineteenth century and was reaching epidemic proportions by the end of the twentieth. A further push is given by the mechanical reproduction of replicas, prints, photographs and the like, which stimulate a desire to see the 'original', or memorialise having done so. Paradoxically, while this commodification naturally increases the fame of a sight or an object, it also tends to devalue the 'aura' which made it canonical in the first place.[4] Furthermore, it is perfectly possible that any given object may have acquired its privileged status largely by accident. For example, the Mona Lisa, while certainly an admired work of art, only acquired its status of incomparable greatness after its spectacular theft from the Louvre in 1911. Until then Raphael's *Fornarina* or the Sistine *Madonna* had enjoyed considerably greater prestige.[5]

'Even under conditions where there is no end of things to see,' writes MacCannell, 'some mysterious institutional force operates on the totality in advance of the arrival of tourists, separating out the specific sights which are the attractions'. Baedeker gave formal expression to this by using his 'star' system in a way that generally avoided eccentricity, at least in so far as it carefully reproduced the scholarly (hence subsequently also the public) consensus of the age. Even when his cultivated friends mocked him for admiring what they regarded as kitsch (for example, Johann Heinrich von Dannecker's Canovian sculpture of *Ariadne Riding a Panther* (1824), which was displayed to maximum erotic effect in Frankfurt's Bethmann Museum), the first Karl Baedeker unrepentantly awarded the sculpture his accolade of two stars. Clearly this reflected its then cult status – which on this occasion happily coincided with Baedeker's personal delight in it. Some sixty-five years later, no less an authority than the Thieme and Becker art lexicon remarked on the astonishing, and by then almost incomprehensible, popularity of the *Ariadne* in its day,[6] such popularity clearly not being explicable purely in terms of aesthetic quality. Nevertheless, the lexicon goes on to say, even if art history has dispossessed the artist of the extraordinary fame he once enjoyed because of it, the work must still be regarded as uniquely paradigmatic of the tendencies of its age.[7]

Later in the history of Baedeker guidebooks, there were to be several instances where an indifferent artefact was considered for a star or stars for reasons that had little or nothing to do with its supposed aesthetic quality. In the 1950s, Karl Friedrich Baedeker is recorded as quarrelling with his co-editor, Hans Baedeker, about the large nineteenth-century bronze of the Goddess of Bavaria that loomed over Munich's Oktoberfest. He wished to award it a single star, justifying this on the grounds that it was a 'famous' sight, whereas 'Hans [who was firmly opposed] approached it purely as a work of art'.[8] In the 1950 edition of the relevant Baedeker it did not get a star, but by 1972 the editors had relented – a small, but not insignificant indication of changing priorities in the canon or sub-canon of touristic sights.

The decision could go in the opposite direction too, as with the Maria Theresia Memorial set up in Vienna in 1888 and intended as a focal point of Gottfried Semper's ambitious and only partly realised *Kaiserforum*. It seemed exciting enough at the time to get a star from Baedeker, but competition from other, seemingly more glamorous attractions seems to have led to the removal of the accolade thirty years later, only to be restored in contemporary Baedekers.[9] Likewise, Theophil Hansen's Heeresgeschichtliches Museum (Museum of Military History, 1856), also in Vienna, got a star in 1896 and was admired by Baedeker for its 'rich Romanesque style' and 'superb vestibule'. By 1929, Austrian Historicism had become highly unfashionable for cultural, historical and political reasons, and the recent devastating military defeat did not exactly inspire enthusiasm for Austria's military history. The standing of the museum's architecture was a casualty of this swing of taste and opinion, which Baedeker faithfully reflects. The museum 'has become a starless building "of a mixed Romano-Byzantine style", and its vestibule, that petrified forest of military effigies, is just a vestibule'.[10]

These examples may serve to show how Baedeker had (and has) his finger on the pulse, both of popular taste and academic opinion; and how his star rating, whether populist or not when awarded, and however perverse its application may appear to later generations, is often vindicated from the point of view of the social historian and art historian, in so far as it accurately signposted contemporary taste. In this respect, the Baedeker editors of the *Handbücher* were really more cautious than John Murray, who indulged John Ruskin in his views on Italian art at a time when these were by no means mainstream.[11] Baedeker's caution can be seen both as a strength and as a weakness: a strength because the users of *Baedekers* actually *wanted* a reflection of the scholarly and public consensus, and welcomed the fact that their own conversational reproduction of it would not be vulnerable to charges of philistinism or ignorance when backed by the authority of Baedeker.[12] The new generation of travellers, as Ivor Brown has wittily observed, were not so much 'explorers' as 'star-gazers'.

On the other hand the weakness of this approach was well expressed (as so often) by that caustic, if erratic, critic William Hazlitt, who wrote: 'A constant reference to the best models of art necessarily tends to enervate the mind . . . and to distract the attention by a variety of unattainable excellence.'[13] The novelist George Eliot, writing to John Blackwood from Florence in 1860, has a slightly different take on the same idea, when she says that she has been 'thrown into a state of humiliating passivity by the sight of so many great things done in the past' and felt 'so completely dwarfed by comparison that I should never have the courage for more creation of my own'.[14] Eliot was a great creative artist and her particular fears might not be shared by mortals whose aspirations were more humble. Nevertheless, Hazlitt's point raises an interesting question in relation to guidebooks. There must be reasons for us to look at works of art beyond the fact that an expert tells us it is the best, or among the best, of its kind; especially as a later generation of experts may not share that view.

Baedeker's delivery of the consensus has the further weakness that some of his descriptions tend to bland reproduction of art historical platitudes, which may ignore other, perhaps equally important factors in the attainment of iconic status. Of Michelangelo's *David* in Florence (two stars, of course) we are first told that it magnificently transcends the limitations of its form; further, our attention is drawn to its air of calm majesty (this an echo of Winckelmann) – notwithstanding that the muscles and limbs are somehow suffused with an inner dynamic, so that the whole body also appears tensed for action.[15] However, there is no word about either the complicated history of the statue's intended and ultimate positioning in the city, nor indeed of the symbolism attached to the subject matter, nor of Michelangelo's politicisation of a biblical commonplace. Some of this may still not have been fully researched at the time (I quote from the 1928 edition of Baedeker), but even Vasari, who gives an ecstatic and spectacularly inappropriate description of the work's 'harmonious proportions', alludes to the *David*'s political symbolism ('[It] was intended as a symbol of liberty for the Palace, signifying that just as David had protected his people and governed them justly, so whoever ruled Florence should vigorously defend the city and govern it with justice').[16]

For the purposes of a guidebook, an *exclusively* aesthetic treatment of such a work is potentially more contentious than one that concentrates on historical and social context; and inevitably it will be more subjective, as can be seen from the lengthy subsequent debate among art historians as to whether Michelangelo may be regarded as an exponent of the High Renaissance, of Mannerism or even a forerunner of the Baroque. Though perhaps only a few, like Hazlitt, would have dared to do so, it was equally possible to see the reverently extolled artistic elements of the work as its very weaknesses: 'The *David* is as if a large mass of solid marble fell upon one's head, to crush one's faith in great names. It looks like an awkard overgrown actor at one of our minor theatres, without his clothes: the head is too big for the body, and it has a helpless expression of distress.'[17] Philip Hensher, reviewing a new book on the *David* in 2002, makes a similar point more acutely: 'A work of art that one doesn't need to look at [because it's a universally acknowledged masterpiece] tends not to be looked at at all.' And he goes on to enumerate the oddities of Michelangelo's statue (the 'drastically out of proportion' hands and head for instance) which flatly contradict the grounds on which much of the received rapture of authorities and laymen from Vasari to the present is based.[18]

The artistic consensus delivered by Baedeker did not only help to entrench the prevailing canonical view of artefacts. In other areas his authority was lent to characterisations that we should now regard as unacceptably stereotypic. Sometimes, as Esther Allen has observed, the cold anthropology of the guides 'sounds like an entry in Flaubert's *Dictionnaire des idées reçues.* Travellers are informed that the inhabitants of Tuscany are "effeminate and refined", Romans are "grave and proud", while the unfortunate Neapolitans are dismissed as "dishonest and perfidious".'[19] If such comments appeared in a guidebook manuscript today, it would be safe to assume they would be subjected to a flurry of rather self-righteous red-pencilling by the editor. The objections to them now seem obvious to most people, not only because they reek of 'ethnic' slurs, but more especially because the less than attractive behaviour of *some* Neapolitans (the pickpockets, the swindlers, the Camorra) is taken to represent the whole. Moreover, the writer seems totally to divorce such behaviour from its context, the centuries of poverty, misrule and political oppression that had helped to make thieving, protection rackets and violence a feature of Neapolitan society. True, some of this background might be touched on in the historical notes on Naples, but from the point of view of the tourist, which was the point of view Baedeker represented, security and personal comfort ranked a long way ahead of trying to understand why the Neapolitan trying to pick his pocket felt compelled to earn his living in this way.

Ethnic generalisations are a staple of earlier guidebooks, some of them clichéd, some simply prejudiced, others pseudo-scientific. Baedeker's use of them should be seen in context, not least because they were still appearing in guidebooks published in the second half of the twentieth century. Take, for instance, J.A. Cuddon's vivid and opinionated *Companion Guide to Jugoslavia* (1968; rev. edn 1974). Written with partisan gusto and romantic empathy for the southern Slavs (particularly the Serbs), the text is often colourful and outspoken to the point of indiscretion. Not untypical is the following passage, the tone of which hovers between a spirited naivety and the bathos parodied so expertly in the writings of the Hungarian George Mikes:

> If there is such a thing as a national character, and if it is instructive to look for it, then I should say South Slavs are intelligent, passionate, individualistic, devoted to principle (to the point of obduracy), impulsive, capable of being very gay and also very sad and reflective. Sometimes they are really sombre. At times they are devious and impenetrable, at others implacably bloody-minded. They are morally and sexually healthy and they usually have beautiful unfussy manners.[20]

It would be impossible to romanticise ethnic groups in this way in a guidebook written today, and not only because the horrors of the Balkan War of the 1990s have made Cuddon's remarks risible *as generalisations*. A 'morally and sexually healthy people' does not go in for ethnic cleansing, and saying that an ethnic group (or for that matter, an individual) is 'devoted to principle' begs the question of which principle, and whether it is a desirable one. Cuddon in fact goes further than most of Baedeker's excursions into ethnic generalisation. But even if his sternest critics might see his remarks as rich mix of cliché, prejudice and naivete, it is also fair to say that ethnic stereotypes do have some relation to a nation's perception of itself and do not arise purely by chance. In articulating the stereotype, the guidebook is performing a function of at least some value, particularly if, as here, the text taken as a whole delves below the surface of the stereotype, and the latter is itself something more than a construct of mere hostility (what the Germans so memorably call a *Feindbild*).

PERCEPTIONS OF BAEDEKER AND THE GERMAN CHARACTER

Not only did Baedeker's guides reinforce the notion of canonic artefacts, they themselves became icons of canonicity, his familiar and dependable *Handbücher für Reisende* achieving a status that soared above the ever-increasing competition. Indeed, 'Baedeker the brand' received the ultimate in terms of recognition: it passed into the language, like Xerox, Hoover, Kleenex and, yes, the more plebeian 'Cook's Tour'.

Not surprisingly, Baedeker's systematisation of sight-seeing was frequently seen as having a specifically German character, thereby attracting the kind of reluctant and ironic admiration often reserved for indispensable cultural products that sweep all before them, including all the local efforts in the same genre. Thus the anonymous reviewer of the *Atlantic Monthly* in 1875 resorts to persiflage that looks very much like camouflaged envy:

> The Germans, who have gone to the bottom of history, philosophy, and religion (and mostly found nothing there), have in Baedeker reduced touristry to a science, and have given the public what there is of it in certain volumes covering the whole area of customary travel in those lands where Germans now keep all the first hotels, and are likely, if they go on with their abominable thoroughness, to gather a main share of the international commerce into their hands and supply the world at last with everything but its wit, grace, beauty, faith and liberty – these trifles being unworthy of their attention.[21]

Such comments may be compared with the view of a scholar of our own age who sees the success of the Baedeker product as emblematic both of contemporary German economic achievements and of a strengthening of German identity. 'That the Baedeker was exported for use on the international tourist market,' writes Rudy Koshar, 'only strengthened the German nation's identification with the standards of economic performance. The tiny guidebook became a symbol of Germany's nineteenth-century "economic miracle".'[22] Clearly, this was the message that had come through loud and clear to Germany's economic competitors, as the waspish comments of the *Atlantic Monthly*'s reviewer implied.

On the other hand, after dispensing his barbed compliments, the same reviewer goes on to praise unequivocally Baedeker's absence of 'sentiment or criticism', its reluctance (unlike Murray) to offer opinions, and its provision of 'all the historical facts necessary to intelligent enjoyment of places and things – points around which the reader can assemble his wandering general knowledge, or with which he can disperse his general ignorance'. The review follows this up by praising a volume in a recently initiated local series of guides to the regions of the United States, that had been conceived 'on the Baedeker plan'. After commending the author of this new guide, a certain Mr Sweetser, for founding his work in autopsy, for his 'careful and pleasant presentation of what may be called tourist-history, no less than for those statistics, directions, and counsels which it is more strictly the business of a guide-book to give,' the reviewer asserts that this is not only a 'conscientious and faithful cicerone' for foreign visitors, but one that is equally so for Americans, as 'we are all necessarily foreigners in nine tenths of our immense territory'.[23]

In other words, the Baedeker approach provides an anchor of rational analysis that enables us to view the components making up the culture and history of our native land just as dispassionately as we might view those components in a foreign country. Baedeker is a product and a methodology that can be applied globally, a brand-name that guarantees solid reliability and detachment, albeit a detachment that has to be seen in a specific cultural context. Behind the apparently disinterested approach to the material lay overarching assumptions –

and sometimes ambivalence – about the nature of culture and progress. Baedeker's general admiration for economic and industrial progress made it acceptable to an American middle class audience: for example, the German Baedekers encouraged travellers, *inter alia*, to visit the factories of the socially innovative firms of AEG and Krupp. On the other hand, Baedeker was 'old European' enough to be sceptical of 'aggressive modernity' and conservative enough to ignore almost entirely the working class districts of Berlin.[24]

BAEDEKER AS LITERARY SHORTHAND

The consequence of an impressive and largely unassailable status was that a whole range of social and aesthetic associations came to be evoked by the Baedeker name. T.S. Eliot wrote a fairly obviously anti-semitic poem in 1920, using Baedeker as a stage-prop (*Burbank with a Baedeker: Bleistein with a Cigar*). Novelists, too, called Baedeker in aid, usually as an ambivalent symbol of the gulf between cultural vitality (the spontaneous creativity that gave birth to what Baedeker describes) and a stagnating civilisation (the 'learned' responses of a Baedeker user). This is more or less its role in a book such as E.M. Forster's *A Room with a View* (1908)[25] or in Samuel Beckett's critical aside in his essay on Proust.

Even more revealing than the final, published text of the Forster novel are its earlier drafts, where the author's satirical bent is given free rein in comparing the aesthetic responses ordained for the visitor to the Santa Croce church by Baedeker, Murray's Handbook, and Ruskin's *Mornings in Florence*: 'Those who trusted to Baedeker began [the tour] in an orderly manner with the right aisle, worked it up to the right transept, where they disappeared into a door leading to the sacristy and . . . chapel, to emerge presently & inspect in turn the chapels to the right of the choir, the choir, the chapels to the left of the choir, the left transept and finally came down the left aisle and departed exhausted and frozen into the warmer air outside.'[26] The heroine, Lucy Honeychurch, is sitting in the left aisle and sees how the attention of the Baedeker acolytes is obviously flagging by the time it gets to her. On the other hand, since she was sitting under the tomb of Carlo Marsuppini (1464, by Desiderio da Settignano), which the 'great purist' Ruskin 'selected as a foil to the excellencies of the sepulchral slab near the door', the Ruskin devotees pass her position first on their tour and can be heard enthusiastically endorsing Ruskin's strictures on the tomb.

Ruskin's book was also intensely ironic at the expense of Murray's Handbook, which was treated as a useful Aunt Sally in order to encourage an approach to the sights that was liberated from Murray's normative text. Yet, as Forster subtly implies, the net effect of all this is to diminish, not increase, the likelihood of authentic personal reactions by the viewer, who is 'forced to be free' by a writer who in turn certainly has his own agenda. Or rather, as James Buzard wittily puts it: 'Forster finds himself at yet another remove from the supposed object of tourist attention, reading Ruskin's reading of Murray's reading (itself the

product of others' readings) of Italy . . . Lucy recognizes the kinship of supposed
enemies by perceiving that Ruskin's and Baedeker's pupils obey their different
masters with the same diligence.'[27] One not totally illogical reaction to this
problem is adopted by Huysmans's reclusive hero in *A Rebours*, who purchases a
Baedeker for a contemplated trip to England, finds the world it evokes
disturbingly ideal and aborts the real journey in favour of the imaginary one.[28]

While there is more than a residual affection evident in E.M. Forster's
treatment of Baedeker, in Thomas Pynchon's novel *V.* (1963), the little red
guidebooks have become the representative image for the vicarious, two-
dimensional world of tourism,

> a curious country, . . . Its landscape is one of inanimate monuments and
> buildings; near-inanimate barmen, taxi-drivers, bellhops, guides: there to do
> any bidding, to various degrees of efficiency, on receipt of the
> recommended baksheesh, pourboire, mancia, tip. As long as the
> Distribution of Time section [is] followed scrupulously, the plumbing of the
> hotel in order ('No hotel', writes Karl Baedeker, 'can be recommended as
> first class that is not satisfactory in its sanitary arrangements, which should
> include an abundant flush of water and a supply of proper toilet paper'),
> the tourist may wander anywhere in this coordinate system without fear. War
> never becomes more serious than a scuffle with a pickpocket . . . depression
> and prosperity are reflected only in the rate of exchange; politics are of
> course never discussed with the native population . . . [the tourists'] Bible is
> clearly written and does not admit of private interpretation . . .[29]

This reflects a fairly widespread attitude and in some respects echoes Roland
Barthes's now celebrated strictures on the Guide Bleu. Both series of guidebooks
had become the victims of their own success, not just as useful books, but as
emblems of middle-class cultural aspirations and (according to critics) devices to
shelter that class from unfiltered contact with rebarbative social, political or
ecological realities.[30] This perception, even if one were to accept it without
qualification, represents a retrospective application of twentieth-century norms
and values to the nineteenth-century's educated middle class, and cultivates the
Marxist's implicit distaste for the bourgeois ethos. For this reason, if no other, it
is worth looking a little more closely at the commercial history of the impressive
dynastic enterprise of Baedeker to identify more precisely the values and
attitudes that ultimately determined the way in which it was carried out.

KARL BAEDEKER: THE FOUNDING FATHER

By any standards and in any age, the first Karl Baedeker (sometimes spelled
'Bädeker') was a remarkable man and indeed he came from a high-achieving
and extremely industrious family. His father, like his father before him, and like
the first two John Murrays, was a scion of the Enlightenment, but with liberal

leanings that reflected the age of Romanticism through which he lived. There was also a recurrent strain of anti-French patriotism that tended to wax and wane according to the state of Prussian-French relations: 'I do not think that [a Handbook to France] would find a rewarding market in Germany,' he wrote to his friend John Murray III in 1844. 'My countrymen . . . journey little in France, with perhaps the exception of Paris. In any case I do not feel inclined to such an enterprise. I do not like France. I have not been to Paris myself, and do not feel moved to do so.'[31]

This attitude, it has been suggested, most likely arose from the cultural milieu of which the Baedeker family were typical products. It was a milieu, writes Rudy Koshar, that 'placed great emphasis on the accomplishments of a specifically German *Kultur*, 'the painting, philosophy, music, poetry, architecture, monuments and scholarship which could potentially be seen as superior to the less authentic "civilization" of other nations, particularly though not exclusively that of France'.[32] The competing notions of French *civilisation* and German *Kultur* is a commonplace of cultural history, with political and social ramifications that exist even today. Baedeker (excluding the embarrassment of the firm's brief and inglorious subjection to Nazi ideology) represented the love of *Kultur* at its best; but at its worst it could be perverted into a kind of sentimental and solipsistic evasion of the very moral engagement it pretended to embrace: everyone has heard the cliché about concentration camp commandants playing scratchy records of Beethoven and Mozart while the camp's inmates were ushered into the gas chambers.

On the other hand, such different conceptions of mediatory cultural roles as probably did exist in the mind of a Karl Baedeker and (for example) that of his approximate French counterpart, Adolphe-Laurent Joanne, should not be taken as implying an undifferentiated or narrowly chauvinistic approach to his own nation on the part of Baedeker. Koshar himself says that Baedeker's obvious pride in German material advances was understated when compared to the Murray guidebooks' effusive praise of English economic might. Furthermore, he concedes that both guidebooks were prepared to offer international comparisons that were even-handed: 'Berlin was a magnificent city, for example, but because of its earlier history as a garrison town and its subsequent rapid and badly planned growth, it lacked the truly ancient and venerable monuments of Paris and London, according to the Baedeker guides. Affirmation, criticism and self-criticism existed side by side in the Baedeker image of the German nation.'[33]

The dynasty had begun as book printers in Bielefeld (Diedrich Baedeker, 1680–1716, was printer to the Prussian court from 1712), but eventually also moved into publishing, bookselling and distribution. Karl's father, Gottschalk Diedrich Baedeker (1778–1841) and his younger brother, Julius, also found the time to edit a liberal-inclined local newspaper (the *Essener Zeitung*, from 1883 amalgamated with the *Westfälischen Zeitung* and known as the *Rheinisch-Westfälischen Zeitung*) as well as attending to the other sides of their business. Gottschalk was active in the community, is credited with having pioneered the concept of the lending library and was instrumental in founding the first

Gymnasium for mixed confessions in Essen. Doctrinal tolerance finds an echo in the decision of the non-Catholic Karl Baedeker in 1836 to publish the *Journal for Philosophy and Catholic Theology*,[34] an organ of the Hermesian group condemned by the Vatican as heretical, and founded with the somewhat quixotic aim of reconciling the philosophy of Kant with Catholic dogma. In the period before the guidebooks were founded, the publishing side of the business was principally concerned with pedagogic, technical and natural scientific literature; no doubt experience in this field facilitated a seamless transition to the 'adult education' supplied by the guidebooks.

Karl Baedeker (1801–59) apprenticed himself to a bookseller in Heidelberg at the age of 16, at the same time enrolling as a philosophy student at the university. Later he worked for the Berlin bookseller Georg Andreas Reimer, who was in constant trouble with the censor for his radical publications (*inter alia*, he attempted to bring out the *Mémoires de Napoléon*). It is unlikely that Baedeker remained unmoved by the radical environment of his apprenticeship, but he again resembled his contemporary John Murray III in the way he preserved a shrewd intellectual and psychological balance, evidently being able to maintain the friendship of men who may have been either much more radical, or much more conservative than himself.[35] He had, therefore, the ideal character traits for a successful (as opposed to a fly-by-night) publisher, as they emerge in the description of him by the poet von Fallersleben: 'honest, liberal-minded, clear-headed and genial'.[36] He was also very hard-working, and in July of 1827 opened a bookshop in Koblenz at his own risk; five years later the first step towards the creation of a guidebook series was taken when he took over the assets of a bankrupt publisher called Röhling who had made a corner in local guidebooks and albums of picturesque views in the surrounding area.

One of Röhling's slightly better selling items (though sales were marginal compared to German, French and English guidebooks to the Rhine) was a guide (1828) for travellers making the by then popular steamboat excursion along the Rhine between Mainz and Cologne. It had been written by a certain Professor J.A. Klein[37] and Baedeker reissued this book in 1835, both in a German and a French version. Such popularity as the original guide enjoyed had owed a great deal to its being the first to cater for a rapidly burgeoning traffic – in the ten years after its inception in 1827, passenger traffic with the Preussisch-Rheinische Dampfschiffahrtsgesellschaft grew from 18,000 to nearly a million annually. However, the book was a rather ponderous scholarly tome of local history coupled with orotund effusions on the beauties of the riparian landscape, old fashioned in style and not very appropriate for its task. Despite its claim to be a *Handbuch für Schnellreisende*, the text was less than ideal for readers and travellers who needed to bone up rapidly, and who might well be side-tracked into time-consuming detours through the thickets of the good professor's prose. Nor was there any practical information in the original edition, a deficiency that Baedeker made good in his version, while also tightening up the prose and extending the text beyond its original narrow focus on the Rhine. The reissue was a success, not quite the 'first Baedeker', but a precursor of the series.

BAEDEKER'S DEBT TO MURRAY AND REFINEMENT OF THE MURRAY CONCEPT

Baedeker was shrewd enough to see that the easy money from Klein's *Rheinreise* had been a lucky stroke, while on the other hand an increasing demand for intelligently organised guidebooks existed if the right kind of formula could be found. From 1836 he was selling John Murray's *Handbook for Travellers on the Continent* in his bookshop (which John Murray, as a gentlemanly quid pro quo, recommended to his readers), and he also noted how popular this guide seemed to be with English visitors to Koblenz, who were to be seen clutching it as they wandered the streets. There was no other serious competition to Murray, although America had produced a sketchy book called *The Tourist in Europe* in 1838. This anticipated the box-ticking lists of later convenience guides for Americans on a whirlwind tour of Europe, and was strongest on matters like accommodation and prices.[38]

From Murray, Baedeker borrowed the format of numbered routes, and later (1844) the 'star' system (asterisks) for highlighting important sights. The approach to content had, of course, similarities, but from the beginning Baedeker developed his own distinctive brand of authoritative information, which at least appeared to be more impersonal, less subjective, and later more concise than Murray's somewhat longer-winded texts. Nevertheless, Baedeker was generous in acknowledging the debt he owed to Murray, which he recorded in the Prefaces of the early books, and in 1839 even called Murray's Handbook 'the most distinguished guide ever published'. This gentlemanly collaboration continued until 1861, when a second generation Baedeker began a direct assault on the British market with Baedekers in English. This seems to have soured relations and Murray was later to complain of plagiarism[39] by his rival and a promotional tendency to airbrush out Murray's role in the inception of the series.

It was in 1839 that Baedeker brought out three volumes that were to be the first of a series which, despite having undergone certain commercial and presentational mutations, is still running today, and which had sold two million copies of eighty-seven guides in three languages by the eve of the Second World War.[40] One volume was the third edition of Klein's *Rheinreise* transmuted into the new format and so heavily revised as to constitute a new book; one covered Holland, and one was for the recently established state (1830) of Belgium. Communications probably determined the choice of areas covered, as it would also have determined the tourist traffic. All three areas were full of historic sights. The Rhine and Holland had opened up to tourism through steamboat travel, while Belgium was early on accessible by rail.

The lion's share of the work on these first books was undertaken by the publisher himself, although he also made use of information from assistants whom he felt he could trust to supply accurate data. Perhaps the most famous anecdote concerning Karl Baedeker's passion for accuracy was related by a fellow German who, in 1847, found himself following a stocky figure up the seemingly interminable steps to the roof of Milan cathedral. The latter kept reaching into his waistcoat pocket, extracting a pea, and transferring it to his trouser pocket. Later the tourist spotted the same gentleman at his hotel and learned that he was Herr Baedeker, the well-known guidebook publisher. Intrigued, he introduced himself and asked the meaning of the ritual on the cathedral steps. A beaming Baedeker explained that he had merely been counting the steps to the roof; after every twenty steps he transferred a pea from his waistcoat to his trousers, so as to be sure he had recorded exactly the right figure for the number of steps at the end of the climb.

After the first three titles, Baedeker continued to research and publish his guides, which at this time still resembled pretty Biedermeier artefacts, having tan covers embellished with emblematic ornamentation. In 1842 *Germany and the Austrian Empire* appeared and in 1844 *Switzerland*, a bestseller for Baedeker as it was for Murray. Swiss tourism, and in particular sophisticated Swiss hotel management,[41] had developed rapidly and the country was well on the way to becoming what Leslie Stephen was to call the 'playground of Europe'[42] for German, British, and later American travellers. Finally, in 1854, apparently in imitation of the product put out by his friend and rival, John Murray III, Baedeker adopted a format similar to that of the latter's Handbooks, including their red covers with gold lettering. To some this was a puzzling move, since Baedeker, it has been claimed, already had the edge on Murray in the race to be market leader; according to Herbert Warren Wind, even German speaking travellers from Britain were saying that the German's series was superior.[43] There may, however, have been marketing reasons behind the decision, since at this time the two firms were still collaborating closely, and the decision would perhaps have facilitated offering prospective buyers something analogous to a Baedeker in a second language.

Like Murray, Baedeker did his own legwork for as long as he could, although (again like Murray) he drew on expertise where necessary, for example, on that of the great classical historian Theodore Mommsen, for descriptions of Roman settlements. Indeed, many of the later contributors to Baedekers were leaders in their field, men like the celebrated architect-archaeologist Wilhelm Dörpfeld, who was to make a significant contribution to Baedeker's *Greece*, or the Dresden art historian Cornelius Gustav Gurlitt. While such figures lent scholarly weight to the text, Baedeker kept his finger on the details of its presentation and on the balance of the guide's contents. Accurate practical information was something of an obsession with him, and in this controlling sense he remained the 'author' of the guides, while the 'experts' were mere contributors and checkers. He remains, wrote Francis Watson, 'deathless and indivisible, as secure as Shakespeare and Homer from the theorists who produce "ghosts" and collaborators. Of the mortality of individual investigators we need take no more heed than of the biographies of Chinese potters. It is Sung, it is Baedeker, it is enough.'[44]

THE AUTHORITY OF THE BAEDEKER NAME AND HIS SOLIDARITY WITH HIS READERS

According to a Hungarian folk tradition, the Renaissance king Matthias Corvinus travelled incognito among his people to discover the realities that the courtiers and councillors would not, or could not, tell him, this being the Hungarians' version of similar myths that exist in many other regions of the world. We also know that, under an assumed name, Emperor Joseph II actually did travel his own realms, as well as many others, to collect reliable and useful information pertinent to the modernisation of the lands he ruled. It is perhaps a pardonable conceit to see this myth-encrusted process, that had begun with a king seeking a way of re-engaging with reality in order to rule more justly, as reaching a mildly absurd apotheosis with the bourgeois businessman Karl Baedeker, who travelled around under *noms de guerre* such as Mueller or Bruncker, the better to serve the interests of travellers and consumers.

A medieval or Renaissance king, once stripped of his disguise, could strike terror into the heart of his unsuspecting subjects; a Murray or a Baedeker, once identified, could have a similarly galvanising effect on innkeepers. 'Throughout Baedeker's career,' says Wind, 'the men who tried to steal the traveller's money were his sworn enemies, and he was tireless in reminding his readers that, say, there was no need to tip the grizzled custodian at the such-and-such museum, even though it was the custodian's unnerving practice to start moaning and continue to moan until a tourist had coughed up twelve or eighteen kreuzer'.[45] On the other hand, Baedeker supplied in admirable detail the going rate for obligatory tips at every turn: a porter in Mannheim should receive twelve kreuzer for carrying a trunk weighing more than forty pounds, eight kreuzer for one weighing less; in Mainz the same pecuniary guidelines applied, but here the threshold weight was fifty pounds (perhaps the men of Mainz were better fed than those of Mannheim and unfazed by the extra ten pounds weight).

Different rates applied in other places, all meticulously noted, though in general Baedeker regarded tipping as a 'wicked practice' to which the traveller had nevertheless to be resigned. His indignant notes on the impositions made on travellers in the Bernese Oberland are quoted by Edward Mendelson and (in slightly different versions) by W.G. Constable and Alan Sillitoe as amusing examples of Baedeker's exasperation getting the better of him:

> Attempts are made on [the traveller's] purse under every pretence and in every form . . . urchins stand on their heads and wave their feet; cretins and cripples implore his aid; . . . Swiss songstresses, neither young nor pretty [but elsewhere described as 'underage'], next appear on the scene; and the nerves of the traveller are often sorely tried by the Alpine horn and the *Ranz des Vaches* [a Gruyères folksong], which though musical at a distance, are objectionable when performed close to the ear. Often a pistol shot is fired off in order to awaken an echo; finally there are the many unavoidable gates, which a half-dozen children expect a gratuity for opening.

And he concludes sadly that 'all this is the inevitable consequence of a massive invasion of foreigners, which has exercised a pernicious influence on the morals of the valley'.[46]

Baedeker's solidarity with his readers, which involved him in the workload of several men, walking the routes of his guides, compiling the information from his notes, trying (with considerable success) to keep the guides up to date,[47] as well as attending to the business side, eventually took its toll on him and he died in 1859 at the comparatively early age of 58. The last guide he worked on was that for Paris (1855). He had perhaps by now overcome the patriotic reservations about the French of his youth and happily did not live long enough to witness the renewed outbreak of hostilities between the two countries. His character, on the surface so clearly etched, fades into enigma when scrutinised more closely. What, for example, were his religious views? From the internal evidence of the guides he would seem to have been a church-going but thoroughly secularised Protestant, his careful listing of Protestant places of worship in Catholic countries simply being part of the Baedeker service to his German Protestant readers. Of Rousseau he says in Baedeker's *Switzerland*, that he possessed 'ability of the highest order, exercised a great influence over the opinions of his age, but their tendency was highly injurious to society and he passed a troubled and agitated life'. This may be a conservative view of Rousseau, but it is hardly an extreme one and would have been widely shared in his day, as it still is by many who have taken the trouble to investigate Rousseau's spectacular hypocrisy.

BAEDEKER AND TASTE

Then again, one has little impression of strong artistic preferences. It is true that Baroque art and architecture often gets short shrift in the guides, but this attitude too faithfully reflects the taste of the age; and when that changed, so did Baedeker's. During the revision of the 1903 German edition of *Central Italy and Rome*, Hans Baedeker had a lengthy argument with his father, which he eventually won, about the necessity of fuller coverage of Baroque architecture and sculpture.[48] Interestingly, this change does not appear to have filtered through to the English Baedekers until much later, which rather confirms Baedeker's claim that the foreign language editions were by no means simple translations of the German prototypes, but were tailored to the interests and tastes of the prospective readership. David Watkin has described how the celebrated art historian Rudolf Wittkower fell under the spell of Baroque architecture as a young man while studying in the Bibliotheca Hertziana in Rome in the 1920s. At this time the contemporary edition (1909) of Baedeker still spoke of 'the degenerate Renaissance known as Baroque', and warned travellers to 'beware of being led captive by art essentially flimsy and meretricious'. 'No one', writes Watkin, 'has been more influential in overthrowing that view than Wittkower. And it was in the pages of Baedeker that he first did so, for he was invited to revise the account of the arts in Rome for a new edition of Baedeker in 1927.'[49]

Indeed, as Francis Watson has pointed out, the 1920s saw the 'emergence from disgrace' of both the Baroque and Rococo styles, as the influence of scholars such as Gurlitt, Wölfflin and Schmarzov percolated into the public arena. The famous Dresden Zwinger, allowed by Baedeker to be 'one of the most pleasing examples of . . . [Baroque] style' in 1877, despite its suspect Rococo leanings, has become by 1925 'the most brilliant and graceful embodiment of the Baroque style in Germany', with its 'happy proportions, distribution of bulk, and profusion of figures of Greek deities, fauns, vases, escutcheons and garlands'. By the 1930s the Amalienburg near Munich, not even mentioned in the 1861 Baedeker, has become 'the most complete expression achieved by the Rococo style in the category of princely pleasure-palaces'. Meanwhile, between 1896 and 1929, Schönbrunn in Vienna is promoted from one star to two, while Sanssouci is in 1877 'a building of one storey', in 1923 'a striking building of one storey', and in 1925 'a beautiful Rococo building of one storey'.[50]

ASSISTING BAEDEKER READERS TO 'STAND ON THEIR OWN FEET'

Baedeker's penny-pinching advice may sometimes appear petty, or petit-bourgeois, but it was given not in the spirit of miserliness for its own sake, but rather to protect his readers from the inevitable and practically universal avarice of those in a position to fleece tourists. Baedeker emerges as an unpretentious man of firm convictions, which were nevertheless subject to the disciplines of an enquiring mind. With his insistence on the virtues of woolly underwear, rigorous hygiene and unruffled politesse, he was a figure the itinerant burgher could identify with. Pleasures such as wine were to be indulged (but partly for health reasons); on the other hand, hardships were to be borne with stoicism. He was enthusiastic about steamship and railway travel, but the best way to see the world was to walk it; or, in a phrase that became identified with him,[51] one should always *sich eine Gegend erwandern* ('get to know a region by hiking through it'). John Murray IV said of his father that 'he regarded a walk as an infallible cure for almost all ills, and [one would] hardly have been surprised to hear him recommend it for a broken leg'. This is also the Baedeker spirit exactly.

Writing in the preface to his guide to Germany and Austria, Baedeker stressed that his 'principal object' was to free his readers from the 'tutelage' of servants, guides, hotel-keepers and the like, and to 'assist him in standing on his *own* feet, to render him *independent,* and to place him in a position from which he may receive his own impressions with clear eyes and lively heart'.[52] If the Baedekers can be said to have a philosophy, this is it, as adhered to by Karl's sons who followed him at the head of the business. The energetic Ernst (part of whose apprenticeship had been served with a London firm called Williams & Norgate, and who issued the first Baedeker in English) lasted only four years before following his father to the grave in 1861. Then Karl Junior managed the publishing house from 1861, until his poor state of health compelled him to hand over the firm's direction to the astute youngest brother, Fritz Baedeker (1844–1925), the junior partner in the business from 1869. Karl, a passionate amateur mountaineer and diligent researcher for the guides on Switzerland and

Tyrol, nevertheless continued to make an important contribution until 1877, but his later years were clouded by mental instability; he was committed to a mental home in 1884,[53] although he died only in 1911.

THE AGE OF BAEDEKER

It was under Fritz's leadership that the guidebooks achieved an absolutely impregnable position as market leaders, reflected in the fact that the overripe age of Edwardian prodigality between about 1870 and 1914 is also sometimes referred to as the 'age of Baedeker'. While the individual volumes had already begun expanding into multiples – *Deutschland und Österreich* was divided into 'north' and 'south' German volumes in 1851, and in 1853 *Österreich and Südbayern und Tirol* got their own volumes – under Fritz the number of countries covered also grew exponentially from the 1870s onwards. Geographically speaking the coverage spread east and south (*Palestine and Syria*, 1875, *Lower Egypt*, 1877, *Upper Egypt*, 1891, *Greece*, 1883, *India*, 1914), as well as north (*Sweden and Norway*, 1879, *Russia*, 1883, *Great Britain*,1887) and finally west (*The United States*, 1893, *Canada*, 1894). Some of these volumes did not even appear in German – the guide to Canada was printed only in English, the part of it dealing with the French regions, only in French – but most were now brought out in three languages, in effect making Baedeker a multicultural publishing empire offering some seventy titles by 1900.

The result of this was that the firm underwent what James Buzard calls 'a Weberian transition from its founder's charismatic "individual authority" to a rational "bureaucracy of editors and agents", thus assuring [its] greater longevity on the tourist business and in the cultural vocabulary of Europe'.[54] The individual volumes were increasingly the product of a cooperative endeavour involving specialists in different fields and authors of different nationalities. For this reason, if for no other, it was vital to develop a strictly imposed house style that reconciled, say, the florid style of a garrulous Scots professor with the desiccated scholarship of a German academic. Thus was born the famous 'corporate identity' of Baedeker, an amalgam of laconic precision, ostensive objectivity and an authoritative manner that sometimes borders on self-parody, as in: 'The torchlight procession presents a fairylike scene (Beware of pickpockets)'.

It was perhaps because of Fritz's single-mindedness and influence that the decks were cleared in 1870 with the sale of the bookshop business and the relocation, in 1872/3, of the publishing activities to Leipzig, which was traditionally the greatest publishing centre of Germany.[55] Business acuteness was ever more necessary in a world of increasing competition[56] and from time to time the Baedeker name had to be defended against abuse. It was a sort of backhanded compliment – but also a clear example of 'passing off' – that a rival firm had put out a 'Baedeker' covering London at the time of the Great Exhibition in 1862; and a more serious problem arose with the publication of a

'Berlin Baedeker' in 1876 by the local Kiessling Verlag. Where possible, the firm met these challenges by printing (or updating) its own volumes to the regions covered, which was usually enough to sort out the competition, and was preferable to getting involved in costly and protracted lawsuits.

Meanwhile, bibliography had acquired a new term, *Baedekeriana*, perhaps the highest tribute to a publisher that the book trade and specialist collectors could pay. Ambivalent tributes were also supplied by novelists or humorists such as Ludwig Thoma, or Arthur Holitscher (author of a *Narrenbaedeker*, 'The Fool's Baedeker'), or Werner Bergengruen, who produced the delightfully titled *Baedeker des Herzens* ('Baedeker of the Heart'): unfortunately, the name of the latter publication had to be changed to *Badekur des Herzens* ('Bathing Cure of the Heart') after an objection by Hans Baedeker was upheld by a Leipzig court. This little book was dedicated by the author to the waiter at the Passau railway station '*der mich "Geehrter Herr Reisender" angeredet hat*' ('who addressed me as 'Esteemed Mr Traveller'), no doubt a sign of the heightened respect resulting from a gentleman travelling with a Baedeker in the hand. R. Schmidt-Cabanis edited a series under the title *Der lustige Baedeker* containing vignettes, jingles and jokes that satirised Baedeker's po-faced asides. Its general tone may be seen from the title of volume 5: *Vollständiger humoristisch-poetischer Führer durch Berlin* (Stuttgart 1890).[57] Even the British humorist Harry Graham, writing towards the end of the glory days of Baedeker in the first decade of the twentieth century, treats Baedeker as an essential prop in his satire on the portly Aunt Maud who yearns to travel ('She often felt that she would choke / If she remained in Basingstoke'). Baedeker is the passport to wide horizons, or actually, as the narrative of Graham's rather feeble poem subsequently reveals, to pseudo-experience. The first stanza makes pretended mockery of stay-at-homes:

> In foreign travel one may find
> A means to exercise the mind,
> To broaden those parochial views
> Which stay-at-homes so seldom lose
> Until with Baedeker in hand,
> They leave their own, their native land.

But the final stanza satirises the lady's hastily acquired expertise:

> I love to hear Aunt Maud enlarge
> On problems of the British Raj;
> On questions that concern the East
> Her talk is a perpetual feast;
> And who so qualified to speak?
> She's lived in India – for a week![58]

By the time Mark Twain published *A Tramp Abroad* in 1880, Baedeker was such a household name that much comedy could be extracted from the famous precision of the guidebook's directions, in this case from Twain's attempt to take a passage down the Gorner Glacier to Zermatt. He tells us that he carefully positioned himself on the middle part ('because Baedeker said the middle part travels fastest'), while putting 'some of the heavier baggage on the shoreward parts, to go as slow freight'.[59]

Another backhanded compliment to Baedeker was the series of guides produced by Piper Verlag after the First World War under the composite title *Was nicht im Baedeker steht*, which covered the main cities of Europe. The image projected by these guides was very much that of the insider's *Geheimtips*, and they also dealt with the more louche and hedonistic aspects of metropolitan life in respect of which Baedeker maintained a lofty reserve – or simply airbrushed out. The authors were often literary figures rather than professional guidebook compilers, and their affectionate and opinionated evocations of the city, coupled with uncensored insider information, made them the forerunners of today's laid-back or uninhibited 'funky' guides to urban fleshpots for cool guys and chicks.[60]

BAEDEKER AND CONTROVERSY, BAEDEKER AT WAR

No publisher dealing in topics with such vast potential for controversy as those covered in a typical Baedeker, whose text was required to be judgemental concerning practical matters while simultaneously being vulnerable to partisan indignation in all other spheres, could hope to escape legal challenge over the years. Baedeker's high profile made it particularly likely that cranks, as well as persons with genuine grievances, should seek to influence the content of the guides. Edward Mendleson quotes one of the more amusing examples concerning Baedeker's 1894 volume on Palestine and Syria, which referred to the eponymous proprietor of Howard's Hotel as 'an Arab' and advised bargaining on the room-price. Howard, 'a Maltese of Syrian ancestry whose name was Awwad', successfully claimed before a British jury that the description of him as an Arab libelled him(!), the offence being compounded by the insulting suggestion of the need to bargain. Baedeker had to remove the reference, but 'Howard' said he would forego any damages if the guidebook would continue to list his hotel. One can imagine the colour rising on Fritz Baedeker's features at the sheer cheek of this, and indeed his magisterial response (in the Preface to the following edition) is *sui generis*: 'Hotels which cannot be accurately characterized without exposing the editor to risk of legal proceedings are left unmentioned.'[61]

The 1906 edition of the resonantly titled *Handbook to Palestine and Syria, with the Chief Routes through Mesopotamia and Babylonia* certainly was free with cultural stereotypes of the type to which Mr 'Howard' was not so much objecting, as saying they were erroneously being applied to him. On the other hand, Baedeker's text here, however amusing and patronising it sounds to us now, also has a clear ethical stance. The stance is situated somewhere between compassion and a necessary vigilance against unreasonable fleecing of the tourist (a certain

amount of skinning was inevitable and had to be accepted philosophically).
'Most Orientals', he writes,

> regard the European traveller as a Croesus, and sometimes as a madman, so
> unintelligible to them are the objects and pleasures of travelling. They
> therefore demand Bakhshîsh almost as a right from those who seem so
> much better supplied with this world's goods. He who gives is a good man . . .
> The custom of scattering small coins for the sake of the amusement
> furnished by the consequent scramble is an insult to poverty that no
> rightminded traveller will offer.
>   Beneath the interminable protestations of friendship with which the
> traveller is overwhelmed lurks in most cases the demon of cupidity . . . It will
> be impossible to avoid extortions or overcharges altogether, and it is better
> to reconcile oneself to this than to poison one's enjoyment by too much
> suspicion.[62]

Less amusing than the run-in with 'Howard' was a dispute between the wars
with two Belgian towns that sued Baedeker for saying that a civilian massacre by
German troops during the First World War had been provoked by sniper fire
from the locals. The German and English editions of the book contained this
assertion, but not the French, which naturally aroused suspicion, though
Baedeker may have deceived himself into thinking that he was just being
tactful.[63]

Fritz Baedeker died in 1925 (just failing to witness the centenary, in 1927, of
the firm his father had founded), and his son Hans took control of the business.
The previous decade had not been easy, what with the disruption of the First
World War (Baedeker lost a fortune patriotically invested in government bonds)
being followed by inflation and restrictions on foreign travel, which, however, the
firm turned to its advantage by developing a series of regional guides for
Germany. Nevertheless, and unlike Murray, which had sold its Handbooks series
in 1901, Baedeker retained its core activity, even if its golden age had closed with
the coming of war and foreign nationals were now hostile to the mere idea of
cultural products emanating from Germany. Compromises were necessary to
survive, one of which was the introduction of advertisements in the guides for
the first time in 1920. Projects had to be abandoned and workers laid off, but the
guides that did emerge were nurtured with undiminished editorial care, notably
the revised *Egypt* of 1929. Aficionados regard this as among the best, if not the
best, guidebook ever compiled, with its 676 pages, its superb maps and plans (an
area in which Baedeker was still head and shoulders above all competitors), the
distinguished scholarship of its historical and cultural essays and its readable
style. In this volume also is to be found the now legendary passage (beloved of
cartoonists) describing how the Great Pyramid of Cheops may be ascended,
assisted by 'two or three of the Beduin . . . with one holding each hand, and if
desired by a third (no extra payment) who pushes behind . . .'. The traveller
should not be hustled by these gentlemen ('Be quiet, or you shall have no fee'),

nor intimidated by demands for bakshish ('it is as well to keep an eye on one's pockets').

But certainly the old Baedeker hegemony had been broken, with Hachette's successor to Joanne, the Guide Bleu, doing good business, together with competition from the new Blue Guides in England (started by a former editor of English-language Baedekers) and the elegant Italian rival of Baedeker put out by the Touring Club Italiano. The situation deteriorated in the 1930s after the Nazis took power, not least in terms of the firm's fabled integrity. Baedeker was a proud name that the Nazis wished to exploit where possible for propaganda purposes, and the subvention granted to the firm in 1934 specified that its task was to increase 'respect for Germany in the world'.[64] Baedeker was unable to avoid completely the insertion of nationalistic and propagandist material, though in fact the propaganda function was more likely to be performed by the exclusion of unwelcome references (for example, to synagogues or military installations) rather than the conspicuous inclusion of officially desired ones. The series was also encouraged to fit in with government-inspired initiatives such as the risible KdF (*Kraft durch Freude*, 'Strength through Joy') programme, which would appear to have impelled the publication of the volume on Madeira (1934).

Government-ordained tasks included producing local guides for German engineers who were preparing defences against an Allied invasion on the Atlantic coast, and a guidebook for the German Army of Occupation in Poland. This last was the most propagandist text the firm was ever to produce, complete with an Introduction of disingenuous bombast by a functionary of the Institut für Deutsche Ostarbeit, according to whom, the 'very great backwardness of all branches of culture' in Poland was due to 'the essence and the race of the local inhabitants and an attitude toward life that is completely alien to German culture'. Damage to railway lines and public buildings was blamed on the unreasonableness of Polish resistance to the German invasion. Polish economic backwardness was attributed to centuries of profiteering by Jewish traders. The decline of Lublin from the eighteenth century was said to be entirely due to large-scale Jewish immigration there, this remark being rounded off with a laconic and chilling parenthesis: 'In 1862 the city had 57 per cent Jews, now it is Jew-free.'[65]

Halfway through the war, the name Baedeker acquired another melancholy association from the retaliation raids of the Luftwaffe in April and May of 1942 on the English cities of Exeter, Bath, Norwich and Canterbury. This was the Germans' answer to the RAF bombing of Cologne and the historic port of Lübeck in March of the same year. Because the targets in Britain were singled out on the basis of the 'two star' cities in Baedeker,[66] these attacks were known as the 'Baedeker raids' (or sometimes the 'Baedeker blitz').

In December 1943 an RAF raid on Leipzig set fire to the Baedeker office building, destroying not only priceless lithographic stones for the famous maps but also the entire archives. This might have been the end of Baedeker, but immediately after the war (1948), in a gesture of proud defiance, the 71-year-old Hans Baedeker brought out a slim guide to the city of Leipzig, now in the

Russian occupation zone. However, the Russians seized the book on the grounds that its Leipzig city plan showed the Russian Kommandatura, and thus supposedly revealed 'military secrets'. In West Germany, the leadership of Baedeker passed to Hans's nephew, Karl Friedrich (1910–79), a great-grandson of the founder, who had been taken prisoner by the Americans and had returned to his home in Schleswig-Holstein. Here he was employed in identifying church bells taken from churches all over Germany preparatory to melting them down for use as munitions. A true Baedeker, he soon set about compiling a guide to the area, his field trips being undertaken by bicycle; the results of his efforts were published in 1949. It was a success, and guides to Frankfurt and Hamburg soon followed. It seemed that the old firm was back in business, all the more so in that, despite some tempting offers from Great Britain and the USA, Karl Friedrich had prudently refused to sell the Baedeker name, which was still an extremely valuable property. However, he did work closely with the London publishers Allen & Unwin, who were the agents for the English Baedekers and who supplied Baedeker with a timely loan in 1950,[67] just as they had done before the war in the late 1920s.

POST-WAR BAEDEKER

Baedeker now moved into the newly fashionable area of motoring guides in collaboration with the oil firm Royal Dutch Shell (which had its own series of guides in Britain) and the Stuttgart printing firm of Mair. The combination of Baedeker's traditional skills in route-building and accuracy of practical detail allied to Mair's production and marketing expertise proved an enduring success. Mair's reorganisation of the guides' contents as an alphabetical gazetteer,[68] prefaced by essays on geography, climate, fauna and flora, history, economy, the arts, famous people and a brief summary of routes, is still the most thorough distillation of information available to travellers, even if the idiosyncrasies of style that endeared the classical Baedekers to their readers have largely disappeared.

The most famous of these quirks was the 'Baedeker parenthesis', as Mendleson aptly calls it, an irresistible parody of which is to be found in E.M. Forster's *Where Angels Fear to Tread*, where we learn that Philip Herriton: 'could never read "The view from the Rocca (small gratuity) is finest at sunset" without a catching at the heart.' To the Baedeker aficionado, entries that refer to 'tonsorial saloons' in the United States, animadversions on the 'shameful defectiveness' of French toilets, devastating one-word or one-line dismissals ('Railway Restaurant, mediocre', or 'Alb. Morino, dirty', or 'the waiter's arithmetic is occasionally at fault') and avuncular reassurance ('There is no cause for alarm when the aircraft "banks" when turning or "dips" owing to gusts of wind, or when the engines slow down, a sign that the pilot intends to fly at a lower height') represent the purest gold, surpassing in poetry even Michelin's genially auspicious topos of '*mérite le détour*'. And if Baedeker sometimes seems to see his readers (and this is also his attitude to orientals) as children who must be indulged, but not too much, this too is productive of some of his most engaging flights of irony, as when he writes the following of the Piazza San Marco in Venice: 'Peas may be bought for the pigeons from various loungers in the Piazza'; furthermore, 'those whose ambitions lean in this direction may have themselves photographed covered with birds'. Such indulgences must be severely rationed, of course, and the traveller must anyway be constantly on his guard against being ripped off: 'not the slightest weight should be attached to the representations of drivers, guides etc.' warns the 1867 Baedeker guide to Italy, drawing attention to an uncongenial local custom of charging foreigners five lira for a cab ride which normally only costs half a lira. One should perhaps salute the genius of the translator, as much as the Baedeker original, who always has such a masterly touch with the 'parenthesis': 'Pleasant walks to the south of the city. Guide 3fr. Adders abound.' (*Baedeker's Southern France*).

These glory days are certainly over, if only because the education system has altered the demands and expectations of later generations of guidebook users. Otto Baedeker, Karl Friedrich's cousin once removed, left the firm in 1971 after some twenty-five years because he felt the 'classical' guidebook had had its day. If by 'classical' is meant the erudite, authoritative vade mecum of the now dissipated class of *Bildungsbürgertum*, he was surely right, even if pockets of resistance to the mass market light bytes survive (Guide Bleu, Blue Guide, Touring Club Italiano). Speaking to Herbert Warren Wind for the latter's 1975 *New Yorker* piece, Karl Friedrich confessed that the word 'Baedeker' had lost its lustre, had indeed become the evocation of a vanished world of the spirit flask and the steamer trunk. He added that the uniqueness of the early Baedekers lay in the readers' conviction that every word could be trusted. Dramatic confirmation of this claim, said Karl Friedrich, came from an anecdote concerning Kaiser Wilhelm I of Germany, whose palace in Berlin stood on Unter den Linden. A visitor in 1880 found his interview interrupted when the Kaiser, noting that it was noon, hurried over to a large corner window to observe the changing of the guard below it. Returning to his visitor, he explained by way of an apology that 'it's written in Baedeker that I watch the changing of the guard from that window, and the people have come to expect it'.[69] For all their merits, it is frankly unlikely that any monarch would now turn out for Lonely Planet or the Rough Guide.

CHAPTER 10

How the Other Halves Lived:
From Cookites and Middle-Class
Excursionists to Dilettante Explorers

A map presents innumerable possibilities; a guidebook supplies a
specific task.
(Esther Allen, 'Money and Little Red Books', 1996)

The opening of a railway in an ignorant or barbarous district is an omen of
moral renovation and intellectual exaltation.
(Thomas Cook, Handbook of a Trip to Scotland, *1846)*

It has been claimed that the first railway excursion was made in 1838, when
some of the good people of Wadebridge in Cornwall were taken to the
neighbouring town of Bodmin to witness the execution of two murderers.
Since the gallows stood in full view of the station, the passengers were able to
watch this entertaining spectacle from the comfort of their carriages, without
even leaving their seats.[1] If nothing else, this macabre little outing demonstrates
that the sightseeing potential of the railway was grasped by its entrepreneurs
almost from its inception. Far more famous than this Bodmin excursion,
however, was the one organised three years later, on 5 July 1841, by Thomas
Cook, founder of the travel firm that bears his name. On that day the Baptist
teetotaller Cook took a party of some 500 people from Leicester to
Loughborough for a temperance convention, having secured from the railway
company a reduced fare of one shilling per head for the round trip.[2] From this
not terribly auspicious beginning was to grow the vast panoply of package tours

catering to all interests and to none. Today it is the lynchpin of a mass industry that keeps airlines, cruise providers, restaurants and thousands of hotels afloat, and supplies employment directly or indirectly to millions. 'It is unimaginable now that a day-trip to Loughborough could be seen as attractive,' writes Michael Bywater. 'Now a man may know Mauritius better than the woods a mile outside his own town; and yet, at the same time, know nothing that is new.'[3]

With the advent of the railway,[4] mass travel became a possibility, and with the advent of the travel entrepreneur, so did mass tourism. At once a gap opened up between those who thought of themselves as independent travellers, cultivated, reasonably affluent and often having mastered a language not their own; and those who were content to leave the travel arrangements to somebody else who was to be responsible for their security and their entertainment. Thomas Cook's *Handbook for a Trip to Scotland* of 1846 floridly proclaimed that 'The opening of a railway in an ignorant or barbarous district is an omen of moral renovation and intellectual exaltation,'[5] but that was not the way that intellectuals and cultural arbiters tended to see it. 'Going by railway I do not consider as travel at all,' opined Ruskin magisterially. 'It is merely being "sent" to a place, and very little different from becoming a parcel.'[6] On another occasion he lamented the 'ferruginous temper' of the age, derisively observing that railways were simply a means whereby 'every fool in Buxton can be at Bakewell in half an hour, and every fool in Bakewell at Buxton'.[7]

Ruskin's comments did not merely reflect the exasperation of a grumpy old man. Like many others he sensed that the new speed of travel would increase the blindness of tourists, an objection that has now become a clichéd sneer of Europeans in regard to shutter-clicking Japanese and bustling American visitors ('If it's Tuesday this must be Brussels'); and this despite the fact that Europeans often behave in exactly the same way in Asia or America. Ruskin was especially withering about those who boasted of 'doing' Europe by train in a week (a tour that was actually on offer from Thomas Cook from 1862 onwards). 'No changing of place at a hundred miles an hour will make us one whit stronger, happier, or wiser. There was always more in the world than men could see, walked they ever so slowly; they will see it no better for going fast. The really precious things are thought and sight, not pace.' In 1864 he rebuked an audience of Mancunian industrialists for their association with railway enterprise:

You have put a railway bridge over the fall of Schaffenhausen. You have tunnelled the cliffs of Lake Lucerne by Tell's chapel; you have destroyed the Clarens shore of the Lake of Geneva; there is not a quiet valley in England that you have not filled with the bellowing fire, nor any foreign city in which the spread of your presence is not marked by a consuming leprosy of new hotels.[8]

The slow progress by carriage, the lingering over a scene with a Claude glass and sketchbook at the ready, the leisurely and random perambulation of a town: these were not things that fitted easily, if at all, into a Cook's railway-based itinerary.

Not everyone saw only the negative side of swifter and cheaper travel. Almost all commentators, however, agreed that the advent of the railway represented a paradigm shift for human society, not simply an incremental technical improvement in transport. The poet Heinrich Heine (writing in Paris) compared the impact of the railway with that of the invention of gunpowder or printing, 'swinging mankind in a new direction . . . space is killed by the railways and we are left with time alone. I feel as if the mountains and forests of all countries were advancing on Paris. Even now, I can smell the German linden trees; the North Sea breakers are rolling against my door.'[9] Thackeray, writing in the *Cornhill*, was the most amusing and eloquent of these observers, asserting hyperbolically that everything pre-railway was the 'old world', stretching back in an unbroken line from the stagecoach to the Ancient Britons. 'We who lived before railways, and survive out of the ancient world, are like Father Noah and his family out of the Ark.' With more prescience than he knew, Thackeray describes, with heavy irony, an acquaintance who had invented a flying machine and 'trembled daily' lest someone else should 'light upon it and patent his discovery,' for the development of which he only needed £500 capital. 'Perhaps faith was wanting; perhaps the five hundred pounds. He is dead, and somebody else must make the flying-machine. But that will only be a step forward on the journey already begun since we quitted the old world.'[10]

Thackeray wonders where the new technologically sophisticated world is heading ('to what new laws, new manners, new politics, vast new expanses of liberties unknown as yet, or only surmised?'). This new dispensation would obviously require a new infrastructure of travel founded on business principles, which Thomas Cook provided, and new ancillary material such as guidebooks, which he also supplied. The multi-volume didacticism of a Eustace and discursive fictive letters of a Keysler or a Misson were hideously inappropriate for the new type of consumer of guidebooks. The bourgeois traveller now began to travel with his densely written 'handbook', while the excursionist took along his no frills basic guide, so that he should have at least some idea of what he was looking at.

GUIDEBOOKS AND GUIDEBOOK PUBLISHERS BEFORE AND AFTER STEAM

Before the advent of steam, before therefore the founding of Cook's, Murray's and Baedeker's guides, there were already a number of handy vade mecums for the prospective British traveller that concentrated on practical information rather than the classic preoccupations of the Grand Tour. Some of these were very successful, for example, Philip Playstowe's *Gentleman's Guide* to France (1766?), written by a retired naval officer and running through ten editions to 1788. The book notably combines thrift with chauvinism, and its popularity does not altogether flatter the image of the John Bulls who used it. On the title page the author asserts that his guide has been written by 'an officer of the Royal Navy, who lately travelled on a principle which he most sincerely recommends to his countrymen, viz. Not to spend more money in the country of our natural enemy, than is requisite to support, with Decency, the character of an English Man.' Constantly expanded in content, and made more handy for travel by reduction from octavo to duodecimo from the fourth edition, the book offered precise rules for an Englishman who wanted to save money. There is also substantial information on travel routes, hotels and restaurants. The later editions are at pains to indicate the places where the English abroad foregathered, and where London newspapers might be read.[11] The idea of travelling in the country of one's 'natural enemy' and denying him, so far as possible, any profit from your travelling is the counterpart of the wiles of the greedy hotelier and grasping restauranteur against whom Thomas Cook was to warn his flock a century later. In truth, neither the image of the excessively mean traveller, nor that of his excessively grasping host, is attractive, although Playstowe's budget guide can be seen as the precursor of many to be published in the twentieth and twenty-first centuries. The attitude of such guidebooks may perhaps be extenuated where the volume of trade from group travel compensates the locals for a parsimonious outlay per individual. Playstowe's ungentlemanly meanness becomes the readily understandable caution of travellers with limited means.

Playstowe's book appeared first with a Quaker publisher, Samuel Farley, and then with George Kearsley, one of the best-known travel publishers of the day. The exponential rise in tourism is indeed suggested by the appearance of several publishers who specialised in guidebooks or published series of them from the mid-eighteenth century onwards – names like George Kearsley,[12] Samuel Leigh, or Sherwood, Neely and Jones may be familiar only to bibliophiles, but they played a significant role in guidebook history. And some of these firms were exceptionally enterprising: Francis Coghlan, for instance, whose series was launched in 1828 with *A Guide to France; or Travellers Their Own Commissioners; Shewing the Cheapest and Most Expeditious System of Travelling with Hints on How to Obtain Their Own Passports*, is thought to have been a travel agent before Thomas Cook more or less patented that profession. His Paris and Belgian guides ran to sixteen editions.[13] Other publishers of guides prospered in the railway age, for example, Alexander Tighe Gregory with his *Practical Guides by an Englishman Abroad* in the 1850s and 1860s, aimed at those pursuing the new fashion of the walking tour, or George Measom, Abel Heywood,[14] Thomas Nelson and Adam and Charles Black, some of whose offerings were very specifically linked to railway travel. The expansion from inland tourism to foreign travel for a wider public can be seen from the list of George Frederick Cruchley, whose series of British guides was extended from 1840 to books for the Levant, Moscow and elsewhere.[15] There was even some self-publishing at the bottom end of the market, for example, the hiking guides produced by the bootmaker Henry Gaze in the 1860s.

Not surprisingly, the travel market boomed with the end of the Napoleonic Wars, boosted also by the first cross-Channel service by steamboat, which was instituted in 1820.[16] However the first guidebooks to be rushed out after the peace were often retreads, like Mariana Starke's work discussed in the previous chapter; and some were inadequately updated, if at all. The new dispensation also encouraged the translation of classic foreign guidebooks such as Ebel's *Switzerland* (1818), Romberg's *Brussels* (1816), Reichard's *Itineraries* (also from 1816) and Mariano Vasi's *New Picture of Rome* (from 1819).[17] Particularly successful was Reichard's extensively illustrated *Itinerary of France and Belgium,* in its second edition by 1822, combining a full account of convenient routes with 'concise description of the Soil, Produce, Manufacturers, Population and Curiosities . . . and occasional Notices of Places Adjacent', and claiming all the advantages of a 'Gazetteer, a Book of Roads and History of France and Belgium that will be found an interesting and useful companion to the British tourist'.

Reichard is partly a digest from other reliable sources (for instance, Boyce on Belgium and Planta on Paris), and he does not offer anything on works of art. On the other hand, his practical information is very thorough (perhaps it is no accident that his guides were put out from the 1820s by Baldwin, Cradock & Joy, publishers to the Society for the Diffusion of Useful Knowledge). For example, he includes tables for calculating the price of entire journeys using the post, which was strictly regulated by the government in France and the Low Countries. Social historians will be interested in his assertion that 'every kind of wearing apparel can be procured cheaper in Paris than at London' (this was in 1822), and in the revelation that the passage from London to Paris by coach and including the sea passage cost '3l. 10s. for an inside coach seat and 2l. 10s. for a cabriolet'.[18] One of the most valuable parts of the book is the information on financing the journey, which at that time meant availing oneself of the 'Circular Exchange Notes' originally instituted by the banker James Herries in the 1770s. These were in fact an early form of traveller's cheques, against which cash was payable at designated correspondent banks on the Continent. In 1874 Thomas Cook was to launch his own 'Circular Notes', which extended the principle to encashment at any location where his other invention, Cook's Hotel Coupons[19] (from 1867), were accepted.[20] In the USA, the American Express introduced its own 'money order' in 1882, and in 1891, its traveller's cheques.

The professionalisation of the travel industry and its ancillary services[21] went hand in hand with the increase in tourism and a wider spectrum of travellers. Intellectuals did not look kindly on this development, and Coleridge even referred to the new breed of tourist as 'Delinquent Travellers' in a poem with this title published in 1824. Even if we accept the contention of Coleridge's biographer[22] that his satire is actually directed at fashionable travellers who indulged in the

> Tour, Journey, Voyage, Lounge, Ride, Walk,
> Skim, Sketch, Excursion, Travel-talk –
> For move [they] must! 'Tis now the rage
> The law and fashion of the Age . . .

his view of the other kind, the less elegant excursionists, is hardly flattering:

Of all the children of John Bull
With empty heads and bellies full,
Who ramble East, West, North and South,
With leaky purse and open mouth,
In search of varieties exotic
The usefullest and most patriotic
And merriest, too, believe me Sirs!
Are you delinquent Travellers!

This is hardly one of Coleridge's best poems, but it reflects, albeit more affectionately, the same mistrust of mass travel, and of a heightened pace of life generally, that is also evident in the objections of Coleridge's fellow Lake Poet, William Wordsworth, in respect of the proposed construction of the Windermere railway link. As usual, there is an undertow of puritanism and snobbery in his attitude, mixed with the nostalgia that Thackeray evokes in the piece quoted above. Pleasures – and hardships – long cultivated by the few are now to be served up for the masses, who will be carried like lords from place to place and will no longer have to sing for their suppers.

THE 'ONEIRIC CHARGE' OF PARIS

Nowhere was more of a beacon for the new tourism than Paris, whose supposedly sybaritic attractions were conveniently close for the Englishman and now attracted the independent middle-class traveller of means. This of course represented the resumption of a long-standing tradition: just before the Revolution, the forerunner of *The Times*, known as *The Daily Universal Register*, in its issue of 29 August 1786, had already thundered its disapproval of such frivolous travel to such a frivolous city: 'To such an amazing pitch of folly is the rage of travelling come, that in less than six weeks, the list of Londoners arrived in Paris has amounted to three thousand seven hundred and sixty, as appears by the register of that city.'[23] Over half a century later, the flood of visitors was, if anything, growing. In Charles Marchal's *Physiologie de l'anglais à Paris* (1841) one reads: 'For the Englishman, Paris . . . represents happiness, a story from *The Thousand and One Nights*, total freedom!' It was again the astute publisher Samuel Leigh[24] who successfully tapped into this enticing image by supplying the most successful text catering to the burgeoning demand for a solid guidebook to Paris. This was Edward Planta's *A New Picture of Paris, or The Stranger's Guide to the French Metropolis Accurately Describing the Public Establishments, Remarkable Edifices, Places of Amusement, and every other Object Worthy of Attention*, which first appeared in 1814 and was continuously revised up to the 1830s. The author laid stress on the title's claim that this was a 'new' picture of the city, remarking that existing guides copied much from old ones and ignored the fact that many of the 'paintings and sculptures, and even buildings' described in them had been 'destroyed during the reign of revolutionary anarchy'.[25] Demand for the book seems to have fallen off in the 1830s: its potential readers were now probably more at home with the *Murray Handbook*, and eventually the English version of *Baedeker's Paris* (1865), while the new 'package' tourist (from 1855)[26] would be catered for by Cook's modest publication prepared for his clients.

Yet, while the success of Planta's guide doubtless traded on the 'oneiric charge'[27] of his subject matter, the guide itself is anglocentric, occasionally chauvinistic in its depiction of Gallic manners and mores, critical of the services available, old maidish in its anxiety regarding the 'prostitutes and gamblers' who might be your neighbouring guests in a café, and sometimes gives the impression that one of the benefits of a stay in Paris is that it prompts you to recall the merits of your own culture and society. At any rate, the dream of Paris has rather collided with reality. This was indeed what Huysmans's hero in *A rebours*, the Duc des Esseintes, feared would happen if he actually travelled to London, as planned. He abandons his trip to England at the last minute, deciding to stick with his dream of its great metropolis (derived from a judicious combination of Dickens and Baedeker), rather than risk a bruising confrontation with the reality of it.[28] As Esther Allen puts it, des Esseintes decides that London itself could not give him 'any more knowledge of the word "London" than he already has . . . for des Esseintes [it] has ceased to exist outside of its representations.'[29]

It was not until the last decades of the nineteenth century and the *belle époque* that some guides allowed themselves to be more open about the physical basis of Paris's 'oneiric charge', namely its fleshpots and nightlife, and above all the availability and professionalism of its prostitutes. A candid publication of 1889 is entitled the *Guide secret de l'étranger célibataire à Paris*, which promises information on '*distractions diurnes et nocturnes, adresses et renseignements sur les établissements de nuit, brasseries servies par des dames bouges [sic], cabarets excentriques, maisons curieuses et renommées*'. With its references to '*maisons speciales, les horizontales du quartier*' and details of rooms available at 35 centimes per night ('*on ne garantit les draps*'), it seems fairly clear what sort of bachelor this book is aimed at – the moneyed gentleman looking for risqué entertainment and commercial sex. Interestingly, the same rue St-Honoré where Planta's little colony of English could feel safe, is lauded for a '*promenoir specialement fréquenté par un public de jolies femmes*'. This publication pioneers a sub-genre of the guidebook, whose candour may have led to it being sold as an under-the-counter article. Openness about sex tourism in more mainstream guidebooks has indeed only come to the fore in the twentieth and twenty-first centuries, particularly in respect of gay culture.

It should not be forgotten, however, that guidebooks to prostitution had existed at least since the eighteenth century. By the nineteenth century, they were articles being sold *sub rosa* to discerning adults, often by the same booksellers who purveyed respectable guides. A not untypical example is *The Swell's Night Guide; or a Peep through the Metropolis under the Dominion of Nox*, which promised information, *inter alia*, on 'The Paphian Beauties', 'The Chaffing Cribs', 'The Singing and Lushing Cribs', 'Fancy Ladies and their Penchants' and so on in London. It was advertised as having 'numerous spicy engravings' and was compiled by a louche character called Renton Nicholson. As we see from this remarkable title, the world of commercial sex had its own complex argot, which the punters would have been familiar with: 'cribs' is slang for brothels, and the phrase 'Paphian beauties' is of course a euphemism for prostitutes (from Paphos on Cyprus, the place where Aphrodite (Venus) stepped ashore after her watery birth, and where her cult flourished in the ancient world). Philip Howell has pointed out how these Victorian guides, more than the lists of courtesans that preceded them and the lists of municipally licensed prostitutes that followed, offered to protect and enlighten their users like a mainstream guidebook, acting as 'etiquette books for male experience in the city'.[30] Renton Nicholson also ran a journal from 1837 to 1842 (*The Town*), which was entirely devoted to a continuously updated 'sexual geography' of the city for the aspirant Lothario.

SPAS: AN OLD TRADITION WITH NEW MARKETABILITY

Spas were exploited in Europe at least from Celtic times: to give one example of many, Roman Aquincum, located in what was later Óbuda[31] on the western shore of the Danube, owed its name to that of an earlier Eraviscan Celtic settlement, whose appellation *Ak-Ink* signified 'Abundant Waters'. Similarly, Bath, which the Romans called Aquae Sulis, is a spa of Iron Age origin. Here and elsewhere the Romans invested heavily, their largest complexes featuring communal pools, changing rooms, warm, tepid and cool halls equipped with basins or pools (*caldaria, tepidaria* and *frigidaria*); latterly there were also wet and dry sweating rooms (*sudaria*). In the early modern period, one of the earliest guidebooks worthy of the name (by one Joannes Elysius, 1475)[32] dealt with the baths at Pozzuoli, near Naples. It is not all that practical, preferring to reprint eulogies of the hot springs by the Latin poets rather than to give solid information; nevertheless, it must be counted as one of the first spa guides. Indeed, it was the progenitor of many successive works of local spa patriotism concerned with the Phlegraean Fields.[33] A popular one seems to have been that by Bishop Pompeo Sarnelli, first published in 1685 and running through six editions over the next 116 years, with French editions in 1702 and 1748. The 1691 edition has a list of rules to be observed by bathers at Pozzuoli. According to Malcolm Letts, later editions claimed on the title page to cover the islands of Capri and Procida. This was a spurious bit of marketing, since there is no trace of the islands in the text itself.[34]

Although many spas were neglected in the Middle Ages, those in Turkish-occupied central and south-eastern Europe were largely preserved, thanks to the highly developed bath culture of the Ottomans, perhaps the only enduring legacy of the latter in the lands they occupied. By the sixteenth century it is clear that the healing properties of many well-known spas were in demand for those who could afford to travel to them – Montaigne set out on his Italian journey with the principal aim of seeking relief for his hereditary ailment of kidney stone by taking the waters. He did in fact spend three months at the attractive Apennine spa of Bagni di Lucca, a place later to be patronised by Browning,

Byron and many British Tuscan residents or travellers.[35] Montaigne's pilgrimage from spa to spa may serve to illustrate the secularisation of a phenomenon that had its origin in ancient religious ritual. Belief in the healing waters of shrines had gradually given way to the scientific application of the same, although Christianity was later to reinvigorate the tradition of miraculous healing at Lourdes.

We have seen that the original motive of Mariana Starke's Italian travels was to accompany a consumptive relative on a convalescent tour, and the nineteenth century saw several spa guides published by doctors such as Edwin Lee (died 1870), Augustus Bozzi Granville (1783–1872) and others. As early as the seventeenth century, a Dr Thomas Johnson had published *Thermae Bathonicae* and Vaughan tells us that more than one hundred different sources of waters with varying properties were discovered between 1660 and 1714.[36] Individual spas like Bath and Tunbridge Wells became fashionable and began to feature in the literature of the period (as in Jane Austen's novels or Christopher Anstey's verse satire, *The New Bath Guide* (1766)). Some authors cast a cold eye on the spas' aspirations to elegance, for example, the actor and composer George Saville Carey, the second edition of whose *The Balnea: Or, An Impartial Description of All the Popular Watering Places in England* had appeared by 1799. Of Margate's supposedly showcase 'Parade' he complains: 'The greatest part of it lies between a noisy stableyard, well furnished with manure, and the common sewer of the contiguous market-place, as well as the lower part of the old town, which frequently yield up the most ungrateful exhalations and unsavoury smells to those who choose to regale themselves in this delicious neighbourhood.'[37]

Nevertheless, the burgeoning civic pride of such places was reflected in the literature they produced for visitors, much of which is aglow with local patriotism. Competition among guidebooks was fierce in a place like Bath, with its captive, bored and relatively wealthy clientele. The size of the market is indicated by the plethora of mid-century publications with titles like *The Original Bath Guide*, *The Invalid's Companion to Bath*, *Gibb's Bath Visitant* and even *Advice to a Young Whist Player*. One might think the field was well covered, but there was still room for a volume aimed directly at traders, *The Bath and Bristol: or the Tradesman's and Traveller's Pocket Companion* (1742 and several subsequent editions.) Thomas Boddely, who published this informative volume, was himself the proud retailer of such exotic wares as 'Quicksilver Girdles for the Itch' and 'France's Female Strengthening Elixir'. Today he would be selling Viagra over the Internet.

Abroad, it was of course not only Italy that offered healing waters, but also Switzerland, Germany (Aachen, Baden), Bohemia (Karlovy Vary/Karlsbad), Hungary, France (Montpellier), the Low Countries (Spa) and Lisbon. The last named had been visited by the novelist Henry Fielding for the cure, and by 1800 there was a guide 'containing directions to invalids who visit Lisbon with a description of the city etc'. Inland spas were soon in competition with seaside resorts, sea-bathing having been given decisive impetus by the publication of Dr Richard Russell's *Dissertation on the Use of Sea Water* (1750). The pleasures of sea-bathing were at first rigorously subordinate to its health-giving potential: it was thought that the water should be entered with closed pores, so a sunless early morning dip was indicated. Feminine modesty was protected through the invention of a bathing machine by a Quaker gentleman from Margate, Benjamin Beale; by means of this elaborate contrivance, the female form was trundled seawards hidden from view, and then enabled to glide securely into the brine, observed only by the odd libidinous seagull. Royal endorsement helped to convince the sceptics and the moralists, like the doctors who prophesied 'immediate death' for their colleague Tobias Smollett when he took to the sea at Nice. George III put Weymouth on the map as a resort by indulging in sea-bathing, which was supposed to cure his fits of madness, though there were those who thought it induced them. 'Majestically' is indeed how he entered the waves to the strains of 'God Save the King' played by some windswept fiddlers in a nearby bathing machine.[38]

By 1803 both seaside resorts[39] and inland spas were so much a part of the culture that the need was felt for an overall guide, which was supplied by John Feltham, who had already written guidebooks to Paris and London, and who now produced his *Guide to All the Watering and Sea-bathing Places*. This could not have been intended for the excursionist, but was more of a celebratory volume in boards with plenty of illustrations – and retailing at a hefty 12 shillings.[40] Guides to individual spas could be as cheap as 1 shilling, with an extra 6 pence being demanded for a city plan. The attractions of the spas were as much social as a medical; they were places that benefited commercially from the hypochondria of gentlemen and ladies of fashion, gradually also from the same phenomenon lower down the social order. A report on the Harrogate spa was candid on this head, remarking that 'nervous ailments are not now confined to the higher ranks, but are spreading rapidly with the extension of knowledge and luxury among the poorer classes', a fact that the surgeon author attributes to 'the anxieties of competition' and 'sedentary habits'.[41] Learned authors hastened to respond to the hunger for scientific backgound on the cures claimed to be available. The previously mentioned Edwin Lee wrote books concerned with 'medical topography and remedial resources' which exhaustively dealt with the composition and curative properties of mineral waters at spas in Britain and abroad; he usually included weather statistics and descriptive passages lifted from local guidebooks.

Dr Granville, a naturalised Englishman of Italian origin, published guides to *The Spas of Germany* (1837) and those of England, together with its sea-bathing places (1841). A rumbustious character, he 'allowed his vigorous prejudices free rein', says Vaughan,[42] and campaigned with some success for the return of art treasures to Italy that had been stolen by the French in the Napoleonic period. His three-volume work *The Spas of England* (1841) is impressive, and includes analysis of the mineral composition of some thirty-six spas together with the physician's view of their medicinal properties. His account of Harrogate is not untypical in its thoroughness, and includes notes on the fashionable season there ('from the end of July to the Doncaster races'), its various wells and the differing benefits that each claimed to provide, the accommodation on offer and the prices thereof, the town's history and topography, and finally critical comments on the lack of capitalistic enterprise displayed by the owners of the springs. In writing of Brighton, the doctor praises the institution of a 'great parallel sewer', accompanying this with a hair-raising description of the sewage discharged directly into the the sea before this measure was undertaken. He notes in passing that Brighton prices are one-third higher than those of London . . .[43] However, there were plenty of cheaper seaside resorts, which became the destination for the typical working class day-trip, particularly after Sir John Lubbock (as Home Secretary) introduced Bank Holidays in 1871 (though none then fell in the summer).

In the second half of the century, Scotland also tried to develop a line in what would now be called 'wellness' tourism, and publications of an informative and didactic nature appeared, such as Charteris's *Guide to Health Resorts at Home and Abroad* (1887), which divided resorts into three categories, sea-bathing, climatic and curative. Sea-bathing in the icy Scottish waters was not exactly to everybody's taste, but it had a long tradition. For example, on the urging of medical friends, Robert Burns went to bathe on the Solway coast in July 1796, which almost certainly hastened his death. In the climatic category Scotland fared better, with many areas (Speyside, for instance) and towns (like Rothesay, on the Isle of Bute) being appreciated for their bracing air. Bidding as curative centres were places like Brodick on the Isle of Arran, whose speciality was the local goat's whey, and mineral spas like Moffat in Dumfriesshire. These regions and towns of course generated their own enthusiastic guidebooks. Although the Moffat spa was successful in the age of Enlightenment, when this 'Cheltenham of Scotland' was patronised by luminaries such as Hume, Boswell and Burns, it was never as fashionable as the famous English spas like Harrogate or Bath. This is rather underlined by the fact that the two local landowners who invested most in Moffat's development, the Duke of Buccleuch and Lord Hopetoun, themselves took the waters at Bath and Buxton respectively.[44] Nevertheless, Moffat compensated by becoming a general holiday resort, as William Wallace Fyfe observed in his *Guide to the Scottish Watering Places: A Visit to Moffat, its Spas, and Neighbourhood* (3rd edn, Edinburgh, 1853). The majority of visitors, he believed, were not invalids, but taking the cure as an ancillary activity, or for pleasure, and as part of their relaxing vacation.

More fashionable than Moffat was Bridge of Allan in Central Scotland, which Baddeley's *Thorough Guide* of 1903 describes in glowing terms, and is claimed by its own guidebook to be the 'Queen of the Scottish Spas'. Major John Henderson developed the spa from spring waters which had flooded a copper mine that had been discontinued in 1807. Another Bridge of Allan guide – admittedly commissioned by Henderson – grandly proclaimed the town to be the 'Montpelier [*sic*] of Scotland'. The author of this latter work of 400 pages was an indefatigable promoter of the resort, raising funds, *inter alia*, for the erection of a monument to William Wallace nearby, since Bridge of Allan unfortunately lacked any tourist sights. Although there was actually nothing to see at the monument, other than a hut and a flagstaff, by the 1890s 36,000 visitors were flocking to it, as opposed to less than 4,000 to the more historically evocative sight of Bannockburn. Bridge of Allan was thus an early example of a resort largely created by good marketing: there were nice touches – the guests were woken each morning to the sound of the pipes – and there were excellent facilities, such as tennis courts, a bowling green, and (from 1895) a golf course.[45]

RAILWAY GUIDES

Dr Granville also turned his physician's spotlight on the implications for public health arising from rail travel, which began to operate commercially from 1830 when the Liverpool–Manchester railway was opened. He is scornful of claims that passengers' health was at risk from the train plunging in and out of tunnels (said to damage the eyes), or from travelling through deep cuttings (said to cause catarrh and agues). On the other hand, he is certainly no covert apologist for the railway companies. Indeed, his complaints of the 'intolerable impertinence' and 'shameful neglect', coupled with the unattractive 'rapacity' displayed by some of the railway companies, led to a public inquiry and remedial legislation. Many of the irritations or worse that have come back to haunt rail passengers since the reprivatisation of the railways in the 1990s were already writ large in the boom years of railway expansion and speculation. With the withdrawal of the stagecoaches, railway tickets, formerly priced to compete with the coach, soared in price as they have today, and for the same reason: each line had effectively a monopoly in its own area, and all the companies together could operate what was effectively a cartel on pricing, though of course this was never admitted. There were also various money-gouging scams, such as extortionate charges for luggage, although baggage should have been much less expensive to carry on a train than in the limited space of a stagecoach. Inevitably, there were also accidents, such as the one that nearly killed Charles Dickens at Staplehurst in Kent in 1865,[46] accidents that rivals to the railway such as canal and coach proprietors made the most of. Often disasters were due to negligence, for example, landslides that were caused by inadequately supported embankments; or they were caused by incompetence and lack of coordination, as with collisions occurring where the lines of different railway companies intersected.[47] There were also instances of stokers falling asleep or getting drunk, with the result that a train ran out of steam.

The biggest bugbear was booking through-tickets for journeys involving lines owned by two or more companies. This was largely solved by the institution in 1842 of a Railway Clearing House for the sale of rail tickets, which made it possible for Thomas Cook to organise his round trips. It was again a Low Church businessman who introduced the other vital component for efficient marketing of railway travel, namely a timetable that enabled passengers to plan their journeys in advance. The first publication in this line was issued in 1839, *The Railway Time Table and Assistant to Railway Travel.* Bradshaw's monthly railway guides were begun by the eponymous Manchester Quaker in 1841, and coverage was extended to the Continent seven years later.[48] Although the books were called 'guides', they chiefly consisted of timetables and maps (George Bradshaw had originally been an engraver of maps and city plans, and had also printed a canal guide),[49] together with advertisements and information on hackney carriage fares or the like. From 1858 steamboat departures and tide charts were also included, so that Bradshaw 'played a large part in making Britain time-conscious'.[50] The thirty-two-page monthly guides gave tables for forty-three railway lines, and publication continued up to 1961.[51] The print was so small that special spectacles were marketed for reading it. In their iconic yellow wrappers, they became a household name, though their contents may often have reflected optimism rather than fact, which is why *Punch* disrespectfully dubbed Bradshaw England's 'Greatest Work of Fiction'.[52] (It is worth noting that Bradshaw provided for provincial travel what had already become indispensable for metropolitan travel. The first recorded timetable for city journeys had been printed in 1829 by George Shillibeer for his horse-drawn omnibus service between Paddington and the Bank of England. The trip took one hour!)[53] Bradshaw was obviously fascinated enough by his product to be a traveller himself, and in fact met an untimely end (1853) from cholera in Norway.

From the 1830s railway guidebooks proliferated, whereby the course of the line through varied environments provided a convenient device for supplying miscellaneous information. *The Tourist's Companion or: The History of the Scenes and Places on the Route of the Rail-Road and Steam-Packet from Leeds and Selby to Hull*, compiled by Edward Parsons in 1835, provides a pleasing example of the cinematic effect achieved by this approach. Topics include bridges, cholera, dissenting and other chapels, Nevison the highwayman, riot in consequence of the dearness of provisions, Statue to Queen Anne, beautiful situation of Selby, gas works, respectability of the inhabitants, and so forth. The Low Church author is at pains to inform his readers about the places of worship available to them; in the list of such for Leeds we find Roman Catholics competing with 'Independents [Congregationalists], Unitarians, Old Connexion Methodists, Protestant Methodists, Friends [Quakers], Inghamites, Primitive Methodists, Female Revivalists (Methodist), the Bethel Union (Sailors), the New Jerusalem [Swedenborgians] and Pro-Methodists'. The doubtless very plain sanctuaries of these various denominations are of course not included for their aesthetic aspects, if any. On the other hand, Parsons does observe tartly of St Mary's on Quarry Hill, presumably an Anglican church, that it is a 'mere specimen of carpenter's Gothic'. Of St John's Church (1634) in Leeds, he is equally dismissive: 'Dr Whitaker says, and there is indubitable truth in his statement, that St John's church has all the gloom and all the obstructions of an ancient church, without one vestige of its dignity and grace.'

Simply using the railway safely and in a manner that could get the most out of it was a sufficiently complex subject to generate it own compendia, notably *The Railway Traveller's Handy Book of Hints, Suggestions and Advice before the Journey, on the Journey and after the Journey*, anonymously published in 1862.[54] This tells the prospective traveller almost all he would need to know about planning a railway journey, and possibly more. It notes that there are two timetables published on the first of each month, the *ABC* and Bradshaw, monthly publication being a necessity as the companies kept changing their schedules. The *ABC* was apparently only useful for 'persons who have only to proceed direct from one point to another, without being doomed to thread the labyrinth of branch lines junctions, etc.', for which Bradshaw would be needed. An explanation is given of the complicated rubric used by the latter, which had 'given rise to innumerable witticisms on its unintelligibility' ('6. A thin line in the middle of the train, thus ∟, represents a shunt, and is intended to show the continuous route of the traveller. 7. Wave lines, thus ~, have a twofold use; first to direct the eye into the the next train; and, second, to show that travellers do not travel past the stations opposite to which the wave line appears.'). As to the advertisements, the reader is warned that 'the glowing terms in which nearly every proprietor speaks of his establishment must not, of course, be interpreted literally'. The author is not without a certain dry humour and cites a joke from *Punch* designed to show how the railway authorities enforced class distinctions. The ticket collector is represented as properly obsequious to first-class passengers ('May I trouble you for your tickets?'). To second-class passengers he is a little more brusque ('Tickets, please'). On entering the third-class carriage, he bawls: 'Now then! Tickets.' There are tips on ventilation, security for females who may be assaulted as the train passes through tunnels, and finally wise advice about leaning out of the window: 'The proper place for the head is inside, not outside, the carriage, and so long as it is kept there, the chances are that it will remain whole.'[55]

This handy guide seems to have been deservedly popular. It was impartial, unlike the little volumes put out from the 1850s by George Measom who produced what he claimed (untruthfully) were the 'official' guides to individual lines, and shamelessly plugged commercial enterprises. It was unpretentious, especially when compared to the 'Plain Rules for Railway Travellers' featured by the insufferably pompous Dr Dionysius Lardner in his book *Railway Economy* (1850). Lardner's rules were somewhat patronising in tone, Rule X, for example, being concerned with the danger of 'yielding to a sudden impulse to spring from the train to recover your hat'. Sombre illustrations of the consequences of doing this are appended: for example, 'Eastern Counties, 4 Mar 1846: Jumping out after hat, hip dislocated. Dublin & Kingstown 19 Dec 1845: Jumped from a train after a parcel which had fallen. Killed.' Other books concentrated on health aspects of railway locomotion, for example, Alfred Haviland's *Hurried to Death: Or, A Few Words of Advice on the Dangers of Hurry and Excitement Especially Addressed to Railway Travellers* (1868). Railway advice continued to drop from the presses up to the turn of the century, acquiring an increasingly populist and irreverent tone, such as in MacCarthy O'Moore's *Tips for Travellers: or, Wrinkles for the Road and Rail* (1899). This concentrated on possible hazards with which unsuspecting travellers could be confronted, including 'Cinder in the Eye', 'Ladies' Huge Hatpins', and the 'Perils of Meat-Pies at Restaurants'.[56] This last caution has a melancholy resonance that echoes down the memory lane of lamentable British Rail cuisine. The latter's ham sandwiches indeed represented a sort of culinary meltdown, and regularly beat off fierce competition from other British products to emerge as the most inedible substances ever offered for human consumption in the civilised world.

THOMAS COOK AND THE RAILWAY AGE

If genius is really 'an infinite capacity for taking pains',[57] both Thomas Cook (1808–92), and his somewhat more adventurous son, John Mason Cook (1834–99), were both geniuses. Like many iconic businessmen, Thomas Cook actually went bankrupt early in his career, in 1846, but recovered to launch one of the most successful business brands ever. The 'brand recognition' of Cook's Tours could be compared not unreasonably with that of subsequent household names like Coca Cola or Microsoft today. Luck, as always, played an important part in his success. He came of age when a market, which, even had it previously existed, could not have been served, was suddenly provided with the means to exploit it through a revolution in transport. Cook was quick-witted enough to take advantage of this and conscientious enough to ensure that his customers were seldom disappointed with what he offered them. As mentioned above, Cook was also swift to exploit the facility for purchasing round-trip tickets, at the same time wringing a volume discount out of reluctant railway companies.[58] This was a major achievement when one considers that a journey from Leicester to Liverpool originally involved buying tickets from no less than six different railway companies! For tours of Scotland and Wales, he devised round-trip combi-tickets that were valid on both steamers and trains. For workers on lower incomes, he devised innumerable round trips to resorts. (It is notable that, of the twenty-six rail destinations listed in the 'Excursion Guide' printed at the end of *The Railway Traveller's Handy Book*, thirteen are to seaside resorts.)

Cook also brilliantly seized on the opportunities afforded by such events as the London and Paris exhibitions of the 1850s and 1860s, providing the first complete package tours for visitors from the provinces who wished to visit them. It is said he arranged tours for some 165,000 people to the Great Exhibition held in London in 1851. This achievement was the result of Cook's genius for successful networking: while taking a party round Chatsworth, he met the Duke's celebrated garden designer, Joseph Paxton, who subsequently designed the Crystal Palace in Hyde Park, where the Great Exhibition was held. It was Paxton who enlisted Cook's help for bringing parties of sightseers from the industrial Midlands and the north, Cook becoming the 'Excursion Manager' for the Midland Railway Company. Workers were encouraged to form travel clubs for the outing and to suscribe for their fares in instalments. Once arrived in London, Cook protected them from sharks claiming to be 'hotel agents' and lodged them in a block of 200 model cottages he had rented in Fulham, where they paid half a crown a day for bed, breakfast and tea. Delegations of workers from Paris, Turin and Germany also lodged there. When Napoleon III held his own Great Exhibition in 1855, Cook organised his first trip to France, no doubt encouraged by his friend Paxton, who had become a protagonist of foreign travel for everyman after accompanying his employer on a Grand Tour.[59] It has been claimed that one of the attractions on offer for this Parisian jaunt was a chance to see an execution by guillotine.[60]

However, as Cook expanded his business to foreign parts, the demographic profile of his clientele changed. He had already been taking middle-class ladies and gentlemen on his Scottish trips, and the foreign ones were chiefly composed of clergymen, doctors, schoolmasters, governesses and 'representatives of the better style of London [and provincial] community'. This was because what Cook termed 'the humbler class of travellers' could not afford or obtain the extended leave that a continental tour entailed. Cook was a democrat at heart, defending his tourists from the repeated attacks made on them by various commentators, such as the novelist Charles Lever, and castigating a Highland grandee who evidently thought that 'places of interest should be excluded from the gaze of the common people'; but he was also a realist. These middle-class excursions abroad also attracted unattached females and seem to have become a discreet marriage market on occasion. Cook was alert to the business value of this development and stressed that the tours were entirely suitable for ladies (who in fact were in a majority of those who signed up for them) and that he himself acted as a 'travelling chaperon'.[61] In all this one sees the mixture of idealism and business acumen that characterised Thomas Cook the entrepreneur, whose democratisation of travel has aptly been called 'philanthopy plus 5 per cent'. The same author remarks that the teetotal Cook 'damned inns as little better than brothels; the tour operator came to terms with them'.[62]

The difference between Cook Senior and Cook Junior, who eventually quarrelled over the firm's business strategy, suggests also a transition from early Weberian capitalism, with its strong underpinning of Protestantism, to the secular liberal capitalism that succeeded it in the second half of the nineteenth century. Cook Senior was a Baptist who took the pledge in 1836 and remained faithful to the Temperance Movement throughout his life.[63] As a publisher and bookseller, he issued temperance tracts, but also his first guidebook, in 1843, the *Guide to Leicester*. This was two years after he had organised his famous excursion from that city to Loughborough to enable Leicester citizens to attend a temperance meeting. His doggedness of character surely owed something to his religious convictions. Only two years after his temperance publishing business collapsed in 1846, he is reported to be trading again as a bookseller, as the owner of a temperance hotel, and even as a 'travel agent' in Leicester. John Mason Cook, on the other hand, believed that business and religion or philanthropy should be kept strictly separate. He was also prepared to get involved in the type of venture that his father shunned. Not only were the 'hotel coupons' his invention, but he also started the banking and foreign exchange side of the business in 1878. In 1887 he even purchased the Mount Vesuvius funicular railway, and later obtained a sole agency from the Khedive in Egypt to run the Nile steamers. At the firm's jubilee celebrations of 1891, which his ageing and now blind father did not attend, he could boast that the company had 84 offices,

85 agencies, 2,692 staff (of which 978 were in Egypt) and 45 bank accounts worldwide. A year later, Cook Senior was dead.

The combination of religion and salesmanship, of missionary work and commerce, was a conspicuous feature of Low Church activity in Britain, and Thomas Cook was not untypical in this respect. After trying his hand as a gardener and wood-turner, he got a job with a printer under contract to the General Baptist Association in Loughborough. He was employed as a book salesman, a post which he combined with Bible reading and missionary work from 1828. In 1829 he actually became a full-time missionary and travelled some 2,700 miles, mostly on foot.[64] (Until a few years ago there was a strong tendency to Non-Conformism among that rather inscrutable tribe known as 'Publishers' Representatives', together with extensive Freemasonry.) Although this was a passing phase, the idea of harnessing business to good causes (or perhaps vice versa?) seemed to have lodged in his brain. Happening to hear that the new railway had come to Leicestershire, he was quick to see its potential for the cause: 'The whole thing came to me as by intuition,' he said. 'The thought suddenly flashed upon me that it would be a capital thing if we could make railways subservient to the interests of temperance.' The next morning he arranged his famous excursion, and the rest, as they say, is history.[65]

Well, not quite. Despite very careful planning, Cook's first package tour of Scotland nearly ended in disaster, and the bad publicity doubtless contributed to the temporary bankruptcy he subsequently suffered. A trip to Wales had been a success (notwithstanding the difficulties encountered in finding English-speaking hosts!), but the railway link to Scotland was not yet complete and in 1846 the excursionists had to take a steamer from Fleetwood (in north-west England) to Ardrossan. The crossing was stormy, many passengers were ill, and Cook had 'overbooked' first-class cabins, so there were not enough for those who had paid for them. And all this after a long train journey in which the passengers, contrary to assurances given before the journey, were trapped for long hours in their carriages and not allowed off for refreshment, or even to relieve themselves. However, things looked up after the party reached Scotland: in Glasgow they were greeted by a salvo of gunfire, a brass band and a civic reception at the town hall. In Edinburgh they were welcomed by the famous publisher William Chambers, who drew a favourable comparison between the peaceful temperance enthusiasts shepherded by Cook and their rather less peaceful ancestors, who had certainly not visited Scotland to see the sights – still less had they eschewed strong drink. Chambers, of course, was not slow to exploit the occasion commercially and produced *The Stranger's Visit to Edinburgh*, which sold like warm haggis at one penny a copy.

THOMAS COOK'S SCOTTISH EXCURSIONS AND THEIR LITERATURE

The Scottish excursions became extremely popular over the next decade, so much so that they aroused the envy of local entrepreneurs. The parties of excursionists also annoyed other travellers when they took up all the available places on transport and or block-booked accommodation. Cook tried to appease his critics by passing the hat round his groups, usually when they were under the influence of some particularly beautiful spot on the classic tour. In this way he was able to finance twenty-four new boats for the fishermen of Staffa and to raise £300 for stocking the library on Iona. This was all to no avail, despite (or perhaps because of) the fact that coach proprietors earned £2,000 from him in 1861, railway companies £4,000 and the steamer companies £10,000; by 1863 the railways were refusing to book any more of his tours, hoping to hoard the business, and the profits, for themselves. Read with hindsight, the handbook for Scottish tours issued by Thomas Cook in 1861 has a somewhat elegiac air about it. *A Guide to the System of Tours in Scotland* outlines the cheap tours that Cook had on offer, the terrain covered being rationally divided into the Lowlands and Edinburgh, the Central Highlands, the Eastern Highlands and the West Coast. The last named included the special offer of a 'Great Highland Excursion' by steamer and coach that looks to have been spectacularly good value at four days' sailing and motoring for a cost of 24 shillings. It began at Glasgow and followed the now classic route via the Kyles of Bute, the Crinan Canal, the Islands of Jura and Scarba, then up to Iona and Staffa. The return leg included Glencoe, the Caledonian Canal and Inverness.

Chambers's support for the original Cook's tours had proved to be a two-edged sword. A long article in *Chambers Edinburgh Journal* of 29 October 1853, proudly quoted in the *Guide to the System of Tours in Scotland*, describes Cook's system and business methods in great detail and with considerable admiration, stressing the desirability of 'English pleasure money getting to the heart of the Highlands'. But the article is also a wake-up call to Scottish transport companies and travel entrepreneurs to seize the opportunities that lay under their noses. It helpfully suggests some potentially money-spinning routes that could be exploited if the locals got their act together – Tweedside with Abbotsford, Roslin and Hawthornden, 'Land o' Burns', Deeside with Balmoral, the lochs and firths of Argyll, the Great Glen and the Northern Highlands. Exploitation would of course require 'railway owners, steamboat owners, coach owners and hotel owners to confer together' (always a problem among fiercely independent-minded proprietors). Economies of scale would make competitively low fares economically viable. The article ends on a note of warning that perhaps give a clue to the reason for Cook's great success in the field: 'Let us all regard a tourist not as a being to be fleeced, but as a man to be pleased.'[66]

In subsequently ganging up on Cook, the Scottish transport and holiday industry no doubt had Chambers's article well in mind. The attitudes of the railway companies, which were not necessarily (wholly) Scottish owned, in part represented myopic business attitudes. Some directors claimed that cheap excursions drew income away from ordinary traffic and represented a loss. When their accountants showed them that profits from excursions were, mile for mile, far in excess of those for ordinary carriage, they simply changed tack and objected to the excursion agent (Cook) taking a share of the profits, which would not have existed without his efforts. Their attitude foreshadows the controversies of the twentieth and twenty-first centuries with which any reader of the reports from Tourist Concern will be familiar. Despite the huge inflows of cash to the host country that it supplies, tourism is seen by many as exploitative in respect of the low wages which, it is claimed, are paid to the local workforce, the repatriation of profits to foreign investors, the destruction of the environment and so forth. The ambivalent attitude to Cook, the uncertainty as to whether he was a carpetbagger taking advantage of them, or an entrepreneur stimulating business and providing employment, was to become a recurring issue in the debate about mass tourism. It is clear that the *coup de main* of the railway companies in 1863 was designed to put Cook out of business, so that local interests could step in and mop up the trade he had created. It very nearly succeeded in this, but the plotters had reckoned without Cook's energy and determination, that turned any such setback into a new challenge to be overcome.[67] Eventually the opposition seems to have fallen away, and Cook was instrumental in bringing parties of Americans to Scotland in 1873, which opened up a whole new and immensely profitable market for the Scots. 'If [Sir Walter] Scott had every claim to be the father of tourism in Scotland,' remarks one Scottish author, 'Cook had no mean role as that of midwife.'[68]

The *Guide to the System of Tours in Scotland* affords other interesting insights into Cook's operation, including the revelation that, of the thousands of tourists carried to Scotland over the previous fifteen years, 'the majority have been ladies'. However, little attempt is made to describe the topography and history of the places visited, for which the reader is referred to other guides, firstly Cook's own *Handbook of a Trip to Scotland*, but also the guides from the well-established firm of guidebook publishers, A&C Black and *Lizar's Guide to the Caledonian Railway* (an illustrated sheet 'not very convenient for the use of the traveller'), or Chambers's *Peebles and its Neighbourhood with a Run on the Peebles Railway*. The last-named, put out by Cook's shrewd Scots admirer, is extensively quoted from, and the purchase of it at a cover price of only 1 shilling is warmly recommended. The willingness to recommend guidebooks published by others is symptomatic of the way that Cook's own guidebook production was placed rigorously at the service of his excursion business. Indeed, much of the varied literature he put out, including the periodical he began in 1864 (*Cook's Excursionist and International Tourist Advertiser*), falls more into the category of 'travel brochure' than that of guide. Such, for example, was the handbook he wrote in 1845 for his first profit-making excursion to Wales (from Liverpool to Caenarfon and Mt Snowdon), which 'resembled in essential respects the modern tour operator's brochure'.[69] Booksellers indeed 'regarded [Cook's guidebooks] as little more than advertisements for Cook's agency', and it was not until 1874 that the firm tried to compete more directly with the mainstream variety.[70] In that year he joined with the publishers and booksellers Simpkin Marshal to produce more comprehensive guides that continued to be published until 1939.[71]

WHAT TO SEE AND HOW TO SEE IT: COOK AND THE GUIDEBOOKS

Facing an impasse in Scotland, and with the enthusiastic support of his friend Joseph Paxton (now a Member of Parliament), Cook turned to continental travel. By 1863 he had already conducted 2,000 visitors to France and 500 to Switzerland. The phrase 'Cook's Tour' soon became proverbial, and Cook was ironically dubbed the 'Napoleon of Excursions', an allusion to the stern discipline he imposed on his groups, though he did not enforce his temperance views on them, which would not have been good for business. (This is in marked contrast to his competitor, John Frame, who tried to impose temperance on the tourists for whom he organised trips from 1881. Cook's business prospered; Frame's struggled.) After France and Switzerland, Cook extended his range to Italy and by 1866 Cook's tourists were visiting the battle sites of the recently ended American Civil War. Four years later he was touring the Holy Land and by 1873 he had conducted the first organised round-the-world trip for tourists. From 1865 he had been in partnership with his son, John Mason Cook, who drove forward the newly christened (1872) 'Thomas Cook & Son' with vigour and vision, the son taking overall control in 1878 after a row with his father. Cook's clients now had the choice of purchasing conducted tours or tickets for independent travel. Round-the-world tickets cost 200 guineas, 1,050 dollars gold. Tickets for the Jerusalem tour cost from 50 to 60 guineas to 300 dollars gold. Clearly, Cook had expanded beyond the market for low cost workers' excursions and was appealing to the moneyed classes. But even so, his tickets seem astonishingly good value.

Cook's clients now included Americans, who soon acquired the fame of being generous, perhaps overgenerous, with their money, and of being easily gulled. That unattractive European habit of milking the American tourist, while simultaneously sneering at his supposed lack of culture, seems to have become quickly established. On the other hand, we find the writer of an article in an American magazine in 1863 blaming his nouveaux riches fellow-countrymen for throwing their money around in Europe ('to show John Bull and the continentals that they [the Americans] belong to the superior class at home'). In arguing that a European trip can be made for a fraction of what the loudmouths claim, he shows how the latter pay heavily over the odds for their callow conceit: 'Nobody cared what they paid or gave away; and the very courier who flattered, or the servants who fawned on them for their money, laughed at them behind their backs.' The guidebooks, he claims, are of little assistance, being based on 'first-class prices and a liberal expenditure. There are no guide books for those who would study economy; who would submit to some privations for the sake of seeing foreign lands and acquiring the desirable knowledge which can only be gained by personal observation.' He recommends Bradshaw for its advertisements for cheap accommodation and gives an interesting breakdown of expenses for a two month tour of the UK and Europe costing only $400. This is an early portent of the great American guides of the twentieth century that explicate a trip to Europe in terms of so many 'dollars a day'. The democratic attitude of most Americans also saved them money. For instance the writer of the article recommends cheap third-class travel on the railway, in the 'parliamentary' carriages (so-called because Gladstone passed legislation compelling the railway companies to introduce them). He points out that there is no difference in comfort between second- and third-class carriages; moreover, your fellow-passengers are unpretentious, talkative and friendly, whereas in first- and second-class they tend to be obnoxious, or 'insolent and encroaching', as he puts it.[72]

As previously remarked, Cook's earlier efforts in the guidebook line were little more than brochures, albeit brochures of some sophistication. As he himself said, they 'excited interest in anticipation [of the excursion]; they [were] highly useful on the spot; and they [helped] to refresh the memory in after days'.[73] In effect they were the first guidebooks for the budget traveller, previous efforts in this line being more akin to road-books. In 1845 he had produced a *Handbook of the Trip to Liverpool: From Leicester, Nottingham and Derby to Liverpool and the Coast of North Wales*, priced at threepence. While *Black's Picturesque Guides* attempted to describe houses and scenery that could be seen from the carriage window, Cook's Preface shows that he is reconciled to 'the impossibility [for travellers] of minutely inspecting the interesting scenes which nature presents or art exhibits' during the railway journey. (On the other hand, he recommends that passengers should change to the other side of the carriage for the return journey, so they can view on the way back the sights they missed when outward bound!) More ambitious was *Black's Picturesque Tourist and Road and Railway Guide* (1854) which provided railway charts in three columns. In the middle is the route showing stations and river bridges; in the left-hand column are the sights seen on the right of the train when coming from London, and in the right-hand column are the sights seen on the left. Typically, the sights featured are towns, villages and mansions, whereby the reader is assured that the names of the owners of the last-named have been painstakingly compiled from Burke's Peerage, Baronetage and History of the Landed Commoners.[74] 'Memorable incidents' connected with the settlements mentioned have been taken from county histories, and the topographical observations from authoritative works on the locality. The populations given are quite up to date, having been culled from the census of 1851. The sights are also given a geographical fix in miles from the final destination, and from the starting point, so that the tables resemble a road-book as applied to the railway.

Unable to compete with this sort of thing, Cook's handbook falls back on quotation from the delightfully titled 'Railway Glances' of the local poet J. Bradshaw Walker, who is hailed as a man of lofty soul and exquisite genius. These qualities are not immediately apparent, however, in the latter's verses on Wakefield, on which the traveller was presumably expected to focus as the train puffed through that only moderately enthralling city:

> 'Hurrah for 'merrie Wakefield!'
> There's Calder rippling clear,
> With its chapel on the bridge
> Built by the fourth Edward. – Where?
> To the left, sir; look again . . .' etc.

This is followed by another rousing number entitled the 'Tunnel Glee', perhaps designed for keeping up the spirits of passengers as they hurtled through the Stygian gloom of the railway tunnels. However, such diversions were probably more worthwhile than the quixotic, but surely doomed, attempt to capture sights from the carriage window. Wolfgang Schivelbusch quotes from an amusing letter written by Victor Hugo in 1837, which gives a tongue-in-cheek description of what the eye actually manages to see from the train:

> The flowers by the side of the road are no longer flowers, but flecks, or rather streaks, of red or white; there are no longer any points, everything becomes a streak; the grainfields are great shocks of yellow hair; fields of alfalfa, long green tresses; the towns, the steeples, and the trees perform a crazy mingling dance on the horizon; from time to time, a shadow, a shape, a spectre appears and disappears with lightning speed behind the window: it's a railway guard.[75]

When it comes to Liverpool itself, the author of Cook's handbook freely admits that his description is cribbed entirely from a local guidebook, *The Stranger's Guide through Liverpool*. Credits at the end of the handbook show that he also drew on Allen's *North Midland Railway Guide* and Parry's *The Steam Packet Companion*. Many such books would soon be available for purchase at the railway bookstalls, which sprang up after 1848. W.H. Smith, which still sells books and newspapers at main UK stations, obtained the exclusive rights to sell such on the Birmingham Railway in 1848, and shortly thereafter for the entire London and north-western system. His very first bookstall was opened on Euston Station. In the early days, many books were lent for a small fee and turned in at the destination. They tended to be novels for middle-class travellers, as published, for example, by Routledge in his Railway Library; Murray, on the other hand, in his list of Literature for the Rail, offered 'works of sound information and innocent amusement'. No doubt guidebooks counted as 'sound information'. Louis Hachette, who emulated W.H. Smith in France from 1852 and who himself published guidebooks, seems to have given them greater emphasis in the stock carried, together with 'books about travel' generally.[76] In both Britain and France the expansion of the railways engendered an expansion of the book market, including guidebooks, and provided ideal locations for selling them to receptive and captive consumers.

Cook was rather slow to tap into the fashion for visiting spas, but by 1885 he had produced a *Tourist's Handbook for Health Resorts of the South of France and Northern Coast of the Mediterranean including Marseilles, Toulon, Cannes, Hyères, Nice, Monaco, Bordighera, San Remo, Genoa and Pisa*. While this handbook concentrates mostly on practical information, with remarks about medical examinations, climate, insurance policies, pensions and so on, it does also feature topics like Mediterranean fauna and flora in a limited way, and further lists the most important sights of Paris. For the more demanding reader it simply recommends Murray's *Central, Southern and Eastern France*, and Black's *South of France*. Not only was there an emphasis on practical advice in Cook's anonymously written works, user-friendliness was valued above comprehensiveness. For example, *The Tourists' Handbook for Palestine and Syria* (1891) boasts that it has been so clearly printed that it can be read without difficulty, either on horseback or in the dim light of the tent. Morover the relevant scriptural passages are reproduced in full, so as to avoid the inconvenience of having to look them up in the Bible. This revealing remark suggests a return to the 'religious geography' of the early pilgrims to the Holy Land (see Chapter 3), whereby 'spirit of place', religious text and the individual's engagement with a particular location of sacred memory come together to create a numinous experience. That this approach can be applied *pari passu* to the secular religion of art is shown by a similar passage in Cook's *Tourists' Handbook for Northern Italy* (1875): 'This book has been printed . . . in clear, legible type,' states the preface, 'with all objects of interest marked conspicuously so as readily to arrest the eye. At a glance any remarkable picture, for example, with the name of the artist and the number in the gallery, can be ascertained without having to search for it in a crowded page of small print, as is too frequently the case in guidebooks.' The pilgrim-sightseer[77] is instantly supplied with the relevant points of reference, from which it is a short step to providing him also with the requisite response.[78]

Thomas Cook took his first group of tourists to Egypt and the Holy Land in 1869, having first done his usual extensive reconnoitre the year before on a trip organised by a rival, the previously mentioned bootmaker and travel entrepreneur Henry Gaze. Cook was a comparative latecomer to this lucrative market, the Egyptian part of which was to be vigorously expanded by his son. As early as 1847, Murray's handbook for Egypt had been published for independent trvellers and we are told that over the next eighty years some 165 guides to the region appeared in England and America. Although exoticism and bargain basement sex was clearly a draw for many Western travellers, Cook of course stressed the once-in-a-lifetime experience offered by a tour of the Holy Land, as he put it 'to trace out sites and scenes immortalised by imperishable events with the Bible in one hand and Murray in the other'.[79] As late as 1858, Murray's guide to Syria and Palestine is advising independent travellers to travel armed and with an escort. A dragoman (interpreter, guide and gofer) was indispensable; but Murray also quotes (more in sorrow than in anger) a contemporary's jaundiced description of these, who were said to come in four different versions: 'the Maltese, or the able knave; the Greek, or the cunning knave; the Syrian, or the active knave; the Egyptian, or the stupid knave'. Often the dragoman looked upon his charges as 'so many well-fledged geese' which it was his bounden duty to 'pluck'.[80] Cook, with his efficient arrangements, removed all these inconveniences at a stroke, and his tours were deservedly popular. The imperialist class in Egypt were of course disdainful, maintaining that 'we have four seasons in Egypt, which we distinguish as follows: first flies; second mosquitoes; third flying bugs; fourth, Cook's tourists'.[81]

As time went on, Cook seems to have realised that simply recommending other people's guides meant a missed business opportunity, although 'Books through

Cooks' was a service that still made available a wide range of travel literature to those of his clients who wanted background reading. His own, relatively modest, guidebooks became money-spinners, selling some 10,000 copies a year for an average price of 5 shillings. Having a captive market of group travellers who could be supplied direct obviously gave them a marketing advantage. The books were no longer always anonymously written – professional authors were sometimes employed to write up the Cook excursion destinations in a more wide-ranging and detailed manner. However, only one of these authors could really compete with Murray's illustrious contributors, namely Sir Harry Luke, whose work on Cyprus (not for Cook) has subsequently been helped to iconic status by Lawrence Durrell's espousal of it in *Bitter Lemons*. Luke revised the *Traveller's Handbook for Palestine and Syria* for Cook in 1924, from which *A Guide to Jerusalem and Judea* was extracted and issued separately at the same time. These later Cook guides were undoubtedly more ambitious volumes than those that had preceded them; on the other hand, they never acquired the authority of Murray and Baedeker, nor were they usually intended to. The only exception was E. Wallis Budge's *Handbook to Egypt and the Sudan*, which weighed in at 812 pages, and supplied everything that was expected from a Baedeker. Budge was himself a heavyweight, the British Museum's Keeper of Oriental Antiquities who obtained for the museum thousands of artefacts in the Near East, often in defiance of laws regulating their export.

The first of the weightier guides appeared in 1874, and covered Switzerland, Holland, Belgium and the Rhine. More than thirty titles,[82] with many revisions, were published up to the outbreak of the Second World War, and the brand name 'Thomas Cook' still appears today on guidebooks, for example, on a series published by the AA. The most prolific author of Cook's guides was one Roy Elston, who revised and rewrote dozens of the existing 'Tourist's' or 'Traveller's' Handbooks. His books are chatty, practical and unpretentious, although the upbeat tone of the travel brochure has infected the style. Thus we are told that the Basses-Alpes contain 'many adorable little villages', where the peasantry

> pursue their eternal round of toil with a picturesque primitiveness that does much to create the atmosphere of other, quieter ages . . . there can be few sights more pleasing than the movement of peasants along the road to Annot, taking their varied produce to the great fair and returning in the twilight with the goods they have bought and failed to sell. Just so, one imagines, did the peasants of the fifteenth century make their way from the remote high-pitched village to the great fair at the town in the valley.

In such passages, the local inhabitants are dangerously close to being reduced to stage figures ambling about for the delectation of an audience well insulated from the harsh reality of their daily lives. This guide, *Rivieras of France and Italy, including the Rhone Valley, Basses and Maritimes Alpes*, published in 1927, is incidentally a treasure trove for the social historian. We learn that intrepid motorists on the Continent in the 1920s were expected to pay 45 per cent of the value of their vehicle on entering France, plus a 'luxury' tax of 12 per cent (the 45 per cent would be refunded on leaving, the 'luxury' tax not). Customs regulations in regard to state monopolies would not have been out of place in the Middle Ages which the author found so picturesque – only 40 grammes of tobacco could be taken into Italy duty free and the French were still levying duties on snuff and tea. We also learn that the London–Paris train service via Folkestone or Dover and Boulogne took 7 hours 20 minutes and went twice daily.

Meanwhile, the brochure function for the business was fulfilled by the *Excursionist*, a magazine that had began publication in 1851 as *Cook's Exhibition Herald and Excursion Advertiser* in order to promote trips to the Great Exhibition. John Mason Cook expanded this early example of infotainment into thirteen overseas editions,[83] its chief function being to inform readers of the services offered worldwide by Thomas Cook & Son. It also contained testimonial letters, travellers' accounts of their tours and editorial comment. In 1902 its name was changed to *The Traveller's Gazette* and publication was to continue right up until 1939.[84] In 1873 the first edition of *Cook's Continental Time Tables & Tourist Handbook*[85] was published, a pioneering work in a pioneering year. For in September 1872, the 63-year-old Thomas Cook led the first round-the-world package tour, lasting 222 days and covering 25,000 miles. Soon the firm was offering 'round-the-world' tickets for '200 Guineas or 1,050 Dollars, gold'.[86]

By a remarkable coincidence an amusing novel by the popular French writer Jules Verne appeared at almost the same time (1873; English translation 1874). It was entitled *Around the World in Eighty Days* and part of its charm was its parody of travel for travel's sake – even if readers, especially younger readers, read it more for the improbable adventures of the protagonists. Phileas Fogg, who wagers he can circumnavigate the world in eighty days, is presented as a curmudgeonly stay-at-home whose servant, Passepartout, has taken a job as his manservant precisely because of his prospective master's settled habits. These are much in evidence on the early part of the trip, which is mostly spent playing whist in ships' cabins, or in planning routes and transport. But soon events overwhelm the pair, who find that the best laid plans cannot ensure against railways that, though optimistically marked on the maps, abruptly terminate in the middle of nowhere like a Sicilian Autostrada; not to mention unforeseen and time-consuming obligations, such as that of rescuing an Indian lady from *sati*. In a final twist, Fogg thinks he has arrived back in London five minutes too late to win his wager, but it turns out that this stickler for detail has forgotten that he has gained a day in travelling from east to west. Fogg's achievement was actually replicated in 1889 by 'Nelly Bly' (the pen-name of Elizabeth Cochrane) who was commissioned by the *New York World* to circle the globe in seventy-five days, and who managed it in seventy-two. Like Fogg, she did not have time to see or experience anything, except through the adventures and mishaps that her pointless, but impressive, project entailed. This was the reverse of 'educational' travel, the aim being to see *as little* of the countries you passed through as possible; the only guidebooks needed were shipping schedules and Bradshaw. Such a journey indeed conformed to the caricature of Cook's tourists promulgated by snobs and cultural critics who depicted the Cookites as 'so many sheep racing mindlessly from one sight to another with little appreciation of what they saw'.[87] The gently satiric side of Verne's delightful novel is often overlooked, but it would have been obvious to contemporaries with a Ruskinian distrust of their fellow men rushing around the continents like headless chickens.[88]

IMPROVED CONDITIONS OF TRAVEL

The experience of travel was traditionally challenging, involving energy, expense and some planning; from the start of organised tourism, however, it also represented a diminution of individuality, a degree of submergence in the group, and hence the tendency to authenticate the experience with a stock response as proof of participation. Clichés or stale anecdotes soon begin to loom large, simply because they are easy to appropriate and recycle. This in turn gives rise to ironic observation on the part of other travellers, who are at pains to disassociate themselves from mere tourists. The remarks by Theodor Fontane in his *Modernes Reisen* concerning a typical tourist outing to an Austrian country house, which were quoted in Chapter 8, could stand for many such sarcastic references ('On a visit to Schloss Reinhardsbrunn, members of a small town rifle club are suitably over-awed to learn that Archduke Ernst killed 50,157 head of game over twenty-five years').[89] One way in which cultivated people could establish their credentials was by ostentatiously adhering to the 'up-market' guidebook.

Group travel pushed prices down through economies of scale and standards up, since it was hard for hoteliers to ignore complaints that threatened a profitable repeat line of multiple bookings. Those who nevertheless thought they could do as they pleased found Thomas Cook a formidable opponent. When the Parisian hoteliers, with traditional Gallic charm, raised their prices by 50 per cent to cash in on the Paris World Exhibition of 1867, Cook simply rented two buildings for his English tourists, one for well-heeled visitors and the other for working men and their families. Not only did he charge an inclusive, transparent price at each of them, he also staffed them with English employees. This did not quite negate the ingenious malice of the Parisians: the municipality delayed permission for using gas in one of the hotels, the water supply proved to be contaminated at the other, and taxes rained down on the entrepreneur, on 'doors, windows, furniture, business and food of all kinds'. More ingeniously, a cheap wine shop was opened opposite the hotel where cognac was sold at two sous a glass, with the doubtless intended result that no less than fifteen of Cook's staff had to be shipped back to England, having succumbed to the lure of bargain-priced alcohol.[90] Still, Cook was not to be defeated and the Parisian venture proved to be a success.

Of course this kind of solution, and the adaptation of continental hotels to English customs and expectations, did rather encourage the inherent insularity of the average British leisure tourist. Travelling in groups could only encourage that insularity – and a tendency to behave rather worse than if one was still at home. This tendency has increased over the years, as anyone who has had the misfortune to be in Faliraki (Rhodes) on a Saturday night in August will know all too well. In the 1930s, however, the worst that could generally be expected of groups of Anglo-Saxons were high spirits and a cheerful indifference to foreign mores, which at least the easy-going Italians took in their stride. There is a delightful passage in Nicky Mariano's *Forty Years with Berenson* (1966) describing an encounter with one such group at the Albergo Nettuno in Pisa:

> We found it full of English people, a whole party of them . . . dining at a long table, exchanging noisy jokes and throwing rolls and oranges at each other. B.B. [Bernard Berenson] was fascinated. 'Who can they be? What are they here for? They are not ordinary tourists and belong to the small bourgeoisie. If they took a trip to Italy at all they would not be spending a night at Pisa.' The next morning he received me with a beaming smile. 'There is only one explanation. They must be undertakers on their way to choose marble for funerary monuments in Carrara or Pietrasanta and have used the occasion to make a jolly party of it. Please go at once to the concierge and ask him.' '*Si Signora*', said the concierge, '*sono partiti or' ora per Pietrasanta a comprar marmi*', 'they have just left for Pietrasanta to buy marble'.[91]

Often the most malevolent resistance to Cook's enterprise came from his fellow-countrymen living or working abroad. Under the pseudonym Cornelius O'Dowd, the British Vice-Consul at La Spezia (Charles Lever, an Irish novelist) used the pages of the influential *Blackwood's Magazine* to launch a swingeing attack on Cook and his tourists in 1865. 'The cities of Italy are deluged with droves of these creatures,' he wrote. 'You see them, forty in number, pouring along a street with their director circling round them like a sheep-dog, the men mostly elderly, dreary, sad-looking, evidently bored and tired, the women somewhat younger, travel-tossed and crumpled, but intensely lively, wide-awake and facetious.' This was unkind enough, but his next idea, that of putting it about that Cook's tourists (known in Italy as '*I Cucchi*') were actually convicted criminals, no more of whom Australia would consent to take, and who were therefore sent off on tours of Europe in the course of which they were conveniently 'lost', was far worse. Lever claimed that this was a joke, but it was received by continentals with as much mirth as caricatures of Muhammad by Muslims, and soon there were incidents of Cook's tourists being stoned in the streets of Italian towns. The British government was obliged to rebut Lever's claims publicly. Cook was robust in his reply: 'Mr Lever would reserve statue and mountain, painting and lake, historical association and natural beauty, for the so-called upper classes and for such Irish Doctors with German degrees[92] as choose to be their toadies and hangers-on. I see no sin in introducing natural and artistic wonders to all.'[93]

Possibly more damaging to Cook than Charles Lever's mockery were the remarks by William Russell, the celebrated *Times* reporter of the Crimean War, who went on a Cook's tour of Egypt that happened to coincide with a visit to the Nile by the Prince and Princess of Wales. Although his subsequent account of his experiences was perhaps intended to be jocular, Russell's self-importance and snobbery largely vitiates what merriment there is, and anyway there is little evidence that Cook had a sense of humour. The reporter accused Cook, *inter alia*, of short-changing his customers with programme alterations and of trying to arrange it so that his vulgar cohorts could catch glimpses of the royal persons as they floated down the Nile. In general he complained that Cook's parties 'filled hotels inconveniently, [and] crowded sites which ought to be approached in reverential silence with a noisy crowd; and they do not tend to inspire the natives with a sentiment of respect for our people'. This was mere snobbery: *Cook's Tourist's Handbook to Northern Italy* (1875) expressly warned its readers to remember that churches were places of worship, remarking that 'English and American travellers [are] the worst about tramping round them with guide-books and opera glasses and disturbing worshippers'.[94] The implication is that the worst offenders were more likely to be the arrogant middle classes bearing their Murrays and Baedekers, not necessarily Cook's carefully invigilated groups, although the tours did allow 'free time', so the instruction was doubtless prudent. From around the 1870s the bulk of Cook's tourists were actually individual travellers using 'circular tickets' issued through the company, and John Mason Cook was frequently at pains to point out in the *Excursionist* that most of his clients travelled quite independently.[95] The spectre of the philistine hordes nevertheless lingered long in the minds of the broadsheet leader-writers.

Russell also complained of the obsessive concern of Cook's tourists about being ripped off, observing that: 'the . . . higgling and bargaining which accompany their ways make one feel uncomfortable'. Cook was unashamed about the 'higgling': his clients were mostly not well off like Russell and his ilk, who could afford lordly gestures and did not need to count their change. Typically, the *Handbook for Northern Italy* (1875) has this advice, oft repeated elsewhere: 'Unfortunately a system prevails in Italy of charging fancy prices, and hotel keepers are not different from their brethren in other branches of business. A bargain must always be made, and even then it is well to have the bill every other day or so, in order to see how things are going.'[96] That this was a necessary precaution is underlined by an interesting study undertaken by Charles Toll Bidwell, Her Majesty's Consul for the Balearic Islands, in 1876. Using official figures, he compared the cost of living in Europe in that year with 1858, and showed that the economies of Europe were 'catching up' with English prosperity, so that the advantage British travellers had previously enjoyed through a strong pound and cheap prices abroad were gradually being eroded. Since 1858 prices in Austria had risen by a third, about the same in Belgium, while between 1858 and 1870 they doubled in Paris, although they fell after the Franco-Prussian War. In Rome they had generally doubled, although 'commodities are less expensive by 33 per cent, in their details'. His survey,[97] ranging from Switzerland to Honolulu, is not very scientific and fails to indicate the extent of British inflation over the same period; nevertheless, the perception seems to be that things are getting remorselessly more expensive for the British traveller, and it was against this that Cook's tourists sought to protect themselves.

Cook, who printed a vigorous pamphlet in his defence against Russell,[98] particularly objected to the latter's description of his charges as 'bears' and to himself as 'continental bear-leader' – either he did not know the provenance of this phrase in the era of the Grand Tour, or by now it had become a mere form of abuse. Although he was sensitive to charges of poor service, he could always draw on the numerous glowing testimonials of his clients. Not untypical was a letter from an American obstetrician and writer on women, Lydia F. Fowler, who rounds off her eulogy by declaring that 'Cook will be remembered as having afforded facilities by which people have been enabled to get away from their daily toil and cares of business to visit remote parts of the country [she had been on a Scottish tour], which action has improved their health, enlarged their minds, and invigorated their spirits.'[99] Cook also had admirers among the politicians of the day: Paxton has already been mentioned, but Gladstone was another. The latter sent a goodwill message to the firm's silver jubilee celebrations in July 1891, in which he acknowledged Cook as a public benefactor, adding, as a good Liberal, that Cook's competitors were 'so many additional witnesses to the real greatness of the service you have rendered'.[100] John Mason Cook, who organised the great pilgrim excursions from India to Mecca, was likewise eulogised by a local newspaper editor in Lahore, one Rudyard Kipling, who spoke of the 'great J.M. [Cook] – the man with the iron mouth and the domed brow'.[101] As for Cook Senior, Lydia F. Fowler is not alone in saluting him as the 'King and Father of Excursions'; others hailed him as the 'Peerless Excursionist', the 'Emperor of Tourists' or, more ominously, as 'the Napoleon of Excursions'.

TOURS AND GUIDEBOOKS TO THE BATTLEFIELDS

The reference to Napoleon is of course an ironic allusion to the stern discipline that Cook imposed on his groups as they moved around Europe. Since we are with Napoleon, this is an appropriate place to mention battlefield tours, a bizarre offshoot of mainstream tourism that flourished in the nineteenth and early twentieth centuries, and which Cook also offered in his programme from 1855. Indeed, one of his prospectuses offered a 'personally conducted tour' of parts of the Low Countries by Cook Senior that included the battlefield of Waterloo, here described by the pacific (if not pacifist) tour manager as 'that interesting field of a feud now past and buried for ever (it is hoped)'.[102] Very soon after the defeat of Napoleon there were organised tours of the site of Waterloo, and indeed a guidebook for the same, the *Stranger's Guide to the Plains of Waterloo*, 'exhibiting on a large scale the position of the armies on the 15th, 16th, 17th and 18th of June, 1815'. We have seen also that Cook's parties were being conducted round the battle sites of the American Civil War only a year after it had ended. However, a veritable boom in battlefield tours was unleashed by the First World War. In

1922 Roy Elston compiled for Cook *Constantinople to Smyrna: Notes for Travellers to Constantinople, Bursa, the Dardanelles, Gallipoli Battlefields and Cemeteries, the Ruins of Troy, the Seven Churches of Asia, Smyrna etc.* Cook's volume on Belgium and the Ardennes (1921) had the following announcement in the Preface: 'Thomas Cook and Son's arrangements comprise tours, escorted and independent, to the battlefields of Belgium, to those of Belgium and France combined, or to those of France, at fares to suit all purses.' The tours were accompanied by an ex-officer, and a special brochure was produced for them, which suggests that they enjoyed considerable popularity. As early as 1919 a more ambitious project was undertaken by Michelin, subsequently one of the most famous of guidebook publishers, which produced a substantial multi-volume guide to the First World War battlefields. The book appears to have mingled sightseeing with propaganda: Rudi Koshar tells us that it is 'as informative as it is moving and filled with anti-German sentiment'.[103]

Whether trips round the killing fields so soon after the event are to be regarded as elegiac, fact-finding, or merely ghoulish, is something that each will decide for himself. The great Viennese satirist Karl Kraus had no doubts about the matter: in 1920 he took his hatchet to an advertisement in the *Basler Nachrichten* promoting motorised battlefield excursions sponsored by that newspaper. The commercial crassness of the advertisement was indeed beyond all parody. Tourists who take up the offer, it boasted, will travel 'an entire day through the battlefields in a comfortable car . . . [enjoying] first class meals, wine'. The highlight of the tour is Verdun 'where perhaps more than 1,500,000 bled to death'. The trip is offered with 'everything included in the price of 117 francs, and with ample meals at first-rate restaurants'. Kraus exploited this unedifying plug to deliver one of his most magisterial denunciations of the press's cynicism, greed and insensitivity. With feline sarcasm, he implies that the mass slaughter of nations, in the eyes of newspaper editors and proprietors, simply presented a convenient opportunity for ghoulish sensation-mongering and financial gain. The battlefield tripper, says Kraus, will gain 'unforgettable impressions of a world in which there is no single square centimetre not rutted by shells and advertisements'. The 'first-class offering of the *Basler Nachrichten*', he further observes, will doubtless succeed in 'fattening up [the newspaper's] list of subscribers using the casualties of Verdun'.[104] It is a characteristically savage indictment, and one that every guidebook writer, as well as every brochure copywriter, would do well to ponder before taking up his pen.

A GUIDE FOR THE INDEPENDENT TRAVELLER AND ONE FOR THE DILETTANTE EXPLORER

To conclude this chapter on the early days of mass travel, it may be appropriate to look briefly at its opposite, which continued to flourish in an age of technical revolution. In the first three decades of the nineteenth century, the independent traveller was still obliged to rely on traditional methods of transportation, and there were books that catered in ever greater detail to his need for precise practical information. A notable, if eccentric, example is *The Traveller's Oracle* by Dr William Kitchiner, who specialised in books of practical information. His efforts included *The Cook's Oracle*, *The Art of Invigorating Life*, *Peptic Precepts* (on digestion) and *Mirth and Motion Prolong Life*. Kitchiner was the son of a coal merchant who claimed to have been to Eton and to have a medical degree from Glasgow. Subtitled 'Maxims for Locomotion, containing Precepts for Promoting the Pleasures and Hints for Preserving the Health of Travellers', Kitchiner's lively and eccentric book (1822) was a mine of useful information, rounded off with 'Seven Songs for One, Two and Three Voices Composed by the author'. The author's achievement may seem all the more impressive, given that he himself had never been abroad.[105] Part II of the *Oracle* consisted of Kitchiner's revision of the *Horse and Carriage Keeper's Oracle* written by 'an old coachman' (John Jervis). It supplied up-to-date information on the costs of 'keeping or jobbing horses and carriages' as well as an 'easy plan for ascertaining every hackney coach fare'.[106]

This Part II of the book cites a couple of doubtless indispensable guides for Londoners and visitors to the city: *Quaife's Hackney Coach Directory* contained some 1,800 standard fares made from precise distance measurements, and *Carey's New Guide for Ascertaining Hackney Carriage Fares* gave the length of every street in the metropolis (in miles, furlongs and poles) as an aid to calculating what the client of a cab should be charged. In a fascinating résumé of the hackney carriage system, Kitchiner reveals the economics of the trade: a driver had to earn 13 shillings a day for the maintenance of his carriages and horses, of which he required a minimum of three, before he would be in profit (this is in *c.* 1827). Expenses of stabling, maintenance, tax and interest on capital amounted to £238 annually. The cabs worked from 9 a.m. until midnight, and the most profitable days for the drivers were Wednesdays and Thursdays, when the greatest number of dinners were given in the city. The cabbie could charge either by time consumed or for the distance covered. The carriage was fitted with a meter, which Kitchiner calls a 'way-wiser' (a mistranslation of *Wegweiser?*), attached to another device ('perambulator') that recorded the distance travelled, and to which a time-piece could be attached, to show the distance travelled per hour. In a footnote, he gives similar details of the Parisian cabs. Using Kitchiner's detailed instructions, and equipped with a good map, the traveller could have worked out the correct fare for any ride he chose to take in London, though it would have been quite complex and time-consuming actually to do so.[107]

Kitchiner begins his main text alarmingly, but sensibly, by advising every prospective traveller to make his will. There follows a list of prudent health precautions and advice on preparing yourself for the journey, for example, by obtaining maps and literature from two of the important guidebook publishers we have already encountered, Leigh in the Strand and Carey in St James. Kitchiner is clearly addressing an educated, but not aristocratic, audience and is inclined to be sententious. This impression is reinforced by his choice of quotations to support his theme, mostly from the luminaries of past ages such as

Sir Philip Sidney and Dr Johnson. Other quotations are evidently intended as light relief; for example, he cites Tertullian, who described how the Cynic Asclepiades made the Grand Tour on the back of a cow, and lived all the while from her milk. Then there is his (Kitchiner's) recommendation that the traveller should be sure of a plentiful and good quality sleep; he illustrates this with the example of Peter the Great, who was accustomed to take a post-prandial nap by resting his head on a servant's shoulder, the unfortunate retainer being obliged to remain stock-still until the great man awoke.

Dietary advice obviously looms large (frequently accompanied by puffs for the author's book on the subject). After admonishing the reader to abstain from 'ragouts, made dishes, puddings, pies' and the like, an admonition that recalls Ben Jonson's aphorism that 'much malice may be vented in a meat pie', he quotes Blackstone's *Commentaries* to the effect that it is possible to take legal action against the proprietor of an inn if the waiter sells you a wine that makes you ill. A hazard of travelling by coach seems to have been what is nowadays identified as an ailment of long-distance flights – deep vein thrombosis. Kitchiner recommends well-fitting shoes. And for constipation the doctor has his own patent remedy, the evocatively named 'Peristaltic Persuader'. Among the more startling pieces of advice is that for the use of a lancet which, claims Kitchiner, if once used in bleeding a person suffering from an infectious disease, may be re-employed for a short time afterwards to inoculate the person who is bled with it from the same disease. We are also told that a razor used to shave a deceased person may be wielded to achieve much the same prophylactic effect on the living. Failing these rather drastic measures, travelling with Pratt's Patent Folding Bedstead may protect the traveller from the contagious diseases of the previous (deceased or not) occupants of beds at the inns. In any case he should carry leather sheets with him, since sheets in the inns are almost invariably damp. If that is not possible, check if the bedding is dry by placing an inverted tumbler between the sheets after heating them with hot coals and observe if there is any steam.

One of Kitchiner's most impressive sections compares the costs of travelling by postchaise with independent travel by private carriage, showing the huge savings (in time as well as money) to be made by using the former. On the other hand, we are warned that the Post Masters connived with the innkeepers to operate a cartel of services and to extract kickbacks and gratuities. The doctor is also hot on security ('in lonesome places . . . if you carry a firearm, it may be well to let the landlord see (as it were accidentally) that you are armed'). He also quotes La Combe's *Picture of London*, which advises travellers to carry a pair [!] of blunderbusses, and to put the muzzle of one out of each window, so they can be seen by the robbers. If firearms are not carried, Kitchiner has various devices to recommend, such as 'cork-screw door fastenings' or simply a portable bolt that may be 'readily attached to any door'. Even if he has these defences, the continental traveller should still place a table and chair against his door and check under the bed and in the cupboards before retiring.[108]

Finally, Kitchiner has second-hand advice (quoted from *Dialogues on the Uses of Foreign Travel*) on appropriate behaviour for those travelling abroad. Travellers are recommended to avoid 'telling the people that the English [customs] are a thousand times better [than theirs] (as my countrymen are very apt to do). Commend their Table, their Dress, their Houses, and their Manners a little more, it may be, than you really think they deserve . . .'. 'Protestants', pursues Kitchiner, 'are too apt to ridicule Catholics, and Catholics to revile Protestants: any ridicule of any Religion, or idle application of sentences taken from the scriptures is a mode of merriment which a Good man dreads for its Profaneness and a witty man dismisses for its vulgarity.' As an impulse for sweet reasonableness in such matters, Kitchiner supplies his own interdenominational hymn at this point, in which 'Christians of all sects may join'. In such emollient passages, he seems to anticipate the ecumenical strivings of the twentieth century, and even the tortured debate about 'offending' religious sensitivities that has taken on such stark dimensions in our own time.

Notwithstanding his admirable calls for tolerance and self-criticism, Kitchiner closes this section of the book in a burst of patriotism, not to say chauvinism. He begins by quoting, apparently with approval, Twiss's *Hints to Travellers* which refers to the 'arbitrary and tyrannic governments [on the Continent], the slavery and poverty of the lower class of people, the pride and ignorance of the opulent, the superstition and bigotry of both'. All these defects are compared unfavourably with '[England's] immaculate climate, fruitful earth, mild government' and 'intelligent inhabitants (of both sexes)', as well as her 'remarkably beautiful women'. Faced with such unavoidable comparisons, the author clearly feels that most of his readers will be all too happy to return from their wanderings and spend the rest of their days in 'Happy England'. The foreign or domestic tour, with its attendant discomforts, dangers and disagreeable encounters, may be successfully negotiated with the assistance of the author's advice. However, the main effect (if not virtue) of such a tour seems to be that it will remind the reader of the considerable advantages to be derived from staying at home.[109]

Kitchiner's remarks, from their tone and content, are clearly addressed to male travellers, but at least by the mid-century there were adventurous female travellers. They were catered for by Miss Davidson's *Hints to Lady Travellers* (1889), which listed twenty-eight medicaments that the well-prepared girl should carry. The inconvenient camouflage of a previous age's feminine fashion now had to give way to convenience wear for travelling. Miss Davidson makes the point succinctly: 'To have to struggle into a gown of complex construction as the breakfast bell is ringing . . . is an experience calculated to make one look with a friendly eye upon the simple feminine toilets of the savage races.' It has already been noted that many of Cook's excursions actually had a majority of women participants, something that Cook greatly applauded. 'The trappings of prevailing fashion', he remarked, 'may sometimes perplex [the ladies] in climbing over precipices, [but they] push their way through all difficulties and acquire the perfection of the tourist character.' Maxine Feifer has listed the amazing range of items that were produced to cater for this new market, everything from an emergency rope-and-pulley fire escape and luminous matchboxes to collapsible baths and Seymour's Patent Magnetic Amyterion for seasickness. And since you were already wondering, gentle reader, there was of course also a portable, mahogany-rimmed chamberpot, disguised as a bonnet box, on sale from Fyfe's Repository of Scientific Inventions for Sanitary Purposes, 46 Leicester Square.[110] Naturally, most female travellers journeyed in groups or were otherwise well chaperoned, but the nineteenth century was also to be the age of intrepid independent lady travellers like Mary Kingsley (1862–1900) and Gertrude Bell (1868–1926), themselves continuing a tradition of female travel pioneered by figures like Lady Mary Wortley Montague (*c.* 1689–1762) and Lady Hester Stanhope (1776–1839).

Where Miss Davidson is unruffled and genteel, the anonymous 'Viator Verax',[111] in his *Continental Excursions: Cautions for the First Tour on the Annoyances, Shortcomings, Indecencies and Impositions Incidental to Foreign Travel*, which is specifically addressed to 'Husbands, Fathers, Brothers and All Gentlemen Going with Female Relations', is blunt and often coarse under the guise of solicitude for the female traveller. Anxious to shield the latter from 'affront, offence, hardship and outrage', Viator Verax supplies a relentless litany of continental rip-offs, ill manners, male chauvinism and lack of hygiene that he claims would never be met with in England. A particular outrage is the peephole bored between adjoining rooms so that voyeurs can spy on ladies dressing. The loos (and foreigners' inability to use them properly) are such that any English gentlewoman would flee them as from a chamber of horrors – even in quite good hotels, they are covered in obscene graffiti. Anyway, foreigners often 'make do' in other ways, for example, French women deposit their business in the opened drawers of a commode! Foreign menus are a snare and delusion, hotel keepers routinely overcharge, extortionate fees at three times the official rate are demanded for luggage carried on trains, where the fellow passengers, more especially the males, are rude and pushy. The last named are inclined to 'rush into the first carriage [they] can climb into'; having bagged a seat, they 'complacently stare out of the window, wondering whether those demoiselles [they] have just shouldered and shoved against, will succeed as well as [they have] done in seating themselves somewhere at their ease'. The author concludes by denying any 'prejudice or illiberal bias', still less any 'senseless pride and pretentiousness' in favour of the English. He is merely telling it as it is.[112]

The most independent traveller of all was the dilettante explorer. From 1855 he (or she) also had a guidebook dedicated to his needs, (Sir) Francis Galton's *The Art of Travel; or, Shifts and Contrivances Available in Wild Countries*. Constantly revised and enlarged, it ran to eight editions between the year of its first issue and 1893. Galton was himself an explorer and his guide, originally designed to appeal to big game hunters in Africa, became more and more of an explorer's manual over the years. The core material was collected during his trip to Egypt and the Holy Land (1845–6), and his exploration of south-western Africa in 1850–1. The advice given was intended to assist 'all who have to rough it, – whether explorers, emigrants, missionaries or soldiers'.[113] In the preface to his book he stressed that he did not 'profess to give exhaustive treatises on each of the numerous subjects comprised in [his] volume, but only such information as is not generally known among travellers'. As an example of what he means by that, he offers his account of the *Dáterám*, an ingenious system for securing tent ropes in loose sand, which was practised by the local inhabitants of only a small area in the southern Sahara. Equally ingenious was his method for measuring the breasts of native women by triangulation (Galton had become fascinated by the outsized bosoms of African ladies).

The *Dáterám* appears entirely practicable, but some of Galton's advice would seem to have required advanced mathematical talent to apply. For example, the directions for finding one's way back to the main party, if lost in the jungle or the desert, begins simply enough with suggestions such as asking oneself the question: 'when I last left the path, did I turn to the left or to to the right?' Over the next three pages, however, the instructions become ever more complex and challenging, accompanied by the sort of graphs and algebraic formulas in which the scientifically minded Galton delighted, but which could surely only have added a further layer of bafflement to that already supplied. By the time the traveller had worked it all out, or (more likely) given up, one strongly suspects he would have expired in the heat or been eaten by a passing predator.

In his Preface, Galton deals crisply with a reviewer who had accused him of copying from an American work entitled *The Prairie Traveller* by one Captain Macy. 'I . . . think it well to remark,' he writes, 'that the first Edition of [Macy's] work was published in 1859, . . . and that the passages in question are all taken from my second Edition published in 1856; part of them are copies of what I had myself written, the rest are reprints of my quotations, as though the Author of *The Prairie Traveller* had himself originally selected them.' In fact, Galton's book, as he is at pains to point out, is a distillation of wisdom, lore and ingenuity collected from many different professional travellers and explorers. Not infrequently this material, much of which had been supplied verbally, was modified by Galton in the light of his attempts to apply the suggested stratagems in the field. Galton adored ingenious devices and his book is a treasure trove of such, often illustrated with etchings that convey the boy scout ethos of the Victorian explorer, as it might be featured in the *Boys Own Paper*. Every page contains a gem of cunning methodology (for example, how to stop an ass braying by tying a heavy stone to his tail – according to the Chinese, 'when an ass wants to bray he elevates his tail, and if his tail be weighted down, he has not the heart to bray'; or how to outwit the sneaky attacks of hostile natives: 'Captain Sturt says, that he has known Australian savages to trail their spears between their toes, as they lounged towards him through the grass, professedly unarmed').[114]

The emphasis throughout the book is on survival through the intelligent application of skills. Galton's great advantage was that he generally observed how the locals actually solved practical problems, or he relied on those of whom he could be sure that they had done so themselves. 'When a Dutchman or a Namaqua wants to carry a load of ostrich eggs to or from the watering-place, or when he robs a nest, he takes off his trousers, ties up the ankles, puts the eggs in the legs, and carries off his load slung round his neck.'[115] To such simple but effective local traditions he added advice on the use of the latest European inventions or techniques. The Royal Geographical Society, to which he was elected a Fellow in 1853 aged only 31, was able to draw on his experience in its *Hints to Travellers – Scientific and General*, the fourth edition of which (1878) was edited by Galton. He was probably the ideal person for such a task, since travel, for him, was meaningful only if it was undertaken in pursuit of scientific aims. The romantic quest – nowadays the pseudo-romantic quest of hideously self-absorbed travel writers – was entirely alien to his cast of mind: he was too busy working out how to avoid the charge of an enraged animal,[116] or how to walk in a straight line through a forest.[117]

There is of course not the slightest hint of humility, still less of what would now be called 'political correctness', in dealing with those he invariably calls 'natives' or 'savages'. Yet the smug dismissal of Galton as no more than a racist, as he would certainly be deemed by today's standards, does less than justice to his quite complex attitudes to native tribes. In a chapter bearing the uncompromising title of 'Management of Savages', he remarks that the latter 'thoroughly appreciate common sense, truth, and uprightness; and are not half such fools as strangers usually account them'. On the other hand, a trouble-making 'savage' is to be treated more as an animal than as a human being, an alarming attitude some sixty years after the official abolition of the slave trade. 'If a savage does mischief,' opines Galton, 'look on him as you would on a kicking mule, or a wild animal, whose nature is to be unruly and vicious, and keep your temper unruffled.' This whole section is a fascinating mixture of ruthlessness and punctiliousness, mingling the self-confident superiority of the Victorian imperialist with the pragmatic attitudes of the survivalist. His remarks on 'Seizing Food' are not untypical: 'If you are hungry, or in serious need of anything that [the natives] have, go boldly into their huts, take just what you want, and leave adequate payment. It is absurd to be over-scrupulous in these cases.'[118]

If the attitude to 'savages' startles the modern reader, Galton's assumptions about the environment and animals are equally without any trace of modern sentimentality or environmental awareness. The nineteenth-century explorer, battling through the jungle and using any effective means to survive, would have had no time for such luxuries. Even so, some of the practices recommended seem to verge on gratuitous cruelty, as in this account of liming crows, quoted from a sage called Mr Lloyd: 'Crows may be killed by twisting up a piece of paper like an extinguisher, dropping a piece of meat in it, and smearing its sides with bird-lime. When the bird pokes its head in, his eyes are gummed up and blinded; and he towers upwards in the air, whence he soon falls down exhausted, and it may be, dead with fright.'[119] This ruthless focus was in keeping with Galton's scientific motivation, though he was said to be of a kindly disposition in his personal relations. His marriage to an intellectual wife, though evidently happy, produced no children; in any case, Galton was absent on his travels for prolonged periods. It was typical of him that he produced a 'Beauty Map' of the British Isles '(compiled on the best statistical principles and showing the prettiest girls in London, the plainest in Aberdeen)'.[120] A cousin of Charles Darwin, Galton had much of the latter's passion for scientific discovery and creative flair. Although his interests were diverse, he is now mostly remembered for his espousal of eugenics, which became something of an obsession. 'His idea of a race perfected by the limiting of marriage to the physically and mentally fit,' observes Dorothy Middleton drily, 'is not one that commends itself to modern thinking.'[121] Nevertheless, he broke new ground in several other areas, including the use of fingerprints for personal identification, the correlational calculus in applied statistics, and the application of the term 'anti-cyclone' (his coinage) in meteorology.

If Galton's readers represent the extreme opposite of the cosseted Cookites, he stood at the threshold of an age where the possibility of independent travel was gradually to become more widespread throughout the social classes. He died in 1911, just before the First World War, which was followed in the twenties and thirties by the first age of independent motorised tourism. A couple of decades after the Second World War, it would become possible for the penniless student to hoist his rucksack onto his back and set off for lengthy travel in foreign parts. Eight years later, in 1973, the first Lonely Planet would be published, to be followed nine years later (1982) by the first Rough Guide. These were volumes specifically aimed at the footloose and youthful independent traveller, who indeed is encouraged to keep them up to date by sending in his corrections and comments. At the same time, package tourism, originally the brainchild of Thomas Cook, would rapidly reach ever greater proportions. But independent and adventure travel in the twentieth century was no longer to be the prerogative of the well-to-do, just as package tours would likewise be offered in all sorts of price brackets, from the bog standard holiday on a Greek beach for lager louts to elegant cultural tours for persons of demanding gastronomic and cultural tastes.

PART V

From Inventory to Ideology: Aspects of the Modern Guidebook

CHAPTER 11

Up-Market, Down-Market:
The Specialist's Bible or an Ariadne's
Thread for Everyman

The travel industry dispossesses cultures in the name of amenity and profit;
it elides idiosyncracy.

(Michael Bywater, 1999)

Always have a glance at the proprietor [of a street vendor's food stall]; if he's
clean and healthy-looking, his food should be too. If he looks as if he's
about to drop dead, eat elsewhere.

(Advice from a Lonely Planet guide, 1994)

THE GUIDEBOOK IN THE ERA OF GLOBALISATION

Writing in the Austrian newspaper *Die Presse* in 2006, the veteran historian Walter
Laqueur remarked that

> some people believe that Europe should get used to its new role, that of
> being a tourist attraction for well-off Chinese and Indians, a sort of Venice in
> gradual decline, but still of great historical interest. 'Here, ladies and
> gentlemen, an important culture once arose, the remains of which we may
> inspect today . . .'. A Europe therefore, of tour guides, translators and
> museum directors. A Europe as theme park, a Disneyland on a high cultural
> level.[1]

Laqueur's provocation points to one significant aspect of the changes wrought by globalisation. Our notions of 'travel', 'tourism' and 'the guidebook' tend to be Eurocentric, tracing their lineage eventually back to Homeric geography. Yet, to take only one aspect of the history of the travel guide, the pilgrimage motif is universal, and stronger in Islam than ever. Guides will always be needed for pilgrims, and some non-Western traditions seem to have featured plenty of such literature. Indeed, Rohun Kagaki's *A Comic Mount Fuji Pilgrimage* of 1861 was a satire on the numerous popular works on pilgrimage, some of which presumably were guides. Then again, a copy of Ibn Battutah's meandering travels dated to 1484 appears from marginal notes to have been used as a guidebook by a Maghribi pilgrim to Mecca.[2]

A widespread ignorance of, and indifference to, the guidebook literature of non-European cultures, except among a handful of scholars, has long been a feature of our European self-preoccupation, and perhaps the present work is another manifestation of it. While we are to a greater or lesser extent familiar with travel writings spanning the centuries from Sir John Mandeville (Ibn Battutah's contemporary) and Marco Polo (his near-contemporary) to Jan Morris and Bill Bryson, as well as great guidebook series like Baedeker, Michelin and the Rough Guide, it is specialists and historians who read the fourteenth-century Ibn Battutah, of whose work the first full English translation was only completed in 1994. Likewise the vivid travel reports of the Turkish scholar (and spy) Evliya Celebi, who travelled the Osman Empire and recorded its topography and the habits of its subject peoples, are known mostly to historians of Central Europe. The achievement and legacy of the great Arab geographers is a commonplace for scholars, but certainly not for the layman. One could multiply the examples.

Walter Laqueur's observations draw attention to the fact that the balance of economic power in the world is beginning to shift, and one day many of the cultural assumptions of European guidebook writers may seem parochial to a global tourist industry deriving much of its income from millions of Chinese and Indians on the move. So long as the domestic market for tourism to Europe remains relatively limited in Asia and the Indian subcontinent, the publishing entrepreneurs of those regions may make do with translations of existing European guides, as the Japanese often seem to do. There must come a time, however, when the Chinese market will sustain plenty of guidebooks to Europe conceived, written and published in (say) Shanghai, which some enterprising publisher in (say) London decides to put out in English. It would be a bold publisher who was the first to do this: as Tzvetan Todorov has pointed out in an essay on travel narratives, colonialism has cast a long shadow over travel-writing and its consumers. 'We are all in favour of people's right to self-determination,' he writes, 'and we all profess the natural equality of races.' Yet today's guidebook writer, consciously or subconsciously, is still negotiating the fact that 'we have not stopped believing in the superiority of our civilization over "theirs"; and why should we, since they all seem to want to imitate us and dream of coming to work in our countries?'[3] An ironic twist is given to Todorov's last remark by the anecdote about the Nigerian anthropologist who decided to study Middle

America in precisely the same inquisitive and scientific manner as countless white American anthropologists have studied Africans. He was nearly lynched for his pains.[4]

Even within Europe, the guidebook has naturally reflected the national identities and cultural assumptions of its authors, although that did not prevent Grand Tour guidebooks from finding a foreign audience, either through a common religious affiliation or the shared values of the Enlightenment (see Chapter 7 for those of Misson and Keysler). Of the nineteenth-century guidebook titans, only Baedeker had sustained success in foreign language editions. This may be attributed to the Baedeker formula that provided a template for the information in a predictable and supposedly objective manner – Murray's guides, superficially similar to Baedeker as a reliable brand, seldom found their way into translation because they were considerably more opinionated in political and social matters, and the opinions were rather obviously those of educated Englishmen. They also used copious literary quotation, something eschewed by Baedeker, a device which may have hidden one type of authorial subjectivity, but arguably replaced it with another, that of the (almost invariably British) authors who were quoted.[5] Modern guidebook series that *are* translated (Eyewitness, Gallimard) tend to be those that strictly adhere to a formula based on a high degree of visualisation,[6] where the concise descriptions are really information capsules designed to accompany the stereoscopic plans and cut-away illustrations. In an online age where the soundbite rules, this is what many people want, as the remarkable success of Eyewitness confirms; but a price is paid in loss of idiosyncracy, also a tendency to blandness, unreflective cliché, or even 'political correctness'.[7]

INTELLECTUAL GUIDES AND AUTHENTIC EXPERIENCE

The first three-quarters of the twentieth century saw the rise and gradual decline of the guide for the educated middle class whose compilers assumed their readers' familiarity with quite sophisticated architectural and artistic terminology, and who were unlikely to be dismayed by the occasional (untranslated) classical quotation. In E.M. Forster's novels, these were the kind of people who got a bad press – dons, clergymen, aesthetes and generally persons whose (over-)education had blunted their emotional authenticity. This of course was unfair as a generalisation, but clearly there was still a market in the mid-twentieth century for the kind of traveller who was mostly interested in accumulating artistic and historical knowledge, and against whose object-obsessed attitudes Heine famously rebelled in 1901, when he resolved to throw away his guide in Florence's Piazza della Signoria. This kind of reader had a natural affinity with the Guide Bleu,[8] the British Blue Guides[9] and Companion Guides, the guides of the Touring Club Italiano (founded 1922),[10] the German DuMont (founded 1968)[11] and the Prestel series. Hovering between the egghead and the middle market was the very successful Michelin guides, whose first volume was *Brittany* in 1926. The series continued with over a hundred titles, also notching up an impressive number of translations including Japanese and Hebrew, the Michelin template evidently being transferable like Baedeker. The English intellectual guidebooks were usually co-published with American firms, thus adequately supplying the US market which, with the notable exception discussed below, has never really produced an equivalent 'heavyweight' guidebook series, excellent though the mainstream Moon, Fodor, Frommer, and others, are.

Notwithstanding the successful translation of the Michelins into English, there is a degree of 'cognitive dissonance' between the American guidebook and the European one which Michael Rowland has explored in a study of Michelin's Guides verts touristiques. He stresses the latter's overemphasis on the past, particularly on medieval France, but even more their penchant for abstract discourse over concrete assistance, something which he sees as characteristically French, or at least un-American:

> The illustrations of religious and historical subjects in the guide vert (a document designed, after all, to assist tourists in the twentieth century) confirm the French predilection for the abstract when confronted with a task that is essentially practical from the American point of view. Touring in this country [France] revolves around the practical concerns of driving and finding tourist attractions, as well as places for eating and sleeping. These challenges do not lend themselves easily to abstract solutions. Reference to the past serves no practical purpose for the American tourist.[12]

Somewhat simplistically, he concludes that the ideal of the American guidebook is 'to see first and then define', while that of the French one is to 'define first and then to see'. And he claims that the 'principal object' of the traveller with Michelin in the hand becomes that of 'confirming the truth of the guidebook, not discovering one's own truth. Discovery is not the goal; validating a preconceived opinion is.'[13] It is a thesis that can be stretched too far, but that there is *some* inherent cultural difference in the approach to guidebook making on each side of the Atlantic is, I think, borne out by even a superficial comparison between the market leaders in the genre of each continent.

To Europeans, the guides started by Arthur Frommer fit the cliché of what an American guide will be like. His passion for writing budget guides started when he was a GI in post-war Europe, and his first effort was *The GI's Guide to Traveling in Europe*, which the US army sold for 50 cents.[14] Discharged from the military, he created the legendary *Europe on $5 a Day* in 1956, and over the next twenty-two years produced fifty-eight budget travel guides until the series was sold to Simon & Schuster in 1978. With over 200 titles, Frommer became the top-selling American travel guide. Its audience is the middle-class American traveller and its strength is its common-sensical advice that helps them spare the pennies so the pounds can take care of themselves – avoid making calls from your hotel room, share a meal between two, do not change money in hotels or in the exchange bureaux at large tranport hubs . . . and so on.

There is, however, an important exception to the rather blunt generalisation that America produces little in the way of intellectual guides, namely a very remarkable series of state and city guides for the domestic market produced in the mid- to late 1930s. Several distinguished American writers participated in this (John Cheever wrote the volume on New York, Nelson Algren most of Illinois). The series was subsidised, as the Federal Writers' Project, under Franklin D. Roosevelt's WPA[15] programme that ran from 1935 to 1943. Derided by conservatives as a charity for mediocre talents, the Writers' Project in fact kick-started the career of authors such as Cheever, Saul Bellow, Ralph Ellison and Richard Wright, while saving established writers like Algren and Conrad Aiken from going under. This did not please the radical Left, however, who regarded the work provided as hush money to prevent the writers from denouncing capitalism.[16] Later, anti-communist zealots also targeted the project, not least because it was frank about the depression, and also delved deeper, and sometimes uncomfortably, into the history and culture of localities than did the bland mainstream guides. Oral history played a significant role in the research (Studs Terkel, later the pope of American oral history, was one of those involved with the project). This somewhat chaotic but altruistic undertaking (W.H. Auden called it 'one of the noblest and most absurd undertakings ever attempted by any state') has not, as far as I know, been replicated anywhere else, but it deserves respect as a state-financed project that allowed its protagonists complete freedom of expression. Ranging from volumes on the California Desert to the Oregon Trail, and covering individual states, as well as most major towns, this was an experiment in presenting America to itself, far more than one aimed at presenting her to outsiders. There is an echo, too, of the cultural distinction drawn by Michael Rowland in comparing the Michelin Guide vert with the American approach: according to the *Rio Grande* regional guide, the series did not seek 'to recreate the past for its own sake but to comprehend the present in terms of the forces that made it'.[17]

While the FWP guides were generally located left of centre (at least in American terms), the reader of the classic European guides was unlikely to be subjected to any alarming political shocks. He could be sure that the guides were well researched on a sound scholarly basis, that they would be slightly conservative in their selection of sights and measured in their appraisal of the same, that they comunicated through words rather than images (though the later DuMont was generally better illustrated than the others), and last but not least that their authors assumed a basic community of taste and values with their potential readers. The compilers of such works were often people on the fringes of academe and indeed academics were an important part of their market. Yet these industrious hacks (as most of them were regarded by snooty reviewers) were hardly ever people who made much of a mark as writers, or even as scholars. 'I know very well', wrote Jonathan Swift in the final chapter of *Gulliver's Travels*, 'how little Reputation is to be got by Writings which require neither Genius nor Learning, nor indeed any Talent, except a good Memory, or an exact Journal'.

Some compilers, like most of the Blue Guide authors, devoted a large part of their lives to successive editions of the standard works they had created, only to see the end of the Net Book Agreement sweep away what modest financial advantage they had derived from steady sellers that paid out royalties. The brands remained respected, but the books became less economic for the publishers; new series with higher production values threatened to sweep the board. Moreover, they were under attack from the Heinerian (and American?) attitude that mistrusted book learning and wanted more an evocation of 'experience'. The new traveller did need advice, of course, but he was more in tune with the Greek sea captains amusingly sketched by E.M. Forster in *Abinger Harvest*: '[They] never will use a chart. They sometimes have one, but it is always locked up in a drawer; for, as they say truly, it is nothing but paper and lines, which are not the least like the sea.'[18] Similarly, Forster has Philip Herriton say in *Where Angels Fear to Tread*: 'Don't, let me beg of you, go with that awful tourist idea that Italy's only a museum of antiquities and art. Love and understand the Italians, for the people are more marvellous than the land.' (It turns out, of course, that he cannot live up to his own slogans.)

THE PROBLEM OF AUTHENTICITY

Lucy R. Lippard remarks in a book about the interaction between tourism, art and place that the 'underlying contradiction of tourism is the need to see beneath the surface, when only a surface is available'.[19] The mainstream contemporary guidebook has lost its innocence in this respect – no longer is there a Baedekerian pretension to authoritative objectivity and depth, either in the selection of sights that are recommended or in the judgements (if any) that are passed upon them. On the other hand, rather than tread directly into the minefield of subjective opinion, most of the mainline guides strive to reproduce what they take to be the consensus view, both in respect of sights worth seeing and in regard to their significance and quality. Strongly subjective (and perhaps critical) judgements are generally reserved for matters like accommodation and restaurants, though even this may be an overstatement, since most guidebooks obviously only wish to feature those hotels and eateries that are considered good or good value. The dissidents among the guidebooks are, or used to be, the Rough Guide and Lonely Planet, the latter being famous for lambasting dreary English seaside resorts and the like. These guides traditionally targeted a young, adventurous backpacking audience (though at least part of that audience has now become middle-aged, possibly a problem for the publishers, who would like to keep such readers without alienating the young). The iconoclastic style was something that went with the territory, and was designed to give the reader a sense of identity that separated him or her from the breakfast flock of package tourists. A Lonely Planet author once described the holidaymakers with whom he had to share Diani Beach in Kenya as 'dreadful. Lobotomised European wage slaves on day release wouldn't be too far from the truth.'[20]

In such judgements, it is the ego of the individual *reader* of the guidebook that is being stroked – savvy, cool, penurious, not like *them* ('the tourist is always the other fellow', as Evelyn Waugh said). The reader of slighting comments about his fellow-men on a Kenyan beach supposedly understands what is authentic in terms of experience, and boasts an authentic identity; he or she belongs to a community of authenticity mediated by Lonely Planet. The greatest task facing today's guidebook is therefore that of identifying and conveying the cultural authenticity of sights and events (as opposed to something 'laid on for the tourists'). In view of the vast sums spent on the commodification of culture by national tourist authorities and the tourist trade, this task becomes harder by the day – there are indeed postmodernists who believe that such an endeavour is anyway misconceived.

Take the example of Vienna, a city that combines a remarkable cultural heritage with a high level of commodification. A few summers back, the distinguished arts festival of the *Wiener Festwochen* was launched with an open-air gala in front of the Rathaus. The show combined popular entertainers (or what the Social Democratic town hall considered to be such) with cosmopolitan and Euro flavours, all washed down with Viennese narcissism. A Johann Strauss number combined a half-hearted csardas with Swan Lake pirouettes and sudden flurries of boot-kicking Cossacks. Though not as bad as an Austrian TV programme that once featured high-kicking Tiller girls in military uniform as an accompaniment to the Radetzky March, the Rathaus gala was nevertheless a grim mélange of ethnic kitsch rivalling the Eurovision Song Contest in awfulness. If Strauss was turning in his grave, the show was also demeaning for the performers and a patronising poke in the eye for the audience, who were evidently assumed to be such wallies that all their cultural consumption had to be served with chips . . . Or possibly not? The square in front of the Rathaus was packed, the TV cameras homed in on smiling faces, the applause was enthusiastic . . . How should the guidebook mediate such events? Ignore them? Patronise them, as I have just done? Or do what the organisers and the Vienna tourist authorities devoutly hoped, namely treat them at face value as splendid examples of Euro-entertainment with 'Viennese flair'?

I deliberately chose the Viennese example, rather than hundreds that could be taken from scenarios such as African dancers performing for tourists, and the whole lugubrious touristic canon of costume, ritual and tradition, known to cynics as 'fakelore'. The vigorous promotion of their respective self-images by Vienna, or Paris, or New York, is an indication that 'autoethnography' is by no means confined to 'backward' cultures trying to cash in on tourism. On the contrary, it is often even more vigorously exploited, though perhaps with more subtlety, in the sophisticated European cultures. What would Venice be without its gondoliers, or London without its beefeaters and superfluous sentries at Buckingham Palace? The guidebooks cannot omit them, yet these are things that belong in the realm of what Dean MacCannell has called 'staged authenticity'. Another author attributes the yearning for authenticity in the individual's travel experiences as a sign of deep-rooted disorientation and dissatisfaction in the busy, fretful and restless life of modern man, an anxiety about the purpose of the individual's life and his or her credibility as a significant person. 'Because our life seems complicated to us, at least that of the Greek fisherman should appear simple. Since we are always changing our partners, friends and homes, the Tuscan peasants need to be apprehended as people who live in stable social conditions.'[21] This accounts for the obsession of guidebook designers with photographs of grizzled old men at café tables, of peasants riding donkeys, of North Africans riding camels and generally with images of 'pre-industrial activities'. 'The technologically dominated present is airbrushed out; the locals who are featured are almost invariably depicted . . . gutting fish or casting nets, harvesting olives, pruning vines, watching over herds of sheep or milking goats.'[22] The trademark cover image of the (generally excellent) Insight Guides was for long a figure in the peasant costume of the country treated by the guide. While the high-quality photographs inside these guides are extremely varied, one is also treated to images like that of the old man in overalls pictured in *Insight Guide Austria* (2001) who might be an old man in overalls anywhere, but who is saddled with the caption: 'Timeless country character.'[23]

'Autoethnography', a phrase coined by the social historian Mary Louise Pratt, appears in her writing as a process whereby the colonised learn to present themselves in the ways which the colonisers expect of them. If one accepts that tourism, like most forms of investment, aid, and other intervention in poor and vulnerable countries, contains an element of witting or unwitting colonialism, then the guidebook will inevitably be complicit in this. An article in the journal of Tourism Concern highlights how this may apply, even at a trivial level, when it asserts that 'The need to find the best bargain is perpetuated by guide books, which highlight budget options. While getting the most out of your travel budget is understandable, I have never seen a guide-book which puts an overly frugal attitude into a cultural context. Locals who work very hard for their living find it difficult to accept that travellers touring the world do not have enough money to pay for their food or their taxi rides.'[24] In reality, the modern tourist may really not have a lot of money in the context of his own society, though he is usually infinitely wealthier, in absolute terms, than the local inhabitants at his holiday resort. His 'meanness' was rationalised in characteristic prose by Baedeker in 1906, when (as quoted in Chapter 9) he wrote: 'Most Orientals regard the European traveller as a Croesus, and sometimes as a madman, so unintelligible to them are the objects and pleasures of travelling.'[25] The 'demon of cupidity', about which Baedeker waxed indignant, may be seen as the inevitable response to tight-fisted visitors, whose egos are pampered by the 'bargains' they manage to secure, just as some natives pride themselves on outwitting and overcharging the ignorant tourists. While money is of course important in absolute terms, the narcissism, self-esteem or plain human dignity of visitor and host are equally in play. Nowadays guidebooks tend to be more concerned than they once were about such things as the economic and environmental impact of the industry of which they are a part, and many seem to recognise that 'the customer' as tourist is not invariably 'right', or that his rights must be properly balanced against those of his hosts.

Quite similar sentiments to those of Baedeker, albeit camouflaged with a veneer of more politically correct language, may still be found lurking beneath the prose of the backpacker's knowing and 'cool' guidebook. A guidebook compiler who lives on the spot may be more sensitive to this kind of issue (and may also be cheaper for the publisher to employ). Yet such are not used as often as one might think, and for a revealing reason. In an article (1995) in *The Author*, guidebook writer Rosemary Bailey explains that, although the knowledge of the region possessed by someone who lives there may be more thorough than that of someone who has been parachuted in, 'this can cause problems with communication, since writers really need to appreciate the particular angle of a series, as well as needing to see a place from the point of view of a visitor'. It is the *visitor*'s idea of authenticity, therefore, that has to be catered for, not that of the local resident or native inhabitant. Bailey goes on to quote the Editorial Director of the Insight Guides: 'ideally we would like to combine writers with local knowledge with our own more objective view. That way you get the best of both worlds.'[26] But this policy statement blurs the difference between a genuinely 'objective' view (if such exists) and one that is imposed, not least to make the text conform to a series format. Nevertheless, the Editorial Director is firmly in the tradition of the Enlightenment: he assumes that he can see the wood for the trees from his external perspective, while the unfortunate natives can only see the trees, and not all of them very well.

CANDOUR IN THE GUIDEBOOKS

Previous chapters of this book have occasionally quoted the hostile comments of travellers as they compare the places and customs they encounter unfavourably with somewhere else, usually their own country (although in the case of the Prussian Archenholz (Chapter 7) Italy is castigated for not being more like England). Now there is a guidebook, or perhaps it is an anti-guidebook, that is entirely devoted to chronicling the most dismaying and bloodcurdling aspects of the world's most dangerous places.[27] According to the authors, this remarkable (and remarkably successful) tome is for 'people who trust other travel guides as much as we trust infomercials', readers whom they categorise as 'adventurers, adrenaline junkies and thrill seekers, intelligence junkies, journalists, expats, the curious and easily amused', and finally, 'Hollywood and the Media'. The principal author, Robert Young Pelton, relates in the Preface that the booksellers, discerning businessmen that they are, reacted with amused incredulity when the book was first presented to them. 'Why would anyone want to buy a book about places they don't want to go to?' they scoffed. Given this kind of enthusiastic endorsement by the trade, it is hardly surprising that the first edition sold out four times in its first year of publication, the second edition three times.

Although *The World's Most Dangerous Places* is not a guidebook in the sense of an itinerary, it certainly is a practical, if one-sided, handbook for travellers to such places, containing pretty much everything the conventional guide fails to mention or skims hastily over. Given that the authors are evidently super-macho Americans, it is perhaps not so surprising (and certainly to their credit) that they list the USA in their formidable list of the world's most dangerous places – earlier editions also featured the USA in the rollcall of criminal places, sandwiched between Russia and Zaire. Stars are awarded for dangerousness – one star for places like the USA ('not really dangerous, but [having] a bad rap for isolated incidents', for example, 'In Wisconsin and Illinois, deranged cannibals lure teenage gay hookers into their homes, decapitate and disembowel them, boil their heads and consume their viscera for dinner'); five stars for 'a place where the longer you stay, the shorter your existence on this planet will be' (Algeria, Sierra Leone, Somalia). Earlier editions featured one of those useful statistical boxes beloved by guidebook publishers, from which we could learn how often the New York City police and others discharge their weapons. In a single year, 928 shots were fired at suspected criminals, though unfortunately 755 of them missed; 155 were fired at dogs, with a more satisfactory score rate of only 44 misses. Suicides were commendably accurate (eight shots, no misses), likewise shots aimed at girlfriends (three shots, each one bang on target).[28] Despite its gallows-humour approach (the illustrative motif heading up the book's different sections features a skull wearing dark glasses and a baseball cap), the work is an astonishingly detailed compendium of real, not imagined horrors. The first section deals with 'What is Dangerous?' (war, terrorism, disease, kidnapping, the drug trade and so on); the second describes in detail the darker sides of thirty-four dangerous countries; and the last is a self-help listing of useful tips for survival, plus details of organisations fighting for a greener world, human rights and the like, as well as information sources on individual issues and countries.

It is an indication of different cultural perspectives on this side of the Atlantic that no European imitation of *Fielding's The World's Most Dangerous Places* seems to exist. Such European anti-guides as there are rely on humour, not to say facetiousness, in serving up the menu of disillusion. Matthias Sommer's *(K)ein Urlaub in Italien* ['(No) Holiday in Italy'] is a case in point, giving would-be humorous tips on how the traveller should deal with everyday irritations in Italy. But the complaints are the same old ones of yore: the avarice of restaurateurs with their *copertino* (cover charges), the dirty streets of Genoa, the swindling rates of exchange and so forth. Even the chapter headed 'The Dangers of the City, or: See Naples and Die' promises a good deal more than it delivers.[29] In any case, the author of a snide guide to Italy is generally not at much personal risk from the environment he whinges about, whereas a book like Karen Dabrowska's now legendary *Iraq: The Bradt Travel Guide*[30] requires real courage and resourcefulness to compile, even if it was written before the invasion of that country and subsequent mayhem. The book is candid about Saddam Hussein's regime, in power at the time it was researched, but neither dramatises nor underestimates the possible dangers, or merely disagreeable experiences, that the tourist might face if he or she ignores the author's sensible, low-key advice. At the same time, it is written with obvious affection for, and understanding of, the Iraqi people and their country's ancient culture, while its account of their often turbulent history is balanced and clear-eyed, for example, about the role of the British and other Western powers in modern times. Bradt stands out from the other guides that make a virtue of being candid on account of its wide perspective (there is much well-chosen quotation from other observers of Iraq over the years), and its lack of self-indulgence (the prose is restrained, but never evasive, coolly penetrating, but never exaggerated or self-glorifying). It is unlikely that anything much better could be produced on such a country at such a time.

Most guidebook readers will benefit from candour of a less dramatic kind than that on offer in the guides to dangerous places; for the (slightly) more prosaic traveller, the Rough Guides, and particularly Lonely Planet, have a reputation for 'telling it like it is', thereby acting as a counterweight to the verbal slurry of the tourist brochure. Fittingly, the founders of Lonely Planet, Tony and Maureen Wheeler, first met on a London park bench, before taking off across Asia in 1972, the journey being financed by their life's savings. Nine months later they arrived (broke) in Sydney. In 1973, stimulated by their friends' curiosity about their experiences, they home-produced *Across Asia on the Cheap*, ninety-six pages of first-hand travel wisdom selling for $1.80. With this unprepossessing first production an industry was born; by 1994 they employed seventy-five editors and cartographers and the firm had an annual turnover of $22 million. Ten years later it had published 650 titles in 118 countries and had annual sales of more than six million guidebooks, about a quarter of all the English-language guidebooks sold.[31] By 2003, gross income was $72 million. The wonderful name was inspired by a Joe Cocker song entitled 'Space Captain' (actually the phrase used was 'Lovely Planet', but Tony fortuitously misheard it as 'Lonely Planet').

The earliest titles were strongly countercultural, with *Africa on a Shoestring* offering tips on how to get hold of marijuana, while another volume even advised on the obtaining of fake student ID cards. As the *Wikipedia* entry for Lonely Planet observes, that kind of thing is unlikely to appear today, especially since the publishers have sought to break into the massive US market, which is 'relatively conservative and prone to litigation'.[32] Since 1981 the raunchy section of the *Japanese Lonely Planet* (the swinging scene, live sex shows) has been trimmed, then eliminated. As Maureen Wheeler revealingly remarked in an interview: 'When we were selling five thousand Japanese guidebooks a year, who cared what we said? At fifty thousand, you have a different responsibility.'[33] The breakthrough came with the *India* guide of 1980, which sold half a million copies and brought Lonely Planet out of the niche into the mass market worldwide. So strong is its footprint that some readers become pathological about the guide and erupt if its information turns out to be wrong – Wheeler has even received death threats from slightly deranged readers who have had a bad hotel experience. It is also widely assumed that he must have died by now through some travelling mishap (a capsized ferry, an Indian train crash), and charming letters of condolence arrive regularly by post.[34] Refreshingly, students from business school, who come to study their operation, say that Lonely Planet contradicts everything they have learned about how to run a company. As with the somewhat analagous Body Shop, the founders have done it *their* way – which includes donating a percentage of revenues to famine relief and other aid projects.

Although Rough Guides might seem to occupy a similar niche to Lonely Planet, there is a significant cultural distinction: by the turn of the millennium the former had been translated into twelve languages, the latter only into French. This would suggest that the Rough Guide has tapped into a more international style of youth culture, though it may also mean that the preponderance of Asian backpackers, at least in the early days, were from Anglophone cultures. The Rough Guide formula was originally devised by Mark Ellingham on a Greek island journey in 1981, when he found no guidebook to bridge the yawning gap between student-oriented efforts, mostly about living on a budget, and heavyweight egghead guides whose authors, like Sir Thomas Mandeville, gave the impression of having travelled no further than the research libraries. Like the Wheelers, Ellingham and some friends decided to write their own guidebook, with snappy, quickly digestible texts on history and culture and bang-up-to-date practical information. Much more attention was paid to matters like the safety of women travelling independently, hitherto hardly an issue for the traditional guides. While that basic formula has remained intact, the guides have expanded and drifted into the mainstream after being taken over by Penguin Books; recommendations now include more expensive accommodation and restaurants at the over 200 destinations covered by the guides. While Lonely Planet mostly stuck to its lathe,[35] Rough Guides has exploited its brand with spin-offs into phrase-books, music guides, CDs, restaurant guides, other reference works and even TV programmes. Ironically, their bestselling item is said to be the Rough Guide to the Internet.

Since both these series are written largely by native speakers of English, who come from an antipodean, American or British background, one might expect their comments to betray certain WASP characteristics, though the authors are clearly at pains to avoid this impression. Here it is interesting to study them on home territory, as it were, to see how the authors position themselves in terms of class, politics and society. As a very broad generalisation, the stance tends to be that of a youngish, independent-minded liberal who is occasionally quite anxious to establish his or her credentials as such. The Rough Guide's opening remark about Glyndebourne is a case in point: 'Glyndebourne, Britain's only unsubsidised opera house, is situated near the village of Glynde, three miles east of Lewes. On one level, Glyndebourne is a repellent spectacle, its lawns thronged with gentry and corporate bigwigs ingesting champagne and smoked salmon – the productions have massive intervals to allow for an unhurried repast.'[36] This passage is quite acute as social observation: in some ways Glyndebourne exhibits the culture of snobbery and corporate perks that is arguably one of the least attractive sides of England; but it is even more revealing about the writer, who is concerned to distance himself from the notion of culture as an adjunct to social or financial status. The Rough Guide is also relentless in its contempt for kitsch, tourist exploitation or heritage fakery. Buckingham Palace is 'a graceless colossus [that] began its days on the site of a notorious brothel', while Stratford-upon-

Avon is 'all but smothered by package-tourist hype and tea shoppe quaintness, representing the worst of "England-land" heritage marketing'.[37] The most interesting aspect of this stance, which runs like a leitmotif through the Rough Guides, is that it demonstrates how the wheel has come full circle since Roland Barthes's castigation of the Guide Bleu. The cultural snobbery of the well-heeled traveller (never 'tourist') between the wars has been replaced by the inverted snobbery of today's itinerant observer, who is equally contemptuous of package tours or of culture washed down with champagne and lobster.

More straightforward are the caustic comments of Lonely Planet, which delights in pointing out that the emperor has no clothes. Although the Wheelers are not themselves Australian, they have made their career in and out of Australia, and the tone of the writing in their guides fits well with the Aussies' reputation for bluntness and plain speaking. Of Cardiff, the guide says: 'Trains and buses deposit you on the edge of one of those faceless shopping centres which make you think the best thing to do would be to get on another bus and head straight out again.'[38] Of Blackpool it comments: 'There are those who visit because they have always done so, those who visit to get pissed and get laid, and those who visit because limited time and money allow them no better option. If you don't fit into one of these categories, give the place a miss.' Essex has 'a serious image problem',[39] while in Edinburgh 'the flip side to the gloss is the grim reality of life in the bleak housing estates surrounding the city, the thriving drug scene and a distressing Aids problem'. This last comment is one that could be made of almost any big city (compare Paris!), though that does not necessarily invalidate it. But the 'real' life of the city, or so the guide seems to be saying, is to be found away from the Royal Mile and Princes Street. Not unreasonably, the Edinburgh tourist office pointed out that they never got complaints about Aids and drugs from tourists, who obviously do not spend their time in grim housing estates. These they can experience vicariously through the bestselling crime novels of Ian Rankin.

SHOCK-HORROR ON THE ITALIAN GUIDEBOOK SCENE

One should not give the impression that only English-language guides are bluntly outspoken. The indignation of official Edinburgh in regard to the Lonely Planet's strictures was mild compared to the hornet's nest stirred up by the distinguished writer Cesare Garboli's preface to *Toscana di alpe e di mare* ('Tuscany of Mountains and Sea'), an officially sponsored quadrilingual insert for Italia Turistica in 2001, which remarked of Lucca: 'Almost all the sins of man, the darkest vices, money, avarice, fraud, lust, gluttony, live in the heart of the Lucchesi, mixed with ambiguous feelings of terror and greed. In Lucca one lives intimately with a corruption that goes deeper than in any other place on earth.'[40] The inhabitants, who still have not forgiven Dante for calling them greedy and placing their city among the damned, were not pleased, especially the representatives of Silvio Berlusconi's Forza Italia, which controlled the municipality of Lucca. One need hardly add that Garboli's effort was sponsored by the regional government, which was under the control of the Centre Left. The Mayor of Lucca demanded huge sums in compensation to the tourist industry for brand contamination and the immediate withdrawal of the 'guide', of which 80,000 copies had been distributed at a cost of 200 million Lire.

This must indeed be a rare example of an *official* tourist publication that was prepared to be abusive about its subject matter, even if the real basis of the huge *scandalo* was that it gave the semi-literate apparatchiks of Forza Italia a wide open goal for scoring against the Left. A feisty Garboli was happy to debate the issue with his critics, and pointed out that 'a publication for tourists should not be limited to celebrating . . . the natural beauties or the well known picturesque attractions of our peninsula, but should provide impulses for reflection, which may at first blush appear ungrateful, but which can help the visitor to a better insight into the spirit and life our cities.'[41] His negative remarks, recycled from something he had written thirty-one years earlier, were of course a literary conceit, more appropriate to a travel book than a guide. Moreover, it turned out that he had compounded his libel on the city (if such it was) with a far greater one which no self-respecting Lucchese could be expected to overlook: he had described the favourite Lucca dessert of *buccellato* as 'austere and grey, almost tasteless'. One's sympathies are instantly with the Mayor.

Standing back a little from this thoroughly enjoyable spat, more pressing objections to Garboli's effort come to mind than the fact that he does not flatter Lucca and the Lucchesi. His is a literary text that plays with generalisations and conceits, which the provincial authority fondly hoped would evoke the region for prospective visitors. Unfortunately, translation plays havoc with such texts, in this case producing hilarious asides in the English version which lend it a unique charm but may not attract tourists: Versilia is rainy with 'debatable geography', and Lucca is 'laborious and lustful', while its inhabitants are mostly 'used car salesmen and estate agents'. Nor is the prospect of a hearty meal of 'lard and pig's bones' in the Garfagnana immediately enticing. It is bad luck on Garboli, whose Italian prose is poetic, nostalgic, sometimes even moving, that it has been applied to the wrong task. The impression given is that things were a great deal more appealing in the days of D'Annunzio and Thomas Mann than they are now: 'Anyone who is over seventy can still remember the clear, clean sea, so transparent that, in the morning one could see on the bottom the sparkling shells of the clams . . .'.[42] *Over seventy?* We had quite forgotten that pollution had been around so long until the brochure so obligingly reminded us . . .

Garboni is probably unique, but his introspective approach to his native land is refreshing for not being narcissistic in the usual way of tourist brochures. Writing a 'warts and all' guide to one's own country may well involve an element of masochism as well as honesty. This is particularly the case if one addresses such an ambivalent case as London, which I have mostly avoided in writing this book, precisely because I partially live there. There is a flipside to the notion of seeing ourselves as *others* see us, so wisely counselled by the Robert Burns, namely seeing ourselves as *we* see ourselves, from which is inseparable a profound admiration for the stamina, tolerance and masochism of foreign tourists visiting contemporary London. This is well captured in an article in the *Observer* by Euan Ferguson,[43] who put himself through the rituals of a foreign visitor to London for a whole day on which, inevitably, it poured with rain. Apart from the horrors of the open-topped bus tour ('On the left is the Royal Academy of Music. This is where Lord Andrew Lloyd Webber, composer of *The Phantom of the Opera*, was once a pupil'), and the resistible delights of the Tower of London gift shop (a Queen's Jubilee loving cup for a mere £12.60), it was the sheer squalor of an environment that he somehow normally took for granted that struck the journalist's eye like an apocalypse. Of Leicester Square, mysteriously a Mecca for tourists, but a place where few Londoners over the age of 25 would wish to linger, he writes the following:

> Turn west into the square proper, where the tourists are drawn, and you will pass, in this order, an Aberdeen Angus Steak House, another homeless teenager, a casino, a shop selling 'sex toys', a café selling the slithery pizza, a huge, flashing, yellow, welcoming sign from the police informing you that you are about to be robbed and – the only thing so far not to do with your money and the getting of it – a small, rather lonely pile of afternoon vomit.

Tacky pubs, overpriced restaurants with indifferent food, monuments stormed by hordes of tourists and gift shops, gift shops, everywhere – why does the foreign tourist put himself through this? In the year that Ferguson was writing (2002), between 20 and 25 million tourists were expected in London 'and 25 million tourists can't be wrong, can they? Oh yes. Very yes. As comprehensively wrong as avocado cheeseburgers [on offer in one particularly dire eatery he had visited with a tourist group].' Yet most of the visitors seemed to take all this in their stride, as if they expected little else, which in itself is revealing. The guidebooks take refuge in extreme brevity of description or talk vaguely of cinemas and neigbouring discos, which is ironic considering the square is probably the most densely thronged three acres of London on an average night. On the other hand, apart from statues of Charlie Chaplin, Shakespeare and Reynolds, there are no real tourist sights in Leicester Square, even if all the tourists go there.

POLITICAL CANDOUR IN GUIDEBOOKS

In the Western democracies guidebook candour represents a welcome critique of the commercial interests of tourism, in which both private enterprise and regional authorities have a stake. Throughout the cold war, a guide written about a country behind the Iron Curtain (and nowadays about ruthless dictatorships) could be critical, bland, evasive, or defiantly defensive; what it could not really be, even if it claimed as much, was neutral. A studiously neutral approach that strove to present politics as a topic that need not be discussed in a land where everything was politicised, though not because the population wanted it that way, inevitably implied a degree of guidebook Finlandisation. The inhabitants knew, even if the guidebook pretended otherwise, that totalitarianism permits no intellectual space that is 'non-political'. As the Czech poet and Nobel Laureate Jaroslav Seifert wrote of his fellow literati under Communism, 'when an ordinary person stays silent, it may be a tactical manoeuvre. When a writer stays silent, he is lying.' In effect, the guidebook compilers had to decide whether to pose as 'ordinary persons' or as 'writers'.

The acid test of a guidebook's honesty was to compare it with a locally produced censored product, though guides in the latter category covered a propagandistic spectrum from the shamelessly mendacious (East Germany) to the subtly obfuscatory and discretely amnesiac (Hungary.) The tone of the officially sanctioned East Bloc guidebook towards the end of the cold war has been delightfully caught by Malcolm Bradbury in his burlesque *Why Come to Slaka* (1986). Written in a perfectly attuned parody of the mangled English found in incompetent guide translations, where you cannot work out which are the translator's errors and which are the printer's, this guidebook to the 'People's Republic of Slaka' caricatures the tone of such works, complete with their linguistic slips that accidentally reveal the truth. For example, the section on Slaka's achievements and political system graciously contributed by the Minister of Culture himself, lauds the 'National Assemblage of the Fatherland', which is responsible for 'policies of revolutionary socialistic emulation, and the advancement of the progress of history. So clear is the will of the people of Slaka that it needs to meet but four days a year.' The 'Assemblage' is composed of 'representatives of all groups: the Committee for State Security, the Counsel of Ministers, our military leaders and even elected representatives. These give their advises to the *Supreme Counsel* ("Politburo"), which decides on executions. The Members of the National Assemblage appoint the Politburo, which appoints the President, who appoints the members of the National Assemblage. This insures coherent policies.' The page where this helpful text occurs is illustrated with a wonderfully shabby black and white photograph featuring what appears to be a Hungarian *csikós* (cowpoke) driving a herd of wild horses towards an electricity pylon. The caption reads: 'Slakan shepherd urges into the future his flock.'[44] Elsewhere, in a passage the Intourist guides would have been proud of, we read that: 'The advanced watercress industry is a miracle of aggro-organization. Our nuclear technology is proud of its piles, and our RMBL Kiev-type reactor, with its spectacular emissions, offers the means of electrifying our entire people.'

In the depths of the cold war, there were not too many Western travel guides to the Communist bloc, for the simple reason that not many people wanted to go there. That left the field largely free for the local publishers to push their wares on the spot. The Corvina 1967 guide to Budapest (in German)[45] is a characteristic example of how the Hungarian Communists handled such material. Most of the rather dull and plodding text is unexceptionable, simply omitting controversial issues. However, the last three paragraphs of the history section present the period from 1947 up to the date of publication as a triumph of five-year-plans, prosperity and progress, all as a result of 'the people' taking command in every sphere of life. The 1956 'counter-revolution' (a nomenclature clung to by the regime almost to its end) was an 'attack against the rule of the people', but happily the Hungarian Socialist Worker's Party was able to restore order (no mention of the Russian intervention), and Budapest soon regained its old lustre . . . Only in the guide's comparatively restrained boasting about the virtually non-existent consumer choice does one detect a faint echo of Bradbury's *Slaka*: '*Die strahlenden Kaufläden beleben nicht mehr allein die zentralen Stadtteile, sondern auch die Außenbezirke*' ('Glittering shops enliven not only the city centre, but also the suburbs.' This of a town where it was quite hard to buy a toothbrush and the placard advertisements for the (only) shoe outlet for the (only) state-owned shoe producer memorably urged the public to: 'Buy shoes at the shoeshop!'[46])

Although the mainstream guides mostly ignored Hungary until the the 1980s, the same year as this Corvina guide appeared also saw the publication of Alan Ryalls's *Your Guide to Hungary*, published by the small firm of Alvin Redman. A decade after the Revolution of 1956, and boasting a foreword by the President of the National Office of Tourism, this guidebook generally reflects the image the Kádár regime sought to project of a land wisely ruled by five-year-plans, helpful officials and smiling traffic policemen (the author seems particularly enamoured of the last named). 'The Hungarian People's Republic', we are told at the end of the history section, 'is carrying on a consistent firm policy for peace to protect its own achievements and to promote peaceful coexistence and cooperation amongst all people'. If this sounds like His Master's Voice speaking, the author volunteers his own assessment as follows: 'I have been asked quite seriously by Britons and Americans whether the "hordes of Soviet troops" stationed in Hungary interfered with my holiday in any way. I can honestly say, throughout my travels in Hungary, I have never come across these "hordes of Soviet troops", though I have occasionally seen a couple strolling in the streets, apparently in harmony with the Hungarians around them.'[47] This is indeed a touching and reassuring picture of a country under 'fraternal' occupation.

Ryall's book, which is full of useful and practical information, but offers minimal coverage of architecture and cultural artefacts, faithfully transmits the Kádár regime's decision to eschew the earlier threatening attitudes of Stalinism ('those who are not with us are against us') in favour of the disarming and reasonable-sounding tone of 'those who are not against us are with us'. One's impression of the author, derived from the somewhat breathless and occasionally naive tone of the book, is that of an idealistic English leftie of the caravanning and camp fire variety. There is no reason to doubt the genuineness of his enthusiasm for Hungary and Hungarians. While he seems a little over-eager to toe the official line in places, it would be wrong to dismiss such a thoroughly useful book as *merely* propaganda. Nevertheless it conjures exactly the air of 'normality' that Kádárism liked to project, and for which, after all, evidence could be adduced if you were ideologically so inclined. By ironically putting the phrase 'hordes of Soviet troops' in inverted commas (twice!), the text also manages to imply that their numbers were greatly exaggerated by ill-informed and possibly ill-intentioned persons, without risking any confrontation with the actual figures. When the Russians were finally persuaded to withdraw their troops in 1989, it turned out that there were 65,000 of them scattered round the country.

Malcolm Bradbury's spoof has had an afterlife in the first parody of a guide to a *demokratura*, an expression used to designate totalitarian states that have become populist, nationalistic and authoritarian during their transition (as we hope) to democracy and the market economy.[48] If Slaka sounds like a Soviet Republic, *Molvania: A Land Untouched by Modern Dentistry* sounds vaguely Balkan (though 'Central Europe' is mentioned), a land where corruption and organised crime, often in the hands of the former Communist *nomenklatura*, constitute a state within a state. However, whereas Bradbury's *Slaka* is a satire on totalitarian absurdities, *Molvania* is primarily a satire on the *Western* travel guide itself, particularly on those that adopt the relentlessly upbeat and patronising tone that seems to have been inspired by infotainment or a CNN feature. 'Molvania prides itself as an environmentally conscious nation,' says the guide, as though awarding Brownie points, 'and all its waste is either sorted and recycled, or dumped over the border in Slovakia.'[49]

The dissonance between *tone* and *content* is one of the perils of formulaic guidebook-writing, and the authors have mercilessly reproduced it, both in the the choice of illustrations and in the heavy-handed use of bold type, a much-loved device of guidebook typographers: 'Molvania prides itself on its attitudes to the disabled and in 1985 it passed legislation allowing them to beg without a permit.' Particularly ingratiating are the examples of sales patter for overlooked 'jewels' and 'gems', a clichéd discourse so dismally familiar from TV advertisements, travel brochures and the like: 'This unique mountain region towering above the mighty River Fiztula has for years been overlooked as a holiday destination. But now, thanks to improved tourist facilities, coupled with a cease-fire in the war with Romania, visitors are beginning to discover the charm of this forgotten jewel.'

The same cheery and persuasive tone pervades the infoboxes, another designer fashion of modern guidebooks inherited from the obsessive techniques of infoflashes, rapid image sequence and soundbites exploited by the broadcasting media in the process of dumbing down their audience. A typical box for a 'Traveller's Tip' reads: 'In many of Vajana's less expensive hotels the breakfast facilities are self-serve. If planning to use the toaster, guests are advised to make sure they are wearing well-insulated footwear.' An infopanel headed The Local Drop . . . runs as follows: 'No-one spends much time in Sasava without being offered a glass of *biljgum*, the locally brewed brandy. This highly scented, thick liqueur is quite unlike anything you've ever tasted – unless you've inadvertently swallowed fabric conditioner – and is generally offered at the end of a meal as a means of prompting guests to leave.' Nor do the captions, which, in many of the highly illustrated mainstream guidebooks, show signs of editorial desperation, escape the authors' horribly accurate satire. A picture of a bosomy and scantily clad dancing girl, with her hand placed on the head of a punter in a nightclub, is captioned: 'The traditional dancers of Lake Vjaza not only entertain but will, for a small extra fee, remove head lice.'

MYANMAR AND THE GUIDEBOOKS

Molvania, however near final implosion as a country, is clearly one determined to attract tourists, and the same could be said of a real country with a far more sinister regime, namely Myanmar (Burma). Its military dictators have tried, with some success, to use tourism both to shore up the regime's finances and as a passport to legitimacy. This is why the heroic, and democratically elected, opposition leader, Aung San Suu Kyi, has urged travellers to boycott her country. Lonely Planet, for many the epitome of independent-minded liberal and humanitarian values, nevertheless chose to publish a guide (albeit a critical one) on Myanmar, and disappointed many of its fans thereby. Its defence is the same as that of other tourist traders doing business in Burma: in the long term, they say, communication and influence through travel exchange helps to unseat undemocratic governments. Unfortunately, this is debatable and at least some businesses are hiding self-serving greed behind such bland optimism, as did many opponents of sanctions against the apartheid regime in South Africa. Lonely Planet published a guide to South Africa too, in which it referred to the government as 'cretins' and 'narrow-minded psychotics'.[50] It is doubtful whether this was more instrumental in toppling the system than sanctions, although the effectiveness or otherwise of sanctions remains a matter of dispute.

However that may be, an honest, critical guide is surely better than the sort of glossy account of 'the Golden Land' that appears in many publications, and not only in the country's official tourist handouts. Reviewing a book of photographs entitled *Back to Mandalay: Burmese Life, Past and Present* by Norman Lewis *et al.* (2006), Victor Mallet remarks in the *Financial Times*: 'This is a remarkable feat: more than 450 colour photographs of Burma and not a single picture of a soldier or a field of opium poppies [the regime also runs the drug trade], let alone a Pepsi bottle, an oil rig, or a hotel building site.' The reader of this book is 'wafted through a quaint and delightful land of Buddhist temples, trained elephants and colourful hill-tribe festivals' – small wonder that the publication turns out to have been sponsored by Japanese and Singaporean participants in Burmese investments, and indeed by the Myanmar government itself. Commercial pressures on tourist literature are insidious, political ones menacing. In an article written in 1984, David Barchard reported that the British Embassy in Ankara had had to intervene to protect the British Institute of Archaeology, which was threatened by the authorities because its ten-year-old guidebook to Ankara had maps of Hellenistic and Roman Asia Minor showing a region called Armenia. Bad consciences make bad history and in countries with little developed tradition of free intellectual discourse, the hope is that intimidation will make unwelcome facts disappear.[51]

The humanitarian argument in favour of unlimited tourism asserts that it provides financial support for the impoverished inhabitants of the world's kleptocracies, which may be true in a limited sense through the provision of seasonal jobs. But as Tourism Concern (quoting Aung San Suu Kyi) has stressed in its criticism of Lonely Planet (whose product is the bestseller of the Burma guides), much, if not most, of the money from tourism in Burma flows directly into the generals' coffers, and thus actually supports the structures of human rights abuse that the guide deplores. Worse still, the generals are known to use slave labour (an estimated two million people) to 'clean up' the country for tourism, and even indulge in ethnic cleansing to establish 'nature reserves'. The argument that 'engagement' circulates more liberal ideas, claim the publisher's critics, is an insult to the oppressed Burmese, since they already have the liberal ideas but want the freedom. 'Lonely Planet is concerned, but it also wants to sell guidebooks,' wrote Nick Cohen in an article in the Observer (2000). 'There's a niche market to corner as the editors of the Rough Guide series, its business rivals, refuse to cover Burma on a point of principle.'

It is an indication of the iconic status of a guidebook like Lonely Planet that the boycott against the firm called for by Burma campaigners was headline news. The founders of the series, Tony and Maureen Wheeler, responded with typical aplomb, seeking to demonstrate that information collected in the field, for which their guides are celebrated, is worth more than posturing abroad. They travelled through Burma in 2001 to find out whether ordinary people supported an economic and tourism boycott, and discovered, or so they said, that they scarcely encountered a single supporter of such measures. Unfortunately, the positive impression that this created was somewhat marred by the return of a cheque the publisher had paid to the Burma Relief Centre in Thailand, whose director accused it of using the Centre's formal letter of thanks for the contribution to justify its line on Burmese tourism: 'We would prefer not to be complicit in any defence [of tourism to Myanmar] your organisation is making.'[52]

The arguments for and against tourism to places like Burma are scarcely reconcilable, and the individual traveller has to make up his own mind on the basis of the widely available facts. Opponents of the boycott, liberals as well as conservatives, have even accused its protagonists of adopting 'totalitarian' attitudes for wanting to interfere with the freedom of others to go where they please. 'Discerning liberal consumers', ripostes Cohen to this assertion, 'are now so self-confident and self-pitying that they pose, without irony, as the victims of Stalin and Hitler when anyone suggests they might make the tiniest moral choice.' There are signs at least that the furore has led guidebook compilers for Burma to enter a defence for their activity. A German author of one such work announces on the cover that all the royalties from the book will go to a Myanmar orphan's home run by monks.[53] The writer, who clearly has a passionate attachment to the land and its people(s), concentrates on the beauty of the landscape, the friendliness and hospitality of the people, the excellent cuisine and all the other themes of the romantic guidebook. On his second journey there, he travelled in a style befitting another age, the age of the Murray Handbook: he tells us that for three weeks he rented 'at a reasonable price' an entire railway carriage, with sleeping quarters, living room, dining room, kitchen and bath, for no more than the price of a hotel room of similar comfort. With this unusual mode of transport he was able to travel all over the country, decoupling the wagon when he arrived at an interesting spot worth a longer stay.

An old Asia hand who has studied in China and Japan and made his first trips as a student backpacker, the writer presents a frank and detailed account of the country's rulers and a longish sympathetic portrait of Aung San Suu Kyi. Interestingly, he feels obliged to counter her call for a tourist boycott head on, and with the usual arguments: 'Perhaps she did not give sufficient consideration to the number of jobs created for ordinary citizens by the tourist business. And she has surely underestimated the far-reaching influence that the presence of foreign tourists can have on any political system. For example, in China tourism has performed a useful service in opening up the country. Contacts, discussion and exchanges of information are inseparable from the presence of foreign visitors – a development that is the last thing a dictatorship would want.'[54] Generally the author presents himself as a realist, pointing out that the generals' firm grip on power is not about to be dislodged by a spied-upon and persecuted population; he seems to favour some sort of compromise involving UN mediation as the only policy likely to improve the position of the opposition and the lot of the Burmese. He is critical of the absolutist stance of the Western media, which he says encourages Aung San Suu Kyi to demand the total capitulation of the generals, something that is not about to happen. The case is persuasively argued. There remains only the question as to whether a German guidebook writer, who travels the country in his personal railway carriage, really knows better what is the right strategy for the benighted Burmese people than a Nobel Laureate who won 80 per cent of the vote in the last free election in Myanmar.

To be fair to Lonely Planet, the ninth edition (2005) of its *Myanmar (Burma)*[55] devotes five even-handed pages to the debate about whether travellers should visit Myanmar at all, something which is probably unique in guidebook history, and the history section is outspoken about the nature of the regime. It gives sensible advice about staying out of trouble and flags up ways in which the tourist can patronise hotels and other services that are not state-run. At a time when Google, supposedly the avatar of freedom of communication, cynically bowed to the will of the Chinese censor in order not to miss out on business in China, Lonely Planet's frank arguing of its case and eschewing of weasel-worded justifications for their actions comes as rather refreshing.

THE IMAGINED PAST: E.M. FORSTER'S ALEXANDRIA

Much of the criticism of guidebooks to countries with oppressive regimes implies a base monetary motive, if not on the part of the author, at least on the part of the publisher, but usually both. This is ironic from an author's point of view, since very few make any more than a paltry living from their labours. Compiling guidebooks has probably always been a labour of love, if not a downright quixotic enterprise, in which financial reward was secondary to the mission to inform. Perhaps the most quixotic of all such guides was also the only one written, one is tempted to say since Pausanias, by a person of real literary stature, namely E.M. Forster. His *Alexandria: A History and a Guide* is one of the cult books in the genre, written during Forster's spell as a 'searcher' for the Red Cross in the city from 1915 to 1919 ('searchers' were employed to visit wounded soldiers in hospital to glean information about men listed as 'missing'). Lawrence Durrell, who drew on the book for his celebrated *Alexandria Quartet* (1960), described it as 'a small work of art', which would have pleased the author, who said that he had 'always respected guidebooks' and indeed used them as a literary touchstone in his own fiction. The critic Bonamy Dobrée claimed that Forster's was 'surely the best guide-book ever written', perhaps because it is as much a guide to cultural memory as it is to the contemporary reality of the place and so appealed to the donnish mind; by the same token, Durrell's *Alexandria Quartet*, an exploration of erotic memory, is the novelistic counterpart of the guide. This is no accident: Forster's first lasting erotic attachments occurred while he was in Alexandria, and he also met, and introduced to the world, the great C.P. Cavafy. Cavafy is the poet of Hellenistic Alexandria, but also of the homoerotic underworld of the city in his own day.

The savagely beautiful Justine in Durrell's eponymous novel (1957) calls Alexandria 'the capital of memory', and another character refers to it as the 'unburied city'. 'The physical city', writes Michael Haag, 'has been embalmed by events, and lacking sufficient opportunity and prosperity, the old has remained in place.'[56] Indeed, the first five sections of Forster's guide comprise an historical periodisation, 'after the fashion of a pageant', as the author said: Greco-Egyptian, Christian, 'The Spiritual City' (on post-Ptolemaic religious thought, and one of the most fascinating chapters), the Arab Period, and finally the Modern Period. The *Guide* proper, illustrated with maps and plans, then follows with eight discursive rambles through Alexandria. It is a guide as much to the unseen as to the seen, Alexandria being a city of the imagination. Forster's allusive, meditative approach to the material is suggested in his introduction to the 1961 edition, published by Doubleday in the USA: 'At the crossing of the two main streets I would erect the tomb of Alexander the Great. I would follow Alexander in imagination to Siwa, the oasis of Jupiter Amnon, where he was saluted as the Son of God. And I would follow the monks too, to the desolate Wady Natrum whence they burst to murder Hypatia.'[57] Finally, the appendices deal with such topics as the death of Cleopatra and the uncanonical gospels. The whole is unrivalled in its ability to evoke a city washed over by civilisations that have given it a unique psychic identity. Forster's achievement, though different in tone, is analogous to the powerful evocation of spiritual decay arising out of an overwhelming past, a past that crowds out the present in the individual's psyche, to be found in Cavafy's memorable poem 'The City'. The latter begins with quiet desperation:

You said, 'I will go to another land, I will go to another sea.
Another city will be found, a better one than this.
Every effort of mine is a condemnation of fate;
And my heart is – like a corpse – buried.

And ends with a brutal reality check:

Always you will arrive in this city. Do not hope for any other –
There is no ship for you, there is no road.
As you have destroyed your life here
In this little corner, you have ruined it in the entire world.[58]

This is by no means Forster's *tone*, which uses different means to achieve the same 'feeling for the poignancy surrounding public and private destiny which "rises from the past"'[59] in Cavafy's poems. His guide is matter of fact, sometimes playful, occasionally Gibbonian:

The Patriarch Cyril . . . having destroyed the cults of Serapis and Isis in the district (AD 389) sent out the relics of St Cyr to take their place. The relics were so intermingling with those of another martyr, St John, that St John had to be brought too, and a church to them both arose just to the south of the present Fort Kait Bey. The two saints remained quiet for 200 years, but then began to disentangle themselves and work miracles, and recovered for the district some of its ancient popularity; indeed many of their cures are exactly parallel to those effected in the temple of Serapis.[60]

Forster cross-referenced his elegant historical sketches to the sights in the guide, thus integrating the sightseeing experience with its intellectual and cultural background. True, there were errors in the history section, gleefully catalogued by one Robert Tracy in a review of the 1961 unaltered reprint of the 1922 first edition, and prompting Forster fans to write in detailing, with equal glee, Tracy's own errors in his piece; but Tracy was alone in describing the book as (by then) 'useless as a guide and of little value as a history'. On the other hand, there was a splendidly Forsterian moment when the author, seven years after the first edition, paid a visit to Alexandria and immediately lost his way as he came out of the railway station, a 'humiliating experience for the author of a guide', as he cheerfully admitted. The 1938 edition was revised somewhat, and annotations to a later reprint of the guide have contextualised some of the factual anachronisms in the book. By 1956 Forster himself believed it to be the 'product of a transitional age, which age is at an end',[61] and remarkably every reissue of the guide after 1938 reverted to the 1922 text, errors and all. Forster's comment points to the book's unique value as a *literary* document, marking a significant phase in the career of one of the century's greatest writers. And it is writers – Durrell, Robert Liddell, Evelyn Waugh, Naguib Mahfouz – who have especially treasured it, while even something so totally of another age and outlook as the Rough Guide was still happy to quote from it in 1996.

The publishing history of what Forster was to call his 'lost guide' deserves a place of honour in the annals of authorial calvaries. True, the firm of Whitehead Morris, with bizarre and surely unbusinesslike generosity, gave Forster a contract stipulating a 25 per cent royalty on the *first* 1,000 copies, and 20 per cent thereafter, instead of a rising royalty as was customary. On the other hand, its Alexandria branch, more accustomed to producing brochures and the like, was out of its depth with a book as well as being dilatory in the extreme. Publication, agreed upon in 1918, was delayed so long (until 1922) that all the British troops who were its intended market had left Alexandria by the time it appeared. In publishing this is known as 'snatching a defeat from the jaws of victory', although to be fair to his publishers, Forster evidently went on revising and altering the copy until shortly before his departure from Alexandria. An even more Dickensian piece of bumbling took place after publication, when the publishers wrote to Forster in 1928 explaining that a fire at their warehouse had destroyed the remaining stock of his book. In their gentlemanly way they enclosed a substantial cheque by way of compensation, part of the insurance pay-out they had received. Shortly afterwards they sent a further letter explaining that, after all, the stock had not been destroyed as had been thought; but since the insurance money had been paid, they had decided themselves to burn it, and this had now been done.

A second edition appeared in 1938 – hardly an auspicious time for such a work – for which the corrections were made by zealous and conscientious Forster supporters in Alexandria. The author, by now a much revered literary figure, merely stipulated that all changes should be '*factual* and not containing any expressions of opinion'. Nevertheless, the latest editor of the work points out that Forster's local helpers 'quietly removed some of the sharp Forsterian asides which might affront modern Alexandria's civic dignity',[62] such excisions representing either a diminution of imperial arrogance (even in the author of *A Passage to India*!), or an early portent of 'political correctness', according to one's point of view. Forster himself, in the introduction to the 1961 edition, calmly observed that 'there are scarcely any national susceptibilities [the *Guide*] does not offend. The only locality it shouldn't offend is Alexandria herself, who in the 2,000 years of her life has never taken national susceptibilities too seriously.'[63]

In 1956 at the Aldeburgh Festival, Forster gave a charming retrospective view of his sojourn in Alexandria and his 'lost' guide, complete with an affectionate but quietly devastating vignette of his publisher, Mr Adamson. The latter had retired in the year the guide was finally published, 'exhausted perhaps by the enterprise, and certainly vowing that he would never be mixed up with authors again'. In this talk Forster laid out his personal ground rules for guidebooks, which his own had admirably incorporated: 'They ought to be dry and not too dry. They ought to stimulate without diffuseness and sustain without boredom.'[64] To these qualities he added the novelist's empathy, an ability to evoke the *genius loci*, of the present, yes, but especially the psychic flavour of past ages. Reading his history and guide, one begins to understand Ibn Dukmuk's extravagant encomium for the city in its ancient greatness: 'If a man make a pilgrimage round Alexandria in the morning, God will make for him a golden crown, set with pearls, perfumed with musk and camphor, and shining from the East to the West.'[65] As James Buzard has pointed out, Forster had produced a sort of anti-Baedeker full of the 'anti-tourist strategies'[66] of his early fiction, demanding of the reader that he or she make an imagined journey, since nothing much remains of the sights discussed; but it must be a journey that is more sensual and alive to the Alexandrian milieu than Baedeker's (by comparison) bloodless recital of objects and artefacts.

ARCHITECTURE AND THE *ZEITGEIST*: 'THE LITTLE GUIDES', PEVSNER AND BETJEMAN

Two biographical vignettes: the first reads: 'His labours were incessant, his memory extraordinary, his system admirable, his clearness of understanding and liveliness of fancy vigorous, his affections warm, his habits exemplary'; and the second: 'The overriding impression . . . is of the breadth of his curiosity, and his ability to communicate enjoyment of his discoveries through an immediate response. Serious discussion of nationally significant buildings is tempered by an engaging sense of the ridiculous. Appreciation is given depth by acute analysis made possible by careful observation.'[67] Were it not for the archaic use of the word 'fancy', these two passages could be descriptions of the same person, but in fact 180 years separates them. The first vignette is of John Britton, the main protagonist of an astonishingly ambitious early nineteenth-century topography entitled *The Beauties of England and Wales* and the sole protagonist of a pioneering *Architectural Antiquities of Britain*. The second vignette is of Sir Nikolaus Pevsner, the founder of the most distinguished series of architectural guides ever produced, the Buildings of England, which began in 1951 and delivered forty-six volumes over twenty-three years. Like Britton's topography, it covered the whole of the country county by county, beginning, in Pevsner's case, with Cornwall and finishing with Staffordshire in 1974. While Britton had a collaborator for the topography, the majority of Pevsner's works were written by the great man himself, who visited each building of each region to investigate its merits, and wrote up his impressions in the evenings in the cheap hotels that he was obliged to use on account of his exiguous travel budget. Small wonder that the term 'Pevsner' is now associated with buildings in the national consciousness as Bradshaw was once associated with the railways.

Of Britton it has been said that his 'ambitions as a scholar far outran his talents . . . [yet] architectural historians have cause to be grateful to the man Beckford once called "that highly ridiculous, highly impertinent Britton, the Cathedral fellow"'.[68] Pevsner, whose talents were admirably suited to his ambitions, was also regarded as an eccentric by some, not least by woolly mastodons lurking in far-flung country houses who regarded their own eccentricity as the criterion of normality. It was a shock to them when they opened their doors one day to a courteous, but inquisitively determined, academic with a slight German accent, who was not to be deterred from inspecting some obscure architectural feature of their ancestral home. Michael Taylor, Pevsner's driver for the research on the Warwickshire volume of the Buildings of England, recalls a response that could have come from a P.G. Wodehouse novel when he telephoned the owner of one venerable pile: 'Want to see the chapel?' boomed this gentleman down the line. 'If you've gone to the bother of phoning, at least I expected you'd want to see the pigs. Come of course, but you'll have to see the pigs.' Another exclaimed, 'Well, the whole house is medieval but I can't imagine what you want to *see* it for.' Institutions, too, could be tricky: when Pevsner wanted to leave Colney Hatch Mental Hospital after an architectural inspection of it, he was confronted by the porter whose functions included making sure that the patients did not escape. His declaration that he was Professor Pevsner failed to impress this functionary, who merely said: 'Well, that's a new one . . .'. Contrary to expectation, such incidents actually seemed to endear the English to the supposedly desiccated Dresden Professor, perhaps because he relished the challenging prospect of politely educating the citizens of his new homeland about the treasures that lay under their very noses. Vivid encounters with cognitive dissonance revealed further aspects of the 'Englishness' on which he was to become something of an authority.

The Buildings of England is indeed what a great series of guidebooks should be, a tool for heuristic education. For this purpose it needs to be opinionated as well as accurate, meticulous about documentation but never afraid to take a stance, often one that contradicted the conventional wisdom. When Pevsner conducted his survey for An Enquiry into Industrial Art in England, the mere fact of his enquiry and the nature of its subject matter had revealed to the English something about themselves, in this case something not very flattering. The directors of one old established firm calmly remarked to him that 'we are not interested in the question of public taste in design', as if that settled the matter. What had happened to the ethos of William Morris and Ruskin? Pevsner responded by quoting the latter: 'Your business as manufacturer is to form the market as much as to supply it.'[69] Pevsner indeed shared with Ruskin a conviction that aesthetics was a matter of ethics, not merely of personal taste, although his critics have pointed out the flipside of this, what one of them calls his 'moralising determinism'.[70] Another castigates him for his apparently unshakeable belief that modernism represented the Zeitgeist, and opposition to it from an unpersuaded public was perverse, or from intellectuals was betrayal.[71]

On the other hand, his belief in modernism stemmed from humanitarian ideals, and when brutalism became fashionable (among architects, never among the public) he was outspoken in condemning its arrogance and inhumanity. The idealistic engagement with human values that was implicit in his guidebook enterprise is stressed by Colin MacInnes, when he writes: 'Never does Dr Pevsner slip for a second into the "aesthetic fallacy" which supposes – as so many architectural authors do – that buildings were built for art historians to contemplate.'[72] This clear-sightedness distinguishes Pevsner from the self-indulgence often lurking in English connoisseurship, and is perhaps the element in his guides that most betrays the mind of a German scholar interested in functionalism, what Simon Jenkins calls 'the Germanic bias [that] sometimes told in judgements of buildings of his own age'.[73] But there the Germanic bias, if not the Germanic approach to his guidebook project, ended. As Ian Buruma has written, 'he arrived in Britain as an apostle of modernism, socialism and European progress and ended up as an admirer of the conservative English "national character". And he did this from a peculiarly German perspective.'[74]

Perhaps it required a sensitive and learned immigrant to identify 'the Englishness in English Art', which is the title of one of Pevsner's most famous books – or perhaps this idea of 'Englishness' is simply a mould into which Pevsner could pour certain aspects of English culture that he felt were sympathetic. Behind the notion of *Volksgeist* or 'national spirit' in art and architecture lay the German Enlightenment and in particular the ideas of Johann Gottfried Herder. Pevsner's own professor at Leipzig, Wilhelm Pinder, had expended much ink on the topic of the German *Volksgeist*, as expressed in art and architecture, with the not entirely unpredictable result that he ended up as a Nazi apologist. Pevsner, a German exile in England whose family was originally of Russian Jewish stock, nonetheless remained true to the idea in its unpolluted essence. Goethe's identification of Germanness with the Gothic of Strasbourg Cathedral, or Ruskin's views on Venetian Gothic, represented its transcendental version, while the notion of the Danish architect, Steen Eiler Rasmussen, that sash windows reflected 'the essence of the practical English character: windows that never quite fit, ventilating rooms with a permanent draft of fresh air',[75] represented . . . well . . . perhaps a generosity of spirit in regard to English joiners? Pevsner privileged the practical, pragmatic nature of English craftsmanship as expressed in the decorative functionalism of the Arts and Crafts Movement, which he forced himself to see as a precursor of Socialistic Modernism such as the Bauhaus. Modernist sympathies found their way into the Buildings of England, for example, when he praised an ugly concrete development around St Paul's Cathedral as 'a brilliant essay in the English tradition of informal planning' (it is noticeable how the phrasing he adopts makes bad modern design sound more palatable by embracing it as quintessentially English). His critics have implied that the Hampstead-dwelling Pevsner was a hypocrite, advocating soulless Corbusier-inspired blocks for the masses while living in leafy bourgeois seclusion himself. Yet Pevsner (fortunately) was more of an idealist than an ideologue, or perhaps too learned to take his principles as far as his critics pretended he did.

Pevsner's initially rather puritan attitudes and his German intellectual rigour were the target of some amusing, but often also unattractive sniping from a group of English polemicists, of which John Betjeman was the leading figure. Betjeman was the General Editor of the Shell Guides, originally published under the auspices of the *Architectural Review*, and his performance as an editor was, to say the least, unpredictable. Pevsner, on the other hand, based his whole system on a legendary series of German artistic and architectural topographies founded by Georg Dehio (1850–1932), and still running today in Germany and Austria. '*Dehio*' was an '*amtliches Inventar*' (official inventory), which nevertheless also took the trouble to describe the *aesthetic* impact of important monuments. The inspiration for Pevsner (which he acknowledged) is clear, and his series of guides did indeed 'describe every structure of account in the country'[76] like a sourcebook. But, with the example of Dehio before him, he also stressed and acted on the principle that 'a training of aesthetic sensibilities and of a historical sense is equally desirable'[77] for those who want to look at architecture profitably. As a result, and despite the caricature of him as an ideologue, he could be appreciative in his guidebook of things that were not really his bag; on the other hand, he could be very critical of self-conscious historicism, even when it served the Arts and Crafts movement he admired, as in this description of the shortcomings of Liberty, the Neo-Tudor Regent Street store: 'Technically there is nothing wrong – but functionally and intellectually everything. The scale is wrong, the symmetry is wrong, the proximity to a classical façade put up by the same firm at about the same time is wrong, and the goings-on of a store behind behind such a façade . . . are wrongest of all.'[78] We are back with Ruskin's *Stones of Venice*, where the guidebook also functions as polemic and moral tract.

There were other architectural guides, notably the very successful Little Guides published between 1900 and 1924, but it is fair to say that Pevsner's achievement trumped them or (in the case of the Little Guides) supplanted them. The more than forty volumes of Little Guides covered every county of England and were mostly researched by their authors on foot, whereas Pevsner had the services of an old banger and a long-suffering driver. Little Guide quality was as variable as its contributors, who ranged from enthusiastic amateurs (clergymen) to more or less opinionated scholars. While they often did supply more local historical context than the Buildings of England (as Pevsner generously conceded in one of his volumes), and also offered some local genealogy (a passion of the class-obsessed English), their aesthetic sympathies were incredibly narrow, 'a conviction that the medieval churches are of far greater interest than any other buildings we possess'.[79] The difference between this blinkered stance and that of the wide sympathies of a Pevsner or a Betjeman is marked: while Betjeman and John Piper described Gayhurst church (1728, Buckinghamshire) as 'one of the classical style treasures of the country' in a Shell Guide, the Little Guide's author (E.B. Roscoe) merely heaped abuse on it: 'a wretched building, showing much 18th century rubbish'. There can be no more dramatic illustration of the way in which guidebooks not only *reflected* changing taste, but were often the main factor in *causing* it to change. The ability to effect what cultural historians like to call a 'paradigm shift' was a talent that both Pevsner and Betjeman shared, the one exercising it by means of encyclopedic scholarship and academic rigour, the other through wit, showmanship and a deft portrayal of the human and social context of architecture – even in his poetry. One of the best-loved Betjeman poems parodies a well-known hymn in its castigation of late Victorian church vandalism masquerading as 'restoration':

The Church's Restoration
 In eighteen-eighty-three
Has left for contemplation
 Not what there used to be.
How well the ancient woodwork
 Looks round the Rect'ry hall,
Memorial of the good work
 Of him who plann'd it all.

. . .

Church furnishing! Church furnishing!
 Sing art and crafty praise!
He gave the brass for burnishing
 He gave the thick red baize,
He gave the new addition,
 Pull'd down the dull old aisle,
– To pave the sweet transition
 He gave th'encaustic tile.[80]

The Shell Guides, founded by Betjeman in 1933, were illustrated topographical histories of counties and 'expressly intended to counteract the antiquarian and mediaeval stance of the Little Guides by drawing attention to the merits of Georgian and and early Victorian architecture, and to the evils of over-restoration'. The same commentator goes on to remark on Betjeman's version of Pevsner's *Volksgeist*, namely 'Englishry', as presented in his polemic *Ghastly Good taste, or a Depressing Story of the Rise and Fall of English Architecture*. While Pevsner was to put forward notions of pragmatism and 'informal planning' as somehow typical of the English character, Betjeman, twenty years earlier, traces its lineaments in religion: 'Do not despise the English Sunday. When it is gone, like the elegant terrace or the simple brick house in the High Street, it will be missed. Sunday is sacred to Protestantism, and Protestantism purified our architecture.'[81] The book ended paradoxically with a paean to modernism – not at all in accordance with the image most people have of a Betjeman nostalgically ironising homely Victorian architecture or Edwardian suburbia. Indeed, in a pamphlet entitled *Antiquarian Prejudice* of 1939, he went further and praised the architecture of Soviet Russia with its 'honest plain structure of steel and glass and/or reinforced concrete'.[82]

Although he later abandoned this position, it can be seen that many of the conflicts between the supposed English sentimentalist Betjeman and the supposedly left-wing, dourly modernist Pevsner, had more to do with good journalistic copy than reality. After all, did not Pevsner, the sworn enemy of 'historicism', end up in 1963 as second President of the Victorian Society (which John Betjeman had done much to bring into existence in 1958)? There is a famous story of Pevsner lecturing on the then extremely unfashionable Victorian designer Matthew Digby Wyatt. Halfway through, he was obliged to administer a stern reprimand to his audience, which had collapsed into helpless laughter, and explain to them that he was entirely serious about Wyatt's virtues. Perhaps there is also a hint of Betjeman's mildly ironic affection for Victorian architecture in Pevsner's quadripartite categorisation of the same into the good, the bad-good, the good-bad and the bad-bad.[83]

While both Betjeman and Pevsner in their different ways were inclined to lament the philistinism of British attitudes, it is notable that both were able to raise sponsorship for their guidebook series, Pevsner from Guinness (the brewers) and the Leverhulme Trust, Betjeman from the oil company Shell. For the most part guidebooks have been purely commercial ventures, not least to avoid compromising their editorial independence – something, as we have seen, to which both Baedeker and John Murray attached great importance. But there seems almost no direct benefit, other than prestige, for the firms associated with the Buildings of England, especially since Pevsner did not enjoy pubs and scarcely mentions any in the guides. In the case of Shell, the link is more obvious, in that the existence of the guides would potentially encourage more motoring, and thereby sell more petrol,[84] but it is a comparatively weak link with few implications for the actual texts of the guides. In an age before 'environmentalism' had become a hot political theme, even Shell's desire to to project an image of environmental awareness and patriotic love of the English landscape would have seemed less disingenuous than activists would now regard it. At the same time, neither venture was embarked upon for personal financial gain, indeed quixotic seems an understatement to describe the attitudes of the series' founders – Betjeman even had part of a routine salary increase for his regular job allocated to the Shell Guide, for which the other authors were being paid £50 per volume.[85] The Buildings of England was actually suspended for three years, so uneconomic had it become for its visionary publisher at Penguin Books, Allen Lane.[86] Yet, even with sponsorship, the achievement and commitment of individual enterprise is magnificent, conjuring the image of the guidebook writer once again as a heroic Ulyssean figure; it has been pointed out that, in the time it took to publish all forty-six volumes of the Buildings of England, the Royal Commission on Historical Monuments managed to produce an inventory of Dorset.[87]

The Shell Guides to England, launched with *Cornwall* in 1934, were a dominant force in the guidebook market for two decades, and particularly successful in the twelve years of austerity after the Second World War, with 'a captive audience and very little competition'.[88] This was despite a shaky start with *Cornwall*, which was badly organised and written before Betjeman had acquired his distinctive tone of voice and approach, one that mingled erudition with ironic affection for English idiosyncracy. It was an irony in itself that Pevsner began *his* series in 1951 with Cornwall, hardly the most promising county of England in respect of interesting architecture, and made a success of it, while Betjeman, who had adored Cornwall from his childhood holidays, made a mess of his first tribute to it.[89] In 1964 he rewrote his *Cornwall* guide in the style that we now associate with him, redolent of social observation, nostalgia for a way of life unsullied by the tourist industry (this in a guidebook!), but also with fascination for the quirks (particularly architectural quirks) thrown up by that industry ('King Arthur's Castle [an hotel!] at Tintagel, the Poldhu at Mullion and the Metropole at Padstow'). 'Farmers' wives specialised in Cornish teas and fishermen rowed the "foreigners" [as the Cornish call visitors] out of the harbour to catch the mackerel they would otherwise be catching for themselves. Farmers on the sea coast started growing bungalows instead of wheat.'[90]

The Shell Guides recovered from an inauspicious start and developed a gazetteer format (except for *Hampshire*, 1937), which seemed admirably to suit the holidaying motorists at whom they were aimed. However, like all guidebook series with multiple authors, the quality of the writing was uneven, which was exacerbated by Betjeman's early preference for roping in his trendy friends from student days at Oxford, whose qualifications for the job were not always apparent. This is how one guide (*Kent*) came to be written by an Anglo-Catholic eccentric known as Lord 'Cracky' Clonmore, a character out of Somerville and Ross, whose full name was William Cecil James Philip John Paul Forward-Howard. Possibly because Clonmore evidently knew next to nothing about his subject and was unable to write (not necessarily a drawback in the book world of the day, if you had the right friends), a lot of his guide was farmed out to others, not that this noticeably improved the text. Even Robert Byron (*Wiltshire*), whose vivid and opinionated travel books are still read, was not at his best in the guidebook genre, displaying a tendency to show off erudition rather than share it with the reader, which is perhaps the one really cardinal sin of a guidebook writer. On the other hand, some guides were distinguished artistically as a result of being written, or co-written and illustrated by talented artists (Paul Nash, John Piper with *Dorset* and *Oxfordshire* respectively).

Direct competition between Pevsner and Betjeman only occurred after the Second World War, when the Buildings of England was launched (1951) and the publisher John Murray decided to pick up the Betjeman Shell Guides, that had lapsed during the hostilities, and turn them into Murray's Guides (Shell were not interested in sponsoring such books when hardly anyone could get hold of much petrol). Although these Murray guides were not a great success, they benefited from the co-editorship of the artist John Piper, who sharpened up Betjeman's prose, too often written hastily under the pressure of alternative commitments, and ensured a certain stylishness of design. By 1951, when the first Pevsners appeared (*Cornwall*, *Nottinghamshire* and *Middlesex*), Murray had given up on the guides, Shell had renewed sponsorship and Betjeman had moved the project to the new publisher (Faber). Chronologically parallel (eventually there were forty-six Pevsners and over thirty Shell Guides) the two series were in most respects complementary rather than competing. Shell Guides really were guidebooks with winsome prose to lure people onto excursions and practical information to assist them, while the Pevsners were architectural reference works arranged in a topographical order (and in recent years, ever more formidably bulky). Briefing Lady Juliet Smith before she began on the *Shell Guide to Northamptonshire* (1968), Betjeman distinguished between Shell and

Pevsner, telling her it was 'no good trying to write a comprehensive, impersonal catalogue. That is already being done in Pevsner's *Buildings of England,* and does not tell you what the place is really like . . . it is the eye and the heart that are the surest guides.'[91] But both series were inspired by a passion for England that can be described as broadly speaking patriotic, the patriotism of a first generation immigrant applying a fresh pair of eyes to what the natives have missed, and the patriotism of an English aesthete who, under the shock of war, grew ever more attached to English qualities in architecture and rediscovered the virtues of a solid middle class as the preserver of those qualities.

As to the much-hyped differences between the rival cicerones, the real distinction was between that of academic professionalism, so revered by the Germans, and secretly admired by those English who mock it, and the gifted amateurism evident in Betjeman's sometimes cavalier, but generally entertaining, approach to his task. Leaving aside professional and academic rivalry and a touch of xenophobia in Betjeman, the two men were chalk and cheese. Pevsner, mocked as 'Herr Professor Doktor' and 'Der Great Categorist', stood for analysis, while Betjeman made a career out of empathy, although in truth a guidebook needs a judicious combination of both. It has been said that what Pevsner feared most was the triumph of emotion over reason;[92] if true, his background probably had something to do with that (his parents were trapped in Germany when the war broke out, and his mother committed suicide to escape the camps). This attitude may also explain one of his best aimed digs at Betjeman (in *London,* volume 2, 1952), which comes in his description of what he knew was the latter's favourite church designed by the camp Anglo-Catholic architect, and the poet's close friend, Ninian Comper: 'There is no reason for the excesses of praise lavished on *Comper's* church furnishings by those who confound aesthetic with religious emotions.'[93] This assertion may be compared with Betjeman's observation in a newspaper article twenty years later: 'I don't think life would be worth living if one were not constantly the prey of one's emotions.'[94]

The Shell Guides are no more, but the the Buildings of England have an afterlife as The Pevsner Architectural Guides under the editorship of Bridget Cherry. Apart from *Lothian* (1978), *Powys* and *North West Ulster* (both 1979), all the volumes on Ireland, Scotland and Wales appeared after Pevsner's death in 1983. The revised editions (Pevsner modestly claimed that the first editions were mere *ballons d'essai* and the project would be justified by the second and subsequent ones), improved by the thousands of comments from obsessive (or sometimes unhinged) readers that Pevsner had invited, march into the future; or actually waddle, since they are getting fatter and fatter. To preserve guidebook portability, a new series of Pevsner inpired paperbacks will cover major cities. The project has modernised in other ways – in the city series, there will be less of the *Kultur des Wortes* (the outward manifestation of Pevsner's German Protestantism), technical terminology and throwaway Latin quotations and more images; and there will even be a website: www.lookingatbuildings.org.uk, featuring a glossary, bibliography and an index of architects.[95] Remarkably influential in his lifetime, Pevsner has cast a long shadow into the future.

Although he was not only a guidebook writer, he is surely unique in being one that changed public perceptions and the priorities of the authorities so significantly, and who became a national institution – as well as the touchstone for ongoing national controversy.

SOME IDIOSYNCRATIC GUIDEBOOKS OF THE TWENTIETH AND TWENTY-FIRST CENTURIES

One result of the huge increase in travel since the twentieth century, and hence the increased demand for travel literature of all kinds, is that guidebooks now extend from the impossibly macrocosmic (*1,000 Places To See Before You Die*) to the obsessively microcosmic, dealing candidly with such hitherto unmentionable topics as *How To Shit In the Woods*.[96] The latter book takes over where Kitchiner and Galton left off (see Chapter 10). The contents page is not without a certain *élan*, featuring chapter titles like 'Anatomy of a Crap', 'Plight of the Solo Poop Packer' and 'Trekker's Trots'. Clearly this entertaining and informative work meets a widespread need, since the strapline on the cover claims over one million copies in print. As the author disarmingly states at the beginning of Chapter 2 ('Digging The Hole'): 'People – corporate lawyers, philandering spouses, presidential candidates – always want to know how to bury their shit. This chapter spells out precisely where and how to dig holes that promote rapid decomposition of feces and prevent contamination of waterways, thereby providing the best protection for the health of humans, the remainder of the animal kingdom, and the planet.' An analogous volume (*Shitting Pretty* by Dr Jane Wilson-Howarth)[97] is by an intellectual heavyweight of the Royal Society of Tropical Medicine and Hygiene, but her approach to the subject is similarly robust; the text is also enlivened with little boxes featuring readers' experiences with mind-boggling solutions to the problems of being caught short (such as the mobile toilets on tricycles of Shanxi Province, China), together with tales of diarrhoea attacks grim enough to deter the most passionate traveller. Richard Dawood's *Traveller's Health* (1986) is the straight man's answer to the faecal jokers and admirably blunt: 'Some 85% of the world's population have never seen a doctor and never will. Many travellers will temporarily be in the same position.'[98] The book is a treasure trove of diseases you never really wanted to know about, including creeping eruption (*larva migrans* and *larva currens*), Ebola, Lassa fever, Marburg virus ('green monkey disease'), Leishmaniasis, Chagas' disease and the guinea worm.

More directly in the tradition of Galton's *The Art of Travel* is *The Worst-Case Scenario Survival Handbook: Travel* (2001),[99] a sequel to *The Worst-Case Scenario Survival Handbook* which *USA TODAY* described as 'an armchair guide for the anxious', and the *Washington Post* endorses as follows: 'Parachute won't work? Open this instead.' Some of the situations examined in the *Worst-Case Scenario* for travel include: 'How to Control a Runaway Camel,' 'How to Treat a Severed Limb' and 'How to Foil a UFO Abduction', this last being as indispensable as a jab against tropical disease for African travellers if you're venturing into places like New Mexico. The UFO abduction advice is perhaps rather prosaic ('Do not panic', 'Firmly tell the extraterrestrial entity (EBE) to leave you alone'), but there is also expertise: 'Go for the EBE's eyes (if they have any) – you will not know what its other, more sensitive areas are.' Although such items might suggest to some that the book is not to be taken seriously (and certainly it is a splendid armchair read), the advice given is sourced in every case to experts. For example, tips on 'How to Survive an Airplane Crash' are offered by William D. Waldock, a Professor of Aeronautical Science, and those on 'How to Jump from Rooftop to Rooftop' are supplied by stuntman Christopher Caso. It is also reassuring that 'How to Deal with a Tarantula' is written by the author of the *Tarantula Keeper's Guide*, who is the President of the American Tarantula Society and the owner of 350 tarantulas. There is even an expert for 'How to Escape from the Trunk of a Car', namely Janet E. Fennell, 'the founder of Trunk Releases Urgently Needed Coalition (TRUNC), a nonprofit [organisation] whose mission is to make sure children and adults trapped in trunks can safely escape'.

NICHE GUIDES AND 'THE BOOK'

The twentieth and twenty-first centuries have also seen the ideological and social fragmentation of the guidebook genre, most obviously in terms of feminism (guides aimed specifically at the independent woman traveller), and homosexuality (for example, *Gay Europe* by David Andrusia, or the decidedly phallocentric *Spartacus International Gay Guide*). One firm entices with a series of guides under the banner of *Horny?*, which is aimed at lustful heterosexuals, though a spin-off line was started in 2003 under the generic title of *Gay and Horny?*[100] There is even a guide designed to help gay and lesbian travellers navigate Disneyland and Walt Disney World,[101] though why gays should require special assistance in confronting Mickey Mouse is something of a mystery. There are also environmentally polemical guides and pioneering works such as *Touring the Black Past*, which concentrates on unknown and neglected landmarks of Afro-American history. Of some 109 presses publishing guidebooks and surveyed in the spring issue of the US *Publishers Weekly* in 2003, nearly half could be described as specialist in some respects, though really only the sex guides fall into the category of social or ideological statement.[102] On the other hand, 2006 saw the publication of a book with a broader public in mind, the first guide to tackle the problems of 'unethical tourism' head-on. *The Ethical Travel Guide*, published for the excellent Tourism Concern, suggests 300 places in sixty countries that can be visited with a good conscience. As Tricia Barnett of Tourism Concern puts it: 'How would you know that a beautiful hotel is on land snatched from fishermen and for which they have not been compensated? [Or that] the water in the pool and shower are depleting local people's resources and their access is limited to two hours a day – as in villages in Goa?' At a time when Thai developers are using the devastation of the recent tsunami to steal land from the locals for new hotels, the relevance of this kind of guidebook hardly needs underlining – perhaps, indeed, it is the guidebook of the future.

The market for such works as *Touring the Black Past*, or even *Dog-Friendly New England*, is necessarily self-limiting, but the same cannot be said of a remarkable alternative text which brilliantly evades the constrictions of the traditional guidebook through being in a state of constant flux, added to or corrected only by its users. Known simply as *The Book*, you cannot buy it in a store and you may not be able to read parts of it, if you do track it down, unless you read Hebrew. Hailed as 'the best unknown guidebook in the world', its genesis may be traced to the El Lobo restaurant in La Paz (Bolivia). It was here, in 1989, that a bored backpacker scribbled down a recommendation for a nearby cheap local hotel. His useful insider's tip was accompanied by the sort of caveats that might deter a more fastidious clientele than that typically addressed by *The Book* ('the rooms don't have windows . . . dark and dingy . . . smelly and dirty' – but of course *cheap*). Patrick Symmes, writing in *Outside Magazine* (2005), gives a vivid characterisation of *The Book* today: 'a set of loosely connected, handmade, decentralized notebooks cached throughout the vagabond meccas of Latin America and Asia – a collective, disorganized stash of travel tips, phone numbers, discount deals, crazed illustrations, conspiracy theories, backbiting marginalia and boozy reminiscence, penned by and for the deeply broke backpackers of the world'. In other words, the text is a sort of palimpsest: additions, deletions and emendations are scribbled both across the existing text of *The Book*, as on its blank pages, wherever it may be found. It is a piece of *sub rosa* counterculture, 'a counterintuitive survivor like the underground postal system in Thomas Pynchon's *The Crying of Lot 49*' (Symmes again).

The main input has been from Israelis, who constitute a tough breed of traveller, having in most cases undergone a spell of military service before their liberation to roam the planet. Volumes of the guide are to be found in such places as a laundromat in San José (Costa Rica), in bars and youth hostels, even in a Chilean butcher's shop run by a Jew. The original book, which had its origins in the Israel of the early 1970s, was only in Hebrew ('In the beginning was the Word'!), but now there is a multi-lingual version. The El Lobo volumes constitute a sort of matrix, and there are some sixteen regional spin-offs. The title recorded on the first page ('International Travel Book') appears in ten or so languages, and a rebarbative user has written at the bottom of the final one: 'Book of the smarmy, conceited been-there-done-that-so-I'm-groovy wankers.' This is a powerful indicator of the fact that *The Book* is as much an ongoing argument as a list of recommendations (lauded sights not infrequently have rude comments added by a later traveller), a refinement never previously attained by the guidebook, though the Internet now makes it technically possible. And through it all runs a darker leitmotif alerting Israeli travellers to South America's less appealing brand of nostalgia – a hotel in Peru run by admirers of the Third Reich, another in Bolivia linked to 'the shadowy rule of that great philanthropist Klaus Barbie'. The mental environment of *The Book* is as immanent as the physical delights and squalor it describes in its own version of beat poetry. As one entry in El Lobo puts it: 'a good experience is not where you go, but inside of ourselves. I've had some of my best experiences fucked out of my brain, and damned superb they were'.[103]

Mind-Travelling and the Survival of the Guidebook

Travel as tourism has become like the activity of a prisoner pacing a cell much crossed and grooved by other equally mobile and 'free' captives. What was once the agent of our liberty has become a means for the revelation of our containment.

(Eric J. Leed, The Mind of the Traveller from Gilgamesh to Global Tourism, *1991)*

So much of who we are is where we have been.

(William Langewiesche)

Some of the more whacky contemporary 'guides' are, however, definitely sailing under false colours, in so far as they cater only for travels in the mind[1] (though of course a good guidebook should cater for the mental journey as much as for the physical one). The guidebook publisher Cadogan includes a *Traveller's Guide to Hell* in its list,[2] the blurb for which is disarming: 'This year, go where the rich and famous are going.' But even the section entitled 'Touring Hell' turns out mostly to be an account of Dante's *Inferno*, whereby one sees the justice of the blurb writer's complaint that Dante was not a travel writer and obviously never visited the place. Still, there is some helpful information for those wishing or expecting to spend a season in hell, typically that you no longer need to remember to take along the fee for Charon. As the guide points out, free admission to hell was one of the first reforms introduced by the Christians. Nor do you need to do much packing, since 'everything necessary for a happy stay in Hell will be supplied by your hosts'. It seems that the service culture of American business has finally reached the nether regions. This is somewhat less the case with heaven, which George Bernard Shaw complained was conventionally depicted as 'a place so inane, so dull, so useless, so miserable, that nobody has ventured to describe a whole day in heaven, though plenty of people have described a day at the seaside'. Leaving aside the fact that a day at the English seaside is often indistinguishable from a day in hell, Shaw's remark reminds us of the difficulty we have in envisaging somewhere so unattractively lacking in mayhem and malice as heaven. Nevertheless, Peter Stanford in his thought-provoking *Heaven: A Traveller's Guide to the Undiscovered Country* (2002)[3] has met this problem head-on and provided some persuasive visions of the place in the course of his metaphorical and spiritual journey there. One could argue that the time is ripe for guides to heaven and hell, since we live in a virtual world where intense experience of a location, imagined or real, can be provided by technology, and there is no need physically to move from one's desk. Indeed, the website Planet Ware ('Time-efficiency distinguishes this website'), while conceived as a journey-planning tool, uses Baedeker base material and hundreds of vivid photographs which almost recreate the travel experience – though it has not yet tackled heaven and hell.[4]

The death of the book – and therefore the guidebook – has constantly been predicted over the last few decades. Despite the technological potential of e-books, text-messaged itineraries, global positioning and the rest, the guidebook stubbornly clings to life and even thrives in some forms. Its death, as Mark Twain said of his own, has been greatly exaggerated. Somehow this is heartening, and suggests that even our apparently jaded and jet-lagged civilisation still has a place for the intellectual stimulation and joy of discovery that a good guidebook can always offer the intelligent user.

THE END: PLEASE LEAVE THIS BOOK AS YOU WOULD HOPE TO FIND IT

Notes

INTRODUCTION

1 The reference to 'tactile values' is one of several sardonic allusions to Bernard Berenson's *The Florentine Painters of the Renaissance* (1896), a book that left Forster distinctly unimpressed.

2 All quotations, both from the novel and the editor's comments, are taken from vol. 3 of the Abinger Edition of E.M. Forster, *A Room with a View*, ed. Oliver Stallybrass, London, 1977. This quotation is from pp. 19–20. The novel was first published in 1908, therefore towards the end of what has been called the 'Age of Baedeker'.

3 *Ibid.*, ix.

4 Maxine Feifer, *Going Places: The Ways of the Tourist from Imperial Rome to the Present Day* (London, 1985), p. 2.

5 Arnold Bennett, *Florentine Journal* (London, 1967; written April–May 1910), pp. 11, 38, 39, 58.

6 Elizabeth Bowen, *A Time in Rome* (London 2003; 1st pub. 1959), p. 65.

7 John Auchard in the Penguin edition of Henry James, *Italian Hours* (London, 1995), xxii–xxiii. The review by Henry James of *Days near Rome* by Augustus J.C. Hare has been reprinted in Leon Edel and Mark Wilson (eds), *Literary Criticism: Essays on Literature, American Writers, English Writers* (New York, 1984).

8 Aldous Huxley, *Along the Road* (London, 1925).

9 Roland Barthes, *Mythologies*, unrevised reprint, tr. Annette Lavers (New York and London, 1972; first pub. 1957), pp. 74–7. While reiterating in the new preface to the French reprint (1970) that the 'essential enemy' remains 'the bourgeois norm', Barthes remarks that 'ideological criticism' of the type propounded in *Mythologies* has subsequently moved on, becoming, *inter alia*, 'more precise, complicated and differentiated'. Under the influence of Saussure, he had believed that 'the pious show of unmasking ["collective representations"] was inadequte; one needed to treat them as sign-systems in order to 'account in detail for the mystification which transforms petit-bourgeois culture into a universal nature' (p. 9).

10 'It's a curious bird, the Oozlum, / And a bird that's mighty wise, / For it always flies tail-first to / Keep the dust out of its eyes!', W.T. Goodge, *Hits, Skits, and Jingles* (1899).

11 This is part of the definition of pilgrimage supplied in F.L. Cross and E.A. Livingstone (eds), *The Oxford Dictionary of the Christian Church* (Oxford and New York, 1997), p. 1288.

12 The French referred to *l'art de voyager*, and the Germans to *Reisekunst* or *Reiseklugheit*.

13 E.S. De Beer: 'François Schott, *Itinerario d'Italia* (London Bibliographical Society, 1942, reprinted from *The Library* in *The Transactions of the Bibliographical Society*, 4th ser., vol. 23, No. 2/3, September–December (Oxford, 1942)).

14   Hayden White, 'The Fictions of Factual Representation', in Angus Fletcher (ed.), *The Literature of Fact: Selected Papers from the English Institute* (New York, 1976), pp. 23 and 43.

15   Hayden White, *Metahistory: The Historical Imagination in Nineteenth Century Europe* (Baltimore and London, 1975), p. 14, n. 7. Obviously one must be cautious about directly comparing historians and the compilers of guidebooks. Nevertheless, White's characterisation of the 'Formist' approach to history (he is using a paradigm taken from Stephen C. Pepper, *World Hypotheses*) has a certain resonance in the guidebook context: '[The Formist] considers an explanation to be complete when a given set of objects has been properly identified, its class, generic and specific attributes assigned and labels attesting to its particularity attached to it.'

16   John Lukács, *Historical Consciousness and the Remembered Past* (New York, 1985), p. 99.

CHAPTER 1

1   E.S. De Beer, 'The Development of the Guide Book until the Early Nineteenth Century', in *Journal of the British Archaeological Association*, 3rd ser., vol. 15 (1952), 36. Richard S. Lambert in *The Fortunate Traveller: A Short History of Touring and Travel for Pleasure* (London, New York *et al.*, 1950), p. 10, describes travel as 'an adjunct to five main classes of human activity; first, war, diplomacy and administration; second, exploration, discovery, colonizing and pioneering; third, migration and commerce; fourth, the spread of ideas, information and knowledge, and fifth, the search for health'. Guidebooks are associated principally, but not exclusively with the fourth and fifth items on this list. Tourism may be said to begin when pleasure becomes the paramount motive for travel.

2   The Book of Joshua, 18: 4–9.

3   Jerome Turler, *The Traveller* (facsimile reprint, Gainsville, FL, 1957, of an anonymous English translation, London, 1575, of *De Peregrinatione, et Agro Neapolitano*, Libri II, 1574 by Hieronymus Turlerus), p. 50. Turler appears to conflate Moses' desire (rejected by the Lord) to 'see the goodly land that is beyond Jordan' in person (Deuteronomy 3: 25), with Joshua's fulfilment of the divine will that the children of Israel should settle the land. According to the Book of Deuteronomy, the Lord said to Moses: 'But charge Joshua, and encourage him, and strengthen him; for he shall go over before this people, and he shall cause them to inherit the land which thou shalt see' [but only from the top of Pisgah or Mount Nebo overlooking Jericho, where in fact Moses is recorded as dying – Deuteronomy 3: 27–8 and 34: 1–7]. See also Numbers 13.

4   The fate of a band of British anoraks who recently went to a military airbase in Greece to indulge their mildly eccentric hobby of 'plane-spotting' may serve to underline the inherent possibilities of cognitive dissonance as between the inquisitive tourist and the local powers. The military did not believe there was a hobby called 'plane-spotting'; and if there was, they could not believe it could be an innocent one.

5   For this and the foregoing examples of merchants and itinerant scholars I am indebted to Frank Santi Russell, 'Information Gathering and Intelligence in the Greek World, ca 800–322 B.C.', unpublished dissertation, University of California, Los Angeles (1994).

6   In the *Oxford Classical Dictionary*, 3rd edn, ed. Simon Hornblower and Antony
    Spawforth (Oxford and New York, 1996), p. 238.

7   Quoted by Denver Ewing Baughan in his introduction to Turler, *The Traveller*, vi.

8   Justin Stagl, *A History of Curiosity: The Theory of Travel 1550–1800* (Chur, 1995), p. 29.

9   Mary Beard and John Henderson, *Classics: A Very Short Introduction*, in the Very Short
    Introductions series (Oxford and New York, 1995), p. 36.

10 Lambert, *The Fortunate Traveller*, p. 11.

11 Herodotus IV.36.

12 E.H. Bunbury, *A History of Ancient Geography among the Greeks and Romans from the
    Earliest Ages till the Fall of the Roman Empire* (New York, 1959; = reprint of 2nd edn,
    1883), vol. 2, p. 145.

13 Strabo's view that geography was 'as much the pursuit of the philosopher as any
    other science' is discussed in an article by William Arthur Heinkel, 'Anaximander's
    Book, the Earliest Known Geographical Treatise', in *Proceedings of the American
    Academy of Arts and Sciences*, 56 (Boston, 1921), 249.

14 Charles William Fornara, *The Nature of History in Ancient Greece and Rome* (Berkeley,
    Los Angeles and London, 1983), p. 13.

15 A somewhat analogous perspective on Roman literature is elegantly written up in
    Claude Nicolet, *Space, Geography and Politics in the Early Roman Empire*, Jerome
    Lectures 19 (Ann Arbor, 1991). On page 8 of his introduction he writes: 'if one
    seeks to study the connection between politics and geography, acknowledged or not,
    one must query all the sources. It is a well-known fact that poetry of varied kinds
    uses evocative names, myths, propaganda, or famous achievements. There is,
    therefore, a geography of Virgil, of Horace, and of Ovid. Indeed nearly all literature
    is open to a geographic reading, particularly history.'

16 An interesting example of perceived reality being made to imitate fiction may be
    seen in Schiller's famous application of the term 'Phaeacians' to the people of
    Austria, thus replicating a recurrent German view of their southern neighbours as
    given over to indulgence and woefully lacking in true Teutonic discipline and rigour.

17 John Elsner, 'From the Pyramids to Pausanias and Piglet: Monuments, Travel and
    Writing', in Simon Goldhill and Robin Osborne (eds), *Art and Text in Ancient Greek
    Culture* (Cambridge and New York, 1994), pp. 226–7.

18 Paul Cartledge, *The Greeks: A Portrait of Self and Others*, rev. edn (Oxford and New
    York, 1993). My reference points and allusions to Cartledge's discourse are taken (in
    the order in which I cite them) from pp. 40, 39, 3, 2, 60, 59.

19 G.E.R. Lloyd (ed.), *Hippocratic Writings*, tr. J. Chadwick, W.N. Mann, I.M. Lonie and
    E.T. Withington (London and New York, 1983), p. 15.

20 Rosalind Thomas, *Herodotus in Context. Ethnography, Science and the Art of Persuasion*
    (Cambridge and New York, 2002), p. 86. For her useful discussion of *Airs, Waters,
    Places*, see chapter 3, pp. 75 ff.

21 e.g. David Landes, *The Wealth and Poverty of Nations* (London and New York, 1999),
    or Jared Diamond, *Guns, Germs and Steel* (London and New York, 1998).

22 Lloyd A. Brown, *The Story of Maps* (New York, 1949; repr. 1977), p. 48.

23 For a clear exposition of Eratosthenes' method and alternative ways of gauging his
    accuracy, see Brown, *The Story of Maps*, p. 29. It is difficult to be precise about the
    exact figure implied by Eratosthenes, because the length of the stade unit of
    measurement that he used is not known with absolute certainty.

24 Bunbury, *A History of Ancient Geography*, vol. 1, pp. 656–7. Aeolus was the ruler of the
    winds who lived on a floating island somewhere in the West. He had the power to

close up the wind in a leather bag. Eratosthenes is being disrespectful at the expense of long-established Homeric lore.

25 Lionel Casson, *Travel in the Ancient World* (Baltimore, 1994), p. 233.

26 Lambert, *The Fortunate Traveller*, pp. 15, 16.

27 Bunbury, *A History of Ancient Geography*, vol. 1, p. 615.

28 See *Oxford Classical Dictionary*, p. 554.

29 Originally it meant the interrogation of witnesses in the law courts (Stagl, *History of Curiosity*, p. 35).

30 Quoted in Brown, *The Story of Maps*, p. 13.

31 *Die Österreichische-Ungarische Monarchie in Wort und Bild* (usually known by its shortened title of *Kronprinzenwerk*), 24 vols (1886–1902).

32 Bunbury, *A History of Ancient Geography*, vol. 2, p. 546.

33 *Ibid.*, p. 553. In a penetrating analysis (pp. 550–636), Bunbury explores in detail the exact nature of Ptolemaean errors and how they seem to have arisen from the sources he used. On the other hand, Brown in *The Story of Maps* nobly defends the the 'select group of men and women who have dared to be wrong' and who constitute the history of science. 'Hundreds of weighty tomes have been written to prove how very wrong were such men as Ptolemy . . . For every page of text, for every map and chart compiled by the pioneers in cartography, a thousand pages of adverse criticism have been written about them by men who were themselves incapable of being wrong because they would never think of exposing themselves to criticism, let alone failure.'

34 Bunbury, *A History of Ancient Geography*, vol. 2, p. 580.

35 See Klaus Albrecht Schröder and Maria Luise Sternath (eds), *Albrecht Dürer*, Exhibition Catalogue (Vienna, 5 September–30 November 2003), p. 274. The reference is to a study by P. Krüger in E. Schneider and A. Spall (eds), *Dürer. Die Kunst aus der Natur zu 'reyssenn'. Welt, Natur und Raum in der Druckgraphik*, Exhibition Catalogue (Schweinfurt, 1997/8), pp. 14–15. The humanist practice of making 'polyhistories' of regions 'explicitly formulated in visual terms', and of '['envisioning'] whole countries through a detailed inventory of their flora, fauna, antiquities and monuments' is discussed by Judith Adler in 'Origins of Sightseeing', *Annals of Tourism Research*, 16 (1989), 13–14.

36 See Pliny, *Natural History: A Selection*, tr. John F. Healy (London and New York, 1991). In the introduction (xvii) Healy comments that 'These figures, however, represent a rather conservative estimate since no fewer than 146 Roman and 327 foreign authors are quoted.'

37 Bunbury, *A History of Ancient Geography*, vol. 2, p. 374.

38 Pliny, *Natural History*, xvii–xviii.

39 *Ibid.*, pp. 4–5.

40 *Ibid.*, p. 6.

41 *Oxford Classical Dictionary*, p. 464.

42 J. Kirtland Wright, *The Geographical Lore of the Time of the Crusades. A Study in the History of Medieval Science and Tradition in Western Europe*, ed. W.L.G. Joerg (New York, 1925), p. 33.

43 *Ibid.*, p. 33. According to the *Oxford Classical Dictionary*, the Greek measure of a *stadion* (stade) was originally the distance covered by a single draught by the plough and contained 600ft, no matter what foot measurement was being used (and there were several different ones). Strabo measures eight and one-third stades to one mile. Other sources approximate the stadium to 607ft (184m).

44   A famous instance of symmetrical geography is found in Herodotus. Of the two greatest rivers known to him, the Ister (i.e. the Danube) and the Nile, he claimed that their mouths were exactly opposite each other across the Mediterranean basin, the former river dividing Europe in the middle, the latter Africa. Moreover, both were of exactly the same length from source to mouth!

45   Sometimes rendered as *Journey Round the World* or *Travels Round the World*; the use of the word *Tour* seems defensible if one thinks of the *Periodos* in terms of a *tour d'horizon*, or a summing up of contemporary geographical knowledge.

46   Fornara, *The Nature of History in Ancient Greece and Rome*, p. 14.

47   The issue has become confused through the application by some scholars of the term *portolan* to what were probably Byzantine *periploi*.

48   O.A.W. Dilke, *Greek and Roman Maps* (London, 1985), p. 134: in the series 'Aspects of Greek and Roman Life', ed. H.H. Scullard).

49   John and Elizabeth Romer give a flavour of it in their *The Seven Wonders of the World* (London, 1995), p. 149: 'From Calameum to the Old Woman's Knee is eight miles. The promontory is rough and on the top there is a rock, and a tree grows on the beach. There is a harbour and water laps right up to the tree. Be careful of the South Wind.'

50   Some scholars say this actually referred to Shetland, others, Norway.

51   Barry Cunliffe, *The Extraordinary Voyage of Pytheas the Greek, the Man who Discovered Britain* (London and New York, 2001). The following quotations are from pp. 42, 43 and 163 respectively.

52   This was Vipsanius Agrippa's *Orbis Terrarum*, made in the years around 10 BC, which has already been mentioned in the context of measuring heights and distances.

53   Brown, *The Story of Maps*, p. 8. According to Suetonius (Book XII), the suffect (i.e. provisional) consul Mettius Pompusanius was executed by Domitian, partly because he possessed a map of the world. Admittedly he was also rumoured to possess an imperial horoscope, which was probably enough to make him a marked man, and his habit of naming his slaves after Carthaginian generals also appears to have gone down badly.

54   Casson, *Travel in the Ancient World*, p. 189.

55   The *Oxford Classical Dictionary*, p. 1151, records the *Peutinger Table* as having been made at Colmar *c.* 1200, being a copy of a fourth-century Roman world-map, itself 'a modification of a 2nd cent. and perhaps even earlier design'.

56   Casson, *Travel in the Ancient World*, p. 187.

57   See Dilke, *Greek and Roman Maps*, pp. 115 ff.

58   See Annalina and Mario Levi, '*Itineraria Picta* – Contributo allo studio della tabula peutingeriana', in *Studi e Materiali del Museo dell' Impero Romano*, 7 (Rome, 1967) for a discussion of this. The suggestion is viewed with scepticism by Nicolet (*Space, Geography and Politics*, pp. 102–3, n. 12). The project to survey the entire Roman world supposedly originated with Julius Caesar just before his death in 44 BC. Either Caesar or Augustus appointed four suitably equipped surveyors, who requested up to thirty-two years for the task!

59   Nicolet, *Space, Geography and Politics*, p. 100.

60   Pliny, *Natural History*, Book III, p. 43.

61   Nicolet, *Space, Geography and Politics*, pp. 113–14. However, the actual *form* of this cartographic (?) monument is much disputed. Suggestions range from a simple cartographical inscription to a mosaic, wall-painting, bronze engraving, marble carving, itinerary map or even globe. It could have been round, oval, rectangular and oriented to the east, north or south. Evelyn Edson, commenting on Kai

Broderson's survey of all the scholarly suggestions as to how the 'map' (if it was one at all) actually looked, concludes: 'His [Broderson's] questions make it abundantly clear that, whether there was a map or not, we have very little concrete idea about its appearance', Evelyn Edson, *Mapping Time and Space: How Medieval Mapmakers Viewed their World* (London, 1997), p. 10.

62 Casson, *Travel in the Ancient World*, p. 294. My account of lost guidebook writers is simply a summary of Casson remarks.

63 Kai Brodersen, *Reiseführer zu den Sieben Weltwundern: Philon von Byzanz und andere antike Texte* (Frankfurt am Main and Leipzig, 1992), p. 59.

64 Pausanias IX.36.3 in Peter Levi (ed. and tr.), *Guide to Greece*, 2 vols (London and Baltimore, 1971), vol. 1, p. 387. The treasure house of Minyas was a *tholos* (tomb) at Mycenae and the walls of Tiryns still stand.

65 The many permutations are given in fascinating detail in Kai Brodersen, *Die Sieben Weltwunder. Legendäre Kunst- und Bauwerke der Antike*, 5th edn (Munich, 2001), to which my summary is heavily indebted.

66 Francesco Albertini, *Septem mirabilia orbis et urbis Romae et Florentinae civitatis* (Rome, 1510).

67 The justification for this is taken from Genesis 42, where Joseph correctly interprets Pharaoh's dream as foreshadowing 'seven fat years and seven lean years'. Under the direction of Joseph, the grain was to be gathered in reserve for the coming famine during the seven fat years. On the strength of this, medieval Christian apologists enlisted the pyramids as 'Joseph's granaries'. Cosmas of Jerusalem, an eighth-century commentator on Saint Gregory of Nazianus, writes that 'The pyramids themselves are the monuments most worth seeing in Egypt. We Christians say that these pyramids were the storehouses of Joseph, where he put the corn from the seven years of plenty. For they are huge buildings, enclosed within the most remarkable precinct. The Greeks, by contrast, among whom is Herodotus, say they are the tombs of kings.' (See: J.-P. Migne, *Patrologia Graeca* (1857–1934), 38.534.)

68 Acts 19: 23–41.

69 Brodersen, *Die Sieben Weltwunder*, p. 18, speaks of wonders that appear '*im Reiseführer zu den Sieben Weltwunder (so eine moderne Bezeichnung für den antiken Text), den ein spätantiker Redner unter dem (Deck) Namen Philon von Byzanz verfaßt hat*'. See also *idem, Reiseführer zu Sieben Weltwunder*.

70 This and the following quotations are taken from the translation by Hugh Johnstone in Romer and Romer, *Seven Wonders of the World*, p. 230.

71 A recurrent campaign to get people to read more in Austria has adopted the slogan *Das Lesen ist Abenteuer im Kopf* ('Reading is adventure in your head').

72 In a fascinating article entitled 'Why Did Herodotus not Mention the Hanging Gardens of Babylon?', something which has long puzzled scholars, Stephanie Dalley has argued persuasively that the Hanging Gardens were not in fact at Nebuchadnezzar's Babylon, but were built by Sennacherib at Nineveh. See Peter Derow and Robert Parker (eds), *Essays from a Conference in Memory of George Forrest* (Oxford, 2003), pp. 171–89.

CHAPTER 2

1 The phrases are those of Domenico Musti, 'La struttura del discorso storico in Pausania', in Jean Bingen (ed.), *Pausanias Historien*, vol. 41 of *Entretiens sur l'antiquité classique* (Geneva, 1994), p. 24.

2   It was compiled by a Dr G. Lolling. The section on Olympia relied heavily on the work of the great German archaeologist Wilhelm Dörpfeld. To Dörpfeld the world has reason to be grateful, as he won the respect of Schliemann and dissuaded him from dismantling the brick walls of the palace at Mycenae. (Schliemann thought they were of recent origin.) Scholars were wont to remark sarcastically that Schliemann's finest discovery was actually Dörpfeld.

3   See John Elsner, 'Pausanias: A Greek Pilgrim in the Roman World', in *Past and Present*, 135 (May 1992), 3–29, for a persuasive and eloquent interpretation of Pausanias as a pagan pilgrim 'evoking a religious identity, deeper than socio-political realities, which lay in the sacred sites and monuments of Greece' (5).

4   The *periegetai* were guides who 'led people around' the sites, and periegetic literature was well established by the time of Pausanias, although it was mostly partial and fragmentary. Dionysius Periegetes ('the Guide') wrote an anachronistic *Geographical Description of the Inhabited World* in hexameters (perhaps for schoolboys) some time in the reign of the Emperor Hadrian, only a few years before Pausanias embarked on his project. He also wrote a *History of Birds* that might have interested our author. A description of Greece attributed to Dicaearchus the Messenian, but probably the work of a later writer between 164 and 86 BC, supplies a lively, not to say scurrilous account of Greece at that time. Pausanias was therefore not the first to write a guide, but he was the first to incorporate most of the modern ingredients, albeit with his own spin on them. For the literature that contributed to the formation of the guidebook genre, see the previous chapter.

5   Ernest Gellner, *Language and Solitude: Wittgenstein, Malinowski and the Habsburg Dilemma* (Cambridge and New York, 1998). The quotation is from chapter 23, 'The Birth of Modern Social Anthropology', p. 116. He concludes: 'This orientation [of Pausanias] already made Frazer into an anthropologist rather than a Classicist, even when he was dealing with documentary material from a literate society.' In the same way, some scholars look upon Pausanias as essentially an ethnologist with antiquarian leanings, though this surely does less than justice to the scope of his work.

6   Elsner, 'Pausanias: A Greek Pilgrim in the Roman World', 10.

7   Pausanias I.32.3 in Peter Levi (ed. and tr.), *Guide to Greece*, 2 vols (Harmondsworth and Baltimore, 1971), vol. 1, p. 93. The actual citations used in the present text may, however, be from other translations, as noted, often the English translation of Pausanias from J.G. Frazer, *Pausanias' Description of Greece*, 6 vols (London, 1898), which is by far the most vivid; also Susan E. Alcock, 'Landscapes of Memory in Pausanias' Histories', in Bingen, *Pausanias Historien*, p. 252.

8   Pausanias I.32.3 in Levi, *Guide to Greece*, vol. 1, p. 93.

9   Alcock, 'Landscapes of Memory in Pausanias' Histories', p. 252.

10   Lionel Casson, *Travel in the Ancient World* (Baltimore and London, 1994), p. 264.

11   It is only fair to add that European Museums have become more flexible regarding opening times in recent years – the Naturhistorisches Museum in Vienna even acquired electric lighting a few years ago for its first-floor showrooms . . .

12   For the sake of convenience and accessibility, textual passages will be sourced to Levi, *Guide to Greece*. The Eurynome passage, referred to here, is in Book VIII, 41.4–6, Levi, *Guide to Greece*, vol. 2, p. 473.

13   Pausanias X.5.5 in Levi, *Guide to Greece*, vol. 1, pp. 416–17.

14   Pausanias X.9.2 in *ibid.*, vol. 1, p. 427.

15   Pausanias X.13.2 in *ibid.*, pp. 438–9.

16 Pausanias X.9.1 in *ibid.*, p. 426.

17 Inscriptions, it is worth noting here, were to become a staple of antiquary-oriented seventeenth- and eighteenth-century guidebooks. Indeed, a few dealt with little else, although supplementary material on coins and statuary was usual.

18 Quoted in Roland and Françoise Etienne, *The Search for Ancient Greece* (London, 1992), p. 31. (Original French edn, Paris 1990.)

19 Levi, *Pausanias: Guide to Greece*, vol. 1, p. 455 comments in a footnote that 'since Pausanias mentioned this [invasion] in [his account of] Athens (Book I, 3.5 ff.), but postponed his full account, he must have had something like a plan of his whole work in mind when he started to write, though he apparently began before the year 160 AD and was not finished until the late seventies or eighties'.

20 The Cnidians were a people inhabiting a long peninsula protruding from Asia Minor into the Gulf of Cos. Their city was famed for its intellectual life.

21 Jacques Lacarrière, . . . *als die Säulen noch standen: Spaziergänge mit Pausanias in Griechenland* (Wiesbaden, 1981), p. 341. (Original French edition, *Promenades dans la Grèce antique*, Paris, 1978.)

22 Lacarrière, . . . *als die Säulen noch standen*, p. 10.

23 Pausanias IX.30.2 in Levi, *Guide to Greece*, vol. 1, p. 371 (I have used Frazer's translation here).

24 For details of the reception and survival of Pausanias I am indebted to the distinguished work of Domenico Musti, *Pausania – Guida della Grecia*, 5 vols (1982–95). He also states that Areta, the Metropolitan of Caesarea in Cappadocia, had a copy of Pausanias made for his library in AD 900.

25 J.G. Frazer, *Pausanias and other Greek Sketches*, pp. 56–63. It has to be said that Frazer himself describes his version of Dicaearchus as a 'free translation or paraphrase', and it is possible that the knockabout quality of the piece, as he renders it, owes quite a lot to Frazer's impish sense of humour. Nevertheless, it is clear that the approach of the text is almost the opposite of that of Pausanias, both in tone and content.

26 *Ibid.*, pp. 22–3.

27 *Ibid.*, pp. 11–12.

28 Levi, *Guide to Greece*, vol. 1, pp. 2–3.

29 For details of these catastrophes see, *inter alia*, *The Oxford Classical Dictionary*, 3rd edn, ed. Simon Hornblower and Antony Spawforth (Oxford and New York, 1996), pp. 1188 and 219–20; and the entry in *Encyclopaedia Britannica* (1994–2000) on 'The Hellenistic Age: The Greek World under the Roman Empire'.

30 Levi, *Pausanias: Guide to Greece*, vol. 1, p. 2.

31 Musti, *Pausania – Guida della Grecia*, vol. 1, xxxv.

32 This illustration is reproduced in a recent book for the general reader, Roland and Françoise Etienne, *The Search for Ancient Greece* (London, 1992), pp. 16–17. The caption states that the artist 'has drawn, with a degree of imagination, the hippodrome of Olympia during the great competitions'. The engraving does partly follow some details of architecture and monuments mentioned by Pausanias.

33 Pausanias VI.20.15 in Levi, *Guide to Greece*, vol. 2, pp. 346–7.

34 Alcock, 'Landscapes of Memory in Pausanias' Histories', p. 249.

35 See Plutarch of Chaeronea (b. before 50 AD, d. after 120 AD) in Robert Flacelière, *Sur les oracles de la Pythie* (Paris, 1937). This is a debate about the role of the Gods and its interpretation by a prophetess, as carried on between five acquaintances on a tour of Delphi. There are references to guides at 395A, 397D and 400D, E, none of them flattering.

36 Pausanias II.23.6 in Levi, *Guide to Greece*, vol. 1, p. 186 (Frazer's translation). Levi translates the last line thus: 'to reverse a majority opinion takes some doing'.

37 Pausanias VI.3.8 in Levi, *Guide to Greece*, vol. 2, p. 292. Compare Herodotus VII.152.3: 'I am bound to repeat what has been said, but I am not bound to believe everything, and this principle holds for every tale (*logos*)'.

38 Norman Douglas, *Old Calabria* (London, 1915).

39 Literally, 'Of all Greeks the most deceitful', but the contemptuous term *Graeculus* encourages a racier gloss, something like 'The dodgiest of all those dodgy Greeks'.

40 Wilamowitz, *Hermes* 12 (1877), 346, quoted in Christian Habicht, *Pausanias' Guide to Ancient Greece*, Sather Classical Lectures (Berkeley, Los Angeles and London, 1998), vol. 50.

41 Wilamowitz, *Hermes* 19 (1884), 463–5, quoted in Habicht, *Pausanias' Guide*.

42 Frazer, *Pausanias' Description of Greece*. This quotation from the commentary, vol. 3, p. 180, quoted in Habicht, *Pausanias' Guide*. The relevant passage is at Pausanias II.17.1 in Levi, *Guide to Greece*, vol. 1, pp. 168–9.

43 Habicht, *Pausanias' Guide*, Appendix 1, 'Pausanias and his Critics', pp. 165–75.

44 Pausanias VI.21.3 ff. in Levi, *Guide to Greece*, vol. 2, pp. 349–435. Levi explains in a footnote that 'Pausanias is entering Eleia from Heraia . . . moving west down the north bank of the Alpheios towards Olympia'; in fairness to Wilamowitz, it must have taken a good deal of close reading and even trial and error to have actually established this.

45 Despite the clear exposition of this in Habicht, *Pausanias' Guide*, the Etiennes can still write the following in 1990: 'In Mycenae in 1874, an error in Pausanias' text led Schliemann to discover a circle of graves inside the acropolis; . . .' (Etienne and Etienne, *The Search for Ancient Greece*, p. 110). The assumed 'error' of Pausanias evidently remains in the literature – but how can an 'error' have led Schliemann to the right answer?

46 Cf. Frazer, *Pausanias and other Greek Sketches*, p. 157: 'In short, if Pausanias copied his descriptions fom a book, it must have been from a book written in his own lifetime, perhaps by another man of the same name. The theory of the copyist Pausanias reduces itself to an absurdity.'

47 Anonymous review in *Atlantic Monthly*, 66/398 (December 1890), 839–44. The book under review was Margaret De G. Verrall, *Mythology and Monuments of Ancient Athens. Being a Translation of a Portion of the Attica of Pausanias*, with an introductory essay and archaeological commentary by Jane E. Harrison. The review is generally positive, but its heavily patronising tone and authoritative display of learning suggest that it was written by a very senior, elderly male professor of the old school.

48 Also, and perhaps more accurately, 'reverse acculturation'.

49 Pliny, *Letters* 8.24, quoted in Susan E. Alcock, *Graecia Capta: The Landscapes of Roman Greece* (Cambridge and New York, 1993), p. 28.

50 A thought-provoking discussion of this issue is to be found in the unconventional essay by Mary Beard and John Henderson entitled *Classics: A Very Short Introduction*, in the Very Short Introductions series (Oxford and New York, 1995), pp. 20 ff. Of Pausanias, the authors remark (p. 38) that: 'Even when they do not mention Pausanias by name, [modern guidebooks] offer the modern visitor much of his information.' Alcock has borrowed the first two words of Horace's aphorism for the title of her fine study: *Graecia capta ferum victorem cepit et artes intulit agresti Latio* (fierce [Rome] has been captured by captive Greece, [who] brought the arts to rustic Latium).

51 Pausanias VII.17.2 in Levi, *Guide to Greece*, vol. 1, p. 268. In a footnote, Levi comments that 'Nero's insupportable speech on this occasion (28 November AD 66)

[i.e. his bombastic proclamation of Greece's liberation] has survived in an inscription built into a church at Karditsa in Boiotia.'

52   Habicht, *Pausanias' Guide*, p. 83, mentions the insulting mock victories awarded to Nero at the 211th Olympiad in AD 67. He points out that Pausanias is our sole witness (Pausanias X.36.4 in Levi, *Guide to Greece*, vol. 1, p. 506 and n. 252) of the fact that these games were the only ones ever to be expunged from the records of the Eleans. This erasure is hardly surprising in view of the fact that, as Levi drily recalls in his note, the emperor 'won' six events, 'including a ten-horse chariot race in which he fell out of his chariot'.

53   On this see, for example, K.W. Arafat, *Pausanias' Greece* (Cambridge and New York, 1996), p. 203. He writes: 'while other sources have much to say of Mummius' personal avariciousness, Pausanias makes no mention of this; he is, however, the only writer to raise the issue of Mummius' impiety.' Nor does Pausanias mention the story illustrating Mummius' legendary philistinism: allegedly he warned those transporting the looted masterpieces from Corinth that, if they destroyed any, they would have to replace them with new ones. It seems his attitude was rather like that of the Russian soldiers to wrist-watches.

54   Pausanias I.20.4 in Levi, *Guide to Greece*, vol. 1, p. 58. It should perhaps be stressed that the extent of Pausanias' opposition to Rome, or lack of it, is a matter of some dispute among scholars. J. Palm in *Rom, Römertum und Imperium in der griechischen Literatur der Kaiserzeit* (Lund, 1959) often implies a relatively positive view of the Romans on the part of the Greeks in general and of Pausanias in particular, or at any rate a differentiated view. Habicht (*Pausanias' Guide*, pp. 120 ff.) vigorously contests this. But he loads the dice a little when he asserts that Pausanias, in the passage quoted, 'does not mean to say that Romans are so noble that Sulla's cruelty is unexpected, but that you would not expect even a Roman to act so viciously'. Apart from the fact that this is surely only one possible interpretation of Pausanias' remark, it seems to ignore another point; namely, that Pausanias' *tone*, here and elsewhere, is notably non-inflammatory, avoiding even the rhetorical clichés that were usual in the descriptions of the sack of cities.

55   Habicht, *Pausanias' Guide*, p. 139, summarises Philostratus' *Lives of the Sophists* treating of these 'learned banqueteers' who were 'famous wealthy, influential, and often vicious'. Like pop megastars on the road from engagement to engagement, they flaunted their fame and money, and were 'accompanied by luggage-carts, horses, slaves and several packs of hounds, while [Polemo] . . . rode a silver-bridled horse'. The contrast with Pausanias, at least as he presents himself in his work, could hardly be more marked.

56   Hornblower and Spawforth, *Oxford Classical Dictionary*. The article on the Panhellenion is on pp. 1105–6, and is written by Antony Spawforth.

57   Paul Cartledge and Antony Spawforth, *Hellenistic and Roman Sparta: A Tale of Two Cities* (London and New York, 1989), p. 209. The same authors remark (p. 207) that the first to the fourth centuries AD saw 'thriving cultural tourism', and that 'such tourism was a recognised cultural activity in the Hellenistic world, generating its own periegetic literature'.

58   The term *epheboi* originally referred to boys who had reached puberty, and ephebic training was a rite of passage to manhood, later (in Athens and Sparta) with a paramilitary aspect for boys who had reached 18 years of age, something akin to 'national service'. The revival of ephebic spectacle and even the institution of a sort of master of ceremonies (*exegetes* or expounder) to explain the ancient Lycurgan

customs to tourists at Sparta is described in Cartledge and Spawforth, *Hellenistic and Roman Sparta*, p. 409.

59   Quoted from G.W. Bowersock in Alcock, *Graecia Capta*, p. 2.

60   For example, the Stadium at Athens (Pausanias I.19.7 in Levi, *Guide to Greece*, vol. 1, p. 56), of which he says: 'Herod of Athens built it, and he consumed most of the Pentelic quarry in the construction'. It would be tempting to think that this was an ironic allusion to Herodes' extravagance, but Pausanias generally seems incapable of irony; as Habicht has pointed out, the only jokes that an alert reader might detect in his work appear to be unintentional, e.g. (Habicht, *Pausanias' Guide*, p. 161) the statement that the Arcadian Aphrodite is called the black Aphrodite 'because men mostly indulge in sexual intercourse at night, instead of, like the beasts, by day' (Frazer's translation, Pausanias VIII.6.5; Levi, *Guide to Greece*, vol. 2, p. 384). Many will doubtless have enjoyed an evening performance at the still existing so-called Odeion of Herodes Atticus on the side of the Athenian Acropolis, which Pausanias (VII.20.3 in Levi, *Guide to Greece*, vol. 1, p. 279 and note) says Herodes Atticus built in memory of his wife who died in AD 160 or 161. Levi cautions, however, that there must be some doubt as to whether this is actually the building that this 'very rich, very generous man, and a builder of discerning taste' dedicated to her.

61   Louis Ebeling, *Classical Weekly* 139 (1913), quoted in Habicht, *Pausanias' Guide*, p. 163.

62   Damophon repaired Phidias' huge chryselephantine statue of Olympian Zeus, an enthroned figure that reached a height of 40ft. According to Pausanias, he also made many other cult statues for the cities of the Achaean Confederacy. The quotation is from Hornblower and Spawforth, *Oxford Classical Dictionary*, p. 428.

63   Pausanias I.28.2 in Levi, *Guide to Greece*, vol. 1, pp. 79–80. Levi mentions in a footnote the tradition recorded in Greek medieval writers that a huge bronze statue by Phidias, probably this one, was carried to Constantinople (perhaps on the orders of Justinian), where it stood on the great square. The same tradition records its destruction: on the eve of the sack of Constantinople (1204) by belligerents of the Fourth Crusade, it was broken up by a drunken mob.

64   According to the legend, Theseus returned from overcoming the minotaur in Crete, but forgot to hoist white sails as he approached Athens. He had set off with black sails, and the white ones were to be the agreed sign to show that he had survived. Theseus' father, King Aigeus, saw the black sails from a spot on the acropolis mentioned by Pausanias to the right of the entrance to the shrine of the Wingless Victory; crazed with grief, he hurled himself down from the heights and was drowned in the sea. This, they say, is how the Aegean got its name. The story is told in Pausanias, I.22.5, Levi, *Guide to Greece*, vol. 1, p. 62.

65   *Ibid*, pp. 9–10.

66   The notion of Pausanias as some sort of pilgrim – by no means universally accepted by scholars, but surely one that supplies useful and powerful insights – is again handled with considerable subtelty by Jas' Elsner in *Art and the Roman Viewer: The Transformation of Art from the Pagan World to Christianity* (Cambridge and New York, 1995), chapter 4, 'Viewing and Identity: The Travels of Pausanias; Or, a Greek Pilgrim in the Roman World', pp. 125–55. On p. 144 he writes: 'with the exception of Pausanias, we possess no text from the pagan world which recounts the process of pilgrimage as a personal journey. Here the contrast between antiquity and the Christian tradition of travel writing is stark. It gives Pausanias' text a unique cultural significance not only as testimony to a specifically *pagan* form and view of pilgrimage but also as a counterpoint to later Christian writing.'

67   On this see Elsner, 'Pausanias: A Greek Pilgrim in the Roman World', p. 23.

68   Lacarrière, . . . *als die Säulen noch standen*, p. 6.

69   In John Elsner, 'From the Pyramids to Pausanias and Piglet: Monuments and Travel
     Writing', in Simon Goldhill and Robin Osborne (eds), *Art and Text in Ancient Greek
     Culture* (Cambridge and New York, 1994), p. 226.

70   T.S. Eliot, 'Little Gidding', the fourth of his *Four Quartets*, Canto V, ll. 242–4 (T.S.
     Eliot, *Collected Poems 1909–1962* (London and New York, 1963, 1964)).

71   Lacarrière, . . . *als die Säulen noch standen*, p. 9.

CHAPTER 3

1   This is according to Eusebius' *Ecclesiastical History*. Melito's other scholarly purpose
     was to establish the exact canon of the Old Testament books.

2   E.D. Hunt, *Holy Land Pilgrimage in the Later Roman Empire AD 312–460* (Oxford and
     New York 2002), pp. 3–4.

3   The actual *omphalos* is today shown to tourists in the Katholikon, the (now) Greek
     Orthodox part of the church of the Holy Sepulchre. It is a marble basin situated
     directly under the dome.

4   Examples of what has been dubbed the *omphalos* syndrome have already been noted
     in Chapter 1, whereby the Greeks placed Delphi at the centre of the world. J.B.
     Harley stresses the role of cartography in [what Sir Ernst Gombrich has called]
     'positional enhancing', 'where a people believe themselves to be divinely appointed
     to the centre of the universe [the *omphalos* syndrome]' and which 'can be traced in
     [world] maps widely separated in time and space, such as those from ancient
     Mesopotamia with Babylon at its centre, maps of the Chinese centred on China,
     Greek maps centred on Delphi, Islamic maps centred on Mecca, and those Christian
     world maps in which Jerusalem is placed as the "true" centre of the world'. J.B.
     Harley, 'Maps, Knowledge and Power', in Denis Cosgrove and Stephen Daniels
     (eds), *The Iconography of Landscape: Essays on the Symbolic Representation, Design and Use
     of Past Environments* (Cambridge, 1988), p. 290. In 1095 Pope Urban II declared that
     'Jerusalem is the navel of the world, the royal city, situated at the centre of the
     world.'

5   Isaiah 66: 15 ff.

6   Rolf Legler, *Sternenstraße und Pilgerweg: der Jakobs Kult von Santiago de Compostela.
     Wahrheit und Fälschung* (Bergisch Gladbach, 2000), p. 80.

7   Sarah Hopper, *To Be a Pilgrim: The Medieval Pilgrimage Experience* (Stroud, 2002), p. 12.

8   Theoderich, *Guide to the Holy Land*, 2nd edn, ed. Ronald G. Musto (New York, 1986),
     p. 78, n. 37. This is a revised reprint of Aubrey Stewart's translation for the Palestine
     Pilgrim's Text Society (1897).

9   The situation is well summed up by Bernhard Kötting: 'An objective differentiation
     between itineraries as travellers' handbooks and itineraries as pilgrims' travel
     literature [*Erinnerungen*] can certainly be made in regard to such books at their
     inception, but after publication the travel accounts [*Erinnerungen*] could be used as
     a guidebook by anyone.' Bernhard Kötting, *Peregrinatio Religiosa: Wallfahrten in der
     Antike und das Pilgerwesen in der alten Kirche* (Regensberg and Münster, 1950), pp.
     350–1.

10   John Wilkinson, *Jerusalem Pilgrims before the Crusades*, 2nd edn (Warminster, 2002),
     pp. 15–16.

11   *Ibid.* provides a translation, pp. 165–6.

12   On the other hand, the Jews believed it to be the place where Abraham was to sacrifice Isaac.

13   Heinrich Fürst, *Im Land des Herrn. Ein Pilgerführer für das Heilige Land* (Werl, 1999), p. 265.

14   Diana Webb, *Pilgrims and Pilgrimage in the Medieval West* (London and New York, 2001), p. 12.

15   Scholarship offers several etymologies for *peregrinatio* and differing definitions of the concept of pilgrimage. Julien Ries in 'Pilgerreisen und ihre Symbolik', in Paolo Cucci von Saucken (ed.), *Pilgerziele der Christenheit: Jerusalem, Rom, Santiago de Compostela* (Stuttgart, 1999), p. 19, derives *peregrinatio* from *per ager* ('across country') and sees it therefore as conjuring the idea of being on the way to somewhere, or of the way itself. The Arabic verb *hajj*, by which Islam designates pilgrimage, means 'to approach something'. In India the word for Hindu pilgrimage is *tîrtha*, meaning the ford at the river that has to be crossed; and in Japan the word used for pilgrimage, *henro*, simply means 'way'. (This last seems close to the European idea embodied in e.g. 'The Pilgrim's Way' or *el Camino*, the 'Way of St James'.)

16   Jas' Elsner, *Art and the Roman Viewer: The Transformation of Art from the Pagan World to Christianity* (Cambridge and New York, 1995), p. 138.

17   The voluntary nature of Christian pilgrimage (except when ordered by a confessor), has often been stressed and compared to Jewish obligations relating to the three annual pilgrimage festivals, and the injunction on every Muslim to visit Mecca once in his life. See e.g. Walter Zander, *Israel and the Holy Places of Christendom* (New York, 1971), p. 1.

18   Quoted from an article in the Saturday Review, the *Guardian*, 4 August 2001.

19   Klaus Herbers, in Yves Bottineau, *Der Weg der Jakobspilger* (Bergisch Gladbach, 1997), introduction, p. 12.

20   Webb, *Pilgrims and Pilgrimage*, p. 8.

21   On this see Legler, *Sternenstraße und Pilgerweg*, p. 29. Legler bases his remarks on the standard work by Kötting, *Peregrinatio Religiosa*. The distinction made by Kötting between *Pilgerreise* and *Wallfahrt* is not however accepted by all scholars.

22   Jonathan Sumption, *Pilgrimage. An Image of Mediaeval Religion* (London, 2002), pp. 45–6.

23   Richard S. Lambert, *The Fortunate Traveller: A Short History of Touring and Travel for Pleasure* (London, New York, *et al.*, 1950), p. 15.

24   Legler, *Sternenstraße und Pilgerweg*, p. 274.

25   Sumption, *Pilgrimage*, p. 29.

26   F.C. Peters, *Jerusalem: The Holy City in the Eyes of Chroniclers, Visitors, Pilgrims and Prophets from the Days of Abraham to the Beginnings of Modern Times* (Princeton, 1985), pp. 313–14.

27   Evelyn Edson, *Mapping Time and Space: How Medieval Mapmakers Viewed their World* (London, 1997), British Library Studies in Map History, vol. I, p. 14.

28   Dieter Richter, *Jean Paul und Italien; mit einem imaginären Reiseführer von Jean Paul Friedrich Richter* (Joditz, 2002), pp. 9–10. Petrarch's guide was entitled *Itinerarium ad sepulcrum Domini nostri Iesu Christi*.

29   The most striking examples of religious 'study tours' to the Holy Land were made by women, such as Egeria the Nun (*c.* 400), and the two patrician Roman ladies (Paula and her daughter Eustochium), whose itinerary of 386 was approvingly written up by St Jerome in 404.

30 Legler, *Sternenstraße und Pilgerweg*, p. 32.
31 Sumption, *Pilgrimage*, p. 68.
32 Norbert Ohler, *Pilgerstab und Jakobsmuschel: Wallfahrten in Mittelalter und Neuzeit* (Düsseldorf and Zürich, 2000), p. 26.
33 Ohler, *Pilgerstab und Jakobsmuschel*, p. 54.
34 Sumption, *Pilgrimage*, p. 13.
35 Dante, *Inferno*, 26.109.
36 '*fatti non foste a viver come bruti / ma per seguir virtute e conoscenza*'.
37 R.W.B. Lewis, *Dante: A Life* (London, 2002), p. 111.
38 John Kirtland Wright, *The Geographical Lore of the Time of the Crusades* (New York, 1925), pp. 106–7.
39 Lewis, *Dante: A Life*, p. 91. However, the ambivalence of Dante regarding the acquisition of philosophical knowledge is already apparent in the *Convivio*, which begins with a siren-like *donna gentile* or Lady Philosophy, who parrots Aristotle's view: '*tutti li uomini naturalmente desiderano di sapere*' ['All men naturally desire to know']. This ambivalence doubtless reflects ongoing uncertainties arising from the expansion of learning during the so-called twelfth-century Renaissance, whereby Christian thought had increasingly absorbed, exploited and partly reinterpreted the wisdom of pagan antiquity. The composition of the *Convivio* in fact spans the beginning of the writing of the *Commedia* (the adjective *Divina* was first added two centuries later, in *c.* 1307).
40 Teodolinda Barolini, *The Undivine Comedy: Detheologizing Dante* (Princeton and Oxford, 1992), p. 111.
41 It was named after the emperor himself (Publius Aelius Hadrianus) and Jupiter Capitolinus. Statues of the emperor and the god were erected in the area of the Temple.
42 Fürst, *Im Land des Herrn*, p. 560.
43 *Ibid.*
44 e.g. the *Onomasticon* appears to be a main source for the famous Madaba mosaic map of the biblical lands, located in a church in a town of the same name in Transjordan some 16 km south of where the Jordan flows into the Dead Sea. The map is literally 'oriented', i.e. the east is at the top, with Jerusalem at the centre, and probably dates to the mid-sixth century. Discovered in 1884, it is the only ancient cartography of Palestine, apart from what appears in the *Tabula Peutingeriana*.
45 Erich Klostermann, 'Eusebius Schrift HEPITON TOPIKOUN ONOMATON TON EN TI THEIA GRAPHI', in *Die Griechischen Schriftsteller der ersten drei Jahrhunderte*, Hrsg. von der Kirchenväter-Commission der Königl. Preussischen Akademie der Wissenschaften. *Texte und Untersuchungen zur Geschichte der Altchistlichen Literatur*, ed. Oscar von Gebhardt and Adolf Harnack, new ser., vol. 2, xxiii, 1 (Leipzig, 1902).
46 See Hunt, *Holy Land Pilgrimage*, pp. 99–100.
47 Herbert Donner, *Pilgerfahrt ins Heilige Land: Die ältesten Berichte christlicher Palästinapilger (4.-7. Jahrhundert)*, 2nd rev. edn (Stuttgart, 2002), pp. 23–4. Donner drily comments that Jerome evidently chose to overlook Judges 9: 7, which records that Jotham stood upon Mt Gerizim to address the people of Shechem (forerunner city of Neapolis): 'He would anyway have been hard to hear; but if Mt Gerizim was next to Jericho, his voice would have had to carry some 50 kilometers from the Jordan valley.'
48 'Der Pilger von Piacenza', in Donner, *Pilgerfahrt ins Heilige Land*, p. 250. The scholarship of this version supersedes an earlier English translation by Aubrey Stewart available in the series published in the nineteenth century by the Palestine

Pilgrims Text Society as *Of the Holy places Visited by Antoninus Martyr* (London, 1885), p. 8. Perhaps one should be cautious of the Piacenza pilgrim's more spectacular assertions, since he remarks elsewhere that 'not even straw and wood will float [in the Dead Sea], but anything thrown into it sinks to the bottom'. (Translated in Wilkinson, *Jerusalem Pilgrims*, p. 136.)

49 Wilkinson, *Jerusalem Pilgrims*, pp. 28–30, 68–9.

50 Donner, *Pilgerfahrt ins Heilige Land*, p. 76.

51 Kötting, *Peregrinatio Religiosa*, p. 356.

52 *Saewulf – Pilgrimage to Jerusalem and the Holy Land*, tr. the Lord Bishop of Clifton, Palestine Pilgrim's Text Society 4 (repr. New York, 1971), p. 10.

53 The site was known as 'Gordon's Calvary' because General Gordon of Khartoum supported its authenticity with characteristic lack of restraint. Jerome Murphy-O'Connor, *Oxford Archaeological Guide to the Holy Land* (Oxford and New York, 1998), p. 141, points out that the Protestants' desire to have a tomb of their own lay behind the keen espousal of the new site and the official endorsement of it by the Anglican Church (later withdrawn). It adds drily that 'in Jerusalem the prudence of reason has little chance against the certitude of piety', an argument that might, after all, be used against many claimed biblical sites. Gordon thought he detected the outline of a skull in the hill behind the tomb.

54 Georgia Frank, *The Memory of the Eyes: Pilgrims to Living Saints in Christian Late Antiquity* (Berkeley and Los Angeles, 2000), pp. 35–6. Frank is dealing specifically with 'tourism' to visit the desert ascetics, whereby holy men and women had themselves become the 'sights', in place of the scriptural *lieux de mémoire*. Accounts of these pilgrimages share with many of the more general itineraries of the Holy Land a one-eyed approach that generally eschews much of what we would now think essential to guidebook content, let alone travel narrative. They indicated the stations on a route that should lead to religious catharsis, but usually the narrator's own spiritual and mundane experiences were left undescribed or alluded to pro forma only. The more lively itineraries (Etheria, the Piacenza Pilgrim) stand out precisely because they reveal something of the narrator's feelings and prejudices.

55 Donner, *Pilgerfahrt ins Heilige Land*, p. 38.

56 *Ibid.*, p. 40.

57 Kötting, *Peregrinatio Religiosa*, p. 353, dismisses the suggestion that the pilgrim was as baptised Jew with the argument that, at the beginning of the fourth century, identified Old Testament sites greatly exceeded New Testament ones in number.

58 Donner, *Pilgerfahrt ins Heilige Land*, is the best source with an extensive critical apparatus for the most important of these texts up to the seventh century, translated by the author. He includes the Bordeaux Pilgrim (333), The Itinerary of the Nun Egeria (*c*. 400), St Jerome's account of the Holy Land journey of two Roman patricians, Paula and her daughter, Eustochium (404), the description of the Holy Land by Bishop Eucherius (after 444), the somewhat erratic assemblage of facts making a topography of the Holy Land by Archdeacon Theodosius (between 519 and 530), the so-called Jerusalem Breviarius (around 550), the itinerary of the Piacenza Pilgrim (around 570) and the journey to the Holy Land by the Anglo-Saxon Arculf (around 680).

59 Wilkinson, *Jerusalem Pilgrims*, p. 4.

60 Klaus Herbers, 'Unterwegs zu heiligen Stätten – Pilgerfahrten', in Hermann Bausinger, Klaus Beyrer and Gottfried Korff (eds), *Reisekultur: von der Pilgerfahrt zum modernen Tourismus* (Munich, 1991), p. 24.

61	Donner, *Pilgerfahrt ins Heilige Land*, p. 214. To prove it, Donner quotes the prospectus and supplies his Latin translation of same.

62	See Peters, *Jerusalem: The Holy City*, p. 156.

63	*Itinerarium Burdigalense*, 17 (Donner, *Pilgerfahrt ins Heilige Land*, p. 58).

64	This translation taken from Peters, *Jerusalem: The Holy City*, pp. 156–7.

65	Theodosius' 'The Layout of the Holy Land' has received a bad press from scholars, chiefly because its geography is jumbled because of different manuscripts being randomly copied. Evidently its main aim was to provide a guide to pilgrims for the holy places, drawing on other guides as well as liturgical works to achieve this. It may in any case be the work of several hands, a sort of encyclopedia of pilgrimage to the East. Despite many errors and confusions and hopelessly inaccurate mileages, Theodosius' olla podrida seems to have been very popular and no less than twelve manuscripts are extant.

66	Donner, *Pilgerfahrt ins Heilige Land*, p. 53, n. 81.

67	Fürst, *Im Land des Herrn*, pp. 288–92.

68	Bede, *Ecclesiastical History of the English People with Bede's Letter to Egbert and Cuthbert's Letter on the Death of Bede*, tr. Leo Sherley-Price, R.E. Latham and D.H. Farmer (London and New York, 1990), p. 295 (v. 15 ff. of the *History*).

69	The edition with a commentary by Paul Mickley (*Arculf. Eines Pilgers Reise nach dem heiligen Lande (um 670)* (Leipzig, 1917) in the series Das Land der Bibel: gemeinverständliche Hefte zur Palästinakunde, Band II, Heft 3 u.4, is especially valuable for the reproductions of the groundplans.

70	Barnabé Meistermann, *Guide de Terre Sainte* (Paris, 1907), ix. This had the official seal of approval from the Roman Catholic Church and appeared in French, English, German, Italian and Spanish.

71	This translation taken from Peters, *Jerusalem: The Holy City*, p. 312. See also Daniel the Abbot, *The Pilgrimage of the Russian Abbot Daniel in the Holy Land*, annotated by C.W. Wilson (New York, 1971); repr. from the Palestine Pilgrims Text Society No. 4, 1895.

72	John Kirtland Wright, *Geographical Lore of the Time of the Crusades* (New York, 1925), p. 115.

73	Peters, *Jerusalem: The Holy City*, p. 298.

74	*Ibid.*, pp. 298–311.

75	Theoderich, *Guide to the Holy Land*, xxii.

76	Wright, *Geographical Lore*, p. 116, has a low opinion of these compendia, ascribing to them a decline in accuracy in guidebooks from the end of the first decade of the twelfth century: 'the decline . . . was hastened by the compilation of standard guidebooks, which may be faintly described as legendary and inaccurate, and from which later pilgrim narratives blindly copy, to the growing exclusion of anything independent or scholarly . . . the *Old* and *New Compendium* are the source of most of the tracts on the Holy Road [from this period] which have been left to us under various names.' In the narrative of Fetellus, Archdeacon of Antioch, the 'desiccating influence of the *Old Compendium* is nearly everywhere apparent'.

77	e.g. in Theoderich, *Guide to the Holy Land*, xxii.

78	*Ibid.*, p. 3.

79	Kurt Wilhelm (ed.), *Roads to Zion: Four Centuries of Travelers' Reports* (New York, 1948), pp. 65–6.

80	See Mukaddasi, *Description of Syria, including Palestine*, ed. and tr. Guy Le Strange (London, Palestine Pilgrims Text Society No. 3, 1886; repr. New York, 1971).

81 For this and the following remarks I have drawn on Richard Barber, *Pilgrimages* (Woodbridge, UK, and Rochester, NY, 1991), pp. 19–29. It should be said that the Franciscan guide of the Commissariat for the Holy Land (see n. 34) takes a less benevolent view, pointing out that Saladin removed some churches from their Christian owners altogether. Absolute objectivity in such matters is well nigh impossible.

82 Barber, *Pilgrimages*, p. 26.

83 They were later more elaborately codified by a British government Commission in 1922. General Allenby himself had entered Jerusalem on foot as a mark of respect.

84 Quoted in Peters, *Jerusalem: The Holy City*, p. 313. Peters in turn has it from a French translation: Abu al-Hasan al-Harawi, *Guide des Lieux de Pèlerinage*, tr. Janine Sourdel-Thomine (Damascus, 1957).

85 Quoted in Peters, *Jerusalem: The Holy City*, p. 316. The incorrect attribution of the mosque to Califf Omar is a memory of the first simple mosque thought to have been built on the site. Abbot Daniel saw the structure initiated by Califf Abd al-Malik and completed in 691, but much restored after earthquakes.

86 *Guide-Book to Palestine (circa A.D. 1350)* [*Innominatus*], tr. J.H. Bernard, Palestine Pilgrims Text Society (London, 1894).

87 *Innominatus*, p. 40.

88 See Clare Howard, *English Travellers of the Renaissance* (New York, 1913), pp. 4–5 and n. 3. Also Sumption, *Pilgrimage*, pp. 185, 186, 190 and 191 for some vivid citations from Wey. *Itineraries of William Wey* were reprinted for the Roxburghe Club from the Bodleian Library manuscript in 1857.

89 See facsimile print of *Informacion for Pylgrymes unto the Holy Londe*, introduced and annotated by Gordon Duff, Edinburgh, 1893.

90 Piers Brendon, *Thomas Cook: 150 Years of Popular Tourism* (London, 1991), p. 8.

91 This and the following quotations are taken from Peters, *Jerusalem: The Holy City*, pp. 427–30, who in turn is using the Palestine Pilgrims Text Society's text: Felix Fabri, *The Book of the Wanderings of Felix Fabri*, tr. Aubrey Stewart, 2 vols (Palestine Pilgrim's Text Society Nos 7–10 (1893); repr. New York, 1971).

92 Karen Dabrowska, *Iraq: The Bradt Travel Guide* (Chalfont St Peter and Guilford, CT, 2003), p. 101.

93 Quoted in Herbers, *Reisekultur*, p. 25.

CHAPTER 4

1 Serafín Moralejo, 'The *Codex Calixtinus* as an Art-Historical Source', in John Williams and Alison Stones (eds), *The* Codex Calixtinus *and the Shrine of St James*, Jakobus-Studien 3, in Auftrag der Deutschen St Jakobus-Gesellschaft, ed. Klaus Herbers and Robert Plötz (Tübingen, 1992), p. 207.

2 The contrast between the guide's religious orthodoxy and its author's evidently earthy character is well analysed in Horton and Marie-Hélène Davies, *Holy Days and Holidays: The Medieval Pilgrimage to Compostela* (East Brunswick, Toronto and London, 1982), pp. 84–8.

3 Walter Starkie, *The Road to Santiago: The Pilgrims of St James* (London, 2003; 1st pub. 1957), p. 6.

4 *Ibid.*, pp. 53–4.

5 Colin Smith, 'The Geography and History of Iberia in the *Liber Sancti Jacobi*' (n. 15), in Maryjane Dunn and Linda Kay Davidson, *The Pilgrimage to Compostela in the Middle*

Ages (New York and London, 2000), p. 40. The same authors have compiled an exhaustive bibliography of the literature of the Santiago pilgrimage: Dunn and Davidson, *The Pilgrimage to Santiago de Compostela: A Comprehensive, Annotated Bibliography*, Garland Medieval Bibliographies 18 (New York, 1994.)

6 Annie Shaver-Crandell, Paula Gerson and Alison Stones, *The Pilgrim's Guide to Santiago de Compostela: A Gazetteer* (London, 1995), p. 163.

7 Yves Bottineau, *Der Weg der Jakobspilger: Geschichte, Kunst und Kultur der Wallfahrt nach Santiago de Compostela* (Bergisch Gladbach, 1987; originally published in French as *Les Chemins de Saint-Jacques*, Paris, 1983), pp. 138, 335–6.

8 Frances A. Yates, *The Art of Memory* (London, 1992; 1st edn 1966), pp. 104, 133.

9 In a Bull entitled *Deus Omnipotens*.

10 See, for example, Edwin Mullins's account of this work in *The Pilgrimage to Santiago* (Oxford, 2000; 1st edn, 1974), pp. 220 ff. Although Mullins uses the term 'proto-Gothic' in inverted commas, conventional guidebooks customarily refer to this work, completed *c.* 1188 by one Maestro Mateo, as Romanesque (e.g. the DuMont Kunstreiseführer, *Der Spanische Jakobsweg*, by Dietrich Höllhuber and Werner Schäfke (Hamburg, 2002), pp. 202 ff.).

11 Dunn and Davidson, *A Comprehensive Bibliography*, xxix, describe this and other Spanish guides of the mid-nineteenth century that combined scholarly historical information with aesthetic and artistic appreciation.

12 *Ibid.*, xxxv and xlvii, n. 30.

13 In the meantime, guidebook literature for the old European routes of 'St James's Way' extends over other countries, notably Italy and Austria. Peter Lindenthal's *Auf dem Jakobsweg durch Österreich* (Innsbruck, 2000) is now in its second edition, and describes itself as a 'cultural guide for hikers in the steps of the medieval St James pilgrims through Austria'. The Confraternity of St James has a website bookshop offering a large number of guides based on historic pilgrim routes for walkers and cyclists, and studies of the routes of earlier well-known pilgrims.

14 G.F. Barwick, 'Some Early Guide-Books', *Transactions of the Bibliographical Society*, 7 (1904), 206.

15 For a detailed and interesting examination of the motives of modern pilgrims, see Nancy Louise Frey, *Pilgrim Stories: On and Off the Road to Santiago. Journeys Along an Ancient Way in Modern Spain* (Berkeley, Los Angeles and London, 1998). This is a sympathetic study based on 'anthropological fieldwork'.

16 William Melczer, *The Pilgrim's Guide to Santiago de Compostela* (New York, 1993), p. 46.

17 *Financial Times*, 15/16 March 2003. The tour was a 'special offer' pitched at the prosperous *Financial Times* readership and 'organised on behalf of the newspaper' by a tour operator.

18 Taken from an essay originally in Bulletin No. 59 of the Confraternity of St James, and now posted in slightly adapted form on the society's website, http://www.csj.org.uk/spirit.htm.

19 Mullins, *Pilgrimage to Santiago*, p. 15.

20 *Ibid.*, pp. 13–14.

21 The supposition is that Salomé, mother of James and John, was the Virgin Mary's sister. The gospels relate that she tried to ensure a privileged place in heaven for her sons, and was rebuked for her hubris.

22 Cf. Numbers 35. For a discussion of this, see Fernando López Alsina, 'Santiago de Compostela', in Paolo Caucci von Saucken (ed.), *Pilgerziele der Christenheit: Jerusalem, Rom, Santiago de Compostela* (Stuttgart, 1999), p. 295.

23 A detailed exposition of the development of the St James cult in terms of documents (several forged) from the eighth century onwards is contained in Robert Plötz's masterly 'Peregrinatio ad Limina Sancti Jacobi', in Williams and Stones, *The* Codex Calixtinus *and the Shrine of St James*, pp. 43 ff.

24 Mullins, *Pilgrimage to Santiago*, p. 5.

25 *Ibid.*, p. 5.

26 Rolf Legler, *Sternenstraße und Pilgerweg: Der Jakobs-Kult von Santiago de Compostela, Wahrheit und Fälschung* (Bergisch Gladbach, 2000), pp. 380, 395. For a discussion of this and other primeval 'starways', see Louis Charpentier, *Spanien: Das Geheimnis der Pilgerstrasse* (Munich, 1991).

27 *Turpini Historia Karoli Magni et Rotholandi.*

28 See López Alsina, 'Santiago de Compostela', pp. 313–14, for the functional modelling of Compostela's church of Santa María de la Corticela on S. Giovanni in Laterano in Rome. The same work discusses the claim to the privileges of an apostolic seat for Compostela (which was resisted by Rome) made in the eleventh century by Bishop Sisnandus I and his successor, Cresconius.

29 Diego Gelmírez was bishop from 1100 and archbishop from 1120; but he was also chancellor to the Count of Galicia and a shrewd politician who cultivated the French connection for tactical gain. This strategy proved useful when Guy, Archbishop of Vienne and brother of the deceased Galician Count, was elected pope as Calixtus II. This is the same Calixtus whose authority is invoked for the *Codex Calixtinus/Liber Sancti Jacobi*. See Melczer, *The Pilgrim's Guide to Santiago de Compostela*, p. 22.

30 See Colin Smith, in Dunn and Davidson, *Pilgrimage to Compostela*, pp. 28–31, for a detailed examination of the fraudulent material of the *Pseudo-Turpin* and its consequences.

31 Shaver-Crandell *et al.*, *The Pilgrim's Guide*, p. 86.

32 The *Codex Calixtinus*, which Shaver-Crandell *et al.* suggest should more accurately be titled *The Pseudo Calixtine Compilation*, exists in twelve versions, all of which include the *Pilgrim's Guide* and other materials relating to the cult of St James, but is sometimes abridged. It is also known as the *Liber Sancti Jacobi* or *Jacobus*, in English *The Book of St James*, in French the *Livre de Saint Jacques*.

33 Starkie, *The Road to Santiago*, p. 40.

34 The extent of Cluniac influence is an extremely contentious matter among scholars. For a detailed survey of the arguments see Raymound Oursel, *Les pèlerins du Moyen Âge: les hommes, les chemins, les sanctuaires* (Paris, 1963), pp. 125 ff.

35 The *Guide*'s apparent internal contradictions seem indeed to have confused scholars in respect of its compiler's intentions. For instance, Melczer (*Pilgrim's Guide to Santiago*, p. 52) first says that its unrealistic reports of mileages are 'at best, the result of a wilfully manipulated calculation . . . meant to attract pilgrims by shortening the road; . . .' But in the following sentence he says: 'Had the motivations for the optimistic reckoning been a propagandistic move towards would-be pilgrims, it would be hard to justify the accounts of banditry and water-related calamities that the Guide provides with a nearly malicious gusto and a gory luxury of details.'

36 Starkie, *The Road to Santiago*, pp. 7–8.

37 Renato Stoppani, in Giorgio Massola, *L'Altro Giubileo: Il Paesaggio Umano del Pellegrino Medioevale* (Bolsena, 1998), introduction, p. 8.

38 Davies and Davies, *Holy Days and Holidays*, p. 85.

39 Serafín Moralejo, 'The *Codex Calixtinus* as an Art-Historical Source', p. 209.

40   Translation in Shaver-Crandell *et al.*, *The Pilgrim's Guide*, p. 95. Hereafter all quotations from Picaud are from this translation.
41   Shaver-Crandell *et al.*, *The Pilgrim's Guide*, p. 62. The authors remark that there is evidence of later alterations, probably in the 1170s.
42   *Ibid.*, p. 81.
43   Klaus Herbers, Robert Plötz (eds), *Die Straße zu Sankt Jakob. Der älteste deutsche Pilgerführer nach Santiago de Composteal* (Ostfildern, 2004).
44   Pierre Barret and Jean-Noël Gurgand, *Auf dem Weg nach Santiago: In den Spuren der Jakobspilger* (Freiburg, Basel and Vienna, 2000) pp. 88–94. This is a revised edition of the 1982 German translation of the French original, *Priez pour nous à Compostelle* (Paris, 1978 and 1999).
45   Shaver-Crandell *et al.*, *The Pilgrim's Guide*, p. 21.
46   *Ibid.*, p. 68.
47   *Ibid.*
48   *Ibid.*, p. 73.
49   *Ibid.*, p. 69.
50   *The Athenaeum*, 30 August 1845. Anonymous review of John Murray, *A Hand-Book for Travellers in Spain and Readers at Home Describing the Country and Cities, the Natives and their Manners, the Antiquities, Religion, Legends, Fine Arts, Literature, Sports and Gastronomy. With Notices on Spanish History*, in two parts. [The author of the Hand-Book was Richard Ford.]
51   The copy in my possession is the German edition of the work, which was of course originally published in Spanish, and is available also in English and French translations: Millán Bravo Lozano, *Praktischer Pilgerführer: Der Jakobsweg* (León, 2002).
52   Hermann Künig von Vach, *Das Wallfahrtsbuch des Hermann Künig von Vach* (1495), Arnold von Harff, *Die Pilgerfahrt des Ritters Arnold von Harff* (*c.* 1500) and Domenico Laffi, *Viaggio in Ponente a San Giacomo di Galitia e Finisterrae* (1673).
53   Lozano, *Praktischer Pilgerführer*, p. 12.
54   Oursel, *Les pelerins du Moyen Age*, p. 100.

CHAPTER 5

1   According to Mauro Lucentini, *Rom: Wege in die Stadt* (Munich, 2000), p. 270, a fragment of this column with its frieze may still be seen lying to the right of the temple of Saturn.
2   *Brewer's Dictionary of Phrase & Fable*, millennium edn, revised by Adrian Room (London, 2000), p. 25.
3   Septimius Severus erected an *Umbilicus Urbis Romae* next to his great arch in the Forum and close to the *milliario aureo* of Augustus. See John R. Curran, *Pagan City and Christian Capital: Rome in the Fourth Century* (Oxford and New York, 2002), p. 7. However, this was primarily conceived as the 'navel of Rome', although by implication that made it the navel of the civilised world.
4   The reference is to the son of Maxentius, not to the founder of Rome.
5   An earlier map of Rome is said to have been engraved on Pompey's impressive portico in the Campus Martius. Marcus Aurelius also had a survey of Rome prepared.
6   See Emilio Rodriguez Almeido, *Forma Urbis Marmorea: aggiornamento generale 1980* (Rome, 1981), with a companion portfolio of fifty-one folded plates, for an update of the research on this remarkable survival from antiquity.

7   The 'temple' became the vestibule of the church. A huge glass window installed in the church of Sts Cosmas and Damian in 2000 enables one to view it. Whether this was actually the temple of Romulus is disputed by modern scholarship. Alternative theories suggest the building may have been the audience hall of the city prefect or a temple of Jupiter. In Vespasian's library of AD 70 it is thought that not only public property registers may have been kept, but also city plans.

8   Fragments are stored in the Antiquarium Comunale, which has long been inaccessible. One piece may be seen in the Crypta Balbi in Palazzo Paganica near the foot of the Capitoline Hill. It shows just the area of the site of the palazzo, which partly occupies that of a Roman theatre built by one Balbus.

9   Arnold Esch, *Wege nach Rom: Annäherungen aus zehn Jahrhunderten* (Munich, 2003), pp. 9–12.

10   Norbert Ohler, *Pilgerstab und Jakobsmuschel: Wallfahren in Mittelalter und Neuzeit* (Düsseldorf and Zürich, 2000), pp. 21–2.

11   The earliest is dated to 334. There is a résumé of similar documents in Cristina Nardella, *Il fascino di Roma nel Medievo: Le 'Meraviglie di Roma' di maestro Gregorio* (Rome, 1996), p. 22, n. 36.

12   Ferdinand Gregorovius, *Geschichte der Stadt Rom im Mittelalter vom V bis XVI Jahrhundert*, 5th edn (Stuttgart and Berlin, 1904), vol. 3, p. 498. For Renaissance palaeographical scholarship dealing with the earliest Roman topography, see e.g. F. Unterkircher (ed.) *Notitiae Regionum Urbis Romae et Urbis Constantinopolitanae*, Codex 162 in the Österreichische Nationalbibliothek, Vienna (Amsterdam, 1960). This listing of the regions of Rome, published by the scholar Janus Parrhasius in 1503, has been traced to a version of an original manuscript from the time of Constantine. Parrhasius invented an author for the manuscript by name of Publius Victor.

13   See Richard Krautheimer, *Rome: Profile of a City, 312–1308*, 2nd edn (Princeton and Chichester, 2000; 1st edn 1980), pp. 13–14.

14   These were know as *scholae* in the Middle Ages and originally referred to associations relating to the different trades. Gregorovius (VIII. 790) points out, however, that many seemed to be formed on ethnic lines – *Anglorum, Francorum, Frisonum*, etc. – which suggests a broader practical and social function.

15   Gregorovius, *Geschichte der Stadt Rom im Mittelalter*, p. 498.

16   Debra J. Birch, *Pilgrimage to Rome in the Middle Ages: Continuity and Change* (Woodbridge and Rochester, NY, 2000), p. 12. She writes: 'It seems unlikely that these guides were written for the use of pilgrims themselves but were instead a record of the churches and sites that pilgrims were already visiting' (p. 97).

17   According to R. Valentini and G. Zucchetti's *Codice Topografico della Città di Roma* (Rome, 1940–53), vol. 2, pp. 49–66, there was an even earlier seventh-century work cataloguing the cemeteries outside the city walls. But this can scarcely be considered a guide.

18   The chains of St Peter are of course displayed at S. Pietro in Vincoli and St Laurence's grid is to be seen at S. Lorenzo in Lucina: believe if you will.

19   Bernhard Kötting, *Peregrinatio Religiosa: Wallfahrten in der Antike und das Pilgerwesen in der alten Kirche* (Regensberg and Münster, 1950), pp. 364–5.

20   William of Malmesbury, *Gesta Regum Anglorum*, IV. 351, p. 402.

21   Walter Map, *De Nugis Curialium*, II.17, ed. M.R. James (Oxford, 1914), p. 82.

22   Codex 326. Mabillon published the Inscriptions and Itinerary in *Vetera Analecta* (vol. 4, Paris, 1685). A recent edition is Gerold Walser (ed.), *Die Einsiedler*

Inschriftensammlung und der Pilgerführer durch Rom (Codex Einsidlensis 326) (Stuttgart, 1987). The Maurists were a congregation of French Benedictine monks founded in 1621 and noted for scholarly work. They adopted St Maurus, a sixth-century disciple of St Benedict, as their mascot.

23 However, Walser (in *Die Einsiedler Inschriftensammlung*), who sees a dominant Christian emphasis in the MS, suggests that some inscriptions may have been misunderstood by the scribe. For example, the puzzlingly long account of the *palmae* and *praemia* awarded to a star Roman jockey may have been assumed by the copyist to have had Christian significance (pp. 10 and 115). Rather the opposite view was taken by Krautheimer in his celebrated *Rome: Profile of a City*: on p. 114 he asserts: '[The text] was written no longer for the pious pilgrim . . . the itineraries through the city . . . list indiscriminately Christian and ancient monuments as they present themselves to the visitor.' However, his next sentence slightly modulates this judgement: 'The guide, then, is meant to appeal to a visitor who is Christian, but has antiquarian interests and knowledge.' This would seem more or less to reflect the present scholarly consensus.

24 Although epigraphs went totally out of fashion from the late nineteenth century, they are making a modest comeback in Rome. The extensive epigraph collection of the Museo Nazionale Romano has been arranged in modern halls on the site of a Carthusian monastery built into the ruins of Diocletian's Baths and was opened at the beginning of the twenty-first century.

25 Walser, *Die Einsiedler Inschriftensammlung*, pp. 159 and ff. Walser's commentary performs the inestimable service of placing the items on the routes in their historical context, identifying (where possible) those that no longer exist, comparing the views of scholars on problematic references and giving a periodisation of names; thus a reader today could revisit the *Itinerary* and enjoy a marvellous historical and archaeological panorama of the city with this work in his hand.

26 Walser, *Die Einsiedler Inschriftensammlung*, p. 205.

27 C. Huelsen, 'La pianta di Roma dell'anonimo Einsidlense', in *Atti della Pontificia accademia romana di archaeologia*, 9 (1907), series 2a, p. 6, quoting R. Lanciani, 'L'Itinerario di Einsiedeln e l'Ordine di Benedetto Canonico', in *Monumenti Antichi*, 1890–2, a cura dell'Accademia dei Lincei, I, coll. 437–552. Huelsen's suggestion, not universally accepted, is that the *Einsidlensis* was the 'truncated and confused epitome of an itinerary much richer in information, which was attached to a plan of the city' (p. 7).

28 Modern scholarship has amalgamated what were originally presented as the separate routes 9 and 10, so older works on the *Einsidlensis* feature thirteen routes.

29 Krautheimer, *Rome: Profile of a City*, p. 114.

30 Walser, *Die Einsiedler Inschriftensammlung*, n. 20.

31 *Ibid.*, p. 165. Huelsen's ('La pianta di Roma', pp. 1–47) influential close reading of the text compares his solutions to various problems of orientation and reference with those of three other important analyses: H. Jordan, *Topographie der Stadt Rom im Altertum* (Berlin, 1878, 1885, 1907; rev. by Huelsen); R. Lanciani, 'L'itinerario di Einsiedeln e l'ordine di Benedetto canonico', in *Monumenti antichi* (Rome, 1891), vol. 1, pp. 439–552; finally, J.B. de Rossi's *Inscriptiones christianae urbis Romae* (Rome, 1888), vol. 2. It is unlikely that all the problems of the *Einsidlensis* will be solved, but the scholarship devoted to it illustrates its significance in a field where documents are sparse. Similarly, for the historian of the guidebook, it provides a rare glimpse of a type of publication of which many more may once have existed.

32   The church escapes the notice of the vast majority of the mainstream guidebooks, including the generally more detailed German language ones such as DuMont, Artemis, etc; it does not even feature in Mauro Lucentini's substantial *Rom: Wege in die Stadt* (Munich, 2000), although it is mentioned in the *Blue Guide*. One of the handful of instances where it is mentioned (p. 106) – and here quite comprehensively described – occurs in a purely religious guide published for the recent Holy Year: *Holy Rome: A Millennium Guide to the Christian Sights*. This book originated with the Touring Club Italiano and was published in an English edition by Fodor in 1999.

33   M. Paul Fabre and L. Duchesne (eds), *Le Liber Censuum*, vol 1. VI.1 (premier fascicle (1889), 2nd ser. (1910), Bibliothèque des Écoles Françaises d'Athènes et de Rome), suggest that this document was originally an administrative survey for the prefecture reporting on the state of the walls after they had been repaired on the emperor's orders.

34   Gregorovius, *Geschichte der Stadt Rom im Mittelalter*, p. 501.

35   Francis Peabody Magoun Jr., 'The Rome of Two Northern Pilgrims: Archbishop Sigeric of Canterbury and Abbot Nikolás of Munkathverá', in *Harvard Theological Review*, 33 (1942), 267–89.

36   W.J. Moore, *The Saxon Pilgrims to Rome and the Schola Saxonum* (Fribourg, 1937), p. 86.

37   The present church on the same site is called S. Spirito in Sassia, dates to the sixteenth century and has a façade by Antonio da Sangallo the Younger.

38   Magoun, 'The Rome of Two Northern Pilgrims', p. 276. Sigeric also left a description of his return route to England along the Via Francigena, which mentions eighty stopping places.

39   *Ibid.*, p. 277.

40   Translations from *ibid.*, p. 280.

41   Averil Cameron, *The Mediterranean World in Late Antiquity: AD 395–600* (London and New York, 1993), p. 76.

42   An example of 'co-opting' was the papal claim to have 'inherited' the mantle of the Caesars. Pope Innocent II (1130–43) was actually addressed as 'Caesar' in panegyrics and was buried in what was believed to be Hadrian's tomb.

43   John Curran, *Pagan City and Christian Capital: Rome in the Fourth Century*, 2nd edn (Oxford and New York, 2002; 1st edn 2000), p. 117.

44   Maurilio Adriani, 'Paganesimo e Cristianesimo nei *Mirabilia Urbis Romae*', in *Studi Romani* (1996), 535–52. This quotation on p. 538.

45   Nardella, *Il fascino di Roma nel Medioevo*, p. 19. Nardella bases this judgement on E. Panofsky, *Rinascimento e rinascenze nell'arte occidentale* (Milan, 1971), pp. 93–4, and M. Adriani, 'Paganesimo e Christianesimo nei "Mirabilie di Roma"', in *Studi Romani*, 8 (1960), 536–9.

46   See, for example, the introductory essay by Cesare D'Onofrio to *Visitiamo Roma mille anni fa: la città dei Mirabilia* (Romana Società editrice, Collana di Studi e Testi per la Storia della Città di Roma, 5, Rome, 1988).

47   Robert Brentano, *Rome before Avignon: A Social History of Thirteenth Century Rome* (New York, 1974), p. 80.

48   In view of the inappropriateness of the title, many scholars follow M. Paul Fabre in using the term *Liber polyptychus* or *Liber polypticus* for this work. It was dedicated to Guido Castello, Cardinal of St Mark, who became Pope Celestine II in 1143. It must therefore have been compiled before that date. As Francis Morgan Nichols points

out (*The Marvels of Rome*, London and Rome, 1889, pp. 157–8, and see nn. 51 ff.) the accounts of papal processions in the *Politicus* (*polypticus*) supply evidence of Roman topography in the twelfth century, and therefore have a bearing on the interpretation of the *Mirabilia*.

49   See Fabre and Duchesne, *Le Liber Censuum*, p. 4.

50   The number given varies, presumably according to which source is being used, though there may also be copying errors.

51   It enclosed the Vatican and St Peter's, creating the so-called 'Leonine City'. Later, a passageway was built connecting it with Castel Sant' Angelo, a place of refuge for popes in times of political turmoil or war.

52   Krautheimer, *Rome: Profile of a City*, p. 237.

53   Fabre and Duchesne, *Le Liber Censuum*, p. 97.

54   *Ibid.*, pp. 98–9.

55   *Ibid.*, p. 99.

56   Compare this with the following passage in the Introduction (p. 35) to Grant Allen's *Historical Guide to Christian Rome* (London, 1911): '*Roma caput mundi regit orbis frena rotundi*' ["Rome, capital of the world, holds the reins of the round orb"]. Such is the legend that has marked the place of Rome in the minds of men for many centuries. If we ask what is the secret of the marvellous and mysterious power of her rule, the reply can only be in the most general terms. She has seldom sought the unattainable, she has seldom mistaken the shadow for the substance; the speculative has always been subordinated to the practical.'

57   Nigel Llewellyn, 'The History of Western Art History', in *Companion to Historiography*, ed. Michael Bentley (London and New York, 2002), p. 833.

58   Jean Baptist de Rossi in *Roma Sotterranea* (Rome, 1864), p. 158, was the first to draw attention to the quasi-official status that the *Mirabilia* acquired by becoming a fixture in the books of the Roman curia.

59   Fabre and Duchesne, *Le Liber Censuum*, p. 104.

60   The detailed classification is laid out in: Ludovicus Urlichs [Charles Ludwig Urlichs] (ed.), *Codex Urbis Romae Topographicus* (Wircebururgi [Würzburg], 1871). The same work supplies a chronological order of earlier and later topographies.

61   Nichols, *The Marvels of Rome*, 2nd edn, with new introduction, gazetteer and bibliography by Eileen Gardner (New York, 1986), xv. The phrase 'the standard guide-book of the more learned visitors to Rome from the twelfth to the fifteenth century' has evidently been taken word for word from Nichols by G.F. Barwick in his article 'Some Early Guide-Books', in *Transactions of the Bibliographical Society*, 7 (1904), 195. Subsequent scholarship has produced little to modify this generalisation, even if guides specifically aimed at Christian pilgrims existed parallel to the *Mirabilia*. Nardella (*Il fascino di Roma nel Medioevo*, p. 17) points out that the *Mirabilia* was certainly not only the standard work for *visitors* to Rome, since a version in Roman dialect appeared in the mid-thirteenth century.

62   Nichols, *The Marvels of Rome*, 2nd edn, xxii. The version offered by Nichols is in fact a fusion of the *Mirabilia Urbis Romae* and the *Graphia aureae urbis Romae*, and he also changed the order of the original *Mirabilia*, as explained on p. xxiii.

63   Gregorovius remarks that the title 'Aurea Roma' was already featured on imperial seals in the time of Otto III (AD 996–1002). The original of *Graphia* is usually dated to the twelfth century.

64   *Il Dittamondo.*

65 A.F. Ozanam, 'Graphia Aureae Urbis Romae', in *Documents inédits pour servir à l'histoire littéraire de l'Italie avec les recherches sur le moyen âge italien* (Paris, 1850), p. 86. The *Graphia* manuscript here discussed is in the Florentine Biblioteca Laurenziana: Plutens LXXXIX.infer.Cod.41.

66 Ozanam, *Documents inédits*, p. 88.

67 Nichols, *The Marvels of Rome*, 2nd edn, even cites the budding export of ruins as building materials, e.g. the the complicated transport of Roman columns to support the roof of Saint Denis in Paris (*ibid.*, xxvii).

68 Eileen Gardner in *ibid.*, xxviii.

69 M. Greenhalgh, '"Ipsa ruina docet": l'uso dell'antico nel medioevo', in *La memoria dell'antico*, 1, p. 146.

70 Nichols, *The Marvels of Rome*, 2nd edn, p. 4. Hereafter all quotations from the text of the *Mirabilia* are from this 1986 reprint of Morgan Nichols.

71 *Ibid.*, p. 46.

72 *Ibid.*, p. 44.

73 *Ibid.*, pp. 33 and 38. *Brewer's Dictionary of Phrase and Fable* says: 'the *Vaticanus Mons* (Vatican Hill) got its name through being the headquarters of *vaticinatores* ("soothsayers")'. The conceit *Caput Mondo* for the Capitoline, emblematic of its historical and geo-political significance, seems to have had a long tradition.

74 Nichols, *The Marvels of Rome*, 2nd edn, pp. 28 and 42.

75 The dating of Master Gregory's visit to Rome and of the composition of his manuscript is not known for sure. The latest scholar to deal with the matter, Cristina Nardella, believes he could have been in Rome under the pontificates of Innocent III (1198–1216), or of Honorius III (1216–27) or of Gregory IX (1227–41): Nardella, *Il fascino di Roma nel Medioevo*, p. 26.

76 Quoted in Brentano, *Rome before Avignon*, p. 5.

77 John Osborne (tr. and ed.), *Master Gregorius – The Marvels of Rome: A Translation of Narracio de Mirabilibus Urbis Romae* (Medieval Sources in Translation for the Pontifical Institute of Mediaeval Studies) (Toronto, 1987), preface.

78 Nardella's translation, *Il fascino di Roma nel Medioevo*, p. 169.

79 Osborne, *Master Gregorius*, points out that Master Gregory refers three times to Pope Gregory I's (590–604) destruction of pagan monuments in the city, and not with approval. In 1162 the Roman Senate announced stiff penalties for anyone caught mutilating Trajan's Column, a sign of a new awareness of the need to protect monuments.

80 *De septem miraculis mundi*, by the 'Pseudo-Bede' (ninth century AD).

81 Pope Boniface IV consecrated it in 609 as Sta Maria ad Martyres, the church of all the martyrs, but Master Gregory uses its popular designation of 'Santa Maria Rotonda'.

82 In the twelth century, the title could imply one of several types of professions with their roots in an academe dominated by the Church – councillors, lawyers or persons of a literary profession. On the dating of the manuscript of the *Marvels* and the possible identity of 'Master Gregory', see Nardella, *Il fascino di Roma nel Medioevo*, pp. 25–9.

83 *Ibid.*, p. 62, points out that the names of the city gates he supplies, which differ from those in the *Mirabilia*, are probably not the original ancient names as Gregory evidently supposes, but those of an ephemeral popular usage.

84 The statue is thought to date from the end of the reign of Marcus Aurelius (AD 161–80) and is first documented from the tenth century. It probably was moved to

the Lateran Hill as early as 782, but from where is not entirely certain. In 1538 it was moved from its position in front of S. Giovanni in Laterano, where Gregory saw it, to the Capitol, which was being remodelled by Michelangelo, who provided it with a simple new plinth. It is currently (since 1997) substituted by a replica while the ancient and fragile original is being restored. Bartolomeo Sacchi da Piadena, a humanist scholar, was the first to propose the now generally accepted attribution of Marcus Aurelius in his biography of Sixtus IV (1471–84).

85 Nardella, *Il fascino di Roma nel Medioevo*, her translation (into Italian) of Master Gregory's *Narracio*, p. 155.
86 Nardella's translation, *Il fascino di Roma nel Medioevo*, p. 157.
87 Some have identified this as the Capitoline Venus, a Roman copy of the Cnidos Aphrodite by Praxiteles, which is today in the Palazzo Nuovo of the Musei Capitolini.
88 According to the Catalogue of Turin.
89 Brentano, *Rome before Avignon*, pp. 85–6.
90 All these may still be seen, although the Veronica is only displayed in San Pietro during Holy Week.
91 Du Cange, *Glossarium Mediae et Infirmae Latinitas*, 10 vols (1883–7), vol. 7, p. 212.
92 Brentano, *Rome before Avignon*, p. 54. A modern parallel to the fanatical zeal of pilgrims and its consequences are the injuries and deaths sustained by Muslims making the *hajj* to Mecca. In 1450 hundreds of pilgrims died on the Ponte Sant' Angelo in the crush of pilgrims trying to cross the Tiber to get to St Peter's.
93 For a thorough examination of the various editions in diverse languages, see: Ludwig Schudt (ed.), *Le Guide di Roma: Materialen zu einer Geschichte der Römischen Topographie, unter Benützung des handschriftlichen Nachlasses von Oskar Pollak* (Farnborough, 1971 = facsimile repr. of 1930 edn), pp. 19 ff.
94 See: Eunice D. Howe, *Andrea Palladio: The Churches of Rome* (Binghamton, New York, 1991), pp. 34–5.
95 See Debra J. Birch, *Pilgrimage to Rome in the Middle Ages: Continuity and Change* (Woodbridge, 1998), p. 14.
96 J.R. Hulbert, 'Some Medieval Advertisements of Rome', in *Modern Philology*, 20/4 (May 1923), 419; see n. 101 below.
97 Charles L. Stinger, *The Renaissance in Rome* (Bloomington, IN, 1985), p. 34. Five *Indulgentiae* were shown at the exhibition in the Bavarian National Museum in 1984 (*Wallfahrt kennt keine Grenzen*). One is a reprint of that printed by Hans Awrl in 1481, probably the first book to be printed with movable type in Munich.
98 Birch, *Pilgrimage to Rome*, p. 179.
99 See, for example, J.C. Furnivall in *Political, Religious and Love Poems*, xvii: '*The Stacyons of Rome* is simply (to me) a puff of the merits of the Papal city as a place for getting pardons and indulgences, in comparison with Santiago and Jerusalem.'
100 Birch, *Pilgrimage to Rome*, pp. 179–80, 199.
101 See the catalogue *Wallfahrt kennt keine Grenzen*, p. 93, Item 129. The figure of seven principal churches and their identities seems to have been fixed quite late in the Middle Ages, sources such as Onuphrius Panvinius citing five churches for ealier periods. On this see Hulbert, 'Some Medieval Advertisements of Rome', p. 405 and n. Hulbert (p. 412) stresses that the *Stacyons* was idiosyncratic, saying nothing of the five or seven principal churches, but starting with St Peter's and discussing the churches in an order determined by topography and an ancient pilgrimage route. On this basis he regards it as much more of a guidebook than the run of the mill *Indulgentiae* (p. 414).

102 E.S. De Beer, 'The Development of the Guidebook until the Early Nineteenth Century', in *Journal of the British Archaeological Association*, 3rd ser., 15 (1952), 40.

103 John Capgrave, *Ye Solace of Pilgrims: A Description of Rome, circa AD 1450, by John Capgrave, an Austin Friar of King's Lynn*, ed. C.A. Mills (Oxford and New York, 1911), viii. John Capgrave, a fifteenth-century prior of King's Lynn and Provincial of the Augustinian Order, was known to have written a description of Rome, but no trace of it was found until this MS surfaced in the Bodleian Library in 1907, its publication four years later being something of a literary sensation.

104 Jonathan Sumption, *Pilgrimage* (London, 2002), p. 263.

105 Capgrave, *Ye Solace of Pilgrims*, pp. 21–2, 25–6. I have modernised the English of the quotations.

106 Capgrave, *Ye Solace of Pilgrims*, p. 28.

107 *Ibid.*, p. 73.

108 Capgrave, *Ye Solace of Pilgrims*, p. 73, and Sumption, *Pilgrimage*, p. 254.

109 Capgrave, *Ye Solace of Pilgrims*, p. 85.

110 *Ibid.*, p. 85.

111 *Ibid.*, pp. 87–8.

112 *Ibid.*, p. 156.

113 Quoted in Robert W. Gaston, 'British Travellers and Scholars in the Roman Catacombs 1450–1900', *Journal of the Warburg and Courtauld Institutes*, 46 (1983), 144–65.

114 Capgrave, *Ye Solace of Pilgrims*, viii.

115 Capgrave, *Ye Solace of Pilgrims*, p. 85. Sumption, *Pilgrimage*, p. 243.

116 Sumption, *Pilgrimage*, p. 224.

117 C. Eveleigh Woodruff (tr. and ed.), *A XVth Century Guide-Book to the Principal Churches of Rome compiled c. 1470 by William Brewyn* (London, 1933). See i–ii, quoting Casimir Oudin's *Commentarium de Scriptoribus Ecclesiasticis* (Leipzig, 1722).

118 Woodruff, *A XVth Century Guide-Book*, iii.

119 The Medici bankers of Florence invented the letter of credit to enable Florentine merchants to circulate easily abroad – and without the danger of carrying a lot of money.

120 See Schudt, *Le Guide di Roma*, pp. 95–6. Albertini was also an enthusiastic collector of inscriptions.

121 Julius Schlosser, *Die Kunstliteratur* (facsimile reprint Vienna 1985 of 1924 edn), pp. 188–9.

CHAPTER 6

1 M.A. Screech (tr. and ed.), *The Complete Essays of Montaigne* (London and New York, 1991), xxxvi.

2 *Ibid.*, xliii.

3 Andrew Hutchinson (ed.), *Travels in Italy: Selections from the* Commentarii *of Pope Pius II* (Bristol, 1988), p. 17.

4 The information and quotations in this paragraph all come from John Hale, *The Civilization of Europe in the Renaissance* (London, 1994), pp. 282, 287.

5 The most extravagant of such panegyrics was a work of propaganda by Manuel Chrysoloras in aid of the then beleaguered Constantinople. Originally written in Greek (1411), the *Laudatio Urbis Romae et Constantinopolis* proclaimed the joint glory

and indivisibility of Rome and 'the new Rome' (Constantinople). Rome, the ancient city, was flatteringly described as forming part of heaven, rather than part of earth. The panegyric was translated into Latin thirty years later and (selectively) exploited by Italian humanists. See Charles L. Stinger, *The Renaissance in Rome* (Bloomington, IN, 1985), p. 73.

6   Cornelia Boumann, 'Philipp von Zesen's Beziehungen zu Holland', Inaugural dissertation, University of Bonn, 1916.

7   See *Deutsche Allgemeine Biographie* (1900), vol. 45, pp. 108 ff.

8   *Ars apodemica* (alternatively *prudentia peregrinandi*) is generally translated as 'the art of travel', and was still current as a concept in the eighteenth century. In French it was *L' art de voyager*, in German *Reisekunst* or *Reiseklugheit*.

9   See Uli Kutter, 'Der Reisende ist dem Philosophen, was der Arzt dem Apotheker. Über Apodemiken und Reisehandbücher', in Hermann Bausinger, Klaus Beyrer and Gottfried Korff (eds), *Reisekultur: Von der Pilgerfahrt zum modernen Tourismus*, 2nd edn (Munich, 1999), pp. 38–47.

10 The two quotations are from Justin Stagl, *A History of Curiosity: The Theory of Travel 1550–1800* (Chur, 1995), pp. 109, 161 and 101.

11 Stagl, *History of Curiosity*, p. 109. My entire discussion of *ars apodemica* leans heavily on this brilliant and indispensable work. Quotations in this and the previous paragraph are from pp. 161 and 109.

12 The full titles are: Hieronymus Turler, *De peregrinatione et agro Neapolitano Libri II* (Strasburg, 1574); Theodor Zwinger, *Methodus apodemica in eorum gratiam qui cum fructu in quocunq; tandem vitae genere peregrinari cupiunt, a Thod. Zvingero Basiliense typis delineata, & cum aliis, tum quator praesertim Athenarum vivis exemplis illustrata. Cum indice* (Basel, 1577; 2nd edn, Strasburg, 1594); Hilarius Pyrckmair, *Commentariolus de Arte Apodemica, seu Vera Peregrinandi Ratione* (Ingolstadt, 1577). Pyrckmair, a Bavarian, was the only Catholic of the three, but (according to Stagl, *History of Curiosity*, p. 65) 'apparently a rather doubtful one'.

13 Frances A. Yates, *The Art of Memory* (London, 2001; 1st edn London, 1966), pp. 230–1.

14 Robert A. Horváth, 'La France en 1618 vue par un statisticien hongrois, Márton Szepsi Csombor', in *Population*, 2, 335–46.

15 Clare Howard, *English Travellers of the Renaissance* (New York, 1913), p. 33.

16 For the matter in this paragraph I have drawn on Stagl, *History of Curiosity*, pp. 71–8. The quotations are from S. Zwicker, *Brevarium apodemicum methodice concinnatum* (Danzig, 1638) and Zwinger, *Methodus apodemica*.

17 Stagl, *History of Curiosity*, pp. 47–8.

18 See entry on Marco Polo in *Encyclopaedia Britannica* (2002).

19 See the excellent introduction to the 1986 facsimile reprint, with commentary, of the first printed edition of *Odorichus. De rebus incognitis/Odorico da Pordenone nella prima edizione a stampa del 1513* [Pesaro], ed. Lucio Monaco and Giulio Cesare Testa (Pordenone, 1986).

20 C.W.R.D. Moseley (tr.), *The Travels of Sir John Mandeville* (London and New York, 1983), pp. 9, 13.

21 This quote and the reference to Lewkenor in Hale, *Civilization of Europe in the Renaissance*, p. 181.

22 Sir John Stradling, *A Direction for Travailers taken out of Iustus Lipsius, and Enlarged for the Behoofe of the Right Honourable Lord, the Young Earl of Bedford, Being Now Ready to Travel* (London, 1592).

23 Judith Adler, 'The Origins of Sightseeing', *Annals of Tourism Research*, 16 (1989), 18.

24 The Habsburg emperor Joseph II (1780–90) imposed on his subjects a paternalistic and severely rational governance which, however, left little room for the accommodation of those aspects of human nature that are not susceptible to sweet (or harsh) reason. Joseph himself was a 'rational' and 'patriotic' traveller, journeying incognito through his own realms, and beyond them, both in order to take the pulse of his peoples and to learn from the experiences of other nations.

25 Berchtold, *Essay to Direct and Extend the Inquiries of Patriotic Travellers with Further Observations on the Means of Preserving the Life, Health and Property of the Unexperienced in their Journies by Land and Sea* (London, 1787–9), p. 11.

26 J.W. Goethe, *Italian Journey* [1786–8], tr. W.H. Auden and Elizabeth Mayer (London and New York, 1970), pp. 44–7.

27 Cited in David Landes, *The Wealth and Poverty of Nations* (London and New York, 1999), pp. 276 ff.

28 'The most common, as well as the most dangerous principles of evil among nations, proceed from the oppression of the peasantry, and from an erroneous system of agriculture, which ought to excite [the traveller] to inquire as minutely as possible into the state of the labouring poor and the different parts of rural and domestic economy, and with the same anxiety as if sent for that purpose by the Government.' Berchtold, *Patriotic Travellers*, vol. 1, p. 15. The book is dedicated, with a eulogy, to Arthur Young.

29 Stagl, *History of Curiosity*, p. 216.

30 Joseph-Jérôme Lefrançais de Lalande, *Voyage d'un François en Italie, Fait dans les Années 1765 & 1766* (Venice, 1769).

31 Hale, *Civilization of Europe in the Renaissance*, p. 181.

32 Attilio Brilli, *Il viaggiatore immaginario: L'Italia degli itinerari perduti* (Bologna, 1997), p. 12.

33 Quoted in E.S. Bates, *Touring in 1600: A Study in the Development of Travel as a Means of Education* (London, New York and Boston, 1911), p. 57.

34 Stagl, *History of Curiosity*, p. 278.

35 Jörg Gail, *Ein neues nützliches Raiß Büchlin der fürnemesten Land und Stett. Durch mich Jörg Gail, Bürger zu Augsburg in truck verfertigt* (Augsburg, 1563).

36 Extract reprinted in Ross and McLaughlin, *The Viking Medieval Reader* (New York, 1949), pp. 487 ff.

37 Monaco and Testa, *Odorico da Pordenone*, p. 11.

38 Georg Pictorius [Jörg Maler], *Raise Büchlin. Ordnung wie sich zu halten / so einaer raisen will in weite und onerfarne Land / unnd wie man allen zufällen / so dem raisenden zustehn mögen / mit guten mitteln der artzney begegnen soll* (Strasbourg and Mühlhausen, 1557).

39 Giles Milton, *Nathaniel's Nutmeg: How One Man's Courage Changed the Course of History* (London, 1999), pp. 18–19.

40 Andrew Borde, *The Boke of the Introduction of Knowledge* (1548; repr. London, 1814), preface.

41 John Chandler (ed.), *John Leland's Itinerary: Travels in Tudor England* (Thrupp, 1993), xxiii.

42 *Dictionary of National Biography*, entry for William Bourne, mathematician (d. 1583).

43 All of these still exist. The pyramid by the Ostian Gate is the funeral monument of Gaius Cestius, an official of the first century.

44 Anthony Grafton, *Leon Battista Alberti: Master Builder of the Italian Renaissance* (Cambridge, MA, 2002), p. 230.

45   *Ibid.*, p. 229.

46   *Ibid.*

47   Both this and the previous quotation are taken from the translation of Bracciolini's
      On the Inconstancy of Fortune (*c.* 1448) in Peter Elmer, Nick Webb and Roberta Wood
      (eds), *The Renaissance in Europe: An Anthology* (New Haven and London, in
      association with the Open University, 2000), pp. 9 and 10. Bracciolini's poetical
      evocation of decay naturally appealed to Gibbon, who supplies a paraphrase of most
      of it in *The Decline and Fall of the Roman Empire* (1776–88). One should perhaps add
      that the collection of inscriptions was not an entirely new activity, since even the
      ninth-century *Einsiedeln Itinerary* shows an interest in inscriptions. But now a more
      systematic and scholarly approach to their collection was adopted, the collectors
      using them to build an historically accurate picture of the topography of the city
      and to combat legend and superstition.

48   Stinger, *Renaissance in Rome*, p. 80. The satirical dialogue was by Andrea Guarna and
      entitled *Simia*; *inter alia*, it wittily tilts at the overweening arrogance of the architect,
      a phenomenon not entirely unknown today.

49   Stinger, *Renaissance in Rome*, p. 37.

50   Herbert L. Kessler, Johanna Zacharias, *Rome in 1300* (New Haven and London, 2000),
      p. 2. In a passage of the *Inferno*, Dante indeed describes a pedestrian management
      system instituted on the Ponte Sant'Angelo to control the pilgrim throng.

51   Stinger, *Renaissance in Rome*, p. 32. To obviate a recurrence of this disaster, Sixtus IV
      had the Ponte Sisto constructed before the Jubilee of 1475, thus providing
      alternative access to the Vatican.

52   The remark was made by Furnivall, who edited the poem for an anthology of
      Political, Religious and Love Poems, and is quoted in J.R. Hulbert, 'Some Medieval
      Advertisements of Rome', in *Modern Philology*, 20/4 (May 1923), 404, from where I
      have extracted it.

53   Stinger, *Renaissance in Rome*, pp. 34, 36. For a detailed account of the relationship of
      the *Libri indulgentiarum* and the *Mirabilia Romae*, see Ludwig Schudt (ed.), *Le Guide
      di Roma: Materialien zu einer Geschichte der römischen Topographie, unter Benützung des
      handschriftlichen Nachlasses von Oskar Pollak* (1971 facsimile reprint of Augsburg 1930
      edn), pp. 19 ff. The earliest *Libri indulgentiarum* are here described as dating from
      between 1470 and 1475.

54   Hulbert, 'Some Medieval Advertisements of Rome', p. 419.

55   Quoted in Rose Marie San Juan, *Rome: A City out of Print* (Minneapolis and London,
      2001), pp. 83–4.

56   Ludwig Schudt, in his edition of Giulio Mancini's *Il Viaggio per Roma* (Leipzig, 1923),
      lists the following editions of *Le cose maravigliose di Roma* that attached Palladio's
      L'Antichità as a separate section: 1563, 1571, 1575 (in Spanish), 1580, 1587, 1589,
      1596, 1615 and 1650. It was also incorporated into Pompée de Launay's very
      popular *Les merveilles de la ville de Rome* from 1628. Elsewhere (in *Le Guide di Roma*
      (1971 facsimile reprint of Vienna and Augsburg, 1930 edn)), Schudt lists some fifty-
      four editions of this astonishingly successful work, including those printed in Rome,
      Venice and Oxford; and in Latin, Italian, Spanish, French and English. The text
      went through all editions unchanged until 1610, when Pietro Martire Felini
      enlarged it by nine chapters for incorporation into his illustrated *Trattato nuovo delle
      cose maravigliose di Roma*. By 1643 it filled out 106 chapters and had acquired the title
      Descritione di Roma Antica e Moderna – an indication of how the requirements of
      readers had shifted from a discourse purely concerned with antiquity.

57 Its full title was *Opusculum de mirabilibus novae et veteris urbis Romae* (1510). In the same year he also published a similar, but less successful book on works of art in Florence. A facsimile reprint of these two works, as well as Palladio's *L'Antichità* and *Le Chiese di Roma* (Rome, 1554), and an anonymous work on Roman palaces and temples (Venice, 1480) was published under the title *Five Early Guides to Rome and Florence*, edited by Peter Murray (Farnborough, 1972). A useful edition of Palladio's *Le Chiese di Roma* is Eunice D. Howe, *Andrea Palladio: The Churches of Rome* (Binghamton, NY, 1991).

58 Schudt, *Le guide di Roma*, lists a total of sixty-three editions between 1554 and 1750. Some years saw up to five different printings, as in 1575, the 'Jubilee of the Counter-Reformation'. It was translated into Spanish in 1589, French in 1608, and into Latin in 1618. A parallel Italian–Latin edition was published at the Sheldonian in Oxford in 1709. As late as 1988, L. Puppi reproduced the guidebooks without commentary in *Andrea Palladio: Scritti sull'architettura (1554–79)* (Vicenza). The latest scholarly English translation of both *L'antichità di Roma* and the *Descritione de le chiese, stationi, indulgenze . . . che sono in la città de Roma* is Vaughan Hart and Peter Hicks, *Palladio's Rome: A Translation of Andrea Palladio's Two Guidebooks to Rome* (New Haven and London, 2006).

59 Deborah Howard, 'Four Centuries of Literature on Palladio', in *The Journal of the Society of Architectural Historians*, 39/3 (October 1980), 225.

60 Murray, *Five Early Guides to Rome and Florence*, p. [8] (unpaginated; introduction).

61 See Hart and Hicks, *Palladio's Rome*, xxv and xli ff., for a detailed account of Palladio's sources, and in particular the influence of Serlio's treatise on the antiquities of Rome.

62 See Howe, *Andrea Palladio: The Churches of Rome*, xiv.

63 Howard, 'Four Centuries of Literature on Palladio', p. 226.

64 Howe, *Andrea Palladio: The Churches of Rome*, p. 37.

65 *Ibid.*, translation of Palladio's *Le Chiese di Roma*, p. 76.

66 This would seem to be a reference to the oratory of S. Sylvestro, which was demolished during the remodelling of the Lateran ordered by Sixtus V in 1586 and undertaken by Domenico Fontana.

67 Both quotations are from Howe, *Andrea Palladio: The Churches of Rome*, translation, pp. 77–8.

68 According to tradition, every Pope up to Leo X (1513–21) had to undergo the testicle inspection by sitting on an open seat (the *sella stercoria*); the Deacon, having verified the necessary appurtenance, called out '*Habet!*' The Roman people, on hearing this, chorused '*Deo gratias!*' For a resumée of the Pope Joan fable see Philip Ward, *A Dictionary of Common Fallacies* (Cambridge, 1978), pp. 201–2.

69 The reference is to the *Liber de vita Christi ac de vitis summorum pontificum omnium* (Venice, 1479), an unsound 'Lives of the Popes' written by the humanist and Vatican librarian Bartolomeo Platina (1421–81). His text deals with this issue in his life of Pope John VIII.

70 Murray, *Five Early Guides to Rome and Florence*, Palladio's *Alli Lettori* ('Address to Readers') preceding the *Descritione de le Chiese & etc. de Roma* (unpaginated).

71 See Ulrich Thieme and Felix Becker, *Allgemeines Lexikon der bildenden Künstler von der Antike bis zur Gegenwart*, vol. 26 (1999 facsimile reprint of Leipzig 1931 edn), p. 164. Also David Watkin, *Abendländische Architektur* (Cologne, 1999), p. 143. Palladio's real name was Andrea di Pietro della Gondola, which he changed to Palladio at the urging of his humanist friend and mentor Giangiorgio Trissino. The eponym

referred also to a guardian angel featured in Trissino's epic poem 'L'Italia liberata dei Goti'. Trissino sponsored Palladio's trips to Rome.

72 Watkin, *Abendländische Architektur*, p. 143.

73 Hale, *Civilization of Europe in the Renaissance*, pp. 257–8. The influence of the Roman baths is supposedly to be seen in the so-called 'thermal' windows of the Redentore.

74 Hart and Hicks, *Palladio's Rome*, xxxix.

75 Claude Moatti, *In Search of Ancient Rome* (New York and London, 1993), pp. 38, 40.

76 Stinger, *Renaissance in Rome*, p. 8.

77 San Juan, *Rome: A City out of Print*, pp. 81–2.

78 Schudt (ed.), *Giulio Mancini*, p. 39.

79 Ludwig Freiherr von Pastor, *The History of the Popes from the Close of the Middle Ages, Drawn from the Secret Archives of the Vatican and other Original Sources*, vol. 29 (London, 1938), p. 515.

80 A reprint of Lauro's book of idealised topographical prints of Rome, *L'Antiquae Urbis Splendor*, ed. Giovanni Alto, appeared in 1637. A facsimile reprint of this has appeared in the excellent series entitled *Collana Vedute d'Italia* (No. 13): Giacomo Lauro, *Meraviglie della Roma antica: Templi, palazzi, terme e stadi. La grandezza della Roma imperiale nelle ricostruzioni ideali dei suoi monumenti.* Una serie di incisioni di inizio '600 inedite da tre secoli' (2nd edn Rome, 1996.) The editors of this volume give Alto's original name as 'Hans Gross of Lucerne'.

81 Pastor, *History of the Popes*, p. 538. San Juan (*Rome: A City out of Print*, pp. 88–9) has a lengthy discussion of the book's title page, which shows Giovanni Alto bestriding images of the city's past. She comments, *inter alia*, that (p. 88): 'This city . . . is defined by its irregularity, both physical and social, and presents no separation between antiquities and contemporary life.' Such a myth, or poetic conceit, was to become a recurrent motif in guides to Rome, and even more so in the depictions of the city.

82 Schudt (ed.), *Giulio Mancini*, p. 45. On Titi, see Joseph Connors and Louise Rice, *Specchio di Roma barocca* (Rome, 1991).

83 Stinger, *Renaissance in Rome*, p. 81. Richard Krautheimer, *Rome: Profile of a City 312–1308* (Princeton, 2000), p. 76. Heinz-Joachim Fischer: DuMont Kunst-Reiseführer, *Rom: Ein Reisebegleiter* (Cologne, 1986, 1989), p. 230.

84 The most important families of the Republican era built grand villas and gardens just beyond the centre of ancient Rome, especially on the Quirinal, Viminal and Esquiline hills. Spectacular finds, including many of the finest statues in the Capitoline collection, were discovered when some of these gardens were excavated at the end of the nineteenth century. I am indebted to my colleague Alta Macadam for detailed information on these '*horti*'.

85 Shakerley is identified in E.J. Baskerville's 1967 Columbia University Ph.D. dissertation, 'The English Traveller to Italy, 1547–1560', which in turn is quoted by Edward Chaney in his erudite *The Evolution of the Grand Tour* (London and Portland, OR, 2000), p. 76, p. 97, n. 79.

86 Howe, *Andrea Palladio: The Churches of Rome*, pp. 116–17.

87 Latterly the Franzini guide was published under the title *Roma antica e moderna*.

88 The material details of these two guides I have taken from Schudt, *Le Guide di Roma*, pp. 26–73; and the same Schudt, *Giulio Mancini*, pp. 25–34 and 41–5. The latter work also contains a useful 'Bibliography of Roman Guides from 1544–1674' (Supplement II, pp. 114–30). Totti also published a *Ritratto di Roma antica* (Rome, 1627).

89 Fourteen times between 1644 and 1700.

90 Henry Cogan (tr.), *The Court of Rome and directions for such as shall travel to Rome, how they may view all rarities* (London, 1654). The first part, 'The Court of Rome', was a translation of Girolamo Lunadoro's *Relatione della corte di Roma*, the rest a translation of Martinelli.

91 This appears in his Bull, *Egregia populi Romani*. The details of the significance of the four, five and seven 'principal churches of Rome' may be found in the *Oxford Dictionary of the Christian Church*, ed. F.L. Cross and E.A. Livingstone (Oxford, 1997), pp. 1231, 1414 and under entries for individual churches or saints. Details of the rituals associated with the five and seven churches have been taken from Joseph N. Tylenda S.J., *The Pilgrim's Guide to Rome's Principal Churches* (Collegeville, MS, 1993.) On basilicas, see *An Irish Pilgrim's Guide to Rome: Great Jubilee of the Year 2000* (Dublin, 1999), pp. 64–5.

92 Gregory Martin, *Roma Sancta* (repr. with an introduction by G.B. Parks, Rome, 1969; 1st edn 1581, pp. 17–19).

93 This was reflected in many guidebooks and topographical studies. Two of the most influential were Onuphrio Panvinio's *De Praecipius Urbis Romae sanctioribusque basilicis* (1570) and Marco Attilio Servano's *De Septem Urbis Ecclesis*, the latter published for the Holy Year of 1575. The first part of Martin's *Roma Sancta* is a sort of guidebook to the seven principal churches.

94 San Juan, *Rome: A City out of Print*, p. 60. However, in keeping with modern scholarship that sees conspiracies of 'control' round every corner, I think she underestimates the way in which these guides sought to address a diverse market. She herself remarks (p. 61) that, while monarchical control of printing was strict in France, 'in Rome the printing trade developed as independent businesses and depended much more on the marketplace'. Notwithstanding this minor caveat, for the observations in the last two paragraphs of this chapter, I am heavily indebted to San Juan's fascinating work on Rome guidebooks.

95 San Juan, *Rome: A City out of Print*, p. 61.

96 *Ibid.*, quoting Stephen Greenblatt in *Renaissance Self-Fashioning*, p. 25.

97 Fioravanti Martinelli, *Roma ricercata nel suo sito e nella scuola di tutti gli antiquarii* (Rome, 1644), p. 180.

98 Pompilio Totti, *Ritratto di Roma Moderna* (Rome, 1638), pp. 176–7.

CHAPTER 7

1 Quoted in the extract from Fynes Moryson's *Travels*, in J.G. Links, *Travellers in Europe: Private Records of Journeys by the Great and the Forgotten from Horace to Pepys* (London, 1980), pp. 163–4.

2 Homer, the *Odyssey*, tr. E.V. Rieu (1946); rev. trans. by D.C.H. Rieu (London and New York, 2003), p. 3. Ascham quoted from a translation by a minor Elizabethan poet, Thomas Watson. In this version, Ulysses 'knew many men's manners, and saw many cities' (*The Scholemaster*, 1570).

3 John Evelyn, *The State of France* (London, 1652), prefatory letter, fol. B 3.

4 Quoted in Gerald Curzon, *Wotton and his Worlds* (ExLibris Corporation, USA, 2003), p. 26. Original source: David Cecil, *The Cecils of Hatfield House* (London, 1973), pp. 80, 84.

5 The emphasis on the role of the aristocracy in the Grand Tour has been diminished, or at least challenged, by recent researchers. See József Börocz, 'Travel-Capitalism: The Structure of Europe and the Advent of the Tourist', in *Comparative Studies in Society and History*, 34/4 (October 1992), 710 (citing John Towner, 'The Grand Tour:

A Key Phase on the History of Tourism', in *Annals of Tourism Research*, 12/3 (1985), 305–8) points out that, for the 151 Grand Tours that have been researched for the period from 1547 through 1840, only 16.6 per cent of the participants were really aristocrats, 'although [this class] represented 2.3 per cent to 2.5 per cent of the population and controlled 14.1 to 15.1 per cent of the national income. The rest – that is, 83.4 per cent – of Grand Tour travellers were classified as gentry, clergy, professionals, merchants, or members of the armed forces.'

6   Konrad (Conrad) Celtis (or Celtes) Protucius (né Pickel or Bickel), *Oratio in Gymnasio in Ingelstadio publice recitata* (1492), from Leonard Foster (ed. and tr.), *Selections from Conrad Celtis 1459–1508* (Cambridge, 1948), pp. 6, 103. A useful translation of Celtis's complete text may be found in Peter Elmer, Nick Webb and Roberta Wood, *The Renaissance in Europe: An Anthology* (New Haven and London, 2000), pp. 295 ff, Conrad Celtis, Inaugural Address to the University of Ingolstadt (1492). The translation offered here is sourced to L.W. Spitz (ed.), *The Northern Renaissance* (Englewood Cliffs, NJ, 1972), pp. 15–23, 25–7.

7   William Congreve, *The Way of the World*, Act III, Scene xv. Locke's views were set forth in *Some Thoughts Concerning Education* (London, 1699), pp. 356–7, 375–7. I have taken these references from Clare Howard, *English Travellers of the Renaissance* (New York, 1968; = repr. of 1914 edn), pp. 186 ff.

8   Turler, *The Traveller* (facsimile reprint, Gainsville, FL, 1957), Preface.

9   Ascham, *The Scholemaster*, quoted in Manfred Pfister (ed.), *The Fatal Gift of Beauty: The Italies of British Travellers. An Annotated Anthology* (Amsterdam and Atlanta, GA, 1996), pp. 78–9.

10   Edward Chaney, *The Evolution of the Grand Tour: Anglo-Italian Cultural Relations since the Renaissance* (London and Portland, OR, 2000), pp. 81, 205. See also R.W. Lightbown, 'The Protestant Confessor, or the Tragic History of Mr Mole', in E. Chaney and P. Mack (eds), *England and the Continental Renaissance* (Woodbridge, 1990), pp. 239–56.

11   There were earlier road-books, of course. See Sir Herbert George Fordham, *The Road Books and Itineraries of Great Britain 1570–1850* (Cambridge, 1924). A French road-book for England was Jean Bernard's *Guide des Chemins d'Angleterre* (Paris, 1579).

12   John Ogilby, *Itinerarium angliæ: or, A book of roads: wherein are contain'd the principal road-ways of His Majesty's Kingdom of England and Dominion of Wales: actually admeasured and delineated in a century of whole-sheet copper-sculps and illustrated with the ichnography of the several cities and capital towns/ by John Ogilby* (London, 1675). Ogilby was the 'King's Cosmographer and Geographic Printer' and one of his achievements was to replace the old British mile of 2,428 yards with a new standard one of 1,760 yards. His great work, constantly reproduced in handier 'Pocket Books', held sway from 1675 to 1794 and was translated into French (1759). While the popular road-books of Paterson (1771) and Owen (1799) still largely relied on Ogilby, *Cary's New Itinerary* (1798) was the first to make new distance measurements. The bibliographical history of Ogilby is fascinatingly set out by Sir Herbert George Fordham in 'John Ogilby (1600–1676). His *Britannia* and the British Itineraries of the Eighteenth century', in *Transactions of the Bibliographical Society*, 2nd ser., vol. 6 of *The Library*, 4th ser. (1926).

13   *Le Voyage de France* (1639). Later editions added the posts and appeared under the title *Le fidèle conducteur pour le voyage de France*, compiled by Louis Coulon (1656).

14   Cary was also a successful cartographer and engraver. He moved to what became his legendary shop in St James in 1820 after a fire destroyed his former premises in the Strand. His *New and Correct Enlish Atlas* (1787) became the standard county atlas.

15 Styrian: from the ancient central-southern Habsburg Crown Land of Steiermark (Styria), which is still one of the nine provinces of modern Austria.

16 Antoni Mączak, *Travel in Early Modern Europe* (Cambridge, 1995), p. 27.

17 Giles Barber, 'The English-language Guide Book to Europe up to 1870', in Robin Myers and Michael Harris (eds), *Journeys through the Market: Travel, Travellers and the Book Trade* (New Castle, DE, and Folkestone, UK, 1999), p. 95.

18 In London, in the early to mid-nineteenth century, Samuel Leigh specialised in guidebooks and initiated the successful series Leigh's Picture of England, which he also published in French for the use of visiting foreigners, together with French–English phrasebooks. There were now other firms concentrating on travel and guides, such as Sherwood or Neely and Jones, all paving the way for the great John Murray to annex the genre.

19 For details of Sir Robert Dallington's *A Survey of the Great Duke's State of Tuscany* (1605), I have drawn on Edward Chaney's informative chapter on this topic in Chaney, *Evolution of the Grand Tour*, pp. 143–60.

20 Mączak, *Travel in Early Modern Europe*, p. 26.

21 Etienne Rey, *Éloge du Mensonge* (Paris, 1925), p. 11.

22 According to vol. 22 of *Biographie Nationale de Belgique* (1914–20), pp. 14 ff., Schott did indeed trace his family back to 'the illlustrious Scottish line of Douglas'. He was born and died in Antwerp, where he was a Senator on the City Council. The success of his *Itinerarii* tempted him to try and repeat the idea with *Itinerarii Italiae, Germaniaeque Libri III. Ad haec iter Galliae et Hispaniae* (Antwerp, 1620), which was a complete failure, perhaps an indication of the extent to which travellers were still focused on Italy.

23 The full title was *Itinerarii Italiae rerumque Romanarum libri tres* (Antwerp, 1600).

24 'Stephanus Vinandus Pighius Campenses' (actually Stephan Wynants Pighe) was an archaeologist when that profession was in its infancy. His biography of his charge, chiefly intended as a memorial for the Cleves ducal archive, was published by Plantin in Antwerp in 1587 as *Hercules Prodicius, seu, principis iuventutis vita et peregrinatio*. It combines an account of the young man's deeds (though he was only 20 when he died), together with a description of their sightseeing together and notes on Pighius' own travels. This work, too, lifted chunks from other authors, chiefly Alberti's *Descrittione di tutta l'Italia*, which first appeared in 1550.

25 E.S. De Beer, 'François Scott's *Itinerario d'Italia*' (London, 1942; repr. from *The Library* in the *Transactions of the Bibliographical Society* (Oxford, 1942), 4th ser., 22/2–3 (September–December 1942).

26 Lorenz Schrader, *Monumentorum Italiae, quae hoc nostro saeculo & a Christianis posita sunt, libri quattuor* (Helmstedt, 1592).

27 The Latin edition had appeared in 1597. The German edition appeared in 1603: J.J. Boissard, *Topographia urbis Romae: Das ist eygentliche Beschreibung der Statt Rom . . .* (Frankfurt, 1603).

28 Ortelius' maps published under this title were the first to be entirely executed in copperplate engravings and went through many editions. See *Old European Cities: Thirty-two 16th Century Maps and Texts from the* Civitates orbis terrarum *of Georg Braun & Franz Hogenburg with a Description by Ruthardt Oehme of Early Map-making Techniques* (London, 1968), p. 10.

29 Fra Leandro Alberti, *Descrittione di tutta l'Italia* (Bologna, 1550; 2nd edn Venice, 1561). *Inter alia*, Alberti included information about important local artists, architects, and occasionally collectors and their collections.

30   A discussion of the individual works that Schottus thought worthy of mention, and
      of the possible influence of Giampaolo Lomazzo's treatise, *Idea del Tempio della
      Pittura* based on the mystical number seven, is to be found in Ludwig Schudt, 'Das
      Itinerarium Italiae des Franciscus Schottus', in *Adolph Goldschmidt zu seinem
      siebenzigsten Geburtstag am 15. Januar 1933* (Berlin, 1935).

31   '*Ein höchst elendes Geschmiere . . .*'. J.J. Volkmann in *Historisch-kritische Nachrichten von
      Italien welche eine genaue Beschreibung dieses Landes, der Sitten und Gebräuche, der
      Regierungs form, Handlung, Oekonomie, des Zustandes der Wissenschaften und insonderheit
      der Werke der Kunst nebst einer Beurtheilung derselben enthalten. Aus den neuesten
      französischen und englischen Reisebeschreibungen und aus eignen Anmerkungen
      zusammengetragen* (Leipzig, 1770), vol. 1, xiii.

32   G.B. Parks (ed.), *The History of Italy (1549) by William Thomas* (Ithaca, NY, 1963),
      xvii–xviii. This is an abridgement of 162 pages of the original's 445, taken from the
      copy in the Folger Shakespeare Library, Washington DC. Thomas also compiled the
      Principal Rules of Italian Grammar, with a Dictionarie (1550), the first such work
      published in England.

33   Parks, *The History of Italy*, p. 50.

34   See Mathis Leibetseder, *Die Kavalierstour: Adlige Erziehungsreisen im 17. und 18.
      Jahrhundert* (Cologne, Weimar and Vienna, 2004), p. 19, for a detailed discussion of
      the origins of the phrase 'Grand Tour'. According to Leibetseder, in the early
      seventeenth century, the English spoke of a *Grand Tour*, the Dutch of a *Grooten Tour*
      and the Germans of the *Grossen Tour* with specific reference to a tour of the French
      provinces.

35   See e.g. the comments of Sara Warneke in *Images of the Educational Traveller in Early
      Modern England* (Leiden, New York and Cologne, 1995), p. 3.

36   R. Rowlands, *The Post. For divers parts of the world, with a description of the antiquities of
      divers famous cities in Europe* (London, 1576).

37   Sir Thomas Palmer, *An Essay of the meanes how to make our Trauailes, into forraine
      Countries, the more profitable and honourable* (London, 1606).

38   Sir John Melton, *A Sixe-Folde Politician* (London, 1609).

39   See Mączak, *Travel in Early Modern Europe*, p. 79.

40   Palmer, *An Essay of the meanes*, pp. 1B and 17, quoted in Warneke, *Images of the
      Educational Traveller*, p. 5.

41   See e.g. Brian Donan, *Ladies of the Grand Tour* (London, 2001).

42   Richard Lassels, *The Voyage of Italy or a Compleat Journey through Italy in Two Parts*
      (Paris, 1670), introduction (unnumbered.)

43   *Ibid.*, Part Two, p. 198, quoted in Mączak, *Travel in Early Modern Europe*, p. 245.

44   *Voyage of the Lady Catherine Whetenhall from Brussels to Italy in the Holy Year, 1650*, which
      mutated into a later work, *The Description of Italy*, both providing raw material for
      Lassels's celebrated summation of his Italian knowledge in a guidebook
      posthumously published and entitled *The Voyage of Italy* (1670). The trip with Lady
      Catherine and her husband ended tragically with her death in childbirth at Padua.

45   Edward Chaney, *The Grand Tour and the Great Rebellion. Richard Lassels and the* 'Voyage
      of Italy' *in the Seventeenth Century* (Geneva, 1988), p. 120.

46   Although Raymond's book has been characterised as the 'the first English
      guidebook to Italy' (*inter alia*, by Chaney in *Evolution of the Grand Tour*, p. 104), all
      agree that it was heavily dependent on existing material and not an original work
      like that of Lassels.

47   E.S. De Beer, 'Richard Lassels', in *Notes and Queries*, 169 (25 April 1931), 292 ff.

48   *The Travels Of An English Gentleman From London to Rome, On Foot* (London, 1704, and several variants).

49   De Beer, 'Richard Lassels'.

50   Giovanni Pietro Bellori (1615–96), *Le vite de' pittore, scultori e architetti moderni* (Rome, 1672).

51   These and the foregoing quotations are taken from the unnumbered Preface of Richard Lassels, *The Voyage of Italy or a Compleat Journey through Italy in Two Parts with the Character of the People, and Description of the Chief Towns, Churches, Monasteries, Tombs, Libraries, Pallaces, Villas, Gardens, Pictures, Statues and Antiquities as also of the Interest, Government, Riches, Force &c of all the Princes. With Instructions Concerning Travel* (Paris, 1670). I have used the copy in the Getty Library, Los Angeles.

52   Chaney, *The Grand Tour and the Great Rebellion*, p. 141.

53   Chaney, *Evolution of the Grand Tour*, p. 113.

54   Joseph Burke, 'The Grand Tour and the Rule of Taste', in R.F. Brissenden (ed.), *Studies in the Eighteenth Century: Papers Presented at the David Nichol Smith Seminar, Canberra, 1966* (Canberra, 1968), p. 235, n. 13.

55   *Observations faites par un voyageur en Angleterre* (1698).

56   Percy G. Adams, *Travelers and Travel Liars, 1660–1800* (Berkeley and Los Angeles, 1962), p. 180.

57   Chaney, *The Grand Tour and the Great Rebellion*, p. 383. The story of 'Pope Joan' was of course a gift for secular propagandists. The most amusing account is the novel by the Greek nineteenth-century writer Emmanuel Royidis (*Papissa Joanna*, Athens, 1886), publication of which caused the author to be excommunicated by the Orthodox Church and the book to be banned until 1920. There is a free English translation by Lawrence Durrell (*Pope Joan*, London, 1960 (rev. edn)).

58   Quoted in Chaney, *The Grand Tour and the Great Rebellion*, p. 427, n. 98.

59   François Maximilien Misson, *Nouveau voyage d'Italie, fait en l'année 1688* (The Hague, 1691). There were further editions in 1694, 1702, 1713 and 1717. The last two-volume English edition was in 1699, thereafter the four-volume edition appeared in 1704, 1714 and 1734. There was a German translation (Leipzig, 1713), and a Dutch translation (Utrecht, 1704). It is hardly surprising that there was no Italian edition.

60   Judith Adler (in 'The Origins of Sightseeing', *Annals of Tourism Research*, 16 (1989), 20) quotes the view of Hermann Harder in *Le Président de Brosses et le voyage en Italie au dix-huitième siècle* (Geneva, 1981) that the fictive letter was an act of homage to the autopsy generally aspired to. 'Even when travels were written up after a journey's completion, their authors often sought to create an impression of authenticity by adopting the literary form of fictive dated letters.' (Adler, p. 20; Harder, p. 70.)

61   In *A New Voyage to Italy*, the English translation of Maximilien Misson (London, 1695), vol. 2, pp. 64–73.

62   Lassels, *The Voyage of Italy*, Preface.

63   Misson, *Nouveau voyage*, vol. 1, p. 289.

64   *Ibid.*, vol. 2, pp. 5–6.

65   See R.S. Pine-Coffin, *Bibliography of British and American Travel in Italy to 1860* (Florence, 1974.) Subsequently a pamphlet, 'Additions and Corrections', was published (1981) as an offprint of an article in *La Bibliofilia*. This indispensable work also contains references to a number of guides translated into English from European languages.

66   Taken from the biographical details in the second German edition, translated by John George Keysler into English as *Travels through Germany, Bohemia, Hungary,*

Switzerland, Italy and Lorrain. Giving a True and Just Description of the Present State of those Countries, their Natural, Literary and Political History; Manners, Laws, Commerce, Manufactures, Painting, Sculpture, Architecture, Coins, Antiquities, Curiosities of Art and Nature etc, 4 vols (London, 1757). I have used the copy in the Getty library, which is illustrated with copper plate engravings from 'drawings taken on the spot'.

67   *Ibid.*, vol. 4, pp. 10, 79–80.

68   *Ibid.*, vol. 1, p. 445.

69   See John Towner, *A Historical Geography of Recreation and Tourism in the Western World 1540–1940* (Chichester and New York, 1996), pp. 107 ff.

70   Thomas Nugent, *Grand Tour Containing an Exact Description of Most of the Cities, Towns, and Remarkable Places of Europe, together with a Distinct Account of the Post-Roads and Stages, with their Respective Distances. Through Holland, Flanders, Germany, Denmark, Sweden, Russia, Poland, Italy, France, Spain and Portugal. Likewise Directions Relating to the Manner and Expence of Travelling from one Place and Country to Another. AS ALSO Occasional Remarks on the Present State of Trade, as well as the Liberal Arts and Sciences, in each Respective Country*, 4 vols (London, 1749), iii.

71   *Ibid.*, vol. 3, p. 64.

72   *Ibid.*, viii.

73   Louis Dutens, *Itinéraire des routes les plus fréquentées, ou journal d'un voyage aux villes principales de l'Europe* (Paris, 1775, London 1782). The indefatigable Dutens (1730–1812) was, like Misson, a Huguenot refugee in England. According to the *Dictionary of National Biography* (*DNB*), he decided to leave France after the Archbishop of Tours forcibly placed his sister in a convent. He entered the British diplomatic service and later acted as bear-leader for the son of the Duke of Northumberland. Converted to Anglicanism, he was given a living in Northumberland, where his French accent and foreign garb excited unfavourable comment, but his passion for billiards seemed to indicate that he was basically harmless.

74   *DNB* (new edition).

75   Nugent, *Grand Tour*, vol. 3, p. 49.

76   John Moore MD (1729–1802) had visited St Cloud and Versailles with the novelist, fellow Scot and fellow doctor Tobias Smollett in 1750. From 1772 he acted as bear-leader to the young Duke of Hamilton on a continental tour lasting five years. In 1779 he published the first fruits of this tour, *A View of Society and Manners in France, Switzerland and Germany*. He met Frederick the Great in Berlin and became well acquainted with Prince Charles Edward Stuart in Florence. Carlyle drew substantially on his account of Paris in 1792 in his history of the French Revolution.

77   In criticising such practices, Moore was evidently pushing at an open door: Grand Duke Leopold of Habsburg-Lorraine shortly thereafter (1786) abolished the death penalty in Tuscany and the instruments of torture were ceremonially burned in the Bargello courtyard. While the influence of the celebrated penologist Cesare Beccaria's denunciation of capital punishment and torture was doubtless crucial, one should not forget that the Grand Duke's mother, Maria Theresia, under the influence of her adviser Sonnenfels and her co-ruling son and Leopold's brother, Joseph, after much hesitation, was finally persuaded in 1776 to abolish torture in the other Habsburg realms, except Hungary. The death penalty was abolished by Joseph II in 1781 after his mother's death, but reintroduced for high treason in 1795, and in 1803 for other serious crimes. Re-abolished in 1919, the interwar corporative state again introduced it. It was not until 1950 that it was finally abolished (for courts martial only in 1968).

78   Volkmann was also the author of several other works written to a similar formula: *Neueste Reisen durch Schottland und Ireland etc* (1784), *Neueste Reisen durch Frankreich* (1787–8), *Neueste Reisen durch Spanien* (1785), *Neueste Reisen durch England etc* (1781–2), *Neueste Reisen durch die Vereinigten Niederlande* (1783).

79   Joseph-Jérôme Lefrançais de Lalande (1732–1807) was Jesuit-educated and trained to be an *avocat*. Finding the law dull, he turned to science and became the most celebrated astronomer of his day, working, *inter alia*, for Frederick the Great. His remarkable *Voyage* was published in 1768 in eight duodecimo volumes, and was quite subsidiary to his oeuvre as a whole (the *Nouvelle Biographie*, while citing numerous scientific works, does not even mention the *Voyage*). Nevertheless, it was more comprehensive than many books that had taken their authors twice as long to compile, '*Contenant l'Histoire & les Anecdotes les plus singulières de l'Italie, & sa description; les Mœurs, les Usages, le Gouvernement, le Commerce, la Littérature, les Arts, l'Histoire Naturelle, & les Antiquités; avec des jugements sur les Ouvrages de Peinture, Sculpture & Architecture, & les Plans de toutes les grandes villes d'Italie.*' It covered the whole of mainland Italy north of Naples. A true son of the Enlightenment, Lalande spent many fruitless days of his sojourn in Rome negotiating with the Vatican to have Copernicus and Galileo removed from the Index. At the same time, the *Biographie Universelle* tells us he was personally pious, an admirer of Charles Borromeo and St Francis of Assisi, and that he robustly refuted many of the allegations against the Roman Church levelled by Protestant writers such as Burnet or Grosley.

80   Joseph-Jérôme Lefrançais de Lalande, *Voyage en Italie*, 3rd edn (Geneva, 1790), vol. 1, p. 23.

81   Volkmann, *Historisch-kritische Nachrichten von Italien*, xx.

82   *Ibid.*, vol 1, xx.

83   Richard Saint-Non, *Voyage pittoresque, ou Description des royaumes de Naples et de Sicile*, 5 vols (Paris, 1781–5).

84   For a detailed and perceptive account of the treatment of Naples in the Grand Tour guidebooks, see Melissa Calarescu, 'Looking for Virgil's Tomb: The End of the Grand Tour and the Cosmopolitan Ideal in Europe', in Jás Elsner and Joan-Pau Rubiés (eds), *Voyages and Visions: Towards a Cultural History of Travel* (London, 1999), pp. 138–61.

85   J.W. Goethe, *Italian Journey*, tr. W.H. Auden and Elizabeth Mayer (London and New York, 1970), pp. 172, 317, 146.

86   Virtuoso: the term was current in English from the seventeenth century and meant a gentleman scholar with superior knowledge and excellent taste. From the Italian *virtù*, Latin *virtus*, the word is associated with 'objects of virtue', i.e. works of art admired for their workmanship, rarity or antiquity.

87   Eduardus [Edward] Wright, *Some Observations made in Travelling through France, Italy &c. in the Years MDCCXX, MDCCXXI, and MDCCXXII*, 2 vols, 2nd edn (London, 1764; 1st edn *c.* 1723), v–x. Compare this with Horace Walpole's remark, admittedly made in jest: 'I am far gone in medals, lamps, idols, prints &c. . . . I would buy the Coliseum if I could', quoted in the leaflet for the Tate Gallery's exhibition 'Grand Tour', October 1996–January 1997.

88   Wright, *Some Observations*, x.

89   De Beer comments that works of art feature prominently in the guides for single Italian towns from the seventeenth century onwards, though some limit coverage to pictures. Early guidebooks to individual buildings include P. Morigia's guide of 1597

to Milan cathedral and G. Stringa's guide to St Mark's in Venice (1610). See E.S. De Beer, 'The Development of the Guide-Book until the Early Nineteenth Century', in *The Journal of the British Archaeological Association*, 3rd ser., 14–16 (1951–53), 42.

90 Mączak, *Travel in Early Modern Europe*, p. 206, comments maliciously: 'If we are to believe the guidebooks published in Catholic countries, he must have been a prolific artist indeed.'

91 Gottfried Wilhelm Leibniz (1646–1716), in *Remarks on the three Volumes entitled 'Characteristics of Men, Manners, Opinions, Times . . .'*, taken from *idem, Philosophical Papers and Letters*, ed. and tr. LeRoy E. Loemker, 2 vols (Chicago, 1956), vol. 2, p. 1031.

92 Sándor Radnóti, 'The Origins of a New Reception of Antiquity: Autopsy and the Transformation of Perception/Vision in Winckelmann' (forthcoming). I am grateful to Professor Radnóti for allowing me to see this article in manuscript.

93 Mr Richardson, Sen. and Jun., *An Account of some of the Statues, Bas-reliefs, Drawings and Pictures in Italy with Remarks* (London, 1722), pp. 3 ff.

94 *Ibid.*, pp. 3 ff.

95 *Ibid.*, p. 3.

96 Radnóti, 'The Origins of a New Reception of Antiquity'.

97 Jonathan Richardson, *Two Discourses* (London, 1719). The quotation is taken from the second discourse, *The Science of the Connoisseur*, as reprinted in Charles Harrison, Paul Wood and Jason Gaiger (eds), *Art In Theory 1648–1815. An Anthology of Changing Ideas* (Oxford, 2000), p. 334.

98 William Aglionby, *Painting Illustrated in Three Discourses* (1685). The quotation is taken from the extract reprinted in Harrison, Wood and Gaiger, *Art in Theory*, pp. 40, 41.

99 Compare Henry Peacham's essay 'Of Travaile' included in his *Compleat Gentleman* (1622), pp. 126–7: 'Would you see a pattern of the funeral pile, burnt at the canonisation of the Roman emperors? Would you see how the Augur's hat and *lituus* [staff] were made? Would you see true and undoubted models of their temples . . .? Repair to old coins, and . . . there shall you find them excellently represented.'

100 Edward Gibbon, *Autobiography* (London, 1911). This quotation taken from Pfister, *The Fatal Gift of Beauty*, vol. 15 in *Internationale Forschungen zur Allgemeinen und Vergleichenden Literaturwissenschaft* (Amsterdam and Atlanta, GA, 1999), p. 83.

101 Joseph Addison, *Some Remarks on Several Parts of Italy etc* (London, 1705). This remark is taken from the 1761 edition and quoted by Towner, *A Historical Geography of Recreation and Tourism*, p. 117.

102 Quoted in E.G. Cox, *Reference Guide to the Literature of Travel* (London, 1948; = repr. of 1938 edn), p. 121. The antiquarian Thomas Hearne (1678–1735) was Assistant Keeper of the Bodleian Library until forced to resign because of his Jacobite sympathies. He published John Leland's *Itinerary* (1710–12) discussed in the previous chapter.

103 Judith Adler, 'Origins of Sightseeing', in *Annals of Tourism Research*, 16 (1989), 18.

104 See Walter E. Houghton Jr., 'The English Virtuoso in the Seventeenth Century' (II), in *Journal of the History of Ideas*, III (1942), 192.

105 Thomas Martyn, *The English Connoisseur; containing an account of whatever is curious in painting, sculpture etc., in the palaces and seats of the nobility and principal gentry of England both in town and country*, 2 vols (London, 1766). This extract quoted in Bernard Denvir (ed.), *The Eighteenth Century: Art, Design and Society 1689–1789* (London and New York, 1983), p. 178.

106 Horace Walpole, *A Description of Strawberry Hill* (London, 1784).

107 Esther Moir, *The Discovery of Britain: The English Tourists 1540 to 1840* (London, 1964), p. 60.

108 Adrian Tinniswood, *The Polite Tourist: A History of Country House Visiting* (The National Trust, 1998), pp. 91–103.

109 Giovanni Pietro Bellori, *L'Idea del pittore, del sculptore, e del architetto*, published as the preface to Bellori's *Le vite de' pittori, scultori e architetti moderni* (Rome, 1672). This quotation is from the translation by Victor A. Velen, in Erwin Panofsky, *Idea: A Concept of Art Theory* (1960; rev. from 1924 edn), tr. Joseph J.S. Peake (Columbia, 1968), Appendix II, pp. 155–72. It is conveniently available in the source book by Harrison, Wood and Gaiger, *Art in Theory*, pp. 96–101.

110 It belonged to the collection of classical statues acquired by Cardinal Ferdinando de' Medici, who bought the Villa Medici on the Pincio in 1576. The Uffizi catalogue states that it was purchased at the beginning of the seventeenth century. I am indebted to Alta Macadam for this information. François Perrier was the first to engrave the Venus in his anthology of statues dating to 1638. Francis Haskell and Nicholas Penny state in their *Taste and the Antique: The Lure of Classical Sculpture 1500–1900* (New Haven and London, 1981) that it may have been acquired from the Palazzo Valle–Rustici–Bufalo, or be the one appearing on a Medici inventory of 1598. They conclude that its provenance remains uncertain.

111 According to Haskell and Penny (*Taste and the Antique*, p. 56), the sculpture was one of several moved to the Uffizi because Grand Duke Cosimo's doctors thought he needed more exercise, so he filled his galleries with suitably improving works to give more point to his daily ramble. This does not imply an over-reverential attitude to the *Medici Venus*. However, the same authors observe that the perceived erotic charms of the sculpture caused embarrassment during the pontificate of the puritanical Innocent XI (1676–89), and that this was why he gave the necessary permission for it to be removed from the papal realms to Florence in 1677. The pope is said later to have regretted giving his permission.

112 The extraordinary development of the *Mona Lisa* cult, which has obvious parallels with the quasi-mythical status of the *Medici Venus* for Grand Tourists, is documented in Donald Sassoon's coruscating *Mona Lisa: The History of the World's Most Famous Painting* (London, 2002). For an idiosyncratic Lacanian look at 'why we look at art and what, indeed, we might be hoping to find', which deals, *inter alia*, with the psychology of mass adoration of this particular picture, see Darian Leader, *Stealing the Mona Lisa: What Art Stops Us from Seeing* (London, 2002). See also Roy McMullen, *Mona Lisa: The Picture and the Myth* (New York, 1975).

113 See also Adams, *Travelers and Travel Liars*, p. 187, for some penetrating observations on the tyranny of contemporary taste.

114 Haskell and Penny, in *Taste and the Antique*, p. 328, quote Guido Mansuelli, *Galleria degli Uffizi: le sculture*, 2 vols (Rome, 1958–61) to the effect that the Venus is 'a copy, perhaps Athenian, and of the first century BC, of a bronze original derived from the type of the Cnidian Venus of Praxiteles by one of the sons or immediate followers of the master'.

115 Napoleon took the *Medici Venus* to the Louvre and commissioned Canova to make a replacement for it, which is now in the Palazzo Pitti in Florence. Earlier the Florentines had turned down an English offer to store it at Gibraltar during the war, and had sent it to Palermo. However, the King of the Two Sicilies agreed, under duress, to hand it over to the French in 1802, and it arrived in the Louvre in 1803.

116 Martin Robertson, *A History of Greek Art* (Cambridge, 1975), vol. 1, p. 549. 'In treatment of body, face and hair, the Medici [Venus] stands closer to Praxiteles than

the Capitoline [Venus], where a rather fifth-century coldness of feature is combined with an ornate hair-style and with matronly forms: heavy breasts and rolls over the hips rendered with some particularity . . . These dull copies, restored and worked over (a version of the Medici in New York is better in these respects) of statues adapted by conventional minds from a creation of great originality, are for us among the most charmless remnants of antiquity. For other ages, more of the original light shone through them than we can detect; and had it not been for such as these, Botticelli's Venus would never have risen quite as she does. They have served a turn in the history of art.'

117 I am indebted to Alta Macadam for pointing this out to me. She also notes that the statue is currently catalogued as a copy of a Greek original of the second century BC. Some other scholars attribute it to the first century BC and are uncertain as to whether it is a copy of a Greek original.

118 Lalande, *Voyage en Italie*, vol. 2, p. 212.

119 John Northall, *Travels through Italy etc* (London, 1766), pp. 57–8.

120 Wright, *Some Observations*, 2nd edn (London, 1764), p. 406.

121 Johann Joachim Winckelmann, *Reflections on the Imitation of Greek Works in Painting and Sculpture* (1755). This quotation is taken from the translation by Elfriede Heyer and Roger C. Norton (1987), reprinted in Harrison, Wood and Gaiger, *Art in Theory*, p. 454.

122 Gibbon, *Autobiography*, quoted in Pfister, *The Fatal Gift of Beauty*, p. 84.

123 The restoration of the arms was credited in the eighteenth century to Bandinelli, in the nineteenth to Bernini, but is now known to have been carried out by Ercole Ferrara after the statue was damaged in transit to Florence in 1677. See Haskell and Penny, *Taste and the Antique*, p. 336.

124 *Ibid.*, p. 99.

125 Tobias Smollett, *Travels through France and Italy*, 2nd edn, 2 vols (London, 1766), vol. 2, pp. 63–4.

126 Laurence Sterne, *A Sentimental Journey through France and Italy* (London, 1768).

127 Perhaps this process had begun somewhat earlier. Haskell and Penny (*Taste and the Antique*, p. 326) draw attention to a marginal note to the English translation of the fifth edition (1739) of Misson's *Nouveau Voyage*, which disowns his purple prose on the subject of the Venus as 'excessive' and adds sharp criticism on the inelegance of the statue's hands and feet.

128 George Gordon, Lord Byron, *Childe Harold's Pilgrimage* (London, 1817), Canto IV.

129 Lady Morgan, *L'Italie*, 4 vols, translated from the English (Paris, 1821) vol. 2, p. 395. The first edition of the English version was also published in 1821, with a second edition in three volumes in the same year. Byron considered it 'a really excellent book', but the conservative establishment was outraged by her pro-French stance.

130 Joseph Forsyth, *Remarks on Antiquities, Arts, and Letters during an Excursion in Italy in the Years 1802 and 1803*, ed. Kenneth Crook [under the title of *Forsyth's Italy*] (Newark, NJ, and London, 2001), p. 28.

131 The modern name is Cape Krio, south-west Turkey.

132 Lalande, *Voyage en Italie*, vol. 2, p. 215.

133 Pliny the Elder, *Natural History: A Selection*, tr. John F. Healy (London and New York, 1991), p. 346.

134 Anna Brownell Jameson, 'Diary of an Ennuyée', in *Visits and Sketches at Home and Abroad* (London, 1834). This quotation taken from Pfister, *The Fatal Gift of Beauty*, p. 151.

135 William Hazlitt, *Notes of a Journey through France and Italy* (1826). The quotation is taken from Pfister, *The Fatal Gift of Beauty*, pp. 151–2.
136 'This author is in fact one of the most inaccurate, unsatisfactory writers that have in our times attained a temporary reputation, and is very seldom to be trusted even when he speaks of objects which he must be presumed to have seen . . . his reader may very fairly esteem all his political portraits and deductions as so much waste paper, the moment they cease to assist, and more particularly if they obstruct, his actual survey . . .' And so on. Lord Byron, *The Complete Poetical Works*, ed. Jerome J. McGann, 'Childe Harold's Pilgrimage' (Oxford, 1980), Byron's notes to the poem, vol. 2, pp. 262, 263.
137 *The Letters of Percy Bysshe Shelley*, ed. Frederick L. Jones (Oxford, 1964), vol. 2, p. 54.
138 The Revd John Chetwode Eustace, *A Classical Tour Through Italy . . . with An Additional Preface and Translation of the Various Quotations from Ancient & Modern Authors*, illustrated with a map of Italy, plans of churches, an index etc., 6th edn, 4 vols (London 1821), vi.
139 *Ibid.*, pp. 66–7.
140 It has been pointed out to me that Eustace's main difficulty here is in accustoming his eye, nurtured on the English romantic style of garden, to the formal layout of Renaissance or baroque gardens. These would have reminded him too much of the formal French gardens, and reawakened his Gallophobic *ressentiment*.
141 C.P. Brand, *Italy and the English Romantics* (Cambridge, 1957), p. 228.
142 Barber, 'The English Guide Book to Europe up to 1870', p. 101.
143 The publication history of Mariana Starke's book, much enlarged and revised is as follows: *Letters from Italy* [written between 1792 and 1798], 2 vols, 1800; the second edition of the same, in which she included accounts of Germany, Portugal, Spain, France, Holland, Denmark, Norway, Sweden, Russia and Poland, 1815; *Travels on the Continent* (John Murray), 1820; *Information and Directions for Travellers on the Continent* (the fifth edition of her original work), 1824. The eighth edition (1833) was entitled *Travels in Europe*. Sicily was included from the sixth edition (1828).
144 Joseph Forsyth, *Remarks on Antiquities, Arts, and Letters during an excursion in Italy in the years 1802 and 1803* (London, 1813; enlarged edn published by John Murray in 1816, 1824 and 1835). The text, with others, was pillaged for *Galignani's Traveller's Guide through Italy* (Paris, 1822). I have used the excellent reprint edited and with a valuable introduction by Keith Crook (Newark, NJ, and London, 2001).
145 Patrick Brydone, *A Tour through Sicily and Malta* (1773) and Henry Swinburne, *Travels in the Two Sicilies 1770–80* (1783–5).
146 He singled out for particular criticism in this respect Mariano Vasi's *Itinerario istruttivo di Roma* (Rome, 1791) and André Mannazale's *Itinéraire instructif de Rome et ses Environs* (Rome, 1802), works which he had used, and found wanting, on his own tour. However, they seem to have been the most successful of the local guides at that time.
147 See Forsyth, *Remarks on Antiquities*, ed. Crook, xxxvii.
148 Quoted in *ibid.*, xvii.
149 Quoted in *ibid.*, xv. Byron's remarks about Forsyth may be found in *Byron's Letters and Journals*, ed. Leslie A. Marchand (London, 1976), 5: 221, 224, 227.
150 Forsyth, *Remarks on Antiquities*, ed. Crook, xlvi.
151 *The Edinburgh Review* was founded by Frances Jeffrey in 1802, and originally allowed both Tory and Whig contributions. *The Quarterly Review*, founded in 1809 by John Murray at the instigation of Walter Scott, was designed, in Crook's words, 'to provide

a Tory and anti-Jacobin answer to *The Edinburgh*'. The latter journal took up the cause of Eustace (though it had to brush aside the fact that he was a Catholic, albeit latitudinarian). Forsyth (from the second edition of his book) was a Murray author, so it was to be expected that *The Quarterly* would treat him favourably. Other journals, such as the High Church *British Critic*, weighed in, but in general it is hard to interpret the differing standpoints in purely ideological terms. Then as now, commerce and literary cliquery appeared to have had as much to do with the judgements handed down, Forsyth's moderate and somewhat ambivalent ideological stance making him a harder target for opponents than Eustace's opinionated and rather pompous text.

152 See Forsyth, *Remarks on Antiquities*, ed. Crook, xxxvi.

CHAPTER 8

1 Murray was also the first to publish a sovereign's letters when the firm brought out a nine-volume edition of those by Queen Victoria between 1900 and 1932.

2 In Disraeli's novel *Sybil* Lord de Mowbray feared that the railways encouraged a 'dangerous tendency to equality' and fostered 'the levelling spirit of the age', quoted in Piers Brendon, *Thomas Cook: 150 Years of Tourism* (London, 1991), p. 15.

3 Robert Gildea, *Barricades and Borders: Europe 1800–1914* (Oxford and New York, 1989), p. 249.

4 *Ibid.*, p. 254.

5 J.A.R. Pimlott, *The Englishman's Holiday: A Social History* (London, 1947; repr. Hassocks, 1976), p. 191.

6 Theodor Fontane, *Modernes Reisen: eine Plauderei* (1873); repr. in *idem, Von, vor und nach der Reise: Plaudereien und kleine Geschichten* (Berlin, 1999, p. 7 and ff.). Visitors to Emperor Franz Joseph's villa at Bad Ischl may enjoy an even more gruesome reminder of the slaughtering zeal of royalty, as they walk up staircases whose walls are densely studded with reproachful-looking chamois heads. Archduke Franz Ferdinand's gamebook, a memorial to woodland bloodbaths, is a highlight of the tour of his country house at Konopiště in Bohemia.

7 Daniel J. Boorstin, *The Image: A Guide to Pseudo-Events in America*, 25th Anniversary Edition (New York, 1985), pp. 85 and 103.

8 For remarks on the terminology of travel literature, see also Giles Barber, 'The English-language Guidebook to Europe up to 1870', in Robin Myers and Michael Harris (eds), *Journeys through the Market: Travel, Travellers and the Book Trade* (New Castle, DE, and Folkestone, UK, 1999), p. 94.

9 Adam Walker, *A Tour from London to the Lakes: Containing Natural, Oeconomical and Literary Observations, Made in the Summer of 1791, By a Gentleman* (London, 1792), quoted in Ian Ousby, *The Englishman's England: Taste, Travel and the Rise of Tourism* (Cambridge, 1990), p. 19. The double standards present in most discussions of tourism were drily summed up in Evelyn Waugh's comment: 'The tourist is the other fellow.' Lucy R. Lippard, in a thoughtful book on the subject (*On the Beaten Track: Tourism, Art and Place*, New York, 1999), remarks (p. 11) that it is 'useless and hypocritical, though not difficult, to be generally "against" tourism' and complains of the 'dyspeptic and melancholy tone in which tourism is most often discussed'.

10 Barber, 'The English-language Guidebook to Europe up to 1870', pp. 94, 102–3.

11 Arthur Sketchley, *Mrs Brown on the Grand Tour* (London, n.d.), p. 95.

12 Another great family firm and famous name in guidebook publishing, A&C Black, lasted almost as long before being taken over by Bloomsbury in 2001. Charles Black was its last Chairman.

13 'The author's always right' proclaimed the last Chairman of the firm before its sale, and it is true that, having carefully chosen an author for its list, the firm almost always displayed great tact in handling its valuable properties.

14 It is a measure of the firm's even-handedness (not without an eye to profitable controversy) that it also published Bishop Wilberforce's attack on Darwin's theories. An indication of the publisher's financial canniness may perhaps be inferred from the indignation of Jane Austen's brother, Henry, who complained in 1815 of Murray's stinginess in paying less for the copyright of *Sense and Sensibility*, *Mansfield Park* and *Emma* than his sister had cleared on 'one very moderate edition of *Mansfield Park*'.

15 Bruce Redford, *Venice and the Grand Tour* (New Haven and London, 1996), p. 115.

16 The firm was also the first to collaborate with a broadcaster when Kenneth Clark's famous series, *Civilisation*, was published in book form in the 1960s. This too was in their travelogue tradition, a survey of the sights by an aesthetically and historically educated eye.

17 Marianna Starke, *Information and Directions for Travellers on the Continent*, new revised and enlarged edn (Paris, 1829), Introduction.

18 Thomas Martyn, in his *Gentleman's Guide in his Tour through Italy* (London, 1787), did occasionally use exclamation marks to highlight exceptional merit, but his system was random and applied almost exclusively to inns.

19 The quotations from Kilvert and Huxley are taken from *Abroad: A Book of Travels* compiled by Jon Evans (London, 1965), pp. 26–7.

20 The edition of 1820 bore the title *Travels on the Continent: Written for the Use and Particular Information of Travellers*. To the Italian core material, the author added routes and information on Germany, Austria, Holland, Spain, Portugal, Scandinavia and Russia. Most of this was written up from secondary sources, and when John Murray himself visited some of these countries for his research, he complained that there were so many errors in Starke as to render the book virtually useless. Unfortunately, Starke now had the bit between her teeth, as the sales and translations of her work multiplied, and rushed out further editions, to the private dismay of Murray.

21 Edmund Boyce, *The Belgian Traveller or a Complete Guide through the United Netherlands* (London, 1815).

22 The first English edition of Johann Gottfried Ebel, *Traveller's Guide through Switzerland* was published in London in 1817, being a bastardisation and plagiarism of Ebel's *Anleitung auf die nützlichste und genußvollste Art die Schweiz zu reisen* (2nd edn, 1804) by one Daniel Wall. Other foreign guides that had been translated around this time included J.B. Romberg, *Brussels and Its Environs* (London, 1816), H.A.O. Reichard's series of itineraries, e.g. *An Itinerary of France and Belgium* (London, 1816) and M. Vasi, *New Picture of Rome* (London, 1816). Home-grown publications included Campbell's *Holland, Belgium and Germany* (1818) and Edward Planta's *Paris* (1814). Specialist publishers had evolved to cater for the guidebook market: before Murray there had been at least three, Samuel Leigh, Neely and Jones, and Sherwood, of which Leigh was the most important and prolific.

23 'The Origins and History of Murray's Handbooks for Travellers', in *Murray's Magazine*, 6 November 1889, p. 113.

24 James Buzard, *The Beaten Track: European Tourism, Literature, and the Ways to 'Culture' 1800–1918* (Oxford, 1993), p. 72.

25   Quoted in John Murray IV, *John Murray III, 1808–1892. A Brief Memoir* (London, 1919), p. 41.

26   Quoted in vol. 2 of Samuel Smiles, *A Publisher and his Friends: Memoir and Correspondence of the late John Murray with an Account of the Origin and Progress of the House, 1768–1843,* 2 vols (London, 1891), p. 460.

27   *Ibid.,* pp. 461 and 477.

28   In the *Handbook for Travellers in Rome* (London, 1869). The quotation is from Gabriele M. Knoll, 'Reisen als Geschäft – Die Anfänge des organisierten Tourismus', in *Reisekultur: Von der Pilgerfahrt zum modernen Tourismus,* ed. Hermann Bausinger, Klaus Beyrer and Gottfried Korff (Munich, 1999).

29   Baedekers are a shade smaller at six and three-quarter inches by four and a quarter. G.F. Barwick, in 'Some Early Guidebooks', *Transactions of the Bibliographical Society,* 17 (1904), p. 194, makes the observation that Murray's adoption of the word *Handbook* for the series beginning in 1836 represented 'the first time the equivalent of the German *Handbuch* was naturalised in England'. And indeed the word *Handbuch,* indicating a manual or compendium of knowledge in a particular field, long preceded Baedeker's adoption of the description *Handbüchlein,* later *Handbuch für Reisende* for his guides. An example is Brockhaus's *Handbuch für Reisende in England* (Leipzig, 1829) from a firm that had already produced other such *Handbücher.* Divided into two parts, it combines general information on England (Part I), with an alphabetical gazetteer of places worth seeing (Part II).

30   Murray himself was pirated in the form of unauthorised French translations. W.B.C. Lister, *A Bibliography of Murray's Handbooks for Travellers* (Dereham, 1993), pp. 1 and 3, lists Belgian pirated editions of the *Handbook for Travellers on the Continent* in 1839 and 1842 and three French ones, but states that 'there may be others'.

31   This notice appears, for instance, facing the title page of *The Handbook for France,* Part I (London, 1877).

32   The *Dictionary of National Biography* tells us that the first of the publishing dynasty, John Mac Murray (or McMurray), was born in Edinburgh in 1745 and served in the marines before coming south and purchasing a bookselling business in Fleet Street in 1768, at which time he dropped the 'Mac' from his name. He was descended from the Murrays of Athol.

33   John R. Gretton, in the Introduction to Lister, *A Bibliography,* ii. Gabriele M. Knoll (*Reisekultur,* p. 343) notes that a French translation of Murray's Rhineland guide of 1842 adds material vital to the French traveller, namely extensive details of the menus available on the steamers. 'The gourmet can go aboard comforted by knowing precisely what are the eight courses that await him in the first class. In the second class there were seven courses, while in the third class one had to be content with four.'

34   The official history of Baedeker put out on the firm's website alludes to these Murray Handbooks in German.

35   Quoted in Alan Sillitoe, *Leading the Blind. A Century of Guidebook Travel 1815–1911* (London, 1996), p. 12.

36   Quoted in Lynne Withey, *Grand Tours and Cook's Tours. A History of Leisure Travel 1750 to 1915* (London 1998), p. 71.

37   Murray's *Handbook for Travellers in Syria and Palestine* (London, 1858) xli, quoted in Withey, *Grand Tours and Cook's Tours,* p. 252.

38   Murray's *Handbook for Travellers in Syria and Palestine* (1868), quoted in Sillitoe, *Leading the Blind,* p. 200.

39 Thirteen years later the controversy seemed to have been forgotten and the establishment had already accepted the books as a classic. *The Times* obituary of Ford said of his *Handbook to Spain*: 'so great a literary achievement had never before been performed under so humble a title'. A (justified?) technical criticism was that the book contained 'in the guise of a manual the matter of an encyclopaedia' and attempts were made to adapt it to the standard Murray formula. It is really a 'one-off' in the series.

40 The information on comparative pricing is taken from Gretton's Introduction to Lister, *A Bibliography*, xxi.

41 '. . . an amalgam of his own observations and blatant plagiarism from others' Guide-books', Gretton, Introduction to Lister, *A Bibliography*.

42 George Paston [pseudonym of Emily Morse Symonds], *At John Murray's: Records of a Literary Circle, 1843–1892* (London, 1932), pp. 164–5.

43 Gretton's Introduction to Lister, *A Bibliography*, xxiii, mentions that when the 1882 edition of the *Handbook for Travellers in Berkshire, Buckinghamshire and Oxfordshire* was being prepared, the Queen herself let it be known through her Private Secretary that she wished to read the proofs for the section on Windsor before it was passed for press.

44 There had previously been four separate volumes on India covering Madras (1879), Bombay (1881), Bengal (1882) and The Punjab (1883). Keatinge's distillation was further reduced by Sir George Forrest, Director of the Imperial Record Office in India. The condensed work was jointly published by Thacker, Spink and Co. of Calcutta and for this reason was excluded from the sale of the Handbooks to Stanford in 1901. Its twenty-second edition was still in print in the 1990s (see Gretton's Introduction to Lister, *A Bibliography*, xiv).

45 Murray's *Handbook for India* (London, 1891), xv–xvi, quoted in Withey, *Grand Tours and Cook's Tours*, p. 283.

46 *A Handbook for Travellers in Greece*, 4th edn, revised and enlarged (London, 1872), p. 159. It is interesting that a subtly different argument was advanced by the Conservative politician and classical scholar the late Enoch Powell, during the agitation regarding the marbles in the 1980s; in an interview he remarked that, if the Greeks were to build a special museum to protect the marbles, then he would have no problem with the idea of returning the latter. Since the Greeks are now doing just that, it will be interesting to see what arguments will now be advanced by those who enthusiastically endorsed the Powellite position.

47 Lister, *A Bibliography*, p. 103.

48 *Ibid.*, p. 114.

49 It is true that the first Professor of the History of Art, Franz Kugler, was appointed to the Berlin Academy in 1833, while Pevsner remarks that the 'history of art, in our sense begins . . . with Jakob Burckhardt', who was still a student under the historian Leopold von Ranke when Kugler published his *Handbook of the History of Art* in 1841–2. However, the Germans were pioneers: not until the late 1860s were the Slade professorships of art established in Britain, and even these reflected the connoisseur tradition, rather than the more academic German approach. The first person to hold a Slade Chair in Oxford was John Ruskin (from 1869). See Vernon Hyde Minor, *Art History's History* (Englewood Cliffs, NJ, and New York, 1994) for a detailed and masterly treatment of this topic, particularly pp. 20 ff.

50 Graham Hough, *The Last Romantics* (London and New York, 1961), p. 9.

CHAPTER 9

1   See also Chapter 1 for a more detailed discussion of the seven wonders of the ancient world and their treatment by pre-Christian and Christian authors.

2   The word first appears as a defined stylistic marker and without pejorative associations in Jacob Burckhardt's *Cicerone* and Wilhelm Luebke's *Geschichte der Architektur*, both published in 1855.

3   'Aura' is here intended as the quality identified by Walter Benjamin in his celebrated essay,'The Work of Art in the Age of Mechanical Reproduction', reprinted in *Illuminations*, ed. Hannah Arendt, tr. Harry Zorn (London, 1999), pp. 211–44, esp. 215.

4   See Dean McCannell, *The Tourist: A New Theory of the Leisure Class* (New York, 1976), pp. 44 ff.

5   On this see Darian Leader's provocative and thought-provoking study, *Stealing the Mona Lisa: What Art Stops us from Seeing* (London, 2002), pp. 4–5.

6   Ulrich Thieme and Felix Becker (eds), *Allgemeines Lexikon der bildenden Künstler von der Antike bis zur Gegenwart*, 37 vols (Leipzig, 1999; = repr. of Leipzig, 1907 and 1908), vols 7–8, entry for Johann Heinrich von Dannecker (1758–1841), p. 370: '*Der "Ariadne" verdankte Dannecker seine einzigartige Popularität und ein Künstlerruhm, den ihm die Kunstgeschichte in der Folge wieder nahm.*'

7   *Ibid.*, entry for Johann Heinrich von Dannecker (p. 370): '*trotz all diesen Harmlosigkeiten behauptet die Ariadne innerhalb der Produktion um 1800 einen Platz, den kein anderes Werk der Zeit charakteristischer ausfüllen könnte*'.

8   See Herbert Warren Wind, 'The House of Baedeker', in the *New Yorker*, 22 September 1975, p. 90.

9   For example, the tenth edition of Baedeker's *Wien* (1999) awards a star to the combined *Maria-Theresien-Platz und-Denkmal*, though all of the quite lengthy description is devoted to the monument. The Heeresgeschichtliches Museum, on the other hand, remains starless.

10   Francis Watson, 'The Education of Baedeker', in the *Fortnightly*, 146 (December 1936), 701.

11   Regarding the revised section on painting for the *Handbook to Italy* (1847), see above, Ch. 8, p. 191.

12   For some, however, Baedeker moved much too slowly and retrospectively. Thus Arnold Palmer, writing in 1949, complains that the 'eighth (1927) edition of Baedeker's *Great Britain* had been, we were told, "entirely rewritten" but it was still breathing the air of its first edition, published in 1887'. Arnold Palmer, 'The Baedeker Firmament', in the *Fortnightly*, 172 (September 1949), 203.

13   William Hazlitt, in 'Fine Arts' (1814), 18:41, quoted in David Lowenthal, *The Past Is Another Country* (Cambridge, 1985), p. 100.

14   George Eliot, *Letters*, 3: 294, quoted in Lowenthal, *The Past Is Another Country*, p. 99. Fortunately, she later recovered her poise.

15   Baedeker, *Oberitalien mit Ravenna, Florenz und Pisa*, 19th edn (Leipzig 1928), p. 564. This volume first appeared in 1861. In the Foreword (p. v) the publisher stresses that historical and art historical aspects of the text have been brought up to date by incorporating the latest scholarship, so that, for example, 'the Baroque period and the Middle Ages are more substantially treated than hitherto'. This would seem to indicate that lack of historical contextualisation was a matter of choice, not oversight.

16   See Vasari, *Lives of the Artists*, tr. George Bull (London, 1987), vol. 1, p. 338. Edward Mendelson, in an excellent article entitled 'Baedeker's Universe' in the *Yale Review* (Spring 1985), writes the following (p. 389): 'In [Baedeker's] descriptions of a place worth visiting, he gave his readers precisely the information they needed to find their way cheaply and conveniently, and precisely the information they needed in order to appreciate what they saw. He trusted them to provide their aesthetic and emotional responses for themselves.' However, as in the case of Michelangelo's *David*, we can see that, with regard to artefacts rather than places, Baedeker was also capable of doing exactly the opposite of what Mendelson so rightly praises.

17   William Hazlitt, *Notes of a Journey through France and Italy, 1826* (London).

18   Philip Hensher reviewing Anton Gill, *Il Gigante: Michelangelo, Florence and the David 1492–1505* in the *Observer*, 28 July 2002, p. 16.

19   Esther Allen, '"Money and the little red books": Romanticism, Tourism, and the Rise of the Guidebook', in *Literature, Interpretation, Theory*, 7 (1996), 223.

20   J.A. Cuddon, *The Companion Guide to Jugoslavia*, 2nd rev. edn (Glasgow and Englewood Cliffs, NJ, 1974), p. 120. George Mikes most famous work parodying and satirising national characteristics is his book on the English entitled *How to be an Alien*. He wrote a number of other volumes in the same vein.

21   However, many comments were less green-eyed. Rudy Koshar in *German Travel Cultures* (Oxford and New York, 2000), p. 26, quotes an American traveller on the 'unfailing Baedeker . . . the true product of the German mind', because always accurate and thorough to a fault.

22   Rudy Koshar, '"What Ought to Be Seen": Tourists' Guidebooks and National Identities in Modern Germany and Europe', in *Journal of Contemporary History*, 33/3 (July 1998), 331.

23   Anonymous review in the *Atlantic Monthly*, 35/2.2 (June 1875), 737–8. The American series of guides referred to were published by Messrs. Osgood & Co. The guide discussed in this review is the second in the series, on the Middle States, the first volume having covered New England.

24   Koshar, *German Travel Cultures*, pp. 49–50.

25   See also the remarks in the Introduction to the present work.

26   E.M. Forster, *The Lucy Novels: Early Sketches for* A Room with a View, ed. Oliver Stallybrass (London, 1977), *Lucy Novels*, 23–4.

27   James Buzard, *The Beaten Track: European Tourism, Literature and the Ways to 'Culture' 1800–1918* (Oxford and New York, 1993), pp. 288–9, 291. And is Mr Emerson being ironic *only* at the expense of the Miss Lavishes of the world when he says to Lucy: 'Baedeker? . . . I'm glad it's that you minded. It's worth minding the loss of a Baedeker. *That's* worth minding.'

28   Roger Clark, 'Threading the Maze: Nineteenth-Century Guides for British Travellers in Paris', in Michael Sheringham (ed.), *Parisian Fields* (London, 1996), p. 28.

29   Thomas Pynchon, *V.* (London, 1995), pp. 408–9. Pynchon has stated he used Baedeker's 1899 guide to Egypt for this chapter.

30   See Rudy Koshar, 'What Ought to Be Seen', p. 332 for a dispassionate corrective to the retrospective critique of Baedeker's more extreme critics, whereby he analyses the content of Baedeker's *Deutschland in einem Bande: Kurzes Reisehandbuch*, 3rd edn (Leipzig, 1913). Koshar gives the following percentages for the proportions of individual subject areas, as applied in the nine-page introductory section entitled 'Main Points of Interest in Germany': Monuments and History, 29.7 per cent; Industry and Commerce, 24.5 per cent; Politics and the Military, 13.5 per cent; Museums, Education

and the Arts, 11.8 per cent; Nature, 10.9 per cent; Resorts and Spas, 9.6 per cent. It is true, of course, that this tells us nothing about *how* these topics are treated, which indeed forms the basis of the objections voiced by Baedeker satirists. Nevertheless, just as it has been pointed out that Murray sometimes included topics such as 'the poor of Amsterdam' which modern commercially oriented guidebooks tend to omit or skate over, so it is probably fair to say that the careful reader of Baedeker could gain rather deeper insights than is implied in the texts of his sharpest cultural critics.

31 Quoted in Clark, 'Threading the Maze: Nineteenth-Century Guides for British Travellers in Paris', p. 21. It is an irony that both Karl Baedeker himself and one of his descendants died while at work on a Baedeker guide to Paris.

32 Koshar, *Travel Cultures*, p. 47.

33 Koshar, 'What Ought to be Seen', 333.

34 *Zeitschrift für Philosophie und katholische Theologie*. It promulgated a system of thought worked out by Georg Hermes (1775–1831), the Professor of Theology at Münster, and was popular in the Rhineland. Shortly after Hermes' death, Rome pronounced against his ideas and some of his works were put on the Index.

35 An example of the latter was his lifelong friend, Ernst Wilhelm Hengstenberg, who began his adult career as a violent propagandist for the *Burschenschaftsidee* (a network of radical and nationalist student organisations), but after studying philosophy and theology in Berlin subsided into a posture of pious Protestantism and bourgeois rectitude.

36 August Heinrich Hoffmann von Fallersleben, *Mein Leben* (Hanover 1868–79), vol. 4.

37 Professor Johannes August Klein, *Rheinreise von Mainz bis Cöln, Handbuch für Schnellreisende* (Koblenz, 1828).

38 See Lynne Withey, *Grand Tours to Cook's Tours: A History of Leisure Travel 1750 to 1915* (London, 1998), pp. 72–3.

39 'The Origin and History of Murray's Handbooks for Travellers', in *Murray's Magazine*, 6 (November 1889), 628–9. The examples he gives certainly seem to suggest that some passages were lifted wholesale.

40 The figure is from an anonymous contribution to *Time*, 9 January 1950, entitled 'Peripatetics: Two-Star Civilization', p. 16.

41 'It may be laid down as a general rule,' recorded Murray, 'that the wants, tastes, and habits of the English are more carefully studied at the Swiss inns than even in those of Germany. Thus, at most of the large inns, there is a late table-d'hôte dinner at 4 or 5 o'clock, expressly for the English; and the luxury of tea may always be had in perfection,' quoted from Murray, 'Switzerland', in Sillitoe, *Leading the Blind*, p. 37.

42 Leslie Stephen, *The Playground of Europe* (1871). Stephen was President of the Alpine Club (1865–8) and wrote another volume in praise of Switzerland in 1862, *Peaks, Passes and Glaciers*. He is however better known as the editor of the *Dictionary of National Biography* (1882–91) and the father of Virginia Woolf. Murray's *Handbook for Switzerland* went through eighteen editions, plus a version put out by the Paris booksellers Galignani in 1839, and sold some 45,000 copies between 1838 and 1891. Baedeker's *Die Schweiz* was no less successful, in its twenty-fourth edition by 1911, and eventually appeared also in an English edition that directly competed with Murray. See John Vaughan, *The English Guide Book c. 1780–1870. An Illustrated History* (Newton Abbot, London and North Pomfret, VT, 1974), p. 47.

43 Wind, 'The House of Baedeker', p. 52. However, he supplies no evidence for this assertion.

44 Francis Watson, 'The Education of a Baedeker', in the *Fortnightly*, 146 (December 1936), 699.

45 Wind, 'The House of Baedeker', p. 52.

46 Mendelson, 'Baedeker's Universe', p. 392; W.G. Constable, 'Three Stars for Baedeker', in *Harper's Magazine*, April 1953, 82; Sillitoe, *Leading the Blind*, p. 44. The last-named includes Baedeker's remark that the abuses were eventually addressed by the authorities, whose advice was 'Give to nobody.' 'The remedy', he wrote, 'therefore lies principally with the travellers themselves.'

47 'No sort of frugality is more ill-suited to a journey,' warned Baedeker gravely, 'than to travel with the aid of an outdated edition of a guidebook', an admonition that all guidebook publishers would surely echo with equal solemnity.

48 Wind, 'The House of Baedeker', p. 64. Likewise, the earlier enthusiastic prescription of opium for stomach upsets and other ailments becomes a stern prohibition in later guides, such are the vagaries of medical fashion.

49 David Watkin, *The Rise of Architectural History* (London, 1983), p. 150. The new edition actually appeared in 1930, according to *Baedeker's Handbooks for Travellers: A Bibliography of English Editions Published Prior to World War II* (Westport, CT, and London, 1975), p. 28. Baedeker's exclusion of Baroque elsewhere sometimes reached absurd proportions. For example, the 1900 ninth edition of the handbook *Austria, Including Hungary, Transylvania, Dalmatia and Bosnia* devotes only eight unimpressed lines to Fischer von Erlach's celebrated Karlskirche in Vienna ('a lofty structure with a dome in the Italian baroque style'), while the architect of the Belvedere ('an imperial château') is not even named, likewise those of the Peterskirche; the church of Maria Treu and the Servitenkirche, both major achievements of the Central European Baroque, are simply omitted.

50 Francis Watson, 'The Education of Baedeker', in the *Fortnightly*, 146 (December 1936), 701.

51 It is possible he invented it, since the earliest example of it quoted from Grimm's *Deutsches Wörterbuch*, compilation of which began in the 1850s, is taken from Baedeker's *Die Schweiz* of 1859. See Wind, 'The House of Baedeker', p. 54.

52 Baedeker's *Deutschland*, 8th edn, 1858, quoted in Mendelson, 'Baedeker's Universe', pp. 387–8. The importance that Baedeker always attached to first-rate cartography and excellent town plans, in which sphere the firm had no rival among the competition, not even Murray, is perhaps another indication of the desire to make the traveller independent of external assistance wherever and whenever possible.

53 His actual illness appears wrapped in mystery. Francis Watson, writing in 1936, merely says that he 'contracted sunstroke in the selfless discharge of his duties in Egypt and had to retire'. But this hardly seems an adequate explanation for mental instability. See, Watson, 'The Education of a Baedeker', 698.

54 Buzard, *The Beaten Track*, p. 73; and quoting Mendelson, 'Baedeker's Universe', p. 393.

55 By 1871 there were, almost incredibly, 114 publishers and 249 bookshops operating out of Leipzig. The city supplied 18 per cent of the total German book production. See Alex W. Hinrichsen, *Baedeker-Catalog. Verzeichnis aller Baedeker-Reiseführer von 1832–1987 mit einem Abriß der Verlagsgeschichte* (Holzminden, 1988), p. 26. During the economic boon of 1869–1872, geographical works and tour guides comprised as much as 24 per cent of total German book production, which twice reached over 11,000 publications in that period. See Hinrichsen, *Baedeker-Catalog*, p. 36.

56 For Switzerland the competition was particularly fierce, one of the more challenging rivals being the series of *Schweizerische Fremdenführer* written by H.A. Berlepsch and published by Weber of Leipzig. Berlepsch's book covering all Switzerland and

published in 1862 was deemed serious competition for Baedeker by independent critics. There were also other less important series (Grieben, Meyer, etc.) in an always crowded market. See Hinrichsen, *Baedeker-Catalog*, p. 24 and elsewhere for detailed discussion of the more or less competing series of guides, few of which, however, could fundamentally challenge Baedeker's dominance, at least of the upmarket scene and over the longer term.

57 This volume was even reprinted in 1985, rather implausibly in Leipzig, a publishing centre then under the not noticeably humorous communist regime of Honecker. Old jokes, like Stalinist leaders, never die.

58 Harry Graham, 'The Traveller', in *When Grandmama Fell off the Boat: The Best of Harry Graham*, pp. 135–8.

59 Mark Twain, *A Tramp Abroad* (London and New York, 1997), p. 293. Twain's pretended indignation at Baedeker's failure to stress in the first sentence of his description that the trip to Zermatt would actually take 500 years should one opt for the glacier as one's mode of transport, recalls the passenger on a cruise ship who is said to have demanded a refund because he lost a day when the ship crossed the international dateline.

60 In this series see e.g. Ludwig Hirschfeld, *Das Buch von Wien* (Munich, 1927), or Eugen Szatmari, *Das Buch von Berlin* (Munich, 1927). Hirschfeld (1882–1945) was a quintessentially Viennese insider, a theatre manager, dramatist, cabaret sketch-writer, operetta librettist, novelist, editor and, last but not least, a writer of that idiosyncratically local literary product, the feuilleton. There has been one recent attempt to revive this type of guide, written by people saturated in the ethos of the city they are describing, but most of today's 'funky' guides (and there are not many) are heavily consumption-oriented. An exception is András Török's remarkable *Budapest: A Critical Guide* (Pallas Athene, London; 4th edn 1998 and several earlier editions published by Corvina and Park in Budapest). This combines witty comment with cultural and historical expertise, and is entirely *sui generis*.

61 Mendleson, 'Baedeker's Universe', 398.

62 I am indebted to John Julius Norwich's *Christmas Crackers* (London, 1982), p. 22, for this quotation, which he reproduces under Baedeker's original heading of 'Intercourse with Orientals'.

63 Mendelson, 'Baedeker's Universe', 402.

64 Hinrichsen, *Baedeker-Catalog*, p. 28.

65 For a detailed examination of this and a similar guide put out by Woerl, see Koshar, *Travel Cultures*, pp. 152–6.

66 Hermann Göring is said to have instructed the Luftwaffe to destroy 'every historical building and landmark in Britain that is marked with an asterisk in Baedeker'.

67 The 'loan' was really an investment by Allen & Unwin in revised editions of Baedekers to London and the regions of Britain.

68 Ironically, this methodology (used from 1979 in a series produced with sponsorship from the Allianz-Versicherungs-AG, a major German insurance company) represents a return to that adopted by the old 'post books' up to the beginning of the nineteenth century. Indeed, it was this form of presentation that had effectively been superseded by the 'routes' of Murray and Baedeker. The division of the Baedeker name at this time between the company in the ownership of Langenscheidt, operating out of Freiburg, and the Baedeker-Autoführer Verlag, operating out of Ostfildern-Kemnat bei Stuttgart, is confusing. The branches were reunited in July 1987 under the name Karl Baedeker GmbH, with offices in Stuttgart

and Munich. On the death of Karl Baedeker's widow in 1984, the connection between the guidebooks and the dynasty that had made them great was finally broken.

69 Wind, 'The House of Baedeker', pp. 91, 49.

CHAPTER 10

1 This bizarre outing is reported by Esther Moir in *The Discovery of Britain: The English Tourists 1540 to 1840* (London, 1964), xv.

2 Piers Brendon, in his engaging *Thomas Cook: 150 Years of Popular Tourism* (London, 1991), p. 6, points out that what you could buy for 2 (new) pence in 1900 would cost about £1 in 1991. In 1990, when Brendon was writing his book, the same trip cost £2.20, since when it has of course increased considerably in price. The cost in old shillings for the same trip had therefore inflated by a factor of about twenty-seven.

3 Michael Bywater, 'Millennial Bestiary: Things We Could Have Done without in the Past 1,000 Years. 12. TOURISM', the *Observer*, 18 April 1999.

4 Between 1801 and 1914, 1,279 companies were authorised by Acts of Parliament to build railways in Britain. See *The Oxford Companion to British Rail History*.

5 T. Cook, *Handbook of a Trip to Scotland including Railway Glances from Leicester via Manchester, to Fleetwood. Views of the Lancashire Coast and the Lakes of Cumberland. Voyage from Fleetwood to Ardrossan. Trip on the Ayrshire, Edinburgh and Glasgow Railways. Scottish Scenery and Descriptions of Edinburgh, Glasgow, etc. etc.* (Leicester, 1846).

6 Quoted in Daniel J. Boorstin, *The Image* (London, 1962), p. 96.

7 Quoted in Brendon, *Thomas Cook*, p. 15.

8 Quoted in Alain de Botton, *The Art of Travel* (London and New York, 2002), pp. 222–3.

9 From *Lutezia*, Part 2, quoted in Wolfgang Schivelbusch, *The Railway Journey – Trains and Travel in the 19th Century*, tr. Anselm Hollo (Oxford, 1980), p. 44; *Geschichte der Eisenbahnreise* (Munich, 1978).

10 William Makepeace Thackeray, 'De Juventute', from the *Roundabout Papers* that appeared in the *Cornhill*. I have taken this quotation from Gerald B. Kauvar and Gerald C. Sorensen (eds), *The Victorian Mind: An Anthology* (London, 1969), pp. 119–20.

11 Giles Barber, 'The English-language Guide Book to Europe up to 1870', in Robin Myers and Michael Harris (eds), *Journeys through the Market. Travel, Travellers and the Book Trade* (New Castle, DE, and Folkestone, UK, 1999), pp. 99–100. Barber refers also to the work on Playstowe by Ron Browne and Maurice Packer in *Factotum* 20 (1985).

12 George Kearsly (*c.* 1739–90, from 1783 spelled Kearsley), seems to fit the caricature of the rascally publisher. As publisher of John Wilkes's *The North Briton*, he was thrown into the Tower for sedition in 1763, but got out by betraying his collaborators. In 1764 he went bankrupt and fled to France, but later returned and continued publishing material as diverse as tax tables and 'The Beauties of Dr Johnson'. See the entry for him in the *Dictionary of National Biography*.

13 Barber, 'The English-language Guide Book to Europe up to 1870', pp. 103–4.

14 Like Kearsley, Abel Heywood (1810–93) was a radical, if somewhat more mainstream. Influenced by the ideas of Robert Owen, he opened a penny reading room for the working class in Manchester in 1831. Later he took over *The Poor Man's*

Guardian, and refused to pay the government stamp duty, for which he suffered three prison terms. His principled opposition to the duty was that it represented a 'tax on knowledge', and he maintained that the working class would always choose good newsapapers over immoral or seditious ones, if they were given the free choice. He eventually became Mayor of Manchester. Successful as a businessman, he built up the largest wholesale newsagency in the country, besides having other publishing interests that included a series of works in local dialects. See the entry for him in the *Dictionary for National Biography*.

15   John Vaughan, *The English Guide Book c. 1780–1870: An Illustrated History* (Newton Abbot, London and North Pomfret, VT, 1974), p. 40. This pioneering work on the history of the guidebook is packed with invaluable detail, although its approach to the topic is primarily bibliographical.

16   Lynne Withey in *Grand Tours and Cook's Tours: A History of Leisure Travel 1750–1915* (London, 1998), p. 9, drawing on several sources, points out that the channel ferries had only begun regular schedules from the 1760s. Even so, 'rough seas and contrary winds could delay sailings for hours or even days. The crossing from Dover to Calais, the shortest route, took at least three hours and more commonly five or six.'

17   Barber, 'The English-language Guide Book to Europe up to 1870', p. 101. Barber further points out that, in the wake of the war, substantial new volumes were also commissioned, which in their turn became classics: Boyce's *Belgian Traveller* (1815), which young John Murray III used (together with Ebel) to prepare himself for his first tour as a guidebook compiler, Campbell's *Holland, Belgium and Germany* (1818), and Edward Planta's *New Picture of Paris* (1814). The publisher Samuel Leigh not only put out important translations (Ebel's *Switzerland*, Vasi's *New Picture of Rome*, Reichard's *Itinerary of France and Belgium*), but also had his own series, *Leigh's New Picture of England*, and the *New Picture of London*. He also published the first named in a French edition for foreign tourists.

18   M. Reichard, *An Itinerary of France and Belgium. Or the Traveller's Guide through these Countries* (London, 1822). It was published in handy duodecimo. Reichard describes himself as 'Privy-Councillor of the Duke of Saxe-Gotha, and Knight of the Saxon Order of Civil Merit'.

19   The hotel coupons were the idea of Cook's son, John Mason Cook, who had a more inventive business brain than his cautious father, and who eventually quarrelled with him over the future strategy of the business.

20   Thomas Cook had launched his hotel coupons in 1868, thereby obviating the need for travellers in his groups to carry large amounts of money or engage in sometimes complicated currency transactions when paying their hotel bills.

21   Britain's first 'family hotel' was opened by David Low in Covent Garden as early as 1774.

22   Richard Holmes in his edition of S.T. Coleridge, *Selected Poems* (London, 1996), pp. 351–2. Holmes, who describes 'The Delinquent Travellers' as 'a surprising humorous coda to the great strange voyage of *The Rime of the Ancient Mariner*', writes that 'Coleridge identifies not with the comfortable fashionable tourists, but with the "delinquent" travellers – bankrupts, criminals, cashiered soldiers, smugglers, exiles, emigrants, all who "go because they cannot stay".' Guidebooks were not on the whole written for such people (except for emigrants), though they doubtless found such works useful. 'The Delinquent Travellers', written in 1824, captures the mania for travel that was a feature of the post-Napoleonic era and the coming of steam power.

23   Quoted in Jeremy Black, *The British and the Grand Tour* (London, 1985).

24   However, he committed suicide by cutting his throat in 1831.

25   Edward Planta, *A New Picture of Paris* (London, 1814), v. This introduction to the book is dated 'London, July 9th, 1814', so it is fair to assume that Planta was first into the post-Napoleonic market with his guide.

26   Cook organised a tour to the Paris Exhibition of that year, which marked the beginning of his continental tours. His excursions to the Great Exhibition of 1851 in Paxton's Crystal Palace, which brought more than 150,000 visitors to London, had effectively launched his 'package tour' business in Britain.

27   This happy phrase is that of Roger Clark in his essay 'Threading the Maze: Nineteenth-Century Guides for British Travellers to Paris', in Michael Sheringham (ed.), *Parisian Fields* (London, 1996), pp. 8–30 (this quotation p. 27). Clark points out that Planta's fulsome recommendation of the City of London Hotel in the rue St-Honoré rests on a 'reassuring avoidance of otherness'. The staff speak English, most of the guests are English and the accommodation is 'completely in the English style'.

28   For an entertaining discussion of the effete des Esseintes and his failed project of travelling to England, see de Botton, *The Art of Travel*, pp. 9–11.

29   Esther Allen, '"Money and the Little Red Books": Romanticism, Tourism and the Rise of the Guidebook', in *Literature, Interpretation, Theory*, 7/2–3 (1996), p. 223.

30   Philip Howell, 'Sex and the City of Bachelors: Sporting Guidebooks and Urban Knowledge in Nineteenth-Century Britain and America,' in *Ecumene* 8/1 (2000), 28.

31   Óbuda, Buda (on the west bank) and Pest (on the east bank) were administratively merged to form 'Budapest' in 1872–3.

32   Joannes Elysius, *Libellus de mirabilibus Civitatis Putheolorum et locorum vicinorum* (Naples, 1475). G.F. Barwick, 'Some Early Guidebooks', in *Transactions of the Bibliographical Society*, 7 (1904), 195, points out that, together with the first printed *Mirabilia Romae* of the same year, this is one of the first books to appear using Gutenberg's invention.

33   See: R.T. Günther, *A Bibliography of . . . the Phlegraean Fields* (1908).

34   Malcolm Letts, 'Some Early Guide-Books to Naples and the Vicinity', in *Notes and Queries*, 12th ser., 3 (3 February 1917), 85–7, particularly 86. Letts says that later versions of Sarnelli bear a suspiciously close resemblance to another Pozzuoli guidebook by Parrino.

35   *Journal de Voyage de Michel de Montaigne*, ed. François Rigolot (Paris, 1992), viii.

36   Vaughan, *The English Guide Book* c. *1780–1870*, p. 16.

37   Quoted in *ibid*, p. 76.

38   Brendon, *Thomas Cook*, p. 11.

39   By the 1830s, Margate and Ramsgate were attracting over 100,000 visitors each year, and Brighton more than 50,000, Brendon, *Thomas Cook*, p. 11.

40   Vaughan, *The English Guide Book* c. *1780–1870*, p. 87.

41   *Ibid.*, p. 128, quoting from Alfred Smith, *The Harrogate Medical Guide; a Popular and Practical Treatise on the Mineral Waters of Harrogate, and the Diseases in Which They Are Useful; with Supplementary Remarks on Diet and Exercise; and Some Select Cases*, 2nd edn (1847), pp. 18, 19.

42   Vaughan, *The English Guide Book* c. *1780–1870*, p. 126.

43   A.B. Granville, *The Spas of England*, 3 vols; *Northern Spas*, vol. 1; *Midland Spas*, vol. 2; *Southern Spas*, vol. 3 (London, 1841). In the same year, Dr Edwin Lee published his *Memoranda on France, Italy & Germany with remarks on Climates, Medical Practice, Mineral Waters etc* (London, 1841).

44   Alastair J. Durie, *Scotland for the Holidays: Tourism in Scotland* c. *1780–1939* (East Linton, 2003), pp. 86–108. I am heavily indebted for the details of Scottish hydros to Durie's chapter on this phenomenon in his fascinating book on Scottish tourism.

45   Durie, *Scotland for the Holidays*, p. 99.

46   The carriage in which Dickens was travelling was the only one that remained on the tracks. The famous novelist helped other passengers to safety before re-entering the carriage to secure the manuscript of *Our Mutual Friend* and his hip-flask of brandy. This close brush with death, and the grisly scene at the crash, made a deep impression on Dickens, who was already suffering from nervous exhaustion due to overwork.

47   Thomas A. Croal in *A Book about Travelling* (London and Edinburgh, 1877) cites a survey by one F.J. Branwell regarding the causes of railway accidents in the 1870s. 58.7 per cent were due to collisions, 12 per cent to trains diverting onto the wrong line, 9.2 per cent to derailments, 9.2 per cent to defects in rolling stock, 4.6 per cent took place on inclines, 1.8 per cent were due to entering stations at too high a speed and 4.5 per cent were due to miscellaneous causes. He concludes that only 35.5 per cent of passengers' deaths were due to factors beyond their personal control. By measuring journeys taken and the number of deaths on the railway, he calculates that there were 11,000,000 journeys for every death.

48   Thomas Cook's own Continental Timetable was first published in 1873.

49   *Bradshaw's Maps of Inland Navigation.*

50   *Dictionary of National Biography* entry on George Bradshaw, 1801–53.

51   *Brewer's Dictionary of Phrase and Fable*, millennium edn, rev. Adrian Room (London, 1999), p. 162, illustrates the way 'Bradshaw' entered the language with a quotation from Conan Doyle's Sherlock Holmes story 'The Adventure of the Copper Beeches' (1892): 'There is a train at half-past nine,' said I, glancing over my Bradshaw. 'It is due at Winchester at 11.30.' 'That will do very nicely.'

52   Brendon, *Thomas Cook*, p. 12. *Punch*, for long the quintessential reading matter for railway journeys, as it was for those waiting their turn in male hairdressing saloons and dentists' waiting rooms, also began publication in 1841.

53   Janice Anderson and Edmund Swinglehurst, *Ephemera of Travel and Transport* (London, 1981).

54   *The Railway Traveller's Handy Book of Hints, Suggestions and Advice before the Journey, on the Journey and after the Journey*, ed. with an Introduction by Jack Simmons (repr. Bath, 1971; originally published anonymously, 1862).

55   *Ibid.*, pp. 21–3, 48, 74.

56   *Ibid.*, pp. 9–10, 13.

57   Jane Ellice Hopkins in *Work amongst Working Men* (1870), but paraphrasing Georges Louis Leclerc Buffon (1707–88): '*Le génie n'est qu'une plus grande aptitude à la patience.*'

58   Edmund Swinglehurst, *Thomas Cook* (Horsham, 1983), p. 47.

59   Richard S. Lambert, *The Fortunate Traveller: A Short History of Touring and Travel for Pleasure* (London, New York *et al.*, 1950), pp. 125–6.

60   The claim is made in an article by Ben Summerskill in the *Observer*, 25 March 2001, 7). However, I have not found independent corroboration of this and the date given for the first of Cook's excursions to France is incorrectly given in the article.

61   Brendon, *Thomas Cook*, pp. 52–3.

62   *Ibid.*, pp. 36 and 44. Withey in *Grand Tours and Cook's Tours*, pp. 142–3, points out that Cook actually lost money on his package tours of the Great Exhibition and his first foreign trips.

63   It was in his capacity as Secretary of the South Midland Temperance Association that Cook organised his famous excursion for temperance movement members from Leicester to Loughborough on 5 July 1841. Some reports maliciously allude to the heightened colour and boisterousness observable in a number of the participants by the end of the day, suggesting that not all were quite as committed to the cause as they claimed. See e.g. Swinglehurst, *Thomas Cook*, p. 12.

64   See Lambert, *The Fortunate Traveller*, p. 119.

65   *Ibid.*, p. 120.

66   *A Guide to the System of Tours in Scotland under the Direction of the Principal Railway, Steamboat and Coach Companies* by Thomas Cook, Tourist Manager, Leicester. With a Series of New Sectional Maps (London, 1861), pp. 31–3.

67   The behaviour of the American railway companies shortly afterwards was even worse. In the long and hypocritical history of American protectionism (demanding that foreign markets be opened up to American business, but obstructing foreign companies attempting to penetrate the US market) Cook's experience was one of the worst. The American railway companies agreed Cook's arrangements for circular tickets and then refused to honour them when the tourists arrived, presumably hoping that such a debacle would knock the business on the head. They too had reckoned without the determination, this time of John Mason Cook, who repeatedly visited New York to circumnavigate this tactic. However, partial success must be ascribed to the Americans, as far fewer tourists subsequently visited the US under the aegis of Cook than the company had expected. See Lambert, *The Fortunate Traveller*, p. 136.

68   Durie, *Scotland for the Holidays*, p. 147. He further comments that 'Scotland may, in fact, have benefited more than Cook's from the fostering of the American connection.' Cook brought 150 Americans, many of them teachers and ministers, to Scotland in 1873 on his first 'Educational Tour of Britain and Europe', and included Melrose Abbey and Abbotsford on the schedule, as well as the Trossachs. On this and his repeat tours there were often American journalists, whose enthusiastic reports stimulated interest in Scotland among their fellow countrymen.

69   *Dictionary of National Biography*, entry for Thomas Cook (1808–92).

70   Rudy Koshar, '"What Ought to Be Seen": Tourists' Guidebooks and National Identities in Modern Germany and Europe', in *Journal of Contemporary History*, 33/3 (July 1998), 330.

71   Edmund Swinglehurst, *Cook's Tours: The Story of Popular Travel* (Poole, 1982), p. 45.

72   'The Cost of a Trip to Europe, and How to Go Cheaply', in *Continental Monthly: Devoted to Literature and National Policy*, 3/6 (June 1863), 730–3. No author is given.

73   Quoted in Brendon, *Thomas Cook*, p. 37.

74   It is amusing, for example, to see some of the entries that might interest social historians, and/or snobs, today. On the right (coming from London), 13 miles from Dover, following an entry for Westenhanger (now Folkestone Racecourse), we read: 'To Hythe 3m. . . . W. Deedes Esq. Saltwood.' This estate has attained a certain currency through the bestselling and indiscreet diaries of ex-minister Alan Clark, who lived there for many years. The reference to 'W. Deedes' is also interesting, since the Saltwood estate was at that time still the family home of the Deedes, W.F. Deedes having been a prominent Conservative politician and subsequently (as Lord Deedes) editor of the *Daily Telegraph*. Thirty-five miles from Dover, Sissinghurst Castle is mentioned, to be seen on the right, if coming from London: 'an ancient mansion now in ruins. It was used during the wars of the last century as a prison for French captives.' It is now better known as a National Trust property that was owned

for many years by another famous diarist, and diplomat, Harold Nicolson, and his wife, the writer Vita Sackville West.

75   Wolfgang Schivelbusch, *The Railway Journey: Trains and Travel in the 19th Century*, tr. Anselm Hollo (Oxford, 1980), p. 59.

76   *Ibid.*, pp. 66–9.

77   According to Brendon, *Thomas Cook*, p. 40, the term 'sightseeing' dates from 1847.

78   It is perhaps worth noting here that one of John Mason Cook's greatest coups was to get a contract for transporting up to 12,000 pilgrims from India to Mecca in the late 1880s. Hitherto this had been a scandalous trade, with overcrowding, overcharging and callous disregard for the welfare of the pilgrims. Pilgrims who could not afford to return home were simply left to starve. Cook reorganised the whole system, slashed the prices of a one-way passage from fifty to thirty rupees, introduced medical supervision and licensed ticket brokers, and generally cleaned the whole thing up. The pilgrims were delighted; their exploiters of hitherto were furious. See Brendon, *Thomas Cook*, pp. 205 ff. for a vivid description of this noble chapter in the history of Thomas Cook & Son.

79   Quoted in *ibid.*, p. 120.

80   *Ibid.*, p. 121.

81   *Ibid.*, p. 136.

82   Although many appeared anonymously as *Cook's Handbook*, or *The Traveller's Handbook*, there was one author (apart from the Egypt specialist, E.A. Wallis Budge and three or four others) whose name recurs on the title pages of the guidebooks, mostly those to countries in Europe. This was Roy Elston, who revised or revamped earlier Cook's or Tourists' Handbooks (e.g. that to Normandy and Brittany) and continually updated them. His name first crops up in 1922 on the flyleaf of *Constantinople to Smyrna: Notes for Travellers to Constantinople, Bursa, the Dardanelles, Gallipoli Battlefields and Cemeteries, Ruins of Troy, Seven Churches of Asia, Smyrna*. The Thomas Cook Archive (which does not have a complete set of the guides) features some fifty-nine titles by Elston, most of them revised editions.

83   *Cook's Excursionist and International Tourist Advertiser*, first published in 1864, later *Cook's Excursionist – European and American Advertiser*. A feature of this publication was its lively advertising for hotels, boarding houses and diverse literature, including guidebooks. The price lists are interesting: in 1869 a three-month tour of the Holy Land, followed by a trip up the Nile, cost £120 (the equivalent of around £2,500 today), and cheap at the price. A purely American edition of *Cook's Excursionist* was published from 1873.

84   Information from the Thomas Cook Archives, prepared by the archivists Paul Smith and Jill Lomer. The collection of this journal in the archives is an invaluable source for documenting the early expansion of mass tourism.

85   It contained details of all the main railway, diligence and steamship routes across Europe. *Thomas Cook's European Timetable* and *Thomas Cook's Overseas Timetable* were still being produced in 2001. (Information from the Thomas Cook Archive.)

86   Round-the-world trips had, of course, been greatly facilitated by the opening of the Suez Canal in 1869.

87   Withey, *Grand Tours and Cook's Tours*, p. 162.

88   For a full and entertaining account of the Verne novel and Nellie Bly's exploit, see *ibid.*, pp. 264–70.

89   Theodor Fontane, *Modernes Reisen: eine Plauderei* (1873), repr. in *idem, Von, vor und nach der Reise: Plaudereien und kleine Geschichten* (Berlin, 1999), pp. 7 and ff.

90   Lambert, *The Fortunate Traveller*, pp. 138–9.
91   Nicky Mariano, *Forty Years with Berenson* (London, 1966), pp. 138–9.
92   Charles Lever (1806–72) was educated at Trinity College, Dublin and studied medicine at Göttingen. From La Spezia he moved on to become British Consul at Trieste, where he died.
93   Quoted in Lambert, *The Fortunate Traveller*, pp. 130–2.
94   *Handbook for Northern Italy*, p. 5.
95   See Withey, *Grand Tours, Cook's Tours*, pp. 159–60.
96   *Cook's Tourist's Handbook for Northern Italy* (London, New York and Rome, 1875), pp. 4–5.
97   Charles Toll Bidwell, *The Cost of living Abroad: Reports and Statistics Showing the Prices of House-rent, Wages, Clerk-hire etc. at the Present Time, and Compared with Those of the Year 1858, at Most of the Principal Places in Foreign Countries. Compiled from Official Returns Laid before Parliament* (London, 1876). Although the main body of the work was aimed at those seeking to *live* abroad, an appendix showed hotel charges 'and other particulars not included in the Official Reports, compiled from the *Queen* Newspaper and published by permission'.
98   The pamphlet was in fact a reprint of a 'Letter to His Royal Highness the Prince of Wales and the Right Honourable the Earl of Clarendon [then Foreign Secretary] by Thomas Cook' (repr. London, 1870).
99   From the Thomas Cook Archive, quoted in Durie, *Scotland for the Holidays*, p. 142.
100 Quoted in Brendon, *Thomas Cook*, p. 219.
101 Quoted in *ibid.*, p. 207.
102 Quoted in Withey, *Grand Tour, Cook's Tours*, p. 142.
103 Koshar, 'What Ought to Be Seen', 336. The book in question is the *Michelin Guide to the Battlefields of the World War*, vol. 1, *The First Battle of the Marne, Including Operations on the Ourcq, in the Marshes of St Gond and in the Revigny Pass, 1914* (Milltown, NJ, 1919).
104 The quotations from the advertisement in the *Basler Nachrichten* for the newspaper's special offer of battlefield tours, and from Karl Kraus's comments on the same, are taken from Frederick Ungar (ed.), *No Compromise: Selected Writings of Karl Kraus* (New York, 1977), pp. 69–74 ('Tourist Trips to Hell', written by Kraus in 1920).
105 See the *Dictionary of National Biography* entry on Kitchiner. He styled himself 'M.D.' – 'as he possessed an extensive library of medical books, this title was not challenged', observes the *DNB* drily.
106 Doctor William Kitchiner, *The Traveller's Oracle or, Maxims for Locomotion, containing Precepts for Promoting the Pleasures and Hints for Preserving the Health of Travellers*. 'Part I Comprising Estimates of the Expenses of Travelling on Foot, on Horseback – in Stages – in Post Chaises – and in Private Carriages; with Seven Songs for One, Two, and Three Voices Composed by William Kitchiner, M.D. Part II: The Horse and Carriage Keeper's Oracle; Rules for Purchasing and Keeping or Jobbing Horses and Carriages; Estimates of Expenses Occasioned thereby; and an Easy Plan for Ascertaining Every Hackney-Coach Fare. By John Jervis, an Old Coachman. The Whole Revised by William Kitchiner M.D. &c.', 2nd edn, 2 vols (London, 1827; 1st edn 1822).
107 *Ibid.*, pp. 296–8, 307, 323.
108 For the preceding three paragraphs, *ibid.*, pp. 16–17, 30, 37, 79, 94, 97, 103, 105, 107, 143.
109 For the preceding two paragraphs, *ibid.*, pp. 165–6, 216.

110   Maxine Feifer, *Going Places: The Ways of the Tourist from Imperial Rome to the Present Day* (London, 1986), pp. 170–1.
111   'Viator Verax' was in fact a clergyman, the Revd George Musgrave, who felt that Murray's Handbooks should stress the dangers of foreign travel to which ladies were exposed far more than they did.
112   Viator Verax, *Continental Excursions: Cautions for the First Tour on the Annoyances, Shortcomings, Indecencies and Impositions Incidental to Foreign Travel*, 4th edn (London, 1863), pp. 7, 20, 33, 36–8, 59, 60.
113   Francis Galton, *The Art of Travel, or, Shifts and Contrivances Available in Wild Countries* (London, 2000 = facsimile reprint of Murray's 5th edn of 1872, with an Introduction (1971) by Dorothy Middleton), xxiii.
114   *Ibid.*, pp. 58 and 313.
115   *Ibid.*, p. 228.
116   *Ibid.*, p. 253.
117   *Ibid.*, p. 293.
118   *Ibid.*, pp. 308–10.
119   *Ibid.*, p. 267.
120   Middleton in *ibid.*, xviii.
121   *Ibid.*

CHAPTER 11

1   Walter Laqueur, 'Dramatische Verschlechterung droht', *Die Presse*, 11 February 2006, p. 41.
2   *The Travels of Ibn Battutah* abridged, introduced and annotated by Tim Mackintosh-Smith (London, 2002), xii. Mackintosh-Smith even refers (xiii) to the first part of the travels as following 'the standard Islamic Grand Tour', and elsewhere (xvii) he alludes to the suspicion that an editor of the *Travels* stuffed it with material from guidebooks, both remarks that indicate a parallel world of guidebook literature in Islamic culture that few of us know about in the West.
3   Tzvetan Todorov, *The Journey and its Narratives*, tr. Alyson Waters, from Chloe Chard and Helen Langdon (eds), *Transports: Travel, Pleasure and Imaginative Geography 1600–1830* (New Haven and London, 1996), p. 295.
4   This anecdote is quoted by Lucy R. Lippard in *On the Beaten Track: Tourism, Art and Place* (New York, 1999), p. 37.
5   See Esther Allen, '"Money and the Little Red Books": Romanticism, Tourism and the Rise of the Guidebook', in *Literature, Interpretation, Theory*, 7/2–3 (1996), 219–20 for a discussion of the use of quotation in the Murray Handbooks. She points out that Murray tended to use authors from his own stable, either those published by him in book form, or contributors to the *Quarterly Review*, which the firm of Murray also published.
6   The success of Michelin guides in foreign translation is an interesting exception to this generalisation, and the Rough Guide has also been translated into a number of languages.
7   A guidebook compiler, writing in *The Author* (Mick Sinclair, 'Way to Go: The Changing World of Travel Guidebook Writing', Winter 1999, pp. 160–1), is candid about the drawbacks of the design-oriented guidebook, of which he evidently has personal experience as a writer: 'For aesthetic reasons, the publisher may also

expect each page to divide neatly into a specific number of paragraphs, sometimes at the expense of grammatical correctness or even literal sense . . . Often there is insufficient space for an item of merit to be given the coverage it deserves (and which the reader might expect.) Conversely, something that really barely warrants being included in the book at all might get significant wordage simply for the sake of the design (again not much of a service for the reader).'

8   The Guide Bleu was the successor to the Guides Joanne, published by Hachette (the last of the Joanne family to be directly involved died in 1922). Originally Hachette entered into an agreement with the Muirheads to translate their Blue Guides into French, and likewise Findlay Muirhead would adapt Hachette's *Paris et ses Environs* for the English market. However, although a distribution agreement between the English Blue Guide publishers and Hachette as publishers of Guide Bleu existed for many years, the two series have in fact been totally distinct since 1933.

9   Blue Guides were one of the most distinguished series (though, as a former Blue Guide author, I should declare an interest). Their chronological trajectory is indicative: first published by Muirhead Guidebooks under the Macmillan Imprint in 1918, they also appeared in France as Les Guide Bleus. From 1932 they were published by Ernest Benn (Rand McNally in the USA until 1982, then W.W. Norton). From 1982 they were published by A&C Black, distinguished publishers of guidebooks in the nineteenth century, which was taken over early in the new millennium by Bloomsbury, the Blue Guides being sold to a small outfit, operating out of Budapest, called Somerset Kft. The Muirhead brothers had originally been responsible for publishing the Baedekers in English, a good business which, however, came to an abrupt halt with the First World War.

10   In 1922 the Touring Club Italiano published its first *Guida d' Italia per Stranieri* ('Guide to Italy for Foreigners'). These earlier TCI guides are collectors' items and were always very environmentally aware, as well as being strong on culture and history. Distinguished geographers like Olinto Marinelli and Giotto Dainelli played an important role in the formulation of the guides.

11   The DuMont Kunstreiseführer remained the intellectual and aesthetic aristocrats of the series, but the publisher branched out extensively into the middle and lower end of the market with several other series such as DuMont direkt, DuMont Reisetaschenbuch, DuMont richtig reisen, DuMont aktiv (a sports guide), and DuMont Reisen für Genießer. DuMont now publishes over 500 titles in seven different series, a comprehensive palette only approached by AA Publishing in the UK.

12   Michael Rowland, 'Michelin's *Guide vert touristique*: A Guide to the French Inner Landscape', in *The French Review*, 60/5 (April 1987), 659.

13   *Ibid.*, 661–2.

14   For information on the founding years of Frommer I am indebted to Kathy Passero, 'Travel Revolutionary Arthur Frommer', in *Biography*, 3/8 (August 1999), 72.

15   WPA was the acronym for the Orwellian-sounding 'Works Progress Administration', basically an employment-creating project by the Federal Government designed to lift the USA out of depression. A useful survey of the guides appears in *The Federal Writers' Project: A Bibliography* by Jeutonne P. Brewer (Metuchen, NJ, and London, 1994.) An appreciative, but rather patronising, review of the series appeared in the *Spectator* of 5 August 1938 from the pen of D.W. Brogan. 'Out-of-work actors were not offered jobs as navvies on the roads, but as actors. Painters were encouraged to

paint in post-offices, which now have tolerable frescoes where we have air mail posters of a devastating competence. And the most bold experiment of all, authors were enrolled by the "Federal Writers' Project" – and one result has been this series of guides.' However, many writers apparently felt ashamed of having had to take money from the state and subsequently airbrushed their contributions out of their biographies.

16   See David A. Taylor, 'A Noble and Absurd Undertaking', in *Smithsonian*, 30/12 (March 2000), 103.

17   Quoted in Elizabeth T. Platt, 'Portrait of America: Guidebooks and Related Works', in *Geographical Review*, 29/4 (October 1939), 663.

18   Quoted in James Michael Buzard, 'Forster's Trespasses: Tourism and Cultural Politics', in *Twentieth Century Literature*, 34/2 (Summer 1988), 168.

19   Lippard, *On the Beaten Track*, p. 8.

20   Quoted in an article by Jeannette Hyde in *The Times*, 5 December 1998, 'Cutting Corners on the World'.

21   Christoph Hennig, *Reiselust: Touristen, Tourismus und Urlaubskultur* (Frankfurt am Main and Leipzig, 1999), p. 172.

22   *Ibid.*, p. 41.

23   *Insight Guide Austria*, 3rd edn (London, 2001), p. 156. In recent years Insight Guides have abandoned the 'folk costume' approach to their covers, and now go for moody cityscapes and the like.

24   Dr Heba Aziz, 'Guide Books Turn Travellers into Package Tourists', in *Tourism Concern*, Winter 1999/2000.

25   Baedeker's *Handbook to Palestine and Syria, with the Chief Routes through Mesopotamia and Babylonia* (1906).

26   Rosemary Bailey, 'Travel Guides', in *The Author*, Autumn 1995, 89–90.

27   Robert Young Pelton, Coskun Aral and Wink Dulles, *Fielding's the World's Most Dangerous Places*, 3rd edn (Redondo Beach, CA, 1998).

28   These and other details of unusual guidebooks were highlighted in an amusing article in the *London Review of Books*, 1 January 1998, by Jeremy Harding ('Best Remain Seated: Jeremy Harding Seeks Travel Guidance').

29   Matthias Sommer, *(K)ein Urlaub in Italien* appears in a series of similar books on other countries. No date or place of publication is given. The credibility of the contents is not greatly enhanced, either by the author's photograph on the back cover, or by the fact that his name is incorrectly spelled on the front cover.

30   Karen Dabrowska, *Iraq: The Bradt Travel Guide* (Chalfont St Peter and Guilford, CT, 2002; corrected edn 2003). Martin Bright, writing in the *Observer* on the eve of the invasion of Iraq (*The Observer Review*, 2 March 2003) describes the guide as 'an eccentric and completely engrossing work, even if most people who read it are unlikely to set foot in the country. [It] has become a word-of mouth bestseller among armchair strategists and concerned peaceniks. The media corps about to be dispatched to the Gulf would be well advised to pack a copy with their chemical weapons suit and gas mask to help them identify which Muslim holy site is about to be turned to dust (and whether it is Shia or Sunni). It is only when Dabrowska turns her attention to the Iraqi holy sites that you realise just how sensitive any lengthy occupation of the country is likely to be.' Strategists and 'experts' turning to a guidebook for reliable information is perhaps the highest tribute that a toiler in the genre can conceive of, though it also recalls the potential for suspicion about the motives of guidebook writers, from antiquity to the 'patriotic travellers' of the

Enlightenment, who were sometimes regarded as spies. In fact Bradt was not the only guidebook used by war planners: *Lonely Planet Iraq* also proved indispensable for drawing up a list of sites that should not be bombed or looted (see Tad Friend, 'The Parachute Artist: Have Tony Wheeler's Guidebooks Travelled too Far?', in the *New Yorker*, 18 April 2005, p. 3).

31   *Wikipedia*, as at May 2006.

32   *Wikipedia* entry for Lonely Planet, as at May 2006.

33   Quoted in Tad Friend, 'The Parachute Artist', p. 15 (of 21 pages).

34   See Jon Krakauer, 'All They Really Wanted was to Travel a Little', *Smithsonian*, 25/7 (October 1994), 135.

35   It does however have a television production company, Lonely Planet Television.

36   *Rough Guide to Britain* (London, 1998).

37   *Ibid.*

38   This and the following two quotes are from *Lonely Planet Britain* (Hawthorn, Victoria, Australia, 1997).

39   *Lonely Planet Scotland* (Hawthorn, Victoria, Australia, 1999) The quotations to which nn. 29–32 refer are all taken from an article by Emma Brockes in the *Guardian* (14 April 1999) entitled 'Do They Mean Us?' which amusingly extracted adverse opinions expressed in Rough Guide, Lonely Planet, Let's Go, Fodor and *The Glasgow Guide*, and solicited comments from the tourist authorities concerned. Of these, mostly reasoned and reasonable responses, that from Stratford-upon-Avon was charmingly candid: 'The majority of people who come here because it is Shakespeares's birthplace don't have expectations of the place beyond a vague idea that it is quaint. They are mostly happy to go to the theatre, sleep through a play and have a wander round.'

40   The full text of Professor Garboli's offending preface was reprinted in *La Repubblica*, 28 February 2001. The passage quoted appeared in an account of the affair by Rory Carroll in the *Guardian* (Europe edn) of 27 February 2001. I have taken the liberty of slightly altering the translation after perusal of the original, and I have also added the next sentence of Garboli's text. I am indebted to Alta Macadam for help in obtaining background material on the controversy: cuttings from *La Repubblica* of 23, 26, 27 and 28 February, 1, 2 and 22 March 2001, and *Metropoli*, 2 March 2001.

41   Quoted in *La Repubblica*, 2 March 2001.

42   The quotations from Garboli's text are taken from the English version. It appeared parallelly in Italian, German and English in *Toscana di alpe e di mare* published by the Provincia di Lucca (Lucca, 2001). The words are printed over a backdrop of stunning photographs.

43   Euan Ferguson, 'Capital Punishment. For Those Who Think It's Hell Living in London, Remember That There is Always Someone Worse Off Than Yourself – the Tourist', in the *Observer*, 3 March 2002.

44   Malcolm Bradbury, *Why Come to Slaka?* (London, Basingstoke and Oxford, 2000), pp. 18–19. This satire is arguably Bradbury's masterpiece, but it caused little stir and is now hard to find.

45   *Budapest: Ein Reiseführer durch die ungarische Hauptstadt*, 3rd edn (Budapest, 1967), pp. 38–9.

46   The slogan was not quite as risible as it appeared: the authorities were campaigning against dastardly and illicit competition from small-scale private enterprise, much favoured by resourceful Hungarians (i.e. most of them).

47   Alan Ryalls, *Your Guide to Hungary* (London, 1967), pp. 36–7. See also the introduction (pp. 15–19) to get an idea of the generally uncritical approach of the whole. My remarks on Budapest guidebooks have been taken from a study of the subject, covering the period from the eighteenth century to the present, that I wrote for the winter number of the *Hungarian Quarterly* (2005), and a longer version of the same (in Hungarian) printed in the March 2006 issue of the Budapest journal *Holmi*.

48   A search of the Web reveals that this term has been extended from its original function of designating countries under authoritarian rule such as Croatia, Slovakia or the Ukraine in the 1990s. Now it is also applied by some to, e.g., England's 'elective dictatorship', where 28 per cent of the electorate can put in place a government with a massive majority, and to other examples of a democratic deficit. However, the more common use is still for states that have moved fom totalitarianism and do not yet meet the criteria of democracy.

49   Santo Cilauro, Tom Gleisner and Rob Sitch, *Molvania: A Land Untouched by Modern Dentistry* (a Jetlag Travel Guide) (London, 2004; 1st edn Australia, 2003), pp. 18, 64, 79, 126, 142.

50   This is quoted in the *Wikipedia* article on Lonely Planet.

51   David Barchard, 'Western Silence on Turkey', in *MERIP [Middle East Research and Information Project] Reports*, No. 121, 'State Terror in Turkey' (February 1984), pp. 3–6.

52   My discussion of the row about the Lonely Planet *Guide to Myanmar* is based on diverse sources as follows: Martin H. Petrich, 'Burmesische Farbenlehre, oder: Wem hilft der Tourismus?', in *Südostasien* 1/2002 (the author is a guidebook author and tour guide in Bangkok); Nick Cohen, 'Burma's Shame', in his 'Without Prejudice' column, in the *Observer*, 4 June 2002; Adrian Levy, Cathy Scott-Clark and David Harrison, 'Burma's Junta Goes Green. Save the Rhino, Kill the People', in the *Observer*, 23 March 1997; Victor Mallet, 'A Blinkered View of Burma' (book review of Norman Lewis *et al.*, *Back to Mandalay: Burmese Past and Present*), in the *Financial Times*, Weekend October 10/October 19 1996; Friend, 'The Parachute Artist'; Tourist Concern bulletins, in particular a debate in the Summer 2003 issue, Number 47, between Glenys Kinnock MEP (against) and the travel writer and broadcaster Peter Hughes (for) on the subject of whether the travel media should promote Burma before democracy is restored; the Lonely Planet entry in *Wikipedia*; internal discussions in the British Guild of Travel Writers on Burma and Human Rights, which are privileged and must remain anonymous.

53   Klaus R. Schröder, *Myanmar/Burma. Reisen im Land der Pagodan* in the Reise Know-How series (Westerstede, FRD, 2002).

54   *Ibid.*, p. 72.

55   Robert Reid and Michael Grosberg, *Myanmar (Burma)* (Footscray, Australia, Oakland, CA, and London, 2005), pp. 17–21 for the discussion of whether you should visit Myanmar.

56   E.M. Forster, *Alexandria: A History and a Guide*, introduction by Lawrence Durrell, afterword and notes by Michael Haag (New York, 1982), p. 241.

57   The introduction was written in 1960 and is reproduced in Miriam Allott (ed.), *E.M. Forster: Alexandria a History and a Guide and Pharos and Pharillon* (London, 2004), p. 5. *Pharos and Pharillon*, a book of historical sketches about Alexandria, was published by Virginia and Leonard Woolf's Hogarth Press in 1923 and was an instant success.

In many ways it complements the commercially unsuccessful *Guide* published the previous year.

58   C.P. Cavafy, *The City*, tr. Rae Dalven in *The Complete Poems of C.P. Cavafy*, with an introduction by W.H. Auden (London, 1961), pp. 27–8. Quoted by Allott in *Alexandria: A History and a Guide*, xlv.

59   *Ibid.*, p. 144.

60   Quoted in Allott, *Alexandria: A History and a Guide*, liv.

61   *Ibid.*, lxxi.

62   *Ibid.*, p. 6.

63   *Ibid.*, p. 356 (reprinted from Forster's talk on 'The Lost Guide' at the Aldeburgh Festival, 1956).

64   Quoted in the afterword by Michael Haag in Forster, *Alexandria: A History and a Guide*.

65   Buzard, 'Forster's Trespasses', p. 176.

66   From the introduction to a selection of Nikolaus Pevsner's architectural comments in the Buildings of England, in Bridget Cherry and Simon Bradley (eds), *The Buildings of England: A Celebration Compiled to Mark Fifty Years of the Pevsner Architectural Guides*, published in a limited edition of 1,500 copies by the Penguin Collector's Society for the Buildings Books Trust (London, 2001), p. 85.

67   Quoted by J. Mordaunt Crook in 'John Britton and the Genesis of the Gothic Revival', in John Summerson (ed.), *Concerning Architecture: Essays on Architectural Writers and Writing presented to Nikolaus Pevsner* (London, 1981), p. 103. The vignette of Britton is taken from the same passage.

68   Quoted by Angus Wilson in his Commemorative Address when Pevsner was awarded an honorary Ph.D. at the University of East Anglia in 1969, and reprinted in Cherry and Bradley, *The Buildings of England*, p. 51.

69   The phrase is Gavin Stamp's in 'Pevsner e l'Inghilterra', in Fulvio Irace (ed.), *Nikolaus Pevsner: La trama della storia* (Milan, 1992), p. 45.

70   e.g. Osbert Lancaster in 'One in the Eye for the Zeitgeist', in the *Cambridge Review*, 3 February 1978, 86, quoted in Gavin Stamp, 'Pevsner e l'Inghilterra', p. 54.

71   Colin Macinnes, 'The Englishness of Dr Pevsner', first published in *Twentieth Century*, January 1960 and reprinted in Cherry and Bradley, *The Buildings of England*, p. 42.

72   Simon Jenkins in the Foreword to Cherry and Bradley, *The Buildings of England*, p. 5.

73   Ian Buruma, *Anglomania* (New York, 2000), p. 238. [First published in UK as *Voltaire's Coconuts, or Anglomania in Europe* (London, 1998).]

74   *Ibid.*, p. 239.

75   *Collins English Dictionary*, 4th edn, updated 2000, p. 1161.

76   A remark in *The Buildings of England: Shropshire* and quoted by John Newman in 'An Appreciation of Sir Nikolaus Pevsner', originally published in an anthology of Pevsner extracts entitled *The Best Buildings of England* (London, 1986), and republished in Bridget Cherry, *The Buildings of England, Ireland, Scotland and Wales: A Short History and Bibiliography*, published by the Penguin Collectors' Society for the Pevsner Memorial Trust in a limited edition of 1,000 copies (London, 1998), p. 51.

77   Newman, 'An Appreciation of Sir Nikolaus Pevsner', p. 60.

78   Alec Clifton-Taylor, 'Architectural Touring with the Little Guides', in Summerson, *Concerning Architecture*, p. 244.

79   John Betjeman, 'Hymn', taken from John Guest (ed.), *The Best of Betjeman* (London, 2006), p. 17.

80 The remarks about the Shell Guides and the quotation from *Ghastly Good Taste* (London, 1933), p. 63, are taken from David Watkin, *The Rise of Architectural History* (London, 1983), p. 134.

81 Watkin, *Architectural History*, p. 134.

82 Newman in Cherry, *The Buildings of England*, p. 66.

83 Ironically, when Pevsner set out to tour Middlesex in a borrowed Wolseley Hornet, after coaxing Allen Lane into the project for the Buildings of England, he needed to be equipped with a permit for 30 gallons of petrol, fuel still being rationed.

84 See Timothy Mowl, *Stylistic Cold Wars: Betjeman versus Pevsner* (London, 2000), p. 56. Betjeman's day job was with the *Architectural Review*, whose director, Maurice Regan, had been persuaded to get involved in publishing the guides once Betjeman had found the sponsor. Betjeman resigned from the *Architectural Review* in disgust at his treatment.

85 In the early 1950s Penguin were losing £3,000 on each paperback volume (Mowl, *Stylistic Cold Wars*, p. 123).

86 Rosemary Hill, 'Positively Spaced Out', in *London Review of Books*, 6 September 2001, p. 30.

87 Mowl, *Stylistic Cold Wars*, p. 57.

88 For an unkind, but well documented, critique of Betjeman's *Cornwall*, see Mowl, *ibid.*, pp. 60–2. The 1964 rewrite, full of delightful things, was the product of Betjeman as the public now knows him, with all his enthusiasms, playful humour and idiosyncratic erudition given full rein.

89 Quoted in Guest, *The Best of Betjeman*, p. 196.

90 Quoted in Mowl, *Stylistic Cold Wars*, p. 137.

91 Ken Powell, reviewing *The Buildings of England: a Celebration*, in the *Independent*, 2001.

92 Quoted in Mowl, *Stylistic Cold Wars*, p. 127.

93 The *Observer*, 1973.

94 Information from Bridget Cherry, 'Fifty Years of the Buildings of England', in *Society of Architectural Historians of Great Britain*, Newsletter No. 73 (Summer 2001).

95 Kathleen Meyer, *How to Shit in the Woods. An Environmentally Sound Approach to a Lost Art*, 2nd rev. edn (Berkeley, CA, 1994.) The quotation that follows is from p. 13.

96 Dr Jane Wilson-Howarth, *Shitting Pretty: How to Stay Clean and Healthy while Traveling* (San Francisco, CA, 2000).

97 Richard Dawood, *Travellers' Health. How to Stay Healthy Abroad* (Oxford, 1986), vii.

98 Joshua Piven and David Borgenicht, *The Worst-Case Scenario Survival Handbook: Travel. How to Survive Runaway Camels, UFO Abductions, High-Rise Hotel Fires, Leeches etc.* (San Francisco, CA, 2001).

99 Published by Really Great Books in the USA.

100 Jeffrey Epstein and Eddie Shapiro, *Queens in the Kingdom: The Ultimate Gay and Lesbian Guide to the Disney Theme Parks* (USA, 2003).

101 See Nataliey Danford, 'All Aboard! Travel Titles for Spring and Summer 2003', in *Publishers Weekly*, 250/3 (20 January 2003). There are a few short reviews in this round-up, notably of *Dog-Friendly New England* and *Canine Oregon*, discussed under the excruciating heading 'The Paws That Refresh'.

102 I am indebted for all the information about *The Book* to Patrick Symmes's article of the same title, which appeared in *Outside Magazine*, August 2005 and is posted on the Web. All the quotations, both from Symmes and *The Book* itself, are taken from this article. I would also like to thank Matt Thompson of Loftus Productions for telling me about this fascinating and unique experiment in guidebook creation.

103 *Ibid.*

EPILOGUE

1   Taoist sages denigrated the physical, or 'external', in favour of the spiritual and intellectual, or 'internal' journey. Lieh Tzu wrote that 'those who take great pains for exterior journeys do not know how to organise visits that one can make inside oneself. He who journeys outside is dependent on exterior things; he who makes interior visits can find in himself everything he needs. This is the highest way to travel; while the journey of the one who depends on exterior things is a poor journey', quoted in Arthur Waley, *Three Ways of Thought in Ancient China* (New York, 1956), p. 43.

2   Michael Pauls and Diana Facaros, *The Travellers' Guide to Hell* (London and Old Saybrook, CT, 1998).

3   Peter Stanford, *Heaven. A Traveller's Guide to the Undiscovered Country* (London, 2002).

4   The publicity for it proclaims that 'navigation is easy and this one resource will deliver in-depth information on: 86 countries, including more than 15,000 towns and cities; 2,200 walking and driving tours; 2,400 maps pinpointing the remotest places; 14,000 high-quality photographs, and no less than 78,500 attractions catering to 150 special interest categories. All of it is on 11,000 pages and all of it is printable.' (Press release, 8 December 2005.)

Index

Note: emboldened page numbers indicate chapters or major sections of text. Sub-entries are arranged alphabetically, except where chronological order is significant.